■ THE RESOURCE FOR THE INDEPENDENT TRAVELER

"The guides are aimed not only at young budget travelers but at the independent traveler; a sort of streetwise cookbook for traveling alone."

—The New York Times

"Unbeatable; good sight-seeing advice; up-to-date info on restaurants, hotels, and inns; a commitment to money-saving travel; and a wry style that brightens nearly every page."

—The Washington Post

"Lighthearted and sophisticated, informative and fun to read. [Let's Go] helps the novice traveler navigate like a knowledgeable old hand."

—Atlanta Journal-Constitution

"A world-wise traveling companion—always ready with friendly advice and helpful hints, all sprinkled with a bit of wit."

—The Philadelphia Inquirer

■ THE BEST TRAVEL BARGAINS IN YOUR PRICE RANGE

"All the dirt, dirt cheap."

—People

"Anything you need to know about budget traveling is detailed in this book."

—The Chicago Sun-Times

"Let's Go follows the creed that you don't have to toss your life's savings to the wind to travel—unless you want to."

—The Salt Lake Tribune

■ REAL ADVICE FOR REAL EXPERIENCES

"The writers seem to have experienced every rooster-packed bus and lunar-surfaced mattress about which they write."

—The New York Times

"A guide should tell you what to expect from a destination. Here Let's Go shines."

—The Chicago Tribune

LET'S GO PUBLICATIONS

TRAVEL GUIDES

Alaska & the Pacific Northwest 2003
Australia 2003
Austria & Switzerland 2003
Britain & Ireland 2003
California 2003
Central America 8th edition
Chile 1st edition **NEW TITLE**
China 4th edition
Costa Rica 1st edition **NEW TITLE**
Eastern Europe 2003
Egypt 2nd edition
Europe 2003
France 2003
Germany 2003
Greece 2003
Hawaii 2003 **NEW TITLE**
India & Nepal 7th edition
Ireland 2003
Israel 4th edition
Italy 2003
Mexico 19th edition
Middle East 4th edition
New Zealand 6th edition
Peru, Ecuador & Bolivia 3rd edition
South Africa 5th edition
Southeast Asia 8th edition
Southwest USA 2003
Spain & Portugal 2003
Thailand 1st edition **NEW TITLE**
Turkey 5th edition
USA 2003
Western Europe 2003

CITY GUIDES

Amsterdam 2003
Barcelona 2003
Boston 2003
London 2003
New York City 2003
Paris 2003
Rome 2003
San Francisco 2003
Washington, D.C. 2003

MAP GUIDES

Amsterdam
Berlin
Boston
Chicago
Dublin
Florence
Hong Kong
London
Los Angeles
Madrid
New Orleans
New York City
Paris
Prague
Rome
San Francisco
Seattle
Sydney
Venice
Washington, D.C.

LET'S GO

COSTA RICA

CHARLENE MUSIC EDITOR

ASHLEY KIRCHER ASSOCIATE EDITOR
BENJAMIN KRUTZINNA ASSOCIATE EDITOR
ERIN SPRAGUE ASSOCIATE EDITOR

RESEARCHER-WRITERS
MEGHA DOSHI
SARAH GOGEL
PHEOBE LITHGOW
NATALIA A. JOSÉ TRUSZKOWSKA

KATHARINE DOUGLAS MANAGING EDITOR
HARRIET GREEN MANAGING EDITOR

NATHANIEL BROOKS MAP EDITOR
CALEB EPPS TYPESETTER

MACMILLAN

HELPING LET'S GO If you want to share your discoveries, suggestions, or corrections, please drop us a line. We read every piece of correspondence, whether a postcard, a 10-page email, or a coconut. Please note that mail received after May 2003 may be too late for the 2004 book, but will be kept for future editions. **Address mail to:**

    Let's Go: Costa Rica
    67 Mount Auburn Street
    Cambridge, MA 02138
    USA

Visit Let's Go at **http://www.letsgo.com,** or send email to:

    feedback@letsgo.com
    Subject: "Let's Go: Costa Rica"

In addition to the invaluable travel advice our readers share with us, many are kind enough to offer their services as researchers or editors. Unfortunately, our charter enables us to employ only currently enrolled Harvard students.

HOW TO USE THIS BOOK

ORGANIZATION. The book starts with **Essentials,** what you need to get to, from, and around the counry, and general cultural information in Life and Times. Coverage is broken down into regional chapters; black tabs on the side of the book should help you navigate. Also consult the map legend at the end of the book.

BEYOND COSTA RICA. Just beyond Costa Rica's borders, southern Nicaragua's Lago de Nicaragua and western Panama's Caribbean Bocas del Toro Archipelago await. Check *Let's Go: Central America 2003* for these amazing, nearby places.

PHONE CODES AND TELEPHONE NUMBERS. Costa Rica's phone numbers have seven digits; there are no area codes. Phone numbers are preceded by the ☎ icon.

WHEN TO USE IT

TWO MONTHS BEFORE. The first chapter, **Discover Costa Rica,** contains highlights of the region, including Suggested Itineraries (see p. 4) to help you plan your trip. The **Essentials** (see p. 11) section contains practical information on planning a budget, making reservations, renewing a passport, health concerns, and other useful tips about traveling in Costa Rica.

ONE MONTH BEFORE. Take care of insurance, and write down a list of emergency numbers and hotlines. Make a list of packing essentials (see **Packing,** p. 25) and shop for anything you are missing. Read through the coverage and make sure you understand the logistics of your itinerary (catching buses, planes, etc.). Make any reservations if necessary.

2 WEEKS BEFORE. Leave an itinerary and a photocopy of important documents with someone at home. Take some time to read the **Life and Times** (see p. 54), which has info on history, culture, flora and fauna, recent events, and more.

ON THE ROAD. The **Appendix** contains a glossary of Spanish terms and Costa Rican slang. Now, arm yourself with a travel journal and hit the road.

PRICE RANGES AND RANKINGS. We list establishments in order of value from best to worst. Our favorites are denoted by the Let's Go thumbs-up (👍). Since the best value does not always mean the cheapest price, we have incorporated a system of price ranges. The table below lists how prices fall within each bracket.

COUNTRY NAME	❶	❷	❸	❹	❺
ACCOMMODATIONS	¢380 -3770	¢3770- 7550	¢7550- 24,500	¢24,500- 37,700	¢37,700- 56,500
	US$1-10	US$10-20	US$20-65	US$65-100	US$100-150
FOOD	¢380- 1150	¢1150- 2650	¢2650- 3800	¢3800- 5300	¢5300- 7550
	US$1-3	US$3-7	US$7-10	US$10-14	US$14-20

A NOTE TO OUR READERS

The information for this book was gathered by *Let's Go* researchers from May through August of 2002. Each listing is based on one researcher's opinion, formed during his or her visit at a particular time. Those traveling at other times may have different experiences since prices, dates, hours, and conditions are always subject to change. You are urged to check the facts presented in this book beforehand to avoid inconvenience and surprises.

CONTENTS

DISCOVER COSTA RICA 1
When to Go 1
Things to See and Do 1
Suggested Itineraries 8

ESSENTIALS 11
Facts for the Traveler 11
Accommodations 26
Keeping in Touch 31
Getting to Costa Rica 36
Getting Around Costa Rica 40
Specific Concerns 45
Other Resources 50

LIFE AND TIMES 54
Land 54
History 58
Costa Rica Today 61
People 64
Culture 65
Additional Resources 72

ALTERNATIVES TO TOURISM 74
Getting Started 74
Studying Abroad 74
Working 78
Volunteering 80

SAN JOSÉ 85
Escazú 104

CENTRAL VALLEY 107
Alajuela 107
Atenas 113
Sarchí 114
Grecia 117
Naranjo 118
San Ramón 120
Palmares 122
Zarcero 122
Heredia 125
Oarva 131
Cartago 132
Orosi 137
Turrialba 141
Near Turrialba 144

NORTHWESTERN COSTA RICA 146
Monteverde and Santa Elena 147
Cañas 154
Near Cañas 156
Tilarán 156
Volcán Tenorio 158
AROUND VOLCÁN MIRAVALLES 159
Bagaces 160
Parque Nacional Palo Verde 161
Reserva Biológica Lomas Barbudal 162
Liberia 163
NORTH OF LIBERIA 168
Parque Nacional Rincón de la Vieja 168
Parque Nacional Guanacaste 172
La Cruz 173

NORTHERN LOWLANDS 176
Ciudad Quesada (San Carlos) 176
Parque Nacional Juan Castro Blanco 179
Puerto Viejo de Sarapiquí 180
Vara Blanca 185
VOLCÁN ARENAL AND AROUND 187
Fortuna 187
Cavernas de Venado 191
San Rafael de Guatuso 192
Upala 194
Los Chiles 196
Refugio Nacional Caño Negro 197

NICOYA PENINSULA 201
Playa Hermosa 201
Near Playa Hermosa 204
Playa del Coco 204
Ocotal 207
Potrero 208
Playa Flamingo 209
Brasilito 211
Near Brasilito 212
Filadelfia 213
Santa Cruz 214
Parque Nacional Marino Las Baulas 216
Playa Tamarindo 218
Playa Junquillal 223
Playa Negra 224
Nicoya 226
Near Nicoya 229
Playa Nosara 229
Nearby Beaches 231
Playa Sámara 234
Playa Carrillo 239
South of Playa Carillo to Mal País 241
Mal Pals and Santa Teresa 244
Montezuma 249
Cabuya 255
Near Cabuya 256
Cóbano 257
Tambor 257
Paquera 260
Near paquera 261

CENTRAL PACIFIC COAST ..262
Orotina 262
Near Orotina 265
Puntarenas 266
Esparza 270
Parque Nacional Carara 271
Jacó 272
Playa Hermosa 279
Parrita 281
South of Jacó to Quepos 282
Quepos 284
Parque Nacional Manuel Antonio 290
Dominical 294
Uvita 297

SOUTHERN COSTA RICA ...300
San Isidro 300
Chirripó and San Gerardo de Rivas 304
San Gerardo de Rivas 304

Buenos Aires 307
Near Buenos Aires 309
Palmar Norte 310
San Vito 311
Near San Vito 313
Ciudad Neily 314
Parque Internacional La Amistad 316

PENÍNSULA DE OSA & GOLFO DULCE 321
Sierpe 321
Bahía Drake 322
Golfito 326
BEACHES SOUTH OF GOLFITO 331
Pavones 331
Pancudo 333
Puerto Jiménez 335
Parque Nacional Corcovado 339

CARIBBEAN LOWLANDS 342
Guápiles 343
Near Guápiles 345
Guácimo 346

Near Guácimo 346
Siquirres 347
Puerto Limón 348
Parismina 351
PARQUE NACIONAL TORTUGUERO 354
Tortuguero Village 354
Oarra del Colorado 362
Cahuita 366
Parque Nacional Cahuita 369
Puerto Viejo de Talamanca 373
SOUTH OF PUERTO VIEJO 378
Gandoca 378
BOCAS DEL TORO, PANAMA 383
Bocas del Toro and Isla Colón 384
Isla Bastimentos 388
Other Islands 389

APPENDIX 398
Climate 398
Language 398

INDEX 405

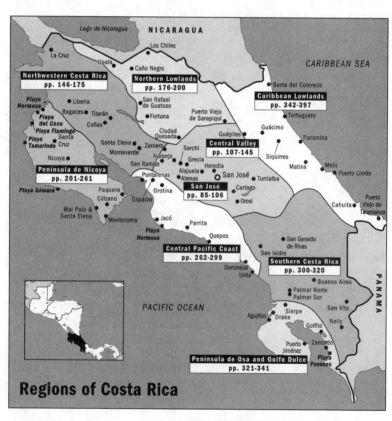

Regions of Costa Rica

RESEARCHER-WRITERS

Megha Doshi   *Central Valley, Caribbean, Central Pacific*

A developing world veteran at *Let's Go*, we knew from day one that Megha would be our *chica* to hunt down the best in Costa Rica. Always up for a challenge, this marathon runner, bioethics major, rugby player, and community service superstar has added "human typewriter" to her list of credits, as her copy was as smooth as her trip through Costa Rica. She was also our last minute godsend for maps and ice cream. *¡Bien hecho*, Megha!

Sarah Gogel   *Northwestern*

We're not sure who fell in love first: Sarah with Costa Rica, or Costa Rica with Sarah. Originally from France, Sarah has spent time volunteering in her "village" of Chaguitillo, Nicaragua. Rest days? Not for this RW! Sarah was so captivated by Costa Rican culture, she has vowed to combine her study of sociology with her newfound passion for tourism. With a little *je ne sais quoi* that is now part *nica* and part *tica*, Sarita is truly as relaxed as the country she researched.

Phoebe Lithgow   *Nicoya Peninsula, Northwestern*

Joining the LG team definitely brought out the inner tiger in this laid-back California gal. On her third trip to Latin America, Phoebe once again shed her usual study of American history and literature for some Latina flair. Although her surfing style might not match her badminton skills, her copy definitely did. Thanks to Phoebe, every mirrored headboard in Costa Rica has now been documented. The only thing we still need to know is: 'tacos as big as your you know what'?!

Natalia A. José Truszkowska   *Osa Peninsula, Southern, Caribbean*

Hailing from Poland, Mexico, and Wisconsin, and having researched for *Let's Go: Eastern Europe 2002*, Natalia decided it was time to give her Latin American roots some attention. Natalia's study of postmodern Hispanic literature was evident in her inquisitive prose. This RW had no qualms about ditching her gear and wading up to her neck through the raging rivers of her jungle route to get the most stellar copy. Natalia loved her *viajera* lifestyle, and we loved her.

CONTRIBUTING WRITERS

Matthew Firestone. A Research Writer for *Let's Go Britain & Ireland 2000*, Matthew honed his traveling and writing skills conducting post-weaning research amongst indigenous populations in Costa Rica. He is currently in Sub-Saharan Africa researching the dietary practices of hunter-gatherer populations inhabiting the Kalahari.

Luis Gamboa. Having received an MBA from the Unversity of Iowa, Luis returned to Costa Rica, where he is now vice-chairman of AMCHAM Costa Rica, and chairman of CINDE (the Costa Rican development authority). He is also a board member of AED, representatives of the United Way in Costa Rica.

Amber Musser. After residing in Costa Rica for four years, Amber is beginning a one year program in women's studies in Oxford in fall 2002.

Oscar Arias. Born and raised in Costa Rica, Oscar is an avid scuba diver and traveler, and now studies applied math and economics at Harvard College.

Melania Cortés. A student of veterinary medicine at Kansas State University, Melania was a long-time volunteer at the Zoológico la Marina working with animals who have been orphaned, injured, or captured illegaly.

Juan Pastor. Born and raised in Costa Rica, Juan studies journalism and international relations at New York University. Juan has interned at the public relations firms of Mark Allen and Company in New York, Sky TV in Britain, and has done public relations work for Nick Junior and MTV.

Rafael Alberto Gamboa. Graduating with a law degree from the University of Costa Rica in 1978, Rafael worked for over ten years as lawyer for the Patronato Nacional de la Infancia, a children's rights advocacy group.

Derek Glanz. Former editor of *Let's Go: Spain, Portugal, and Morocco 1998*, Derek is a freelance journalist, having completed his post-graduate studies in international relations.

Shannon Music. A native Costa Rican, Shannon interned at the Interamerican Court of Justice in San José, and worked the summer of 2002 at the Ethos Institute of Business and Social Responsibilities in São Paulo, Brazil. She is a psychology concentrator at Harvard College.

Maria Isabel Gamboa. A primary school teacher in San José, Maria Isabel studied English at Northwest Missouri College and got a Masters in preschool education from the University of Costa Rica.

Eugenia Cortés. Eugenia is currently studying Architecture at the Universidad del Diseño in San José, and is interested in photography.

ACKNOWLEDGMENTS

LET'S GO

We thank: The rock star RWs: Megha, Natalia, Phoebe, and Sarah for their phenomenal efforts toward this new book; Kate and Harriett for the constant guidance and focus; our marvelous mapper Nathaniel Brooks; Megha Doshi, Jay Gardner, and Adam Grant for last minute help; Prod; the typists; and all the contributing writers. Thank you, *gracias*, Costa Rica, working with you was *pura vida*.

Ben thanks: Ashley, Charlene, and Erin—the only women in my life—for motivating me to come into the office (literally) every day, and for their dedication, patience, and humor. Marlene por haberme dejado con tanta afición por Centroamérica. Hermann, Ursula, Jan, and Jenny for always caring about me. Everybody else who has been supportive.

Ashley thanks: The elusive semicolon, fantastic Charlene, Erin, and Ben, who kept me laughing, groaning, and hard at work, the fam, Linda and John for weekend getaways, Sam and Scott for late-night parties, ghetto-fabulous Dave, and Marla. Thanks to Starbucks for taking half my paycheck. *Besos* to Jay for your help, support, and Leo's breakfasts.

Charlene thanks: Costa Rica, my homeland and inspiration. Meat and cheese. You kept me alive. Ben for the finest execution of "cheap, foreign labor" I've ever seen—wait, after *me*, that is! Erin and Ash for the fun and hard work. AEs rock. Kate, our salvation. Mom, Dad, and Shannoncita for ALL your help and for keeping me laughing late at night. Abe, for the love, motivation, and best times I had this summer.

Erin thanks: Ben for the late nights and humorous anecdotes, appleless Ashley for honesty and fun, and of course carnivorous Charlene for her incredible devotion and *tica* charm. Kato, Lauren, Lindsey, Moud, Nalina, and XC teams—you're the best. My family- Mom, Dad, Colleen, Cara, Kevin, Nanny, and the Harkins- *mucho amor como siempre!*

Editor
Charlene Music
Associate Editors
Ashley Kircher, Benjamin Krutzinna, Erin Sprague
Managing Editors
Kate Douglas, Harriett Green
Map Editor
Nathaniel Brooks

Publishing Director
Matthew Gibson
Editor-in-Chief
Brian R. Walsh
Production Manager
C. Winslow Clayton
Cartography Manager
Julie Stephens
Design Manager
Amy Cain
Editorial Managers
Christopher Blazejewski, Abigail Burger, D. Cody Dydek, Harriett Green, Angela Mi Young Hur, Marla Kaplan, Celeste Ng
Financial Manager
Noah Askin
Marketing & Publicity Managers
Michelle Bowman, Adam M. Grant
New Media Managers
Jesse Tov, Kevin Yip
Online Manager
Amélie Cherlin
Personnel Managers
Alex Leichtman, Owen Robinson
Production Associates
Caleb Epps, David Muehlke
Network Administrators
Steven Aponte, Eduardo Montoya
Design Associate
Juice Fong
Financial Assistant
Suzanne Siu
Office Coordinators
Alex Ewing, Adam Kline, Efrat Kussell

Director of Advertising Sales
Erik Patton
Senior Advertising Associates
Patrick Donovan, Barbara Eghan, Fernanda Winthrop
Advertising Artwork Editor
Leif Holtzman
Cover Photo Research
Laura Wyss
President
Bradley J. Olson
General Manager
Robert B. Rombauer
Assistant General Manager
Anne E. Chisholm

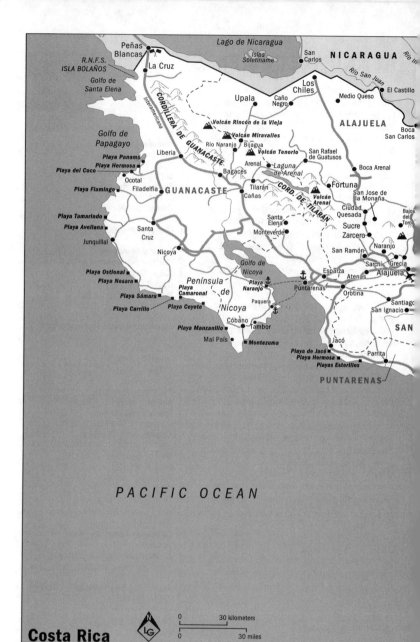

Costa Rica

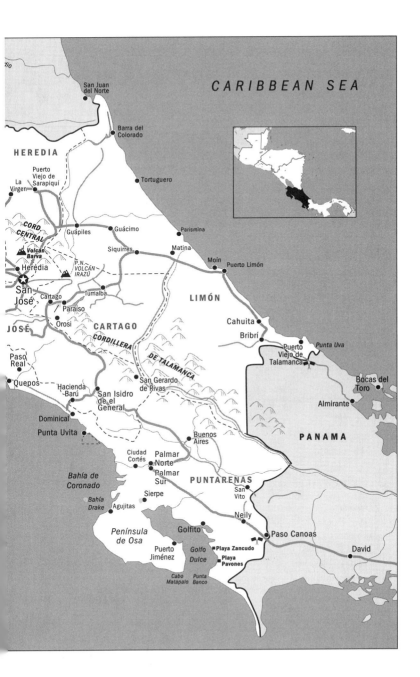

CARIBBEAN SEA

HEREDIA

San Juan del Norte

Barra del Colorado

Puerto Viejo de Sarapiquí

La Virgen

Tortuguero

CORD. CENTRAL

Guápiles

Guácimo

Parismina

Volcán Barva

Siquirres

Matina

P.N. VOLCÁN IRAZÚ

Heredia

Moín

Puerto Limón

San José

Cartago

LIMÓN

JOSÉ

Paraíso

Turrialba

Orosi

CARTAGO

Cahuita

Bribrí

CORDILLERA

Punta Uva

Paso Real

DE TALAMANCA

Puerto Viejo de Talamanca

Quepos

Hacienda Barú

San Gerardo de Rivas

San Isidro de el General

Bocas del Toro

Almirante

Dominical

PANAMA

Punta Uvita

Buenos Aires

Ciudad Cortés

Palmar Norte

Bahía de Coronado

Palmar Sur

PUNTARENAS

San Vito

Bahía Drake

Sierpe

Agujitas

Neily

Península de Osa

Golfito

Paso Canoas

David

Puerto Jiménez

Golfo Dulce

Playa Zancudo

Playa Pavones

Cabo Matapalo

Punta Banco

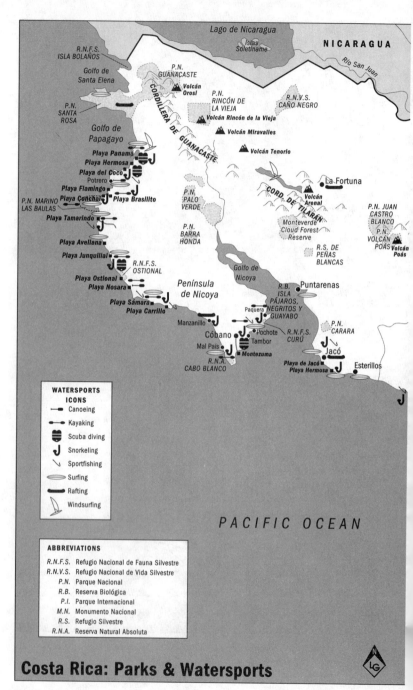

Costa Rica: Parks & Watersports

WATERSPORTS ICONS
- Canoeing
- Kayaking
- Scuba diving
- Snorkeling
- Sportfishing
- Surfing
- Rafting
- Windsurfing

ABBREVIATIONS

R.N.F.S. Refugio Nacional de Fauna Silvestre
R.N.V.S. Refugio Nacional de Vida Silvestre
P.N. Parque Nacional
R.B. Reserva Biológica
P.I. Parque Internacional
M.N. Monumento Nacional
R.S. Refugio Silvestre
R.N.A. Reserva Natural Absoluta

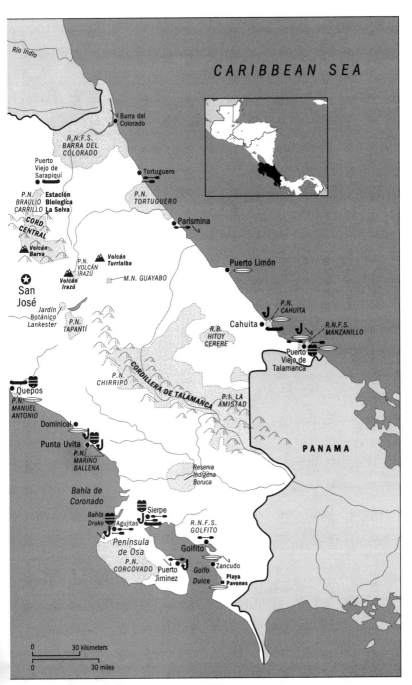

CARIBBEAN SEA

Río Indio

Barra del
Colorado

R.N.F.S.
BARRA DEL
COLORADO

Puerto
Viejo de
Sarapiquí

Tortuguero

P.N.
TORTUGUERO

P.N.
BRAULIO   **Estación
CARRILLO** **Biológica**
            La Selva

CORD
CENTRAL

Volcán
Barva   **Volcán**
          P.N.   **Turrialba**
          VOLCÁN
          IRAZÚ   Parismina
      Volcán
      Irazú   *M.N. GUAYABO*   Puerto Limón

San
José

*Jardín
Botánico
Lankester*   P.N.
                P.N.   CAHUITA
                TAPANTÍ   **J**
                                                            J
                                    R.B.   Cahuita   R.N.F.S.
                                    HITOY   MANZANILLO
                                    CERERE
                                                          Puerto
                                                          Viejo de
                                                          Talamanca
                    P.N.
                    CHIRRIPÓ   *CORDILLERA DE TALAMANCA*

Quepos   P.I. LA
                                          AMISTAD
P.N.
MANUEL
ANTONIO   PANAMA

Dominical

Punta Uvita   **J**

          P.N.
          MARIÑO
          BALLENA

                              *Reserva
                              Indígena
                              Boruca*

*Bahía de
Coronado*

Bahía   Sierpe
Drake **J**
      Agujitas
  J   R.N.F.S.
                    GOLFITO
*Península
de Osa*   Golfito
      P.N.
      CORCOVADO   **J**
              Puerto   Zancudo
              Jiminez *Golfo*
                       Dulce   **Playa
                                  Pavones**

0   30 kilometers

0   30 miles

XV

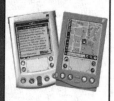

DISCOVER
COSTA RICA

From warm, turquoise waves, red, oozing magma, and dripping cloud forests, to awe-inspiring churches and bustling markets that come alive with the colors of tropical fruit and bright hand-painted oxcarts, Costa Rica, a haven of peace and stability in Latin America, offers endless opportunities to experience and explore. Although it covers only 0.03% of the world's territory, this tiny country managed to capture some of the earth's most unique sites and natural wonders—it holds 6% of its plant and animal life—and its rich culture and friendly people magically charm people into staying for years.

Costa Rica has no army and the government has made public health and education its priorities, endowing Costa Ricans, also know as *ticos*, with one of the best health care systems and highest literacy rates in Latin America. The *ticos* are proud of their country's strong democracy and outstanding social security system and will warmheartedly share their beautiful country with whomever cares to join them in relaxing, kicking back, and living la *pura vida*. Inexpensive and compact, yet splendid and diverse—Costa Rica welcomes a broad range of travelers, from bold adventurers, to budget travelers, or those simply seeking comfort and convenience.

WHEN TO GO

The most important climatic factor to consider when planning a trip to Costa Rica is the **rainy season,** or *invierno* (winter), which generally falls between May and November. The rest of the year is the **dry season,** or *verano* (summer). On the Pacific Coast and in the highlands, the seasons are quite distinct, while on the Caribbean Coast, some rain should be expected regardless of season. Temperature is determined by altitude rather than season; the highlands experience moderate highs and pleasantly cool nights while the coastal and jungle lowlands swelter. For a temperature chart, see the **Appendix** (p. 398) in the back of the book.

Dry season is "high season" for tourists—larger crowds and higher prices. The budget traveler may wish to consider a rainy season visit. Even then, the sun generally shines for much of the day, and most afternoon rainstorms are furious but fleeting. Dry season travel is key only for visitors in search of a dark tan or isolated areas where roads and trails can be washed out for weeks on end.

Many of the year's best parties happen during **Semana Santa,** the week-long Easter holiday, and from **Christmas** to the end of the year.

THINGS TO SEE AND DO

THE WILD LIFE

Waterfalls thundering over a lush valley. Cloudforests laced with climbing orchids, blanketed in mist. Fuming volcanoes. Miles of white-sand beach. Costa Rica may be small in terms of land mass, but its biodiversity is astounding.

Blessed with one of the most breathtaking and extensive park systems in the world, Costa Rica is a nature-lover's paradise. The diversity of the region's national parks caters to every whim—whether you seek to stroll along well-maintained trails to the soothing voice of an expert guide or machete and wade your way through thousands of kilometers of jungle, Costa Rica is sure to please.

Costa Rica established its national park system in 1970, and today approximately ¼ of the land has been protected in reserves, parks, and refuges. Thus far, tourism and the precious ecosystems have coexisted harmoniously, and ecotourism has been a huge boost to the Costa Rican economy. These natural wonders are just a hop away from the capital city of San José. Get the best of both worlds in **Puerto Viejo de Sarapiquí** (p. 180), by first cruising along the Sarapiquí river and if you're super hard core, later hiking through not one, but two, peaks in **Parque Nacional Braulio Carrillo** (p. 129). For some Caribbean flavor, head to **Parque Nacional Tortuguero** (p. 354), where appropriate to its namesake, you can witness one of the most important turtle spawning sites on the eastern coast. Cross the country to the Pacific Ocean, where the Nicoya Peninsula and northwestern Costa Rica are a heavenly mix of beach and brush. Boil in the mud pits at **Parque Nacional Rincón de la Vieja** (p. 168), spelunk through the mysterious caves of **Parque Nacional Barra Honda** (p. 229), and watch more turtle nesting at **Parque Nacional Santa Rosa** (p. 170). A bit farther inland are the toucans, sloths, and howler monkeys of the **Monteverde Cloud Forest Reserve** (p. 147), and if sparks of hot magma turn you on, check out **Volcán Arenal** (p. 190). Fly away to **Refugio Nacional de Vida Silvestre Caño Negro** (p. 197), near the border of Nicaragua, where an amazing array of migratory birds making this mangrove marsh their temporary home. Finally, southern Costa Rica and the border with Panama offer a more remote bout with mother nature. **Golfito** (p. 326) and **Bahía Drake** (p. 322) are clean and green, while **Parque Nacional Corcovado** (p. 339), the gem of the region a bit farther south, is a virtual garden of Eden.

SEX ON THE BEACH

OK, maybe not for everyone. But beach-hungry travelers will find that Costa Rica has everything else they might desire: snorkeling, diving, surfing, sunbathing. **Playa Tamarindo** (p. 218), on the Pacific, offers the perfect combination of gorgeous beach days and wild tropical nights, while **Jacó** (p. 272) is a party-going surfer's paradise. In **Manzanillo** (p. 380), the long, pristine stretch of Caribbean is hemmed in by rainforest and coral reef. For a change of pace, visit the isolated beaches of **Parque Nacional Santa Rosa** (p. 170), famous for surfing and turtle-watching, the algae-carpeted tide pools of **Playa Avellana** (p. 226), or the marine biological spectacle of the beaches of **Uvita** (p. 380). Surfing is at its best on the endless waves of **Pavones** (p. 331). Avid surfers and non-surfers alike flock to **Playa Hermosa** (p. 279)—not to be confused with the upscale beach of the same name on Península Nicoya—for a relaxed atmosphere, hot black sand, and exhilarating waves. An appealing blend of surfing and swimming exists at **Playa Bonita** (p. 348), 4km northwest of Limón. **Zancudo** (p. 333), a weekend vacation destination for many *tico* families, offers a taste of culture, as well as unparalleled sportfishing, 5km of black-sand beach, and swimming. Congo and white-faced monkeys scamper across the coconut palms and smooth sand of **Cahuita** (p. 366), where horseback riding tours are an option. No trip to Costa Rica is complete without following the beaches of **Montezuma** (p. 249) to magnificent waterfalls, wildlife, and waves.

LIVIN' LA VIDA (URBANA)

For the less nature savvy out there, fear not. Pumas and jaguars are not going to be jumping out of the skyscrapers of Costa Rica's modern, fast paced urban centers. These ferocious felines may be lacking in the *ciudades*, but *tico* warmth and culture definitely are not. Starting at the capital of **San José** (p. 85), you might have to dig around a little for treasures like the National Theater, the Jade and Gold Museums, and the National Center of Art and Culture. Much easier to find will be the Costa Rican college crowed, and the frequent parties in the suburbs of **Heredia** (p. 125), **Cartago** (p. 132), **Alajuela** (p. 107), and **San Pedro** (p. 95). Heredia is the site of an old fort and beautiful gardens, while Cartago is a center of religious worship, with La Basílica de Nuestra Señora de los Ángeles, where thousands of devout Costa Ricans take their annual pilgrimage. Past the butterfly farms and zoos of Alajuela is **Sarchí** (p. 114) with a craft center for your inner creative genius. Don't be fooled by the name of nearby **Centro Comercial El Pueblo** (p. 100), this diverse hot spot is more of a disco than a shopping center. The chic **Escazú** (p. 104) is another option for a classier night of bar hopping. While cities become more remote and green heading away from San José, **Liberia** (p. 163) and **Santa Cruz** (p. 214) are good bets for urban comfort in the northeast, and **San Isidro** (p. 300) in the south.

PEOPLE AND CULTURE

Interactions with Costa Rica's people are the highlight of many trips to the region. Come to the Central Valley on August 2nd and witness the most impressive annual pilgrimage that thousands of Catholic *ticos* make on *El Día de la Virgen* to **Cartago**'s (p. 132) Basílica de la Señora de los Ángeles, or visit San Joaquín de **Heredia** (p. 125) not far west from the center of town, for the *Semana Santa* processions. Go to **San José** (p. 85) at the end of the year and party through Christmas and the New Year with *ticos* that come from all over the country to enjoy the sound of live music, fireworks, bull riding and traditional fares in **Zapote**. **Santa Cruz** (p. 214), in the Nicoya Peninsula, is officially *La Ciudad Folklórica de Costa Rica*, steeped in history and traditions that come to life every January with indigenous and folk dances, bull riding, fares, and horse shows, all to the tune of folkloric bands. You can also enjoy the safe and relaxing pace of life at **San Ramón** (p. 120), "the city of presidents and poets," where some of Costa Rica's greatest political and literary figures were born. Traditional Catholic families, proud of the role San Ramón once played in the country's fight for democracy, education, culture, and the rights of the poor, will give you a warm welcome and show you around the town. Finally, go to **Puerto Viejo de Talamanca** (p. 373), 61km southeast of Puerto Limón, to experience the eclectic mix of Afro-Caribbean, Spanish, and indigenous cultures of Costa Rica's west coast. Puerto Viejo is also the most commercially venturous of the Caribbean towns, with colorful craft markets and handmade souvenir shops sprinkled throughout the city. In general, Costa Ricans are known for their warmth and hospitality. Travelers who stop to chat will find locals truly excited to show what their hometowns have to offer.

COME FOR A WEEK, STAY FOR A YEAR

It's not unheard of: unsuspecting travelers get tangled up in the web of *tico* allure, and, well, just can't leave. And who would want to? For many, Costa Rica has *it*: that one spot where the scene is just right—the people are friendly, scores of fascinating beaches and parks await exploration, and the food and culture make life a dream. Idyllic spots abound in Costa Rica, whether in a cloud forest, coral reef, kareoke bar, luxury resort, or Spanish school. Lounge in a hammock, or better yet a hot spring, in **Arenal** (p. 190). Learn why black-sand **Playa Hermosa** (p. 201) deserves its name, and then continue your beach bum life from sea to shining sea. Party like a rock star with the college kids in the suburbs of **San José** (p. 85). Major cities have national parks within walking distance, with national wonders like the phenomenal turtle spawning of **Parque Nacional Tortuguero** (p. 354). If you don't want to spend your days twiddling your thumbs in paradise, there are numerous volunteer, work, and study options in Alternatives to Tourism.

■ LET'S GO PICKS

BODACIOUS BEACHES: Where to begin? **Punta Uva**'s (p. 380) calm waters are perfect for swimming, and its palm- and mango tree-lined shores are perfect for relaxing. Enjoy some of the most spectacular waterfalls, wildlife, and waves at **Montezuma** (p. 249). For untouched tranquility, expansive waters, and verdant islands, head to breathtaking **Ocotal** (p. 233), and don't miss the warm, powdery white sands and pristine blue waters of **Sámara** (p. 234).

BEST DIVING AND SNORKELING: Visit **Cahuita** (p. 366) to enjoy the largest coral reef on Costa Rica's Caribbean coast. Uncover the secrets of **Playa del Coco**'s (p. 204) waters and its many lush islands. Also visit **Playa Hermosa** (p. 201), another of Costa Rica's best scuba beaches.

BEST SURFING: Dominical (p. 294) and **Playa Pavones** (p. 331), in southern Costa Rica are essential stops on true surfers' itineraries. **Playa Negra** (p. 224) and **Playa Tamarindo** (p. 218), with its endless silvery waters, are also celebrated by surfers of all skill levels.

BEST PLACES TO GET YO' FREAK ON: For a taste of *tico* revelry, hit the *Calle de la Amargura* in **San Pedro** (p. 101). Spend another wild night at **Centro Comercial El Pueblo** (p. 100) nearby, or in the classy suburb of **Escazú** (p. 104). Spice up your nightlife with the sun, waves, and parties of **Jacó** (p. 272), and add a pinch of Caribbean flavor at **Puerto Viejo de Talamanca** (p. 373).

BEST HOT SPRINGS: Soak in the Volcano's shadow at **Tabacón**, while you bear witness to **Volcán Arenal**'s (**p. 190**) flares of molten rock.

BEST NATIONAL PARKS: Boat through **Refugio Nacional de Vida Silvestre Caño Negro** (p. 197), an aquatic wonderland with labyrinths of mangroves and lots of wildlife. Explore, hike through lush wilderness, and stay overnight at the **Monteverde Cloud Forest Reserve** (p. 151), or mimic monkeys in **Parque Nacional Corcovado** (p. 339). Get a natural high on **Cerro Chirripó** (p. 305), Costa Rica's tallest peak.

BEST PLACES TO GET STEAMROLLED BY PIPING HOT MAGMA: Volcán Arenál (p. 190), froths lava nightly above the town of Fortuna, or hike through a boiling landscape at the foot of **Rincón de la Vieja** (p. 168).

BEST PLACE TO BUILD YOUR BATCAVE: At **Cavernas de Venado** (p. 191), spiders, bats, and rushing water are all that keeps you from an underground waterworld. **Parque Nacional Barra Honda**'s (p. 229) limestone caves form breathtaking stalactite and stalagmite forests.

BEST PLACES TO SHED YOUR SHELL: Don't miss **Parque Nacional Tortuguero** (p. 354) the most important nesting site for marine turtles in the entire Western Hemisphere. Also visit **Parque Nacional Marino Las Baulas** (p. 216), **Playa Hermosa** (p. 201), and **Playa Tamarindo** (p. 218) in the Nicoya Peninsula.

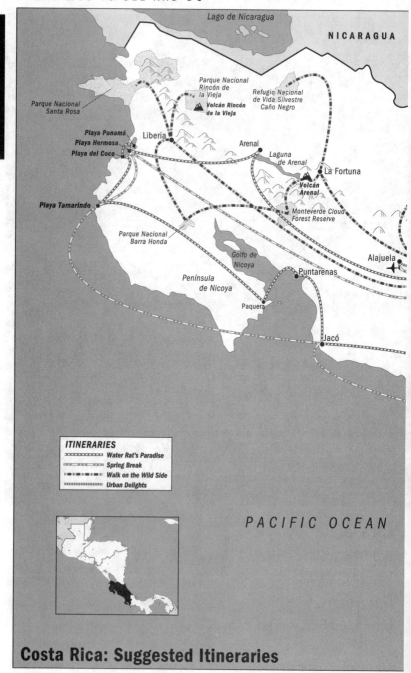

Costa Rica: Suggested Itineraries

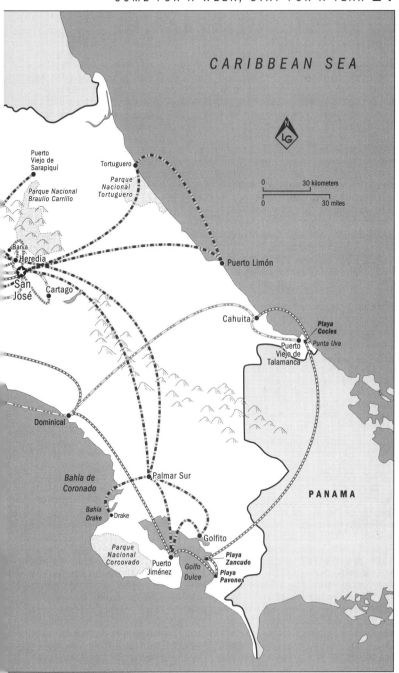

CARIBBEAN SEA

PANAMA

Puerto
Viejo de
Sarapiquí

Tortuguero

Parque
Nacional
Tortuguero

Parque Nacional
Braulio Carrillo

0   30 kilometers

0   30 miles

Barva

Heredia

San
José

Cartago

Puerto Limón

Cahuita

Playa
Cocles

Punta Uva

Puerto
Viejo de
Talamanca

Dominical

Bahía de
Coronado

Palmar Sur

Bahía
Drake   Drake

Parque
Nacional
Corcovado   Puerto
Jiménez

Golfo
Dulce

Golfito

Playa
Zancudo

Playa
Pavones

SUGGESTED ITINERARIES

DISCOVER

WATER RAT PARADISE Wait! Don't head for the coast just yet. From **San José** (**p. 85**), catch a bus and get ready to set sail at **Laguna Arenal** (**p. 156**). Windsurf the day away and spend the night loosening up in natural hot water springs while you bear witness to **Volcán Arenal's** (**p. 190**) flares of molten rock, and gather strength for your upcoming adventures. From Volcán Arenal, the long ride to the **Nicoya Peninsula** (**p. 201**) will be proved worthy by the warm sand and tame tides of **Playa Hermosa** (**p. 201**), one of Costa Rica's best scuba beaches. You need not go far from here to enjoy beautiful and deserted **Playa Panamá** (**p. 204**), just north of Playa Hermosa, where the serene waters make kayaking, water-skiing, windsurfing, snorkeling, and scuba diving a dream come true. Then go south along the coast, past Playa Hermosa to scuba dive, snorkel, and uncover the delightful secrets of **Playa del Coco's** (**p. 204**) waters or tour its many lush islands. Further south, cosmopolitan **Playa Tamarindo's** (**p. 218**) endless silvery waters are celebrated by surfers and treasured by snorkelers. To head back to the **Central Pacific** (**p. 262**), catch a ferry from **Paquera** (**p. 260**). From **Puntarenas** (**p. 266**), head straight for **Jacó** (**p. 272**) for surfing in dangerous waters and nights taken over by young crowds, parties, and music. Move to the south of the country and arrive at surfer's paradise, **Dominical** (**p. 294**), another nightlife hotspot. Next, head for **Golfo Dulce** (**p. 321**), where thriving marine wildlife makes for ideal snorkeling. You can take a rest at **Puerto Jiménez** (**p. 335**) and enjoy the dazzling views of Costa Rica's untamed nature. When you're ready, cross the gulf. Bronzed bodies and board shorts will signal your arrival at **Playa Pavones** (**p. 331**), an essential stop on any true surfer's itinerary. North of Pavones, the peaceful **Playa Zancudo** (**p. 333**) has World Record sports fishing. You now have a long journey ahead of you. **Punta Uva** (**p. 380**), all the way over on the Atlantic coast, makes for perfect body surfing. Finally, before heading back to San José, make sure to visit **Cahuita** (**p. 366**), where howler monkeys and turquoise waves call snorkelers and scuba divers to enjoy the largest coral reef on Costa Rica's west coast.

WALK ON THE WILD SIDE Head out from **San José** to **Liberia** (**p. 163**), in the **Nicoya Peninsula** (**p. 201**). Lots of smiles will greet you at this dusty *sabanero* region and the lively town with colonial architecture is great for bouncing off to some very exotic destinations. Nearby **Parque Nacional Rincón de la Vieja** (**p. 168**) has an active volcano, sulfuric lagoons, boiling mud pits, thermal waters, and is celebrated by bird watchers. Also visit **Parque Nacional Santa Rosa** (**p. 170**), famous for turtle watching. Further down the Peninsula, **Parque Nacional Barra Honda** (**p. 229**) is a paradise of wildlife with breathtaking limestone caves that form stalactite and stalagmite forests. From Barra Honda, take the ferry across the **Golfo de Nicoya** and head inland toward the **Monteverde Cloud Forest Reserve** (**p. 147**), where you can explore, hike through the lush wilderness, and stay at the refuge overnight. After that, head to **Volcán Arenal** (**p. 190**) and stay for a day or two. Hike by day and, by night, loosen up in thermal waters with dazzling views of oozing magma and the flaming rocks that fly from the volcano's crater. In the morning, go to **La Fortuna** (**p. 187**), a nice little town west of Arenal, from which you can explore the Fortuna Waterfalls and the stunning mineral formations of Las Cavernas de Venado. Guided boat tours can take you to **Refugio Nacional de Vida Silvestre Caño Negro,** an aquatic wonderland with labyrinths of mangroves, rivers, and lakes; a haven for over 250 species of birds, 30 species of mammals, and rare fish species, like the prehistoric gaspar. Head back to **Heredia** (**p. 125**), in the central valley. From here, make a day trip to **Puerto Viejo de Sarapiquí** (p.

180), in the **Northern Lowlands** (p. 176), to cruise through the wildlife of the Sarapiquí River and walk the lush trails of **Parque Nacional Braulio Carrillo** (p. 129). Back in Heredia, you can drive to **Palmar Norte** (p. 310) or fly there from **San José.** From Palmar Sur you have two options—or you can do both trips if you can fit them in your itinerary. You can head to **Bahía Drake** (p. 322) in the **Osa Península** (p. 321), the perfect place for the nature-loving adventurer, where monkeys drip off mango trees and waves crash into jungle coasts. The other option is to head south to **Golfito** (p. 326), the free-trade zone, take a ferry across the **Golfo Dulce** to **Puerto Jiménez** (p. 335), and visit **Parque Nacional Corcovado** (p. 339), referred to as a Garden of Eden by many and as "the most biologically intense place on earth" by National Geographic. Head back to **Palmar Sur** and drive or fly back to **San José.** From San José, fly to **Tortuguero** (p. 354), a small but increasingly popular sea-side village accessible only by boat or plane. Be sure to explore the nearby **Parque Nacional Tortuguero** (p. 360) for hiking, boating, and turtle spying. Leaving, catch a boat to **Puerto Limón** (p. 348), then head back to **San José.**

VIVA SPRINGBREAK! Party, Party, Party! Twist this itinerary around and around; turn it inside out. No matter what you do, you'll find the fountain of youth at all of these vibrant hotspots. **SAVOR THE CITY.** By day, take advantage of your time in the Central Valley to relax and visit the small villages and towns around **San José** (p. 85), such as **Heredia** (p. 125), **Cartago** (p. 132), and **Alajuela** (p. 107). By night, the tropical music in **San José** will keep you hopping. For a taste of *tico* revelry, hit the *Calle de la Amargura* (Street of Bitterness) in **San Pedro** (p. 95). From pumping raves and Spanish rock to karaokes and more laid-back locales, this bar-stacked side road is the heart of the Costa Rican college scene. Spend another wild night at **Centro Comercial El Pueblo** (p. 100) nearby. More of a disco town than shopping center, you'll find ticos, gringos, and the most random

mix of crowds, old and young, at the bars, restaurants, and discos that flood it. For more upscale and classy outings, head out to **Escazú** (p. 104). The mix of fast foods and finer dining, casual bars and chic discos, draw young crowds from the whole metropolitan area.

BRONZED BOOTY AND BEACHES Hit the **Nicoya Peninsula** (p. 201). For sun worshippers, few beaches match **Playa Hermosa**'s (p. 201) warm, soothing sands, and its tame tides and clear waters make it great for water sports. Try kayaking, waterskiing, snorkeling, and windsurfing. You can also visit **Playa del Coco** (p. 204) and **Playa Panamá** (p. 204) nearby. Further south, cosmopolitan **Playa Tamarindo's** (p. 218) endless silvery waters are prized by surfers. Scenery, sunbathing, snorkeling, shopping and the high season's thumping nightlife make it a great place to visit. Now you're ready to head out to the **Central Pacific** (p. 262). Catch a ferry across the **Golfo de Nicoya** and head straight to **Jacó** (p. 272) for surfing in dangerous waters. Wild young crowds make this beach an ongoing party where the music never stops thumping and the beer never stops flowing. Heading further south along the coast, you can join **Dominical's** (p. 294) young surfers at a beach where relaxed, quiet evenings develop into pounding dance parties. If you want to experience the **Caribbean** (p. 342), you have a long journey ahead of you, but it's more than worth it. Follow the howler monkeys to **Cahuita** (p. 366), on the Atlantic shores. Scuba dive or snorkel your way through the turquoise waters of the largest coral reef on Costa Rica's west coast and enjoy the hot nightlife and parties of **Puerto Viejo de Talamanca** (p. 373) before you return to **San José.**

URBAN DELIGHTS (THE BEST OF THE CITIES) Don't dart straight for the beaches and jungle-enshrouded isolation. Explore the **Central Valley** (p. 107) for a week and experience Costa Rica's true magic—its rich culture and warm-hearted people. Upon your arrival at the airport in **Alajuela** (p. 107), stay in this city for a day or two. Visit **Sarchí** (p. 114), the nation's biggest crafts center, famous for its brilliantly decorated, multi-colored ox-carts. Alajuela is also home to the **Butterfly Farm** (p. 112), Latin America's oldest butterfly exporter, and **Zoo Ave** (p. 112), where you will be fascinated by exotic species in their natural habitats. **Heredia** (p. 125), your next destination, is only a short 15-20min. ride from Alajuela and will only take a day to visit. Right in the town's *parque central,* is the **Fortín de Heredia,** an old fort which used to guard a prison in the 1800s. You will also see the **Jardines de la Inmaculada,** some lovely church gardens dedicated to the Virgin Mary. A few blocks away is the **Universidad Nacional,** where you can meet lots of young people and get a taste of the Costa Rican college scene. Head north from Heredia and visit the little town of **Barva** (p. 130), with its typical colonial architecture and adobe houses, and the **Museo de Arte y Cultura Popular** in **Santa Lucía.** You can now head for **San José** (p. 85), Costa Rica's capital. It might not be the most attractive city, but once you've found the treasures that hide amidst its crowded streets, you'll want to stay for 2 or 3 days. Enjoy cultural shows or a concert by the Sinfónica

Nacional under high-ceiling frescoes and among sculpted gold banisters at the **Teatro Nacional** (p. 98). For a look at Costa Rica's history, don't miss the **Museo Nacional's** (p. 98) collections of pre-Columbian art and exhibits on the country's colonial life, archaeology, and geology. You will also be fascinated by the **Museo de Jade** (p. 98), which holds the world's largest collection of American jade, and captivated by the sparkling pre-Columbian gold exhibits at the **Museo de Oro** (p. 98). Finally check out the calendar of artistic and cultural activities at the **Centro Nacional de Arte y Cultura** (p. 99) for exhibits, dance performances, and other Costa Rican arts. You're now ready to go to **Cartago** (p. 132), home of the most famous place of worship in Costa Rica-**La Basílica de Nuestra Señora de los Ángeles.** Every year, on August 2, El Día de la Virgen, thousands of ticos make a pilgrimage to this church to visit the Patron Saint. Finally, don't miss **Las Ruinas de la Parroquía,** the ruins of the first church of Cartago, built in 1575 and destroyed by various earthquakes.

ESSENTIALS

FACTS FOR THE TRAVELER

ENTRANCE REQUIRMENTS

Passport (p. 12). Required of all visitors. Passports must be valid for at least 6 months after date of entry.

Visa (p. 12). Not required for citizens of Australia, Canada, Ireland, New Zealand, South Africa, UK, US, or members of the European Union.

Tourist Card. Available upon entry for US$4. Valid for 90 days; renewable at the Dirección de Migración in San José (p. 91).

Onward/Return ticket. Required of all visitors.

Inoculations and Medications (p. 20). None required.

Work Permit (p. 12). A valid **Employment Authorization Document** (EAD) is required of all foreigners planning to work in Costa Rica.

Driving Permit (p. 45). Valid foreign license and photo ID required. Vehicle permits are issued at border crossings into Costa Rica.

Airport Departure Tax. US$17. Cash only.

EMBASSIES & CONSULATES

COSTA RICAN CONSULAR SERVICES ABROAD

Australia Embassy: Piso 11, 30 Clarence St, N.S.W. 2000 Sydney (☎612 9261 1177; fax 9261 2953). Open M-F 10am-5pm.

Canada Embassy: 325 Dalhousie St., Ste. 407, Ottawa, Ontario, Canada K1N 7G2 (☎613-562-2855; fax: 562-2582). Open M-F 9am-5pm.

South Africa Embassy: P.O. Box 68140, Bryanston 2021, South Africa (☎27 11 705 3434; fax 11 705 1222). Open M-Su 8am-6pm.

UK Embassy: Flat 1, 14 Lancaster Gate, London W2 3LH (☎171 706 8844; fax 171 706 8655)

US Embassy: 2114 "S" St., NW, Washington, D.C. 20008 (☎202-234-2945; fax 202-265-4795; www.costarica-embassy.org). Open M-F 9am-5pm. **Consulate:** 2112 S St. NW, Washington, D.C. 20008 (☎202-328-6628; fax 202-265-4795). Open M-F 10am-1pm.

CONSULAR SERVICES IN COSTA RICA

Australia, Ireland, and New Zealand don't have embassies in Costa Rica.

Canada Embassy: (mailing address: Apdo. 351-1007, Centro Colón, San José), Oficentro Ejecutivo, Edificio #5—detrás de la Contraloría, Sabana Sur, San José (☎296 4149; fax 296 4270; canadacr@racsa.co.cr; www.sanjose.gc.ca). Open M-Th 8am-4:30pm, F 8am-1:30pm.

UK Embassy: (mailing address: Apdo. 815-1007, San José), Centro Colón (11th flr.), San José, Costa Rica (☎258 2025; fax 233 9938; britemb@racsa.co.cr).

US Embassy: (mailing address: Apdo 920-1200, San José), Calle 120, Av. Central, Pavas, San José, Costa Rica (☎220 3939; after hours 220 3127; fax 220 2305; www.usembassy.or.cr). Open M-F 8am-4:30pm. Call for detailed hours of services.

TOURIST OFFICES

Instituto Costarricense de Turismo (ICT), (mailing address: Apdo. 777-1000, San José), Av. 4, Calles 5/7, 11th flr., San José (☎223 1733; fax 223 5452; info@tourism-costarica.com or mailus@tourism-costarica.com; www.tourism-costarica.com). **Branch location:** Av. Central/2, Calle 5, Plaza de la Cultura. The national tourist bureau. Free maps and helpful hints. Publishes a comprehensive listing of tour companies and lodgings. Information in the **US:** (☎800-343-6332). Open M-F 8am-8pm EST.

Costa Rican National Chamber of Tourism (CANATUR), (www.tourism.co.cr or www.canatur.org). Extensive tourism information.

DOCUMENTS & FORMALITIES

PASSPORTS

REQUIREMENTS. Citizens of Australia, Canada, Ireland, New Zealand, South Africa, the UK, and the US need valid passports to enter Costa Rica and to re-enter their home countries. Costa Rica does not allow entrance if the holder's passport expires in under six months; returning home with an expired passport is illegal and may result in a fine.

NEW PASSPORTS. Citizens of Australia, Canada, Ireland, New Zealand, the UK, and the United States can apply for a passport at any post office, passport office, or court of law. Citizens of South Africa can apply for a passport at any office of Foreign Affairs. Any new passport or renewal application must be filed well in advance of the departure date, although most passport offices offer rush services for a very steep fee.

PASSPORT MAINTENANCE. Be sure to photocopy the pages of your passport with your photo and entry stamp as well as your visas, traveler's check serial numbers, and any other important documents. Carry one set of copies in a safe place, apart from the originals, and leave another set at home. Consulates also recommend that you carry an expired passport or an official copy of your birth certificate in a part of your bag separate from other documents.

If you lose your passport, immediately notify the local police and the nearest embassy or consulate of your home government. To expedite its replacement, you will need to know all information previously recorded and show ID and proof of citizenship. In some cases, a replacement may take weeks to process, and it may be valid only for a limited time. Any visas stamped in your old passport will be irretrievably lost. In an emergency, ask for immediate temporary traveling papers that will permit you to re-enter your home country.

VISAS & WORK PERMITS

VISAS. As of August 2002, citizens of Australia, Canada, Ireland, New Zealand, South Africa, UK, or US do not need visas to enter Costa Rica. For detailed information on visa regulations (see **Alternatives to Tourism,** p. 74).

Double-check on entrance requirements at the Costa Rican nearest embassy or consulate (see **Embassies & Consulates Abroad,** p. 11) for up-to-date info before departure. US citizens can also consult the website at www.pueblo.gsa.gov/cic_text/travel/foreign/foreignentryreqs.html.

WORK PERMITS. Admission as a visitor does not include the right to work, which is authorized only by a work permit. Entering Costa Rica to study requires a special visa. For more information, see **Alternatives to Tourism,** p. 74.

IDENTIFICATION

When you travel, always carry two or more forms of identification on your person, including at least one photo ID. Make sure your passport is always with you, as police sometimes stop buses and demand proof that you are a legal tourist. Many establishments may require several IDs in order to cash traveler's checks; banks require only a passport. When carrying important documents on your person, keep them out of sight and reach, under your clothes (in a money belt or pouch) if possible. Never carry all your forms of ID together; split them up in case of theft or loss. An **international health card,** a record of all your immunizations available from your doctor, is another good thing to take along.

TEACHER, STUDENT & YOUTH IDENTIFICATION. The **International Student Identity Card (ISIC),** t he most widely accepted form of student ID, provides discounts on sights, accommodations, food, and transport; access to 24hr. emergency helpline (in North America call ☎877-370-ISIC; elsewhere call US collect ☎715-345-0505); and insurance benefits for US cardholders (see **Insurance,** p. 24). The ISIC is preferable to an institution-specific card (such as a university ID) because it is more likely to be recognized and honored abroad. Applicants must be degree-seeking students of a secondary or post-secondary school and must be of at least 12 years of age. Because of the proliferation of fake ISICs, some services (particularly airlines) require additional proof of student identity, such as a school ID or a letter attesting to your student status, signed by your registrar.

The **International Teacher Identity Card (ITIC)** offers teachers the same insurance coverage as well as similar but limited discounts. For travelers who are 25 years old or under but are not students, the **International Youth Travel Card** (**IYTC;** formerly the **GO 25** Card) also offers many of the same benefits as the ISIC.

Each of these identity cards costs US$22 or equivalent. ISIC and ITIC cards are valid for roughly one and a half academic years; IYTC cards are valid for one year from the date of issue. Many student travel agencies (see p. 36) issue the cards, including STA Travel in Australia and New Zealand; Travel CUTS in Canada; usit in the Republic of Ireland and Northern Ireland; SASTS in South Africa; Campus Travel and STA Travel in the UK; and Council Travel and STA Travel in the US. For a listing of issuing agencies or for more information, contact the **International Student Travel Confederation (ISTC),** Herengracht 479, 1017 BS Amsterdam, Netherlands (☎+31 20 421 28 00; fax 421 28 10; istcinfo@istc.org; www.istc.org).

CUSTOMS

Upon entering Costa Rica, you must declare certain items from abroad and pay a duty on the value of those articles if they exceed the allowance established by Costa Rica's customs service. Check with the nearest Costa Rican embassy for details. Note that goods and gifts purchased at **duty-free** shops abroad are not exempt from duty or sales tax; "duty-free" merely means that you need not pay a tax in the country of purchase. Upon returning home, you must similarly declare all articles acquired abroad and pay a duty on the value of articles in excess of your home country's allowance. In order to expedite your return, make a list of any valuables brought from home and register them with customs before traveling abroad, and be sure to keep receipts for all goods acquired abroad. Visitors leaving Costa Rica will have to pay the official airport tax/exit fee of US$17. Credit cards and traveler's checks are not accepted.

MONEY

CURRENCY & EXCHANGE

The currency chart below is based on August 2002 exchange rates between local currency and Australian dollars (AUS$), Canadian dollars (CDN$), Irish pounds (IR£), New Zealand dollars (NZ$), South African Rand (ZAR), British pounds (UK£), US dollars (US$), and European Union euros (EUR€). Check the currency converter on financial websites such as www.bloomberg.com or www.xe.com, or any major newspaper for the latest exchange rates.

AUS$1 = ¢204		¢100 = AUS$0.52
CDN$1 = ¢242		¢100 = CDN$0.44
IR£1 = ¢464		¢100 = IR£0.23
NZ$1 = ¢176		¢100 = NZ$0.61
ZAR1 = ¢35		¢100 = ZAR3.09
US$1 = ¢377		¢100 = US$0.28
UK£1 = ¢574		¢100 = UK£0.19
EUR€1 = ¢366		¢100 = EUR€0.29

(COLONES (¢))

As a general rule, it's cheaper to convert money in Costa Rica than at home. While currency exchange will probably be available in your arrival airport, it's wise to bring enough foreign currency for the first 24-72 hours of your trip.

When changing money abroad, try to go only to banks or *casas de cambio* that have at most a 5% margin between their buy and sell prices. Since you lose money with every transaction, **convert large sums** (unless the currency is depreciating rapidly), **but no more than you'll need.**

If you use traveler's checks or bills, carry some in small denominations (the equivalent of US$50 or less) for times when you are forced to exchange money at disadvantageous rates, but bring a range of denominations since charges may be levied per check cashed. Store your money in a variety of forms; ideally, at any given time you will be carrying some cash, some traveler's checks, and an ATM and/or credit card. All travelers should also consider carrying some US dollars, as they are the most widely accepted foreign currency.

TRAVELER'S CHECKS

Traveler's checks are one of the safest and least troublesome means of carrying funds. **American Express** and **Visa** are the most widely recognized brands. Many banks and agencies sell them for a small commission. Check issuers provide refunds if the checks are lost or stolen, and many provide additional services, such as toll-free refund hotlines abroad, emergency message services, and stolen credit card assistance. Ask for the toll-free refund hotline number and the location of refund centers when purchasing checks, and always carry emergency cash. In order to collect a **refund for lost or stolen checks,** keep the checks' receipts separately from the checks themselves and store them in a safe place. Record check numbers when you cash them, leave a list of check numbers with someone at home, and ask for a list of refund centers when you buy your checks.

Most banks in Costa Rica change traveler's checks but require your passport, proof of purchase, and often another picture ID with matching signatures and names. If all else fails, ask politely but firmly for the *gerente* (manager), who can often help you out. Try several banks, as different branches of the same bank can be very in policy. Only in the most touristed areas will local businesses and shops accept traveler's checks. Order smaller denominations (US$20-100). Never countersign your checks until you actually cash them, and always bring your passport and proof of purchase with you when you do so.

American Express: Checks available with commission at select banks and all AmEx offices. US residents can also purchase checks by phone (☎888-887-8986) or online (www.aexp.com). *Cheques for Two* can be signed by either of 2 people traveling together. For purchase locations or more information contact AmEx's service centers: In the US and Canada ☎800-221-7282; in the UK ☎0800 521 313; in Australia ☎800 25 19 02; in New Zealand ☎0800 441 068; elsewhere US collect ☎+1 801-964-6665; in Costa Rica ☎220 0400 or 204 7400.

Visa: Checks available (generally with commission) at banks worldwide. For the location of the nearest office, call Visa's service centers: in the US ☎800-227-6811; in the UK ☎0800 89 50 78; elsewhere UK collect ☎+44 020 7937 8091.

Travelex/Thomas Cook: In the US and Canada call ☎800-287-7362; in the UK call ☎0800 62 21 01; elsewhere call UK collect ☎+44 1733 31 89 50.

CREDIT, DEBIT, AND ATM CARDS

Where they are accepted, credit cards often offer superior exchange rates—up to 5% better than the retail rate used by banks and other currency exchange establishments. Credit cards may also offer services such as insurance or emergency help and are sometimes required to reserve hotel rooms or rental cars. That said, many budget hotels and restaurants in Costa Rica won't accept cards, and it's best not to count on them except in some of the larger cities.

Credit cards may be used for **cash advances,** which allow you to withdraw money from associated banks and ATMs throughout Costa Rica. For this purpose and in general, **Visa** is the most useful card to have, followed by **MasterCard**; **American Express** cards work at AmEx offices, major airports, and some ATMS.

If you do plan on advancing money on your card, you'll need to get a **personal identification number (PIN)** from your credit card company and be prepared to pay a hefty transaction fee. To receive cash advances you must activate your account and establish your PIN. To do so contact your credit card company. If you're traveling from the US or Canada, memorize your PIN code in numeral form; machines often don't have letters on their keys. If your PIN is longer than four digits, ask your bank whether the first four digits will work, or whether you need a new number. Check with your bank before you leave to see if your card will be of use in Costa Rica. You may also need to show your passport.

The use of **ATM cards** is fairly widespread in Costa Rica, but not all are connected to international networks. Depending on the system that your home bank uses, you can most likely access your personal bank account from abroad. ATMs get the same wholesale exchange rate as credit cards, but there is often a limit on the amount of money you can withdraw per day (around US$500), and computer networks sometimes fail. There is typically also a surcharge of US$1-5 per withdrawal.

Debit cards are as convenient as credit cards but have a more immediate impact on your funds. A debit card can be used wherever its associated credit card company (usually Mastercard or Visa) is accepted, yet the money is withdrawn directly from the holder's checking account. Debit cards often also function as ATM cards and can be used to withdraw cash from associated banks and ATMs throughout Costa Rica. Ask your local bank about obtaining one. Both ATM and Debit cards also require PINs.

The two major international money networks are **Cirrus** (to locate ATMs call ☎800-424-7787 in the US, or visit www.mastercard.com) and **Visa/PLUS** (to locate ATMs call ☎800-843-7587 in the US go to www.visa.com).

GETTING MONEY FROM HOME

If you run out of money while traveling, the easiest and cheapest solution is to have someone back home make a deposit to your credit card or cash (ATM) card. Failing that, consider one of the following options.

WIRING MONEY. It is possible to arrange a **bank money transfer,** which means asking a bank back home to wire money to a bank in Costa Rica. This is the cheapest way to transfer cash, but it's also the slowest, usually taking several days or more. Note that some banks may only release your funds in local currency, potentially sticking you with a poor exchange rate; inquire about this in advance. Money transfer services like **Western Union** are faster and more convenient than bank transfers—but also much pricier. Western Union has many locations worldwide. To find one, visit www.westernunion.com. In Costa Rica call ☎ 777-7777. In the US ☎ 800-325-6000, in Canada ☎ 800-235-0000, in the UK ☎ 0800 83 38 33, in Australia ☎ 800 501 500, in New Zealand ☎ 800 27 0000, in South Africa ☎ 0860 100031. If a town has a Western Union, it will be listed in that section's Practical Information. Money transfer services are also available at **American Express** (p. 15).

US STATE DEPARTMENT (US CITIZENS ONLY). In dire emergencies only, the US State Department will forward money within hours to the nearest consular office, which will then disburse it according to instructions for a US$15 fee. If you wish to use this service, you must contact the Overseas Citizens Service division of the US State Department (☎ 202-647-5225; nights, Su, and holidays ☎ 202-647-4000).

COSTS

The cost of your trip will vary considerably depending on where you go, how you travel, and where you stay. If you spend a lot of time in heavily touristed areas—or travel during peak tourist seasons like Christmas and Easter—you'll wind up spending more. The rainy season (May-Nov.) typically brings the best deals. Transportation in very remote areas can also be expensive. Your most significant expense will probably be your round-trip (return) **airfare** to Costa Rica (see **Getting to Costa Rica: By Plane,** p. 36). Before you go, spend some time calculating a reasonable per-day **budget** that will meet your needs.

STAYING ON A BUDGET. To give you a general idea, a bare-bones day in Costa Rica (camping or sleeping in hostels/guesthouses, buying food at supermarkets) would cost about US$20 (¢7600). A slightly more comfortable day (sleeping in hostels/guesthouses and the occasional budget hotel, eating one meal a day at a restaurant, going out at night) would run upwards of US$30 (¢11300). For a luxurious day, the sky's the limit. Also, don't forget to factor in emergency reserve funds (at least US$200) when planning how much money you'll need.

TIPS FOR SAVING MONEY. Some simple ways of traveling cheaply taking advantage of opportunities for free entertainment, splitting accommodation and food costs with other trustworthy fellow travelers, buying food in supermarkets rather than eating out, and doing your laundry in the sink (unless you're explicitly prohibited from doing so). With that said, don't go overboard with your budget obsession. Though staying within your budget is important, don't do so at the expense of your health or a great travel experience.

TIPPING & BARGAINING

Tipping and especially bargaining in the developing world is quite a different practice from what you are probably accustomed to; there are many unspoken rules to which tourists must adhere. In tourist and upscale restaurants, a 10% tip is common.

In some establishments, a 17% sales and service tax is already included. In smaller restaurants frequented by locals, tipping is rare. Tour guides generally appreciate something extra; small change is appropriate for porters in hotels and restaurants. Taxi drivers are not tipped. In general, particularly good service may deserve an extra tip of 5% or so.

At outdoor markets, handicraft markets, and some handicraft shops, bargaining is expected and essential. On the other hand, prices at supermarkets and most indoor stores are not negotiable. Bargaining for hotel rooms is often a good idea, but only at cheaper establishments, and more in the low season (or if the hotel simply isn't full.) For more on bargaining, see **The Art of the Deal,** p. 17.

TAXES

There is a 13% **sales tax** on all purchases. In addition, restaurants charge a 10% **service charge** on all bills. There is also a 3.39% **tourism tax** in addition to the sales tax on hotel rooms. Usually these charges will be included in the prices cited, but ask beforehand to be sure.

E S S E N T I A L S

THE ART OF THE DEAL

Bargaining in Central America is a given: no price is set in stone, and vendors and drivers will automatically quote you a price that is several times too high; it's up to you to get them down to a reasonable rate. Successful merchants enjoy the haggling (just remember that the shopkeepers do this for a living and have the benefit of experience). With the following tips and some finesse, you might be able to impress even the most hardened hawkers:

1. Bargaining needn't be a fierce struggle laced with barbs. Quite the opposite: good-natured wrangling with a cheerful smiling face may prove your biggest weapon.

2. Use your poker face. The less your face betrays your interest in the item the better. If you touch an item to inspect it, the vendor will be sure to "encourage" you to name a price or make a purchase. Coming back again and again to admire a trinket is a good way of ensuring that you pay a ridiculously high price. Never get too enthusiastic about the object in question; point out flaws in workmanship and design. Be cool.

3. Know when to bargain. In most cases, it's quite clear when it's appropriate to bargain. Most private transportation fares and things for sale in outdoor markets are all fair game. Don't bargain on prepared or pre-packaged foods on the street or in restaurants. In some stores, signs will indicate whether *precios fijos* (fixed prices) prevail. When in doubt, ask tactfully, *"Es su mejor precio? (Is that your lowest price?)"* or whether discounts are given.

4. Never underestimate the power of peer pressure. Try having a friend discourage you from your purchase—if you seem to be reluctant, the merchant will want to drop the price to interest you again.

5. Know when to turn away. Feel free to refuse any vendor or driver who bargains rudely, and don't hesitate to move on to another vendor if one will not be reasonable about the final price he offers. However, to start bargaining without an intention to buy is a major faux pas. Agreeing on a price and declining it is also poor form. Turn away with a smile and *"gracias"* upon hearing a ridiculous price—the price may plummet.

6. Start low. Never feel guilty offering what seems to be a ridiculously low price. Your starting price should be no more than one-third to one-half the asking price.

7. Give in. In the final blows of the deal when you are fighting over the last five *colones,* give in. The vendors are trying to make a living and the small difference is probably just tiny loss for you that can go a long way for them.

SAFETY AND SECURITY

PERSONAL SAFETY

EXPLORING. You might not be able to look like a local, but looking like you know what you're doing makes a world of difference. Dress conservatively (see **Packing,** p. 25). Familiarize yourself with your surroundings before setting out, and carry yourself with confidence; if you must check a map on the street, duck into a shop. Traveling with a buddy is always recommended, particularly at night or in more remote areas. However, If you are traveling alone, be sure someone at home knows your itinerary; never admit that you're unaccompanied. Find out beforehand which areas are unsafe; tourist offices, consulates and other travelers are good sources. Try to avoid nighttime travel, and be wary of streets in the big cities at night. Be aware of red light districts and ares that are not tourist-friendly.

SELF DEFENSE. There is no sure-fire way to avoid all the threatening situations you might encounter when you travel, but a good self-defense course will give you concrete ways to react to unwanted advances. **Impact, Prepare, and Model Mugging** can refer you to local self-defense courses in the US (☎800-345-5425). Visit the website at www.impactsafety.org for a list of nearby chapters. Workshops (2-3hr.) start at US$50; full courses run US$350-500.

DRIVING. If you are using a **car,** learn local driving signals and wear a seatbelt. Most cars are standard, so make sure you are comfortable driving a stick shift. Children under 40 lb. should ride only in a specially-designed carseat, available for a small fee from most car rental agencies. Study route maps before you hit the road, and if you plan on spending a lot of time on the road, you may want to bring spare parts. If your car breaks down, wait for the police to assist you. For long drives in desolate areas, invest in a cellular phone and a roadside assistance program. Be sure to park your vehicle in a garage or well-traveled area, and use a steering wheel locking device in larger cities. **Sleeping in your car** is one of the most dangerous (and often illegal) ways to get your rest. For info **hitchhiking,** see p. 45.

TERRORISM. Terrorism is not of special concern in Costa Rica. The country is firmly democratic and has been politically stable for decades. For information on Costa Rica's current events, see **Costa Rica Today,** p. 61. The box on travel advisories (p. 18) list offices to contact and web pages to visit to get the most updated list of your home country's government's advisories about travel.

TRAVEL ADVISORIES. The following government offices provide travel information and advisories by telephone, fax, or the web.

Australian Department of Foreign Affairs and Trade: ☎ 13 0055 5135; faxback service 02 6261 1299; www.dfat.gov.au.

Canadian Department of Foreign Affairs and International Trade (DFAIT): In Canada and the US call ☎800-267-6788, elsewhere call ☎+1 613-944-6788; www.dfait-maeci.gc.ca. Call for their free booklet, *Bon Voyage...But.*

New Zealand Ministry of Foreign Affairs: ☎04 494 8500; fax 494 8506; www.mft.govt.nz/trav.html.

United Kingdom Foreign and Commonwealth Office: ☎020 7008 0232; fax 7008 0155; www.fco.gov.uk.

US Department of State: ☎202-647-5225, faxback service 202-647-3000; http://travel.state.gov. For *A Safe Trip Abroad,* call ☎202-512-1800.

PROTECTING YOUR VALUABLES. There are a few steps you can take to minimize the financial risk associated with traveling. First, **bring as little with you as possible.** Second, buy a few combination **padlocks** to secure your belongings either in your pack or in a hostel. Third, **carry as little cash as possible.** Keep your traveler's checks and ATM/credit cards in a **money belt**—not a "fanny pack"—along with your passport and ID cards. Fourth, **keep a small cash reserve separate from your primary stash.** This should be about US$50 sewn into or stored in the depths of your pack, along with your traveler's check numbers and important photocopies.

CON ARTISTS & PICKPOCKETS. In large cities **con artists** often work in groups, and children are among the most effective. Beware of certain classics: sob stories that require money, rolls of bills "found" on the street, mustard spilled (or saliva spit) onto your shoulder to distract you while they snatch your bag. **Don't ever let your passport and bags out of your sight.** Beware of **pickpockets** in city crowds, especially on public transportation in markets, and on the beach at night. Also, be alert in public telephone booths: If you must say your calling card number, do so very quietly; if you punch it in, make sure no one can look over your shoulder.

ACCOMMODATIONS & TRANSPORTATION. Never leave your belongings unattended; crime occurs in even the most demure-looking hostel or hotel. In hotels, double-check all locks. It may be a good idea to bring along a **padlock** to use in lieu of the one some budget places give you. Don't leave valuables in your room.

Travelers using public transportation are usually requested to store their larger pieces of luggage on top of or below the bus. Though this a considered to be a relatively safe practice, luggage locks might help protect the contents of your outer pockets. Consider carrying your backpack in front of you and keeping it in your lap, where you can see it. When traveling with others, sleep in alternate shifts. Buses can get quite crowded, particularly in rural areas. What Westerners might consider to be a two-person seat may be used to squeeze four. If traveling by **car,** don't leave valuables (such as radios or luggage) in it while you are away.

DRUGS & ALCOHOL

Penalties for possession, use, and trafficking in illegal drugs in Costa Rica are strict, and convicted offenders can expect lenghty jail sentences and fines. People may try to sell you everything from marijuana to cocaine (*cocaína*); use your head, and don't buy it. Your home embassy will be of minimal assistance should you get into trouble. Remember that you are subject to the laws of the country in which you travel, not those of your home country; it is your responsibility to familiarize yourself with these laws before leaving. If you carry **prescription drugs** while you travel, have a copy of the prescriptions themselves and a note from your doctor. Avoid public drunkenness; in certain areas it is against the law, and can also jeopardize your safety and earn the disdain of locals. Costa Rica also has **dry laws,** prohibiting the sale of liquor on the day prior to, of, and following elections.

ROAD RULES. Roads and highways throughout Costa Rica can be narrow, hilly, winding, and not always in the greatest state of repair. Government regulations and their enforcement concerning the maintenance of public transport vehicles vary from country to country. **Traveling by night on a bus should be avoided at all costs.** If traveling on a bus that is too fast for comfort, it is considered to be well within acceptable social boundaries to politely ask the driver, "*Más despacio, por favor*" (Could you please drive more slowly).

HEALTH

Common sense is the simplest prescription for good health while you travel. Drink lots of fluids to prevent dehydration and constipation, and wear sturdy, broken-in shoes and clean socks.

BEFORE YOU GO

In your **passport,** write the names of any people you wish to be contacted in case of a medical emergency, and list any allergies or medical conditions. Matching a prescription to a foreign equivalent is not always easy, safe, or possible, so carry up-to-date, legible prescriptions or a statement from your doctor stating the medication's trade name, manufacturer, chemical name, and dosage. While traveling, be sure to keep all medication with you in your carry-on luggage. For tips on packing a basic **first-aid kit** and other health essentials, see p. 26.

The names in Costa Rica for common drugs are: *aspirina* (aspirin), *paracetamol* (acetaminophen), *penicilina* (penicillin), and *antihistimínico* (antihistamine/allergy medicine). Brand names such as Tylenol, Advil, and Pepto Bismol are also well known.

IMMUNIZATIONS AND PRECAUTIONS

Travelers over two years old should make sure that the following vaccines are up to date: MMR (for measles, mumps, and rubella); DTaP or Td (for diptheria, tetanus, and pertussis); OPV (for polio); HbCV (for haemophilus influenza B); and HBV (for hepatitis B). In addition, adults traveling to Costa Rica on trips longer than four weeks should also consider the following immunizations: Hepatitis A vaccine and/or immune globulin (IG), an additional dose of Polio vaccine, and typhoid and cholera vaccines, particularly if traveling in remote areas. For recommendations on immunizations and prophylaxis, consult the CDC (see below) in the US or the equivalent in your home country and check with doctors for guidance.

USEFUL ORGANIZATIONS & PUBLICATIONS

The US **Centers for Disease Control and Prevention (CDC;** ☎877-FYI-TRIP; toll-free fax 888-232-3299; www.cdc.gov/travel) maintains an international hotline and an informative website. The CDC's comprehensive booklet *Health Information for International Travel,* an annual rundown of disease, immunization, and general health advice, is free online or US$25 via the Public Health Foundation (☎877-252-1200). Consult the appropriate government agency of your home country for consular information on health, entry requirements, and other issues for various countries (see the listings in the box on **Travel Advisories,** p. 18). For quick information on health and other travel warnings, call the **Overseas Citizens Services** (☎202-647-5225; after hours 202-647-4000), or contact a passport agency, embassy, or consulate abroad.

INOCULATION RECOMMENDATIONS

There are a number of inoculations recommended for travel in Costa Rica:
Hepatitis A or immune globulin (IG).
Hepatitis B, particularly if you expect to be exposed to blood (e.g. health-care workers), have sexual contact, stay longer than 6 months, or undergo medical treatment. Hepatitis B vaccine is now recommended for all infants and for children ages 11–12 years who did not receive the series as infants.
Rabies, particularly for travel in rural areas or for people expecting to come into contact with animals.
Typhoid, particularly for travel in more rural areas.
As needed, booster doses for **tetanus-diphtheria** and **measles.**

US citizens can send a self-addressed, stamped envelope to the Overseas Citizens Services, Bureau of Consular Affairs, #4811, US Department of State, Washington, D.C. 20520. For information on medical evacuation services and travel insurance firms, see the US government's website at http://travel.state.gov/medical.html or the **British Foreign and Commonwealth Office** (www.fco.gov.uk). The **Pan American Health Organization,** a sub-group of the World Health Organization, 525 23rd St., NW, Washington, D.C. 20037, USA, provides public health information specific to Costa Rica (☎ 202-974-3000; fax 974-3663; www.paho.org).

For detailed information on travel health, including a country-by-country overview of diseases, try the **International Travel Health Guide,** by Stuart Rose, MD (US$19.95; www.travmed.com). For general health info, contact the **American Red Cross** (☎ 800-564-1234; www.redcross.org).

ESSENTIALS

MEDICAL ASSISTANCE ON THE ROAD

Costa Rica has one of the best health care systems in Latin America. For major medical problems, San José has well-equipped facilities and more English speaking doctors (p. 92). Private clinics often offer higher quality care than public social security hospitals. In emergency situations, social security hospitals will treat people, including international travelers, free of charge, but the quality of assistance can vary. Medical services in rural areas tend to be basic. It's generally a good idea to be prepared to treat minor health concerns yourself.

If you are concerned about obtaining medical assistance while traveling, you may wish to employ special support services. The *MedPass* from **GlobalCare, Inc.,** 2001 Westside Pkwy., #120, Alpharetta, GA 30004, USA (☎ 800-860-1111; fax 770-677-0455; www.globalems.com), provides 24hr. international medical assistance, support, and medical evacuation resources. The **International Association for Medical Assistance to Travelers (IAMAT;** US ☎ 716-754-4883, Canada ☎ 416-652-0137, New Zealand ☎ 03 352 20 53; www.iamat.org) has free membership, lists English-speaking doctors worldwide, and offers detailed info on immunization requirements and sanitation. If your regular **insurance** policy does not cover travel abroad, you may wish to purchase additional coverage (see p. 24).

Those with medical conditions (such as diabetes, allergies, epilepsy, heart conditions) may want to obtain a **Medic Alert** membership (first year US$35, annually thereafter US$20), which includes a stainless steel ID tag and a 24hr. collect call number. Contact the Medic Alert Foundation, 2323 Colorado Ave, Turlock, CA 95382, USA (☎ 888-633-4298; outside US ☎ 209-668-3333; www.medicalert.org).

ONCE IN COSTA RICA

ENVIRONMENTAL HAZARDS

Heat exhaustion and dehydration: Heat exhaustion can lead to fatigue, headaches, and wooziness. Avoid it by drinking plenty of fluids, eating salty foods (e.g. crackers), and avoiding dehydrating beverages (e.g. alcohol and caffeinated beverages). Continuous heat stress can eventually lead to heatstroke, characterized by a rising temperature, severe headache, and cessation of sweating. Victims should be cooled off with wet towels and taken to a doctor.

Sunburn: Bring a high SPF sunscreen (at least SPF 30) with you, and apply it liberally and often to avoid burns and risk of skin cancer. Protect your eyes with good sunglasses, since ultraviolet rays can damage the retina of the eye after too much exposure. If you get sunburned, drink lots of fluids and apply an aloe-based lotion or vinegar.

Hypothermia and frostbite: A rapid drop in body temperature is the clearest sign of overexposure to cold. Victims may also shiver, feel exhausted, exhibit slurred speech or poor coordination, hallucinate, and/or suffer amnesia. **Do not let hypothermia victims fall asleep,**

ESSENTIALS

or their body temperature will continue to drop and they may die. To avoid hypothermia, keep dry, wear layers, and stay out of the wind. In wet weather, wool and synthetics such as fleece retain heat; cotton will make you colder.

High altitude: Keep in mind the added difficulty of less oxygen when exerting yourself. Note that alcohol is more potent and UV rays are stronger at high elevations.

INSECT-BORNE DISEASES

Many diseases are transmitted by insects—mainly mosquitoes, fleas, ticks, and lice. Be aware of insects in wet or forested areas, especially while hiking and camping; wear long pants and long sleeves, tuck your pants into your socks, and buy a mosquito net. Use insect repellents such as DEET and soak or spray your gear with permethrin (licensed in the US for use on clothing). Travelers have also reported success with ingesting garlic and/or vitamin B12 to prevent insect bites.

Malaria: Transmitted by *Anopheles* mosquitoes that bite at night. The incubation period varies from 6-8 days to as long as months. Early symptoms include fever, chills, aches, and fatigue followed by high fever and sweating, sometimes with vomiting and diarrhea. See a doctor for any flu-like sickness that occurs after travel in a risk area. To reduce the risk of contracting malaria, use mosquito repellent and fans, particularly in the evenings and when visiting forested areas, and take oral prophylactics, like **mefloquine** (sold under the name Lariam) **doxycycline,** or **chloroquine** (ask your doctor for a prescription). Be aware that these drugs can have very serious side effects, including slowed heart rate and nightmares. Malaria in Costa Rica occurs year-round in rural areas below elevations of 500m. The main **areas of risk** are the provinces of Alajuela, Limón, Guanacaste, and Heredia. Note that these are the names of the provinces, not the cities of the same name—cities are generally malaria-free.

Dengue fever: An "urban viral infection" transmitted by *Aedes* mosquitoes, which bite during the day rather than at night. Dengue has flu-like symptoms and is often indicated by a rash 3-4 days after the onset of fever. Symptoms for the first 2-4 days include chills, high fever, headaches, swollen lymph nodes, muscle aches, and, in some instances, a pink rash on the face. If you experience these symptoms, see a doctor, drink plenty of liquids, and take fever-reducing medication such as acetaminophen (Tylenol). **Never take aspirin to treat dengue fever.**

Other insect-borne diseases: Filariasis is a roundworm infestation transmitted by mosquitoes. Infection causes enlargement of extremities. There is no vaccine. **Leishmaniasis** is a parasite transmitted by sand flies. Common symptoms are fever, weakness, and swelling of the spleen. There is a treatment, but no vaccine. **Chagas' disease (American trypanomiasis)** is another relatively common parasite transmitted by the cone nose and kissing bug, which infest mud, adobe, and thatch. Its symptoms are fever, heart disease, and later on an enlarged intestine. There is no vaccine and limited treatment.

FOOD- & WATER-BORNE DISEASES

Prevention is the best cure: be sure that your food is properly cooked and the water you drink is clean. Peel fruits and veggies and avoid tap water (including ice cubes and anything washed in tap water, like salad). Watch out for food from markets or street vendors that may have been cooked in unhygienic conditions. Other culprits are raw shellfish, unpasteurized milk, and sauces containing raw eggs. Buy bottled water or purify your own by bringing it to a rolling boil or treating it with **iodine tablets;** note however that some parasites such as *giardia* have mechanisms that resist iodine treatment, so boiling is more reliable. Always wash your hands before eating or bring a quick-drying purifying liquid hand cleaner.

Traveler's diarrhea: Results from drinking untreated water or eating uncooked foods. Symptoms include nausea, bloating, and urgency. Try easily digestible, high energy foods keep your strength up and lots of juice and soda. Do not drink milk. Over-the-counter anti-diarrheals (e.g. Imodium) may counteract the problems. The most danger-ous side effect is dehydration; drink 8 oz. of water with ½ tsp. of sugar or honey and a pinch of salt, try uncaffeinated soft drinks, or eat salted crackers. If you develop a fever or your symptoms don't go away after 4-5 days, consult a doctor. Consult a doctor immediately for treatment of diarrhea in children.

Dysentery: Results from a serious intestinal infection caused by certain bacteria. The most common type is bacillary dysentery, also called *shigellosis.* Symptoms include bloody diarrhea (sometimes mixed with mucus), fever, and abdominal pain and tender-ness. Bacillary dysentery generally only lasts a week but is highly contagious. Amoebic dysentery, which develops more slowly, is a more serious disease and may cause long-term damage if left untreated. A stool test can determine which kind you have; seek medical help immediately. Dysentery can be treated with the drugs norfloxacin or cipro-floxacin (commonly known as Cipro). If you are traveling in high-risk (especially rural) regions, consider obtaining a prescription before you leave home.

Cholera: An intestinal disease caused by a bacteria found in contaminated food. The dis-ease has recently reached epidemic stages in Central America. Symptoms include diar-rhea, dehydration, vomiting, and muscle cramps. See a doctor immediately; if left untreated, it may be deadly. Antibiotics are available, but the most important treatment is rehydration. Consider getting a (50% effective) vaccine if you have stomach problems (e.g. ulcers) or will be living where the water is not reliable.

Hepatitis A: A viral infection of the liver acquired primarily through contaminated water. Symptoms include fatigue, fever, loss of appetite, nausea, dark urine, jaundice, vomit-ing, aches and pains, and light stools. The risk is highest in rural areas and the country-side, but it is also present in urban areas. Ask your doctor about the vaccine (Havrix or Vaqta) or an injection of immune globulin (IG; formerly called gamma globulin).

Parasites: Microbes, tapeworms, etc. that hide in unsafe water and food. **Giardiasis,** for example, is acquired by drinking untreated water from streams or lakes. Symptoms include swollen glands or lymph nodes, fever, rashes or itchiness, and digestive prob-lems. Boil water, wear shoes, and eat only cooked food.

Schistosomiasis: Also known as bilharzia; a parasitic disease caused when the larvae of flatworm penetrate unbroken skin. Symptoms include an itchy localized rash followed in 4-6 weeks by fever, fatigue, painful urination, diarrhea, loss of appetite, and night sweats. To avoid it, do not swim in fresh water. If exposed to untreated water, rub the area vigorously with a towel and apply rubbing alcohol.

Typhoid fever: Caused by the salmonella bacteria; common in villages and rural areas in Central America. While mostly transmitted through contaminated food and water, it may be acquired by contact with another person. Early symptoms include fever, headaches, fatigue, loss of appetite, constipation, and sometimes a rash on the abdomen or chest. Antibiotics can treat typhoid, but a vaccination (70-90% effective) is recommended.

OTHER INFECTIOUS DISEASES

Rabies: Transmitted through the saliva of infected animals; fatal if untreated. By the time symptoms (thirst and muscle spasms) appear, the disease is in its terminal stage. If you are bitten, wash the wound thoroughly, seek immediate medical care, and try to have the animal located. A rabies vaccine, which consists of 3 shots given over a 21-day period, is only semi-effective.

ESSENTIALS

Hepatitis B: A viral infection of the liver transmitted via bodily fluids or needle-sharing. Symptoms may not surface until years after infection. A 3-shot vaccination sequence is recommended for health-care workers, sexually-active travelers, and anyone planning to seek medical treatment abroad; it must begin 6 months before traveling.

Hepatitis C: Like Hepatitis B, but the mode of transmission differs. IV drug users, those with occupational exposure to blood, hemodialysis patients, and recipients of blood transfusions are at the highest risk, but the disease can also be spread through sexual contact or sharing items like razors and toothbrushes that may have traces of blood.

AIDS, HIV, & STDS

For detailed information on **Acquired Immune Deficiency Syndrome (AIDS)** in Central America, call the **US Centers for Disease Control's** 24hr. hotline at ☎ 800-342-2437, or contact the **Joint United Nations Programme on HIV/AIDS (UNAIDS),** 20, ave. Appia, CH-1211 Geneva 27, Switzerland (☎ +41 22 791 3666; fax 22 791 4187). Costa Rica does not screen tourists who stay up to 90 days for AIDS. Travelers planning extended visits for work or study may or may not be tested for AIDS. Contact the consulate of Costa Rica for information.

Sexually transmitted diseases (STDs) such as gonorrhea, chlamydia, genital warts, syphilis, and herpes are easier to catch than HIV and can be just as deadly. **Hepatitis B** and **C** can also be transmitted sexually (see p. 24). Though condoms may protect you from some STDs, oral or even tactile contact can lead to transmission. If you think you may have contracted an STD, see a doctor immediately.

WOMEN'S HEALTH

Women traveling in unsanitary conditions are vulnerable to **urinary tract** and **bladder infections,** common and very uncomfortable bacterial conditions that cause a burning sensation and painful (sometimes frequent) urination. Over-the-counter medicines can sometimes alleviate symptoms, but if they persist, see a doctor.

Vaginal yeast infections may flare up in hot and humid climates. Wearing loosely fitting trousers or a skirt and cotton underwear will help, as will over-the-counter remedies like Monostat or Gynelotrimin. Bring supplies from home if you are prone to infection, as they may be difficult to find on the road.

INSURANCE

Travel insurance generally covers four basic areas: medical/health problems, property loss, trip cancellation/interruption, and emergency evacuation. Although your regular insurance policies may well extend to travel-related accidents, you may consider purchasing travel insurance if the cost of potential trip cancellation/interruption or emergency medical evacuation is greater than you can absorb. Prices for travel insurance purchased separately generally run about US$50 per week for full coverage, while trip cancellation/interruption may be purchased separately at a rate of about US$5.50 per US$100 of coverage.

Medical Insurance (especially university policies) often covers costs incurred abroad; check with your provider. **US Medicare** does not cover foreign travel. **Canadians** are protected by their home province's health insurance plan for up to 90 days after leaving the country; check with the provincial Ministry of Health or Health Plan Headquarters for details. **Homeowners' insurance** (or your family's coverage) often covers theft during travel and loss of travel documents (passport, plane ticket, etc.) up to US$500.

ISIC and **ITIC** (see p. 13) provide basic insurance benefits, including US$100 per day of in-hospital sickness for up to 60 days, US$3000 of accident-related medical reimbursement, and US$25,000 for emergency medical transport.

Cardholders have access to a toll-free 24hr. helpline (run by the insurance provider **TravelGuard**) for medical, legal, and financial emergencies overseas (US and Canada ☎ 877-370-4742, elsewhere call US collect ☎ 1 715-345-0505). **American Express** (US ☎ 800-528-4800) grants most cardholders automatic car rental insurance (collision and theft, but not liability) and ground travel accident coverage of US$100,000 on flight purchases made with the card. Other credit card companies may also offer insurance benefits; call for details.

INSURANCE PROVIDERS. Council and **STA** (see p. 38) offer a range of plans that can supplement your basic coverage. Other private insurance providers in the US and Canada include: **Access America** (☎ 800-284-8300); **Berkeley Group/Carefree Travel Insurance** (☎ 800-323-3149; www.berkely.com); **Globalcare Travel Insurance** (☎ 800-821-2488; www.globalcare-cocco.com); and **Travel Assistance International** (☎ 800-821-2828; www.europ-assistance.com). Providers in the **UK** include **Columbus Direct** (☎ 020 7375 0011). In **Australia**, try **AFTA** (☎ 02 9375 4955).

ESSENTIALS

PACKING

Lay out only what you absolutely need, then take half the clothes and twice the money. If you plan to do a lot of hiking, see **Camping & the Outdoors**, p. 28.

LUGGAGE. If you plan to cover most of your itinerary by foot, a sturdy **frame backpack** is unbeatable. (For the basics on buying a pack, see p. 30.) Remember that packs will be left on top of buses and otherwise exposed to the elements, so bring along a waterproof pack cover or sturdy trash bags. Toting a **suitcase** or **trunk** is fine if you plan to live in one or two cities and explore from there, but a very bad idea if you're going to be moving around a lot. Many travelers leave their bags in storage at hostels as they make their way down the coast. In addition to your main piece of luggage, a **daypack** (a small backpack or courier bag) is a must.

CLOTHING. No matter when you're traveling, it's always a good idea to bring a good **rain jacket** (Gore-Tex® is both waterproof and breathable), sturdy shoes or **hiking boots,** and **thick socks. Flip-flop** or waterproof sandals are must-haves for grubby hostel showers. Hiking sands such as Tevas or Reefs are great for water sports. You may also want to add one outfit beyond the jeans and T-shirt uniform and maybe a nicer pair of shoes if you have the room. If you plan to visit any religious or cultural sites, remember that you'll need something besides tank tops and shorts to be respectful. A wide-brimmed **hat** keeps the sun at bay. Costa Rica's highlands get quite cold at night—be sure to take a sweater or medium weight **fleece.** Costa Ricans generally value a neat and clean appearance and appreciate visitors who do likewise. This is particularly useful when dealing with businesses and officials. Not all local women dress conservatively but the female visitor is advised to do so. For information on local dress, see **Customs & Etiquette**, p. 66.

CONVERTERS & ADAPTERS. The standard current is 110V AC—the same as the US, Canada, and Mexico. The outlets take two-pronged US plugs. Visit a hardware store for an **adapter** (which changes the shape of the plug) and a **converter** (which changes the voltage). Don't make the mistake of bringing only an adapter.

TOILETRIES. Toothbrushes, towels, cold-water soap, shampoo, talcum powder (to keep feet dry), deodorant, razors, tampons, and condoms are often available but are very expensive and may be difficult to find, so bring extras along. **Contact lenses,** are also expensive and difficult to find, so bring enough extra pairs and solution for your entire trip. Also bring your glasses and a copy of your prescription in case you need emergency replacements. If you use heat-disinfection, switch temporarily to a chemical disinfection system (check first to make sure it's safe with your brand of lenses), or buy a converter to 110V. Sunscreen and insect repellent are essential. Many travelers also suggest taking pre-moistened anti-bacterial wipes.

FIRST-AID KIT. For a basic first-aid kit, pack: bandages, pain reliever, antibiotic cream, a thermometer, a Swiss Army knife, tweezers, moleskin, decongestant, motion-sickness remedy, diarrhea or upset-stomach medication (Pepto Bismol or Imodium), an antihistamine, sunscreen, insect repellent, burn ointment, and a syringe for emergencies (get an explanatory letter from your doctor).

FILM. Film and developing in Costa Rica are easy to find but expensive to buy, so consider bringing along enough film for your entire trip and developing it at home. Less serious photographers may want to bring **disposable or waterproof cameras** rather than an expensive permanent one. Despite disclaimers, airport security X-rays *can* fog film, so buy a lead-lined pouch at a camera store or ask security to hand-inspect it. Always pack film in your carry-on luggage, since higher-intensity X-rays are used on checked luggage. Find out before whether it is appropriate to take pictures, especially in religious sites and indigenous reserves and villages.

OTHER USEFUL ITEMS. For safety purposes, you should bring a **money belt** and small **padlock**. Basic **outdoors equipment** (plastic water bottle, compass, waterproof matches, pocketknife, sunglasses, sunscreen, hat) may also prove useful. **Quick repairs** of torn garments can be done on the road with a needle and thread; also consider bringing electrical tape for patching tears. If you want to do laundry by hand, bring detergent, a small rubber ball to stop up the sink, and string for a makeshift clothes line. **Other things** you're liable to forget: a **mosquito net,** an umbrella, sealable **plastic bags** (for damp clothes, soap, food, shampoo, and other spillables), an **alarm clock,** safety pins, rubber bands, a **flashlight** in case of power outages, earplugs, garbage bags, and a small **calculator.**

IMPORTANT DOCUMENTS. Don't forget your passport, traveler's checks, ATM and/or credit cards, and adequate ID (see p. 13). Also check that you have any of the following that might apply to you: a hosteling membership card (see p. 13), international driver's license (see p. 13), and travel insurance forms.

ACCOMMODATIONS

HOTELS AND HOSPEDAJES

WHAT TO EXPECT. Rooms in Costa Rica can cost as little as US$5 or so per night, though US$10-15 may be a better general figure. Accommodations go by many different names. *Hospedaje, hotel, pensión, posada,* and *casa de huéspedes* are all common terms; the differences between them are by no means consistent. Standards vary greatly, but generally speaking, for a basic room expect nothing more than a bed, a light bulb, and perhaps a fan; other amenities are a bonus. The very cheapest places may not provide towel, soap, or toilet paper. For a slight price jump you can get a room with private bath, and for a modest amount above that you might find a place with some character and charm.

AMENITIES TO LOOK FOR. In sea level areas, try to get a room with a fan (*ventilador* or *abanico*) or a window with a nice coastal breeze. In more upscale hotels, air conditioning may be available. Also look for screens and mosquito netting. At higher elevations, a hot-water shower and extra blankets will be most welcome. Make safety an extra priority in urban areas; you can often get more comfort and security for only a couple extra dollars. In isolated, non-touristed areas, accommodations will usually be basic but friendly. If you plan on staying well off the beaten path, your own mosquito net, toilet paper, towel, and flashlight are a must.

BATHROOMS. *Let's Go* quotes room prices with and without private bath. Note that "with bath" means a sink, toilet, and basic shower in the room, not an actual bathtub. Shared baths are typically the same sort of thing, just off the hall. Hot shower is a relative term in Costa Rica: "hot" can often be tepid at best. Quite frequently, the heating device will be electric coils in the shower head. Such devices work best at low water pressure. The electrical cord should be an easy reminder that water, electricity, and people do not mix well, so be sure to avoid touching the shower head or other metal objects during a shower. Toilets in Central America often do not have toilet seats. Moreover, the sewer systems generally cannot handle everything thrown in them. As a rule, do not flush used toilet paper, tampons, or other waste products. Instead, use the receptacle (usually) provided. Toilet paper always seems to be missing when you most need it; it is wise to carry some on you wherever you go.

GETTING A GOOD PRICE. Hotels in Costa Rica charge a hotel tax (16.39% cumulative sales and tourism tax); double-check if this has been included in the rate. Rooms shared with other travelers usually cost less per person. Often a hotel will first show you the most expensive room. Ask if there's anything cheaper (*¿Hay algo más barato, por favor?*). You can sometimes bargain for a lower rate at hotels, particularly during the low season, on days when there are vacanies, or if you're staying for several days.

HOSTELS

HOSTELLING INTERNATIONAL

Joining the youth hostel association in your own country (listed below) automatically grants you membership privileges in **Hostelling International (HI),** a federation of national hosteling associations. Roughly two dozen HI hostels are scattered throughout Costa Rica. HI's umbrella organization's web page (www.iyhf.org), which lists the web addresses and phone numbers of all national associations, can be a great place to begin researching hostelling in a specific region. HI hostels in Costa Rica can be found at www.hicr.org. Other comprehensive hostelling websites include www.hostels.com and www.hostelworld.com.

Most student travel agencies (see p. 36) sell HI cards, as well as the national hosteling organizations below. Prices listed below are valid for **one-year memberships**.

Australian Youth Hostels Association (AYHA), Level 3, 10 Mallett St., Camperdown NSW 2050 (☎02 9565 1699; fax 9565 1325; www.yha.org.au). AUS$52, under 18 AUS$16.

Hostelling International-Canada (HI-C), 400-205 Catherine St., Ottawa, ON K2P 1C3 (☎800-663-5777 or 613-237-7884; fax 237-7868; info@hostellingintl.ca; www.hostellingintl.ca). CDN$35, under 18 free.

An Óige (Irish Youth Hostel Association), 61 Mountjoy St., Dublin 7 (☎830 4555; fax 830 5808; anoige@iol.ie; www.irelandyha.org). IR£10, under 18 IR£4.

Youth Hostels Association of New Zealand (YHANZ), P.O. Box 436, 193 Cashel St., 3rd Floor Union House, Christchurch 1 (☎03 379 9970; fax 365 4476; info@yha.org.nz; www.yha.org.nz). NZ$40, under 17 free.

Hostels Association of South Africa, 3rd fl. 73 St. George's St. Mall, P.O. Box 4402, Cape Town 8000 (☎021 424 2511; fax 424 4119; info@hisa.org.za; www.hisa.org.za). SAR45.

ESSENTIALS

Scottish Youth Hostels Association (SYHA), 7 Glebe Crescent, Stirling FK8 2JA (☎01786 89 14 00; fax 89 13 33; www.syha.org.uk). UK£6.

Youth Hostels Association (England and Wales) Ltd., Trevelyan House, 8 St. Stephen's Hill, St. Albans, Hertfordshire AL1 2DY, UK (☎0870 870 8808; fax 01727 84 41 26; www.yha.org.uk). UK£12.50, under 18 UK£6.25, families UK£25.

Hostelling International Northern Ireland (HINI), 22-32 Donegall Rd., Belfast BT12 5JN, Northern Ireland (☎02890 31 54 35; fax 43 96 99; info@hini.org.uk; www.hini.org.uk). UK£10, under 18 UK£6.

Hostelling International-American Youth Hostels (HI-AYH), 733 15th St. NW, #840, Washington, D.C. 20005 (☎202-783-6161; fax 783-6171; hiayhserv@hiayh.org; www.hiayh.org). US$25, under 18 free.

CAMPING & THE OUTDOORS

Costa Rica's extensive national park system provides good hiking and camping opportunities, but not all parks offer camping facilities. Many parks have short looping trails that can be easily completed as daytrips. To experience some of the most impressive parks to their fullest, consider camping there. There are restrictions on how many people can be in a given park at the same time, and camping outside of official camping areas is usually not permitted. In some cases it is required to be accompanied by a guide; inquire at the local MINAE offices in advance to get the most out of your trip. Outside of national parks and a few private campsites, camping on beaches or on people's property (usually for a small fee) is possible, but always check with locals beforehand. Some cheaper, hostels allow travelers to camp outside and use their indoor facilities; always agree upon a price before setting up camp. Camping should be avoided in populated areas; hotels are almost as cheap and much safer.

An excellent general resource for travelers planning on camping or spending time in the outdoors is the **Great Outdoor Recreation Pages** (www.gorp.com).

USEFUL PUBLICATIONS & RESOURCES

A variety of publishing companies offer hiking guidebooks to meet the educational needs of novice or expert. For information about camping, hiking, and biking, write or call the publishers listed below to receive a free catalog.

Sierra Club Books, 85 Second St., 2nd fl., San Francisco, CA 94105, USA (☎415-977-5500; www.sierraclub.org/books). Publishes general resource books on hiking, camping, and women traveling in the outdoors as well as books on hiking specifically in Central America, including Costa Rica.

The Mountaineers Books, 1001 SW Klickitat Way, #201, Seattle, WA 98134, USA (☎800-553-4453 or 206-223-6303; fax 223-6306; www.mountaineersbooks.org). Over 400 titles on hiking, biking, mountaineering, natural history, and conservation.

WILDERNESS SAFETY

THE GREAT OUTDOORS. Stay warm, stay dry, and stay hydrated. The vast majority of life-threatening wilderness situations can be avoided by following this simple advice. Prepare yourself for an emergency by always packing raingear, a hat and mittens, a first-aid kit, a reflector, a whistle, high-energy food, and extra water for any hike. In high elevations dress in wool or warm layers of synthetic materials designed for the outdoors; never rely on cotton for warmth, as it is useless when wet. For more information, consult *How to Stay Alive in the Woods,* by Bradford Angier (Macmillan Press, US$8).

Check **weather forecasts** and pay attention to the skies when hiking, since weather patterns can change suddenly. Always let someone, either a friend, your hostel, a park ranger, or a local hiking organization, know when and where you are hiking. Do not attempt a hike beyond your ability—you may be endangering your life. See **Health**, p. 20, for information about basic medical concerns.

SNAKES. Snakes usually don't attack people unprovoked, and only a small number of Costa Rica's snakes is venomous. Overall, you will be very unlikely to have any close encounters. The best way to prevent snake bites is to hike with a guide, wear hiking boots and long pants, stay on trails, and keep your eyes open. Don't grab any branches without looking for snakes before, and keep your tent and bags closed in the wilderness.

The most dangerous snake, the **fer-de-lance,** or common lancehead, is named for its triangular and pointed head, and is an aggressive and highly venomous pit-viper that lives in the forests and agricultural lands of Costa Rica. They are up to 2m long and are well camouflaged with a gray, brown, olive or green coloration, with a large triangle pattern whose tips meet along the top of their backs.

Venomous **coral snakes** have a red, black, and yellow coloration. If the red and yellow of the coloration touch, then you are indeed looking at a coral snake. On average, they are 60cm long and live in a wide variety of habitats. Fortunately, they are rather shy, so you are not very likely to encounter them.

If you are bitten by a snake, don't panic. Try to figure out what the snake that bit you looks like, but to avoid more bites keep your distance and don't try to kill or capture it. Don't do anything to the bite wound: don't cut, suck, or ice it. Immobilize the bitten area and put on a bandage two to four inches above the bite, but don't cut off the blood flow (you risk losing your limb). It should be loose enough to slip a finger under the bandage. Keep the bitten limb lower than your heart. Most importantly, get to a hospital immediately.

SPIDERS. Spiders and scorpions are overall much less dangerous than people think, although some species' bites can be rather painful and severe, and require medical attention. Bites are best avoided by checking your shoes and clothes before putting them on, by wearing shoes, and by checking under toilet seats. Also avoid reaching into dark places (such as under furniture or rocks).

CROCODILES. The large American crocodile kills about one person each year in Costa Rica. Rangers and guides know where the habitats of crocodiles are, and uncomfortably close encounters with these creatures are easily avoided by not swimming in waters where they are known to live.

CAMPING AND HIKING EQUIPMENT

WHAT TO BUY...

Good camping equipment is both sturdy and light. Camping equipment is generally more expensive in Australia, New Zealand, and the UK than in North America.

For lowland camping, a hammock and mosquito net are usually enough shelter, and both are readily available in Costa Rica. If using a hammock, bring along a generous length of rope to reach and get around any tree and a plastic tarp to keep you out of the rain. If you plan on camping at higher elevations, for example en route to a peak or volcano, a sleeping bag and other cold-weather gear will be essential. Because fuel supplies are inconsistent, buy multi-fuel camping stoves. Camping supplies can be difficult to find once there; in general, you're much better off purchasing equipment before you arrive.

Sleeping: Most sleeping bags are rated by season ("summer" means 30-40°F at night; "four-season" or "winter" usually means below 0°F). They are made either of **down**

(warmer and lighter, but more expensive, and miserable when wet) or of **synthetic** material (heavier, more durable, and warmer when wet). Prices range US$80-210 for a summer synthetic to US$250-300 for a good down winter bag. **Sleeping bag pads** include foam pads (US$10-20), air mattresses (US$15-50), and Therm-A-Rest self-inflating pads (US$45-80). Bring a **stuff sack** to store your bag and keep it dry.

Tent: The best tents are free-standing (with their own frames and suspension systems), set up quickly, and only require staking in high winds. Low-profile dome tents are the best all-around. Good 2-person tents start at US$90, 4-person at US$300. Seal the seams of your tent with waterproofer, and make sure it has a rain fly. Other tent accessories include a **battery-operated lantern**, a **plastic groundcloth**, and a **nylon tarp**.

Backpack: Internal-frame packs mold better to your back, keep a lower center of gravity, and flex adequately to allow you to hike difficult trails. **External-frame packs** are more comfortable for long hikes over even terrain, as they keep weight higher and distribute it more evenly. Make sure your pack has a strong, padded hip-belt to transfer weight to your legs. Any serious backpacking requires a pack of at least 4000 in^3 (ca. 66 liters), plus 500 in^3 (ca. 8 liters) for sleeping bags in internal-frame packs. Sturdy backpacks cost anywhere from US$125-420—this is one area in which it doesn't pay to economize. Fill up any pack with something heavy and walk around the store with it to get a sense of how it distributes weight before buying it. Either buy a **waterproof backpack cover**, or store all of your belongings in plastic bags inside your pack.

Boots: Be sure to wear hiking boots with good **ankle support.** They should fit snugly and comfortably over 1-2 pairs of wool socks and thin liner socks. Break in boots over several weeks first in order to spare yourself painful and debilitating blisters.

Other necessities: Synthetic layers, like those made of polypropylene work best, and a **pile jacket** will keep you warm even when wet. A **"space blanket"** helps you to retain your body heat and doubles as a groundcloth (US$5-15). Plastic **water bottles** are virtually shatter- and leak-proof. Bring **water purification tablets** for when you can't boil water. Although most campgrounds provide campfire sites, you may want to bring a small **metal grate** or **grill** of your own. For places that forbid fires or the gathering of firewood, you'll need a **camp stove** (the classic Coleman starts at US$40) and a propane-filled **fuel bottle** to operate it. Also, don't forget a **first-aid kit, pocketknife, insect repellent, calamine lotion,** and **waterproof matches** or a **lighter.**

...AND WHERE TO BUY IT

The mail-order/online companies listed below offer lower prices than many retail stores, but a visit to a local camping or outdoors store will give you a good sense of the look and weight of certain items.

Campmor, 28 Parkway, P.O. Box 700, Upper Saddle River, NJ 07458, USA (US ☎888-226-7667; elsewhere US ☎+1 201-825-8300; www.campmor.com).

Discount Camping, 880 Main North Rd., Pooraka, South Australia 5095, Australia (☎08 8262 3399; fax 8260 6240; www.discountcamping.com.au).

Eastern Mountain Sports (EMS), 1 Vose Farm Rd., Peterborough, NH 03458, USA (☎888-463-6367 or 603-924-7231; www.shopems.com).

L.L. Bean, Freeport, ME 04033 (US and Canada ☎800-441-5713; UK ☎0800 891 297; elsewhere, call US ☎+1 207-552-3028; www.llbean.com).

Mountain Designs, 51 Bishop St., Kelvin Grove, Queensland 4059, Australia (☎07 3856 2344; fax 3856 0366; info@mountaindesigns.com; www.mountaindesigns.com).

Recreational Equipment, Inc. (REI), Sumner, WA 98352, USA (☎800 426-4840 or 253-891-2500; www.rei.com).

ENVIRONMENTALLY RESPONSIBLE TOURISM. The idea behind responsible tourism is to leave no trace of human presence behind. A campstove is the safer (and more efficient) way to cook than using firewood, but if you must make a fire, keep it small and use only dead branches or brush rather than cutting vegetation. Make sure your campsite is at least 150 ft. (50m) from water supplies or bodies of water. If there are no toilet facilities, bury human waste (but not paper) at least 4 in. (10cm) deep and above the high-water line and 150 ft. or more from any water source and campsites. Always pack your trash in a plastic bag and carry it with you until you reach the next trash receptacle. For more information on these issues, contact one of the organizations listed below.

Earthwatch, 3 Clock Tower Place #100, Box 75, Maynard, MA 01754, USA (☎800-776-0188 or 978-461-0081; info@earthwatch.org; www.earthwatch.org).

International Ecotourism Society, 28 Pine St., Burlington, VT 05402, USA (☎802-651-9818; fax 802-651-9819; ecomail@ecotourism.org; www.ecotourism.org).

National Audubon Society, Nature Odysseys, 700 Broadway, New York, NY 10003 (☎212-979-3000; fax 212-979-3188; webmaster@audubon.org; www.audubon.org).

Tourism Concern, Stapleton House, 277-281 Holloway Rd., London N7 8HN, UK (☎020 7753 3330; fax 020 7753 3331; info@tourismconcern.org.uk; www.tourismconcern.org.uk).

YHA Adventure Shop, 14 Southampton St., Covent Garden, London, WC2E 7HA, UK (☎020 7836 8541; www.yhaadventure.com). The main branch of one of Britain's largest outdoor equipment suppliers.

ORGANIZED ADVENTURE TRIPS

Organized adventure tours offer another way of exploring the wild. Activities include hiking, biking, canoeing, kayaking, rafting, climbing, surfing, snorkeling, scuba diving, horseback riding, diving, photo safaris, and archaeological digs. Tourism bureaus can often suggest parks, trails, and outfitters; other good sources for info are stores and organizations that specialize in camping and outdoor equipment like REI and EMS (see above).

Specialty Travel Index, 305 San Anselmo Ave., #313, San Anselmo, CA 94960, USA (☎800-442-4922 or 415-459-4900; fax 415-459-9474; info@specialtytravel.com; www.specialtytravel.com). Tours worldwide.

KEEPING IN TOUCH

BY MAIL

SENDING MAIL HOME FROM COSTA RICA

Airmail is the best way to send mail home from Costa Rica. **Aerogrammes,** printed sheets that fold into envelopes and travel via airmail, are available at post offices. Write *par avion* or *correo aéreo* on the front. **Surface mail** is by far the cheapest and slowest way to send packages. It takes one to three months to cross the Atlantic and two to four to cross the Pacific—good for items you won't need to see for a while, such as souvenirs or other articles you've acquired along the way that are weighing down your pack. These are standard rates for mail from Costa Rica to:

Australia and New Zealand: Allow 8 days for regular airmail. Postcards/aerogrammes/letters up to 20g cost ¢170 (Costa Rican colones); packages up to 0.5kg ¢2440, up to 2kg ¢9640.

Canada: Allow 10 days for regular airmail. Postcards/aerogrammes/letters up to 20g cost ¢110; packages up to 0.5kg ¢1370, up to 2kg ¢5420.

UK and Ireland: Allow 6 days for regular airmail. Postcards/aerogrammes/letters up to 20g cost ¢130; packages up to 0.5kg ¢1630; up to 2kg ¢6430.

The US: Allow 5-6 days for regular airmail. Postcards/aerogrammes/letters up to 20g cost ¢90; packages up to 0.5kg ¢1370, up to 2kg ¢5420.

SENDING MAIL TO COSTA RICA

You can mark envelopes "air mail," "par avion," or "correo aéreo," but it's not essential. In addition to the standard postage system whose rates are listed below, **Federal Express** (www.fedex.com; Australia ☎ 13 26 10; US and Canada 800-247-4747; New Zealand 0800 73 33 39; UK 0800 12 38 00) handles express mail services from most countries to Costa Rica; for example, they can get a letter from New York to Costa Rica in 2 business days for US$45.61 and from London to Costa Rica also in 2 business days for UK£31.

Australia: Allow 7-8 work days for regular airmail to Costa Rica. Postcards and letters up to 20g cost AUS$1; packages up to 0.5kg AUS$13, up to 2kg AUS$46. **EMS** can get a letter to Costa Rica in 4-5 working days for AUS$32. (www.auspost.com.au/pac.)

Canada: Allow 5-15 days for regular airmail to Costa Rica. Postcards and letters up to 20g cost CDN$1.25; packages up to 0.5kg CDN$10.65, up to 2kg CDN$35.55. (www.canadapost.ca.)

Ireland: Allow 8-10 days for regular airmail to Costa Rica. Postcards and letters up to 25g cost IR£.57. Add IR£3.40 for Swiftpost International. (www.anpost.ie.)

New Zealand: Allow 1 week for regular airmail to Costa Rica. Postcards NZ$1.50. Letters up to 20g cost NZ$2-3; small parcels up to 0.5kg NZ$16.38, up to 2kg NZ$49.34. (www.nzpost.co.nz/nzpost/inrates.)

UK: Allow 4 days for airmail to Costa Rica. Letters up to 20g cost UK£0.65; packages up to 0.5kg UK£4.55, up to 2kg UK£17.30. **UK Swiftair** delivers letters a day faster for UK£3.50. (www.royalmail.co.uk/calculator.)

US: Allow 4-7 days for regular airmail to Costa Rica. Postcards/aerogrammes cost US$0.70. Letters under 1 oz. cost US$0.80. Packages under 1 lb. cost US$14; larger packages vary in price (around US$20). **US Express Mail** takes 2-3 days and costs US$24.75 (0.5/1 lb.). **US Global Priority Mail** delivers small/large flat-rate envelopes to Costa Rica in 3-5 days for US$5-9. http://ircalc.usps.gov.

RECEIVING MAIL IN COSTA RICA

There are several ways to pick up letters sent to you by friends and relatives while you are abroad. Mail can be sent via **poste restante** (General Delivery; *Lista de Correos*) to almost any city or town in Costa Rica with a post office. Address *poste restante* letters as follows:

Charlene MUSIC
Lista de Correos
Correo General
City, Costa Rica

The mail will go to a special desk in the central post office, unless you specify a post office by street address or postal code. It's best to use post offices in big cities, since mail may be sent there regardless. It is usually quicker, though more expensive, to send mail express or registered. Bring your passport (or other photo ID) for pick-up; there may be a small fee. If the clerks insist that there is nothing for you, have them check under your first name as well. *Let's Go* lists post offices in the **Practical Information** section for each city and most towns.

American Express travel offices throughout the world offer a free **Client Letter Service** (mail held up to 30 days and forwarded upon request) for cardholders who contact them in advance; address the letter to the AmEx office. Some offices will offer these services to non-cardholders (especially AmEx Travelers Cheque holders), but call ahead to make sure. *Let's Go* lists AmEx office locations for most large cities in **Practical Information** sections; for a complete list, call ☎800-528-4800.

BY TELEPHONE

CALLING HOME FROM COSTA RICA

A **calling card** is probably your cheapest bet. Calls are billed collect or to your account. You can frequently call collect without even possessing a company's calling card just by calling their access number and following the instructions. **To obtain a calling card** from your national telecommunications service before leaving home, contact the appropriate company listed below (using the numbers in the first column). Also try **www.justphonecards.com** for cheap rates. To **call home with a calling card,** contact the operator for your service provider in Costa Rica by dialing the appropriate access number (listed below in the second column).

COMPANY	TO OBTAIN A CARD, DIAL:	TO CALL ABROAD, DIAL:
AT&T (US)	800 361-4470	0800-011-4114
British Telecom Direct	800 34 51 44	0800 044 1044
Canada Direct	800-561-8868	0800-015-1161
Ireland Direct	800 40 00 00	+353 1 661 4808
MCI (US)	800-444-3333	0800-012-2222
New Zealand Direct	0800 00 00 00	0800-064-1064
Telkom South Africa	10 219	0800 113 366
Telstra Australia	13 22 00	+61 9491 2303s

You can usually also make **direct international calls** from pay phones using prepaid phone cards (see below), but they are less cost-efficient. (See the box on **Placing International Calls** for directions on how to place a direct international call.)

To use an ATM/MCI phone card, use a **blue** pay phone and be persistent, as busy signals are common. Nice hotels usually have phones with better service. Placing a **collect call** through an international operator is even more expensive, but may be necessary in case of emergency. You can place collect calls through the service providers listed above even if you don't have one of their phone cards.

CALLING WITHIN COSTA RICA

Coin-operated phones are not as available as they once were, since most have been replaced by the more efficient **prepaid phone card** phones (cards are widely available at news stands, convenience stores, and bookstores). The cards carry a certain amount of phone time depending on their denomination, and usually save time and money in the long run. The **CHIP card** can only be used on the new blue computerized payphones, which will tell you how much time, in units, you have left on your card.

ESSENTIALS

ESSENTIALS

 PLACING INTERNATIONAL CALLS. To call Costa Rica from home or to call home from Costa Rica, dial:

1. The **international dialing prefix.** To call out of **Costa Rica,** 00; **Australia,** 0011; **Canada** or the **US,** 011; the **Republic of Ireland, New Zealand,** or the **UK, 00; South Africa,** 09.
2. The **country code** of the country you want to call. To call **Australia,** dial 61; **Canada** or the **US,** 1; the **Republic of Ireland,** 353; **New Zealand,** 64; **South Africa,** 27; the **UK,** 44; **Costa Rica,** 506.
3. The **city/area code.** Let's Go lists the city/area codes for cities and towns in Costa Rica opposite the city or town name, next to a ☎. If the first digit is a zero (e.g., 020 for London), omit the zero when calling from abroad (e.g., dial 20 from Canada to reach London).
4. The **local number.**

The **Colibrí** and **Viajera** cards are the other two brands of prepaid telephone cards that come with a Personal Identification Number (PIN) and a toll-free access number (197 and 199 respectively). They are sold at most grocery stores and have reasonable rates. Instead of inserting the card into the phone, dial the 3-digit access number followed by the 7-digit phone number if it is a national call or 00+country code+area code+number for international calls. These cards can be used from any phone in the country. Only card denominations of ₡2000 and ₡3000 can be used to make international cards; CHIP cards cannot. If you have any problem with your phone card or need more information, you can call the toll-free number 800-220-9220 for help. Phone rates typically tend to be highest in the morning, lower in the evening, and lowest on Sunday and late at night. Call ☎ 113 for information.

TIME DIFFERENCES

Costa Rica is six hours behind **Greenwich Mean Time (GMT),** equivalent to Central Time in North America. Costa Rica is one hour behind New York, two ahead of Vancouver and San Francisco; nine behind Johannesburg; and 16 hours behind Sydney. Costa Rica ignores **daylight savings time,** so fall and spring switchover times vary.

BY EMAIL AND INTERNET

Internet service is plentiful and speedy in Costa Rica. Service is provided by Radiográfica Costarricense, a government owned subsidiary of the ICE (Instituto Costarricense de Electricidad), and Internet cafes are scattered throughout the country. Most charge approximately US$1 per hour, though in smaller cities, it can run up to US$5 per hour. You can also rent computer time in ICE offices.

Though in some places it is possible to forge a remote link with your home server, in most cases this is a much slower (and thus more expensive) option than taking advantage of free **web-based email accounts** (e.g. www.hotmail.com and www.yahoo.com). Travelers with laptops can call an Internet service provider via a **modem.** Long-distance phone cards specifically intended for such calls can defray normally high phone charges; check with your long-distance phone provider to see if it offers this option. **Internet cafes** and the occasional free Internet terminal at a public library or university are listed in the **Practical Information** sections of major cities. For lists of additional cybercafes in Costa Rica, check out www.cibercentro.com/costarica and cybercaptive.com.

GETTING TO COSTA RICA

BY PLANE

When it comes to airfare, a little effort can save you a bundle. If your plans are flexible enough to deal with the restrictions, **courier fares** are the cheapest. Tickets bought from consolidators and standby seating are also good deals, but last-minute specials, airfare wars, and charter flights often beat these fares. The key is to hunt around, be flexible, and ask persistently about discounts. Students, seniors, and those under 26 should never pay full price for a ticket.

AIRFARES

Airfares to Costa Rica peak from December to April and from July to September; holidays, especially Christmas and Easter, are also expensive. The cheapest times to travel are between mid-September and November or April and July. Midweek (M-Th morning) round-trip flights run US$40-50 cheaper than weekend flights but are generally more crowded and less likely to permit frequent-flier upgrades. Not fixing a return date ("open return") or arriving in and departing from different cities ("open-jaw") can be pricier than round-trip flights. Patching one-way flights together is the most expensive way to travel. Flights between cities within Costa Rica will be much cheaper (see **San José Flights,** p. 85).

If Costa Rica is only one stop on a more extensive globe-hop, consider a **round-the-world (RTW) ticket.** Tickets usually include at least five stops and are valid for about a year; prices range US$1200-5000. Try **Northwest Airlines/KLM** (US ☎ 800-447-4747; www.nwa.com) or **Star Alliance,** a consortium of 14 airlines including United Airlines (US ☎ 800-241-6522; www.staralliance.com).

Fares for roundtrip flights to San José from the US or Canadian east coast cost around US$600 in the off season (May-Nov.) and US$1150 in the high season (Dec.-April); from the US or Canadian west coast approximately US$800-$1300; from the UK, UK₤550-₤1100; from Australia AUS$3000-AUS$3500; from New Zealand NZ$3000-NZ$3800.

BUDGET & STUDENT TRAVEL AGENCIES

While knowledgeable agents specializing in flights to Costa Rica can make your life easy and help you save time and energy, they may not spend the time to find you the lowest possible fare—they get paid on commission. Travelers holding **ISIC** and **IYTC cards** (see p. 13) qualify for big discounts from student travel agencies. Most flights from budget agencies are on major airlines, but in peak season some may sell seats on less reliable chartered aircrafts.

usit world (www.usitworld.com). Over 50 **usit campus** branches in the UK, including: 52 Grosvenor Gardens, **London** SW1W 0AG (☎0870 240 1010); **Manchester** (☎0161 273 1880); and **Edinburgh** (☎0131 668 3303). Nearly 20 **usit NOW** offices in Ireland, including 19-21 Aston Quay, O'Connell Bridge, **Dublin** 2 (☎01 602 1600; www.usit-now.ie), and **Belfast** (☎0289 032 7111; www.usitnow.com). Offices also in Athens, Auckland, Brussels, Frankfurt, Johannesburg, Lisbon, Luxembourg, Madrid, Paris, Sofia, and Warsaw.

Council Travel (www.counciltravel.com). Countless US offices, including branches in Atlanta, Boston, Chicago, L.A., New York, San Francisco, Seattle, and Washington, D.C. Check the website or call ☎800-2-COUNCIL (226-8624) for the office nearest you. Also an office at 28A Poland St., Oxford Circus, **London** W1V 3DB (☎020 7437 7767). As of May, Council had declared bankruptcy and was subsumed under STA. However , their offices are still in existence and transacting business.

CTS Travel. Offices accross Italy and in Paris, London, and now New York. Call toll-free 877-287-6665. In **UK**, 44 Goodge St., London W1T 2AD (☎020 7636 0031; fax 7637 5328; ctsinfo@ctstravel.co.uk).

STA Travel, 7890 S. Hardy Dr., Ste. 110, Tempe AZ 85284, USA (24hr. reservations and info ☎800-781-4040; www.statravel.com). A student and youth travel organization with over 150 offices worldwide (check their website for a listing of all their offices), including US offices in Boston, Chicago, L.A., New York, San Francisco, Seattle, and Washington, D.C. Ticket booking, travel insurance, railpasses, and more. In the UK, walk-in office at 11 Goodge St., **London** W1T 2PF or call ☎020 7636 0031. In New Zealand, Shop 2B, 182 Queen St., **Auckland** (☎09 309 0458). In Australia, 366 Lygon St., **Carlton** VIC 3053 (☎03 9349 4344).

Travel CUTS (Canadian Universities Travel Services Limited), 187 College St., **Toronto,** ON M5T 1P7 (☎416-979-2406; fax 979-8167; www.travelcuts.com). 60 offices across Canada. Also in the UK, 295-A Regent St., **London** W1R 7YA (☎020 7255 1944).

COMMERCIAL AIRLINES

The commercial airlines' lowest regular offers are the **Advance Purchase Excursion (APEX)** fares, which provide confirmed reservations and allow "open-jaw" tickets. Generally, reservations must be made seven to 21 days ahead of departure, with seven- to 14-day minimum-stay and up to 90-day maximum-stay restrictions. These fares carry hefty cancellation and change penalties (fees rise in summer). Book peak-season APEX fares early; by May you will have a hard time getting your desired departure date. Use **Microsoft Expedia** (msn.expedia.com) or **Travelocity** (www.travelocity.com) to get an idea of lowest published fares, then use the resources outlined here to try and beat them. Low-season fares should be appreciably cheaper than the **high season** (July-Sept. and Dec.-Apr.) ones listed here.

TRAVELING FROM NORTH AMERICA

From the US, the largest gateways for flights to Costa Rica are Miami and Houston, with other flights originating from Atlanta, Boston, Chicago, L.A., New York, Newark, and Washington, D.C. Basic round-trip fares to San José, Costa Rica range from US$500-1200. Standard commercial carriers like **American, Continental,** and **United** offer the most convenient flights, but might not be the cheapest, unless you grab a special promotion or airfare war ticket. Charter flights sometimes run from Canada, but scheduled flights are routed through the US. You might find cheaper fares by flying on a Latin American airline like Lacsa, Taca, Copa, or MartinAir. Otherwise, check online or consult a travel agent about discount airfares.

TRAVELING FROM EUROPE

No Irish airlines provide service to Costa Rica. **British Airways** flies from London to San José. **Iberia** flies from Spain with direct connections to San José. **Alitalia** flies from Italy to Miami, Caracas, and Santo Domingo, and **Taca** provides passengers with a connecting flight. **LTU** provides services from Germany.

TRAVELING FROM AUSTRALIA & NEW ZEALAND

From Australia or New Zealand, the least expensive route is via Los Angeles or Miami. In order to complete a trip, you must change airlines.

STANDBY FLIGHTS

Traveling standby requires considerable flexibility in arrival and departure dates and cities. In addition, it is especially difficult to find room on flights to Costa Rica. Companies dealing in standby flights sell vouchers rather than tickets, along with the promise to get to your destination (or near your destination) within a certain window of time (typically 1-5 days). You call in before your specific window of time to hear your flight options and the probability that you will be able to board each flight. You can then decide which flights you want to try to make, show up at the appropriate airport at the appropriate time, present your voucher, and board if space is available. Vouchers can usually be bought for both one-way and round-trip travel. You may receive a monetary refund only if every available flight within your date range is full; if you opt not to take an available (but perhaps less convenient) flight, you can only get credit toward future travel. Carefully read agreements with any company offering standby flights, as tricky fine print can leave you in the lurch. To check on a company's service record in the US, call the Better Business Bureau (☎212-533-6200). It is difficult to receive refunds, and clients' vouchers will not be honored when an airline fails to receive payment in time.

TICKET CONSOLIDATORS

Ticket consolidators, or **"bucket shops,"** buy unsold tickets in bulk from commercial airlines and sell them at discounted rates. The best place to look is in the Sunday travel section of any major newspaper (such as the *New York Times*), where many bucket shops place tiny ads. Call quickly, as availability is typically extremely limited. Not all bucket shops are reliable, so insist on a receipt that gives full details of restrictions, refunds, and tickets and pay by credit card (in spite of the 2-5% fee) so you can stop payment if you never receive your tickets. For more info, see www.travel-library.com/air-travel/consolidators.html.

TRAVELING FROM THE US & CANADA
Travel Avenue (☎800-333-3335; www.travelavenue.com) searches for best available published fares and then uses several consolidators to attempt to beat that fare. Other consolidators worth trying are: **Interworld** (☎305-443-4929; fax 443-0351); **Pennsylvania Travel** (☎800-331-0947); **Rebel** (☎800-227-3235; travel@rebeltours.com; www.rebeltours.com); **Cheap Tickets** (☎800-377-1000; www.cheaptickets.com); **Travac** (☎800-872-8800; fax 212-714-9063; www.travac.com). Consolidators on the web include **Internet Travel Network** (www.itn.com); **Orbitz** (orbitz.com); **Travel Information Services** (www.tiss.com); **TravelHUB** (www.travelhub.com); **The Travel Site** (www.thetravelsite.com). Keep in mind that these are just suggestions to get you started; *Let's Go* does not endorse any of these agencies. As always, be cautious and research companies before you hand over your credit card number.

TRAVELING FROM THE UK, AUSTRALIA, & NEW ZEALAND
In London, the **Air Travel Advisory Bureau** (☎0207-636-5000; www.atab.co.uk) can provide names of reliable consolidators and discount flight specialists. From Australia and New Zealand, look for consolidator ads in the travel section of the *Sydney Morning Herald* and other papers.

CHARTER FLIGHTS

Charters are flights a tour operator contracts with an airline to fly extra loads of passengers during peak season. They fly less frequently than major airlines, make refunds particularly difficult, and are almost always fully booked. Schedules and itineraries may also change or be cancelled at the last moment (as late as 48 hr. before the trip and without a full refund), and check-in, boarding, and baggage claim are often much slower, but can also be cheaper. There are several options available out of Montreal, Toronto, and Vancouver in Canada. **Discount clubs** and **fare brokers** offer members' savings on last-minute charter and tour deals. Study contracts closely; you don't want to end up with an unwanted overnight layover.

BY BOAT

Costa Rica's natural beauty and exotic beaches have also made it a celebrated stop-along-the-way for many cruise lines. **Windstar Cruises** depart from Barcelona, Istanbul, Venice, and many other European ports (www.costa-rica-cruises.com); and **Royal Caribbean, Carnival,** and **Princess Cruise Lines** depart from the USA, Mexico, and Canada. Costa Rica is usually on the way to one of their main destinations.

BORDER CROSSINGS

NICARAGUA. There is one land crossing at **Peñas Blancas/Sapoa** (p. 172), 75km north of Liberia and near Rivas, Nicaragua. There is also a crossing at Río San Juan near **Los Chiles** (p. 196), south of San Carlos, Nicaragua.

PANAMA. There are three land crossings; **Paso Canoas** (p. 318) is 18km southeast of Ciudad Neily, Costa Rica, near David, Panama. **Sixaola/Guabito** (p. 383) is on the Caribbean coast 1½hr. from Puerto Viejo de Talamanca, near Changuinola, Panama. A third crossing at **Río Sereno,** east of San Vito, is rarely used.

GETTING AROUND COSTA RICA

A word of advice: ask. *Ticos* are extremely friendly, and signs in Costa Rica are very limited, so if you have any doubts, or carrying a map isn't helping, just stop and ask. People are quick to help. Landmarks are the way of the wise in most of Costa Rica. Most mid-range and larger towns have streets in an orderly grid of *calles* (streets) and *avenidas* (avenues); the *calles* run north-south and the *avenidas* east-west (exactly the opposite of the Nicaraguan paradigm). Usually odd-numbered *calles* lie to the east of the grid's center and even-numbered *calles* to the west, while odd-numbered *avenidas* increase in number to the north and even-numbered to the south. The grid is usually centered on a *parque central* (central park), and its axes are usually Av. Central and Calle Central. An address given as Calle 2, Av. 3/5 means the building is on Calle 2 between Avenidas 3 and 5. Locations are often specified by a certain number of *metros* from the *parque*. *Metros* here refers to portions of city blocks, not actual meters; *100 metros al norte del parque central* indicates a building one block north of the *parque*. When it comes to walking, remember that cars have the right of way, not pedestrians, so look twice before crossing the street even if you have a crosswalk.

BY PLANE

Two airlines, **Sansa** (☎231 9414 or 443 3555; fax 257 9444; sansa@costaricabureau.com; www.grupotaca.com) and the pricier but more reliable **Travelair** (☎220 3054 or 296 2317, 800 948 3770 in US or Canada; travelair@centralamerica.com; www.travelair-costarica.com), have **flights** connecting San José with destinations throughout Costa Rica (see p. 85). Both have several years of experience and reach many destinations. Children ages 2-12 get a 25% discount on Sansa. One-way trips for adults cost US$45-70 depending on destination, and round trips are US$85-130. (☎506 .) Children ages 2-11 pay 50% of the regular fare on Travelair. One way trips for adults cost around US$45-95 and round trips US$115-185.

BY BUS

The **bus** system is thorough, cheap, and reliable; from San José, you can travel almost anywhere in the country for under US$6. However it's not always immediately clear where they arrive, when they leave, or how much they cost. Just ask around; people will know. The bus system is labyrinthine; although every destination is served by a different company, and each company is located in a different part of town. Note, however, that a seemingly microscopic, direct distance between two points on a map often translates into hours on a bumpy, windy road. You can find the most accurate bus information, including detailed schedules and maps at the **Instituto Costarricense de Turismo** (**ICT**; ☎506 223 1733 or 800-343-6332 from North America), along Av. 2 in San José (see **San José: Buses,** p. 86). You can also find ICT representatives at the base of the stairs just before you exit the airport.

BY CAR

If you're traveling by **car,** you'll have a good network of highways at your disposal. A seat belt must be used by the driver and any front-seat passenger. Although the government has been working on paving and fixing roads, road conditions still vary and tend to be quite rough (by international standards) in some places. Random potholes and bumps might make it hard to relax while driving, and watch out for open manholes along side roads, especially after hard rains. In general, it is always key to be careful and drive defensively.

Many places do require **four-wheel-drive (4WD)** vehicles, especially during the rainy season, so it might be a good idea to know where you're going and what roads are like before you rent your car. Car rental agencies might be able to help you out with information on road conditions. Before traveling, you can visit the **Association for Safe International Road Travel** (**ASIRT**; www.asirt.org) regarding safe road travel.

RENTING

Renting a car in Costa Rica is a great idea if you're planning on leaving the city. Most tourist destinations are only a few hours away, and you will definitely enjoy the scenery and beautiful countryside as you drive. If you're staying in the city, however, it could be a hassle, since parking and traffic make it more difficult to drive than walk or use public transportation, which isn't very expensive. When choosing a car, it is important to consider that cheaper cars tend to be less reliable and harder to handle on difficult terrain. In addition, although many places can be accessed without 4WD during the dry season, road conditions can change drastically during the rainy season. If you're planning on visiting Monteverde, any place south of Golfito, the southern Nicoya Peninsula, or the Osa Peninsula, a 4WD vehicle is recommended regardless the time of year. Less expensive 4WD vehicles in particular tend to be more top-heavy and more dangerous when navigating particularly bumpy roads. Knowing how to drive standard cars is essential.

RENTAL AGENCIES. You can generally make reservations before you leave by calling major international offices in your home country. However, the price and availability information they give sometimes doesn't jive with what the local offices in Costa Rica will tell you. Try checking with both numbers to make sure you get the best price and accurate information. Local desk numbers are included in town listings; for home-country numbers, call your toll-free directory.

To rent a car from most reantal agencies in Costa Rica, you need to be at least 21 years old. Some agencies require renters to be 25, and most charge those aged 21-24 an additional insurance fee (around US$20 per day) and at least double the credit card deposit. Policies and prices vary from agency to agency. Small local operations occasionally rent to people under 21, but be sure to ask about the insurance coverage and deductible, and always check the fine print. Rental agencies in Costa Rica include:

Adobe Rent a Car (☎506 258 4242; fax 221 9286; www.adobecar.com/index1.html). Prices range from US$40 per day for a sedan to US$79 for a 4WD (during the low season). Min. age 21. Valid license and passport required. As part of the Special Car and Driver Program, get a bilingual chauffeur for a whole day for US$174.

Hertz Rent a Car (☎506 221 1818; fax 233 7254; www.hertzcr.com). Prices range from US$22 per day for a sedan to US$71-$115 for a 4WD. Min. age 25. Valid license and passport required. Portable cellular phones available at US$1.95 per min.

Budget Rent a Car (☎506 667 0126; fax 442 2495; www.budget.co.cr/pagecreator/home.cfm). Prices range from US$24 per day for a sedan to US$63 for a 4WD. Valid license and passport required. If you present your Taca boarding pass within 24hr. of arrival, you can get a free day of rental and triple the miles of your distance program.

COSTS & INSURANCE. Rental car prices start at around US$19 a day from national companies, US$22 from local agencies. Expect to pay much more for larger cars and 4WD vehicles. Cars with **automatic transmission** can cost up to $10 per day more than standard manuals (stick shift), and in some places, automatic transmission is completely unavailable. It is virtually impossible, no matter where you are, to find an automatic 4WD. If you rent a car, chances are you're planning to leave the city, in which case you will need a **stick shift** car to battle Costa Rica's rough and hilly roads.

Many rental packages offer unlimited kilometers, while others offer a limited number of kilometers per day with a small surcharge for every kilometer after that. Return the car with a full tank of petrol to avoid high fuel charges at the end. Be sure to ask whether the price includes **insurance** against theft and collision. Remember that if you are driving a conventional vehicle on an **unpaved road** in a rental car, you are almost never covered by insurance; ask about this before leaving the rental agency. Beware that cars rented on an **American Express** or **Visa/Mastercard Gold or Platinum** credit cards in Costa Rica might *not* carry the automatic insurance that they would in some other countries; check with your credit card company. Insurance plans almost always come with an **excess** (or deductible) of around US$750 for conventional vehicles; excess ranges up to around US$950+ for younger drivers and for 4WD. This means you pay for all damages up to that sum, unless they are the fault of another vehicle. The excess you will be quoted applies to collisions with other vehicles; collisions with non-vehicles, such as trees ("single-vehicle collisions"), will cost you even more. The excess can often be reduced or waived entirely if you pay an additional charge, around US$15-25 per day.

National chains often allow one-way rentals, picking up in one city and dropping off in another. There is usually a minimum hire period and sometimes an extra drop-off charge of several hundred dollars.

ON THE ROAD. The speed limit on the highway is 100km per hr. and varies from 40-60km per hr. in urban areas. Around school zones, hospitals, and clinics, it is 25km per hr. **Petrol (gasoline)** prices vary but average about US$2.26 per gallon throughout the country.

Driving on the beaches is prohibited everywhere, except when there is no road or path that connects two towns. All car passengers must wear seatbelts, and you must pull over if police ask you to do so. Never forget your personal documents and the vehicle's registration papers. Some travelers report that police may ask for a small fee instead of issuing a ticket; as tickets rarely exceed US$30, it's a good idea to just pay the ticket instead of risking getting in trouble and encouraging a bad practice.

DRIVING PRECAUTIONS. When traveling in hot areas (i.e. the coastal areas), bring substantial amounts of water (a suggested 5L of **water** per person per day) for drinking and for the radiator. For long drives to unpopulated areas, register with the police before beginning the trek and again upon arrival at the destination. When traveling for long distances, make sure tires are in good repair and have enough air, and bring good maps. A **compass** and a **car manual** can also be very useful. You should always carry a **spare tire** and **jack, jumper cables, extra oil, flares, and flashlight.** If you don't know how to **change a tire,** learn before heading out, especially if you are planning on traveling in deserted areas. Blowouts on dirt roads are common. If you do have a breakdown, **stay with your car;** if you wander off, there's less likelihood trackers will find you.

DANGERS. The most important rule is to be confident and stay alert. In general, roads in Costa Rica are not very wide and can be quite curvy and dangerous in the outskirts of the country, especially when leaving the Central Valley to reach the coasts. There are few road signs and many blind curves. Don't pass other cars when you don't have perfect visibility, and if someone is passing, just let them cut in line. When driving in the city, keep your doors locked and, at night, your windows shut. If you get into an accident, drive to the nearest lit, public area and call the police for assistance.

CAR ASSISTANCE. If you are involved in an **accident,** wait until the police arrive to move your vehicle so that an officer can prepare a report. You can report an accident by calling ☎911 or 800 012 3456.

DRIVING PERMITS & CAR INSURANCE

INTERNATIONAL DRIVING PERMIT (IDP). If you plan to drive a car while in Costa Rica, you must be over 18 years old. Your country's driver's license is valid for 90 days, but proof of entry to the country is also required for a police officer to accept it, so carry your passport. It may be a good idea to just get an **International Driving Permit (IDP)** anyway, in case you're in a situation where the police don't know English. Information on the IDP is printed in 10 languages.

Your IDP, valid for one year, must be issued in your own country before you depart. An application for an IDP usually needs to include one or two photos, a current local license, an additional form of identification, and a fee. To apply, contact the national or local branch of your home country's Automobile Association.

CAR INSURANCE. By law, all vehicles in Costa Rica must be insured against personal injury to third parties. Insurance against material damage to other cars, on the other hand, isn't mandatory.

Most credit cards cover standard insurance. If you rent, lease, or borrow a car, you will need a **green card** or **International Insurance Certificate** to certify that you have liability insurance and that it applies abroad. Green cards can be obtained at car rental agencies, car dealers (for those leasing cars), some travel agents, and some border crossings. Rental agencies may require you to purchase theft insurance in countries that they consider to have a high risk of auto theft.

BY BOAT, MOPED, BICYCLE, ETC.

Boat transportation is only necessary to enter and exit Parque Nacional Tortuguero (see p. 354). Public boat transport is available daily out of Limón, but is not always reliable. It might be best to stick to prearranged packages set up by your hotel or by tour operators. When it comes to bikes, Costa Rica is a wonderful country for mountain biking, and you can find tours for any level of skill that allow you to explore the country at your own pace. However, riding on most main roads can be dangerous, as they have no shoulders and there are many reckless drivers.

BY THUMB

 HITCHHIKING AND SAFETY. *Let's Go* urges you to use common sense if you decide to hitch and to consider all the risks before you make that decision. The information listed below and throughout the book is not intended to reccomend hitchhiking. We do not consider hitchhiking a safe means of transportation

Tourists report that hitchhiking is generally safe, but *Let's Go* strongly urges you to consider the risks before you choose to hitchhike. In Costa Rica, hitchhiking is not too common and is discouraged on main roadways and urban areas. In rural areas it is considered safer.

SPECIFIC CONCERNS

WOMEN TRAVELERS

Women exploring on their own inevitably face some additional safety concerns, but it's easy to be adventurous without taking undue risks. If you are concerned, consider staying in hostels which offer single rooms that lock from the inside or in religious organizations with rooms for women only. Stick to centrally located accommodations and avoid solitary late-night treks or metro rides. Always carry extra money for a phone call, bus, or taxi. **Hitchhiking** is never safe for lone women, or even for two women traveling together. Look as if you know where you're going and approach older women or couples for directions if you're uncomfortable.

Generally, the less you look like a tourist, the better off you'll be. Trying to fit in can be effective, but dressing in the style of an obviously different culture may cause you to feel ill at ease and a conspicuous target. Dress conservatively. Stick to pants or long skirts in the city, even if it's too warm. Similarly and especially in the rural areas, don't let shorts get too short, especially if you're traveling alone. Wearing a conspicuous **wedding band** may help prevent unwanted overtures.

Your best answer to verbal harassment is no answer at all; feigning deafness, sitting motionless, and staring straight ahead at nothing in particular will do a world of good that reactions usually don't achieve. The extremely persistent can sometimes be dissuaded by a firm, loud, and very public "*Déjame en paz* (leave me alone)" in Spanish. Don't hesitate to seek out a police officer or a passerby if you are being harassed. Memorize the emergency numbers in places you visit, and consider carrying a whistle on your keychain. A self-defense course will both prepare you for a potential attack and raise your level of awareness of your surroundings (see **Self Defense,** p. 18). Also be aware of the health concerns that women face when traveling (see p. 24).

TRAVELING ALONE

There are many benefits to traveling alone, including independence and greater interaction with locals. On the other hand, any solo traveler is a more vulnerable target of harassment and street theft. As a lone traveler, try not to stand out as a tourist, look confident, and be especially careful in deserted or very crowded areas. If questioned, never admit that you are traveling alone. Maintain regular contact with someone at home who knows your itinerary. For more tips, pick up *Traveling Solo* by Eleanor Berman (Globe Pequot Press; US$17) or subscribe to **Connecting: Solo Travel Network,** 689 Park Road, Unit 6, Gibsons, BC V0N 1V7, Canada (☎604-886-9099; www.cstn.org; membership US$35). **Travel Companion Exchange,** P.O. Box 833, Amityville, NY 11701, USA (☎631-454-0880, in the US ☎800-392-1256; www.whytravelalone.com; US$48), links solo travelers with companions with similar travel habits and interests.

OLDER TRAVELERS

Senior citizens might be eligible for discounts on transportation, museums, movies, theaters, concerts, restaurants, and accommodations. If you don't see a senior citizen price listed, ask, and you may be delightfully surprised. The books *No Problem! Worldwise Tips for Mature Adventurers*, by Janice Kenyon (Orca Book Publishers; US$16) and *Unbelievably Good Deals and Great Adventures That You Absolutely Can't Get Unless You're Over 50*, by Joan Rattner Heilman (NTC/Contemporary Publishing; US$13) are both excellent resources.

ElderTreks, 597 Markham St., Toronto, ON M6G 2L7, Canada (☎800-741-7956; www.eldertreks.com). Adventure travel programs for the 50+ traveler in Costa Rica.

Elderhostel, 11 Ave. de Lafayette, Boston, MA 02111, USA (☎877-426-8056; www.elderhostel.org). Organizes 1- to 4-week "educational adventures" in Costa Rica on varied subjects for those 55+.

ESSENTIALS

The Mature Traveler, P.O. Box 15791, Sacramento, CA 95852, USA (☎800-460-6676). Deals, discounts, and travel packages for the 50+ traveler. Subscription$30.

Walking the World, P.O. Box 1186, Fort Collins, CO 80522, USA (☎800-340-9255; www.walkingtheworld.com), organizes trips for 50+ travelers to Costa Rica.

BISEXUAL, GAY, & LESBIAN TRAVELERS

Legally, all Costa Rican citizens are considered equal, regardless of their sexuality, and consensual homosexuality and bisexuality are not a crime. In addition, recent legal rulings that prohibit bar raids and allow gay establishments to operate have largely eliminated incidents such as police harrassment in gay locales. In general, the government, media, and citizens of Costa Rica are much more open about homosexuality than they were 10 years ago, yet the traditional Roman Catholic family and the *machista* culture might still make gay and lesbian life uncomfortable. People are usually tolerant of gays and lesbians as long as they are not affectionate in public. Listed below are contact organizations, mail-order bookstores, and publishers that offer materials addressing some specific concerns.

Out and About (www.outandabout.com) offers a bi-weekly newsletter addressing travel concerns and a comprehensive site addressing gay travel concerns.

Gay's the Word, 66 Marchmont St., London WC1N 1AB, UK (☎+44 20 7278 7654; www.gaystheword.co.uk). The largest gay and lesbian bookshop in the UK, with both fiction and non-fiction titles. Mail-order service available.

Giovanni's Room, 1145 Pine St., Philadelphia, PA 19107, USA (☎215-923-2960; www.queerbooks.com). An international lesbian/feminist and gay bookstore with mail-order service (carries many of the publications listed below).

International Lesbian and Gay Association (ILGA), 81 rue Marché-au-Charbon, B-1000 Brussels, Belgium (☎+32 2 502 2471; www.ilga.org). Provides political information, such as homosexuality laws of individual countries.

Purple Roofs Gay and Travel Directory: Costa Rica provides information on gay/lesbian-friendly lodging throughout the country (http://www.purpleroofs.com/centralamerica/costarica/costaricaregion.html).

FURTHER READING: BISEXUAL, GAY, & LESBIAN.
Spartacus International Gay Guide 2001-2002. Bruno Gmunder Verlag (US$33).
Ferrari Guides' Gay Travel A to Z, Ferrari Guides' Men's Travel In Your Pocket, and *Ferrari Guides' Inn Places.* Ferrari Publications, US$16-20. Purchase the guides online at www.ferrariguides.com.
Gente 10. Bimonthly publication by Design and Communications J&D S.A.; the first magazine directed at Costa Rica's gay and lesbian community. It includes a directory of gay and lesbian hot spots and can be found at bookstores, hotels, and health clinics in the country. 1 year international subsription US$30. www.gaycostarica.com/gente10/ingles.html.

TRAVELERS WITH DISABILITIES

Independent travel for people with disabilities can be extremely difficult in Costa Rica. Public buses don't have the necessary provisions to carry wheelchairs, and only the newer constructions have been designed with ramps and wider spaces to suit wheelchair use. Braille signs for the blind are rare, and the special phone service for the hearing impaired is not readily available. However, **Ley No. 7600,** an Equal Opportunities for Disabled Persons Law, has raised the population's awareness and respect for the disabled and has made integrating the disabled into the country's development one of the government's priorities. There is a toll-free phone number (☎800 266 7356; open daily 8am-4pm) to call for any information about services and rights of the disabled. In case of an emergency, however, it is always better to call ☎911. Those with disabilities should inform airlines and hotels of their disabilities when making reservations; some time may be needed to prepare special accommodations. Call ahead to restaurants, museums, and other facilities to find out if they are handicap-accessible. **Guide dog owners** should inquire about the quarantine policies of Costa Rica.

USEFUL ORGANIZATIONS

Mobility International USA (MIUSA), P.O. Box 10767, Eugene, OR 97440, USA (voice and TDD ☎541–343-1284; www.miusa.org). Sells *A World of Options: A Guide to International Educational Exchange, Community Service, and Travel for Persons with Disabilities* (US$35).

Society for Accessible Travel and Hospitality (SATH), 347 Fifth Ave., #610, New York, NY 10016, USA (☎212-447-7284; www.sath.org). An advocacy group that publishes free online travel information and the travel magazine *OPEN WORLD* (US$18, free for members). Annual membership US$45, students and seniors US$30.

TOUR AGENCIES

Directions Unlimited, 123 Green Ln., Bedford Hills, NY 10507, USA (☎800-533-5343). Books individual and group vacations for the physically disabled; not an info service.

TRAVELERS WITH CHILDREN

Family vacations often require that you slow your pace and always require that you plan ahead. If you plan on renting a car, it is best to bring your child's seat with you since rental companies don't always have them. **Be sure that your child carries some sort of ID** in case of an emergency or in case he or she gets lost.

Museums, tourist attractions, and accommodations often offer discounts for children. Restaurants might not have kids' meals, but don't worry about splitting a meal between two children or a child and an adult; it is perfectly acceptable. Children must pay a full fare on public buses if they occupy a seat but not if they sit on their parent's lap. Children under two generally fly for 10% of the adult airfare on international flights (this does not necessarily include a seat). International fares are usually discounted 25% for children ages 2-11.

In general, *ticos* are especially welcoming, friendly, and even captivated by travelers with children; note, however, that businesses that want to keep peace and quiet simply avoid misunderstandings by not allowing children under a certain age. For more information, consult one of the following books:

Backpacking with Babies and Small Children, Goldie Silverman. Wilderness Press (US$10).

How to take Great Trips with Your Kids, Sanford and Jane Portnoy. Harvard Common Press (US $10).

Have Kid, Will Travel: 101 Survival Strategies for Vacationing With Babies and Young Children, Claire and Lucille Tristram. Andrews McMeel Publishing (US$9).

Adventuring with Children: An Inspirational Guide to World Travel and the Outdoors, Nan Jeffrey. Avalon House Publishing (US$15).

Trouble Free Travel with Children, Vicki Lansky. Book Peddlers (US$9).

ESSENTIALS

DIETARY CONCERNS

One word: **diarrhea.** Don't let yourself be frightened, though; it is not as atrocious as it seems. Diarrhea and stomach aches are just common symptoms most travelers experience while adjusting to a Costa Rican diet, and usually they go away after a little while. You can avoid some indigestion by drinking bottled water—unlike Costa Ricans, travelers sometimes aren't immune to the country's tap water. The **water** in Costa Rica, however, is generally safe to drink, especially in larger cities and touristed areas. Places you should be particularly careful about water quality are: Parque Nacional Corcovado, some parts of the Osa Peninsula, and the Northern Caribbean. Veggie-eaters should watch out, as salads washed with tap water can make you sick, especially in lower budget, rural restaurants, and *sodas*. In general, vegetarians and vegans shouldn't have a hard time finding tasty foods. Although there might not be many exclusively vegetarian restaurants (although a growing number of healthy vegetarian establishments are springing up in the Central Valley and Central Pacific, most offer rice and beans (staple foods), fresh fruits, and cooked vegetable dishes. If you think you have food poisoning, feel comforted by the fact that Costa Rica's health care system is one of the best in Latin America. The **North American Vegetarian Society,** P.O. Box 72, Dolgeville, NY 13329, USA (☎518-568-7970; www.navs-online.org), publishes information about vegetarian travel, including *Transformative Adventures, a Guide to Vacations and Retreats* (US$15).

For more info, visit a bookstore, health food store, or library, and consult *The Vegetarian Traveler: Where to Stay if You're Vegetarian, Vegan, Environmentally Sensitive,* by Jed and Susan Civic (Larson Publications; US$16).

Travelers who keep **kosher** should contact synagogues in larger cities for information on kosher restaurants. You can contact the **Centro Israelita Sionista de Costa Rica** (☎233 9222; fax 233 9321) for more information on Costa Rica's Jewish community. If you are strict in your observance, you may have to prepare your own meals on the road. A good resource is the *Jewish Travel Guide,* by Michael Zaidner (Vallentine Mitchell; US$17).

OTHER RESOURCES

Let's Go tries to cover all aspects of budget travel, but we can't put *everything* in our guides. Listed below are books and websites that can serve as jumping-off points for your own research.

USEFUL PUBLICATIONS

The Tico Times, San José, Costa Rica (☎258 1558; fax 233 6378; info@ticotimes.net; www.ticotimes.net). Central America's leading English-language newspaper covers news, business, and cultural development in Costa Rica and Central America.

La Nación, San José, Costa Rica (☎247 4664; fax 247 4481; www.nacion.co.cr). Costa Rica's leading Spanish newspaper.

Actualidad Económica, San José, Costa Rica (☎224 2411; fax 225 7365; ibarboza@actualidad.co.cr; www.miactualidad.com). Learn about economics, banking, finance, and entrepeneurship in Costa Rica.

Costa Rica Explorer, San José, Costa Rica (☎ 247 4664; fax 247 4481; www.nacion.co.cr). Useful news and info for travelers. Published every 2 months.

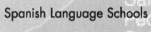

TRAVEL PUBLISHERS & BOOKSTORES

Hippocrene Books, Inc., 171 Madison Ave., New York, NY 10016, USA (☎718-454-2366; www.hippocrenebooks.com). Publishes foreign language dictionaries and language learning guides.

Hunter Publishing, 470 W. Broadway, 2nd. floor, South Boston, MA 02127, USA (☎617-269-0700; www.hunterpublishing.com). Has an extensive catalog of travel guides and diving and adventure travel books.

Rand McNally, P.O. Box 7600, Chicago, IL 60680, USA (☎847-329-8100; www.randmcnally.com), publishes road atlases.

Adventurous Traveler Bookstore, P.O. Box 2221, Williston, VT 05495, USA (☎800-282-3963; www.adventuroustraveler.com).

Travel Books & Language Center, Inc., 4437 Wisconsin Ave., NW, Washington, D.C. 20016, USA (☎800-220-2665; www.bookweb.org/bookstore/travelbks). Over 60,000 titles from around the world.

WORLD WIDE WEB

Almost every aspect of budget travel is accessible via the web. Within 10min. at the keyboard, you can make a reservation at a hostel, get advice on travel hot spots from other travelers who have just returned from Costa Rica, or find out exactly how much a ticket would cost.

Listed here are some budget travel sites to start off your surfing; other relevant websites are listed throughout the book. Because website turnover is high, use search engines (such as www.google.com) to strike out on your own.

OUR PERSONAL FAVORITE...

■ **Let's Go:** www.letsgo.com. Our constantly expanding website features photos and streaming video, online ordering of all our titles, info about our books, a travel forum buzzing with stories and tips, and links that will help you find everything you ever wanted to know about Costa Rica.

THE ART OF BUDGET TRAVEL

How to See the World: www.artoftravel.com. A compendium of great travel tips, from cheap flights to self-defense to interacting with local culture.

Lycos: cityguide.lycos.com. General introductions to cities and regions throughout Costa Rica, accompanied by links to applicable histories, news, and local tourism sites.

Rec. Travel Library: www.travel-library.com. A fantastic set of links for general information and personal travelogues.

INFORMATION ON COSTA RICA

Atevo Travel: www.atevo.com/guides/destinations. Detailed introductions, travel tips, and suggested itineraries.

CIA World Factbook: www.odci.gov/cia/publications/factbook/index.html. Tons of vital statistics on Costa Rica's geography, government, economy, and people.

Costa Rica Tourism and Travel Bureau: www.costaricabureau.com. Offers background information about the country as well current facts about transportation and accomodations. Also offers travel tips and suggests tours and activities.

Costa Rican National Chamber of Tourism: www.tourism.co.cr. Travel tips and requirements for visitors as well as information on national parks, adventure, ecotourism, hotels, car rentals, and real estate.

Embassy of Costa Rica: www.costarica-embassy.org. Vital information on travel requirements, updates on current events, and links to relevant websites.

Foreign Language for Travelers: www.travlang.com. Provides free online translating dictionaries and lists of phrases in Spanish.

Geographia: www.geographia.com. Highlights, culture, and people of Costa Rica.

MyTravelGuide: www.mytravelguide.com. Country overviews, with everything from history to transportation to live webcam coverage of Costa Rica.

World Travel Guide: www.travel-guides.com/navigate/world.asp. Helpful practical info.

ESSENTIALS

LIFE AND TIMES

Endowed with dripping cloud forests, red-hot active volcanoes, lush flora and fauna, and a generous, welcoming culture, Costa Rica captivates all who dare to explore it. The only real risk facing most travelers is becoming so hopelessly wrapped up in its beauty that they never want to go home. This tiny country unfolds new and more vibrant colors at every turn. Its national parks and preserves comprise more than 25% of its area, and despite the fact that the whole country makes up only 0.03% of the world's territory, it is home to 6% of Earth's biodiversity. Awe-inspiring surroundings, combined with endless recreational opportunities from climbing and rafting to surfing and diving, easily explain why more and more curious visitors trickle in every day.

Yet far too many visitors dart right for the jungle-enshrouded isolation, missing out on much of the country's true magic—its culture and people. Costa Ricans, also known as *ticos*, are proud of their country's strong democracy and outstanding social institutions. They are incredibly warmhearted, and it is this striking friendliness and easy, comfortable *manera de ser* (way of being) that often entices people to stay and live here forever.

Public health and education are the government's top priorities. Many infectious diseases have been nearly eradicated, and since Costa Rica has no army, it spends an outstanding 23% of the national budget on education, compared to the 3% it spends on its civil police force. While Costa Rica is a haven of political and economic stability, it is the warm hearts and smiling faces of the *ticos* that will prove worth your visit. Between all the exploring, take some time to enjoy the people, to kick back, and to internalize the essence of the Costa Rican mantra, *¡Pura vida!*

LAND

Costa Rica contains an immense variety of landscapes within its compact area. The country is dominated by a massive arc of highlands that include more than 60 volcanoes, eight of which are active, in four distinct chains. From northwest to southeast, the chains are **Cordillera de Guanacaste, Cordillera de Tilarán, Cordillera Central,** and **Cordillera de Talamanca,** the last of which is non-volcanic. Generally, as one proceeds southeast along the isthmus, the mountains become higher and the cordilleras broader, culminating in Costa Rica's highest point, Mount Chirripó (3820m), in the Cordillera de Talamanca. Between Cordilleras Central and Talamanca lies the high Central Valley, or Meseta Central, whose fertile soil is home to over half of Costa Rica's population.

The mountain ranges also affect the country's **climate** significantly. On the Pacific side, west of the cordilleras, there is increasing precipitation from north to south, with a rainy season from May to October in the north and from April to December in the south. Costa Rica's Caribbean side, east of the cordilleras, experiences rainfall year-round. Temperatures vary mostly by elevation, ranging from the hot, humid lowlands to the warm, temperate climates in medium elevations to the chilly heights of Costa Rica's tallest peaks.

The Pacific lowlands are narrower, drier, and over four times longer than the Caribbean lowlands. In contrast to the Caribbean, the Pacific coastline is a long, broken series of rocky peninsulas, bays, and white-sand beaches, a product of

plate tectonics. Sizable portions of these points of land, most notably the Península de Osa and the Península de Nicoya, were originally islands driven into the mainland by the collision of two tectonic plates. The convergence of tectonic plates off Central America's Pacific coast makes Costa Rica prone to both **earthquakes** and **volcanic eruptions.** An earthquake of magnitude 6.7 struck 89km south of San José in August 1999. Though tremors were felt throughout the country, damage was minimal and much less harmful than the repercussions of the massive 1991 earthquake. The biggest potential risk stems from volcanic eruptions, as several active volcanoes line the densely populated Central Valley. **Hurricanes** tend to pass the country to the north, such as Hurricane Mitch, which caused tremendous destruction in Nicaragua and Honduras, but left Costa Rica unaffected. Occasionally, though, a hurricane does strike the country, as in 1997 when Hurricane Cesar caused widespread damage, especially in the south of the country.

FLORA & FAUNA

Costa Rica is world-renowned for its incredible wealth and diversity of plant and animal life. Situated on the Central American isthmus that connects North and South America, flora and fauna endemic to both the southern and northern hemispheres thrive here. In fact, Costa Rica serves as the major intersection point for species from these two continents, which had evolved separately for 140 million years on their respective continents before the formation of the Central American land bridge. This unique geography and ecology, combined with the country's relative economic stability and its aggressive protection and preservation efforts, have laid the ground for Costa Rica's enormous, evergrowing ecotourism industry. Roughly 25% of Costa Rica's territory is protected in an extensive system of national parks, biological reserves, forest reserves, and wildlife refuges; no other country in the world protects a greater portion of its territory.

PLANTS

The natural vegetation of Costa Rica is forest; 99% of the country used to be covered by trees. Deforestation, especially over the past century, has reduced the expanse of forests in Costa Rica to around one quarter of the land. Yet an overwhelming variety of plants have survived, amounting to over 10,000 plant species, including over a thousand different types of orchids and hundreds of tree species. The distribution of vegetation is mostly shaped by climatic factors including the amount of rainfall and the average temperatures, both of which are closely tied to altitude, and of course by human intervention, for example through agriculture.

VEGETATION ZONES. Starting along the coast, one would either find sand of different shades on the beautiful beaches, or in parts of the Caribbean and the Golfo de Nicoya and Golfo Dulce areas, dense, saltwater-resistant **mangroves.** Moving inland, Costa Rica's lowland **tropical rainforests** and **evergreen forests** on the lower mountain slopes harbor a vegetation strongly resembling that of their South American equivalents. Ascending further, evergreen oaks and laurels, orchids, and bromeliads form the moist, dripping **cloud forests** for which Costa Rica has become famous. At higher elevations in some areas, **conifers** form a significant part of the forest landscape. Above the treeline, the vegetation resembles that of the Andean highland **moors,** with evergreen shrubs, berries, herbs, and mosses. The country's drier northwest has some **savannas** and **deciduous forests.**

ENDANGERED PLANTS. Despite the great variety and lush appearance of Costa Rica's vegetation, some well-known plants have significantly reduced populations, including many insect-eating plants, ferns, cacti, palms, and orchids (some of which are even on the verge of extinction). Please take pictures and fond memories of Costa Rica's natural beauty, but don't take any plants or pick any flowers in the wilderness. Stay on marked trails in national parks and ask your guide and the park rangers for specific tips on how to respectfully enjoy the plant life.

DANGEROUS PLANTS. The tropical diversity of plants brings with it a whole new variety of exotic, edible fruits, vegetables, and other plants. While in restaurants and markets it is often exciting and rewarding to experiment with these new flavors, it is much safer to refrain from such experiments when out in nature. Don't eat anything unless you're absolutely certain that what you're about to eat is safe. If you have even the slightest doubt, consult with a knowledgeable local or even better, don't eat it. Generally, though, "look, don't touch" is a good rule of thumb, saving you from the plants and the plants from you. If you do come into contact with a plant that produces an unpleasant reaction, or which you know to be poisonous, the best treatment is simply washing your hands, changing any clothes that touched it, and avoiding touching your eyes and other sensitive membranes.

INTERESTING PLANTS. Of all things green, some of the most spectacular are the **epiphytes**—plants that obtain both their nutrients and their moisture from the air and rain, and that often grow on other plants and trees (in a non-parasitical manner). Costa Rica is also home to an incredible variety of **trees** found nowhere else. What birds are to the animal aficionado, **orchids** are to the plant lover—the flashy, sometimes elusive and hard-to-spot flowers come in a stunning variety of well over a thousand different species. Since Costa Rica has it all, you can kill two (even three) birds with one stone (only figuratively, of course)—many orchids are epiphytes, and many epiphytes grow on trees.

ANIMALS

Costa Rica is home to an overflowing abundance of animals, mainly a mix of South and North American species. In total, there are over 240 known mammal, 850 bird, 180 amphibian, and 230 reptile species identified within the country. In addition, there is an abundance of insects.

MAMMALS. Costa Rica is home to four types of **monkeys,** all hailing from South America: howler monkeys, spider monkeys, capuchin monkeys, and squirrel monkeys. Other South American immigrants to Costa Rica include **anteaters, sloths,** and **armadillos.** There several different wildcats, such as **jaguars, pumas,** and **ocelots.** There are also a few grazing ungulates, such as deer, peccaries, and **Baird's tapir,** Latin America's largest and perhaps its shyest land mammal. There are also many more commonly known mammals such as otters, weasels, foxes, coyotes, raccoons, and opossums.

BIRDS. The most numerous vertebrates in Costa Rica are birds, making Costa Rica a prime birdwatching location—bring a pair of binoculars, patience, a silent travel companion, and lots of luck to spot beauties like the ever-elusive resplendent **quetzals, toucans, macaws, hummingbirds,** or even the world's most powerful bird of prey, the monkey-eating **harpy eagle.** Of course, many of these species are both scarce and skittish; the chances of spotting some of them are remote at best. The harpy eagle, for example, hasn't been spotted in such a long time that it is assumed to be extinct now in Costa Rica, though it is said to still live in Panama.

AMPHIBIANS AND REPTILES. Costa Rica's beaches are visited by large numbers of **turtles** who mysteriously return to their ancient nesting grounds for the *arribada*

You can help these animals survive by not buying them or any products made from them, and by staying on trails in parks. If you're considering buying a souvenir, don't necessarily trust the vendors, as they may tell you that a product is "safe" or from a legal, non-endangered species, even if that's not the case. Also be aware that the trade with endangered species is regulated internationally, and that you can be fined and jailed for carrying protected animals or products made from them.

every year. A good number of **snakes** live in Costa Rica, but fortunately, 75% of them are non-venomous colubrids. **Boas,** including boa constrictors, (but not the giant anaconda) are impressive representatives. There are also **crocodiles**, alligators, and caimans, and their smaller terrestrial cousins, the **lizards,** such as iguanas and geckos. If you don't feel like you're in wonderland yet, look for the cover-famous **tree frogs,** brightly colored **poison-dart frogs,** and the rare **golden toads.**

MARINE LIFE. While the Central American isthmus represents a confluence of two separate worlds for terrestrial species, for marine life it acts as a sharp barrier dividing the Pacific ecosystem from the Caribbean. The Pacific is much colder, more turbulent, and nutrient-rich, and supports large populations of open-water fishes like tuna, mackerel, jacks, and billfish. In contrast, the Caribbean is much more stable, shallow, and nutrient-poor, encouraging the growth of coral reefs, seagrasses, and mangroves. Both the Caribbean and Pacific teem with life, and aside from countless species of fish, including many **colorful reef fish** and the occasional **shark,** there are a number of marine mammals. **Manatees, whales,** and **dolphins** can all be found in the oceans around Costa Rica.

INSECTS AND SPIDERS. Insects abound, especially along bodies of freshwater. In contrast to the obligatory annoyance of mosquitoes and sandflies, the iridescent colors and patterns of **butterflies,** dragonflies, and countless moths will heighten your appreciation of flying insects—until they flutter off just as you try to capture them on film. Don't miss the ambitious **leaf-cutter ants**, fierce **army ants,** and impressive **beetles** on the ground. **Spiders** in Costa Rica come in all shapes, colors, and sizes, ranging from your standard harmless house spiders to giant **tarantulas** and **golden orb spiders.**

ENDANGERED ANIMALS. Unfortunately, many of Costa Rica's most remarkable animals are endangered. Over 200 animal species are endangered, and another 40 face extinction in Costa Rica. The list of these unfortunate creatures reads like a "who's who" of Costa Rican wildlife. These include the harpy eagle, red-and-green macaws, some monkeys, giant anteaters, manatees, Baird's tapir, several wildcat species, including the jaguar, puma, and ocelot, several turtle species, the American crocodile, golden toads, and the boa constrictor.

DANGEROUS ANIMALS. As one would expect from a tropical nature paradise, Costa Rica also has a few not-so-cute venomous animals. While some of these animals can be quite intimidating, none of them are malicious and out to prey on humans. Most fear humans and will flee if possible. A few things can greatly reduce the risk of any unpleasant encounters. Venomous snake bites are usually the most dangerous, but don't occur very often. Watch out especially for **coral snakes** and the aggressive **fer-de-lance.** However, most of Costa Rica's snakes are not venomous and rarely attack humans. Wearing sturdy shoes (ideally covering your ankles), staying on trails, and keeping your eyes open virtually eliminate the risk of getting bitten by a snake. In addition to snakes, there are a number of nasty crawling creatures including **spiders, scorpions, caterpillars,** and **centipedes.** Scorpions and spiders generally like dark places, so check shoes and toilet seats.

If you're camping, try to keep your bags closed and check your items before putting them on. **Mosquitoes, sandflies** and similar flying insects are mostly a nuisance, but can transmit dangerous diseases such as malaria and dengue. Long-sleeved clothes, insect repellent and mosquito netting are a good defense. Stray dogs and vampire bats can transmit rabies, but only rarely to humans. Vampire bats can be easily avoided by sleeping in a tent. Lastly, poison-dart frogs have the most powerful toxin of all animals, but the poison is only effective if it enters the bloodstream or mucus membranes, so don't grab them or put them in your nose. The best rule with unknown animals is **"look, don't touch."** Think of them as pop-stars—best admired from a distance.

HISTORY

THE COLONIAL PERIOD

1502 was the year that **Christopher Columbus** landed on Costa Rica's eastern shores and decidedly called it "rich coast." Spanish missionaries, however, surely disagreed and more likely felt that it was the devil they encountered when they arrived. They were set back by the rough environment, assailed by tropical disease, and defied by hostile **Chibcha,** natives who fiercely resisted colonization. And much to their surprise, there wasn't even enough wealth to make Costa Rica worth their efforts. In 1562, **Juan Vásquez de Coronado** finally managed to successfully establish himself in the central valley and founded the city of Cartago.

During the colonial period, Costa Rica became part of the viceroyalty of Mexico, New Spain, as part of the kingdom of Guatemala. Unlike most of its Central American neighbors, however, Costa Rica's remoteness from the capital and its lack of mineral wealth made it a forgotten land and gave it the opportunity to develop with the least colonial influence. Furthermore, the country was unique in that the native population wasn't large enough to be subjugated and turn into a labor force, which forced the Spaniards to turn to subsistence farming and prevent the extremes of wealth and poverty from developing to the same degree they did in most of Latin America.

INDEPENDENCE AND GROWTH OF THE REPUBLIC

Costa Ricans claim that the way the country attained its independence is just another example of Costa Rica's arbitrary but frequent strokes of *buena suerte*, or providence, and is characteristic of its long history of peace and harmony. In the beginning of the 19th century, Mexico revolted against Spain, and on September 15, 1821, Guatemala declared its independence and incited its sister states to do the same. Costa Rica was far away, and this news didn't reach the country until one month later, so without any need for warfare or uprisings, Costa Rica simply accepted its independence and had its first peaceful elections. It became a member of the **United Provinces of Central America,** yet was one of the first states to strike out on its own when it dissolved in 1838. By 1848, Costa Rica was recognized for its export crops and coffee market, in which Great Britain invested heavily; and since most arable land had already been divided on a small and equitable scale, the increased income didn't lead to the stratified system of land-owning elites and working peasants that characterized its Central American neighbors.

Although Costa Rica has had a stable political history, it hasn't always been a perfect democracy. For most of the 19th century, literacy requirements restricted voting to about 10% of the population. Also, between 1824 and 1899 the presidency was unstable, and numerous presidents resigned before the end of their terms. **General Tomás Guardia,** the first and one of Costa Rica's few dictators, seized power in 1870. During his 12 years in power, this iron-fisted leader's ambitious policies by and large actually benefited and modernized the country, and while it did cost Costa Ricans their civil liberties and a sizable trade deficit, he established the base for future economic progress. A new constitution was drafted in 1871, and the crop base expanded to coffee, sugar, and bananas. This expansion demanded improvements in infrastructure, which led to better roads and to the construction of the railroad to the Caribbean with the help of **Minor Keith,** the North American entrepreneur who formed the **United Fruit Company.** Tomás Guardia also instated free and compulsory primary education for all citizens, which allowed Costa Rica to reach a high level of literacy early on. After his dictatorship, the country saw a peaceful transition back to democracy, and in 1890, Costa Rica conducted the first legitimate, large-scale elections in Central American history, in which **José Joaquín Rodríguez** won the presidency.

STRAYING FROM PEACE

Only twice has Costa Rica strayed from its peaceful tradition. The first time happened in 1856, when **William Walker,** from Tennessee, attempted to turn Central America into a slave state of the United States. Costa Ricans had never fought before, yet the *ticos* raised arms to defend their freedom and force the American filibusters out of the country. To fight the war, the citizens formed an army of 9000 men, and the first troops headed out to Guanacaste, where they fought and won their first battle, **La Batalla de Santa Rosa,** at the Casona de Santa Rosa. Walker's men fled to Rivas, Nicaragua. Motivated by their triumph and in an effort to defend their Central American neighbors, the Costa Ricans followed them, and Costa Rica's national hero was born out of the **Batalla de Rivas,** the second battle waged against William Walker. Most enemy forces were concentrated in a big house in Rivas, Nicaragua, called the Mesón de Guerra, a strategic location from which the *filibusteros* could give shooting signals and were guaranteed control of the battle. **Juan Santamaría,** a young Costa Rican from Alajuela, sacrificed his life and ran across the battlefield with a torch, setting the Mesón on fire, which forced enemy forces to surrender. Costa Ricans now celebrate the day Juan Santamaría burned the Mesón de Guerra and won freedom on April 11, 1856.

The second violent event took place almost 100 years later, when incumbent **Rafael Angel Calderón Guardia** claimed an electoral fraud and refused to give up the presidency to Otilio Ulate, who had won by a small margin. Calderón's leftist presidency in the 1940s had brought important land and social reforms to the country, and the establishment of a minimum wage. However, it had also led to widespread discontent from the elites and opposing factions. The tension had been accumulating, and it finally blew up with the War of National Liberation in 1948. This civil war was led by **José Figueres Ferrer,** a wealthy coffee farmer and intellectual. Don Pepe, as the people called him, appealed to the people and headed a populist, anti-authoritarian uprising that demanded respect for democracy. As head of the new **Founding Junta of the Second Republic,** Figueres banned the communist party, gave women and blacks the right to vote, and revised the constitution in 1949 establishing a presidential term limit of four years, creating an **Electoral Tribunal** to oversee elections, and abolishing the Costa Rican military. All that remains of the army today is the country's civil guard, a government police force of only 8400 members. After 18 months in power, Figueres kept his promise and stepped down from the interim junta, handing over the presidency to **Otilio Ulate,** the man who had originally won the elections and wasn't even on his Figueres' party. Figueres was much admired for his actions, and in 1953 was elected president. Once in office, ironically, he imposed many leftist reforms similar to those that motivated the civil war in the first place, like nationalizing banks and utilities.

MOVING INTO THE 20TH CENTURY

Costa Rica's transition into the 20th century was rather ungraceful. The annexation of Guanacaste and boundary disputes with Panama created a volatile situation in Costa Rican politics, and the US intervention on Panama's behalf did nothing to improve the situation. During this period of instability Costa Rica had another dangerous flirtation with autocracy when **Alfredo González,** winner of the 1913 elections, was overthrown by the reactionary **General Federico Tinoco.** His dictatorship, however, was unpopular and brief, and the decades to follow were smooth and prosperous. The US antagonism toward Tinoco restored its popularity among *ticos.* From this period on, the nation's democratic and educational structures flourished, even as dependence on foreign trade increased.

SO LONG, SOLDIERS

Since the army was abolished in 1949, Costa Rica has enjoyed peace, political stability, and a relatively high degree of economic comfort. In addition, it has become Latin America's most democratic country. Most of Costa Rica's non-financial problems in the second half of the 20th century have been partly because of civil strife in other Central American nations, especially in El Salvador and Nicaragua. As many as 500,000 **refugees** (some Salvadoran, mostly Nicaraguan) have poured across the border since the late 1970s. This overflow has caused internal problems including unemployment swells, higher illiteracy rates, and mounting tensions between *ticos* and their new neighbors. Today this is still a complex and unresolved issue.

The 1980s were a tough period for Costa Rica. In addition to the internal economic crisis of devaluation, soaring welfare, and oil costs, the plummeting prices of coffee, sugar, and bananas, the war between the left and right in Nicaragua brought additional instability to the region. In 1987, however, former president **Oscar Arias Sánchez** earned the **Nobel Peace Prize** when he achieved a consensus among all Central America leaders with the *Plan de Paz Arias,* a peace plan that brought long-lasting stability. He negotiated a sustained cease-fire agreement and laid the groundwork for a unified Central American Parliament. In 1988, he increased his commitment to democracy when he created the **Arias Foundation for Peace and Human Progress.** Since then, Costa Rica has strived to be an oasis of peace and prosperity amidst an often chaotic and conflict-torn isthmus.

The more recent president **José María Figueres** (1994-1998), son of the original Figueres, had intentions to improve health care and education in Costa Rica, to protect the environment, and to reduce poverty. However, he became increasingly unpopular, and his term was plagued by strikes and general economic instability. In 1998, Costa Ricans elected economist **Miguel Angel Rodríguez** of the Social Christian Unity Party, who also attempted to lower inflation, poverty, and unemployment in addition to privatizing and improving the country's services.

In recent years, Costa Rica has seen declines in its education, welfare, and social programs. However, the government is persistent in its efforts to improve the country. Today, Costa Rica continues to have one of the highest literacy rates in the world, high standards of living, the best reputation for health care, the second lowest birth rate, one of the highest life expectancies, and the safest, most reliable public transportation system of Central America.

DID YOU KNOW...

— That all the profits from the *Parque de Diversiones* go to the *Hospital Nacional de Niños?* It is the only amusement park in the world that donates all of its profits to a charitable cause.

— That the zoológico La Marina in San Carlos is the only place in the world where tapirs have been bred in captivity? Doña Alba, the owner of this refuge for wounded and confiscated animals, is to be credited for this feat.

— That the world's toughest mountain bike race takes place in Costa Rica? In La Ruta de los Conquistadores, every October, riders start the trajectory on the Pacific coast and go though gusty winds, knee-high mud, rough terrain, abandoned railroad bridges, and extreme heat and cold to finish on the Atlantic coast, all in three days.

— That many of the outstanding international tennis players played as juniors in the *Copa del Café?* This internationally known "Coffee Bowl" takes place every January at the Costa Rica Country Club in Escazú.

— That the first Latin American astronaut to orbit the earth is from Costa Rica? Franklin Change, an admired *tico*, holds the world record for spending the longest number of hours on board a space shuttle.

— That one of the humpback whale's migration routes ends in the Pacific waters of Costa Rica, a unique place for the reproduction of these singing cetaceous travelers from the Antarctic (18,000 km away)?

— That on average every three days a scientific work is published based on research conducted at one of the O.T.S. (Organization of Tropical Studies) biological stations: La Selva in Sarapiquí, Las Cruces in San Vito, and Palo Verde in Guanacaste? This nonprofit consortium includes 64 universities and research institutions mostly from the United States and Costa Rica.

LIFE AND TIMES

COSTA RICA TODAY

Costa Rica is one of the most prosperous countries in Latin America today. It has been and continues to be politically stable, and its well-educated population maintains a strongly democratic spirit and an awareness for many environmental, political, and social issues. Economically, the country has experienced relatively stable growth and a slow reduction in inflation. While the challenge of reconciling debt-management and a diversifying, liberalizing economy with a welfare state persists, Costa Rica is experiencing generally positive trends. Some challenges, such as unemployment, informal sector employment, and poverty still trouble the country, but to a lesser degree than in most of Latin America. The government and population seem generally willing and determined to tackle these issues.

ECONOMIC CHALLENGES AND OUTLOOK

Costa Rica's export-oriented economy relies primarily on **tourism** and on a high-tech sector that took off in the late 1990s with US chip-manufacturer Intel's opening of a large chip-processing plant in San José. Agriculture continues to be important, but with a worldwide overproduction of coffee and Ecuadorian bananas selling below their production price, competition is fierce, and the cultivation of Costa Rica's two principal crops is becoming increasingly less profitable. Costa Rica pursues a rather cautious strategy when it comes to exploiting its natural resources like wood and minerals. In a move to protect Costa Rica's environmental wealth, as the basis for a flourishing tourism industry, the government halted all approvals of further open-pit mining in Costa Rica and plans to terminate licenses for existing open pit mines.

KNOCK ON WOOD Portico, a large exporter of wood, has struck an alliance with Fundecor, a non-governmental organization promoting environmentally sustainable development, to cut trees in a socially and environmentally sustainable fashion. Consumer insistence on certified wood, governmental regulations, and a high level of awareness among Costa Ricans have contributed to the innovative way of doing business. Trees are cut selectively, taking into account regeneration periods, and Portico/Fundecor buys wood from the owners of small patches of wood which allows them to make a livelihood without having to wipe out or sell their patches of forest. Although regulations are lax enough to allow wood exporters like Portico to cut a significant portion of their trees from non-regulated areas in whichever way they desire, efforts are made to create and expand such innovative and productive cooperations between business and conservation interests.

President Pacheco, just shortly after his election, reiterated that tourism is a viable economic avenue for Costa Rica, and thus its development strategies have been geared increasingly toward environmental and social sustainability, as tourists mainly come to Costa Rica for two reasons—its vast, unspoiled nature and its reputation for convenience and safety.

"COSTA RICA—NO ARTIFICIAL INGREDIENTS"

As the official slogan of Costa Rica's tourist industry, the message reveals just how important Mother Nature has been to the country's success. **Ecotourism,** essentially a Costa Rican invention, has made the country famous worldwide, and continues to be a huge draw for foreign tourists. In 1998, Costa Rica passed a unique **biodiversity law,** regulating the use and protection of Costa Rica's natural and genetic resources, protected areas, and encouraging environmental education. In 2001, over 1.1 million visitors came to Costa Rica, generating over US$1.2 billion in revenues, making tourism the single most significant contributor to Costa Rica's economy. Although Intel's investment in the high-tech sector temporarily took the throne for the single largest pillar of Costa Rica's foreign revenues, President Abel Pacheco and proposed a close cooperation of public and private sector institutions to foster the country's tourism industry. Their joint marketing efforts run under the label "Costa Rica—no artificial ingredients."

But not everything is sunshine in Costa Rica's tourism industry—while the government has plans to steer tourism in the direction of high-end, luxury ecotourism, trying to attract more affluent, comfort-seeking travelers, and toward a sustainable form of "sea, sand, and sun" tourism, conservation groups are concerned that larger facilities will put too heavy a burden on Costa Rica's precious ecosystems.

COMPUTER, INFORMATION, AND COMMUNICATION TECHNOLOGIES

Costa Rica is technologically rather modern, with a large computer hardware industry and a growing software industry. A modern European style GSM cell phone network is expected to be established by November 2002, making Costa Rica compatible with many other countries' cell phone networks. Internet use is also more widespread than in other Latin American countries, and the country has an unusually large and diverse media culture, with a wide array of broadcasters.

In 1998, by opening a chip-processing plant in Belén, near San José, micro-chip manufacturer Intel made the single largest foreign investment in the history of Costa Rica. Just a year later, exports from the Intel plant were the largest source of foreign currency revenue in the country. By 2001 it became apparent, however, that the Intel investment had not had the anticipated spillover effects.

COSTA RICA IN THE WORLD

Costa Rica is open to economic integration of the greater region, being a member of the Central American Common Market (CACM), subscribing to a uniform external tariff and to free-trade internally. It also supports the Puebla-Panama plan, initiated by Mexico's president Vicente Fox, which intends the "Mesoamerican" integration of Mexico's struggling southern states and all seven Central American countries. Costa Rica does currently not advocate/support the political integration of Central America, as it considers the other countries' democracies as not sufficiently developed yet for such a step.

Since 1948, Costa Rica has not had a military, and despite severe turbulences and civil wars in Central America and border conflicts with Nicaragua and Panama, Costa Rica has successfully maneuvered itself through these times. Key factors in this success have been Costa Rica's neutrality, trade integration, and use of OAS (Organization of American States) mechanisms to defuse minor conflicts with Nicaragua. Costa Rica continues without a military, having only a police force totaling 8,400 (and an elite anti-terrorism force of 750). An increasingly important area of activity for Costa Rica's police forces is to strengthen control of the vast territorial and international waters surrounding Costa Rica to combat drug-trafficking. The government has taken steps to strengthen the sea and air divisions of its police force to tackle this task. Costa Rica also signed a bilateral maritime counter-drug agreement with the US, in effect since late 1999.

COSTA RICA AND NICARAGUA

Two issues continue to strain Costa Rican-Nicaracuan relations: the conflict over the use of the bordering Río San Juan and massive illegal immigration from Nicaragua. Dating back to 1858, the **Cañas-Juarez Treaty** established that the San Juan River between Costa Rica and Nicaragua constituted the border and belonged to Nicaragua, but that Costa Rica was granted free and perpetual commercial access to the river. In 1998—140 years later—Nicaragua became irritated because Costa Rican police were using the river to reach border posts. Negotiations continue as both countries try to come to a consensus on what constitutes commercial use of the river. The issue receives a great deal of attention in both countries and has resulted in heated diplomatic exchanges, though military conflict seems unlikely. The border regions of both countries are paying the price for the tension and uncertainty, as the conflict impedes necessary investment and development.

The issue of migration between the two countries remains. Costa Rica is better off economically than Nicaragua, which has led to massive illegal immigration by Nicaraguans to Costa Rica. Many educated Nicaraguans come to work illegally for the better job opportunities. Close to 300,000 foreigners (about 8% of the population) live in Costa Rica, many lacking legal status. Successive governments have attempted to address the issue by having amnesties, the last one in 1999, for illegal immigrants. The problem of illegal migration persists, with Costa Rican border police returning up to 150 illegal Nicaraguan migrants per day.

LIFE AND TIMES

THE UNSPECTACULAR RECORD ELECTIONS OF 2002

In the lackluster election in February 2002, 31% of Costa Ricans didn't go to the polls to elect their new president. For the first time ever in Costa Rican history, the first round of elections did not turn up a clear winner. Many voters decided to withhold their votes from the traditionally strongest parties **Partido Unidad Social Cristiana (PUSC)** and **Partido de Liberacion Nacional (PLN),** and voted for a third party candidate. **Abel Pacheco** finally won the presidency in the run-off election on April 7. This second round yielded a record-low voter turnout, with a 39% abstention rate. It also marked the first time in the history of modern Costa Rica that the incumbent party returned to power. This marked voter turnout took a dive in the 1998 presidential elections, with an abstention rate of 30%, which remained high throughout the 2002 elections.

INSTITUTIONAL CHALLENGES

Costa Rica's health care, education, and welfare systems all are in need of a boost to maintain or improve standards. However, this must be accomplished while keeping inflation and unemployment low. Another major challenge for Costa Rica and already a priority on the political agenda is poverty. Despite Costa Rica's overall well-developed welfare system, over 800,000 Costa Ricans, or nearly 20% of the population, are classified as poor. In conjunction with tourism, the ugly face of poverty and social stratification becomes manifest in increasing levels of crime and sex tourism. It will take more than just increased policing to tackle these problems at their roots.

While Costa Rica does not have much trouble with organized crime (drug trafficking being the major activity in that realm), corruption and cronyism continue to be problematic, though to a lesser degree than in other countries.

In 2000, despite overall positive economic trends, there was increased civil unrest, including the largest demonstrations in Costa Rica in 30 years. People expressed their discontent with an energy bill that was seen as providing loopholes for Costa Rica's two main parties to divide the spoils between them. The bill was later declared unconstitutional by the Costa Rican Supreme Court, but the case illustrates the challenge posed by opening up monopolies. In addition school teachers protested because they suspected the government was not going to follow through on its promise to pay them for the extra days of the extended length of the school year.

PEOPLE

DEMOGRAPHICS

Anything that ends with the diminutive *tico* is just the right size for Costa Ricans. They turned the word *chiquito*, which means small, into *chiquitico*, and they use this different ending so often that *"ticos"* has become a term referring to Costa Ricans in general. Out of nearly 3,900,000 inhabitants, **indígenas** comprise less than 1% of the population, and those of **African** descent make up only 3% and are concentrated on the Atlantic coast. The region's largest remaining indigenous groups are the **Bribrí** and **Cabecar.** Except for **Guanacaste,** where people have darker skin due to the mix with the Cabecares, 94% of the population is of European descent.

Most *indígenas* in Costa Rica who maintain their traditional ways live on one of 22 reserves that are scattered throughout the country. However, the reserve boundaries are often disrespected, and indigenous lands are constantly threatened. Generations of other ethnic groups, including Germans, Americans, Italians, and Chinese, have also immigrated to Costa Rica and over the past 150 years have established small communities. Monteverde, for example, was founded in the 1950s by a group of Alabama **Quakers** and is now home to a Quaker community that works producing different types of cheeses and other milk products.

LANGUAGE

Spanish, with a characteristic *tico* twist in accent and usage, is the official language. Blacks along the Caribbean coast also speak English, and indigenous groups like the Bribrí speak Spanish in addition to their native tongue. The country's most unique and popular phrase is *pura vida* (cool, awesome) and you'll probably laugh at the fact that *tuanis*, which has a similar meaning, was what became of the English phrase "too nice" after Costa Ricans used it for a while. Some other fun words and phrases unique to the country are: *mae* (dude), *quedarse bateado* (remain stupefied or baffled), and *atarantado* (wound-up). Accent varies by region as well. The Spanish of the Guanacaste province bears more resemblance to that of Nicaragua than that of the Central Valley.

RELIGION

Costa Rica is a politically secular country, with a weak link between church and state. **Roman Catholicism** is the official religion and is practiced by about 90% of the population. Catholic churches exist in nearly every town in the country, and they are often at the center of cultural and religious events. Holy Week, which culminates in Easter Sunday, is a fervent balance of piety, pilgrimage, prayer, and partying. Nonetheless, there *is* religious freedom in Costa Rica as written in its constitution. The majority of blacks on the Caribbean Coast are Protestant, though the religion has yet to gain the ubiquity found in other Central American countries. You may also encounter Jehovah's Witnesses, Jews, Menonites, Quakers, and other denominations.

CULTURE

FOOD AND DRINK

If it doesn't have rice and beans, it isn't *tico!* Rice and black beans are everyday staple foods and part of every Costa Rican's diet, whether *gallo pinto* (fried rice and beans cooked with spices) for breakfast, a *casado* for lunch, or a black bean soup for dinner. The word *casado* literally means married man, and it is the name given to a big, hearty plate of rice and beans with meat, *macarrones* (noodles), *maduros* (sweet plantains), and cabbage and tomato salad, which wives would prepare for their husbands to take when they worked the fields. *Tamales* and *chicharrones* (deep-fried pork rind) are also typical foods. **Comida típica** (native dishes) in Costa Rica can best be described as tasty, not spicy. *Salsa Lizano* has become Costa Rica's number one condiment and you're almost guaranteed to find it on every table if it's not spicing up your meal already. *Sodas*, the small diners you can find at almost every corner, will become your best friend if you're looking for flavorful, home-style cooking at inexpensive prices. *Restaurantes* are larger and generally more expensive.

SLANG Just as common as *hola* is *adios* when people pass each other by on the street in Costa Rica. Don't get confused, either, if you're a girl walking with a guy friend and a man calls him *cuñado*, which means brother-in-law. The cat-caller is pretending you are his girlfriend, and your male escort merely your brother. Likewise, if he calls your mother *suegra* (mother in law), you can be certain this cat-caller has a thing for you. Speaking of family, friends sometimes use *primito* (little cousin) as a term of endearment for each other. Finally, the ubiquitous slang word *mae* is the *tico* counterpart of man or dude, derived from the Spanish *maje* (which actually means stupid) and shortened when spoken fast with a lilting tone: *¡Pura vida, mae!*

Fruits include pineapple, banana, melon, strawberries, and papaya, but you can also find the more traditional *tamarindo, guayabas, cases,* and *marañones* (the fruit of cashews), which are often used to make *frescos* (drinks) and ice cream. You will also find the more exotic *pejiballe,* a fleshy fruit that grows on palm trees, which is boiled, flavored with salt, and usually eaten with mayonnaise. The Atlantic Coast has a much stronger Caribbean influence than the rest of the country, and here you will find everything, including *gallo pinto,* chicken, and a meat-and-vegetable Carib stew called *rondon,* cooked in coconut milk.

Empanadas (turnovers), *batidos* (fruit shakes), and *frescos* (milk or water based fruit drinks) are everywhere. Don't be surprised when you see *ticos* from age 5 to 80 enjoying a big glass of Costa Rica's world-class coffee (usually mixed with milk) more than once a day. Along with coffee, *horchata,* a cornmeal drink flavored with cinnamon, and *agua dulce,* a traditional drink made with boiled water and brown sugar, are traditional drinks popular in the country. *Pipas,* green coconuts with chopped-off tops full of refreshing coconut water, are also popular and sold at roadside stalls. *Guaro,* the local liquor, is a clear, cheap moonshine that mixes nicely with anything, and is the *campesino's* drink of choice. Finally, when it comes to beer, anyone who's not a fan of Imperial, the Costa Rican beer, is liable to be chased out of the country.

CUSTOMS AND ETIQUETTE

BEING COSTA RICAN. The ideals of peace and democracy are also widespread, all Costa Ricans share a strong character regarding civil rights and liberties, and are always willing to stand up against whomever threatens these ideals. *Ticos* are very **family-oriented.** Kids live with their parents through their college years and don't leave home until they get married. Close, extended families are common, and the peace and stability of the country add to their innate warmhearted nature, They are mostly very relaxed and helpful, and willing to lend a hand, or even a home, in times of need.

PUBLIC DISPLAYS OF AFFECTION. In general, *ticos* are very affectionate and are often physically expressive. It isn't unusual to see couples holding hands or walking arm in arm. Also, in public places like bars and discos, it isn't bad manners for couples to hug, kiss, or even for girls to sit on their boyfriend's lap. When dancing, it is usual to dance close together; however, "grinding" is frowned upon.

HOUSEGUEST MANNERS. Thankfulness is a very admirable quality in house guests. Say thank you often. Middle- and upper-class families often have an *empleada,* a young girl or woman who lives in the house and gets paid to help with house chores. Nonetheless, your hosts will be very grateful if you offer to help serve others or clean after a meal is over, especially if they're doing the work.

AGAIN, FOR THE LAST TIME! When a party is winding down, be it a high school prom, New Year's celebration, or just a fun gathering, there comes a point when everyone knows the fat lady has sung. However, more often than not, when a *zarpe* (literally translated as "take-off" or "leaving") ensues, everyone feels they should have done what they wanted to early on, whether it was another drink or another dance. *Ticos* love *fiestas*, and more often than not, the last zarpe becomes the first. So get ready to party, knowing that a *zarpe* may mean the night is just starting.

TABLE MANNERS. When having a meal, it is good manners to wait until everyone has their food before you start eating. You should place your napkin on your lap at fancier restaurants, always eat with a fork, and use a knife to cut meat or butter bread. Although unusual, if you're far from the city, you could find yourself at a small *soda* where they only give you a spoon. This is because *campesinos*, the people who live in very rural areas and work the fields, often eat with a spoon. Don't be embarrassed to ask for a fork and knife. Many meals come with bread or corn tortillas, both of which you can hold and eat with your hand. Finally, if the food is good and you're hungry, eat everything on your plate. *Ticos* don't believe in leaving a little bit just because it's good manners.

HOW TO BE POLITE. When speaking Spanish, in Costa Rica there is an important distinction between *usted* and *vos*. Use *usted* when you're talking to a stranger or someone who is older; it is more formal and respectful. You may use *vos* when talking to friends. It is important to use *Don* or *Doña* before an older person's name. For example, call your friend's father *Don* Alberto and not just Alberto.

When it comes to gender relations, *machismo* has left its mark, yet women still appreciate the chivalry it has taught men. Out of tradition, men are very gentlemanly and courteous and they will always protect and care for girls. It is considered good manners for men to open doors for women and help carry their bags.

GREETINGS. When saying hi to someone you know, young or old, it is routine to kiss the person once, on the cheek. You can also hug someone when you're saying hi; it will always be well-received and considered warm and friendly.

TABOOS. Although times are changing, most people in the country are committed Catholics, and their religious beliefs make **sexual relations before marriage** an ongoing taboo, especially among older generations. **Homosexuality** is another hot topic, and although in general people are more open about it, public displays of affection is usually uncomfortably accepted.

DRESS CODE. Costa Ricans are always very conscious about looking presentable and tidy when they go out. Although the climate is warmer than in many countries, when they aren't at the beach, they don't dress as if they were. Men usually wear slacks, jeans, t-shirts, polo shirts, or button-down shirt. Women try to look elegant and usually wear pants, jeans, or skirts in the city. You can wear shorts; however, short shorts aren't appropriate unless you're at the beach. People usually dress more stylishly to go out to clubs and bars, but they don't wear anything too flashy, so save the sparkled tube-top for another country.

THE ARTS

Long before Columbus set foot on the soil he aptly named the "rich coast" in 1502, the indigenous populations of the area were living in cultures that left a record of their sophistication in form of impressive works craftmanship and art. Typical artifacts include **statues** in **gold, jade,** and **stone.** Another impressive set of artifacts,

LIFE AND TIMES

whose mystery is only exceeded by its sophistication, are the almost perfectly spherical **Diquís stones**, mainly found in southern Costa Rica (especially around Palmar). Some of the stones are 1600 years old, arranged in geometric formations that point to the earth's magnetic north. 130 of the stones have been catalogued, and many remain to be examined. With the arrival of the Spanish colonial rulers, Costa Rica's arts and culture were dominated by European ideals for the following centuries. Today, however, Costa Ricans take pride and an active interest in their pre-Columbian history and culture.

Prior to the 20th century, Costa Rican literature drew primarily from folk tales and colloquial expression in a movement known as *"costumbrismo."* The nation's working people were represented through *El Moto* and *Las Hijas del Campo* by **Joaquín García Monge**. Despite the strength of this early movement, Costa Rican literature didn't fully bloom until 1900, when it began to give voice to political and social criticism. **José Marín Cañas's** *Infierno Verde*, a depiction of the Chaco War between Paraguay and Bolivia, bolstered developing anti-imperialist sentiment. Similarly, **Oreamuni's** *La Ruta de su Evasión* confronts tensions stemming from Latin American *machismo* and between generations. Playwrights **Alberto Cañas** and **Daniel Gallegos** accompanied the so-called "Circle of Costa Rican Poets" in an attempt to unite the nation's thinkers against the sociopolitical cruelties of the twentieth century. Many *ticos* revere two of the country's contemporary authors: **Fabián Dobles**, winner of the Premio Nacional, Costa Rica's highest distinction for artistic and intellectual achievement; and **Carlos Salazar Herrera**, painter, poet, professor, and the author of *Tres Cuentos de Angustias y Paisajes*.

The rule of thumb in Costa Rican popular culture, especially with teenagers, is a simple conditional: if it's *norteamericano*, it's cool. TVs across the country emit canned laughter from *The Fresh Prince of Bel Air* (in Spanish, *Príncipe del Rap*), and Britney and Justin (Spears and Timberlake) double-team many *discotecas* with a teenybopper music invasion. Traditional *salsa* and *merengue*, while harder to find on the radio, are often played in nightclubs. Internationally popular groups originating in Spanish-speaking countries also find their way into Costa Rica, including the Mexican rock group *Maná* and Puerto Rican star Ricky Martin.

The Spanish-language **newspapers** *La Nación* (www.nacion.co.cr) and *La República* (www.larepublica.net) represent alternative views of the two main political parties in Costa Rica. In English, the *Tico Times* (www.ticotimes.net) offers extensive summaries of cultural events, hotels, restaurants, and current events. The *Tico Times'* publication *Exploring Costa Rica* is an invaluable guide to the country's tourist attractions and cities.

SPORTS AND RECREATION

Costa Rica is renowned for the diversity and affordability of its outdoor adventures, and many travelers come for its high-quality offerings. Activities run the gamut from scenic to strenuous, including **sportfishing, surfing, scuba diving, snorkeling, kayaking, white-water rafting, mountainbiking,** and **golf.** (Yes, golf: Costa Rica boasts the best 18 hole courses in Central America.) While tour groups and guides are more common than *típico* food, this results in competitive prices for the budget traveler, as well as more stringent safety requirements.

Sportfishing is an increasingly popular activity, especially as many towns begin to expand their services to cater to big-game fishermen. Many new luxury fishing lodges offer guides, full service, and the newest boats and technology. Consistent with their conservationist philosophy, many companies are only catch-and-release. A fishing license is required for both salt- and freshwater fishing; some packages include one in their price, but be sure to ask. Around the Central Pacific region dorado, tuna, snapper, wahoo, mackerel, and yellowfin abound. On the Carribbean coast, catches include Atlantic sailfish, dorado, tuna, barracuda, kingfish, grouper, and jacks. Billfishing (sailfish and marlin) is best from Dec-April. Freshwater sportfishing offers a different experience. Lake Arenal, the largest inland fishing lake and the only one open year-round, has mainly *guapote* (rainbow bass). *Bobo* (a type of mullet), *machaca* or *sabalito* ("little tarpon"), and *guatpote* run in the freshwater rivers. Río Frío, in Los Chiles, has some of the largest tarpon, as well as snook, drum, and *guapote*.

Surfers come from round the globe to ride the waves of the Pacific and Caribbean beaches. Many of the best surfing beaches are around a four-hour drive from San José, where waves range from fast and hollow to consistent lefts and rights. Jacó, Playa Dominical, and Limón are among the best areas to begin lessons or hone your skills. The best surfers head to Pavones and Playa Negra for the most challenging waves. Costa Rica hardly suffers from a lack of marine life, reefs, or guides; as such, **scuba diving** and **snorkeling** are extremely popular among travelers looking to explore the waters beyond their beach chair. However, many experienced divers report somewhat decreased visibility, particularly during the rainy season. Cahuita has large, beautiful reefs, as do Punta Gorda and Isla del Coco.

Further inland, **white-water rafting** and **kayaking** are fun ways to see biodiversity first-hand. Costa Rica's rugged terrain, drainage network, and amount of runoff result in ideal conditions for paddling. Rapids range from Class II to Class V depending on physical and technical ability. Some of the best sites are Quepos, Fortuna de San Carlos, Parque Nacional Santa Rosa, and Puerto Viejo de Sarapiquí. **Mountain biking** has become popular only in the last decade, and is a great way to see the country and take advantage of the mountainous terrain, dirt trails, and beach roads. Guided trips cater to all ability levels. Some of the best biking is reputed to be around Turrialba, Volcán Arenal, Orosi Valley, and El Rodeo near Cuidad Colón. First introduced in 1944, **golf** in Costa Rica today has the lucky combination of being world-renowned and uncrowded. In the 1970s, the Cariari Country Club, between San José and the International Airport built the first and only golf course in the country for over two decades. Today, high-ranking Garra de León Resort and Valle del Sol in the Central Valley are also challenging courses.

COSTA RICA'S FESTIVALS (2003)

DATE	NAME & LOCATION	DESCRIPTION
mid-Jan.	Fiestas Patronales de Santa Cruz, Guanacaste	History and traditions are revived in honor of Santo Cristo de Esquipulas. Folk dances, *marimba* music, rodeo, and bull-fighting celebrate the Costa Rican culture.
Jan. 14-24	Fiestas de Palmares	Fairgrounds are set up in town. Dances, concerts, fireworks, food, music, and bullfighting. The festival also hosts sporting events like mountainbike races.
2nd Su in Mar.	Día del Boyero, Escazú	Day of the ox-cart driver. Beautiful ox-cart processions proceed down the streets of San Antonio de Escazú.
Mar. 19-23	University Week, San José	Crowning a queen, sporting events, parades, concerts, lectures, open-air art shows, and hundreds of free activities on the campus of the University of Costa Rica
Mar./Apr.	Semana Santa	Holy week. Celebrated with religious processions throughout the country.
2nd Su in June	Father's Day	A family-oriented day celebrating fatherhood.
June 29	Día de San Pedro y San Pablo	Many religious celebrations in and around San José.

DATE	NAME & LOCATION	DESCRIPTION
last week of August	Semana Afro-Costarri-cense, San José and Limón	A week to celebrate and rescue the values and traditions of the Afro-Costa Rican culture; featuring lectures, panel discussions, craft and artwork displays, parades, floats, dancing, and festivals. Aug. 28 – election of the *Black Beauty* queen Aug. 30 – family and cultural recreational activities Aug. 31 – *Día de la Cultura Negra* parade
Aug. 31	Día de San Ramón	Colorful processions celebrate the *tico* culture and the town of San Ramón.
Dec. 8	Fiesta de los Negritos	Costumed dancing and celebrations of Boruca indigenous traditions.
Dec. 26 (daytime)	Tope Nacional, Paseo Colón, San José	Nearly a century-old tradition, the street of Paseo Colón is made free game for a parade of more than 3000 of the country's finest horses and their riders.
Dec. 26 (nighttime)	Festival de la Luz, Paseo Colón, San José	A Light Festival with floats and colorful light and designs that run down two of San José's main streets. Beautiful fireworks light up the country's capital.
Dec. 27	Carnaval Nacional, Paseo Colón	A carnival celebrating the end of the year. Colorful floats compete for prizes; costumed people join the parade and dance to live bands and music.
Late Dec.	Fiestas de Zapote, a suburb southeast of San José	Every year, a big fair is set up in Zapote to celebrate the Christmas season and the New Year. Costa Ricans from all over the country come to enjoy the live music, fireworks, food, and especially the non-fatal *tico* bullfights.
Dec. 31	Día de los Diablitos	A Boruca indigenous celebration.

COSTA RICA'S OFFICIAL HOLIDAYS

DATE	NAME & LOCATION	DESCRIPTION
Jan. 1	New Year's Day	Celebrated with a big dance in San José's *parque central*.
Apr. 11	Juan Santamaría Day	Commemorates the day Costa Rica's only national hero, Juan Santamaría, burned down the filibusters' fort and helped Costa Ricans win the Battle of Rivas (1856).
Mar./Apr.	Good Thursday and Friday	Holy Week; paid holidays celebrated with religious processions, especially in Tres Ríos, Cartago and San Joaquín de Flores.
May 1	Día de los Trabajadores	Labor Day. National paid holiday for all workers.
July 25	Anexión del Partido de Nicoya	Celebrates the day in 1824 when the province of Guanacaste willfully became part of Costa Rica. Civic activities take place in every school and there are musical and folkloric festivities throughout the country, especially in Santa Cruz, Liberia, and San José.
Aug. 2	Virgen Mary Queen of Angels	People from all over the country make a religious pilgrimage to the Basílica de los Ángeles cathedral in Cartago.
Aug. 15	Mother's Day	A family-oriented holiday celebrating and recognizing motherhood.
Sept. 15	Costa Rican Independence Day, San José	Costa Rica's independence from Spain in 1821 is celebrated with parades, marching bands, and parties throughout the country. At 6pm, student runners finish a relay with the Freedom Torch that starts in Guatemala. Lantern-lit child parades and marching bands bring streets to life at night.
Oct. 12	Día de la Raza/Día de las Culturas	Formerly known as Columbus Day, Costa Rica celebrates this day with a cultural party. A big multi-day carnival takes place in Limón the week prior to Oct. 12.
Nov. 2	All Soul's Day	Church processions and pilgrimages to the cemeteries.
Dec. 25	Christmas Day	Family-oriented celebrations with dinners, trips to the beach, and lots of parties.

THE HAND OF HISTORY
Molding the *tico* character

Costa Rica is a beautiful country crossed by high mountains and volcano peaks. In a few hours you can go from the coolness of the mountains to the warmth of its beaches and small rural towns cling from the hillsides and hide in the valleys. People often wonder how Costa Rica manages to safeguard democracy and freedom, how this tiny country and its people have sheltered peace even at times when its neighbors are plagued by conflict, corruption, and upheaval. To many, the answer lays in the character of the *ticos*. Time and history ingrained the values of peace and democracy in their hearts, making *ticos* independent, tolerant, and friendly; yet sharp, perceptive, and vigilant in matters concerning their peace and freedom.

When the news of the Declaration of Independence arrived from Guatemala in 1821, Costa Ricans opted, in an open council, to show signs of prudence and wait for the uncertainties to settle. The truth is that independence arrived unexpectedly, without firing a single shot.

In 1883, Dr. Eusebio Figueroa, the minister of external affairs, died in a duel defending his honor. The President, Don Próspero Fernández, headed the funeral procession, followed by relatives, friends, townspeople, and government officials. When they reached the cemetery, however, they found the gates closed and chained because the church refused to give a Christian burial to anyone killed in a duel. The President gave an order for the soldiers to tear down the gates and Dr. Figueroa was finally buried. Because of this and other incidents, in 1884, President Fernández expelled the Catholic Bishop and the Jesuits from the country. While this was happening in Costa Rica, the rest of Latin America and Spain were still enduring the oppression of the Holy Inquisition.

The disregard for power was exemplified in the second half of the XIX Century, when, in the absence of the President, the next man designated to govern rejected the appointment and hid in a farm far away from the capital. The soldiers found him there and brought him back to the presidential house, where they had to force him to stay and rule.

At the beginning of the 20th Century, there was a small, armed conflict with Panama due to a boundary disagreement. General Volio, a priest and revolutionary, managed to pacify the soldiers, who were demanding their pay and a war spoils, with a phrase that would be famous: "If there is pay, there is no glory, and if there is glory, there is no pay."

During World War II, Costa Rica declared war on the Axis powers (Germany, Japan, and Italy) before the United States and other great powers. They say, although it hasn't been confirmed, that Hitler had to find a map to locate the small country.

In 1949, President José Figueres Ferrer, revolutionary, statesman, philosopher, victorious general, and possibly the greatest man Costa Rica ever produced, abolished the army. During his third presidential term, Figueres launched an ambitious plan to supply the small local municipalities with trucks and tractors. He also decided to put together a first class symphony orchestra. When the opposition leaders challenged and criticized his musical ideas, he replied with one of his famous phrases, "What good are tractors without violins?" Today Costa Rica's symphony orchestra is akin to the best in the world and is a source of national pride.

Ticos have a great natural vocation for peace, democracy, and liberty; they despise what is contrived and deceptive, and they make fun of the ones in power. Many things have changed, but the heart and motivation of the simple peasant of colonial times is entrenched in the soul of this great, small country. As former president of Uruguay, Julio María Sanguinetti, once said during an American presidential summit in San José, *"Donde hay un costarricense, esté donde esté, hay libertad."* (No matter where they are, where there's a Costa Rican, there is liberty.)

Rafael Alberto Gamboa was born and raised in Costa Rica. He studied law at the University of Costa Rica and currently practices in his own firm in Heredia. He maintains an active interest in Costa Rican History.

ADDITIONAL RESOURCES

HISTORY

Costa Rica: Quest for Democracy (Westview Profiles Nations of the Contemporary Latin America) by John A. Booth. Published 1998.

A Holy Alliance?: The Church and the Left in Costa Rica, 1932-1948 (Perspectives on Latin America and the Caribbean) by Eugene D. Miller. Published 1996.

Hostile Acts: U.S. Policy in Costa Rica in the 1980s by Martha Honey. Published 1994.

FICTION AND NON-FICTION

The Ticos: Culture and Social Change in Costa Rica by Mavis Hiltunen Biesanz, et al. A typical guidebook that instructs visitors on the politics, history, culture, economy, and ethnicity of the country through fictional stories.

Costa Rica: The Last Country the Gods Made. by Colesberry, A. A glimpse at the art, indigenous culture, feminism, and religion among other aspects of Costa Rica.

When New Flowers Bloomed: Short Stories by Women Writers from Costa Rica and Panama. Edited by Enrique Jaramillo Levi. A representative segment of recent fiction, rich in imagination, from Central America.

Costa Rican Tales. By Ricardo Guardia.

The Children of Mariplata: Stories from Costa Rica. By Miguel Benavides; translated by Joan Henry. Eleven short fictional stories.

Costa Rica: A Traveler's Literary Companion. By Oscar Arias. Editor Bárbara Ras. Twendy-six short fictional stories provide a different perspective and reveal the true soul of Costa Rica's politics, history, culture, economy, and ethnicity.

EDUCATION

Children of the World: Costa Rica. by Ronnie Cummins. Published 1990. The cultural, social, and economic life of the country is explored through observations of everyday activities of children.

FILMS AND VIDEOS

Exploring Costa Rica - Colors, Creatures, and Curiosities. Trailwood Films, PO Box 1087, Shelbyville, KY 40066. (☎800-75-TRAIL.) 82min. video US$24.95.

An Introduction to Ecological Economics. Griesinger Films. 7300 Old Mill Road, Gates Mills, OH. 44040 USA. 45min. video US$25.

Investing in Natural Capital. Griesinger Films. 7300 Old Mill Road, Gates Mills, OH. 44040 USA. 42min. video US$29.95.

Conversation for a Sustainable Society. Griesinger Films. 7300 Old Mill Road, Gates Mills, OH. 44040 USA. 43min. video US$25.

Costa Rica Counts the Future. Griesinger Films. 7300 Old Mill Road, Gates Mills, OH. 44040 USA. 45min. video US$39.95. Study Guide included.

Costa Rica: Child of the Wind. A film by Jim Burroughs and Ceil Sutherland. Red Ribbon, American Film and Video Festival, 1988. 58 min. Video. $295.

TRAVEL BOOKS

Costa Rica: The Last Country the Gods Made. By Adrian Colesberry. Essays on a variety of topics, ranging from religion, the politics of coffee, and indigenous issues.

Breakfast of Biodiversity: The Truth about Rain Forest Destruction. By John Vandermeer, Ivette Perfecto, and Vandana Shiva. Examines the relationships between agriculture, ecology, global warming, and economic progress in the Costa Rican ecosystem.

LIFE AND TIMES

ALTERNATIVES TO TOURISM

Traveling from place to place around the world may be a memorable experience. But if you are looking for a more rewarding and complete way to see the world, you may want to consider Alternatives to Tourism. Working, volunteering, or studying for an extended period of time can be a better way to understand life in Costa Rica. This chapter outlines some of the different ways to get to know a new place, whether you want to pay your way through or just get the personal satisfaction that comes from studying and volunteering. In most cases, you will feel that you partook in a more meaningful and educational experience—something that the average budget traveler often misses out on.

Alternatives to tourism are particularly appealing to backpackers traveling through Central America and spending at least three to four weeks in each country, as well as high school and college-age students interested in cultural immersion and Spanish language instruction. Most volunteers gravitate to Costa Rica's diverse environmental work opportunities and conservation projects, which range from very well-organized and structured programs that must be prearranged months in advance to smaller, regularly changing assignments that are offered as work is needed and can be set up easily once you are in Costa Rica. Though popular with travelers on all types of budgets, most of Costa Rica's volunteer and language school opportunities require a payment to cover basic expenses like food and lodging. If just traveling through the country and looking for an interesting alternative to tourism, read newspapers, hotel information boards, and fliers posted on the streets in touristed areas for local opportunities. And regardless of whether you find yourself repairing trails at a national park for a few days, rafting and hiking through the jungle, or learning Spanish from natives in a small village, you're bound to have a unique and culturally intense experience, not to mention plenty of stories to bring home with you.

GETTING STARTED

For an extensive list of "off-the-beaten-track" and specialty travel opportunities, try the **Specialty Travel Index,** 305 San Anselmo Ave., #313, San Anselmo, CA 94960, USA (☎ 800 442 4922 or 415 459 4900; fax 415 459 4974; www.specialtytravel.com). **Transitions Abroad** (www.transitionsabroad.com) publishes a bi-monthly on-line newsletter for work, study, volunteering, interning, and specialized travel abroad. **Business Enterprises for Sustainable Travel** (www.sustainabletravel.org) supports travel that helps communities preserve natural and cultural resources and create sustainable livelihoods. The website has listings of local programs, innovative travel opportunities, and internships.

STUDYING ABROAD

Study abroad programs range from basic Spanish language and culture courses to a diverse range of college-level classes, often for credit. In order to choose a program that best fits your needs, find out what kind of students participate in the program and what sort of accommodations are provided. In programs that have large groups of students who speak the same language, there is a trade-off. You may feel more comfortable in the community, but you won't have the same opportunity to practice a foreign language or to befriend other international students. For accommodations, dorm life provides a better opportunity to mingle with fellow students, but there is less of a chance to experience the local scene. Homestays with local families have potential to build lifelong friendships with natives and to experience day-to-day life in more depth, but conditions can vary greatly from family to family. Cost, duration, and availability of extracurricular programs are a few of the other variables worth considering.

Those relatively fluent in Spanish may find it cheaper to enroll directly in a university abroad, although getting college credit may be more difficult. Some American schools still require students to pay for credits they obtain elsewhere. Most university-level study-abroad programs are meant as language and culture enrichment opportunities and, consequently, are conducted in Spanish. Still, many programs do offer classes in English and beginner- and lower-level language courses. A good resource for finding programs that cater to your particular interests is **www.studyabroad.com,** which has links to various semester abroad programs based on a variety of criteria, including desired location and focus of study. The following is a list of organizations that can help place students in university programs abroad or have their own branch in Costa Rica.

STUDY PROGRAMS

NORTH AMERICAN PROGRAMS

American Field Service (AFS), 310 SW 4th. Ave., #630, Portland OR 97204, USA (☎800 237 4636; fax 503 241 1653; afsinfo@afs.org; www.usa.afs.org), offers summer, winter, semester, and year-long homestay exchange programs in Costa Rica for mostly high school students and graduating seniors. Financial aid available. Check website for regional offices.

American Institute for Foreign Study, College Division, River Plaza, 9 W. Broad St., Stamford, CT 06902, USA (☎800-727-2437, ext. 5163; www.aifsabroad.com). Organizes programs for high school and college study in universities in Costa Rica.

Council on International Educational Exchange (CIEE), 633 3rd Ave., 20th fl. study (Spanish and English language), volunteer, academic, and internship programs in Costa Rica.

School for International Training, College Semester Abroad, Admissions, Kipling Rd., P.O. Box 676, Brattleboro, VT 05302, USA (☎800-336-1616 or 802-257-7751; www.sit.edu). Semester- and year-long programs in Costa Rica run US$10,600-13,700. Also runs the **Experiment in International Living** (☎800-345-2929; fax 802-258-3428; www.usexperiment.org), 3- to 5-week summer programs that offer high-school students cross-cultural homestays, community service, ecological adventure, and language training in Costa Rica and cost US$1900-5000.

REGIONAL PROGRAMS

There are numerous opportunities to study in metropolitan Costa Rica as well as on the outskirts of the country, rainforests, and beaches. Some programs specialize in Spanish and academics, while others focus more heavily on field research. Below are some examples, but for more information go to www.studyabroad-links.com/search/Costa_Rica/ or www.westnet.com/costarica/education.html.

VISA INFORMATION
Citizens of the Canada, the UK, and the US do not need a visa for visits to Costa Rica of 90 days or fewer, only a stamp, sticker, or insert in your passport specifying the purpose of your travel and the permitted duration of your stay. Australian, Irish, New Zealand, and South African citizens are allowed a 30 days' stay with no visa. Purchase visa extensions for around US$50 at **La Oficina de la Migración** (see p. 91) during the first week in the county; alternatively, just leave the country for 72 hours when your visa expires and return for another 90 days. A valid **passport** not expiring for at least 6 months after date of entry is required of all travelers; **carry a copy of your passport** (the page with your photo on it and the page with the stamp) with you at all times.

Most **short-term** study, work, and volunteer programs do not require special visas; standard tourist visas (see p. 12) are valid for the given period of time. Foreign students registered in recognized public or private educational institutions planning to study in Costa Rica for an extended period of time (e.g. 6 months or more), may apply for temporary residence (US$100 deposit required, can be waived under special circumstances) at the embassy upon entering the country (see www.costarica-embassy.org/Student%20Visa.htm. for more information). **Long-term** programs that require special entry documentation often handle the documentation procedures for the participants. US citizens can take advantage of the **Center for International Business and Travel (CIBT; ☎800-925-2428)** and **G3 Visas and Passports** (☎888-883-8472 or 703-276-8472; www.g3visas.com), which secure visas for travel to almost every country for a variable service charge. Double-check on entrance requirements at the nearest embassy or consulate for up-to-date information before departure. US citizens can consult www.pueblo.gsa.gov/cic_text/travel/foreign/foreignentryreqs.html.

Cultural Experiences Abroad, (world: 480 557-7900, fax 557-7926; USA: ☎800 266-4441; www.gowithcea.com; info@GoWithCEA.com) Earn college credit at Veritas University, one of the most recognized private universities in Costa Rica. Offers language courses and business, ecology, and environment electives. Includes housing (homestay available), meal plan, excursions, medical insurance, internship, scholarship, and financial aid opportunities. Semester US$5800-6000; summer US$2600-3500; intensive month US$2300.

Instituto Monteverde, Apdo. 69-5655, Monteverde, Puntarenas (☎/fax: 506 645 5053; mvi@mvinstitute.org; www.mvinstitute.org). "Education for a sustainable future." This non-profit association provides educational and cultural resources for the local community. 10-week programs in tropical ecology, biology, architecture, landscaping, and planning. 6-week and 16-week programs also available. Accredited by CIEE and the University of California Education Abroad Program.

University of Costa Rica Field Ecology (www.educationabroad.com; contact: Academic Coordinator Gerardo Avalos, ☎506 207-5392, fax: 207-5392; gavalos@ns.biologia.ucr.ac.cr). A tropical field ecology program for English speaking undergraduates at Costa Rica's main national university. Students take Spanish lessons and stay with Costa Rican families, receiving 16hr. of college credit. US$8500.

LANGUAGE SCHOOLS

Unlike American universities, language schools are frequently independently-run international or local organizations or divisions of foreign universities that rarely offer college credit. Language schools are a good alternative to university study if you desire a deeper focus on the language or a less rigorous courseload. These programs are also good for younger high school students that might not feel comfortable with older students in a university program. Some good programs include:

A2Z Languages, 5112 N. 40th St., Suite 103, Phoenix, AZ 85018, USA (☎800 496 4596; info@a2zlanguages.com; www.a2zlanguages.com), offers 1-week to 6-month language programs for all levels and arranges educational and cultural tours. US$315-US$1000 per week, including homestay, 2 meals, airport pickup, and 4-6hr. daily instruction.

Academia Latinoamericana de Español S.A., Apdo. 1280-2050 San Pedro Montes de Oca, San José, Costa Rica(☎224 9917; fax 225 8125; recajhi@sol.rasca.co.cr; www.alespanish.com). Spanish taught in small groups. Classes start every M.

AmeriSpan Unlimited, P.O. Box 40007, Philadelphia, PA 19106, USA (☎800 879 6640 or 215 751 1100; fax 215 751 1986; info@amerispan.com; www.amerispan.com), offers 1-week to 6-month language immersion programs in Alajuela, Heredia, Manuel Antonio, Monteverde, Playa Flamingo, San José, and San Joaquín de Flores. Classes start every M. College credit available. US$100 registration fee. Classes start at US$355 per week and include 4hr. daily classes, airport pickup, homestay, meals, and excursions.

Cascada Verde, Apdo. 888, 8000 San Isidro P.Z. Costa Rica (cascadaverde@hotmail.com; cascadaverde@cascadaverde.org; www.cascadaverde.org). See **Volunteering, Community Service, p. 82**).

Comunicare, 12086 SJO 1601 NW, 97th Ave., PO Box 025331, Miami, FL 33102-5331, USA, or Apdo. 1383-2050 San Pedro Costa Rica (☎/fax 506-224-4473; comunica@rasca.co.cr; www.comunicare.co.cr). A non-profit organization offering Spanish classes, cultural and Central American studies, and volunteer opportunities working with the community around San José.

Costa Rican Language Academy, P.O. Box. 1966-2050, San José, Costa Rica (US ☎866-230-6361, worldwide ☎506 280-1685 or 280-1739; fax 280-2548; crlang@crlang.co.cr; www.spanishandmore.com). Language and cultural study custom tailored for individual students. Homestays and weekend excursions plus lessons in Latin dance, Costa Rican cooking, Spanish music, and conversation.

Escuela Idiomas d'Amore, P.O. Box 67, Quepos, Costa Rica (☎/fax 777 1143; in the US ☎/fax 262-367-8598 or 310-435-9897; damore@sol.rasca.co.cr; www.escueladamore.com). "Immerse yourself in Spanish on the beaches", halfway between Quepos and Parque Nacional Manuel Antonio. Participants are primarily adults in high season, college students in low season. A percentage of tuition goes to the World Wildlife Fund.

Forester Instituto Internacional, P.O. Box 6945, 1000 San José, Costa Rica (☎225 3155; fax 225 9236; forester@rasca.co.cr; www.fores.com). Spanish language programs in the nation's capital.

La Escuela del Mundo (☎643 1064; www.schooloftheworld.org). 50m east of Panadería Tosso in Jacó; look for a blue sign. Offers 1-week (US$390), 2-week (US$735), and 4-week (US$1275) programs in Spanish, ecology, surfing, drawing and painting. Students in all programs take weekly field trips to hike, kayak, and horseback ride.

Languages Abroad, 413 Ontario St., Toronto, Ontario M5A 2V9, Canada (☎800 219 9924 or 416 925 2112; info@languagesabroad.com; www.languagesabroad.com), offers 2 to 12-week language programs for all levels in San José, Heredia, Monteverde, Manuel Antonio, Playa Flamingo, and San Joaquin de Flores. Min. age. 18.

Language Immersion Institute, 75 South Manheim Blvd., SUNY-New Paltz, New Paltz, NY 12561-2499, USA (☎845 257 3500; www.newpaltz.edu/lii). 2-week summer language courses and some overseas courses in Spanish. Program fees are around US$1000 for a 2-week course.

Montana Linda Spanish School, 250m oeste del Bar la Primavera, Orosi, Cartago, Costa Rica (☎/fax 533 2153 or 533 3640; info@montanalinda.com; www.montanalinda.com), set in the beautiful Orosi Valley about 1½hr. from San José. Offers some of the cheapest Spanish classes around. Package prices include dormitory-style accommodation in the charming Montana Linda Hostel, 3hr. daily instruction in small classes, and breakfast and dinner daily. 4 classes (5 nights) US$99, 5 classes (6 nights) US$120, 10 classes (13 nights) US$225. Private room additional US$2.50 per night, homestay additional US$5 per night.

OTHER INTERESTING PROGRAMS

Archaeological Institute of America, 656 Beacon St., Boston, MA 02215, USA (☎617-353-9361; www.archaeological.org). The *Archaeological Opportunities Bulletin* (US$20 for non-members) lists field sites in Central America. Purchase the bulletin online from Oxbow/David Brown Books (www.oxbowbooks.com) or by phone at ☎800-791-9354.

Costa Rica Rainforest Outward Bound School, P.O. Box 243, Quepos, Costa Rica (☎ 777 1222; www.crrobs.org), offers several adventure, surf, and water intensive programs with a Spanish language emphasis. Spanish programs generally run 30 days, and participants may be eligible for academic credit.

Peace Studies and Peace Journalism, (☎249 1821, fax 249 1095; info@rfpi.org; http://www.rfpi.org/ipc.html). Sponsored by Radio for Peace International and the International Center for Human Rights in Media. 10 week immersion course on Peace Studies, Journalism, Ethics, and an optional Spanish course. Cost includes classes, materials, food, lodging, laundry, field trips and special events. US$3850.

WORKING

There are two main schools of thought. Some travelers want long-term jobs that allow them to get to know another part of the world in depth (e.g. teaching English, working in the tourist industry). Other travelers seek out short-term jobs in the service or agricultural sector to finance their travel, working for a few weeks at a time to finance the next leg of their journey. Paid work can be exceedingly difficult to find in Costa Rica. The country is generally reluctant to give up precious jobs to traveling foreigners. It's not impossible, though, and making friends with locals can help expedite work permits or arrange work-for-accommodations swaps. This section discusses both short-term and long-term opportunities for working in Costa Rica. Make sure you understand Costa Rica's **visa requirements** for working abroad. See the box on p. 76 for more information.

For US college students, recent graduates, and young adults, the simplest way to get legal permission to work abroad is through **Council Exchanges Work Abroad Programs** (☎888 COUNCIL; www.councilexchanges.com/work/cr.htm). Fees are from US$300-425. Council Exchanges can help you obtain a three- to six-month work permit/visa and also provides assistance finding jobs and housing.

LONG-TERM WORK

If you're planning on spending a substantial amount of time (more than three months) working in Costa Rica, search for a job well in advance. Note that many jobs require previous experience and/or some knowledge of Spanish. International placement agencies are often the easiest way to find employment abroad, especially for teaching English. Some helpful online jumping-off points are: **Electronic Network for Latin American Careers and Employment** (www.lanic.utexas.edu/enlace/),

ALTERNATIVES TO TOURISM

Escape Artist.com (http://jobs.escapeartist.com/Openings/Costa_Rica/), **International Career Employment Center** (www.internationaljobs.com), **Jobs Abroad** (www.jobsabroad.com), **The Monster Board Global Gateway** (http://globalgateway.monster.com/), **Overseasjobs** (www.overseasjobs.com), and **Saludos** (www.saludos.com).

Internships, usually geared toward college students, are a good way to segue into working abroad. Although they are often unpaid or poorly paid, many say the experience is well worth it. Be wary of advertisements or companies that claim the ability to get you a job abroad for a fee—often the same listings are available online or in newspapers, or even out of date. It's best, if going through an organization, to use one that's somewhat reputable. Some good ones include:

AmeriSpan Study and Work Abroad—Costa Rica, 5 Spiros Way, Menlo Park, CA, 94025, USA (☎215 751 1100; fax 215 751 1986; www.amerispan.com/volunteer_intern/). Offers volunteer/internship placements in addition to Spanish immersion programs.

Intern Abroad, 8 E. 1st Ave., Suite 102, Denver, CO, 80203, USA (☎720 570 1702; www.internabroad.com/CostaRica.cfm), has numerous postings for recent semi-temporary and long-term job opportunities and internships.

SUNY Brockport International Education (☎585 395 2119; fax 637-3218; www.studyabroad.com/suny/brockport/; overseas@brockport.edu). Contact to numerous internship positions in the country.

TEACHING ENGLISH

English instruction is probably the most easily available profession for foreigners looking to stay in Costa Rica for the long haul. Teaching jobs abroad are rarely well-paid, although some elite private American schools can pay somewhat competitive salaries. Volunteering as a teacher in lieu of getting paid is also a popular option, and even in those cases, teachers often get some sort of a daily stipend to help with living expenses. Jobs aren't hard to find if you are a native English speaker, especially if you're North American.

In almost all cases, you must have at least a bachelor's degree to be a fullfledged teacher, although college undergraduates can often get summer positions teaching or tutoring. Native English speakers working in private schools are most often hired for English-immersion classrooms where no Spanish is spoken. Those volunteering or teaching in public, poorer schools are more likely to be working in both English and Spanish.

Many schools require teachers to have a **Teaching English as a Foreign Language (TEFL)** certificate. Not having one does not necessarily exclude you from finding a teaching job, but certified teachers invariably find higher paying jobs. The TEFL is, however, usually required to teach English in most businesses or organizations. Many accredited 4-year universities offer TEFL certification courses. The **Boston Language Institute,** 648 Beacon St., Boston, MA 02215, USA, offers helpful information about the TEFL, certification courses for both native and non native English speakers, and overseas job placement services. (☎877 998 3500 or 617 262 3500, ext. 228; tefl@boslang.com; www.teflcertificate.com. Homestay available. 4-week full time program or 12-week part-time program US$2500.)

Placement agencies or university fellowship programs are the best resources for finding teaching jobs in Costa Rica. The alternative is to contact schools directly or just try your luck once you get there. If you are planning on trying the latter, the best time of the year is several weeks before the start of the school year, which begins in early February or March. The following organizations are extremely helpful in placing teachers in Costa Rica:

Amity Institute, Amity Volunteer Teachers Abroad Programs, 10671 Roselle St., Suite 100, San Diego, CA 92121-1525, USA (☎858 455 6364; fax 858 455 6597; www.amity.org). Offers both full-year and semester-long positions. US$25-50 processing fee and US$500 placement fee. For anyone with at least 2-3 years' teaching experience, AVTA also offers positions with **Teacher Workshops Abroad,** a program that conducts pedagogical workshops for local teachers. Min. age 21.

Fulbright English Teaching Assistantship, US Student Programs Division, Institute of International Education, 809 United Nations Plaza, New York, NY 10017-3580, USA (☎212 984 5330; www.iie.org). Competitive program sends college graduates to teach in Costa Rica.

International School Services, 15 Roszel Rd., P.O. Box 5910, Princeton, NJ 08543, USA (☎609 452 0990; fax 609 452 2690; iss@iss.edu; www.iss.edu), maintains a list of almost 200 international schools accredited by the International Recruitment Center, runs a recruitment and placement service for experienced teachers who wish to teach abroad, and post job vacancies online.

Office of Overseas Schools, US Department of State, Office of Overseas Schools, Washington, D.C., 20522-0132, USA (☎202 261 8200; overseasschools@state.gov; www.state.gov/www/about_state/schools) has information on worldwide American-sponsored elementary and secondary schools overseas and current fact sheets on the 182 American international schools.

WorldTeach, Inc., Center for International Development, Harvard University, 79 John F. Kennedy St., Cambridge, MA 02138, USA (☎800 483 2240 or 617 495 5527; fax 617 495 1599; www.worldteach.org). Fees range from US$4000-6000. Sends students and recent college graduates for one-year, six-month, and summer positions to Costa Rica to teach English, math, science, and environmental education.

SHORT-TERM WORK

Traveling for long periods of time can get expensive; consequently, many travelers try their hand at odd jobs for a few weeks at a time to make some extra cash to carry them through another month or two of touring around. Short-term work in Costa Rica, however, is quite limited and not regularly offered. Travelers looking for jobs in Costa Rica end up asking around at local business if foreign help is needed and taking whatever positions are available. English-speakers are often hugely in demand, so flaunt this skill if you can. Popular types of employment include: tourist agencies/tour guides, Spanish-English translators, bartenders, and waiters/waitresses. Another popular option is to work several hours a day at a hostel in exchange for free or discounted room and/or board. Most often, these short-term jobs are found by word of mouth or by simply talking to the owner of a hostel or restaurant. Another good resource for temporary job offerings is the classified section in *The Tico Times.*

One mutually beneficial way to earn a bit of extra money is freelance English tutoring. Many Costa Rican natives are eager to learn English from a fluent or native speaker in order to make themselves more competitive on the job market. Depending on the region of Costa Rica, tutoring sessions can pay anywhere from US$2-10 per hour. Advertising in a local paper or posting flyers in highly visible areas may net a small group of inquiries quite quickly. Just bear in mind that leaving in a hurry after teaching a few lessons may leave your students in the lurch.

VOLUNTEERING

Volunteering can be one of the most fulfilling experiences you can have while traveling through Costa Rica; not only is it an excellent way to immerse yourself in local culture and become familiar with the people and language, but it's also a great way to give back to the country and its diverse needs. Moreover, it is far easier to find volunteer positions than paid work.

Many volunteer services charge you a fee to participate in the program, and these fees can be surprisingly hefty (although they frequently cover airfare and most, if not all, living expenses). Try to do research on a program before committing—talk to people who have previously participated and find out exactly what you're getting into, as living and working conditions can vary greatly. Different programs are geared toward different ages and levels of experience, so be sure to avoid taking on too much or too little. The more informed you are and the more realistic expectations you have, the more enjoyable the program will be.

Most volunteers choose to go through a parent organization that takes care of logistical details and frequently provides a group environment and support system. There are two main types of organizations—religious (often Catholic), and non-sectarian—although there are rarely restrictions on participation for either.

COMMUNITY SERVICE

NORTH AMERICAN PROGRAMS

Alliances Abroad, 2423 Pennsylvania Ave., NW, Washington, D.C., 20037, USA (☎ 866 5ABROAD; infola@alliancesabroad.com; www.internshipsabroad.com). One month of intensive language classes followed by 1-11 months of volunteer work in social services, humanitarian organizations, women's services, health care, environment, national parks. Fees start US$895 for 2 months plus US$100 application fee.

Amigos de las Americas, 5618 Star Lane, Houston, TX 77057, USA (☎ 800 231 7796; fax 713 782 9267; www.amigoslink.org). Sends high school and college students in groups of 2-3 to work in rural Latin American communities for up to 8 weeks. One year of Spanish instruction required. Costs average US$3500, including airfare.

Cross-Cultural Solutions, 47 Potter Ave., New Rochelle, NY 10801, USA (☎ 800 380 4777 or 914 632 0022; fax 914 632 8494; www.crossculturalsolutions.org). Operates 2-week to 6-month humanitarian programs helping people with disabilities and in health and child care, education, and social development. Dormitory-style accommodations and all meals included. Fees range from US$2100-4200.

Global Routes, One Short St., Northampton, MA 01060 (☎ 413 585 8895; fax 413 585 8810; mail@globalroutes.org; www.globalroutes.org). Sends college and high school students (age 17+) for 3 months to teach English, promote environmental awareness, and construct health clinics, playgrounds, and schoolhouses. Many adventure excursions included. 2-year Spanish study required. US$3500 plus airfare for 4 weeks.

Habitat for Humanity International, 121 Habitat St., Americus, GA 31709, USA (☎ 229 924 6935 ext. 2551; www.habitat.org). Volunteers build houses for anywhere from 2 weeks to 3 years. Short-term program costs range from US$1200-1800.

International Volunteer Programs Association, 71 W. 23rd St., 17th fl., New York, NY 10010, USA (☎ 212 807 8686, ext. 150; ivpa@volunteerinternational.org; www.volunteerinternational.org), an up-to-date search engine of hundreds of volunteer and internship opportunities around the world.

Languages Abroad, 413 Ontario St., Toronto, Ontario M5A 2V9, Canada (☎ 800 219 9924 or 416 925 2112; info@languagesabroad.com; www.languagesabroad.com), offers several English-teaching, volunteer, and work abroad opportunities programs in Costa Rica. Check website for specific program fees and details.

Peace Corps, Office of Volunteer Recruitment and Selection, 1111 20th St., NW, Washington, D.C., 20526, USA (☎800 424 8580; www.peacecorps.gov). Opportunities in agriculture, social development, sustainable communities, and health care in 70 developing nations, including Costa Rica. 2 year min. commitment. plus 3 months training.

Service Civil International Voluntary Service (SCI-IVS), SCI USA, 3213 W. Wheeler St., Seattle, WA 98199, USA (☎/fax 206 350 6585; www.sci-ivs.org). Arranges placement in work camps in Costa Rica for those 21+. Registration fee US$65-125.

REGIONAL PROGRAMS

▓ **Punta Mona Center,** (puntamona@hotmail.com), located 5km south of Manzanillo on the southern Caribbean coast, is a 30-acre organic farm and educational retreat center dedicated to sustainable agriculture using innovative permaculture technology. Surrounded on one side by pristine rainforest and the other by the coconut-fringed Caribbean, Punta Mona is an extremely popular getaway for international backpackers looking to escape Costa Rica's more touristed and developed locales. Volunteers spend their days and nights picking (and eating!) the over 120 varieties of tropical fruit, observing huge marine turtles nest on the beach, living in houses built completely of fallen trees, and using solar powered eco-friendly energy. American Stephen Brooks started the project in 1995 with a group of North American high school students, and the farm, since grown to an active environmental educational center and volunteer facility. Volunteers just need to show up and ask for Steve. US$20 per day to stay at the farm, US$10 per day for volunteer-work exchange program. All meals included.

Cascada Verde, Apdo. 888, 8000 San Isidro P.Z., Costa Rica (cascadaverde@hotmail.com; cascadaverde@cascadaverde.org; www.cascadaverde.org). This non-profit organic permaculture farm and retreat offers voluntary work exchange programs at Playa Uvita on the southern Pacific coast. In an alternative setting between rainforest and beach, guests can take Spanish classes (US$75 per week or US$100 for 10 private 90min. lessons); learn about permaculture and sustainable living; and participate in guided yoga, massages, wood and stone carving, basket weaving, painting, and teaching. The Cascada Verde Foundation is also involved in stopping clear cutting for monocrop plantation and runs a program to start a nursery, enrich soil, plant native trees, repair trails, and create a permaculture water management system. Interested volunteers can bring tents or sleep on the wooden floor of the old farmhouse with access to a compost toilet, clear spring water, and an open fireplace. Those who want to stay at the primary farm can camp out for free in exchange for work or pay for lodging with hot bath, kitchen and laundry facilities, excellent vegetarian and vegan meals, workshop classes, and organic bananas (US$27 per day). Any volunteer who teaches something (eg. art, music) receives 33% off food and accommodations.

Centro de Educación Creativo (Creative Learning Center), Apdo 23-5655, Monteverde, Puntarenas, Costa Rica (☎/fax 645 5161 or 645 5147; cec-clc@sol.racsa.co.cr; www.cloudforestschool.org). A private elementary and middle school English immersion program also works on environmental education. Volunteers assist teachers in the mornings; afternoon activities are flexible. 3-month min. commitment. Short-term (1 week or more) volunteers can work on special projects but not in the classroom. For information, contact Director Todd Beane.

Centro de Nutrición y Educación (CEN), (☎464 1020) San Carlos de Guatuso. Main location in Guatuso is a yellowish house with Mickey Mouse in front, 50m north of Coocique on the main street. This amazing program, with numerous locales around the country, was created 25 years ago by the Costa Rican Ministry of Health to provide food and basic education to children 2½-5½ years old, milk every month to babies, and medical attention to pregnant women. Volunteers help cook food and sing with the 78 permanent children or the kids who walk in from time to time. Ask for an internship with Marjulie, the head of a group of 5 women who permanently work at the Center. Open M-F 7am-3pm.

CONSERVATION WORK

NORTH AMERICAN PROGRAMS

Earthwatch, 3 Clocktower Pl. Suite 100, Box 75, Maynard, MA 01754, USA (☎800-776-0188 or 978-461-0081; www.earthwatch.org). Arranges 1- to 3-week programs in Costa Rica to promote conservation of natural resources, advance cutting edge scientific research, and test exciting hypotheses. Volunteers work with the giant marine turtles on the Caribbean coast or in the tropical forest in Costa Rica's Guanacaste region. Fees vary based on program location and duration. Costs average $1700 plus airfare.

Elderhostel, Inc., 11 Avenue de Lafayette, Boston, MA 92111-1746, USA (☎877 426 8056; fax 877 426 2166; www.elderhostel.org). Sends volunteers age 55 and over around the world to work in construction, research, teaching, and many other projects. Costs average $100 per day plus airfare.

REGIONAL PROGRAMS

Arenal Conservation Area ASOPA and ULIMA, apt. 113384 1000 San José, Costa Rica (☎/fax 233 4989; asvo89@racsa.co.cr). Go directly to the village and talk to Geovanny Galeano or to the conservation area's volunteer association ASVO (Asociacion de Voluntarios) in San José to sign up for this program to investigate, develop, and sustain ecotourism in the northern zone of the Arenal Conservation area near Parque Nacional Caño Negro. **ASOPA** is a fishing project that only takes place in March and April (driest season). Help the community members fish in the *lagunetas* (many little lagoons formed by the drying of the big lagoon), and then classify, count, and report the project to MINAE. Another interesting project is the ULTIMA, which classifies, samples, and protects the eggs of the freshwater Jicota turtle. Other various jobs include cleaning up the environment and taking inventory of the fish and lake species. These projects are 1-2 weeks long; housing is provided by MINAE; food is US$12 per day.

Asociación Preservacionista de Flora y Fauna Silvestre (APREFLOFAS), P.O. Box 917 2150, Moravia, San José, Costa Rica (☎506 240 6087; fax 236-3210; preserve@so.racsa.co.cr; www.preserveplanet.org). A non-profit volunteer organization that promotes reforestation, works to guard Costa Rica's natural resources from illegal exploitation, and provides a wealth of information on ecotourism in Costa Rica's parks.

ASVO, Asociación de Voluntario de Areas Protegias Silvestres, Calle 1, Av. 10/12, San José, Costa Rica (☎233 4989; 256 8467 ext. 27; asvo89@rasca.co.cr). Your link to virtually every national park in Costa Rica. Although some parks prefer that volunteers contact their conservation areas directly, you can always reach a specific park through this office. Live and work in the same conditions as the park rangers.

Avancari Eco-Camp, Las Juntas, Costa Rica (☎662 1655; ecocampavancari@yahoo.com). In the tropical forest near Monteverde Cloud Forest lies Avancari Eco-Camp, a conservation project looking for volunteers to help with reforestation, ecological studies, environmental education, trail creation, and agricultural projects. Volunteers stay in comfortable dormitory accommodations, can take tours of the nearby gold mines and waterfalls, and ride the zip lines in the forest canopy. Meals included.

Comisión Salvemos Las Tortugas de Parismina; (☎798 1246, ask for Jason, Miguel, Jenry, Rick, or Vicky or leave a message in Spanish; www.costaricaturtles.com). Volunteers of all ages assist with turtle conservation efforts in Parismina, a tiny hamlet on the banks of the Río Parismina on the northern Caribbean coast. They help patrol the beach at night to watch for poachers, collect turtle eggs, re-locate them to the association's hatchery, and return hatchlings to the sea. It's recommended that volunteers stay for anywhere from a few days to a few weeks, although shorter visits can be arranged. Even without prior arrangements, travelers can arrive in Parismina and almost be guaranteed some kind of volunteer activities; just ask anyone in town to direct you to Dona Vicky's house. The association arranges homestays for US$15 per day with 3 meals a day.

Finca Lomas (☎ 224-3570; fax 253 7524; anaicr@rasca.co.cr; www.anaircr.org/finca/en/finca_lomas.html), in the Talamancan Lowland Rainforest. Works to establish sustainable economic and environmental groups and encourage community self-sufficiency. 1-month min. for volunteers.

Herrera Botanical Garden and Reforestation Project at Escondido Trex (☎ 735 5210; osatrex@racsa.co.cr; www.herreragardens.com). Volunteers needed on the 30-hectare Botanical Garden near Puerto Jiménez to help garden, reforest cattle pastures, plant flowers and trees, and repair trails in secondary forest. Herrera is also developing an animal sanctuary to give the wildlife a larger track of forest to habitat. Volunteers must stay for a minimum of 4 days and work for 5½hr. per day. Accomodations are provided for free in the Herrera Campground or for US$1.50 per day for simple "*tico*-style" lodging. A simple kitchen is available, or 3 meals per day are provided for US$10. Volunteers who work for 2 weeks have access to canoes for free.

Programa Voluntarios para la Conservación del Ambiente (PROVCA), P.O. Box 085-3007, Heredia, Costa Rica (☎ 222 7549 or 395 0412; mam271@racsa.co.cr). PROVCA volunteers participate in national park and turtle conservation activities in four modalities: organized groups, individual participation, research projects, and social work/thesis writing. Tasks include developing specific projects within a park, doing administrative work, researching environmental impact on certain areas, beach cleaning, trail repair, and in-depth research. Volunteers must stay for a min. of 2 weeks and be at least 18 years old. US$10 per day covers meals and lodging at the volunteer site.

WIDECAST Foundation, Snail Mail Apdo. 170-2070, Sabanilla, San José, Costa Rica (☎ 224 3570; fax 253 7524; tortugas@sol.racsa.co.cr). Marine biologist Didher Chacón coordinates volunteering at Refugio Nacional de Vida Silvestre Gandoca-Manzanillo to help save the area's endangered leatherback turtles. Volunteers usually alternate taking 6hr. hatchery shifts to guard eggs from poachers. The patrols are in charge of tagging the turtles, installing microchips, taking tissue samples, measuring females who emerge from the sea to lay eggs, camouflaging the nest, and relocating the eggs to the hatchery. An investigative assistant provided by ANAI oversees all volunteer efforts.

SAN JOSÉ

Truth be told, San José (pop. 300,000) can be a disappointing starting point for travelers beginning to explore the serenity and vibrant natural beauty of Costa Rica. The streets are crowded and chock full of car honking, seemingly suicidal drivers, the air is clogged with diesel fumes, and *"Americana"* is a word seen all too often on storefronts. But then again, San José never promised anyone nature or calm. Most travelers grumble about the city, enduring the long bank lines and dodging umbrellas during the rainy season on their hurried way through the capital. However, those who stay a few days longer get to know a much livelier and charismatic version of San José and its inhabitants. In addition to offering all the amenities a traveler could want, Costa Rica's bustling capital is draped with a distinct *tico* flair personified by its laid-back and diverse residents, who truly make the city's personality. They linger with their families and loved ones in the beautiful plazas and parks, listening to the live bands that often play on the weekend afternoons, delay their work days to gather under San José's roofs and park domes to escape rain storms, and thrive on a camaraderie that echoes throughout the country.

Surrounded by mountains and perched 1182m above sea level, San José was first settled in 1736, but spent much of the colonial era as a sleepy tobacco-farming town. In 1823, the capital was moved here from Cartago and the city became a focal point for the Costa Rican coffee economy. Since the 1950s, San José has grown rapidly and it is now *the* transportation hub of Costa Rica, with buses and planes to just about every destination in the country, and home to two major universities. Its cooler and more tolerable weather, convenient transportation, fantastic nightlife, and sights make it a worthy stopover between the two coasts.

✈ INTERCITY TRANSPORTATION

FLIGHTS

Juan Santa María International Airport, about 15km northwest of San José in Alajuela, is most cheaply accessible by bus from San José to Alajuela (see **Buses,** below). Taxis from San José charge US$10. **Grayline Tours** (☎232 3681 or 220 2126) runs an airport shuttle that picks up from many mid-range and top-end hotels around town for US$6. Call for more info. Airlines flying to **international destinations** include **American** (☎257 1266), **Continental** (☎296 4911), **Copa** (☎222 6640), **Delta** (☎257 2433), **Iberia** (☎227 8266), **Lacsa** (☎296 0909), **Mexicana** (☎257 6334), **SAM** (☎233 3066), **Taca** (☎222 1790), **TWA** (☎221 4638), **United** (☎220 4844), **Varig** (☎257 0094). **Sansa** (☎221 9414; www.flysansa.com) offers scheduled flights **within Costa Rica.** The following are daily high season departures and one-way fares for Sansa:

Barra del Colorado (30min., 6am, US$55); **Carillo** near **Sámara** (75min., 8:10 and 11:50am, US$66); **Golfito** (1hr.; 6, 10:30am, 2:15pm; US$66); **Liberia** (50min., 5:15 and 11:50am, US$66); **Nosara** (1hr., 11:50am, US$66); **Palmar Sur** (55min., 9:30am, US$66); **Puerto Jiménez** (55min., 6am and 2:05pm, US$66); **Punta Islita** (55min., 8:10am, US$66); **Quepos** (30min., 6 per day 7:45am-4:25pm, US$44); **Tamarindo** (50min., 6 per day 5:15am-3:50pm, US$66); **Tambor** (35min., 10:25am and 4:25pm, US$55); **Tortuguero** (35min., 1 per day 6am, US$55).

Tobías Bolaños Airport, in Pavas, serves **Travelair** (☎220 3054 or 888 535 8832 in US for reservations; www.travelair-costarica.com) domestic flights. Travelair is a bit pricier and somewhat more reliable than Sansa (though Sansa is improving.) Daily high season departures and one-way fares for Travelair include:

Barra del Colorado (30min., 1 per day 6:15am, US$60); **Carillo** near **Sámara** (75min., 8"30am and 1pm, US$73); **Golfito** (1hr.; 6, 8:30am, 2:30pm; US$76); **Liberia** (50min.; 6, 8:30, 11:30am, 1:30pm; US$73); **Nosara** (1hr., 1pm, US$73); **Palmar Sur** (55min., 9 and 9:15am, US$66); **Puerto Jiménez** (55min.; 6, 8:30, 11am, 2:30pm; US$76); **Punta Islita** (55min.; 8:30am and 1pm, US$73); **Quepos** (30min., 6 daily 6am-4pm, US$45); **Tamarindo** (50min., 4 per day 6am-3pm, US$73); **Tambor** (35min., 8:30am and 1pm, US$60); **Tortuguero** (35min., 6:15am, US$60).

BUSES

Buses to almost every destination in the country arrive and depart from one of the city's many stops and terminals. Many cluster around **Terminal Coca-Cola,** site of an old bottling plant between Av. 1 and 3, Calles 16 and 18. The latest schedule is available at the **Instituto Costarricense de Turismo (ICT)** at the Museo de Oro (see **Tourist Information** below).

Alajuela-Airport: TUASA, Av. 2, Calles 12/14. (☎222 5325. 30min.; every 10min. 5am-10pm, every 30min. after 10pm; ¢210.)

Cahuita and Puerto Viejo de Talamanca: Terminal Caribe, Av. 13, Calle Central. (☎257 8129. 4hr.; M-F 6 and 8am, 4 per day 10am-4pm; return 5 per day 7:30am-4:30pm; ¢1750.)

Cariari: Terminal Caribe, Calle Central, Av. 13. (2hr.; 5 per day 6:30am-7pm, return 4 per day 5:30am-5:30pm.)

SAN JOSÉ

San José Center

▲ ACCOMMODATIONS
Casa León, 26
Casa Ridgway, 30
Costa Rica Backpackers Hotel, 27
Gran Hotel Imperial, 11
Hotel Balmoral, 14
Hotel Bienvenido, 3
Hotel Boston, 28
Hotel El Descanso, 21
Hotel Nuevo Almeda, 9
Hotel Príncipe, 24
Pensión de la Cuesta, 12
Pensión Otoya, 2
Tica Linda, 33
Toruma Youth Hostel, 15

● FOOD
Churrería Manolos, 16
Deli City, 19
News Cafe, 17
Nuestra Tierra, 22
Padrísimo, 25
Rest./Bar La Embajada, 5
Shakti, 31
Soda Flor de la Carmen, 10
Soda el Parque, 23
Spoon, 13
Tin Jo, 29
Rest. Vishnu Vegetariano, 6

♪ NIGHTLIFE
Acapulco, 18
La Avispa, 32
El Cuartel de la Boca del Monte, 8
Déjà Vu, 34
Bar Esmerelda, 20
Infinito Discoteque and Twister Club, 1
Salidas Orbital 2000, 7
Salsa 54, 4

N

0   200 meters
0   200 yards

TO ALAJUELA (15km)

Río Torres

Parque Zoológico Simón Bolívar

Centro Comercial El Pueblo

Museo de los Niños

PASO DE LA VACA

OTOYA

AMÓN

COCA COLA

MERCED

SANTA LUCIA

CARMEN

SOLEDAD

BELLA VISTA

Parque Nacional

Asamblea Legislativa

Biblioteca Nacional

Museo de Crimen

Museo Nacional

Museo Nacional de Arte Cultura

Centro Nacional de Arte y Cultura

PLAZA DE LA DEMOCRACIA

Serpentarium

Museo de Jade

Parque Morazán

Parque España

Parque Nacional

Museo de Oro

Teatro Nacional

PLAZA DE LA CULTURA

Mercado Central

Farmacia Fischel

BanCrecen

La Casona

Librería Lehmann

7th St. Books

Fiesta Casino

Clínica Bíblica

Cine Omni

Más X Menos

Parque Central

Parque de la Merced

Red Cross

Hospital San Juan de Dios

Hospital Nacional de Niños

Museo de los Niños

Buses to Volcán Irazú

Buses to Guadalupe

PLAZA DE LAS GARANTÍAS SOCIALES

To Nicaragua, Panamá, Guatemala, Honduras

To Puerto Limón, Cahuita, Puerto Viejo de Talamanca, Cariari, Siquirres, and Guápiles

To Fortuna (Arenal), Monteverde

To Playa Sámara, Carrillo

To Golfito, Playa Nosara & Garza, Tamarindo

To Poás, Alajuela

To Escazú

To Jacó, Manuel Antonio, Quepos

To Puntarenas

To Cartago

To Moravia, Guadalupe

To San Pedro

To Turrialba

TO LA SABANA, MUSEO DE ARTE COSTARRICENSE (1km)

TO LA UNIVERSIDAD DE COSTA RICA, SAN PEDRO (5km)

Juan Santa María

Paseo Colón

Av. Central
Av. 1
Av. 3
Av. 5
Av. 7
Av. 9
Av. 11
Av. 13
Av. 2
Av. 4
Av. 6
Av. 8
Av. 10
Av. 12
Av. 14
Av. 16
Av. 18
Av. 20

C. Central
(railroad not in use)

Cartago: SACSA from Calle 5, Av. 18/20. (☎233 5350. 50 min., every 10min. 5am-midnight.) Also from Calle 1/3, Av. 2. (10:30pm-midnight; ¢210.)

Fortuna: Terminal Atlántico Norte, Calle 12, Av. 7/9. (☎256 8914. 5hr.; 6:15, 8:40, 11:30am; return noon and 2pm; ¢2300.)

Golfito: TRACUPA, Av. 3/5, Calles 14. (☎222 2666. 11hr.; 7am and 3pm, return 5am and 1pm; ¢3100.)

Guápiles via Parque Nacional Braulio Carillo/Quebrada González: Terminal Caribe, Av. 13, Calle Central. (80min., every 30min. 5am-9pm, ¢470.)

Heredia: Transportes Unidos 400, Calle 1, Av. 7/9; Av. 2, Calle 10/12; Calle 4, Av. 5/7; Av. 7, Calle 13. (25min., every 10min. 5am-10pm, ¢180.)

Jacó: Transportes Morales, La Coca-Cola, Av. 3, Calle 16. (☎223 1109. 2½hr.; 7:30, 10:30am, 3:20pm; return 5, 11am, 3pm; ¢650.)

Liberia: Pulmitan, Av. 5, Calle 24. (☎256 9552. 4hr., 11 per day 6am-8pm, ¢1410.)

Limón: Caribeños, Terminal Caribe, Av. 13, Calle Central. (☎221 2596. 2½hr., every hr. 5:30am-7pm, ¢1005.)

Monteverde: Autotransportes Tilarán, Atlántico Norte Terminal, Calle 12, Av. 7/9. (☎222 3854. 4½hr., 6:30am and 2:30pm, ¢1330.)

Playa Nosara and Garza: Alfaro, Calle 14, Av. 3/5. (☎222 2666. 6hr.; 6am and 2:45pm, return 1pm.)

Playa Panamá and Hermosa: Tralapa, Calle 20, Av. 3. (☎221 7202. 5hr.; daily 3:25pm, return 5am.)

Playa Sámara and Carillo: Calle 14, Av. 5. (6hr.; M-Sa 12:30pm, return 4am, Su 1pm.)

Playa Tamarindo: Alfaro, Calle 14, Av 3/5. (☎222 2666. 5½hr.; daily 3:30pm, return 6:45am.) Tralapa, Av. 3, Calle 20. (4pm, return 7am.)

Playas del Coco: Calle 14, Av. 1/3. (☎666 0138. 5hr.; 8am and 2pm; return 9am and 2pm.)

Puntarenas: Empresarios Unidos de Puntarenas, Av.12, Calle 16. (☎222 0064. 2½hr.; every 40min. 6am-5pm, return 4:15am to 7pm; ¢855.)

Quepos and Manuel Antonio: Transportes Morales, Terminal Coca Cola, Av. 1/3, Calles 16/18. (☎223 5567. Direct 3½hr.; 6am, noon, 6pm; return 6, 9:30am, noon, 5pm; ¢1375. Indirect 5hr.; M-F 5 per day 7am-5pm, Sa and Su 4 per day 7am-4pm; return daily 5, 8am, 2, 4pm; ¢780.) Only direct buses continue to Manuel Antonio.

Siquirres: Terminal Caribe, Av. 13, Calle Central. (1½hr.; 6:30 and 8:30am, then every 2hr. until 6pm.)

Turrialba: Transtusa Av. 6, Calle 13. (☎591 4145. 1½hr.; 5 from 5:15-8am, then every hour until 8pm; ¢605.)

Volcán Irazú: Av. 2, Calle 1/3. (2hr.; Sa and Su 8am, return 12:30pm; round-trip ¢1500.)

Volcán Poás: TUASA Av. 2, Calle 12/14. (☎222 5325. 2hr.; daily 8:30am, return 2:30pm.)

International Buses: Guatemala: TicaBus, Calle 9, Av. 4 (☎221 8954). 60hr. with one night in Nicaragua and one night in El Salvador (6 and 7:30am, ¢10,000). **Honduras:** TicaBus. 48hr. with one night in Managua (6 and 7:30am, ¢9700). **Managua:** TicaBus (11hr.; 6, 7:30, 10am; ¢3000). TransNica, Calle 22, Av. 3/5. (☎223 4242. 11hr., 5:30 and 9am.) NicaBus, Terminal Caribe, Calle Central, Av. 13. (☎256 4248. 11hr., 1 per day 6am.) Panaline, Calle 16, Av. 3/5. (☎256 8721. 11hr., daily 4:30am.) **Panamá City:** TicaBus (16hr., 1 per day 10pm, ¢7000); Panaline (16hr., 1 per day 1pm, ¢8500).

✦ ORIENTATION

San José follows the traditional Costa Rican grid, with *avenidas* running east-west and *calles* running north-south. **Avenida Central** (called **Paseo Colón** north of Calle 22) is the main drag, with a shopping and eating area blocked off to traffic between Calles 2 and 5. Just west of the city center is the frantic **Mercado Central**, bordered by Av. Central/1 and Calle 6/8. Four blocks further west of the market is **Terminal Coca-Cola**, on Av. 1, Calle 16/18.

Within the city center, **Barrio Amón,** northeast of Av. 5 and Calle 1, and **Barrio Otoya,** slightly east of Amón, are the most architecturally interesting. West of downtown past Calle 42, **La Sabana** is home to the large **Parque Metropolitano La Sabana.** The quiet, hilly suburb of **Escazú,** with a few gorgeous bed and breakfasts and some of San José's most ritzy restaurants, lies 5km further west. East of downtown past Calle 35, is upscale **Los Yoses,** followed by student-oriented **San Pedro,** home to the University of Costa Rica and some of the city's best entertainment.

 As Central American cities go, San José is comparatively safe, yet theft, prostitution, and drugs make some areas a little shaky. Problem spots include Terminal Coca-Cola, south of Av. 8 between Calles 2 and 12, Av. 4 to 6 between Calles 4 and 12, and north of the *mercado central*. Generally, areas beyond a couple of blocks from San José center pose more of a threat after dark. The safest way to get around after dark, especially for single women, is by taxi.

⎛ LOCAL TRANSPORTATION

Bus: Local buses run about every 5-10min. from about 5am-10pm and go all over San José, including to the suburbs and the airport. There are no official printed schedules. Instead, ask a local, taxi or bus driver, or read the signs on the front of the bus. Most bus stops are marked with the destination they serve. As local destinations generally run no more than ¢200, it's best to carry small change. Major bus stops include: **Escazú** (Calle 16 and Av. 1/Central); **Guadalupe** and **Moravia** (Av. 3, Calle 5/7); and **San Pedro** (Av. 2, Calle 11/13 and Av. Central, Calle 9/11).

Private Bus: Grayline Tours (☎232 3681 or 220 2126) offers "fantasy buses" to and from popular destinations all over Costa Rica for US$21-25 one-way. Buses run once or twice daily between **Arenal, Jacó, Liberia, Manuel Antonio, Playa Hermosa, Playa Tamarindo, Puerto Viejo de Talamanca,** and **San José.** Most leave daily between 7-8:30am. Call for reservations.

Car Rental: Prices range from US$19 (for a small sedan) to $105 (for a 4X4) per day. Minimum age to rent is 21, although many companies require drivers to be at least 23. Some companies will rent to those between 18-21 but require double or triple the deposit. Passport, valid driver's license, and major credit card required; International Driver's Permit not necessary for rentals less than 3 months. **Avis Rent a Car,** at the Hotel Corobicí, north of the Parque La Sabana on Calle 42 (☎232 9922, at the airport 552 1321). **Budget,** Paseo Colón, Calle 28/30 (☎223 3284, at the airport 441 4444). Open 7am-6pm; airport office open daily 24hr. **Economy** (☎231 5410, at the airport 442 8100). **Europcar** (☎257 1158, at the airport 440 8257). Open M-F 7:30am-6pm, Sa 8am-4pm, Su 8am-3pm; airport office open daily 6am-10pm. **Hertz,** Paseo Colón, Calle 36/38 (☎258 4343, at the airport 443 2078). Open 7am-6pm. **National Car Rental,** (☎290 8787, at the airport 440 0085, toll-free from US 800-227 -7368), also at the Hotel Jade and Hotel Real Intercontinental in San José.

Motorcycle Rental: Wild Riders, Calle 32, Paseo Colón (☎256 1636). US$40 per day, US$180 per week, includes basic insurance and helmet. Major credit card and valid driver's license required. Open 7am-10pm.

Bike Rental: EuroTours S.A. and **L&M Tours** (☎282 6817 or 282 6653; http:// mltours.cjb.net), rent mountain bikes, helmets, and bicycle carriers for US$12 per day, $56 per week. Also run mountain bike tours including round-trip transportation from your hotel. (3½hr. of mountain biking with a guide, fruit drinks, and lunch US$49.)

SAN JOSÉ

THE INSIDER'S CITY

Av. 7
Av. 5
Av. 3
Av. 1
Av. Central

Parque España
Parque Morazán

6 **4** **5** **3** **1** **2**

C. Central
C. 1 C. 3 C. 5 C. 7 C. 9

ARTGALLERY HIGHLIGHT MAP

Hidden among San José's ceaseless bustle and commercialism is a cultural wonderland of art galleries, many of which cluster around Calle 5, Av. 1/3. The galleries listed below are casual and do not require prior appointment to visit, although many more elegant galleries in San José hold frequent public openings advertised in *The Tico Times*. Artwork varies from intricate woodcarvings to enormous abstract paintings, and the prices vary just as much; you can walk away with a US$20-30 small painting or have the gallery ship your US$5000+ masterpiece anywhere in the world. If you'd rather spend your money traveling, check out La Casona, on Calle Central, Av. Central/1, for much cheaper but equally beautiful souvenir-type artwork.

1 Marvel at **Arte Latino's** wide selection of bright surrealist and abstract paintings, including Javier D'avalo's captivating images of *campesino* children. (☎258 3306. Open daily 9am-7pm.)

2 Get knick-knack happy at **Sebastián Gallery**, where you can select from a reasonably-priced collection of hand-painted ceramics, dishware, and wooden and metal jewelry. (☎257 4557. Open daily 9am-6pm.)

⁊ PRACTICAL INFORMATION

EMBASSIES

Australia (☎224 1152, ext. 111), has no embassy, but an official representative can be found on the 2nd fl. of Building B of the Plaza del Este in front of Centro Comercial. Visa forms are available in the office or can be downloaded (www.immi.gov.au/allforms/form-list.htm). All forms must be sent to the Australian embassy in Mexico. Open M-F 8am-5pm.

Canada (☎296 4149), in Sabana Sur, Oficentro Ejecutivo building #5, behind the Contraloría. Visa and passport service before noon. Open M-Th 8am-4:30pm, F 8am-1:30pm.

UK, Av. Central, Calle 35 (☎258 2025, emergency 225 4049), Edificio Colón, 11th fl. Consular services available. Open M-Th 8am-noon.

US, Av. Central, Calle 120 (☎220 3939 or 220 3050, emergency 220 3127), in front of the Centro Comercial. Open M 8-11:30am and 1-3pm, Tu 8-11:30am, W-F 8am-4:30pm.

TOURIST AND FINANCIAL SERVICES

Tourist Information: Instituto Costarricense de Turismo, main office Av. 4, Calle 5/7 (☎223 1733, 24hr. cell 389 7258, info service 800-012-3456, from US 800-343-6332). Also at Calle 5, Av. Central/2, next to El Museo del Oro, and Av. Central, Calles 5/7, 2nd fl. (☎257 3857). Free country and city maps, intra-city bus schedules, and brochures. Open M-F 8am-5pm, Sa 8am-noon.

Guided Tours:

Costa Rica Expeditions, Av. 3, Calle Central (☎257 0766; fax 257 1665; costaric@expeditions.co.cr), 1 block east of the San José post office. Single and multi-day tours throughout the country.

Ecole Travel, Calle 7, Av. Central/1 (☎223 2240), inside 7th Street Books, is a reputable and relatively inexpensive tour company. Tours to Tortuguero (2 days US$95, 3 days US$125), Volcán Arenal and Monteverde (4 days US$260), Río Sierpe (3 days US$145), and Jacó (4 days US$169-215).

Costa Rica Nature Escape, Calle 5, Av. Central/1 (☎257 8064; www.crnature.com), has fantastic student rates for all sorts of adventure, rest, and eco-tourism packages, including a 3 day and 2 night Tortuguero deal for US$175. Open M-F 7:45-4pm. Travelers short on time would benefit from the **Highlights Tour** offered by **Ecoscape Nature Tours** (☎297 0664 or 240 5106; www.ecoscapetours.com). A 1-day tour of Poás Volcano and Cloud Forest, La Paz and San Fernando Waterfalls, Selva Verde Rainforest Lodge, a boat ride on the Río Sarapiquí, and a drive through Braulio Carillo National Park is US$79 per person including lunch.

Whitewater Rafting: Aventuras Naturales (☎225 3939).
Open daily 7am-6pm. Class III and IV on the Río Pacuare for
US$95 per person, students $75. **Ríos Tropicales** (☎233
6455). Open M-F 8am-7pm, Sa 8:30am-noon. Class III and
IV on the Río Pacuare for US$95 per person and Río Reven-
tazón for US$75 per person. **Costa Rica Expeditions**
(☎257 0766). Open M-Sa 8am-5pm. Class III and IV on the
Río Pacuare for US$95 per person; 10% student discount.
Costa Rica Nature Escape, Av. 5, Calle Central/1 (☎257
8064). Class III on the Río Reventazón or Río Sarapiquí from
US$65. Class IV on the Río Pacuare from US$85 per day, 2
days/1 night all-inclusive US$245. Much cheaper rates for
students available.

Kayaking: Ríos Tropicales (☎233 6455). Experience
required. US$25 per hr. **Costa Rican Expeditions** (☎257
0766).

Bungee Jumping: Latin America's oldest and safest bungee
company is **Tropical Bungee** (☎232 3956'; www.bun-
gee.co.cr). Jumps offered daily from 9am-4pm at the 80m
(265 ft.) Colorado River Bridge. No reservations necessary.
US$40 per jump. The truly adventurous should try their Full
Adrenaline Tour, a day of bungee jumping, paragliding, and
climbing.

Immigration: Dirección de Migración (☎220 0355),
on the Autopista General Cañas Hwy., the road to the
airport. Take the red bus to Alajuela from Av. 2, Calles
12/14 or Calles 10/12, and get off at *La Oficina de
Migración.*

Banks: There are dozens of banks all over San José and
nearly all of them have 24hr. Cirrus/Plus/V ATMS. All
require photo ID to change cash, and most require
passport and charge 1% commission to cash traveler's
checks.

Banco Central, Calle 2, Av. Central/1 (☎243 3333). Open M-
F 8:30am-3:30pm.

Banco de Costa Rica, Av. 2, Calle 2/4 (☎287 9000). Open
M-F 8:30am-3pm, Sa 7am-2pm.

Banco Nacional, Calle 4, Av. 1/3 (☎223 2166). Open M-F
8:30am-7:30pm.

Banco de San José, Calle Central, Av. 3/5 (☎295 9595).
Open M-F 8am-7pm.

BanCrecen, Av. 1, Calle Central. Later hours. Can only change
traveler's checks early in the day on weekdays. Open M-F
9am-9pm, Sa 9am-2pm.

Banco Popular, Calle 1, Av. 2/4. Open M-F 8:15am-7pm, Sa
8:15am-noon.

American Express: Calle Central, Av. 3/5 (☎257
1792), across from Banco de an José. Lost or stolen
card hotline ☎0 800-011-0271 or 0 800-012-3211.
Passport needed for check cashing. Open M-F 8am-
4:15pm.

Western Union: Av. 2/4, Calle 9 (☎800-777-7777).
Open M-F 8:30am-5pm, Sa 9am-12:30pm.

3 Puzzle over Ana Barientos' energet-
ically mysterious abstract paintings
or take a gander at some of Barry
Biesanz' renowned wood carvings
at Atmósfera. (☎222 4322. Open
daily 9am-6pm.)

4 Review a wide variety of large Latin
American canvases, including J.R.
Serrano's famous *campesino*
women and Rojelio Chávez' intricate feather paintings, at **Amir Art
Gallery,** . (☎221 9128. Open daily
8:30am-6:30pm.)

5 Browse through **Galería Diana's**
varied mix of traditional paintings,
unique wood figures, pre-Columbian artifacts, vibrant bird sculptures, and souvenirs. (☎256
9972. Open daily 9:30am-
6:30pm.)

6 Get a lesson on traditional Costa
Rican life at ◪**Galería Namú,**
which specializes in original indigenous and folk art. The knowledgeable English-speaking managers
will explain the background behind
each item, many hand-made by
campesino women and members
of the Bribrí, Boruca, Chorotega,
and Huetar tribes. Namú purchases all its artwork from artistis
themselves, not on consignment
like some other galleries, so a
splurge on some unique pieces
here is well-worth it. (☎256 3412.
Open M-Sa 9am-5pm.)

LOCAL SERVICES

English Bookstores: 7th Street Books, Calle 7, Av. Central/1 (☎256 8251). New and used books to delight the reader weary of romance novels in hostel exchange piles. Classics like Vonnegut, Tolstoy, and Twain as well as popular fiction, natural history, and travel books on Costa Rica. Some foreign newspapers. New books ¢5000-8000, used ¢900-2000. Open daily 9am-6pm. AmEx/D/MC/V. **Librería Lehmann,** Av. Central, Calle 1/3, has a small selection of light reading. Open M-F 8am-6:30pm, Sa-Su 9am-5pm. To trade in old reads, head to the **Internet/laundry** facility on Calle 1, Av. 2, one story below street level in the small strip mall on the northwest corner. Bring 3 books and get 2 free, bring 2 and get 1 free. Buy used books for US$2+.

Gay-Lesbian Organizations: Triángulo Rosa (☎234 2411). **Casa Yemaya** (☎661 0956) organizes all-female excursions throughout the country. Very friendly staff is knowledgeable about challenges for female travelers.

Supermarkets: Más X Menos, Av. Central, Calle 11/13. Open M-Sa 7am-midnight, Su 8am-9pm.

Laundry: Lavandería, Calle 8, Av. Central/1, next to Gran Hotel Imperial. ¢2000 per normal load, ¢2300-2500 per big load. Open M-F 8am-6pm, Sa 8am-5pm. **Sixaola,** Av. 2, Calle 7/9. Same-day service if brought in by 10am. ¢700 per kilo. Open daily 8am-6pm. **Lavandería,** Calle 1, Av. 2, one story below street level in the small strip mall on the northwest corner. Wash ¢1100, dry ¢700. Open daily 7am-11pm.

EMERGENCY AND COMMUNICATIONS

Emergency: ☎911.

Police: ☎911. To report a theft, contact the **Organismo de Investigación Judicial** (OIJ), Av. 6/8, Calles 17/19. Main office at Av. 4, Calle 6. (☎295 3000). English spoken.

Pharmacies: Farmacia Fischel, Av. 1, Calle 2 (☎257 7979), near the center of town. Huge selection. Attentive service. Open M-Sa 8am-7pm, Su 9am-5pm. AmEx/D/MC/V.

Hospitals: Hospital San Juan de Dios, on Paseo Colón, Calles 14/18 (☎257 6282). Large white building where Av. Central turns into Paseo Colón, after Calle 14. 24hr. emergency service. **Clínica Bíblica,** Calle 1, Av. 14/16 (☎257 5252). 24hr. emergency care, 24hr. pharmacy. English spoken.

Telephones: Card and coin phones all over town; most phones take ¢5 and ¢10 coins. Otherwise, buy a ¢500, ¢1000, ¢2000, or ¢3000 card from Más X Menos (see **Supermarkets,** above) or one of the many street vendors. **Radiográphica,** Av. 5, Calle 1 (☎287 0489). US$3 for collect calls. Also has AT&T Direct, MCI, and Sprint service. International calls only. Open daily 7:30am-9pm. Directory assistance ☎113. **Instituto Costarricense de Electricidad (ICE) office,** Av. 2, Calle 3 (☎257 7743). Open M-F 7:30am-7pm, Sa 8am-7pm.

Internet: Mostly clustered on Av. Central between Calle 7 and 13. **Internet Café,** Av. Central, Calle 7/9, 4th fl. ¢300 per hr. Open daily 8am-midnight. **Café Internet,** Av. Central, Calle 11/13, 2nd. fl., across from Más X Menos. ¢300 per 30min., ¢400 per hr. Open daily 7am-11pm. **Eyes Internet,** 50m down the first side street past Calle 11 walking east on Av. Central. ¢200 per hr. Open daily 8:30am-1am.

Post Office: Calle 2, Av. 1/3, in the large green building. San José has no street mailboxes, so all mail must be sent from here. Open M-F 7:30am-6pm, Sa 7:30am-noon.

Postal Code: 1000.

ACCOMMODATIONS

San José has hundreds of accommodations for every imaginable budget. That said, it's best to steer clear of the cheapest lodgings; paying the relatively "pricey" $10-12 for a dormitory bed is a trade-off for comfortable, clean lodgings and a friendly atmosphere. Staying slightly outside the city center is well worth the inconvenience to escape the noise, grit, and potentially dangers of the city center. The accommodations listed below are divided into four categories. **East** of the *parque central* is highly recommended for safe, comfortable, and affordable accommodations. Hotels **south** of the *parque central* are generally reasonably priced, but often louder and less charming. Try to avoid places **north** and **west** of the *parque central* which, although inexpensive, tend to be in the most dangerous areas with higher concentrations of prostitutes, drug problems, and people stumbling out of bars after dark. A pleasant alternative to staying downtown is **San Pedro**, a 10min. bus ride away, and the pleasant suburb of **Escazú**, a 20min. bus ride, which offers beautiful B&Bs that merit a splurge.

EAST OF THE PARQUE CENTRAL

Costa Rica Backpackers Hostel, Av. 6, Calle 21/23 (☎221 6191; www.costaricabackpackers.com). Brand new to San José's hostel scene, this inexpensive backpacker magnet has the feel of a luxurious college dorm. It's a bit of a walk from the city center, but the spotless rooms, hot water in the shared bathrooms, night watchman, free Internet, big communal kitchen, TV room with cable, tons of tourist info, and swimming pool will make you want to stay forever. Baggage storage ¢50 per bag per day. Laundry ¢2000. Check-out 11am. No phone reservations. Dorms ¢2500 per person. ❶

Casa Ridgway, Av. 6/8, Calle 15 (☎222 1400, fax 233 6168; friends@racsa.co.cr), in the short, dead-end street between and running parallel to Av. 6 and 8. An active Quaker peace center, this friendly, immaculately-kept home is popular with backpackers and volunteer groups. Sitting area with communal kitchen, dining area, and a large library is available to guests. Bathrooms are spotless and there is plenty of hot water to go around. Ask Flor, one of the owners, for a taste of her out-of-this-world *gallo pinto*. Public phone (☎255 6399), laundry (US$5), and storage available. Quiet hours 10pm-7am. Dorms US$10 per person; a few singles US$12; doubles US$24. ❶

Casa León, Av. 6, Calles 13/15. (☎222 9725). Turn right onto Calle 15 from Av. 2 and go up the first set of stairs to your right. Though small, Casa León is homey and clean with laid-back owners and bright, comfortable lodgings. Well-maintained rooms and appliances. Public phone, laundry (¢2000), and communal kitchen available. Two shared hot baths. Popular with traveling students. Up to 6 people in a dorm. Dorms US$10; singles US$15; doubles US$25. ❶

Pensión de la Cuesta, Av. 1, Calle 11/15 (☎256-7946). A wonderful, inviting B&B with a beautiful kitchen and dining area. Rooms and hallways decorated with eclectic artwork painted by the owners themselves. Breakfast included. Jan.-Feb. singles US$23; doubles US$33; triples US$43; quads US$53. Mar.-Apr. US$20/US$30/US$40/US$48; June-Dec. US$18/US$31/US$41/US$49. AmEx/MC/V. ❷

Tica Linda, Calle 7, Av. 10 (☎222 8432). Marked by a tiny nameplate on the door. A backpacker favorite and an ideal spot to get hints from veterans. Not much private space, but it has a very cozy feel and an absolutely hilarious owner. Warm water in the communal bathroom. Dorms ¢1300; singles ¢1500. ❶

Hotel Balmoral, Calle 7, Av. Central (☎222 5022, fax 221 7826; www.balmoralco.cr). An upscale place with tons of luxurious perks. Gorgeous, modern rooms with A/C and private hot baths, cable TV, and wall-to-wall carpeting; some with balconies and safe deposit boxes. 30min. of free Internet per day and access to the gym and sauna.

FROM THE ROAD

CAN'T GET ENOUGH OF THAT *TICO* LOVE

One thing you'll notice right away upon arriving in Costa Rica is how affectionate *ticos* are. Coming from a culture in which love and relationships are much more private, it was quite a shock to see *tico* couples, young and old alike, kissing in parks, holding hands in grocery store lines, and cuddling on the seats of the public bus.

It wasn't too difficult to get used to this rather refreshing show of love, but what I was more uncomfortable with were the catcalls and unwanted attention I received from many *tico* men. Now, don't get me wrong—I wasn't a unique target of their attention; pretty much any girl there will definitely be noticed in a very deliberate way. At first, their calling me *cariño, mi amor,* and *linda* were a bit unsettling; and more than once, I shot back angry looks and nasty *"dejame en paz"* utterings under my breath. As my naturally dark skin got more and more bronzed, *morenita* became the nickname of choice. To me, this attention was definitely unwarranted, especially as a female traveling by myself.

I guess it wasn't until I was wandering through the market in San José, as every fruit and vendor asked me *Que puede ofrecerle, linda?* that I finally realized how harmless and in fact friendly their intentions were. Though the literal translations can be quite coarse, Costa Ricans use them very casually and affectionately, and extremely few women ever experience anything beyond the nicknames. After a while, actually, I really grew to love the cute phrases the *ticos* use. It's just one more example of their constant efforts to be friendly and courteous.

—Megha Doshi

Check-out 2pm. Rooms start at US$60 per night plus tax. AmEx/D/MC/V. ❹

SOUTH OF THE PARQUE CENTRAL

Hotel Boston, Av. 8, Calles Central/2 (☎257 4499 or 221 0563). Spacious, mint-green rooms with sturdy wooden beds, TVs, and clean private bathrooms. Most rooms have hot water. Laundry service and phone available. Singles ¢3500; doubles ¢5000; triples ¢6000; quads ¢7000. AmEx/MC/V. ❶

Hotel Príncipe, Av. 6, Calles Central/2 (☎222 7983; fax 223 1589), 1 block north of Hotel Boston. The racket from the surrounding bars may be a bit bothersome, but quiet hours after 10pm help you sleep. The big rooms are a bit worn but have bright sheets, comfy beds, and private hot-water baths; rooms on the upper floors have a sparkling view of San José. Attached bar and small lobby with cable TV. Each floor has a sitting room. Safety deposit box available M-F 8:30am-8pm. Singles ¢4000; doubles ¢5500; triples ¢7000. ❷

NORTH OF THE PARQUE CENTRAL

Gran Hotel Imperial, Calle 8, Av. Central/1 (☎222 8463; fax 257 4922). True backpackers rough it and crash in one of Imperial's 80 less-than-luxurious rooms, yet the friendly atmosphere and many extras will make your stay more enjoyable. Dirt-cheap restaurant/bar, laundry (¢1500), book exchange, TV in the lobby, Internet (¢200 per 30min., ¢300 per hr.), public phone, bag storage (¢50 per bag per day), and hot water in the mornings. Guests gather for beers and stories in the evening on the balcony overlooking the *mercado central.* No smoking or visitors after 10pm. Restaurant open M-Sa noon-8:30pm; bar until 11pm. Singles ¢1500; doubles ¢3000, with bath ¢5000; triples ¢4500; quads ¢6000. ❶

Pensión Otoya, Calle 1, Av. 3/5 (☎221 3925). Spacious, bright rooms with yellow walls and wall-to-wall carpet. Hot baths are a bit worn. Pleasant sitting area is perfect for reading or chatting. Laundry ¢1000. Free baggage storage. Singles ¢2700, with bath ¢3700; doubles ¢2500/¢3500; triples ¢2300/¢3300. ❶

Hotel Nuevo Almeda, Calle 12, Av. Central/1 (☎233 3551). A good value with clean rooms, huge windows, wall-to-wall carpet, and private, spotless hot-water baths. Check-out noon. Singles US$15; doubles US$14 per person; triples and quads US$10 per person. Ask for special discounts for low season and long stays. ❷

Hotel Bienvenido, Calle 10, Av. 1/3 (☎233 2161). Pay a bit more at this large hotel for clean rooms, large hallways, and hot water in the private bathrooms. Beautiful common area with TV and small restaurant. Phone calls US$0.50 per min. Baggage storage US$2 per bag per day. Safety deposit box $2. Check-out 2pm. Singles and doubles US$18; triples US$27; quads US$26. AmEx/MC/V. ❷

WEST OF THE PARQUE CENTRAL

Hotel El Descanso, Calle 6, Av. 4 (☎221 9941), entrance on Calle 6. Safe, classy, calm lodgings with comfy beds, TVs, and clean, private hot baths. Very professional staff. The rooms and hallways are spacious. Check-out noon. Singles US$10; doubles US$20. ❶

SAN PEDRO

▨ **Toruma Youth Hostel (HI),** Av. Central, Calles 29/31 (☎/fax 224 4085; reca-jhi@racsa.co.cr). Take the San Pedro bus (¢105) from Av. Central, Calles 9/11, and get off at Kentucky Fried Chicken. Toruma is the stately yellow building directly across the street. A backpacker magnet with over 80 clean single-sex rooms and shared hot baths. Bright, spacious lobby with sofas, cable TV, and lockers. Visitors fill the common area and share stories. English spoken. Breakfast included 7:30-9am. Free Internet and luggage storage for guests. Reception daily 7am-10pm. Reservations recommended. Dorms US$13, US$11 with HI card; singles US$26; doubles US$28. AmEx/MC/V. ❷

❏ FOOD

SAN JOSÉ

Black beans, rice, and fried chicken are San José's staples. Western culture has left its mark, however, and fast-food joints abound downtown, especially around Av. Central, Calle 1-3. More authentic *tico* fare like *casados* and *gallo pinto* can be found at the hundreds of *sodas* dotting the city. Most have cheap lunch and dinner specials (¢600-1200 for a complete meal). An even cheaper option is to head to the **mercado central,** where you can snag a tasty, inexpensive, variety-filled meal or buy fruits, veggies, and meats to cook in your hostel's kitchen. Most of the higher-quality and more pleasant *sodas* and restaurants are in the vicinity of Av. Central.

▨ **Soda el Parque,** Calle 2, Av. 4/6. El Parque's round-the-clock hours invite both suit-clad business men for lunch and late-night revelers who are addicted to the delicious and inexpensive *comida típica.* Medium-sized breakfasts ¢650-1000, large ¢950-1400. *Casados* ¢1000. Open 24hr. AmEx/MC/V. ❶

▨ **Tin Jo,** Calle 11, Av. 6/8, is *the* place to splurge on a delicious meal. Exotic, elegantly presented Chinese, Thai, Indian, Japanese, Indonesian, and Burmese cuisine hits the spot when you tire of rice and beans. Indoor water fountain and perfectly-set tables exude a royal atmosphere. Veggie-friendly menu. Sushi ¢1800-3000; curries ¢2800-4500; meat dishes ¢3000-4000; noodles ¢2000-3000. Open M-Th 11:30am-3pm and 5:30-10:30pm, F-Sa 11:30-3pm and 5:30-11pm, Su 11:30am-10pm. AmEx/MC/V. ❸

▨ **Restaurant Vishnu Vegetariano,** main branch at Av. 1, Calles 1/3. (☎290 0119.) Other locations include Av. 4, Calle 1 (next to the Banco Popular), Av. 8, Calles 11/13, and Calle 14, Av. Central. Locals and tourists alike swarm here for yummy food and quick service that makes the heart and wallet very happy. Fresh fruits and veggies decorate both the dining area and your delicious meal, which might be *gallo pinto* (¢800), a veggie hamburger (¢550) or the belly-stuffing *plato del día* (soup, dessert, fruit drink, rice, salad, and veggie entree ¢1150). Whatever they put in the lasagna (¢1250) is so delicious, you'll be pleading for their secret recipe. Don't leave without trying the *morir soñando* (die dreaming; ¢450). Main branch open M-Sa 8am-9:30pm, Su 9am-7:30pm; other locations close a few hours earlier. ❶

FROM THE ROAD

A LEAGUE OF THEIR OWN

Never having been a serious fan of professional sports, the last place I expected a sudden surge of spirit for a national sports team was in a foreign country. But in the midst of the *futbol manía*, it was impossible not to get drawn into the wild Costa Rican enthusiasm for their heroic *jugadores*. It was World Cup season here, and, as one *tico* put it to me simply, soccer was "la pura vida." For days leading up to the game against the talented Brazilians, *ticos* patriotically dressed in the bright red-and-blue jerseys of the national team, Costa Rican flags waved proudly from every shop window and car antenna, and all anyone would talk about was the big game. Somehow, I started getting just as revved up and nervous about the game as everyone else.

That Wednesday night before the game started, I found myself in Centro Comercial El Pueblo. The narrow sidewalks were rocking and screaming with packs of red and blue—and not just clothes. Most fans had their faces and chests painted in Costa Rican colors. I was slightly intimidated, since I was by myself and not Costa Rican. But no one seemed to care, I realized, as a loud DJ-type asked me why my face wasn't painted and excitedly threw me in line with the rest. I then went to All Stars, a San Pedro sports bar, where the scene was just as intense. I grabbed a seat in front of the huge TV. The game began with "oohs" and "aahs" and signs and loyal fans from every corner of the country screaming "Sí se puede!"

Nuestra Tierra, Av. 2, Calle 15. Burlap sacks, candle-lit tables, wooden tables, *vaquero*-uniformed waiters, and meals served on palm leafs transport you 70 years back to authentic, country-style cooking in rural Costa Rica. The place is elegantly rustic. *Plato del día* ¢750, *casados* ¢1100. Open M-Sa noon-10pm. ❶

Deli City, Av. 2, Calle 1, 1 story below street level in the small strip mall on the northwest corner of the intersection. Nothing here is really authentic, but after tasting the delicious hot sub sandwiches (¢600), pizza (¢400 per slice), and spaghetti (¢800), you really won't care. Locals on their lunch breaks are especially fond of the great lunch specials (pizza, sandwich, or pasta with fruit and shake for ¢1000), and the breezy outdoor sitting area is a fantastic place to enjoy them. Open daily 7am-11pm. ❶

Spoon, Av. Central, Calles 5/7. More than 17 locations in San José area, including one in the San Pedro Mall. This Latin American chain restaurant is always a safe option. The huge menu includes sandwiches (¢1000), cake (¢800), salads (¢2000), try the Thai salad with chicken, spinach, and cheese), some standard Mexican dishes (chicken quesadilla ¢1600) and breakfast dishes (¢800). Open daily 9am-9pm. AmEx/MC/V. ❷

Churrería Manolos, Av. Central, Calle 2 and Av. 1, Calles 11/13. Famous for its fresh, cinnamon-crispy, melt-in-your-mouth-good *churros*. Flavored *dulce de leche* ¢150; dip it in chocolate for ¢50 more and get an extra taste of heaven. Menu also includes standard lunch and dinner meals (rice dishes ¢900-1500). Upstairs bar draws a post-drinking crowd all night long. Main location open 24hr. ❶

Padrísimo, Calle Central, Av. 6/4. A Mexican restaurant with adobe walls, bright tapestries, and tablecloths, and cheese oozing out of every hot bite. Plenty of veggie options, and they'll substitute beans for meat in just about every dish. Bean and cheese burrito ¢1150; chicken enchilada ¢1300; fajitas ¢2200. Imperial ¢550; Corona ¢1000; margarita ¢700. Open daily noon-9pm. MC/V. ❷

Shakti, Av. 8, Calle 13. Bright yellow walls on the outside hide the dimly lit, soothing haven of health and wholesome goodness inside. Daily specials are the best deal, with *platos del día* for ¢1000, but the hearty *casados*, salads, veggie burgers, and creative pasta dishes have fancy touches like walnut sauces and raisin garnishes. Very popular at lunch. Open irregularly for lunch and dinner. ❶

Restaurant/Bar La Embajada, Av. 1, Calles Central/2. Locals fill the long bar almost every night for the camaraderie, cheap beer, and TV. Large portions of hearty *típico* dishes served all day. Rice dishes ¢1200. Local beers ¢400. Open daily 8am-11pm. ❶

News Cafe, Av. Central, Calle 7, attached to the Hotel Presidente. A slightly up-scale American cafe/bar packed with tourists craving good ol' bar food (buffalo wings ¢1000-1500) and California-influenced pastas, salads, meats, and wraps. Don't miss the amazing breakfast buffet (¢2500), complete with fruit bar, *tico*, and American dishes, fresh pastries, and made-to-order omelets. Excellent chocolate chip cookies (3 for ¢400). Beer ¢550; cocktails ¢1000. Open daily 6am-11:30pm. AmEx/MC/V. ❷

SAN PEDRO

The heart of San José's bustling student scene, San Pedro is replete with good, inexpensive cafes and restaurants. From San José, catch a bus to San Pedro from Av. Central, Calle 9/11 (10min., every 5-10min., ¢105), ride past Mall San Pedro, and get off when you see the Outlet Mall to your right. This main drag into San Pedro is Av. Central, and the street running directly perpendicular is Calle Central. Walk north down Calle Central with the Parque John F. Kennedy to your left and the Outlet Mall behind you. The first street on your right leads to Calle 3 (better known as **Calle de la Amargura**); a left on Calle 3 leads to the University campus, and a right leads back down to Av. Central. This loop is packed with students during the school year.

Restaurante Il Pomodoro, 100m north of JFK Park on Av. Central. The aroma of garlic spills into the street, enticing the pasta-deprived into this authentic Italian jewel of a restaurant. Generous portions of crispy thin-crust pizzas (small ¢1200-2400, medium ¢1800-3000, large ¢2400-4000) and pastas (¢1700-2000). Beer ¢550; wine ¢750. Open M-Th 11:30am-11pm, F-Sa 11:30am-midnight. AmEx/D/MC/V. ❷

Restaurante Vegetariano, 200m north of JFK Park on Av. Central. The bright yellow walls embellished with animal paintings might remind you of nursery school, but the vegetarian snacks and entrees will make you forget. Veggie burger ¢700; burrito ¢750; falafel ¢1000. Kitchen open M-F 10am-5:15pm. ❶

Jazz Café, 150m east of Calle 3 on Av. Central, is a more upscale place to get your toes tapping, with live jazz almost every night. Dine on salads (¢900-2000) or pasta (¢1900-2600). Cocktails attract a large late-night crowd. Open daily from 6pm. ❷

Cool Running, Av. Central, Calle 5. Dreadlocked waiters nodding to Bob Marley beats bring you plates of plantains, yucca, cassava rolls, rice and beans, and rasta salads. Most dishes ¢800-1300. M-Sa 11am-9pm. ❶

It wasn't until I stepped outside for some air, however, that I realized the full scope of the *tico* passion for the game. The main streets from San José to San Pedro were completely blocked off to traffic, now funneling a steady stream of crazed fans, their eyes locked on the enormous screen set up across from Mall San Pedro. Even the police teams were getting into the action, "authoratatively" discussing the game and cheering with the hundreds of fans. What a rush—the whole country was, at that very instant, watching the game, each and every person's face cringing and heart beating wildly with every bad call or near-miss block.

This wasn't just about winning the game; it was part of the culture and patriotism that holds the *ticos* together, a source of national pride and faith. The love for the game was an equalizer, and suddenly, as long as you were a fan and swore by the last ball that would slide by the Brazilian goalie, you were everybody's friend. That night was a huge tragedy when Costa Rica lost to Brazil, and what followed was almost a national day of mourning. However, loyal fans still donned the ubiquitous jerseys, and one street vendor told me that he sold more "Vamos ticos!" T-shirts that day than before the game. At the heart of every town I visited, no matter how small, I could always count on finding a large soccer field in the center of town and catching a casual game of pick-up. Sure, the World Cup wasn't theirs to polish and treasure this year, but the sport, national pride, and love of the game will always be in the halls of *tico* fame.

—**Megha Doshi**

Mazorca, on a small side street off Calle 3, 100m north of Av. Central. A dim, earthy restaurant specializing in natural vegetarian cuisine. Delectable homemade dishes include veggie pizza (¢1300), baked cannelloni (¢1300), and Caribbean soup (¢800). Open daily 11am-7pm. ❶

�◉ SIGHTS

TEATRO NACIONAL. Built in 1897 using taxes imposed by the Costa Rican government in response to a national desire for more cultural venues, the *Teatro Nacional* (National Theater) is a source of national pride for Costa Rican citizens whose efforts the theater represents. The extravagant theater is graced with sculpted banisters overlaid in 22.5 carat gold, marble floors, and high-ceiling frescoes. Italian sculptor Pitro Bulgarelli's statues personifying Dance, Music, and Fame adorn its facade. Deeper inside the lobby is Costa Rica's most famous **mural,** a beautiful collage of bananas and coffee, the country's livelihood at the turn of the 20th century. A grand staircase inspired by the Paris Opera ascends toward bright overhead reliefs. Performances, which include opera, dance, drama, and music, are a real treat. (*Av. 2, Calles 3/5, off the Plaza de la Cultura.* ☎ *221 1329. Open M-F 9am-5pm, Sa 9am-noon and 1-5pm. Tours ¢600. Tickets ¢2000-5000.*)

MUSEO NACIONAL. This museum offers a glimpse into every aspect of Costa Rican life. In the past 50 years, it has been transformed from the Cuartel Bellarista, a military headquarters, to the home of an eclectic collection of artifacts. Now housing collections of pre-Columbian art and exhibits on Costa Rican history, colonial life, archaeology, and geology, it is a tribute to the continued efforts in scientific research and education that defend the country's natural and cultural heritage. The museum was built in an old Costa Rican fort and bullet holes from the 1948 Revolution mark the walls. Don't miss the view from the museum's gazebo. (*Calle 17, Av. Central/2.* ☎ *257-1433. Open Tu-Su 8:30am-4:30pm. ¢200, students free.*)

MUSEO DE JADE. The 11th floor of Costa Rica's Social Security building is an unlikely location for this stunning collection of artifacts, reportedly the world's largest collection of American jade (pronouced *ha-day* in Spanish). The emerald colored mineral was of distinct importance to Costa Rica's indigenous groups, and many tools, pots, jewelry, religious figures, and weapons dating back to pre-Columbian and Maya times are on display. Recently renovated, the exhibitions are well-lit and accompanied with English and Spanish explanations. Don't miss the spectacular, panoramic ▨birds' eye view of San José from the museum window. (*11th fl. of INS Building, Av. 7, Calles 9/13. ¢1200.*)

MUSEO DE ORO. Established in 1950 by the Central Bank of Costa Rica to help preserve Costa Rican cultural heritage, the Museo de Oro, underneath the Plaza de Cultura, houses a three-part exploration of Costa Rican culture. One floor has a permanent gold exhibit, with pre-Columbian items dating from 500 AD to the 16th century. Another exhibit houses bills, coins, and *boletos de café* (coffee tokens) from the 16th century. The final hall is used for a range of rotating fine arts and archeological exhibits. (*Av. Central, Calle 5.* ☎ *243 4202. Open Tu-Su 10am-4:30pm. Admission ¢1500, students and children ages 7-12 ¢300.*)

SERPENTARIUM. This miniature snake garden houses a collection of native reptiles, amphibians, insects, and spiders. Descriptions printed in English and Spanish describe their behaviors and geographical ranges. Avid reptile fans may be the only ones who think the steep entrance fee is worth it. (*Av. 1, Calles 9/11.* ☎ *255-4210. Open M-F 9am-6pm, Sa-Su 10am-5pm. ¢1500, children under 13 ¢500.*)

PARQUE DE ESPAÑA AND PARQUE MORAZÁN. Complete with well-manicured lawns, benches, and a majestic dome perfect for enacting your own version of a Shakespearean romance, these neighboring parks are a tranquil and cool place to rest aching feet. Sudden downpours draw a crowd of students, couples, and business men, who crowd under España's dome to stay dry. *(Av. 3/5, Calles 5/13. Free.)*

MUSEO DE ARTE COSTARRICENSE. Housed in a terminal of San José's old airport, this small museum is filled to the brim with over 3200 works of Costa Rican nationalist art from the 19th and 20th centuries. The walls of the Salón Dorado are carved and painted to look like gold with the history of Costa Rica depicted in one fluid sweep around the four walls. *(Paseo Colón, Calle 42, on the eastern edge of Parque La Sabana. ☎ 222 7155. Open Tu-Sa 10am-4pm, Su 10am-2pm. ¢400, students free.)*

CENTRO NACIONAL DE ARTE Y CULTURA. The large, tan-colored center, between Parque de España and the National Library, offers a calendar of artistic and cultural events and some of Costa Rica's oldest earthquake-surviving edifices. Stop by to see if there's a performance running. *(Av. 3, Calles 15/17. ☎ 257 7202.)*

PARQUE ZOOLÓGICO Y JARDÍN BOTÁNICO NACIONAL SIMÓN BOLÍVAR. Although run down, it may be worth a stop to see the otherwise elusive jaguar and squirrel monkeys. Costa Rican agoutis, reptiles, a lion, jaguar, and tapirs are on display. *(Av. 11, Calle 7, 300m north and 175m northwest of Parque Morazán in Barrio Amón. ☎ 256 0012 or 233 67017. Open daily 8am-5pm. ¢700 per person, children under 3 free.)*

MUSEO DE CRIMEN. This peculiar crime station features a small collection of weapons, drug paraphernalia, criminal evidence, and accompanying explanations entirely in Spanish. The most bizarre exhibits show fascinating preserved aborted fetuses and diseased organs. Not exactly a tourist destination but a worthwhile stop if you're into scientific criminology. *(Calle 17, Av. 6/8, on the 2nd fl. of the Supreme Court of Justice (OIJ). ☎ 295 3581. Open M-F 7:30am-noon and 1-5:30pm, although the museum sometimes closes a bit earlier. Free.)*

ENTERTAINMENT

Probably in response to the increased number of thick-walleted tourists, a number of 24hr. casinos have opened up in San José, many in hotels clustering on Av. 1 near Calle 5. **Fiesta Casino**, Av. Central, Calle 7/9, has a good mix of tables and slots if you want to try your luck. You must be over 18 to gamble. Several movie theaters throughout San José show recent US releases with Spanish subtitles. In the center of downtown is **Cine Omni**, Calle 3, Av. Central/1 (☎ 221 7903), in the Edificio Omni (¢1100). **Sala Garbo** (☎ 223 1960) and **Teatro Laurence Olivier** (☎ 222 1034), in the same building on Av. 2, Calle 28, 100m south of the Paseo Colón Pizza Hut, show a more artistically varied selection of older films from Latin American countries and North America (¢850). **Multicines San Pedro** (☎ 280 9585), in San Pedro Mall, has 10 modern theaters with digital sound (¢1200, ½ price on W). For tons of fun on wheels, head to **Salón de Patines Music**, 200m west of the JFK park in San Pedro, where you can roller skate the day away, listen to great music, and meet lots of young people. (Open M-F 7-10pm; Sa, Su, holidays 1-10pm.)

SHOPPING

San José's sheer size and tourist following makes buying anything from basic necessities to souvenirs and art work easier—and sometimes cheaper—than in other Costa Rican towns. You'll find the best selection of Costa Rican art, woodwork, jewelry, clothing, hammocks, and other souvenirs in a strip of vendors on Av. 2, Calle 13/15 near the Museo Nacional. (Most vendors open M-Sa 8am-6pm, some open Su.) Another option is **La Casona,** Calle 1, Av. Central/1, a collection of many souvenir stores under one roof. (Most stores open daily M-Sa 9:30am-6:30pm, some open Su.) Serious art collectors should check out San José's many wonderful art galleries, many along Av. 1 between Calle 5 and 13. For a standard Western selection of clothing and sportswear, take a San Pedro-bound bus to **Mall San Pedro** or **Outlet Mall.**

▨ NIGHTLIFE

San Pedro pulses with life at night: the dance is salsa and merengue, the drink is either ice-cold *cervezas* or *guaro* sunrise cocktails, and the scene varies from *ticos* belting out Latin tunes in karaoke bars to American sports bars packed with tourists playing pool and chatting in English. **Calle de la Amargura** is always hopping and has the best casual atmosphere for meeting young *ticos;* **El Pueblo** is the best dancing scene; and **San José center** caters to a slightly older crowd of both locals and foreigners. Most bars and clubs charge ¢1000 for cover, sometimes higher for men, but cover usually includes a couple of drinks. Dress is usually casual; jeans and sandals are fine in San Pedro bars, but you might want to throw on some dressier threads to go to El Pueblo and San José clubs. It's a good idea to bring your **passport** with you to most clubs and bars because the bouncers will require a good ID (18+) to let you in.

CLUBS

CENTRO COMERCIAL EL PUEBLO

Any *tico* will confirm that El Pueblo, a 15min. ride north of San José center, is *the* place to be for a wild night of dancing and drinking till the wee hours of the morn. Shockingly similar to the raging Cancún spring break scene, this expanded courtyard filled with narrow stone paths contains gift shops, bars, and dance clubs that usually get going between 10:30 and 11pm. Although most easily accessible by taxi (¢500), you can take a bus to Calle Blancos from Av. 9, Calle 3 (until 11pm, ¢70). The area's affluence and high security make El Pueblo a safe, contained area. Just don't wander too far outside the boundaries.

▨ **Infinito Discotheque** (☎221 9134), the most popular spot in El Pueblo. Warm and exciting interior with dark wood walls, red leather furniture, and lamps that throw shafts of color everywhere. A fish tank lights up the bar and makes the liquor sparkle tantalizingly. The larger dance room is geared to the college crowd and plays danceable pop and trance. Cover ¢800; W and Su ladies free; F-Sa ladies free before 9pm. Open M-W 6pm-4am, F-Su 6pm-6am. Another room plays "romantic music" for the 45-plus crowd. Cozy rooms and bars span the distance between the two. Fairly high gringo count in the high season. Cover Su-Th ¢450, F-Sa ¢500, including first drink. Open daily 6pm-5am.

Twister Club (☎222 7562), towards the back and on the left of El Pueblo, attracts a late-20s crowd where the music is loud, people are dressed to impress, and the line forms early. House beats on the dance floor keep the bodies moving. Open daily 6:30pm until the crowd dies out..

NEAR THE CITY CENTER

San José's center is crawling with bars and clubs, many of which remain hidden between *sodas* and shops to all but the observant eye. At many, you'll find a wide range of ages chatting over drinks, while others blast popular Latin hits for expert dancers. Most places seem to have a little bit of both.

A NIGHTLIFE FOR EVERYONE
For those in search of music, drinks, and a good time in the city, there are three main night-life options you can choose from in the San José area.

San Pedro is most commonly known for *La Calle de la Amargura* (Street of Bitterness, see p. 97), which is the main hangout for students from the Universidad de Costa Rica. This street consists of an assortment of small bars and pool places. The most popular ones right now are Caccio's (especially on Tuesdays), Tavarúa, Pueblo Viejo, and Mosaikos. A lot of young people gather here to drink, dance with friends to pop and reggae music (no merengue and salsa here!), and if the time is right, enjoy a soccer match on really big screens. Prices are cheap, people are friendly, and there is no need to dress up. Very important: the action here starts early, from 3-5pm, when most classes have ended.

If you're in search of the preppy scene and classier bars, **San Rafael de Escazú** (p. 104) is the place to go. Bars like Frankie Go, Tabú, Bamboleo (especially on Thursdays), Fandango (in the Centro Comercial Trejos Montealegre), and Sambuka (in La Rambla) are all near the main drag. They offer a wide array of cocktails and dance music, and you're basically guaranteed an enjoyable night. Prices here are higher however; you usually have to pay a cover of ₡1000-2000 colones.

Want to shake your hips to some merengue and salsa? Go to **El Pueblo** (p. 100). This *centro comercial* is filled with bars of all shapes and sizes with live music and several lively restaurants. These places generally start filling up after 1am. People of all ages, places, and ideals come here, so come with an open mind and be sure to bring a lot of energy; this party lasts until the sun comes up!

—Melania Cortés is a student of veterinary medicine at Kansas State University, Melania was a long-time volunteer at the Zoológico la Marina working with animals who have been orphaned, injured, or captured illegaly.

Acapulco, Av. Central, Calles 17/19 (☎222 1070), 1 block east of the northeast corner of the Museo Nacional. A strong local following gathers early for drinks and chats at one of the many bar tables. Later in the night, flashing lights and thumping music attract a varied crowd, many outstanding in the arts of *salsa* and *merengue.* Cover ₡1000, ₡3000 for men on F. Open bar for women arriving early (7-9pm) and all night on F for men and women. Open Th-Su starting at 5pm.

Salsa 54, Calle 3, Av. 1/3 2nd fl. (☎223 3814), is a meeting place for the mature who are still young enough to boogie to a mix of love songs, 60s hits, and *salsa.* Many of the dancers are experts, but don't let that stop you from joining in. Tu and W fills with pool and karaoke fans. *Salsa* and *merengue* lessons every Sa 10am and noon (₡5000 for 4 lessons). Tu and W no cover, Th-Su ₡1000. Open Tu-Su 7pm-2am.

Salidas Orbital 2000 (☎233 3814), right next door to Salsa 54. A younger crowd dances to pop, tango, *salsa,* and *merengue* on 3 small stages amid a sea of red plush cocktail tables. Karaoke every night 6-8pm. Male and female models wearing next to nothing dance in the Model Revue. Cover ₡1000. Open W-Su 7pm-2am.

SAN PEDRO

El Cuartel de la Boca del Monte, Av. 1, Calles 21/23, in between San José and San Pedro. One of San José's hottest spots for the burgeoning 20s scene. A welcoming atmosphere featuring live local bands with Latin rhythm on M evenings and no cover for ladies. Cover ₡1200 for live music, otherwise free. Open daily 6pm-2am.

Fuera de Control, Av. Central, Calle 5 (☎253-8062). Flashy lights, a raised stage, and karaoke in English and Spanish let every sing along queen and king have their 15min.-of-fame fantasy. The daily happy hour and 2-for-1 specials help the shy overcome their performance phobias. Karaoke Su-Th 9-11pm, live music F, hip hop and rave Sa. Beer ₡450; 2 for ₡750 6-9pm and all night Sa. Cocktails ₡850. Open daily 4pm-2am.

Planet Mall, Mall San Pedro, 4th fl. (☎280 4693). Mingle with a very young crowd on the huge dance floors as you gaze down on the bright lights of San José through the floor-to-ceiling windows. Cover ₡1500. Open Th-Sa 8:30pm-2:30am.

BARS

The enormous bar scene near the University of Costa Rica in **San Pedro** is student-oriented, but casual and diverse enough to accommodate just about anyone seeking a good time. People and loud music overflow into the streets, making the area relatively safe, but take precautions. Calle 3 north of Av. Central, known as **Calle de la Amargura** (Street of Bitterness; see **San Pedro,** p. 97), is the heart of the college scene. There are relatively few tourists, making it easier to meet the fun-loving and outgoing *tico* students. Places to try include: **Caccio's** (beer ₡450; no cover; open M-Sa 10am-2am), **Mosaiko's** for a more laid-back atmosphere (hip hop M, reggae Tu, electronic W, rock, pop, alternative Th-Sa; free tequila for girls Sa 8-10pm; beer ₡450; cover ₡1000; open 11am-2am), and **Bar Tavarúa,** a surf and skate bar which pumps out the beat and opens up a back room for dancing on crowded nights (beer ₡450; cover ₡1000, ladies free Th; open M-Sa 11am-2am). Bars closer to San José center tend to be populated by older men and their girlfriends or female escorts. To avoid such an uncomfortable setting, check out the following:

▧ **Raíces,** Av. 2, Calle 45, across from the Mall San Pedro and around the corner from All Stars Bar. A *tico* favorite, this reggae bar draws a young, alternative student crowd who worship everything Jamaican. Dreadlocked teens and their surfer counterparts jam to Fugees and Bob Marley, while the mellower chill on the outskirts, Red Stripe in hand. Beer ₡450. T and W 7-9pm 2-for-1 drinks. Cover ₡1000, includes 2 drinks. Open W-Sa 7pm till the crowds leave.

Bar Esmeralda, Av. 2, Calles 5/7 (☎221 0530). Caters to an older crowd. Mariachi music offers a soothing alternative to pop. Open daily 7pm-1am.

GAY/LESBIAN NIGHTLIFE

Déjà Vu, Calle 2, Av. 14/16 (☎256 6332). The clientele of this chic and classy nightclub love to glitter and shine. A fantastic mix of trance and reggae keeps the scantily-clad patrons moving till dawn. Don't miss the flamboyant Sa drag show. Cover Th ₡2000, F ₡1500, Sa ₡3000. Open bar 9-11pm. Open M-Sa 8pm-6am.

La Avispa, Calle 1, Av. 8/10 (☎223 5343), an attractive setting with tons of space for ultimate enjoyment: 3 dance floors, a courtyard, and pool tables (₡200 per game). Dress in your most outrageous threads. Singles night 2nd W of the month, ladies night last W of the month. Th karaoke. Cover ₡700. Open Tu and Th-Su 8pm-2:30am.

NEAR SAN JOSÉ

INBIOPARQUE

From San José, take a bus from Calle Central, Av. 7/9 to Santo Domingo (20min., ₡170); tell the driver you want to go to INBio parque. From the drop-off point, walk 250m west (to your right) along the main road; the complex will be on the left. ☎244 4730; www.inbio.ac.cr/inbioparque. Open daily 7:30am-4pm. US$12, students US$9. AmEx/MC/V.

If you're in San José for a few days before heading off to the more adventurous national parks and wildlife refuges, a visit to INBioparque will prep you with a wealth of information about Costa Rica's national park system, various species of flora and fauna, and the importance of biodiversity. Though it has the distinct feel of a field trip excursion, visitors of all ages will benefit from the easy-to-understand and informative English/Spanish explanations. The visit starts

GUILT-FREE PLEASURES Back in the early 50s when there was no children's hospital, Costa Rica had a terrible polio epidemic. At that time a group of Costa Rican citizens, aided by embassies from various countries, started an annual fair to collect funds for the construction of the Children's Hospital.

Following the construction of the hospital, polio cases dwindled, and the annual fundraising fair gtadually became the **Parque Nacional de Diversiones,** Costa Rica's national amusement park. Today this park features modern attractions like roller coasters, water rides, an arcade building, a simulator, and many places to sit, relax, and eat. One of its main attractions, however, is **Pueblo Antiguo,** an educational replica of San José in the 1900s; a town filled with typical restaurants, ox-carts, old stores, souvenir shops, cows, horses, and actors all come together to rescue Costa Rica's culture and traditions. What makes this amusement park an especially outstanding source of pride for the ticos, however, is that it is the only amusement park in the world that donates all of its profits to help support the Children's Hospital the most advanced of its type in Latin America.

The Parque Nacional de Diversiones is located 2km west of Hospital México in La Uruca, San José. (☎231 2001, fax 296 2212; parque@parquediversiones.com. Entrance ¢3000. Open W-Th 9am-5pm, F-Sa 9am-8pm, Su 9am-7pm.)

with an introductory video on the scope and value of biodiversity followed by a large exhibition hall with colorful and interactive displays on the geological history and evolution of life on Earth, including a brief sound and light show of Costa Rica's protected areas. Then you'll have a chance to amble along the park's petite and wheelchair-accessible trail network through three forest habitats: central valley forest, humid forest, and dry forest. The trails are mostly easy cement paths sprinkled here and there with information about the biodiversity and the many plant species, including orchids, bromeliads, and *guarumos*. The trails also wind through a small butterfly garden and exhibitions on tarantulas, frogs, bullet ants, and marine animals. A typical Costa Rican restaurant, restrooms, and gift shop are also available. Touring the facilities on your own can take anywhere from 1½-2½hr., depending on how long you spend reading the explanations. Free guided tours (2¼hr.) are also offered every hour, although they may be booked in advance by large groups.

MORAVIA

Once engulfed by coffee plantations, the small suburb of Moravia, northeast of San José, now interests most travelers for its extensive souvenir and artwork selection. For the best selection, take a bus from San José, Av 3, Calle 5/7, and tell the driver to drop you off at **La Calle de la Artesanía.** Here you'll find a street lined with souvenir shops peddling everything from Cuban cigars and woven bags to hand-carved wooden sculptures, jewelry, and the *típico* ox carts so characteristic of Costa Rican country life. Near the middle of the strip is **Hidalgo la Rueda,** a family-run leather store that gives brief tours of its on-site factory. Some of their machines date back to WWII, and they give most of the scraps to schools for arts and crafts projects. (Open M-Sa 8am-5pm, Su 10am-6pm.) At the end of the strip down a side street to the left (near the *parque central*), is the huge **Mercado de Artesanía Las Garzas,** a complex of several souvenir and handicraft stores, convenient for those who need to get lots of shopping done in a hurry. (Open M-Sa 9am-6pm, Su 10am-4pm.) Bargaining down the price about 15-20% is common at most of the stores on this strip, and discounts are often offered for payments *en efectivo* (in cash).

ESCAZÚ

Though just 10km west of San José, the tranquil and cozy suburb of Escazú seems worlds apart in character. Rolling hills and greenery take the place of the capital's towering buildings and grimy air, enticing increasing numbers of retired Americans and Europeans who want both the serenity of a small town and convenience of being near the city. Though the town center is simple with a classic colonial feel, the lush green hills on the outskirts hide some fantastically relaxing and luxurious bed and breakfasts, while some of San José's classiest restaurants are scattered along the road to San Rafael de Escazú, 1km northeast.

■ ★ ORIENTATION AND PRACTICAL INFORMATION

From San José, buses to Escazú leave from the stop at Calle 16, Av. Central/1 (about every 15min., ¢125) and drop passengers off on Av. Central at the north side of the **parque central.** The **church** is on Calle Central on the east side of the *parque.* The road to **San Rafael de Escazú** starts from Calle 5, three blocks east of the *parque,* and continues 1km northeast. Many restaurants are along this stretch of road. Local services include: **Banco de Costa Rica,** at the northeast corner of the *parque* (open M-F); **Banco Nacional,** at the southwest corner of the *parque* (open M-F 8:30am-3:45pm); **Palí** supermarket, 100m north and 50m west of the bank (open M-Th 8am-7pm, F-Sa 8am-8pm, Su 8am-1pm); and the **post office,** one block north of the bank. (Open M-F 8am-5pm.)

■ ACCOMMODATIONS

Many of Escazú's growing number of foreign residents maintain wonderfully relaxing and cozy bed and breakfasts just outside the town center. Most guests have cars to make commuting to nearby restaurants and San José a bit easier, but public transportation and walking is not too difficult.

■ **Costa Verde Inn** (☎ 228 4080; www.costaverdeinn.com), just outside the town center, is nestled snugly in the hills near a cow pasture. Sit in the lap of luxury at this secluded, small country inn, which is more like a resort, with spectacularly comfortable rooms with king size beds, private stone baths, tastefully decorated walls, hot tub, jacuzzi, a sun deck, and living room with fireplace. The hotel also offers lighted tennis courts, tour service, and gourmet breakfast in the tropical gardens. Internet ¢80 per min. Laundry ¢250 per piece. Singles US$45; doubles US$55. ❸

■ **Villa Escazú Bed and Breakfast** (☎ 289 7971; www.hotels.co.cr/vescazu.html), just down the hill, is run by superb chef and New York native Inez Chapman. The wooden house affords lovely views of the central valley, and has 6 airy rooms with sparkling shared hot baths, laundry service, and parking. The best part is the delicious breakfast Inez whips up using only the freshest ingredients (sometimes picked right off her own trees) and rich, tasty coffee. Breakfast included. Singles and doubles US$26-60. ❸

■ **Casa de las Tías** (☎ 289 5517; www.hotels.co.cr/casatias.html), in San Rafael de Escazú, is another charming and homey yellow and turquoise B&B. Friendly and funny owners Javier and Pilar maintain an immaculate Victorian-style house close enough to the town to easily walk to several wonderful restaurants, but set back from the main road just enough to allow true indulgence in the many amenities and pretty tropical gardens. The house has four bedrooms and one junior suite with kitchenette, each decorated with its own unique style and with good views. Amenities include: ceiling fans, private hot bath, laundry service, TV, tour service, and full gourmet breakfast on a pleasant balcony. Javier promises an extra breakfast to any guest who can spot more than

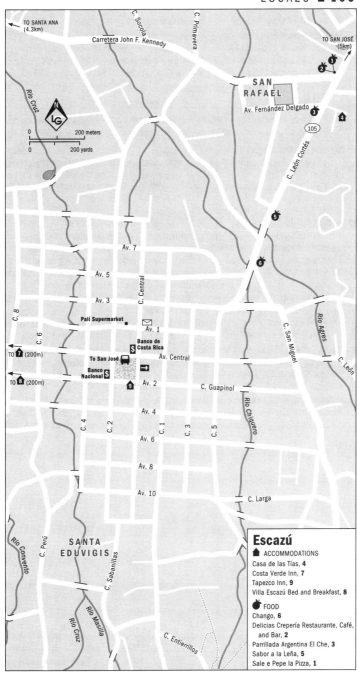

Escazú

⌂ ACCOMMODATIONS
Casa de las Tías, **4**
Costa Verde Inn, **7**
Tapezco Inn, **9**
Villa Escazú Bed and Breakfast, **8**

🍎 FOOD
Chango, **6**
Delicias Crepería Restaurante, Café,
  and Bar, **2**
Parrillada Argentina El Che, **3**
Sabor a la Leña, **5**
Sale e Pepe la Pizza, **1**

his record of seven species of birds simultaneously in the huge tree outside. Singles US$54; doubles US$65; triples US$75. AmEx/MC/V. ❹

Tapezco Inn (☎228 1084), smack in the town center, at the southeast corner of the *parque*, is a charming place with hillside views, jacuzzi, small restaurant, and nicely decorated rooms with private hot-water baths. Singles US$40; doubles US$50. ❸

🛇 FOOD

Escazú boasts some of the country's most elegant dining options. Most come at a price, but tired travelers craving an exotic flavor won't regret the splurge.

▨ **Chango,** on the road to San Rafael de Escazú, is very popular and recommended by Escazú natives. The dining area, with rich mahogany wood tables, earthy decor, and large windows overlooking lush green tress, looks like something from a cozy country club, the perfect atmosphere to dine on exquisitely prepared steak, ribs, and Mediterranean entrees. Fried calamari ¢2300; capellini ¢2700; shish kebobs ¢3500-¢4800; grilled tenderloin ¢5300; baklava ¢1500. Open daily 11:30am-2am. ❸

▨ **Parillada Argentina El Che,** at the end of the road to San Rafael de Escazú, is a favorite with local businessmen and foreign residents. Waiters bustle around in the small, rustic open-air restaurant that will make any carnivore's mouth water. An array of meats, from beef, pig, tongue, sausage, and kidney, are grilled to perfection and flavored with authentic Costa Rican and Argentine flavors. Salads ¢1300-¢1500. Most entrees ¢4000-8000. Wine ¢650 per glass. Open daily noon to 10pm. ❸

Sabor a la Leña, on the road to San Rafael de Escazú, is less damaging to your wallet and almost as tasty. Delicious pizzas (personal ¢1200-1300) in creative flavors like Tex-Mex, Popeye, Picante, and Mexicana. The foccaccia (¢730) makes a great appetizer to your garlic-heavy meal. Delivery available ☎228 1941. Open daily noon-midnight. ❷

Sale e Pepe la Pizza, in the strip mall at the end of the road to San Rafael de Escazú, is an intimate and elegant pizzeria that incorporates gourmet ingredients like gorgonzola, salami, salmon, and fresh artichokes into its thin crust Italian pizzas (¢1750-4000) and pastas (¢2800-¢3500). Open daily noon-3pm and 6-11pm. ❸

Delicias Crepería Restaurante, Café, and Bar, in the strip mall, whips up fresh and unique veggie and seafood crepes (¢1400-¢1700), sweet crepes with nutella (¢1000), and pasta dishes like spinach ricotta ravioli (¢2200). Open daily 10am-10pm. ❷

CENTRAL VALLEY

The Central Valley, or Meseta Central, is a high and vast region cordoned off to the north and south by the great volcanic mountain ranges that divide Costa Rica in two, the Cordillera Central and the Cordillera de Talamanca. Many of the volcanoes, including towering Volcán Irazú and Volcán Poás, are still active and have caused the valley's residents heartache more than once, but the ash has also blessed these temperate plains and rolling hills with enough fertile soil to cultivate crops and rich coffee for several nations. It's no surprise that almost two-thirds of all *ticos* live in this valley and that four of Costa Rica's five largest cities mark its center. Many travelers skip over the landlocked Central Valley and rush to the more typical vacation spots on either coast, just a half-day's journey away in either direction, but that doesn't mean the country's metropolitan areas are lacking in wildlife, adventure, and authentic *tico* culture. Even the largest cities like San José and Cartago are surrounded by tiny agricultural communities like Sarchí and Grecia and rugged national parks and monuments like Parque Nacional Tapantí and Monumento Nacional Guayabo. Visitors will find they can sample a taste of urban life while keeping unearthly volcanos, butterfly gardens, and the country's wildest rafting rivers a daytrip away.

ALAJUELA

Alajuela, 3km from the country's international airport and 17km northwest of San José, is the home of national hero Juan Santamaría, who died burning down the fort of the US military adventurer William Walker in 1856. Although the town is often overlooked by travelers on their way to the beach or the capital, its shaded *parque central* in front of the large, colonial, red-domed cathedral is a good place to sit and relax and is in itself a fine reason to stay and visit. Except for the colorful central market, which takes up an entire block 200m west of the park, the west side of the town goes literally and figuratively downhill. In all other directions however, Alajuela has a sunny character and the people are always friendly. The town also serves as a convenient base for excursions to the Butterfly Farm, Zoo Ave, Volcán Poás, Sarchí, and other exotic destinations.

▣ TRANSPORTATION

From the TUASA station, Av. Central/1, Calle 8 (☎442 6900), 300m west of the southwest corner of the *parque central*, **buses** go to **San José** (45min., every 5min. 4am-10pm, ¢220) and **Volcán Poás** (1½hr., M-Sa 9:15am, return 2:30pm). Buses to **Sarchí** depart from 100m west of the station (1¼hr.; M-Sa every 25-30min., 5am-10pm, Su every 25min., 6:10am-10pm; ¢275).

▣ ▣ ORIENTATION AND PRACTICAL INFORMATION

Arriving at the TUASA bus station, Av. Central/1, Calle 8, walk to the left to the end of the block, then right for three blocks to reach the **parque central,** boxed in by Av. Central/1 and Calle Central/2. Look for the white **catedral** on the far end and a white dome-like shelter over a stage. The streets of Alajuela form the standard

Costa Rican grid, but street signs are rare and often point in the wrong direction, so it's best to count the blocks in your head or use landmarks, as locals do. To complicate things, both Av. 9 and Calle 12 are called **Calle Ancha.**

Banks: Banco Nacional, Av. Central/1, Calle 2. Open M-F 8:30am-3:45pm. **Banco Interfín,** Av. 1/3, Calle 2. Open M-F 8am-5pm, Sa 9am-1pm. Both have 24hr. MC/V **ATMs.** Banco Interfín changes Citibank and Visa traveler's checks. **Banco San José,** Av. 3, Calle Central/1 changes American Express traveler's checks for a US$1 fee. Open M-F 8am-7pm, Sa 9am-1pm.

Supermarket: The most popular is **Palí,** 4 blocks west and 1 block south of the southwest corner of the *parque central.* Open M-F 8:30am-8pm, Sa 7:30am-8pm, Su 8:30am-6pm.

Market: The enclosed **mercado central,** 2 blocks west of the *parque,* is a crowded collection of meat, cheese, fruit, and vegetable stands, as well as a variety of other shops. Open M-F 7am-6pm, Sa 6am-6pm.

Police: (☎443 4511 from 9am-5pm; ☎911) 1 block north and 3 blocks east of the *parque's* northeast corner, around the corner from the fire station. Limited English. Open daily 24hr.

Hospital: Av. 9, Calles Central/1, (☎443 4042; emergency ☎440 1333), 5 blocks north of the northeast corner of the *parque* on Calle Central, facing *Parque de las Palmeras.* Open 24hr.

Telephones: At the *parque,* Av. Central/1, Calles Central/2.

Internet: Cafes are scattered across the city. Try **Tropicafé S.A.,** Av. 3, Calle 1. ₡300/hr. for Internet use; also serves coffee. Open M-Sa 8am-10pm, Su 1-9pm.

Post office: Av. 5, Calle Central, 2 blocks north of the northeast corner of the *parque.* **Fax** available. Open M-F 8:00am-5:30pm, Sa 7:30am-noon. **Postal code:** 4050.

▐ ACCOMMODATIONS

▧ **Villa Real Hostel,** Av. 3, Calle 1 (☎441 4022; villareal@hotmail.com). 1 block north and 1 block east of the northeast corner of the *parque.* This small bright blue hostel always has its coffee brewing in the cozy, earthy common room with cable TV where guests can socialize with English-speaking Diego, the man behind the counter who has friends all over the world. Two common bathrooms serve all the rooms. Kitchen available. Rooms US$12 per person; US$10 for a shared room with 3 other people. AmEx/MC/V. ❷

Hotel El Mango Verde, Av. 3, Calles 2/4 (☎441 7116 or 441 6330; fax 443 5074; mirafloresbb@hotmail.com). Like a mango, this inviting hotel is best on the inside: it offers a miniature garden courtyard, open-air sitting areas with couches, cable TV, a patio, and a communal kitchen (bring your own food). Tropical colors abound and the rooms are clean and simple. The helpful manager lives in front with his family and speaks some English. Reservations recommended. Singles US$10, with bath US$15; doubles US$15/25. Cash only. ❶

Pensión Alajuela (☎441 6251; pension@racsa.co.cr; www.pensionalajuela.com), is 4 blocks north of the *parque,* across the street from the judicial court and the hospital. The bamboo bar is frequented by flocks of US tourists. The rooms are decorated with flashy tropical murals. TV and towels available. Internet ₡500 for 30min. Checkout noon. Reservations recommended. Singles US$18, with bath US$28; doubles US$25/32; triples US$30. Credit cards accepted with 10% surcharge. ❷

Hotel Alajuela, Calle 2, Av. Central/2 (☎441 6595; fax 441 7912), south of the southwest corner of the *parque central.* A central location with the perks and without the noise—but you pay for it. Rooms with private bathroom, a phone, and a fan. Cable TV in the common area. Check-out noon. Singles US$24; doubles US$34. ❸

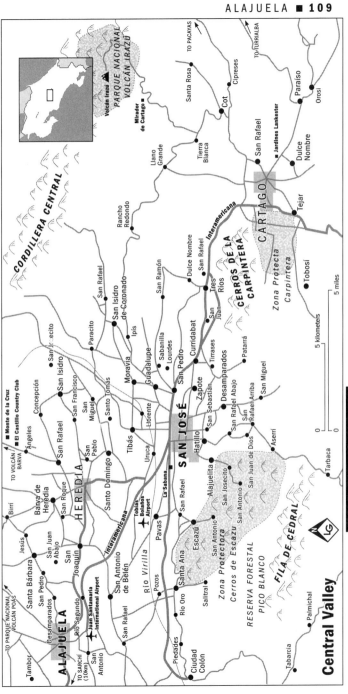

Central Valley

Alajuela

🏠 ACCOMMODATIONS
El Cortez Azul, **3**
La Guaria Inn, **13**
Hotel Alajuela, **11**
Hotel El Mango Verde, **6**
Hotel Pacandé, **4**
Pensión Alajuela, **1**
Villa Real Hostel, **5**

🍴 FOOD
La Mansarada Bar
& Rest., **12**
Soda Alberto, **8**
Soda Don Hernán, **9**
Soda El Fogón del Pollo, **7**
La Tacareña Bar & Rest., **2**

🍸 NIGHTLIFE
Cugini Bar & Rest., **10**
Monkey Shots, **15**
Spectros, **14**

La Guaria Inn, Av. 2, Calles Central/1 (☎440 2948; fax 441 9573; laguariahotel@netscape.net). This self-titled bed and breakfast, named after the national flower, is more delicate and feminine with private bathrooms, fans, and hot water, as well as breakfast included. If privacy and comfort are what you're looking for, it's worth the extra money. Singles US$30; doubles US$35. ❹

El Cortez Azul, Av. 5, Calles 2/4 (☎443 6145; cortezazul@latinmail.com). Upon entering the common area, a dramatic wooden sculpture carved by the manager himself immediately reveals the artistic talent of your friendly host, who lives upstairs. Kitchen available. Services include mountain bike rental (US$20) and guided tours around Volcán Poás and the area around Alajuela. Singles with shared bathroom US$10; rooms of varying sizes with private bathroom US$12-15. ❷

Hotel Pacandé, Av. 5, Calles 2/4 (☎443 8481; www.hotelpacande.com). Spacious rooms with wood-tiled floors and big closets. Owners are eager to bargain on the prices. Singles US$20; doubles US$25-30; triples US$30, with bath US$35. ❸

🍴 FOOD

La Mansarada Bar and Restaurant, 25m south of the southeast corner of the park, on the second floor, has a casual, airy ambience ideal for leisurely dinner, and the food is worth the wait. Fresh fish beautifully presented, with zingy shrimp ceviche (₡1700) and a steamy *sopa de mariscos* (seafood soup, ¢1200). It's worth buying wine for. Open daily 11am-11pm, usually an hr. later on F and Sa. ❷

La Tacareña Bar and Restaurant, Av. 7, Calle 2 (☎442 1662). A low-lit place of refuge from the rain or a stressful day, the atmosphere here is warm, the service quick, and the portions hearty. Burgers and sandwiches average ¢700. Entrees range from ¢950 to ¢2500. Open daily 10:30am-11pm. V. ❶

Soda El Fogón del Pollo, Calle 4, Av. 1/3 (☎443 1362; luvihe@yahoo.com). Owned by an Argentinian who knows his chicken. Delicious *casados* with *pollo asado* (¢850); french fries (¢350); and pork ribs (¢1200). Open M-F 7am-8pm. ❶

Soda Don Hernán, on the northeast corner of the *parque*. A local soda-meets-burger joint that pleases everyone's tastes. Sandwiches at ¢600. Fries, drinks, and ice cream to top off the meal. Open daily 8am-10pm. Major credit cards accepted. ❶

Soda Alberto, Calle 4, Av. 1/3. Neighborly service guaranteed with your *plato del día* (¢800 with *refresco*). Open daily for breakfast and late lunch from 7am-4:30pm. ❶

▣ NIGHTLIFE

Alajuela doesn't have a hopping nightlife. Not too many people go out, but those who do scatter themselves through the town's restaurants for beers and TV. Cugini Bar recently replaced popular Taberna Peppers and promises to be as lively.

Cugini Bar and Restaurant, (☎440 6893) 2 blocks east of the southeast corner of the *parque central*, is a new place owned by a "half-Irish, half-Italian, half-tico, half-gringo" American. Brilliantly decorated with a bit of everything (NASCAR, baseball, classic mob movie posters, and even miniature classic American cars). Classic is indeed the key word: the restaurant upstairs will serve a blend of southern Italian and American cuisine. The bar offers creatively named cocktails (like "The Godfather") priced ¢700-2500. Open M-Sa noon-midnight; happy hours Tu-F after 4:30pm.

Spectros, about 550m south of the park's southwest corner, is a dark, gigantic disco with karaoke on Su, M, and W nights, live music Th nights, and "ladies night" from 8pm-10pm on F, when only women are allowed in for half-price and free drinks (plus exotic male dancers). Open daily 8pm-4am, except Tu.

Monkey Shots, south of Spectros, is a half-outdoor, half-indoor bar. If you don't like strippers, don't come W nights (when men dance) or Sa nights (when ladies do). Occasional live music costs money, but there is no cover charge. Open daily 6pm-6am.

▣ DAYTRIPS FROM ALAJUELA

VOLCÁN POÁS

To get to Poás, take one of the buses that depart daily from San José's TUASA station, Av. 2, Calles 12/14 (2hr., 8:30am, ¢600). They stop at the TUASA station in Alajuela at 9:15am and arrive at Volcán Poás at approximately 10:30am. The return bus leaves the park at 2:30pm. Bring something to do, as you may finish sightseeing before the bus is ready to leave. Park open Dec.-Apr. daily 8am-4:30pm, May-Nov. 8am-3:30pm. US$7.

Fifty-five kilometers northwest of San José, **Parque Nacional Volcán Poás** is a cloud forest easily accessible by trails full of moss, palms, orchids, and a dangling ceiling of bromeliads. A national park since 1971, Poás receives the most visitors of any park in the country, largely due to its proximity to San José and Alajuela. The area's highlight is the steam-belching crater of active Volcán Poás (2574m). Inside the crater (1320m across and 300m deep), there is a turquoise acid pool and *fumaroles* (vents in the earth's crust) that audibly release bursts

CENTRAL VALLEY

THE LOCAL STORY

NINE DAYS OF MOURNING

When there is a death in small, rural Aserri, everybody goes to the wake, dressed in solid black, pale and wearing no makeup, especially the women. They whisper, fearful of waking up the corpse, lying in his gray, velvet casket, parked in the middle of the big living room, amongst white candles and natural and artificial flower bouquets with written messages of "deepest condolences" and "sharing your pain and loss." "He was such a good boy, so young and handsome, an excellent son, with such a great future... and a lot of 'dough."

They pray the rosary several times and drink lots of coffee to stay awake. The next day, they walk in procession to the cemetery—through streets and avenues and obstructing traffic—where they bury him.

And then the *novenario*, nine evenings of rosaries and singing and foods. The last day, the eating and drinking becomes a party. Tortillas topped with potato, picadillo (seasoned, cooked vegetables), and chayote, corn *empanadas* (turnovers), *tamales*, fried yucca, rice with chicken, *chicharrones* (deep fried pork rind) with tortillas, and sweet homemade bread. And to drink? There is lots of coffee, black or with milk, *aguadulce* (water-based sugar cane drink), *horchata* (rice water and cinnamon drink), and lemonade. An entire banquet for the neighbors and mourners.

That is why there are always people who never even knew the person that died at the wakes and *novenarios*.

of volcanic steam. The cone itself looks like a rainbow carved into the terrain, with vibrantly colored layers of gray, white, and red earth that trace the history of the volcano's eruption.

A **Visitors Center** has a small museum to educate guests about preservation and appreciation of the surrounding environment. There is also a souvenir shop and a *café* with good coffee and a smattering of lunch items and pricey pastries. The most direct route to the crater is a 10min. walk up a gentle, paved path from the Visitors Center. Laguna Botos, a 15min. walk beyond the crater, is the collapsed cone of another volcano, now filled with rain water but too acidic to sustain life.

Poás is most enjoyable in the morning, especially from May to Nov., when noon-time clouds and rain obscure the view. Try to avoid visiting on Sundays, when the park is usually packed.

FINCA DE LAS MARIPOSAS (BUTTERFLY FARM)

Call ahead at ☎438 0400 and the farm will provide transportation from San José or Alajuela; or take the blue and white "Guácima" bus from the corner of Av. 2 and Calle 8 in Alajuela (45min.; about every 1½hr., 8:30am-4:30pm; ¢85). Return about every 30min. 11:15-11:45am and 1:15-5:15pm. Open daily 9am-5pm. Tours begin at 9, 11am, 1, 3pm, and last about 2hr. US$15 includes English-speaking tour, US$9 with ISIC, US$7 for children ages 4-12; tours with transportation from San José US$25 per person. Call ahead to find out reduced rates for groups larger than 10.

Southwest of Alajuela in La Guácima lies the renowned Finca de las Mariposas, a pleasant, rural garden that is home to countless fluttering butterflies, exotic and ordinary. The four acre farm is Latin America's oldest exporter of the delicate creatures, selling more than 70 different species all over the world. Genuine butterfly lovers will show you flowers and butterflies you won't see anywhere else. Come early during the rainy season; butterflies hide during afternoon showers.

ZOO-AVE

☎433 8989. In Alajuela, buses leave from the lot south of Calle 8, Av. Central/2. A visit takes about 45 minutes. Open daily 9am-5pm. ¢2900, children 2-10 ¢500.

The biggest bird reproduction center in Central America, Zoo-Ave breeds and rehabilitates birds, reptiles, and mammals before reintroducing them to nature. Visitors can see 100 species of birds, including quetzales, falcons, and owls, plus some playful monkeys and crocodiles.

ATENAS

It's hard to find tourists in the quiet village of Atenas, 25km down the road west of Alajuela, and the villagers like it that way. Atenas is a good "time out" stop on a busy itinerary—Volcán Poás and Manuel Antonio are one and three hours away, respectively, and both the Butterfly Farm and Zoo-Ave are en route to the village from Alajuela. Luxurious hotels some kilometers out of town offer exhilarating views of the valley, and signs on buses brag of the best climate in the world. For reference, the church is on the *parque's* south side

If you're looking for a place to stay, **Ana's Place B&B ❷**, 200m east of the Acueductos y Alcatarillados (AyA) water company behind the church, offers the only lodgings available in the town itself, at the bottom of a hill. Rooms with big beds, quiet fans, and lots of closet space look onto a yard with chirping birds. (☎446 5019; anaplace@sol.racsa.co.cr. ¢4000 per person, ¢4500 with breakfast.) Other accommodations are all in **Santa Eulalia,** north of town (take a bus or taxi). **El Cafetal Inn ❹** treats guests to early-morning breakfasts on a hillside patio, below which are trails leading to a river and a four-leaf-clover-shaped pool. The tastefully decorated rooms offer iridescent blue and magenta bedspreads, comfy chairs, and huge windows looking onto coffee plantations or the vast valley. Breakfast is included. (☎446 5785; www.cafetal.com. Dinner with wine and dessert US$25. Nature tours available; horseback riding US$15. Singles US$70; doubles US$85; tower room with curved wall of windows US$99; additional bed US$15.) With an even more dramatic view, **Hotel B&B Vista Atenas ❸** offers bright white rooms and a Franco-Belgian restaurant. There's also a cliff-side pool and two cabins with kitchens. (☎446 4272; vistaatenas@hotmail.com. Singles US$35; doubles US$40. Cabins for two people US$45. No credit cards.) German-owned **Apartamentos Atenas ❸** offers no view, but slightly lower prices. The roomy cabins, all with kitchens, cluster in forest landscaping. (☎446 5792; apatenas@sol.racsa.co.cr. Breakfast US$5. Singles US$30; doubles US$35; quad with two rooms US$60.) Eight rooms with tinted sliding glass doors and kitchenettes make up **Hotel Colinas del Sol ❷**, which also has a big pool and arranges airport transportation for US$14. (☎446 4244; fax 446 7582; info-hcs@hotelcolinasdelsol.com. Breakfast US$6, request day before. Doubles US$32; up to two extra cot beds, US$5 each.)

If you are hungry, head for **Soda Tío Mano ❶**, just west of the *parque's* southwest corner, a typical *soda* with a wide variety of desserts. (Burgers ¢450;

But it all serves some purpose—although they never knew that person in life, the dead now brings them good memories of food and drink, and sometimes even aguardiente (a potent unrefined liquor) and a party to them.

These customs of praying to the dead for nine days straight, with big reunions and banquets, take place throughout Costa Rica, in the capital and all of its provinces. There are even rural places where they still kill a cow or a pig to feed the many relatives, friends, and guests of the dead, and even those who, uninvited, are the first to arrive and pray and the last to leave, just to go home with a full stomach and a contented heart.

—María Isabel Gamboa is a primary school teacher in San José. María Isabel studied English at Northwest Missouri College and recieved a Masters in preschool education from the University of Costa Rica.

peach-and-strawberry cheesecake ¢275. Open daily 7am-9pm.) They also serve good food at the **Internet** cafe **K-puchino's Coffee Shop ❶**. (☎446 4184. Internet ¢300 per 30min., ¢500 per hr. Salad ¢800. Open Tu-Su 7am-11pm.) Chinese food is as much the rage in Atenas as elsewhere in Costa Rica, and **Restaurante Don Tadeo ❶**, next to the Internet cafe, whets that Asian appetite. (☎446 5158. 2-person wonton, chicken, vegetables, mixed rice meal ¢8500; *casados* ¢1100. Open daily 11am-11pm, later on weekends.)

SARCHÍ

Those who charge Costa Rica with the decay of its national culture will be stymied by this town. Meaning "wide open jungle space" in the indigenous language of Huetar, Sarchí was inhabited by Indians until 1640, and is one of the oldest settlements in the Western Valley. The nation's biggest crafts center, Sarchí, a small village 30km from San José, a 25min. drive from the International Airport, keeps an old tradition alive in the form of brilliantly decorated *carretas* (wooden oxcarts). Once purely functional as coffee transporters, the famous *carretas* began to be painted in the early 1900s to bring families to *fiestas* in style, and became a status symbol. In addition to their traditionally red-orange patterns, the carts are valued for the "music" they make as they rattle along the path. Legend has it that families were able to recognize each other by each cart's distinctive sound. Though miniature knock-off carts appear throughout Central America, and are often cheaper, the originals are worth the visit. You can also visit the more than 200 workshops where they are made, and talk with the artisans. (Typical carts ¢51,000-91,000; minicarts ¢1050. Shipping to the US US$48-82.)

In 1930, the first *fotingo* car arrived, and not long after, in 1935, the national road system cut through the region. As a result, the *carretas* lost their value as a means of transport, and began to fade in importance. However, the advent of tourism saved the economy and the tradition; in 1977, the first high school of the region began imparting knowledge of the craft in a plan called *Plan de Estudios para la Modalidad Artesanal del Colegio Francisco J. Orlich*, and ox-cart "souvenirs" began to be produced in great quantities. In 1988, former President Don Oscar Arias declared the *carreta* a national worker's symbol. People such as Don Chaverri and Don Alfaro were pioneers in the crafts field, and proudly display their factories today.

On top of being the cradle of Costa Rican crafts, Sarchí is situated in the fertile and rich *cantón* of Valverde Vega, in between Volcán Poas and Volcán Barva. Nearby natural wonders include Bajos del Toro Amarillo, 40min. away, with waterfalls, trout fishing, and Parque Nacional Juan Castro Blanco. Though it is easy to slip into the tourist shuttle bus mentality of buying national crafts in large tour groups, Sarchí is more than a half-day destination spot. It is an opportunity to dance with the locals, visit waterfalls, and get to know local artisans.

▐ TRANSPORTATION

Buses to **Los Ángeles** (6 per day 5am-6:30pm) pass by **La Luisa** and **San Pedro,** as do buses to **Trojas** (5:40, 10:45am, 1:30, 3:45pm) and **San Juan** (9 per day 6am-5:40pm). To **Naranjo** (5km), **Grecia,** and **Alajuela,** buses pass by every 25min. (6am-11pm). Buses go to the capital, **San José** (1½hr. direct, 5, 5:30, 6am; return 12:25, 5:15, 5:55pm). Indirect buses from San José to **Sarchí** leave from Av. 5 and Calle 18 (7 per day 5:30am-6pm, ¢350). Buses run less frequently on the weekends. Buses leave in front of the tourist office in Sarchí Sur for **Bajos del Toro Amarillo** (3:15, return the next day at 5:30am). **Taxis** (☎454 4028) can be found around the *parque* (6am-midnight).

◪ 🔢 ORIENTATION AND PRACTICAL INFORMATION

Sarchí is divided into **Sarchí Norte** and **Sarchí Sur**. Sarchí Norte has mainly furniture stores, while Sarchí Sur has more handicrafts and ox-cart vendors. About 1km separates the two; public buses pass by often, or you can walk between the two.

Tourist Information: Information can be found at newly opened **Costa Tica Tours** (☎454 4146, fax 454 3870; costaticatour@hotmail.com), across from the Joaquín Chaverri factory and the *Plaza de Artensanía* in the little blue and white booth. The **Revista Sarchí Guide** has good maps, history, and up-to-date info about the town.

Banks: Banco Nacional (☎454 4126) is in front of the soccer field on the main road, Sarchí Norte. (Open M-F 8:30am-6pm.) **Banco de Costa Rica** (☎454 1100), 50m southeast of Sarchí Norte on the main road. (Open M-F 8:30-3pm.)

Markets: Supermercado El Pequeño Super (☎454 4136), 50m northeast of the *parque central* in Sarchí Norte on the main road. (Open daily 7am-9pm.) **Supermercado El Parque** (☎454 4120), in front of the west side of the *parque central* in Sarchí Norte. (Open daily 7am-8pm.)

Police: Fuerza Pública (☎454 4021), at the end of La Eva part of town. Open 24hr.

Red Cross: (☎454 4149, emergency 911), 50m north of the Banco Nacional Sarchí Norte. Open 24hr.

Pharmacy: Farmacia Valverde Vega (☎454 4842 or 454 1418), next to the west corner of the *parque central* in Sarchi Norte. Open daily 8am-8pm. **EBAIS Health Center** (☎454 4054 or 454 4910), 25m west of the gas station on the main road in Sarchí Norte. Open M-F 6am-4pm. The closest **hospital** is in Grecia (see Grecia, p. 117).

Internet: Ask Giovanni at **Costa Tica Tours** about using his Internet.

Post Office: (☎454 4533, fax 454 4300), 125m west of *parque central* in Sarchí Norte. Open M-F 8:30am-5:30pm.

🏠 ACCOMMODATIONS

Cabinas Mandy (☎454 2397), 400m north of the fire station in Sarchí Norte. Owned by friendly Gerardo Campos. There are 5 rooms with TV, private hot-water baths, and parking. Rooms ₵3500-₵5000. ❶

Cabinas Fantasía (☎454 2007), on Calle Trojas, 1km north of the San Pedro church, has 7 rooms with TV and private hot-water baths. 3 rooms have kitchen facilities. ₵5000-₵6000 per cabin. ❷

Cabinas Paraíso Río Verde (☎454 3003), 100m east and 100m south of the catholic church in San Pedro, about 3km from Sarchí Sur. Rooms, cabins, a pool, and panoramic views. Rooms US$25, US$35, US$45. ❷

Hotel Villa Sarchí (☎454 3029), on Calle Rodríguez in San Juan de Sarchí. Rooms have cable, private hot-water baths, and a pool. Rooms US$25-US$45. ❸

🍴 FOOD

Las Carretas (☎454 1636), next to the Joaquin Chaverri factory in Sarchí Sur, is the most famous restaurant in the area, and serves up great *típica* for ₵2200-₵3000. Open daily 11am-5pm. ❸

Super Mariscos (☎454 4330), 200m northeast of the *parque central* in Sarchí Norte, serves up good seafood, meat, and cheeses. ₵1500-₵5000. ❷

Restaurante Típico La Finca (☎454 1602), behind the *cooperativa de artesanos* in Sarchí Norte, offers great views and *típico* food. Open daily 10am-5pm. ❶

Restaurante El Río (☎454 4980), next to the bridge of Río Trojas in Sarchí Norte, has comforting pastas, and sells crafts in its *centro turístico*. Open daily 10am-6pm. ❶

Cafetería y Panificadora Super Pan (☎454 4121), on the southeast side of the *parque* in Sarchí Norte. Delicious homemade breads and cakes. ❶

Bar y Restaurante El Kiosko (☎454 3130), in front of the beneficio Trojas in Sarchí Norte, serves up delicious food and fun karaoke. Open Th-Su 11am-midnight. ❶

Restaurante Helechos (☎454 4560), to the left of the entrance inside the Plaza de Artesanía in Sarchí Sur, has tasty tacos and other Mexican eats (chicken taco ¢1300; hamburger ¢800; milkshake ¢600), as well as very good coffee. Open daily 10am-7pm. Credit cards accepted. ❶

👁 🛈 SIGHTS AND SHOPPING

PLAZA DE ARTESANÍA. A shopping center packed with arts and crafts of different types, including leatherwork, jewelry, woodwork, textiles, ceramics, paintings, and furniture. This area caters to tourists; though it is quite commercial, it's worth a gander. Inside the plaza, Grettel and Henry's **Fábrica El Rancho Sarchiseño** makes and sells *carretas*. (☎454 3430, fax 454 2396. Small ox-cart US$181, largest US$1000; shipping US$60-70. *Let's Go* readers get a 20% discount with cash.)

MUEBLERÍA QUISAMO. This workshop specializes in Genisaro, Cedo, and Guanacaste work, and is very open to answering questions from visitors. The biggest furniture exhibition in Sarchí is at **Mueblería San Judas,** which exports its products. (Quisamo ☎454 4062. 800m south of Trojas bridge in Sarchí Norte coming from Naranjo. San Judas ☎454 4208; 300m south of Trojas bridge.)

FABRICA DE CARRESTAS JOAQUÍN CHAVERRI. Dating to 1903, this is one of the biggest factories and showrooms in the country. Watch specially selected artists paint the days away in an open-air workshop while woodcutters deftly wield the massive parts. Enjoy music, coffee, fruits, and juices, and ask master craftsman Carlos Chaverri (the son of Joaquin) to autograph his work. (☎454 4411, fax 454 4944; artchaverri@costaricaexporta.com; www.sarchicostarica.com. Also sells in the Plaza de Artesanía, Local 17, 21, and 25. Open daily 8am-6pm.

JOYERÍA MONSE'S. One of the only jewelry stores in the region that makes pre-columbian replicas with fine stones. (In the Plaza de Artesanía, Local 12. ☎/fax 454 4722; joarca@racsa.co.cr.; www.joyeriamonses.com.)

🎵 ENTERTAINMENT

Disco Scratch (☎454 4580), upstairs from Restaurante Helechos (see **Food,** above), is a great place to see the interesting local dance scene. Cover ¢500. Happy Hour before 10pm. Open F-Su 8pm-late.

Bar La Troja del Abuelo, has pool tables and a TV. Have a beer (¢450) and watch sports. The attached restaurant has expensive, sophisticated dishes. Tomato cow tongue ¢2100; T-bone steak ¢3100. Open daily 6pm-2am. Upstairs bar opens at 4:30pm.

Bella Vista Sarchi Discoteque y Restaurante, 2km north of the stadium in La Luisa in Sarchí Norte. Fast and international food, pools and waterslides, and dancing at night.

GRECIA

Forty-five kilometers northwest of San José and 9km southeast of Sarchí is the historical and cultural center of the *cantón* of Grecia. Numerous locals and tourists come to admire the national heritage, a unique, metallic red iron church, which was transported by boat from Belgium to Puerto Limón 106 years ago, and then to Grecia by oxen. It sat 10 years in the plaza before being reconstructed in French neogothic style to its present elegance. Grecia's international claim to fame has been its election as the cleanest city in Latin America in 1989. Recycling bins still abound today. The cultural town and nearby serpentarium, butterfly gardens, and Volcán Poás (35 min. away) make Grecia a great site to visit for a few days.

▐▀ TRANSPORTATION

From **San José,** catch the **bus** between Calle 18 and Av. 5. (30min., M-F, 5am-10pm, 250¢.) From **Naranjo** catch the bus on Edificio San Judas street, across from the Paraíso Infantil store (1hr.; M-F, 6 per day every 25min. 4:55am-10pm, Sa-Su less frequent; ¢170). The bus terminal in town is anout 400m west of the main plaza past the **mercado.** Buses depart to northern regions from the street perpendicular east of the station, where **taxis** pass by frequently as well. Most hotels here can arrange transportation if you call in advance.

◪ ▒ ORIENTATION AND PRACTICAL INFORMATION

The bus station you arrive at is about 400km west of the church, which faces west. The *casa de la cultura* and the, even more visible, the *municipalidad* is north.

Tourist information: MINAE of the Cordillera Volcánica Central and sub-region of Grecia, (☎ 494 0065, 494 5240; fax 494 5580), next to the Red Cross. **Hotel Aero Mundo** (see **Accommodations,** below) has a tourist office/travel agency offering hotel reservations around Costa Rica, flight bookings, and information on Grecia.

Tours: Posada Mimos Hotel (see **Accommodations,** below) also gives tours in and around the cantón. German Marcel and Lucrecia of **El Mundo de los Serpientes** (the World of Snakes), 1km towards Alajuela on carretera vieja in front of *aserradero* El Poró, are waiting for those avid snake and reptile-lovers to come discover the 40 species they have in a rural setting. (☎/fax 494 3700. ¢1300; children ¢500. Open M-Su 8am-4pm.) Another animal haven is Luis Davila's **Mariposario Spirogyra,** 150m south of the church on the dead end of Calle Blancos, which also exhibits art galleries and is part of a conservation project at the basin of Torres river. Open M-Su 8am-5pm; ¢850-2000. **Brothers Oscar and Carlos Alberto Maroto** (☎ 494 3296), 25km north of Mutual Alajuela) are great sources for those interested in the detailed history of Grecia. Spanish only. You might be able to visit the **liquor factory** FANAL if you ask around.

Municipalidad (☎ 494 4111), on the north side of the *parque.*

Banks: Banco de Costa Rica, on the south side of the church and **Banco Nacional,** on the west corner of the *parque* (☎ 444 6857), and **Banco Popular** (☎ 494 1055; fax 494 3013) all keep normal bank hours and services. **Mutual Alajuela,** 50m south of the southeast side of the *parque,* has a **Western Union** (☎ 494 4874). Open M-F 8am-5pm, Sa 8am-noon.

Pharmacy: Farmacia Grecia (☎ 444 5160), on the west side of *parque.*

Hospital/Medical Services: Hospital (☎ 494 0033), 200m east of northeast side of church. Open 24hr. **Red Cross** (☎ 494 2205), 50m north and 50m west of the northeast side of the church.

CENTRAL VALLEY

Emergency: Police (☎ 494 5379), 500m south of the bus terminal at the corner with the cemetery. **Tránsito** (☎ 494 4111), 800m south of the church and 350m east.

Internet Access: Agencia de Viaje Aero Mundo, 100m south and 175m southeast of church. (See **Accommodations,** below. US$1 per 30min., US$2 per hr. Fax available.)

Post Office: 100m north and 50m east of church.

ACCOMMODATIONS

Hotel Aero Mundo (☎ 494 0094, fax 494 6060; aerotess@recsa.co.cr), 100m east of the Banco de Costa Rica, is the closest accommodation to the center of town. Family-run, 8 rooms available, all with cable TV, carpeting, hot water, and fans. Singles US$25; doubles US$35; triples US$45; quads US$55; taxes not included. For longer stays there are three apartment-style rooms with mini-kitchens and other supplies for 2, 3, and 4 people (2 nights US$60, discounts possible). Reservations preferred. ❸

Healthy Day Country Inn Resort and Spa (☎ 444 5903), 1.5km from the center of town, on the way in from Sarchí Sur to your right. Lose weight or just get back into shape with their various treatments. Considerably fair prices for such a central location and nice rooms. Standard US$43 per person per night. ❹

Posada Mimosa (☎ 494 5868; fax 494 2295; mimosa@mimosa.co.cr; www.mimosa.co.cr), 2km north of **Fanal** in the town of **Rincón de Salas,** on the road from San Ramón to Grecia; follow the yellow signs. In the suburbs of Grecia 15min. from the city center and set on 17 acres of jungle, rivers, sugar cane fields, and coffee planations, this place offers a beautiful retreat in the wild for a couple of days at an altitude of 750m. Breakfast included. Rooms US$50-80; tax not included. ❹

FOOD AND NIGHTLIFE

Delicious **Restaurante Tarire** ❶, 100m north of northeast corner of *parque,* serves meat and seafood for ¢1400-1800. (☎ 244 4389; open M-F 4pm-2am, Sa-Su 11am-midnight.) **Soda y Restaurante Oasis** ❶, on the southwest corner of the *parque,* serves fast-food (¢600) and good *típico* meals. (☎ 494 6303. Meals ¢1300-1800. Credit cards accepted) Picnic at **Tropical,** 400m north of the church. It has two pools, a parking lot, basketball courts, ranchos, *parrillas,* and dancers on Sundays. (¢500 during the week, ¢800 Su, children ¢500. Open daily 8am-5pm.) In El Poró, on the road to Alajuela (1.2km from Grecia), is **Rancho Bello Horizonte** with good music and food (☎ 218 1045 or 398 7151). **Bar Ándale,** 500m west of hospital, and **Bar El Lago,** 1km east of church, are where the locals hang out on weekends.

NARANJO

In 1838, in honor of the city's distinctive and omnipresent orange trees, pioneer Don Judas Tadeo Corrales it *Los Naranjos de Púas.* Part of the *cantón* (small town) of Grecia, Naranjo is home to many natural havens such as the nearby protected El Chayote. El Cerro del Esperitu Santo, at a height of 1353m, affords a panoramic view of the entire Central Valley, the Cordillera Volcánica Central, the Cordillera de Guanacaste, and Volcán Arenal. Naranjo is famous for it's production of sugar cane, beans, maiz, chile, jalapeños, and coffee. Numerous coffee mills and plantations (*cafetales*) surround the city, infusing the land with picturesque sights and appealing odors. Those seeking relaxation can indulge in the plentiful *balnearios* (hot springs), like that of Las Estufas in the poblado of Palmitos. More stomach-plummeting activities include bungee jumping off the world-renowned Colorado bridge. The 22.76km district is mainly rural, but abundant boutiques hint at the proximity of the country's capital.

 TRANSPORTATION. Buses to **Sarchí, Grecia** and **Alajuela** leave from across from the Paraíso Infantil store. (About every 30min. 4:55am-10pm.) Another terminal (☎451 3655) is located on the east side of the *mercado* with frequent buses to **San José** (every 15 min. 4:25am-8am, every 40min., 8am-8:30pm; ¢12,000.) Weekend schedules change slightly. Check in the blue office at the exit of the market on the right for updates. Groups of 50 or more can call Martín (☎451 0235) for a special bus. **Taxis** are available 6am-11pm (☎450 0083).

 ORIENTATION. The **zona protectora El Chayote** is north of Naranjo, between the protected zone of Río Toro and the cantones of Alfaro Ruiz and Valverde Vega, between the Parque Nacional Juan Castro Blanco and the Parque Nacional Volcán Poás. The **Cerro del Espíritu Santo** is southeast of Naranjo, the *mirador* **Piedra Grande** is in the district of San Miguel in the cerro Las Palmas and **Las Estofas** is in Palmito, 6km west on the road toward Palmares. In town, the church faces west toward the *parque* (notice the sculpture on the northeast corner). This town operates on the standard Costa Rican **grid system,** with Calle Central in between the *parque* and the church, and Avenida 0 in between the church and the market.

 PRACTICAL INFORMATION. Supermarket Bolanos (☎451 4071) is 10m east of the *casa comunal.* **Palí** is 50m north and 25km east of the gas station (☎451 1920; open daily 7am-8pm). The public **library** is next to the *casa de la cultura* (open M-F noon-6:30pm, Sa 9am-1:30pm). **Banco Nacional** is south of the bus stop on the corner of Edificio San Judas street. A Mutual Alajuela **ATM** machine and **Western Union** are located 10m west of the Banco de Costa Rica. **BanCrecen,** on the corner of Edificio San Judas Street, also has an **ATM. Police stations** are located both in the market and in front of the football stadium (☎450 0051). The **Red Cross** is at the entrance of town (☎450 0297 or 911). There are three **pharmacies: Colonial,** west of Banco de Costa Rica (☎450 0074; open M-Sa 8am-noon and 1:30-9:30pm); **Elizabeth,** on the side of the basilica church (☎451 5317; open M-Sa 7am-8pm, Su 8am-2pm.); and **Naranjo,** in front of the west side of the municipal market (☎450 0108; fax 450 0483; open M-Sa 8am-7:30pm). **Internet** at **Café Webcam,** diagonal to the Banco de Costa Rica on the second floor. (☎451 6061. ¢150C per 5min.; ¢250 per 30min.; ¢400 per hr. Burner, scanner, printer ¢100 per black and white page, ¢150 per color page. *Refrescos* and *bocas* are served.) The **post office** is 100m east and 50m north of the *municipalidad.* (☎/fax 450 0644. Open M-F 7:30am-6pm.)

 ACCOMMODATIONS. There are no official, recommended hostels in town, but many Naranjeños are very open to let you stay in their houses if you call in advance. The engineer **Eliomar Solis ❶,** 300m north of the Judas Tadeo Corrales school in Candelaria, rents out one 2-person room with private bath. (☎451 5631. Room ¢2000, breakfast ¢500 extra.) **Cabañas San Miguel ❶,** has six rooms out of town (☎451 1302) and Arturo Sibaja's fancy **Cabañas Vista del Valle Plantation Inn Rosario Naranjo ❺,** on the road toward San Ramón, past the Puente Grande de Rafael Iglesias, 1km toward Naranjo and a right turn at the entrance of the bungee jumping site, has 14 rooms available. (☎/fax 451 5631; www.vistade.valle.com; mibrejo@racsa.co.cr. Breakfast included. Budget rooms for 2 US$115.)

 FOOD AND ENTERTAINMENT. Food of the mountains typically abounds with *picadillo de chayote, papa, arracache* (cooked vegetables), *pan dulce* (sweet bread), *sopa de mondongo* (tripe soup), *arroz con leche* (rice pudding), and *cajetas de leche y coco* (sweet milk and coconut nugat). The market in town is actually quite clean, safe, and pleasant to eat in. Other choices are: **Soda y Restaurante La Chiminea ❶,** 25m south of church. (☎451 3821. *Casados* ¢900;

cantonese and chicken rice ¢1125; specialty pizzas ¢2350. Open daily 10am-11pm.) **Soda y Restaurante Don Taco ❶**, 100m south of the church and 50m east, serves fast food (¢500-700), *chuletas* (¢1500), and shakes (¢350). (☎450 0825. Open daily 11am-3am.) Have some ice cream at the **Heladería La Cascada ❶**, on the north side of the *parque;* open M-F 9am-7pm, Sa-Su 9am-9pm. If you like karaoke, **Paraíso 2000,** on the northwest side of the *parque*, opens its doors daily from 4pm-midnight for you to sing the night away (☎451 5222).

◙ SIGHTS. This region is home to the coffee producers and exporters **Coopronaranjo, R.L.** (☎450 0138; coffee@coopronaranjo.com), which you can visit between December and March to see and help the *cogedores de café* (coffee pickers) collect the ripe fruit. If you have a group of six people or less, you can go **ballooning** over the coffee and sugar cane mountains of Naranjo with a very reliable tour group called **Serendipity.** Call in advance to find out where to be picked up. (☎558 1000, fax 558 1010; http://www.serendipityadventures.com/ballooning.htm;costarica@serendipityadventures.com.) Become an adrenaline addict by jumping off the 81m, 120 yr. old Colorado bridge with **Tropical Bungee** (☎/fax 248 2212), on one side of the bridge or **Costa Rica Bungee** (☎494 5102 for Spanish; ☎393 3249 for English) on the other. Guides are experienced and jumps are usually around US$20.

SAN RAMÓN

San Ramón, 13km west of Sarchí, retains some of the humanistic spirit that made it "the city of presidents and poets." On Sundays families relax in the park after worshiping at the elegant cruciform church, rebuilt after the earthquake of 1924. Placards marking the birthplaces of great political and literary figures—among them five former presidents including José Figueres Ferrer and *costumbrista* poets like Lisímaco Chavarría Palma (1878-1913) and Féliz Ángel Salas Cabezas (1908-1948)—are scattered throughout the modern town. The part the town played in the fight for democracy, education, culture, and the rights of the poor in Costa Rica is memorialized in its museum. Elderly people here have a quiet pride for their humble yet revolutionary history, while the town's youth, more oblivious to its history, simply refer to it as a close-knit city with a safe, slow pace of life.

◤ TRANSPORTATION

Buses arrive at the **station** northwest of the *parque* (the church is on the *parque's* eastern side). From the **terminal** 100m north and 175m west of the northwest corner of the *parque*, buses depart for **Puntarenas** (1½hr., M-F 12 per day 5:15am-11:45pm; Sa-Su and holidays 11 per day 5:15am-11:30pm; ¢385) and **San José** via **Alajuela** (1¼hr.; M-F 13 per day 4:30am-10:15pm; Sa-Su and holidays 11 per day; ¢475). Regional buses leave from the station that runs through the block northwest of the *parque* to: **Fortuna** (2¾hr.; 5:30, 9am, 12:30, 4pm; ¢650); **Naranjo** (25min., about every 40min. 5am-10:10pm, ¢155); **Palmares** (20min., every 15-30min. 6am-7:10pm, ¢95); **Zarcero** (1hr., 7 per day 5:55am-5:30pm, ¢210). The **taxi** stand is on the west side of the *parque*.

◪ PRACTICAL INFORMATION

Banco Nacional, 100m south of the church, exchanges currency. (Open M-F 8:30am-3:45pm.) The **ATM** across the street at Mutual Alajuela accepts the broadest range of credit and debit card networks. If you're in a money pinch on the weekend, try **Banco Popular,** 75m east of the northeast corner of the church (open M-F 8:30am-5pm, Sa 8:30am-noon). The **mercado** takes up the block north of the park and is busiest on Fridays and Saturdays. (Open M-Sa 6am-6pm, Su 6am-noon.) **Supermercado Peribásicos** is off the northeast corner of the church. (Open M-Sa 7am-10pm, Su 7am-9pm.) Contact the **police** at ☎445 5127 or dial 911 in an emergency. **Hospital Carlos Luis Valverde Vega** is 400m north of the park (☎445 5825). **Milenium C@fe Internet,** 100m east and 25m south of Banco Nacional, has fast and cheap **Internet** access. (¢400 per hr. Open M-Sa 9am-9pm, Su 10-7pm.) The **post office** is 100m south and 100m west of the park. (Open M-F 8am-noon and 1-5:30pm.)

▟ ACCOMMODATIONS

▨**Hotel la Posada** (☎445 7359 or 447 3131), 400m north and 50m west of the east side of the church, is by far the best in town. The Polynesian-meets-Victorian reception area is full of antique *tico* furniture, ancient cooking instruments, and tropical plants. Rooms have wood cabinets, private baths, TV, full mirrors, and fridge. Breakfast is included. Simple, spare singles US$15. Matrimonial suite US$30-40. ❷

Gran Hotel (☎445 6363), 100m south and 250m west of the southwest corner of the park, is more on the budget side with small but interesting rooms, some of which have views of the indoor courtyard with mildly tacky pink leather sofas around a TV and a chandelier hanging from a high ceiling. Singles with shared bath ¢2000; matrimonial bed with private bath ¢3000; doubles and triples with private bath ¢4000. ❶

Nuevo Hotel Jardín ❶ (☎445 5620), 100m west and 50m north of the northwest corner of the park, has basic two-toned rooms and small private baths. Singles ¢3000; doubles ¢6000; triples ¢7500.

Hotel San Ramón (☎447 2042), 300m west and 25m south of the northwest corner of the park, is pricier but more spacious and comfortable. Cable TV with jumbo remotes and private baths. Singles ¢5000; doubles ¢7000. Open 24hr. ❷

▟▟ FOOD AND ENTERTAINMENT

Mino Arias, 25m south of the southwest corner of the *parque,* is where *Ramonenses* point to for dinner. The popular place is tranquil, with mood lighting and an excellent menu. Chavelona steak and chicken cordon bleu ¢2450 tax included. Open M 11am-3pm, Tu 11am-7:30pm, W-Th 11am-8pm, Fri-Sa 11am-10pm, Su 11am-8pm. ❸

La Colina Centro, around the corner, 50m west of the *parque's* southwest corner, has a basic self-serve buffet, but the uniformed waitresses will wait on you. Filling *plato del día* with beef or chicken ¢1100. Open daily 8am-10:30pm. ❶

El Buho perches on the hill north of the *parque,* 100m south of the tall green church. Seafood is the specialty and the bar is a comfortable kick-back spot. *Patacones* ¢500; fish fillet ¢1200. Open daily 11am-midnight. ❶

Pizzería Grace (☎447 1871), 100m south and 125m west of the southwest corner of the *parque,* is a great pizza parlor. The supreme is mighty meaty. Delivery available. 1 slice ¢500, 12-piece pizza ¢3750. Open daily 11am-11pm. ❶

Greco's, across the street, is a bar whose second story is open for dancing Th-Sa and which takes Friday night karaoke seriously. Open daily 6pm-2:30am.

▟ SIGHTS

MUSEO DE SAN RAMÓN. on the north side of the *parque,* traces the town's history since prehistoric times and includes a life-size reproduction of a *campesino* home with homemade *ramonense* mannequins at work (making cigars, harvesting, collecting wood). The tender loving care that went into these displays makes the experience worthwhile, and visitors get a sense of the famous liberal politicians, artists, and educators who hail from here. There is also an interesting section on earthquakes and a rotating exhibition of contemporary art. (☎ 437 9851. Open M-F 1-5pm, W and Sa 8:30-11:30am. Hours disrupted the 2nd week of July. Free.)

LOS ÁNGELES CLOUD FOREST RESERVE. This reserve is only accessible by taxi through ex-president Rodrigo Carazo's Hotel Villablanca (¢3700 one-way from San Ramón), unless you want to walk 10km from the bus stop. The hotel itself consists of 48 meticulously decorated, colorful adobe cabins complete with bathtubs, fire places, refrigerators, and rocking chairs. The expansive property is perpetually veiled in mist and the trails around it (two short 2km and two 6km trails, one is only available with guide) are muddy and beautiful. (☎/fax 661 1600. Singles US$68; doubles US$85; family room US$140. Non-guest forest entrance US$15. Guided walks US$20. Zip-line canopy tour US$38.50 per person. Horseback riding US$12 per hr. Lunch and dinner in the hotel restaurant US$12. Open daily noon-2pm and 7-9pm.)

PALMARES

Driving west on the **Interamericana,** before San Ramón, one finds a turn-off leading south to the town of Palmares. All Costa Ricans know that Palmares is synonymous with *"fiesta"* for 10 days starting on Jan. 14. The town starts planning its annual party, *Las Fiestas de Palmares,* in July the year before, and the payoff is tremendous. The festival is welcoming, well-organized, and fun for everyone, especially the young people. The *tope*—a procession of purebred horses—kicks off the week; fairgrounds north of the town center are then transformed by fireworks, roller-coaster rides, concerts (such as Eddy Herrera and Calle Ocho), and sporting events like mountain-biking races. There is also a bullfighting ring where Palmares hosts its own running of the bulls and bullfights, in which the bulls never die. Try, try, try to make it to Palmares during this week. The palm-filled park and gray stone church (made with whole slabs and a special eggshell cement) are here year-round, but otherwise, there's not much more for visitors to see.

The only hotel in Palmares is **Cabinas Sueca ❷,** 1.5km towards San Ramón on the highway. You should reserve before Dec. 15 if you plan on staying in Palmares during Las Fiestas. Rooms are simple, with a mirror and private bath. (☎/fax 453 3353. ¢4000 per person; ¢3500 in groups of 4 or more.) It might be a better idea to stay in San Ramón (see **Accommodations,** p. 121) and commute to the fairgrounds. While there is plenty of food to go around in the January fairs, there aren't many places to eat in town. **Soda del Río ❷,** 200m north of the park on the highway, has a standard menu and gets crowded during the lunch hour. (*Casados* ¢1850. Open daily 9am-11pm.) Another favorite is **House Pizza ❸,** 500m north of the park's northeast corner. (☎453 5050. Large pizza ¢4600. Open daily 11am-11pm except Tu.)

ZARCERO

Sweet Zarcero (pop. 4500) winds its way through narrow hills, abutting cheese factories. Named after the aromatic *zarzaparilla* fruit found in the region, it was erected as a city in 1918, but was inhabited long before by indigenous people. Zarcero, head city of its *cantón* Alfaro Ruiz, is home to a famous wooden, gothic, and renaissance parish church constructed in 1895, dedicated to the archangel of San Rafael. The *zarcereños* take much pride in their divine symbol, which stands decorated in front of world-renowned topiary creations (bulbous bushes clipped in fantasy shapes like dancing animals and double arches). Tourists come just to see these botanical creations; however, there is much more to discover in the region, said to be the *cuna* (cradle) of organic agriculture. In this picturesque region, under the fog and mist natural to its cloudy forest climate, hide 3 protected ares: Parque Nacional Juan Castro Blanco to the northeast, Zona Protegida Río Toro to the east, and Zona Protegida El Chayote to the southeast. Many natural trails open to the public in nearby towns boast orchids, bromeliads, vibrant wildlife, and incredible vistas from the Central Valley, spinning out from the plains of San Carlos to Guanacaste, to the Gulf of Nicoya. The high-altitude weather—fresh, clean, and cold for Costa Rica—helps preserve Zarcero's charm.

▛ TRANSPORTATION

On winding, steep mountain passes, Zarcero lies on the road connecting the northern plains of Costa Rica to the capital, and as a result has very good transportation running in between **San José** and **Cuidad Quesada.** Catch the **bus** in front of Tienda Elizabeth on the main road to go to **San José** (2 hr., 17 per day 5:30am-8pm, ¢600). Coming from San José, take a bus headed to **Cuidad Quesada;** you will be dropped off at the yellow bus stop "Solidez y Confianza" on the main road, in front of the shoe store. This is also the departure point for buses headed north to **San Carlos** (☎256 8914; 45min., 7, 8:15, 9:15am) via **Upala** (13 per day 10am-9pm, ¢400). Buses leave from in front of the beige building near the taxi stand, on the south side of the *parque* to **San Ramón** (☎445 6251; 20min., 8 per day 5:55am-7pm, ¢300), **Brisa** (6am, 11:55am, 5pm; ¢150) and **Palmira** (7, 11am, 4pm; ¢100). From **San Ramón,** regional buses leave for Zarcero from the station that runs through the block northwest of the *parque*, for **Naranjo** (1hr. 7 per day 5:55am-5:30pm, ¢210). **Taxis** (☎463 2161) line up in front of the pizzeria on the south side of the *parque.* Taxis run to: **Laguna** (¢600); **Bajo del Toro** (¢6000); **La Brisa** (¢1200); **Pueblo Nuevo** (¢1200); **San José de la Montaña** (¢20000); **Naranjo** (¢4000); **Sarchí** (¢5000); **Grecia** (¢6000); and **San Carlos** (¢6000).

▣ ▨ ORIENTATION AND PRACTICAL INFORMATION

Zarcero is a linear town with all its shops on the main street. Facing the church, right is south and left is north. **Tourist information** is at the newly formed **Camara de Turismo of Zarcero (CATUZAR),** in the yellow building 50m north of the high school. (☎463 2120, fax 463 2726; catuzar@costarricense.com.) **Banco de Costa Rica** is 100m north and 10m of the plaza (☎463 3333, fax 463 3232; open M-F 8:30am-3pm); **Coocique** has a **Western Union** across from the Red Cross on the main road (☎463 3815; open M-F 8am-5pm, Sa 8am-noon). **Supermercado Osman González** is in front of the *parque* (☎463 3101; open M-Sa 7am-7pm, Su 8am-noon). The **police** (☎463 3231) and **fire station** (☎463 3281) are 10m north of the northeast corner of the plaza. **Farmacia Zarcero** is on the south side of the *parque.* (☎463 3855. Open M-Sa 7am-8pm, Su 8am-noon. All credit cards accepted). **Red Cross** is next to Coocique (☎463 3131). **Hospital de San Ramón** (☎445 5823). **Internet** access at **Mulitcomputo Costa Rica**, 50m south of the southwest corner of the *parque* (☎463 1595; ¢300 per 30min.; open M-F 8am-noon and 1:30pm-6pm, Sa 9am-noon and 2-5pm). **Post Office** on the *parque.* (☎436 3276. Open M-F 8:30am-noon and 1-5:30pm).

▛ ACCOMMODATIONS

Should you decide to stay the night, options are limited. On one side of the budget spectrum is **Gladys' house** ❶ (lacking an official name), a right turn at the bottom of the hill on the north side of town. (☎463 3484. ¢1500 per person.) **Hotel Don Beto ❸,** on the north side of the church, is owned by well-traveled Flory and son Luis, and has 8 beautifully designed rooms with great views. Reserve in advance in high season.

(☎463 3137. Singles US$20; doubles US$25, with private bath US$30.) They also run vans with lunch included to the nearby **Bajo del Toro** and **Termales del Bosque** nature attractions that are hard to get to on one's own. (US$30 by taxi; US$100 for Don Beto's van independent of number of passengers.) Outside of Zarcero, 3km north of the *parque* (¢600 by taxi), a yellow house is the reception for **Cabinas Pradera ❷**, a potentially good deal for large groups who want temporary isolation in cabins with one matrimonial bed, two individual beds, and a fireplace. (☎463 3558 or 463 3959. ¢7000 per cabin, with kitchen and fridge ¢8000.) 4km from Zarcero in the small town of **Laguna**, there are a few more accommodations. **Cabinas La Pradera ❶**, 100m north and 350m east of the *salón comunal*, has 5 cabins, and runs horseback riding tours to nearby waterfall Palmira. Email for prices. (☎/fax 463 3959; luisblan@racsa.co.cr.)

◨ FOOD

Don't miss these typical Zarcero foods: *queso tierno* (¢750/kg), *natilla* (¢300), *bizcocho casero* (¢250), *cajetas de leche* (small, sugary squares made with boiled milk and sugar, ¢300), and *toronjas rellenas* (stuffed grapefruits) from the factory at La Esperanza. An excellent place to buy and try them is at **Soda Super 2**, on the west side of the *parque*. (☎463 2047. Open daily 8am-6pm.) Next door is Isidro's **Restaurante El Heguirón ❶**, which serves great fast food (☎463 1708; fried chicken ¢500; tacos ¢400; open daily 6:30am-8pm). Head to **Restaurante Soda el Zarchereño ❶**, in front of the San Carlos bus stop on the main road, for the pre-cooked but fresh buffet. Entrees include *yuca, camote, madur, picadillos de arracache, and ayote*. (☎463 1460. Buffet ¢850-¢950. Open daily 7am-9pm.) For delicious bread and sweets, try **Panadería la Marinita**, 150m north of the northwest side of the garden, and **Panadería Berrocal**, on the southwest side of the *parque*. For dessert, sample donuts, *bizcochos*, and *cajetas* from **bakeries** along the main street. There are also *sodas* scattered around; the yellow counter at **Jiffy** is popular. (Super taco with chicken and beef ¢400. Open 10:30am-11pm.)

◉ SIGHTS

For local entertainment, people flock to the large **pool** and **jacuzzi** in **APAMAR**, 860m west of the *parque* on the road to Guadalupe, for relaxation and rehabilitation. (☎463 3674, fax 463 1274. Restaurant sometimes open.) Next door is Bernardita and Gustavo's **Cow's Country** (☎463 1211), where if you call enough in advance, lunch can be prepared for you. Here you can observe the milking process, go trout fishing, horseback riding, and buy locally made products. You can also trout-fish and eat your catch on-site at **Ecoturístico Los Quetzales**. On the road going north toward San Carlos, turn at La Brisa and go 1km until you see the sign for "Ecoturistico La Reina." The site is 1km beyond. There there are 3km of natural trails for birdwatching. (7km from Zarcero in the village of Legua.) Learn about organic cultivation at Rodolfo's **Jugar del Valle**, on the road toward San Carlos, turn at Laguna, 500m from its center. (☎463 2622.) The **Toro Amarillo** waterfall in this area is 120m tall. **Coopebrisas** is one of two cheese factories outside of Zarcero, less than 20min. north. To get there, take a taxi (¢3000 round-trip) and, once there, ask to see the production manager. He will answer all of your questions and show you the process. You can put on protective gear—to protect you and the cheeses from each other—and get a closer look at the mixing vats. (Open M-Sa 7am-5pm.)

HEREDIA

Perched on a hilltop 11km north of San José, the university town of Heredia (pop. 30,000) retains the cosmopolitan air of the capital while leaving the smog and frenzy behind in favor of a more relaxed atmosphere. The city lagged behind Cartago in wealth and stature through the colonial era and, following Mexico's independence from Spain in 1821, Heredia's residents campaigned to have Costa Rica annexed by Mexico—to the rest of the country's overwhelming dissent. In the 1830s, Costa Ricans briefly chose Heredia as their capital, but soon reconsidered and sent the government to San José. A popular suburb for commuters working in the capital, Heredia attracts visitors with its friendly atmosphere, vibrant student scene, and proximity to both the airport and Braulio Carrillo National Park.

TRANSPORTATION

Taxis: Flag one down or call ☎ 260 3307. **Taxis** run throughout town, but some are reluctant to give short rides. The 15min. taxi ride from the airport to Heredia is about ¢2500.

Buses: Most **buses** disembark near the *parque* or the *mercado,* although a few leave from the **Parque Los Ángeles** (currently undergoing construction), two blocks west of the *mercado's* western boundary, and others from across the **Universidad Nacional** on Calle 9.

Heredia

● FOOD
Café-Heladería Azzura, **5**
Fresas, **2**
Restaurante Nuevo Viena, **8**
El Restaurante Sabroso, **12**
Vishnu Vegetarian/
   Mango Verde, **3**

■ ACCOMMODATIONS
Hotel América, **9**
Hotel Colonial, **11**
Hotel Heredia, **1**
Hotel Las Flores, **14**
Hotel Manolo, **13**

■ NIGHTLIFE
Bar Oceano, **7**
Bulevar, **4**
Metamorphosis
   Champs, **10**
Miraflores Disco
   y Tropicales
   Taberna, **6**

TO VOLCÁN
BARVA (3km)

Printed schedules are scarce, but most taxi drivers know when and from where buses leave, so you can ask them. Purchase tickets upon boarding. Carry small change. From the bus stop in front of the Universidad Nacional, Av. Central, Calle 9, buses go to **Alajuela** (20min., about every 15min. 6am-10pm, ¢95). Across from the Supermercado Palí near the south side of the Mercado Mercantil on Av. 8, is the stop for buses to **Armonía, La Aurora, Barva, Cahuites, Cinco Esquinas, Pasito, Santa Paula.** A schedule is posted on the wall outside the supermarket (most buses every 10-30min. 5:15am-11:30pm). From Av. 6 between Calles 6 and 8, buses go to **Mercedes Sur, San Joaquín, Santa Bárbara, Santa Cecilia, Santa María.** From Calle 4, Av. 6/8, across from the west side of the Mercado Municipal, buses go to **Paso Llano** via **San José de la Montaña** (1hr.; M-F 6:25am, noon, 4pm; Sa 6:25, 11:15am, 4pm; Su 6:45, 11am, 4pm; ¢210). Buses leave from the bus stop in front of the Universidad Nacional, Av. Central, Calle 9 to **Puerto Viejo de Sarapiquí** via **Vara Blanca** (3½hr.; 11am, 1:30, 3pm; ¢920). Along Calle Central, between Av. 2 and 4, are the buses to **San José** (30min., every 5min. 4:50am-midnight, ¢105). Night buses (30min.; every hr. M-Th midnight-4am, every 30min. F-Su midnight-4:30am; ¢130).

■■ ? ORIENTATION AND PRACTICAL INFORMATION

Heredia is organized in a simple grid system, with *calles* running north-south and *avenidas* running east-west. However, few streets are labeled, so it's best to start exploring from the **parque central,** Heredia's hub. The *parque* is boxed in by Calle Central to the east, Avenida Central to the north, Calle 2 to the west, and Avenida 2 to the south. From the central arteries, odd-numbered *calles* and *avenidas* extend east and north of the park, while even-numbered *calles* and *avenidas* extend to the west and south. The town's few sights are located near the *parque central,* and the **Universidad Nacional** lies five blocks east of it, just beyond *Calle 9.* Two blocks southwest of the *parque's* southwest corner is the bustling **Mercado Municipal,** bordered by Calles 2 and 4 and Avenidas 6 and 8.

Banks: Most of Heredia's banks change cash and traveler's checks for a 1-2% commission rate. **Banco Nacional,** Av. 2/4, Calle 2. Open M-F noon-6pm. The branch at Av. 6, Calle 6 is open M-F 8:30am-3:45pm. For weekend transactions, head to **Banco Cuscatlán,** Av. 2, Calles 4/6. Open M-F 9am-6pm, Sa 9am-noon. Both of these banks have 24hr. **ATMs.** MC/V.

Market: Many covered butcher shops, fruit and vegetable stands, and small, inexpensive *sodas* are set up at the **Mercado Municipal,** Av. 6/8, Calles 2/4. Open M-Sa 6am-6:30pm, Su 7am-noon.

Supermarket: Enormous **Más X Menos,** Av. 6, Calles 4/6, carries house ware, clothing, a wide variety of foods, and some medicines. Open M-Sa 7am-midnight, Su 7am-9pm. AmEx/MC/V. **MegaSuper** on Av. 4, Calles Central/1, down the *avenida* from Farmacia Fishel, sells a good variety of snacks and beer. Open daily 8am-9pm. AmEx/MC/V.

Laundry: No self-service, but **Martinizing Dry Cleaning,** Av. 1, Calle 2, will clean shirts for ¢950, pants for ¢1000. Open M-F 7:30am-6pm, Sa 8am-12:30pm. AmEx/MC/V.

Emergency: ☎911.

Police: Av. 5/7, Calle Central (☎237 0011), 4 blocks north of the *parque.*

Medical Services: Many clinics and basic pharmacies around town. **Farmacia Fishel,** corner of Av. 4 and Calle Central (☎261 0994). Open M-Sa 8am-8pm; Su 10am-6pm. AmEx/MC/V. **Farmacia Imperial,** Av. 8, Calle 8/10 (☎260 7825). Open M-F 8am-8:30pm, Sa 8am-8pm. AmEx/MC/V.

Hospital: Hospital San Vincente de Paul, Calle 14, Av. 6/10 (☎261 0001), has an adjoining pharmacy for prescriptions.

Telephones: Card and pay phones cluster the northeast and southwest corners of the *parque,* at the northwest corner of Av. 3/Calle 6, and near the Universidad Nacional on Av. Central. Purchase a phone card from **Soda El Testy,** at the *parque's* southwest corner. Open 7am-10pm.

Internet: Plenty around town. A few minutes from the *parque central* is **PlanetWeb,** Av. 1, Calle 6/8, next to the barber. ¢200 per hr. Open daily 9am-10pm. **Cosmos Internet Café,** Av. 2, Calles 5/7. ¢300 per hr., ¢200 per 30min. Open daily 8am-10pm. **Internet Café,** Av. Central, Calles 7/9. ¢350 per hr. Open M-Sa 24hr.

Post Office: Telégrafo Gobernación Correo, Av. Central, Calle 2, across the street from the northwest corner of the *parque.* Mail a postcard to almost anywhere in the world for ¢150. **Fax** available. Open M-F 8am-5:30pm, Sa 7:30am-2pm. **Postal code:** 3000.

ACCOMMODATIONS

Heredia sees relatively few tourists but maintains several good and inexpensive accommodations. Even the ones outside the city center are relatively loud, however; barking dogs and cars blasting loud music will serenade you to sleep or keep you from it. All listed accommodations provide linens, towels, and soap.

Hotel Las Flores, Av. 12, Calles 12/14 (☎261 8147). A gem in budget accommodations. Gleaming white marble floors, pleasant owners, bright rooms, and private, high pressure, hot water showers make the10min. walk from the *parque* worth it. Rooms have large window, comfy bed, and large mirror, and the owners make beds and clean bathrooms every day. Singles US$11; doubles US$18; triples US$24. AmEx/MC/V. ❷

Hotel Colonial, Av. 4, Calle 4/6 (☎237 5258). This central hotel has a tranquil, inviting atmosphere, complete with a cute puppy and a sitting room. Tile floors, hot water in shared baths, and mid-sized rooms with varnished wood paneling make it luxurious for the price. Singles ¢2000; doubles ¢3500. ❶

Hotel Manolo, Av. 12, Calle 2/4 (☎226 3508 or 237 0476). Family-run with bright, colorful interior, Manolo offers 8 somewhat bare but large and well-kept rooms. Singles and doubles with private hot showers and fans ¢6000 per night, with TV and music ¢8000. Student discounts available. AmEx/MC/V. ❸

Hotel América, Calle Central, Av. 2/4 (☎260 9292), near the *parque central.* A gorgeous winding staircase leads to a hallway of small but spotless rooms with large fans and private hot-water showers. Laundry available and a 24hr. restaurant/bar downstairs. Singles US$29; doubles US$41; quads US$111. AmEx/MC/V. ❹

Hotel Heredia, (☎238 0880) just north of Av. 3 on Calle 6. Though staffed by a helpful family, Hotel Heredia is a last resort. Basic singles and doubles, private cold-water baths, and no locks on doors. Singles US$10; doubles US$18. ❷

FOOD

Sodas serving inexpensive burgers, basic rice and meat dishes, and ice cream line every street. Some nicer cafés surround the *parque central,* while a few more expensive sit-down restaurants are near the Universidad Nacional. A handful of American fast food joints (Taco Bell, Burger King, McDonald's, KFC, and Papa John's) are just south of the Universidad near Av. 2, Calle 9.

Vishnu Vegetarian/Mango Verde, Av. Central/1, Calle 7. A vegetarian chain, Vishnu offers a welcome break from greasy *soda* fare. The *plato del día,* with rice, entree, salad, soup, fruit drink, and dessert, is a steal at ¢1150. Healthy veggie burgers (¢550), pita sandwiches (¢800), and pasta dishes (¢1250) are best washed down with a *refresco natural* (¢350). Open M-F 9am-6pm, Sa 9am-5pm. ❶

Fresas, Av. 1, Calle 7. Fresas does wonders for fresh fruit salads (¢260-550), fruit drinks (¢350-800), and fruit desserts (strawberries with ice cream or nutella ¢1700). The large, open dining area is ideal for a comfortable evening meal. Tacos ¢700, spaghetti ¢1500, *casado con huevos* ¢1200-2000. Open daily 8am-midnight. ❷

Café-Heladería Azzura, on Calle 2, Av. Central/2, at the southwest corner of the *parque central*. A cozy outdoor sitting area offers a great view of the *parque* as you eat a club sandwich (¢1200) or devour one of the mouthwatering flavors of Italian-style gelati. (¢400-600). Breakfast available. Open daily 7am-10pm. ❷

El Restaurante Sabroso, Av. 6, Calle 6/8, next to the Banco Nacional. Enter through a red pagoda into one of Heredia's many Chinese restaurants. Enjoy your wontons (¢1400), chicken wings (¢1500), *carne asada* (¢1900), or rice and seafood dishes (¢1500-2200) in the quiet dining area. Open daily 11am-midnight. ❷

Restaurante Nuevo Viena, Av. 2/4, Calle Central. Escape Heredia's bright sun to join the locals at this dark, cool, TV-lit diner. Many meat options. Hamburgers (¢500-1500) and rice dishes (¢800-1300). Adventurous beef tongue (¢1000-2000). Open 24hr. ❷

◔ SIGHTS

Overlooking the east side of the *parque* is the weathered, gray stone **Iglesia de la Inmaculada Concepción.** The church celebrated its 200th birthday in 1997—an amazing feat considering the many earthquakes it has survived. (Open M-W and F 6am-7pm, Th 3-4:30pm, Sa 4 and 7pm, Su 9, 11am, 4, 7pm.) Many *ticos*, especially school children, find refuge in shaded **Jardines de la Inmaculada,** church gardens dedicated to the Virgin Mary, tucked into the northeast corner of the *parque*.

El Fortín de Heredia, north of the *parque* near the post office, is a crumbling 13m high fort constructed in 1876 as a sentinel to guard a prison long since demolished. Now a historic monument, the tower's loopholes, originally designed to maximize defensive rifle range and minimize exposure to enemy bullets, serve as a reminder of the relatively politically unstable past of the now peaceful, army-free Costa Rica. Surrounding the Fortín is a small park with several monuments to past Costa Rican leaders and a stage where concerts are held. The **Palacio Municipal** next door will not let visitors go up because of the fort's shaky staircase, but check out the secretary's office and flip through a binder full of town history and folklore.

To the casual visitor, the **Universidad Nacional,** five blocks from the Fortín on Av. Central, Calle 9, resembles a large garden interrupted by classrooms. Stroll under the roofed pathways that cross the campus to peek in on Costa Rica's college life. Young *tico* couples chat and cuddle near the center of the University at the popular *Casa Estudiantil*, which offers Costa Rican style cafeteria food. (*Casado* ¢400-¢650.) Next door is a bookstore selling mostly Spanish school books and school supplies. (Open M and W-F 8am-5pm, Tu 9:30am-5pm.)

◐ NIGHTLIFE

Though the town itself seems to die down after 7pm, bars bustle with foreigners and *ticos* until 2am. Most students, however, go into San José or Barva for a night on the town or head to the *parque* and other venues for impromptu concerts. Check the postings all over the Universidad for current info. In addition to establishments listed below, both Costa Rican and international students frequent **Bulevar,** an open-air bar *terraza* on Av. Central, Calle 7, and **Metamorphosis Champs,** a disco with frequent concerts at 8pm on Av. 4, Calle 9 (students with ID ¢500). Current hot spots include **Delire** (reggae) and **Av. 51;** ask any student for more specific directions.

Want to polish your moves before hitting the dance floor? **Merecumbé** dance instruction, on Av. 4/6, Calle 9, offers dance lessons in merengue, salsa, and swing. (☎237 0857. US$30 for 8 group classes; US$11 per hour for private classes.)

Bar Oceano, Av. 2/4, Calle 4 (☎260 7809). Taunting the landlocked with surfboards, fishing nets, and watersports videos, cozy Oceano is a popular spot for foreigners and locals alike. During the week the crowd is mostly *ticos* and the music is alternative rock, while the weekends bring in a more varied crowd eager for classic rock and reggae. Beer ¢350. No cover. Open daily 6pm-midnight.

Miraflores Disco y Tropicales Taberna, Av. 2, Calle 2/4 (☎237 1880). On the 2nd floor "Tropical Tavern" try out some Karaoke (Su and M) or listen to live local music (Tu-Th). Head up one more flight to one of the city's oldest and most popular discos. Locals merengue to Costa Rican classics played upon request. Cover ¢500. Beer ¢500. *Taberna* open daily 7pm-3am; disco open F-Su 8pm-3am.

⚑ DAYTRIPS FROM HEREDIA

PARQUE NACIONAL BRAULIO CARRILLO

*You can access Braulio Carrillo National Park from the road just north from Heredia to Sacramento, or from the San José-Puerto Limón highway (Rt. 32). To reach Volcán Barva from Heredia, take a bus headed for Paso Llano via San José de la Montaña, which departs from Calle 4, Av. 6/8, on the west side of the Mercado Municipal (1hr.; M-F 6:25am, 12:15, 4pm; Sa 6:25, 11:15am, 4pm; Su 6:45, 11am, 4pm; ¢210). Try catching the earliest bus—the temperature will be much more bearable for the long hike ahead. If you miss the three daily buses, don't take the buses that run on the hour from that spot; they'll leave you with an additional 7km to trudge up a steep, un-shaded road. Ride the bus as far as the driver will go to Paso Llano (Porrosatí), where you'll be dropped off across from Champo's Bar. Three buses a day return to Heredia from the stop outside Champo's Bar (M-F 7:50am, 1:30, 5:15pm; Sa 7:50am, 12:30, 5:15pm; Su 8am, 1, 5:15pm). To access the **Quebrada Ranger Station** near the Rainforest Aerial Tram (see below) from Heredia, catch a bus to San José, then another to Guápiles (every 30min., 6am-9pm). Ask the driver to let you off near the ranger station. No buses make regular stops at the ranger station or tram, but they pass by every 30min. and you can flag one down.*

About 25km northeast of Heredia lies **Parque Nacional Braulio Carrillo,** 45,900-hectares of land named after Costa Rica's third chief of state. In 1978, when Rt. 32, the road through the forest from San José to Puerto Limón, was constructed, the park was born from conservationists' efforts to save the area's biodiversity.

Despite the improved access to the forest via the highway, this national park remains largely unexplored and untouristed. The park's rugged landscape is dramatically interrupted by sweeping mountains and gorgeous rippling rivers. Combining forces with the 4.5m of rain that the park sees annually, Braulio Carrillo's varied terrain lends itself to hundreds of rushing waterfalls and river canyons. The park comprises two dormant volcanoes, **Volcán Cacho Negro** and **Volcán Barva.** Volcán Barva, one of the few accessible areas of the park, is an excellent, moderately strenuous day-hike destination. Although a good portion of the "trail" to the volcano is a paved road surrounded by farms and the occasional dairy cow, a trek up the dormant volcano offers pure, isolated forests, few crowds (you'll likely be the only one), gorgeous views, and a glimpse at Costa Rican country life. A few shrouded *lagunas* sit near the top of the volcano, but be sure to stay on the marked path because visitors have been known to go missing for days.

Apart from Volcán Barva, the trails near the northeastern corner of the park are the only easily accessible, hikeable areas of the forest, although rangers report that car theft and armed robberies on the trails are not uncommon. It's best to go in a group. *Let's Go* does not recommend hiking these trails alone or after dark.

VOLCÁN BARVA

About 25m back from the bus stop in Paso Llano is a paved road marked with signs to Volcán Barva. This road climbs 4km to the tiny village of Sacramento, where you can refuel at a small bar/restaurant on the left side of the road (look for the Pilsen sign). From Sacramento, it's another 4km uphill to the ranger station and entrance to the park. One kilometer out of town the road turns rough and rocky. The park entrance and ranger station (☎283 5906) awaits at the end of the road (open daily 8am-4pm; admission US$6, students US$1).

The 8km uphill walk to the ranger station, where the main trail to Volcán Barva begins, takes an exhausting 1½-2hrs., but idyllic cow pastures, lush tree canopies, and stunning views of the valley below, combined with the feel of the soothing, crisp air, make the journey up a worthy hike of its own. The main trail is a 2km, 45min. uphill hike along a shaded, well-maintained trail to three lagoons at the volcano's summit, though detours along the way warrant extra time to explore. About 300m down the trail, **Sendero Álvaro,** a 1.8km path, veers off to the right. Another 300m leads to a 900m turnoff for **Mirador La Vara Blanca.** If it's clear (not too likely in the wet season), you can see the Caribbean from this lookout. Back on the main route, the trail slowly transforms from its modest beginnings to a beautiful moss-covered Costa Rican cloud forest. Surrounding the trail are thick layers of *brome-liads*, *robles*, and the huge *gunnera insignis* plants, nicknamed *sombrillas de pobre* (the poor man's umbrella) for their wide, round leaves. These plants (up to 1.5m high) are noticeable by their bright red, heart-like centers.

About 35min. up the trail, bear left (there's a sign) to ascend the remaining 200m to the edge of **Laguna Barva.** Creep through the mess of foliage for the best view of the lagoon. An acidic pool cupped in an extinct volcano, Laguna Barva (70m across, 8½m deep, with an average temperature of 11°C) is too harsh an environment for fish, but its waters suit a variety of aquatic insects. Shrouded with trees extending 100m up to the rim, the lagoon is secluded and magical. A second well-marked trail leads another 2km up to **Laguna Copy** (40m across). This path is especially muddy and difficult in the rainy season. The third lagoon, **Laguna Danta** (500m across), is rather inaccessible by foot. To see the view from the rim of the volcano, fork right at the sign and turn left at the trash can when the trail ends. This is Barva's highest point (2.9km).

The dense, evergreen forest around Volcán Barva is habitat for over 6000 species of plants (roughly half the total in Costa Rica) and 500 species of animals, among which reside jaguars, coyotes, pumas, ocelots, kinkajous, poison arrow frogs, and the bushmaster, Costa Rica's largest venomous snake. Fortunately for visitors, the innocuous white-tailed deer, the resplendent quetzal (the "phoenix of the forest"), and the park's three species of monkeys—the howler, white-faced, and spider monkey—are the most likely sightings on the slopes of Barva.

From start to finish, the hike from Paso Llano to the summit and back takes about 5½hr. at a moderate pace. If you take the 6:30am bus from Heredia, you should have time to climb to the top, see both lagoons, and descend the volcano to catch the 1:30pm bus. Since the volcano is 2.9km (9500 ft.) above sea level, cold rain and wind should be anticipated. It is not advisable to stray from the trails.

🎦 **CAMPING.** Although camping is prohibited elsewhere in the park, it's allowed near the ranger station at Volcán Barva. Ask the ranger to show you where to camp and notify him when you leave. The facilities have space for 10 tents and provide access to potable water and toilets, though campers should bring their own drinking water in March and April and their own tents year-round. (Call 1 week ahead. Camping or 4-person cabin US$2 per person.)

BARVA

Usually, travelers pass straight through this small colonial village (3km north of Heredia) on their way to Volcán Barva or Poás. However, students from San José and Heredia know the sweet charm of this town, and so should you. Barva mainly offers a place to escape crowds and relax in the peaceful *parque*. It is also home to an impressive church, constructed in honor of San Bartolomé between 1568-1575; August 24 is the annual celebration for this patron saint. Barva, nominated in 1972 to be the historical and cultural center of the *cantón* of Barva (the 2nd and smallest of Heredia), has two excellent museums: the **Museo de Cultura Popular,** and the **Museo del Café.** To the north is Volcán Barva (2906m), a picturesque ride from Barva to Sacramento. There are also thermal baths and soap factories.

▐ TRANSPORTATION

There are two **bus stops** around the *parque.* Buses on the northeast side of the *parque* head north; buses on the southwest side head south. Buses head north to **San José de la Montaña** (10min., daily 4:45-10:30pm, ¢90); **Paso Llano** via **Sacramento,** the entrance to **Parque Nacional Braulio Carrillo** (30min., ¢120). Buses head south to **Heredia** on Ruta 422 (10min.; every 7min. M-Sa, every 10min. Su, 4:45-11pm; ¢70). Buses from Heredia to Barva leave from the college's gymnasium (4:55-11pm). For more bus information call **Transportes Barveños** (☎262 1839). **Taxis** line up on the south side of the *parque.*

▐ ▐ ORIENTATION AND PRACTICAL INFORMATION

The church on the *parque central* faces west. North of the *parque* with the health center and school. South is the chicken restaurant.

Tourist Information: Alejandro Villalobos at **EcoTours Express** (☎262 3424; fax 237 4298; ecoexpress@sol.racsa.co.cr), 3 blocks west and 1 block south of the *parque,* is very helpful. The calm office has great info about many tours in Costa Rica. Open M-Sa 8am-5pm.

Tours: Café Britt (☎260 2748, fax 260 1456; info@cafebritt.com; www.cafebritt.com), is up the hill from the Universidad Nacional de Heredia; follow the signs. Offers many tours deconstructing the coffee process. Also has tours to the La Guácima butterfly farm, the rainforest aerial tram at Braulio Carrillo National Park, and to Volcán Poas.

Municipalidad: (☎260 3292), the colonial house to the right of the police station.

Banks: Banco Nacional (☎262 2571), is 200m west and 50m north of the church.

Markets: Mi Mercado Barva Heredia (☎238 2619), in front of the bus stop on the southwest corner of the *parque.* (Open M-Th 8am-7pm, F-Sa 8am-8pm, Su 8am-1pm.) **Frutas y Verduras Mata Express** (☎261 5866), 125m south of the church, is the place to buy and eat many kinds of fresh-picked fruit. (Open M-Sa 7am-6pm, Su 8am-1pm.)

Police: (☎237 0835), on the west side of the *parque.* Open 24hr.

Red Cross: (☎237 1600), 200m east of the church up the hill, in the house behind the white bars on the right.

Pharmacy: Farmacia Mansay (☎262 5718), diagonal to the *casa de cultura,* in the shopping center complex. Open M-Sa 8am-9pm, Su 10am-6pm. **Farmacia San Barto-lomé** (☎260 2858), 50m south of the church. Credit cards accepted.

Medical Services: Clínica de Barva (☎237 5627 or 262 0185) runs along the north-west side of the *parque.* Open M-Th 7am-4pm, F 7am-3pm, emergencies daily 4-7pm.

Internet: Internet Café (☎ 260 7123), on the southeast corner of the *parque,* has 10 computers with speedy connections (¢200 per 30min., ¢350 per hr.). They also have **fax** and **photocopy** service. Open M-Sa 7:30am-10pm.

Post Office: 200m south of the southeast corner of the *parque* on the left, across from the new bank. Open M-F 8am-noon and 1-5:30pm.

ACCOMMODATIONS

There are no lodging options in the town proper of Barva. However, Heredia is only 10min. away (see **Heredia: Accommodations,** p. 127). There are a few other interesting options in the Barva proximity.

Cabañas de Montaña Cypresal (☎ 237 4466; fax 221 6244), 5km north of Barva in the charming village of Birri, has 24 rooms. Singles US$35; doubles US$41. ❸

Hotel Chalet Tirol, in nearby San Rafael, has a range of rooms. They also offer horse-back rides and a French restaurant. Chalet rooms US$65; luxury suites with continental breakfast, fireplace, and cable TV US$75. ❹

El Portico Hotel (☎ 260 6000 or 237 6022), in San José de la Montaña, 4km east of the road entering Bibri. There is easy bus access to this hotel from Barva, which is a 4 star resort with prices to match. ❺

FOOD AND ENTERTAINMENT

Soda La Cuchara, 25m south of southwest corner of the *parque,* is a super option for *típico* food. Large *casados* with dessert and juice (¢800). Open M-Sa 7am-7pm, Su 10:30am-5pm. ❶

Refugio del Chef Jacques (☎ 261 5319), 3.5km north of the *parque* in San José de la Montaña, serves excellent French cuisine (¢1200-¢5850). Open W-Su 11am-11pm. ❷

Restaurante Wong Ko (☎ 261 8839), 250m west of the southwest corner of the *parque,* serves good Chinese food (¢750-¢2000). Open daily 11am-midnight. ❶

Soda Marcela (☎ 261 5104), across from Restaurante Wong Ko, has good fast food. Try the *comida criolla* with natural *frescos* (¢850). Open daily 6am-8pm. ❶

Heladería Kela, on the northeast side of the *parque,* has delicious ice-cream fruit salads (starting at ¢400). Open daily 9:30am-9:30pm. ❶

Pooles K-Cha, has 6 pool tables and serves food in a great atmosphere. Soda open daily 8am-10pm; pool tables available M-F 3pm-midnight.

Bar Tabu/Cueva Club, 250m north of the church, has swimming pools, sport courts, and a spacious, trendy, second floor bar. Open Tu-Th 5pm-midnight, F-Su 5pm-2am.

Complejo Villa Barva (☎ 261 5234), 500m north and 300m west of the church, has a bar, restaurant, and live music on weekends. *Bocas* (appetizers) ¢500. Open Tu-F 4pm-late, Sa-Su 11am-late.

CARTAGO

Cartago (pop. 30,000) had its stint of importance when it served as the nation's capital from 1563 until 1823, before the seat of power shifted to San José, 22km northwest. Its size, power, and remarkable colonial architecture have since suffered from frequent earthquakes and volcanic eruptions, reducing the once crowded and busy urban center to a quiet town with a suburban feel. Cartago's most famous sights, La Basílica de Nuestra Señora (The Basilica of Our Lady),

Las Ruinas de la Parroquia (The Parochial Ruins), and the nearby Lankester Botanical Gardens, are easily visited on a daytrip from San José, although a smattering of rather overpriced hotels can provide a solid base for visiting nearby Volcán Irazú or Parque Nacional Tapantí.

▐ TRANSPORTATION

Bus departure points are scattered about town. There are no printed schedules, but bus and taxi drivers are a good source of information for bus schedules and departure points. Buses from Calle 6, Av. 1/3 depart to **Orosi** (40min.; M-Sa about every 30min. 5:30am-10:30pm, Su about every 30min. 7am-10pm; ¢215); from Av. 5, Calles 4/6 to **Paraíso** for **Lankester Botanical Gardens** (15min., every 10min. 5am-10pm, ¢85); from Av 4, Calle 2/4 to **San José** (SACSA ☎551 0232; in San José ☎233 5350. 40min.; every 10min. M-Sa 4:45am-11pm, Su 5-11pm; ¢180); from Calle 4, Av. 6/8 to **Tierra Blanca** (30min.; every hr. M-Sa 5:30am-10pm, Su 7am-10pm; ¢180); from Av. 3, Calles 8/10 to **Turrialba** (1½hr., daily every hr. 6am-10pm, ¢325). For information on getting to **Volcán Irazú**, see p. 136. **Taxis** line up at the west side of the *parque central* on Calle 4, Av. 1/2.

▐ ORIENTATION

Unlike most Costa Rican towns whose main drags are Av. and Calle Central, Cartago is anchored by Av. and Calle 1, which form the southern and western edges of the *parque central*. Just east of the *parque* stand **Las Ruinas,** the ruins of a cathedral destroyed by an earthquake, while the stately **La Basílica de Nuestra Señora de los Ángeles** is at the west end of town. Another good landmark is the *mercado central*, bounded by Calle 1/3 and Av. 4/6 slightly northwest of the *parque central*. **Volcán Irazú** soars 32km northeast of town, and the **Jardín Botánico Lankester** is about 8km southeast. Though the city is relatively safe, don't wander too far north or west of the *mercado central*, and take taxis whenever possible at night.

▐ PRACTICAL INFORMATION

Banks: Banco Popular, Av. 1, Calles 2/4, and **Banco Nacional,** Av. 4, Calle 5, will change traveler's checks and cash, give cash advances, and have **24hr. ATMs.** Banco Popular open M-F 8:15am-5pm, Sa 8:15-11:30am. Banco Nacional open M-F 8:30am-3:45pm.

Laundromat: Lavandería Fabimar, Av. 2, Calle 11. ¢475 per kg. Open M-F 8am-noon and 1-6pm, Sa 9am-3pm.

Market: Palí Supermarket is on Av. 4, Calle 6. Open M-Th 8:30am-7:30pm, F-Sa 8:30am-8pm, Su 8:30-6pm.

Police: On Av. 6, Calle 2/4 (☎551-0455), in the yellow building.

Red Cross: On Av. 5, Calle 1/3 (☎551 0421).

Medical Assistance: Farmacia Central, on Av. 1, Calle 2 (☎551 0698), south of Las Ruinas, is well stocked. Open M-Sa 8am-8pm. You can get medical care at **Hospital Dr. Max Peralta Jiménez,** on Av. 5/9, Calles 1/3 (☎550 1898).

Internet Access: You'll find **Internet** access at **Cafe Internet,** Av. 4, Calle 6/8. ¢300 per 30min., ¢500 per hr.; open daily 10am-10pm. There's also **Internet Cafe Las Ruinas,** on Av. 2, Calle 4. ¢400 per hr. Open M-Sa 9am-9pm, Su 1-7pm.

Post office: On Av. 2, Calle 15/17. Open M-F 7:30am-6pm, Sa 7:30am-noon.

Postal code: 7050.

CENTRAL VALLEY

CENTRAL VALLEY

Cartago

ACCOMMODATIONS
Hotel Dinastía, **1**
Los Angeles Lodge, **4**

FOOD
La Puerta del Sol, **5**
Restaurante y Taberna La Calzada, **2**
Soda y Restaurante Friendly's, **3**

TO IRAZÚ

Basílica de
Nuestra Señora
los Angeles

CARAVACA

PLAZA DE
LA BASÍLICA

C. 16
C. 14
C. 12
C. 10
C. 8
C. 6
C. 4
C. 2
C. 1
C. 3
C. 5

Av. 6
Av. 4
Av. 2
Av. 1
Av. 3
Av. 5
Av. 7
Av. 9

TO PARAISO (8km),
TURRIALBA (35km)

ANGELES

Tribunales
de Justicia

To Turrialba

TO SAN
FRANCISCO

Café en
Línea

To Tierra
Blanca

Pali

To San
José

Las
Ruinas

To Oresi

Los Capuchinos

To Irazú

To Paraíso,
Lankester
Gardens

Parque
Central

Pharmacy

TAXI

MERCADO

Old Train
Station

Banco Nacional
de Costa Rica

PLAZA
COLEGIO

PLAZA
COLEGIO

TO SAN
JOSÉ (22km)

TO (200m)

TO TEJAR

200 meters
200 yards

ACCOMMODATIONS

Cartago's lack of safe, inexpensive accommodations makes San José or Orosi better places to stay, although there are a couple of quality lodgings in town.

Hotel Dinastía, on Calle 3, Av. 6/8 (☎551 7057), just north of the *mercado central,* is a good choice. The small wood-paneled lobby has a comfy sitting area with TV and sofas. Singles and doubles with fan and shared bath ₡4500, with TV and private hot shower ₡6500; triples with private hot shower ₡9000-10,000. ❷

Los Ángeles Lodge Av. 4, Calle 14/16 (☎551 0957), is attractive and a bit more expensive, but in a safer and more scenic location overlooking the Basílica. Spotless, well-equipped rooms come with private bath, and the sunlit sitting area is perfect for watching TV or admiring the Basílica. Full breakfast included 7:30-9am. Singles US$20; doubles US$30; triples US$40; quads US$50; quints US$70. MC/V. ❷

FOOD

La Puerta del Sol, next door, serves good standard food in a large, friendly dining area with yellow and blue booths. *Gallo Pinto* with eggs ₡1000; sandwiches ₡400-900; *casados* ₡1300; *platos fuertes* ₡1400-2000. Open daily 8:30am-11pm. ❷

Soda y Restaurante Friendly's, on Calle 4, Av. 1/3, is one of the tastiest and most inexpensive options for a quick bite to eat. Burgers ₡350-1000; *gallo pinto* ₡550; sub sandwiches ₡550-800. Open daily 8am-11pm. ❶

Restaurante y Taberna La Calzada, Av. 1, Calles 1/2, across from the ruins has good food and a laid back local bar scene. Mexican, American, Costa Rican, and Chinese entrees ₡1200-2000. Heineken 2 for 1 ₡650. Open daily 10am-2am. ❷

SIGHTS

LA BASÍLICA DE NUESTRA SEÑORA DE LOS ÁNGELES. La Basílica de Nuestra Señora de Los Ángeles, Costa Rica's most famous and sacred place of worship, stands at the far east end of town. Thousands of *ticos* make an annual pilgrimage to this awe-inspiring cathedral on August 2 for *El Día de la Virgen* to worship the statue of La Negrita, an indigenous image of *La Virgen,* said to have great healing powers. The legend dates back to 1635, when an *indígena* woman found the statue on a stone while searching for firewood. She brought it home with her but it was gone the next day. She went back, found it on the same stone, and brought it home a second time. The statue miraculously reappeared on the stone three more times, prompting the local priest to declare the spot a holy place and to order a church built around it. La Negrita was declared the patron saint in 1824, about 100 years before the Basílica was destroyed by an earthquake and later rebuilt in the beautiful Byzantine style in which it currently stands.

The interior of the church, decorated with stunning stained glass windows, intricately carved pillars, walls emblazoned with biblical scenes, and a remarkable golden altar, is even more striking than the carefully constructed exterior. The church's real treasure, however, is hidden in the small room to the left of the main altar that is crammed full of offerings to the Virgin. Glass cases line the wall, displaying hundreds of miniature metal body parts offered to the Virgin as appreciation for her magical blessings that the givers believe helped cure their malady. A shelf at the front of the room is filled with medals, miniature house models, and even graded school exams, testament to the *tico*'s widespread faith in La Negrita's powers.

From this room, two sets of stairs lead down to the **Cripta de la Piedra** (Crypt of the Stone), which contains the boulder where La Negrita is said to have been first sighted. *(Open daily 5:30am-8pm. Free.)*

LAS RUINAS DE LA PARROQUIA. The crumbling walls of **Las Ruinas de la Parroquia,** Av. 1/2 and Calles 2/4, at the east side of the *parque central,* are the remains of Cartago's first parochial church. First built in 1575 and dedicated to Apostle Santiago of Spain, the cathedral stood unharmed until 1841, when an earthquake almost completely destroyed it. The cathedral was later reconstructed, only to be damaged by another tremor in 1910. Now enclosing an overgrown garden, the ruins and adjacent *parque central* are excellent for an afternoon picnic and nap.

NEAR CARTAGO

JARDÍN BOTÁNICO LANKESTER

*To get to the Garden from Cartago, take a Paraíso **bus** from Av. 5, Calles 4/6 (15min., every 10min. 5am-10pm, ¢85) and ask the driver to let you off at Restaurante Casa Vieja. Buses between Orosi and Cartago will also stop here. From the drop-off point in front of the restaurant, you'll see a sign for Jardín Lankester. Walk down the wide gravel road and turn right at the first road; it's a 15min. walk. ☎ 552 3247, fax 552 3151. Open daily 9am-3:30pm. US$5, students US$3.50.*

Located 6km southeast of Cartago near the small town of Paraíso, the lush tropical garden more closely resembles a fairy tale landscape from Alice in Wonderland than the manicured flower beds more typical of botanical gardens. Several self-guided trails wind through the garden's 10 hectares of tropical premontane forest, nourishing vegetation including bromeliads, heliconias, gingers, banana plants, cacti, ferns, and trees, among which flutter over 100 species of birds. The garden's intense mix of life, which requires such different climates and habitats yet exists in the relatively small and enclosed gardens, is truly astounding. Well, but not overly, maintained trails are replete with informational signs and labels, making the trip enjoyable for both nature lovers as well as casual hikers.

Founded in the 1950s by British naturalist Charles H. Lankester and now operated by the University of Costa Rica, the garden's real treasure is its internationally famed collection of epiphytes, including its spectacular orchids. Epiphytic orchids grow on other plants in soil generated from decaying organic matter. This means that instead of leeching minerals and water from their hosts, these plants grow their own roots (which can be seen hanging from tree branches), and don't damage other wildlife. The best time to see the 800 species of orchids bloom is Feb.-May, but there is always something flowering. Brochures are available in English, Spanish, German, French, and Italian. The garden also runs field courses in tropical biology and offers a **volunteer program.**

VOLCÁN IRAZÚ

*The best time to see Volcán Irazú is on weekends; getting there during the week is difficult without private transportation. A bus leaves **San José** from 2 Av., 1/3 Calles, across the street from the Gran Hotel Costa Rica (1½hr.; Sa and Su 8am, return bus 12:30pm; round-trip ¢1500). It stops in **Cartago**, 100m south of the southeast corner of the ruins, across the street from Iglesia Los Capuchines (8:30am, ¢800 round-trip from Cartago). During the week take a taxi from Cartago or Tierra Blanca (¢7000 one-way, ¢15,000-20,000 to have the taxi wait a few hours and drive you back), or a bus to **Tierra Blanca**, then hike the remaining 20km uphill. Buses leave from the Tierra Blanca stop in Cartago for **San Juan de Chicua**, 6km from the peak. (☎ 219 7187; call ahead for confirmation. 1hr., M and Th 11am, ¢350.) Returns are only early morning, so to get back, call a taxi. Park open daily 8am-3:30pm. Admission US$7.*

With an elevation of 3432m, Volcán Irazú is Costa Rica's tallest active volcano. The name commemorates the indigenous village Iztarú that once perched daringly on the shoulder of the capricious volcano. Appropriately, the village name means "mountain of quakes and thunder." It first erupted in 1723 and has recorded 15 eruptions since, the most recent on Dec. 8, 1994. However, its most famous eruption occurred on March 9, 1963, the day John F. Kennedy arrived in Costa Rica for an official visit. The blast severely damaged the agriculture in the Central Valley, destroyed some 300 homes, and transformed parts of the surrounding forest into the gray, dusty wasteland they remain today. Though sulfurous fumaroles continue to roll off a few of the volcano's five craters, Irazú is relatively inactive and is one of the rare volcanoes that can be observed from up close. Just like out of a sci-fi movie, Irazú seams unearthly with its moon-like terrain and craters covered in black ash. If you're lucky—mornings in the dry season are best—you can see the Atlantic Ocean, Pacific Ocean, and Lago de Nicaragua from the summit. For the best view, follow the paved road from the ticket office to the top and turn left on the small path that turns off to the right before the parking lot. Past the lot is the cement path that leads to Irazu's three main craters.

The expansive **Cráter Playa Hermosa,** a big playpen of volcanic ash, is the first crater on the left. To the right is the **Cráter Diego de la Haya** (690m wide, 100m deep), named after the Cartago mayor who recorded the volcano's first eruption. Straight ahead is the **Cráter Principal** (1050m wide, 300m deep), the only active crater, which boasts an enormous cauldron. Both Diego de la Haya and Principal cradle sulfurous iguana-green lakes, the color resulting from the chemicals produced by gases emitted into the water by the volcano.

Be sure to bring rain gear and a few extra layers of warm clothes, since temperatures range from a high of 17°C to a bone-chilling low of -3°C, and rainfall averages almost 2200mm annually. A small *cafetería* serves overpriced snacks, hot drinks, and souvenirs. There is no camping or lodging.

OROSI

Regretfully overlooked by most travelers scurrying away to the more touristed coasts, small and tranquil Orosi (pop. 8000) teems with surprises close and exciting enough to warrant at least a couple days' excursion from San José. Cozy lodgings and a friendly, colonial town atmosphere make Orosi the perfect retreat to escape the Central Valley's urban sprawl. You can visit the nearby nature reserves, hot springs, coffee farms, and raging rivers, all hidden snugly in the rolling hills and luscious waterfall-laden rainforest of the Orosi Valley.

▐▀ TRANSPORTATION

Buses to Orosi leave Cartago from Calle 6, Av. 1/3 (40min.; M-F every hr. 5:30am-10pm, Su about every 30min. 7am-10pm; ¢215) and return to **Cartago** from the northeast corner of the soccer field on the main road (40min.; every 45min. 4:45am-9:10pm, Su 5:45am-7:15pm; ¢200). **Taxis** also leave from the northeast corner of the soccer field. (☎ 533 3343.)

▐ PRACTICAL INFORMATION

Despite the lack of street names, Orosi is easily navigable if you keep in mind a few landmarks and directions. Buses and taxis arrive on the main drag, which runs from north to south through town; you'll be traveling south along this road past the soccer field. **La Iglesia de San José Orosi** is at the west side of the field. **Parque Nacional Tapantí** and **Purisil Park** are about 10km east of town along the main drag.

The tourist office, **Oficina de Información Turística,** 200m south of the southeast corner of the soccer field on the main drag, arranges tours to Parque Nacional Tapantí, Volcán Irazú, Purisil Park, Casa Soñando, and also rents mountain bikes. (☎533 3825, cell 382 4195. Bikes US$1 per hr., US$7 per day.) Many accommodations in town also arrange tours and rent bikes (See **Accommodations** below). If by chance you're in town on a Friday, **MINAE Orosi,** at the northwest corner of the soccer field, can provide information on nearby national parks. (☎533 3082. Open F 8am-5pm.) Groceries, fax, and photocopy service are available at **Super Anita #2,** 250m south of the southeast corner of the soccer field, where they might change US dollars if you buy something. (Open daily 7am-8pm. MC/V.) Other local services include the **police station,** directly north of the soccer field(☎533 3082), and the **medical clinic,** next to the police. (☎533 3052. Open M-F 8:30am-4pm.) You'll find **Internet** access at **PC Orosi,** 100m south of Super Anita #2 (¢300 per 30min., ¢500 per hr.; open M-Sa 9am-7pm) and **Vallenet Internet,** 100m south and 20m west of the southwest corner of the soccer field. (¢250 per 30min., ¢500 per hr. Open M-Sa 9:30am-7:30pm.)

ACCOMMODATIONS

■ **Montaña Linda** (☎533 3640; fax and international ☎(506) 533 2153; info@montanal-inda.com), 200m south and 200m west of the southwest corner of the soccer field. Wake up to roosters and cows at this eclectically decorated tree house-like hotel. The young Canadian and Dutch owners attract backpackers with the fun hostel-like atmosphere, spotless communal bathrooms (with hot water), shared kitchen (US$1), and delicious breakfasts and dinners (US$2-3.50). Spanish classes (US$99-205 with meals and lodging) are offered. If you seek the luxury of private baths and killer mountainside views, try their **Bed and Breakfast** up the street. Laundry US$4. Dorms US$5.50; singles US$8; doubles US$12. Bed and Breakfast rooms US$25-35. All prices add 16% sales tax. **Camping** US$2.50 per person, US$3.50 renting a tent. ❶

Cabinas Media Libre (☎533 3838), 300m south and 25m west of the southeast corner of the soccer field, is a luxurious bargain for a group of three but a bit pricey for the solo guest. All gleaming modern triples (you can squeeze in 4) are equipped with TV, fridge, phone, private hot water bath. The hotel has a restaurant. Laundry ¢1000. Singles US$20; doubles and triples US$30. AmEx/MC/V. ❷

Hotel Río Palomo (☎533 3128), about 4km out of town on the Río Palomo. A quiet, family-friendly lodge. Walk about 25min. east along the main road, past the Balneario Los Patios; turn left when you see a sign for the hotel and walk another 15min. Comfortable cabins with private hot water baths, fans, and furniture. Some have full kitchens. Large pool, horseback trail, trout stream, and restaurant. Cabins for 1-3 people ¢7000; large cabins with kitchen for 4 ¢10,000. AmEx/MC/V. ❷

Orosi Lodge (☎533 3578; www.orosilodge.com), 400m south and 100m west of the southwest corner of the soccer field. A charming, colonial-style, German-owned hotel. Modern rooms with fridge, coffee maker, ceiling fan, orthopedic mattresses, and private hot water bath. Private balconies and views of the nearby volcanoes. The lodge's attached cafe offers a small selection of pastries and snacks. **Internet** access ¢750 per 30min. Doubles US$35, in high season US$40; triples US$45/50. AmEx/MC/V. ❸

FOOD

Soda Luz, 100m north of the northwest corner of the soccer field, serves some of the heartiest, most inexpensive meals in town. Burgers ¢400; spaghetti ¢800; *casados* ¢800-1000. Open M-Th 7am-4pm, F-Su 7am-8pm. ❶

Bar Restaurante Orosi, at the northeast corner of the soccer field, offers good food in a relaxed, tropical setting. Rice dishes ¢800-1200; shrimp cocktail ¢1100; bacon with cassava ¢2100. Local beer ¢380. Open daily 10am-10pm. ❶

👁 SIGHTS

LA IGLESIA DE SAN JOSÉ OROSI. Built in 1743, this is one of Costa Rica's oldest churches still in use, having remarkably withstood earthquakes that have wiped out nearby villages. Defying tradition, the church is also reputed to be Costa Rica's only church that faces east instead of the customary westward orientation. The worn, whitewashed walls, red terra cotta-tiled roof, and ornately carved antique wooden altar confirm its colonial roots and make Sunday mass (10am, 6:30pm) with upbeat Padre Carlos Alfaro a truly memorable experience. Adjoining the church, the **Museo Franciscano** houses a collection of Christian relics from the early 18th century, including several wooden replicas of Christ, dusty gowns, and fancy candelabras. *(At the west of the soccer field. Open Tu-Sa 1-5pm, Su 9am-noon and 1-5pm. US$1, children ¢100.)*

BALNEARIO TERMAL OROSI. The closer of Orosi's two hot mineral baths, this facility has two simple pools at 35°C, a drastic drop from the scalding 60°C water at the source. Basic showers and a reasonably priced restaurant are available. *(☎ 533 3009. 300m south and 100m west of the southwest corner of the soccer field, next to Orosi Lodge. Open daily 7:30am-4pm. ¢500.)*

BALNEARIO DE AGUAS TERMALES LOS PATIOS. Slightly farther and more scenic than Balneario Termal Orosi, Los Patios has a few more warm mineral pools and a cold one. *(☎ 553 3009. 2km south out of town along Orosi's main road. Open Tu-Su 8am-4pm. ¢700.)*

LA CASA DEL SOÑADOR. This old-fashioned, intricately designed "Dreamer's House" is the masterpiece of late Costa Rican sculptor Macedonio Quesada, who built the bamboo and wooden *casita* in 1989. Now maintained by Quesada's sons Hermes and Miguel, and a handful of assistants who seem to be constantly working away in the workspace downstairs, the house is filled with nativity scenes and *campesino* figures with Latin American, indigenous, and East Asian influences. Everything in the house, from the doors to the window shuttles, is intricately chiseled and drafted. *(1km from Orosi on the road to the town of Cachí. From Orosi, walk east along the main road past the Balneario Los Patios until you see a sign for Hotel Río Palomo. Turn left and walk another 15min. to the hotel; make another left and continue 4.5km past the hotel to La Casa del Soñador. Most Cartago-Orosi buses will go as far as the town of Palomo. From there it's a 4.5km walk. A taxi from Orosi costs ¢2500-3000.)*

LAS RUINAS DE UJARRÁS. The small village of Ujarrás was abandoned after it was virtually destroyed by a flood in 1833, but the ruins of the town's 17th century church draw a constant flow of tourists, mostly on organized tours arranged by Orosi hotels. Set in a well-kept park surrounded by coffee plantations, the church is said to have been built when an Indian found a wooden box in a river, which he brought to Ujarrás. Upon opening it, the Indian found a statue of the Virgin and was no longer able to move it from Ujarrás. The statue, known as **La Virgen de Candelaria,** has since been moved to the town of Paraíso, along with the rest of Ujarrás' residents, who continue to celebrate their sacred Virgen by holding an annual parade from Paraíso to Ujarrás in late March or early April. *(To get here from Orosi, catch a bus to Paraíso from the northeast corner of the soccer field. 20min., every 30min. 4:45am-9:15pm, ¢120. From Paraíso, buses leave every 20-30min. for La Represa de Cachí. From there it's a 1km walk to the ruins; ask the driver to point you in the right direction. To return to Orosi, confirm with the driver for a bus that can pick you up from the drop off point at Cachí. Open daily dawn to dusk. Free.)*

⬛ GUIDED TOURS

Many Orosi hotels and the tourist office arrange tours of the nearby attractions and provide equipment for you to fully enjoy the views. The **Montaña Linda** hotel (see **Accommodations** above) offers guided tours of Orosi valley, Volcán Irazú, Monumento Nacional Guayabo, and white water rafting. *(Orosi tour US$5. Irazú US$12, not including park fee. Monumento Nacional Guayabo US$25, including park fee. Rafting US$70.)*

For awesome panoramic views of the Orosi and Cachí Valley, check out the 3-4hr. "Yellow Church Walk." Montaña Linda offers directions. The **Orosi Lodge** leads combined tours of Volcán Irazú, Mirador Orosi, and La Basílica de Nuestra Señora de los Ángeles (US$40); Parque Nacional Tapantí (US$45); and Orosi Valley, a sugar cane mill, La Casa del Soñador, and the Lankester Botanical Gardens (US$40). The lodge also rents mountain bikes and canoes. *(Bikes US$3 per hour, US$10 per day. Canoes US$25 per 6hr.)*

⬛ DAYTRIPS FROM OROSI

PARQUE NACIONAL TAPANTÍ

The lengthy 12km hike from Orosi to Parque Nacional Tapantí passes through rolling coffee plantations. Head south along the main road from Orosi; the first half of the hike is fairly flat, but the road gets rockier as it proceeds uphill to the park. If you're short on time or energy, you can take a cab (one-way ¢3000), and either walk back down or arrange for the cab to pick you up. ☎ 771 5116 or 551 2797. Open daily 7am-5pm. US$7.

Twelve kilometers away from central Orosi is a 61 sq. km wildlife refuge turned national park Tapantí, famed for having the highest average rainfall (6.5m per yr.) in Costa Rica. The resulting 150+ rivers and streams intersect a pristine rainforest inhabited by an enormous diversity of wildlife: 45 species of mammals, including tapirs, pacas, jaguars, and kinkajous; 260 species of birds, including scoli robins, orioles, hawks, and falcons; 28 species of reptiles and amphibians, including two types of vipers; and an average 80-160 species of trees per hectare. The huge amounts of rainfall that Tapantí receives are used to generate hydroelectric power for most of San José's population. From the main road, **Camino Principal** (1.6km) leads to the **ranger station,** where the park's three trails begin—the **Oropéndola** (1.2km), **La Pava** (400m), and the **Árboles Caídos** (2km), in increasing order of difficulty. The last has some steep inclines but can be finished within 1-1½ hr. Oropéndola leads up to a pool in the Río Grande de Orosi, where swimming is possible. Although camping is not permitted, the park offers very basic **rooms.** (¢1000 per person; call in advance to secure a bed.) The communal showers have warm water. Bring a sleeping bag and food to cook in the kitchen. Spanish and English maps (¢200) are available at the ranger station.

PURISIL PARK

Getting to Purisil, located 10km east of Orosi along the main drag, involves quite a bit of hiking, unless you take a taxi (¢3000, one-way). Most Cartago-Orosi buses go as far as the town of Palomo, from where it's a 7km uphill walk. Walking from Orosi means hiking 10km east along the main road to the park entrance. If you don't want to walk down for the return trip, hire a cab in advance to pick you up or have the park call you one. Central office ☎ 228 6630, park office 381 3895. Open daily 8am-5pm. US$5, students US$2.

Located 10km east of Orosi, the Purisil Park nature reserve provides 171 peaceful hectares of cloudy rainforest and trout streams to enjoy en route to or from Parque Nacional Tapantí, just 2km further east. The park's name originates from an indigenous word that means "crystal clear" or "pure waters," quite fitting for the park's several immaculate trout streams. Fishing is appropriately one of the park's most popular attractions; they provide fishing equipment, charge US$5 per kg of fish, and will even cook your catch at their excellent **restaurant,** Las Ortencias. Non-fishermen can hike on the two short trails (350m and 1200m) through primary and secondary forest, squint to spot the elusive quetzal and toucan, or learn about conservation efforts and the park's history at the interactive museum.

TURRIALBA

Often bypassed by travelers either uninterested in adventure tours or on too limited a budget to afford them, relatively small and suburban Turrialba, at the confluence of the Ríos Colorado and Turrialba, generally keeps to itself. What has brought the town international recognition, however, is its proximity to the Ríos Reventazón and Pacuare, both packed with Class III-V rapids and some of the world's best river runs. Whitewater rafters and kayakers of all abilities splash through during the rainy season while other travelers stay a night or two on the way to Costa Rica's most significant archaeological site, Monumento Nacional Guayabo.

▐ TRANSPORTATION

Turrialba has two main bus stations. From the bus station 100m west of the southwest corner of the *parque* (☎556 0159), buses leave for **San José** (direct: 1¾hr.; every hr. 5am-4pm, 5:30pm; indirect: 2¼hr.; every 1½hr. 5am-9pm; ¢605) via **Cartago** (1½hr. ¢350) and **Siquirres** (2hr.; Tu-Th every 2hr. 6am-6:15pm, F-M every hr. 6am-7pm; ¢470) via **CATIE** (10min.; ¢80). An additional free private bus shuttles passengers to and from CATIE; pick it up at the stop opposite the Red Cross. On weekends and in the high season, you might have to buy tickets to San José in advance to ensure a seat. From the other station, 100m south and 50m west of the southwest corner of the *parque*, buses leave for **Monumento Nacional Guayabo** (1hr.; M-Sa 11am and 5:15pm, return 12:50; Su 9am, return 5pm; ¢155).

▐▐ ORIENTATION AND PRACTICAL INFORMATION

Turrialba, 62km east of San José, is arranged in a fashion similar to most Costa Rican cities. Most streets have names, but no one uses them. With the *parque central* as a reference point, things aren't too tough to find. As you exit the bus station (coming from San José or Cartago), the **parque** is on the next block to your left (east), and the **church** is just south of the *parque*.

> **Tourist Information:** No official office, but Doña Blanca at **Hotel Interamericano** (see **Accommodations,** below), will gladly help with info about the town and nearby sights.
>
> **Banks: Banco de Costa Rica,** 200m south and 100m east of the southeast corner of the *parque*. Open M-F 8:30am-5pm. **Banco Nacional** (open M-F 8:30am-3:45pm) and **Banco Popular** (open M-F 8:15am-5pm, Sa 8:15-11:30am) are just a few meters west of Banco de Costa Rica.
>
> **Western Union** (☎ 556 0439), 100m south and 50m east of the southwest corner of the *parque*. Open M-Sa 8am-6:30pm.
>
> **Police:** (☎556 0030, ☎117 for emergencies), 200m north of the northeast corner of the *parque*.
>
> **Hospital:** (☎556 1133), 300m west of the northeast corner of the *parque*.
>
> **Red Cross:** (☎556 0191), 100m west and 50m south of the northwest corner of the *parque*.

Supermarket: Supermercado Compramás, at the northeast corner of the *parque.* Open M-Sa 8am-8pm.

Pharmacy: Farmacia (☎556 0379), 100m south of the southeast corner of the *parque.* Open M-Sa 8am-8pm, Su 8am-6pm. V.

Internet: Turrialba.net Cafe Internet, in the Centro Comerical Yel, 100m west and 50m south of the southwest corner of the *parque.* ¢250/30min., ¢400/hr. Open M-Sa 9am-9pm, Su 1-7pm.

Post Office: 200m north of the northeast corner of the *parque.* Open M-F 7:30am-5pm, Sa 7:30am-noon.

Postal code: 7150.

ACCOMMODATIONS

Turrialba has a good number of budget places, although you'll be hard-pressed to find many dirt-cheap places often available in other towns. Although most of Turrialba's hotels are a touch pricier, they usually offer a few much-missed comforts like hot water and comfy beds.

Hotel Interamericano (☎556 0142; www.hotelinteramericano.com), the yellow building 200m south of the southwest corner of the *parque.* What makes Interamericano's small but comfortable and airy rooms extra special is owner Blanca Vasquez, a native *tica* who lived in New York City for 20 years. Doña Blanca has tons of information about sights and restaurants, knows just about everyone in town, and can recommend good guides for all sorts of water sports. Amenities include hot showers, breakfast (entrees US$3), luggage storage, laundry (¢2000), and a large sitting area with English magazines, Internet, and cable TV. Singles US$10, with bath and TV US$20; doubles US$18/US$30; triples US$27/US$40; quads US$35/US$50. ❶

Hotel La Roche (☎556 7915), 150m north of the northeast corner of the *parque.* Its semi-secluded location on the banks of the Río Turrialba gives La Roche a quiet, homey feel. A few small doubles with sinking beds, pink and turquoise walls, and clean cold baths open up to a pleasant courtyard. Ask for a room upstairs if you'd like a little balcony. Singles and doubles ¢3500. ❶

Hotel Kardey (☎556 0050), 200m west and 50m south of the southwest corner of the *parque,* is a great place for groups of 3 or 4. A friendly owner maintains a few spotless rooms with wall-to-wall carpeting, private hot baths, and pretty balconies. Singles ¢7000; doubles ¢8000; triples ¢9000; ¢2000 per each additional person. ❷

Hospedaje la Esmerelda (☎556 5312), 100m north and 200m west of the northwest corner of the *parque,* has 10 homey, wood-panelled rooms with private hot bath, TV, and fan. A few have carpeting, but the rest have clean tile floors. Singles ¢3500; doubles ¢5000; triples ¢7500; quads ¢10,000. ❶

Hotel Wagelia (☎556 1566; www.wagelia.com), 150m west of the southwest corner of the *parque.* One of Turrialba's more upscale places, Wagelia boasts 18 comfortable rooms with A/C, private hot bath, cable TV, phone, safe deposit box, and a large dressing area. The attached bar and restaurant serves decent, moderately-priced entrees, and laundry and tour service are available. Breakfast and taxes included. Singles US$55; doubles US$69; triples US$76. AmEx/MC/V. ❸

Whittingham Hotel (☎550 8927), 200m west and 150m south of the southwest corner of the *parque,* is another decent option for budget travelers. Some of the rooms are a bit dark, but all have fans, sinks, and clean tile floors, and some even have TVs. Singles and doubles with shared bath ¢2500, with private bath ¢3500; triples ¢4200. ❶

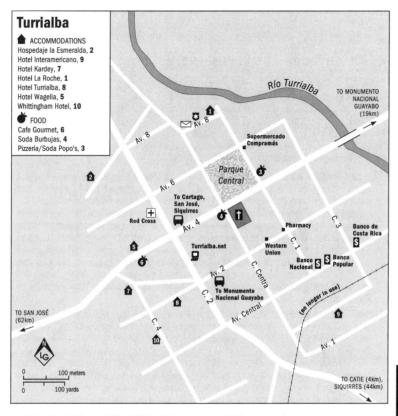

Turrialba

ACCOMMODATIONS
Hospedaje la Esmeralda, **2**
Hotel Interamericano, **9**
Hotel Kardey, **7**
Hotel La Roche, **1**
Hotel Turrialba, **8**
Hotel Wagelia, **5**
Whittingham Hotel, **10**

FOOD
Cafe Gourmet, **6**
Soda Burbujas, **4**
Pizzería/Soda Popo's, **3**

Río Turrialba

TO MONUMENTO
NACIONAL
GUAYABO
(19km)

Av. 8

Supermercado
Compramás

Parque
Central

Av. 6

To Cartago,
San José,
Siquirres

Red Cross

Av. 4

Pharmacy

C. 3

Banco de
Costa Rica

Turrialba.net

Western
Union

C. 1

Banco
Nacional

Banco
Popular

Av. 2

To Monumento
Nacional Guayabo

C. 2

C. Central

(no longer in use)

Av. Central

TO SAN JOSÉ
(62km)

C. 4

Av. 1

0   100 meters
0   100 yards

TO CATIE (4km),
SIQUIRRES (44km)

Hotel Turrialba (☎556 6396), 100m south and 150m west of the southwest corner of the *parque,* is a bit pricey for solo travelers but makes a decent value for pairs. All the rooms are simple but clean with wood-panelling, private hot bath, and a couple fans. Laundry ¢2000. Singles ¢6500; doubles ¢9000. ❷

🍴 FOOD

Food in Turrialbe is much less exciting than the raging rivers that rush past it; choices are limited to basic sodas and pizza places.

Pizzería/Soda Popo's (☎556 0064), on the east side of the *parque,* is a popular place for good, inexpensive food in a simple atmosphere. They'll even deliver to your hotel if a day of rafting has you too tired to walk over here. Pizzas ¢1000-1500, *plato del día* ¢750, burritos ¢400. Open M-Sa 11am-11pm, Su 5-11pm. ❶

Cafe Gourmet, 150m west of the southwest corner of the *parque.* Boasting the motto "Coffee without caffeine is like a sea without sun, like wine without alcohol," Cafe Gourmet is every coffee imbibers heaven. The burlap coffee sacks decorating the walls and drinks and desserts guaranteed to make you swoon make it the perfect place to catch up on your reading, postcard-writing, or journaling. Apple pie ¢500, *pinto* ¢600, chocolate mint espresso drink ¢600. Open M-Sa 7am-7pm. ❶

Soda Burbujas, diagonally across the street from the southwest corner of the *parque,* is a casual, dimly lit place popular with river rafters and kayakers. Sandwiches ¢350-500, *gallo pinto* ¢550-700, *casados* ¢800-900. Open daily 7am-8pm. ❶

⚑ ⬙ OUTDOOR ACTIVITIES AND GUIDED TOURS

Capitalizing on Turrialba's legendary rafting and kayaking opportunities, several tour operators offer adventure trips for all abilities. A day on the raging rapids will cost you a pretty penny, but the experience is unforgettable. If you have your own equipment or rent from one of the tour companies, Hotel Interamericano (see **Accommodations,** p. 142) will help arrange truck transport to nearby rivers. The hotel will also set you up with information about the nearby **serpent farm** (10km away), **Volcán Turrialba,** and the **Aguiares waterfall.**

Costa Rica Rios Aventuras (☎556 9617; www.costaricarios.com), 150m north of the northeast corner of the *parque,* is the most reputable rafting and kayaking operator and owns the largest fleet of water sports equipment of any Central American company. Co-owners Ray McClain and Tom Foster have been at the sport for over 20 years and are among the world's best rafters and kayakers, each having earned several distinctions at the national level. Ray, a Wisconsin native, opens his cheerful home for some pool and grub after exciting expeditions. The company's small size and experienced staff means you'll have a safe and personable trip. Although they specialize in pre-booked multi-day trips, a number of full-day and half-day options are available. Kayaking US$41-90, mountain biking US$25-55, canyoning US$38-105, rafting US$63-150. Just stop by Ray's house for information or reservations.

Rainforest World (☎556 2678; www.rforestw.com), inside the shoe repair shop 100m west and 50m south of the northwest corner of the *parque.* Experienced rafter, kayaker, and owner Phil Coleman offers everything from tame "scenic float trips" on the Río Pejibaye (no white water) for US$45 to the hard-core Class V, "extreme" rafting and kayaking trips for the experienced river runner (average US$65-90). Horseback rides, tours to Parque Nacional Tapantí and Monumento Nacional Guayabo, and volcanic lake snorkeling trips accommodate the less adventurous spirits. Booking through Hotel Interamericano (whether or not you're a guest) may earn you a sweet discount.

Loco's (☎556 6035 or 396 8079; riolocos@whiteh20.com). Definitely not one of Turrialba's largest companies, but likely one of the friendliest. They prefer small groups, but they can accommodate groups of up to 24 with advance notice. Class III-IV plus rafting on the Pacuare and Reventazon US$60 half-day, US$90-125 full-day; horseback tour US$65 full-day; Volcán Turrialba US$85; trip to Monumento Nacional Guayabo US$40; waterfall tour US$25.

NEAR TURRIALBA

▛ MONUMENTO NACIONAL GUAYABO

*Buses to the park entrance station leave from the local bus terminal in **Turrialba** at Av. 2, Calles Central/2 (1¼hr.; M-Sa 11am, 5:15pm, Su 9am; ¢140). There is one snag: buses return from Guayabo at 5:30am and 12:30pm only, so a same-day trip requires either a very quick visit to the ruins or a 4km walk downhill to the main paved road where buses pass more frequently (7am, noon, 1:30, 4pm). Alternatively, you can hire a cab to the monument (¢4000-4500) and take the 12:30pm bus back. Getting there is easier on Sundays, when the bus leaves Turrialba at 9am and does not return from the park until 4pm, although you'll have completed your visit hours before the return bus leaves. Monument ☎556 9507. Open daily 8am-3:30pm. US$6, children under 12 free.*

Located 19km northeast of Turrialba, Monumento Nacional Guayabo is Costa Rica's most important archaeological site, its only declared National Monument, and an interesting daytrip for those with extra time in Turrialba. The park itself covers 218 hectares, although the archaeological site is just 20 hectares, and only four of those 20 have been excavated. Much remains unknown about the civilization that built and eventually abandoned the site, believed to have been inhabited from 1500BC to 1400AD by about 10,000 people. Some scientists say that the Guayabo people migrated to Columbia, and, in fact, many indigenous Colombians claim to have northern ancestors of similar traditions. The mysterious first inhabitants did leave a record of some of their technological advances. Their houses were built on large *montículos* (circular foundations), and they constructed a bridge, *calzadas* (long causeways), and an impressive aqueduct system that still works. The vague remnants of these structures, at the end of an easy 1.4km trail through rainforest, are the focal point of the site, though you will pass a monolith, coffin graves, and several intricate petroglyphs on the way. As there are no official guided tours, it's worth asking the rangers for a quick briefing or shelling out ¢200 for a pamphlet. Another 1.1km trail from the park entrance leads to a rushing stream with potable water. Both trails, especially the shorter one, get extremely muddy in the rainy season; be sure to bring proper footwear and rain gear. Though the ruins are interesting, there's not much else to see, and fast hikers who take the 11am bus from Turrialba and only do the 1.4km trail to the ruins can make it back to the entrance just in time to catch the 12:30 bus back to town. If you want to stay overnight, there's a **campsite** in the monument (US$2 per person) that has a toilet, a cold shower, a clearing for tents, and barbecue pits.

CENTRAL VALLEY

NORTHWESTERN COSTA RICA

Two mountain chains stretch across northwestern Costa Rica, guarding some of the country's most famous attractions. The world-famous Monteverde Cloud Forest Reserve protects the cloud forest that once covered the entire Cordillera de Tilarán. The volcanic Cordillera de Guanacaste, to the north, holds three spectacular national parks. Superbly situated between these ranges is Volcán Arenal, Central America's most active volcano. Meanwhile, arid, lowland Guanacaste contrasts sharply with these lush regions, but offers a cowboy charm all its own. Here, rugged coast (preserved by the lovely Parque Nacional Santa Rosa), flowering shrubs, and traditional folklore make the region an eclectic delight.

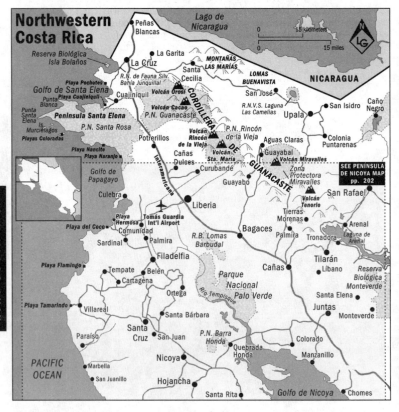

SEE PENINSULA DE NICOYA MAP pp. 202

MONTEVERDE AND SANTA ELENA

The Monteverde area, 184km northwest of San José and due north of Puntarenas, is the sole reason for many travelers to come to Costa Rica. Several private reserves adjoining Monteverde and neighboring Santa Elena, including the famous **Monteverde Cloud Forest Reserve,** protect some of the last remaining primary cloud forest. In 1951 a group of 44 US Quakers, some of whom had been sentenced to jail time, exiled themselves to this town, protesting the peacetime draft before the Korean War. The group set aside a section of its land for the benefit of the entire community. In 1972, this watershed was expanded and made into the now-famous reserve. With its mystical cloud forests now carefully protected, Monteverde is in no danger of losing its title as Costa Rica's primary tourist attraction. Luckily, conscientious locals and a set of specialists—biologists, planners, and educators—are also committed to controlling tourism's effects on the area.

Centered around a triangle of short blocks, **Santa Elena** feeds and houses tourists who have made the pilgrimage up the jarring, unpaved roads towards tranquil Monteverde. People appreciate Santa Elena for the facilities it provides, yet the town is pleasant on its own merit. We often think nature lies on the outskirts of a town; in this case, Santa Elena is certainly a town on the outskirts of nature.

▐ TRANSPORTATION

Direct **buses** to Santa Elena and Monteverde run from **San José, Puntarenas,** and **Tilarán.** Coming from **Liberia,** you can take a San José-bound bus as far as Lagarto, and take a bus to Monteverde from there (9:30am, 3, 5pm). All buses make a stop in **Santa Elena** and many continue along the road through Monteverde until the cheese factory, 2.5km from the reserve. Leaving Monteverde, buses head to: **San José** (4½hr., 6:30am and 2:30pm, ¢1475); **Puntarenas** (3½hr., 1 per day 6am, ¢795); **Tilarán** (3hr., 1 per day 7am, ¢620). Buy return tickets from Monteverde in advance at the Marza Transport ticket office located half a block south of Banco Nacional in Santa Elena. (☎645 5159. Open daily 5:45-11am and 1-4pm.)

▟ ORIENTATION

Arriving buses stop in the town of **Santa Elena,** which has most of the local services, budget hotels, and budget restaurants. From here, an unpaved road heads 6km southeast to the famous **Monteverde Cloud Forest Reserve.** The actual Quaker settlement of **Monteverde** is strung along this road, as are restaurants and hotels. The **Santa Elena Reserve** is 5km northeast of the Santa Elena town. Unless otherwise noted, the following services are in Santa Elena.

▐ PRACTICAL INFORMATION

Information/Tour Companies: Camino Verde Information Center (☎645 5916 or 645 6296) is across from the bus stop. They book reservations to the Santa Elena reserve, Monteverde canopy tours, and more. Save yourself time by dropping by **Desafío Tours** (☎645 5874), across the street from the supermarket in Santa Elena, under Morphos, to book a taxi and boat combo or a horseback ride to Fortuna. Group and student rates. Open 8am-8pm daily.

Bank: Banco Nacional, northwest of the bus stop, changes traveler's checks and US dollars and gives cash advances on Visa. ATM only accepts local cards. Open M-F 8:30am-3:45pm.

Supermarket: Supermercado La Esperanza, on the corner at the south end of the road from Banco Nacional. Well-stocked with food, bakery goods, and toiletries. Open M-Sa 6am-8pm, Su 6am-2pm.

Bookstore: Librería Chunches (☎645 5147), half a block southwest from Banco Nacional. US newspapers and magazines, new and used books and music, local information, and coffee. Open M-Sa 8am-6pm.

Laundry: Available at **Librería Chunches,** see above. ¢1700 per load.

Emergency: Red Cross (☎128 or 645 6128).

Police: (☎645 5127; emergency ☎117), at the south end of the road from Banco Nacional. Open 24hr.

Pharmacy: Vitosi (☎645 5004), next to the police station. Open M-Sa 8am-7:30pm, Su 9am-1pm.

Medical Services: Clínica Monteverde (☎645 5076), 50m west and 150m south of the sports field (north of the center). Open M-F 7am-4pm, Sa-Su 7am-7pm.

Telephones: A block south of Banco Nacional in front of the church, and outside Supermercado La Esperanza. Closer to Monteverde, next to La Pizzería Johnny, outside the grocery store next to CASEM (see **Other Sights and Activities,** below), as well as in the Visitors Center at the reserve.

Internet Access: Available at **Desafío Tours** (☎645 5874), across the street from the supermarket in Santa Elena, under Morphos. US$2.50 per hr.

Post office: Up the first hill on the way to Monteverde, beyond the Serpentarium. **Fax** available. Open M-F 8am-noon and 1-4:30pm, Sa 7:30am-noon.

Postal code: 5655.

█ ACCOMMODATIONS

Basic lodging is available at the Monteverde Reserve and, with more planning, at the Bosque Eterno de los Niños. Expensive and moderate hotels line the road to the Monteverde reserve; most budget places are in or near Santa Elena.

SANTA ELENA

▓ **Pensión Santa Elena** (☎645 5051). Bright rooms, a friendly staff, and a porch teeming with backpackers. Communal kitchen, hot water, Internet, and informative signs plastering the walls. Dorms US$5 per person; singles with private bath US$12; doubles with private bath US$15. ❶

▓ **Cabinas Tina's Casitas** (☎645 6321). Southwest of town, set back from the road, on the water. Bungalow-style, clean and spacious rooms have beds made of branches. Laundry available. US$7 per person, with bath US$10. High season US$10/US$20. ❶

Pensión el Tucán (☎645 5017). The warmest, coziest, and most comfortable beds in budget Monteverde. Rooms and hot-water baths are small but spotless. Breakfast 5:30-9am, dinner 6-9pm. US$5 per person, with private bath US$10. No credit cards. ❶

Pensión Colibrí (☎645 5682), down the hill from Banco Nacional and behind Pensión Santa Elena. Warm and colorful rooms and an open-air sitting area with flowers climbing the porch railing. Breakfast ¢750, dinner ¢1000. Rooms ¢2000 per person, with private bath ¢3900. No credit cards. ❶

Hotel el Sueño (☎/fax 645 5021), down the hill from the pharmacy on the opposite side of the street. The outside is unappealing but rooms are clean and beds soft. Internet US$4 per hr. Breakfast US$3. Rooms US$7 per person, with bath US$10. ❶

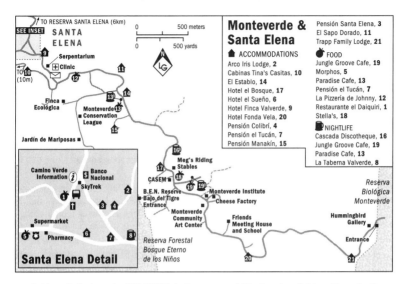

Monteverde & Santa Elena

🏠 ACCOMMODATIONS
Arco Iris Lodge, **2**
Cabinas Tina's Casitas, **10**
El Establo, **14**
Hotel el Bosque, **17**
Hotel el Sueño, **6**
Hotel Finca Valverde, **9**
Hotel Fonda Vela, **20**
Pensión Colibrí, **4**
Pensión el Tucán, **7**
Pensión Manakín, **15**

Pensión Santa Elena, **3**
El Sapo Dorado, **11**
Trapp Family Lodge, **21**

🍴 FOOD
Jungle Groove Cafe, **19**
Morphos, **5**
Paradise Cafe, **13**
Pensión el Tucán, **7**
La Pizzería de Johnny, **12**
Restaurante el Daiquirí, **1**
Stella's, **18**

🌙 NIGHTLIFE
Cascada Discotheque, **16**
Jungle Groove Cafe, **19**
Paradise Cafe, **13**
La Taberna Valverde, **8**

Cabinas Sol y Luna (☎ 645 5629), in the same neighborhood as Cabinas Tinas Casitas. Seven rooms of good value facing the outskirts of Santa Elena. Matrimonial beds with tiled private baths, hot water, and a small porch US$10 per person. ❶

Hotel Finca Valverde (☎ 645 5157; fincaval@racsa.co.cr), just down the road from Santa Elena's center. Bouncing bridge over a river, views of the coffee plantation behind the hotel, a restaurant, and large, comfortable rooms. Some have lofts and are arranged cabin-style, making this a good family option. Singles US$35, high season US$46; doubles US$52/US$64; triples US$64/US$75. ❹

Arco Iris Lodge (☎ 645 5067; fax 645 5022; arcoiris@racsa.co.cr; www.arcoiris-lodge.com). The high end of Santa Elena lodging, removed up the hill past Pensión Colibrí. Gorgeous wood cabins. Breakfast buffet US$6.50. Singles US$35-40; doubles US$45-50; triples US$55-60. Budget bunk room US$15, high season US$20. Family cabin for 4 US$75. AmEx/MC/V. ❹

MONTEVERDE

🖼 **Pensión Manakín** (☎ 645 5080; fax 645 5517; www.monteverdeforever.com; manakin@racsa.co.cr), about 1.5km from Santa Elena toward the Monteverde Reserve. Inviting lounge with TV and VCR and chess tables. Comfortable rooms in various sizes face the forest, where white-faced monkeys wait for bananas from the owner. Veggie meals, horse tours, and Internet. Meals US$5. Rooms US$10 per person, US$15 with private bath; prices vary by season. Cabin with kitchen and refrigerator US$50 per person; long-term rental available. V. ❶

🖼 **Hotel el Bosque** (☎ 645 5158 or 645 5221; fax 645 5129; elbosque@sol.racsa.co.cr), across from Stella's (see **Food,** below) and next to CASEM (see **Other Sights and Activities,** below). Pleasant and private rooms, all with private bath and some with fridge and TV for the same price. Spread out over a large property that strikes a natural balance between garden and forest. Also on-site: two 2km trails and an Italian restaurant. Friendly and unobtrusive family owners. Doubles US$20, high season US$32; triples US$32/US$37. ❷

El Sapo Dorado (☎ 645 5010; fax 645 5180; sapo@cool.co.cr; www.sapodorado.com). These "mountain suites" are the only ones around with fireplaces. Cabins of rich, dark wood with inviting chairs, big unscreened windows, and a luxurious ambiance of isolation. Romantic restaurant with vegetarian options open to public. Three levels of accommodation: "classic" doubles US$74, high season US$89; "sunset terrace" doubles (with gulf-view terrace and minifridge) and "fountain" doubles (two rooms) US$84/US$99. US$17-19 per additional person. ❺

El Establo (☎ 645 5033; establo@racsa.co.cr; www.hotelestablo.com), across from the turn-off to the butterfly farm on the road to Monteverde. Feels like a ski lodge, with long stone-paved hallways, couches gathered around fireplaces, and communal TV rooms. High-occupancy rooms have a king, a queen, and a twin bed plus loft. Junior suites up the hill have views and separated showers and bathtubs. Pool and restaurant. Singles US$30-70; doubles US$50-90; triples US$90. AmEx/MC/V. ❹

Trapp Family Lodge (☎ 645 5858; trappfam@sol.racsa.co.cr). The closest to the Monteverde Cloud Forest Reserve, and it feels that way. Tall ceilings, huge windows, and a feeling of spaciousness complementing the vastness of the surrounding nature. Big rooms with sofa chairs facing the forest. Hot-water private baths. Restaurant and bar open until 9 or 10pm. Singles US$55; doubles US$65; triples US$75. AmEx/MC/V. ❹

Hotel Fonda Vela (☎ 645 5125 or 645 5114; fax 645 5119; info@fondavela.com; www.fondavela.com). A guest's written comment "love the statues, restaurant, and foggy vibe" minimizes the opulence of this hotel. 5 buildings of rooms with fancy lamps, phones, and stained-wood bars, some with TV and lofts, sprawl across grassy landscaping and forest trails. The view varies, but the level of comfort does not. 2 restaurants. Standard doubles US$85; junior suites with king, queen, or sofa bed US$94 for 2 people; US$9 per extra person. ❺

FOOD

SANTA ELENA

▨ **Pensión el Tucán** has a restaurant as peaceful as the hotel itself. Simple dishes. Pancakes US$5, hearty *casados* US$5, veggie plate US$5. ❷

▨ **Morphos,** across the street from the supermarket in Santa Elena, offers sub-style sandwiches (¢800-1450) and fresh dinners with hearty vegetables and potatoes (daily special including wine or beer ¢1800-2500) in a candlelit, funky-butterfly interior. Open daily 11:30am-9:30pm. V. ❷

Restaurante el Daiquiri, on the main Street of Santa Elena, has prices on the high side. Inattentive service, but very good food. Sea bass in mushroom or hearts-of-palm sauce ¢2500, *casados* ¢1500. Open 11am-9:30pm. AmEx/MC/V. ❸

MONTEVERDE

▨ **Jungle Groove Cafe** (☎ 645 6270), down the turn-off next to Stella's. Even if you visit during an off-hour, you'll catch the casual vibe. (See **Nightlife,** below). Garlic calamari stuffed with cassava ¢2800; drinks ¢800-1000. Open for food noon-10pm. Reserve 2hr. ahead for groups of more than 5. ❸

Paradise Cafe (☎ 645 6081) is a haven for vegetarians and a rainbow of local performers, who stun guests with "dinner theater" W and Su nights. (See **Nightlife,** below.) Spicy potato wedges ¢600, veggie burger ¢1800, homemade granola with yogurt ¢1250. Open daily 7am-8pm. ❸

Stella's (☎ 645 5560), 3.25km from Santa Elena on the road to Monteverde, is a slice of heaven. Freshly baked pies (blackberry ¢757). Colorful, organic salads (¢1146) and sandwiches (¢450-875) in an art-filled eatery. The paintings are Stella's own, and you may see some of the portrait subjects around. Open daily 6am-6pm. V.

La Pizzería de Johnny (☎ 645 5066), a landmark on the Monteverde road close to Santa Elena, serves flavorful wood-fired pizza and other Italian dishes. Try the delicious "Monteverde" pizza. Small US$5; medium US$11; large US$19. Pasta US$5. Reserve ahead. Open 11:30am-9:30pm. V. ❷

NIGHTLIFE

La Taberna Valverde (☎ 645 5883), 300m from Banco Nacional on the road to the Reserve, has a bar and a dance floor hopping seven nights a week, with good and not-so-good dancers, locals and tourists, and a similar range of music, from danceable *salsa* to what-the-hell?! Open daily 11am-1am.

Cascada Discotheque, a big disco with a waterfall in its parking lot, 2km from Santa Elena toward the Reserve, spouts danceable Latin and pop music. Often hosts live bands. Cover ¢2000 on some nights. Open Tu-Sa 8pm-2am, Su 8pm-midnight.

Jungle Groove Cafe (☎ 645 6270), is down the turn-off next to Stella's in Monteverde. Huge social tables surround an elevated catwalk-style stage, where the Cuban dueña sings Latin to Sadé in live-music jams with the locals, then serves creative drinks at the bar. There's also fire dancing. Open for fun until midnight Tu-Su; live music F 7:30pm.

Paradise Cafe (☎ 645 6081) hosts "dinner theater" W and Su nights. Performances include breathy yogic dancing and an amazing fire juggler, set to abstract, rhythmic music played on instruments such as jaw-harps, rain sticks, and even a didgeridoo.

THE RESERVES

RESERVA BIOLÓGICA MONTEVERDE

*The reserve is 6km uphill from Santa Elena. Walk, take a taxi, or take a public bus that leaves Santa Elena at 6:25am and 1:15pm and returns from the reserve at 1:15pm and 4pm (45min., M-Sa). Visitors Center ☎ 645 5122, or 645 5112 for guided tours only; fax 645 5034; www.cct.or.cr. Open daily 7am-4pm. US$12, with student ID or under 12 US$6, children under 10 free. The center provides general info, maps, and binoculars. 3hr. **guided tours** daily 7:30am (with slideshow), 8am, and 1pm (US$15 per person); proceeds benefit an environmental education program geared towards rural schools and communities. Call the night before. Night hikes 7:15 and 9:30pm (US$13; no reservations required). Some local hotels arrange private tours. To spend the night, the Visitors Center has **dorms** with bunks, communal showers, and three meals (US$26). Inside the reserve are 3 **shelters** with cooking areas, water, and showers. Reserve in advance. Bring sleeping bag and food. US$3.50-5 per night.*

Positioned on the continental divide and extending down both the Caribbean and Pacific slopes, this enthralling private reserve encompasses 10,500 hectares and houses 2500 species of plants, more than 600 species of animals, and thousands of species of insects. Although Monteverde's wildlife includes jaguars, mountain lions, and peccaries, the most commonly seen animals include *pizotes*, white-faced monkeys, and howler monkeys. Birds include the emerald toucanette, the bananaquit, and the elusive quetzal. It can be hard to see animals in the dense cloud forest, so visitors who expect too much are sometimes disappointed. However, guides' trained eyes and ears will help enhance the experience by interpreting your exotic surroundings. You can also explore marked **trails** on your own—highlights include **La Ventana lookout** and a long **suspension bridge.**

N.W. COSTA RICA

RESERVA SANTA ELENA

Reserva Santa Elena is 5km northeast of Santa Elena village. Walk on the road north from Banco Nacional, take a taxi (¢2500 one-way) or catch the reserve's minibus in front of Banco Nacional. (6:45, 11am, 2pm; ¢700. Return 10:30am, noon, 3pm; ¢500). Make reservations for buses after 6:45am. (☎ 645 5390; rbnctpse@racsa.co.cr.) US$8; with student ID or age 10-12 US$4.50; children under 10 free. Open daily 7am-4pm. Guided tours available. Day tour, 7:30 and 11:30am, US$15 per person not including entrance fee; night tour, 6:30pm, US$15 per person including entrance fee. The reserve information center in town is 200m north of the bank and there is a also a Visitors Center at the entrance.

The Monteverde cloud forest is amazing, but don't overlook the Santa Elena Reserve, established in 1992 to relieve the burden of excessive tourism from Monteverde. Home to the same flora and fauna, this impressive alternative gives its proceeds to the town's high school. The peaks within the reserve are the highest in the area (some over 1700m). There are four principal **trails,** all short enough (1-5km) to be done as day hikes. From some lookouts you can see Volcán Arenal, 19km away. **Guided tours** can be arranged a day in advance.

RESERVA FORESTAL BOSQUE ETERNO DE LOS NIÑOS

Contact Monteverde Conservation League ☎ 645 5003; fax 645 5104; acm-mcl@sol.racsa.co.cr. The Bajo del Tigre entrance is open daily 8am-5pm. US$5, students US$2. Lodging US$20 per person, US$40 with meals. Student and group discounts.

Under-appreciated Bosque Eterno de los Niños is the nation's largest private reserve. The "Children's Eternal Rain Forest" is named for Swedish school children who contributed to the Monteverde Conservation League for land preservation. The lower-elevation Bosque Eterno covers 22,000 hectares, twice that of Monteverde Reserve, and less foliage makes for better bird watching and views. The **Bajo del Tigre** entrance is just 3.5km southeast of Santa Elena along the road to Monteverde and offers short 4km hikes through premontane forest. The Visitors Center is very welcoming of children, and one of the **trails** is designed for them. Farther away, two **field stations, San Gerardo** and **Poco Sol,** have accommodations available. (Arrange with the League two weeks in advance.)

👁 🎒 OTHER SIGHTS AND ACTIVITIES

FINCA ECOLÓGICA DE MONTEVERDE. The banana and coffee plantations that used to operate here are now private reserve land. Loop trails pass the old plantations as well as lookouts and two cascading waterfalls, and can be hiked in anywhere from 30min.-3hr. Animals you may see in the premontane forest include agoutis, coatimundis, sloths, monkeys, and many birds. Printed guides are available at the Visitors Center. *(The well-marked turn-off from the Monteverde road is between Pizzeria Johnny and Paradise Café, almost 1km from Santa Elena. ☎ 645 5554; fax 645 5363; fincaecologica@racsa.co.cr. Open daily 7am-5pm. US$7, US$5 with student ID and for Costa Rican nationals, US$3 for children ages 6-12. Guides recommended. Call a day ahead. Guides US$15 for 2½hr tour. Night tour 5:30-7:30pm US$14 including entrance fee; arrive around 5pm. Night tour frequently features porcupines, sloths, and kinkajous.)*

JARDÍN DE MARIPOSAS (BUTTERFLY GARDEN). This biodiversity center focuses on the study of all sorts of insects, from the elegant to the nasty, not just the popular butterflies. Young and energetic volunteer guides give a 1hr. tour of the four separate butterfly habitats, which recreate the conditions of three different elevations and the forest understory. Hand-raised insects on-site include a colony of leaf-cutter ants, a variety of beetles, walking sticks, and tarantulas. Special cameras zoom in on their fascinating activities. *(Turn off the Monteverde road about 1km from Santa Elena; signs will direct you. ☎ 645 5512; www.best.com/~mariposa. Open daily 9:30am-4pm. ¢2500, with student ID ¢2000, children ¢1000. Call about volunteer opportunities. Guided tours included in entrance fee.)*

CANOPY TOURS. Three firms offer zip-lines that speed from platform to platform high above the forest canopy. The original, **Canopy Tour,** based at the Cloud Forest Lodge 7km northeast of Santa Elena, has 8 lines and 2 repelling systems. Their Santa Elena office is across from the supermarket. **Sky Trek,** across from the Banco Nacional in Santa Elena, offers a similar 2½-3hr. of zipping ecstasy along 11 longer lines, and also a tamer **Sky Walk,** a stroll along five suspension bridges in the Santa Elena Reserve. **Selvatur,** formerly known as Monteverde Canopy, is located across from the bus stop. *(Canopy Tour: ☎645 5243; www.canopytour.com. Office open daily 6am-8pm. 2-2½hr. US$45, students US$35, children US$25. Prices include transport. Reservations required. Sky Trek: ☎645 5238; info@skywalk.co.cr. Office open daily 6am-9pm. US$35, students US$28, children US$24. Transportation US$1 each way. Reservations required. Selvatur: ☎645 5929. US$35, students US$30, children US$25.)*

SERPENTARIUM. This is a recently expanded showcase of the snakes, frogs, iguanas, and turtles of the Monteverde area. But beware—11 of the 17 venomous snakes of Costa Rica are here. *(Just outside of the village on the road to Monteverde. ☎645 6002 or 6003. Open daily 9am-5pm. US$7, students US$5, children under 7 free.)*

RANARIO (THE FROG POND). Twenty-six species of frogs are on display in terrariums here; a tour guide will help spot postcard-famous amphibians like the gauche leaf frog and the poison dart frog on a 45min. tour included with the entrance fee. *(Near the Monteverde Lodge, on the road south of the southern edge of the Santa Elena "triangle." ☎645 6318; ranariomv@racsa.co.cr. Open daily 9am-8:30pm. US$8, with student ID US$5.)*

HUMMINGBIRD GALLERY. The patio hosts hundreds of hummingbirds; the species present depend on the season. Nature photos by renowned Michael and Patrice Fogden are on display in the attached art gallery, and watercolors by Sarah Dowell are on sale. *(Just before the entrance to the Monteverde Reserve. ☎645 5030. Open daily 8:30am-4:30pm. Slide shows on the natural history of the reserve. Entrance US$3.)*

HORSEBACK RIDING. There are many opportunities for horseback riding in the area. **Meg's Stables,** 2.5km from Santa Elena, next to Stella's (Stella is Meg's mom), offers 2hr. rides (US$23) and a 5hr. ride to an 80 ft. waterfall (US$45). *(☎645 5560 or 645 5419; night 645 5052. Call ahead for reservations.)*

CASA DE ARTESANOS. Founded in 1982 to provide economic opportunities for women in the area, Casa de Artesanos de Santa Elena de Monteverde **(CASEM)** now has 92 artisans selling their handmade crafts. *(3.25km from Santa Elena on the road to Monteverde. ☎645 5190. Open M-Sa 8am-5pm.)*

MONTEVERDE COMMUNITY ART CENTER. The studio offers week-long classes with local artists specializing in crafts ranging from stained glass to creative storytelling. Reservations for workshops must be made in advance. *(Across the road and over the bridge from the cheese factory. ☎645 6121. Shop open daily 9am-5pm. Classes US$235 per week, US$30-40 per day.)*

CHEESE FACTORY. The most stable business in the Monteverde community was started by Quakers (once they got the cows up the hill) as a logical way to make their milk productive—plain milk turned sour before reaching the bottom of the mountain, but not cheese! Watch the production process through an observation window as you enjoy delicious ice cream and milkshakes, sold in the store along with 16 kinds of cheese. *(Southeast along the road, about 500m from Stella's. www.monteverde.net. Open M-Sa 7:30am-5pm, Su 7:30am-12:30pm. Milkshakes ¢1500.)*

MONTEVERDE FRIENDS MEETING HOUSE AND SCHOOL. The friends welcome visitors to their biweekly meeting (Su 10:30am, W 9am) in a warm, wooden room with pews in a circle, as per Quaker tradition. The meetings tend to be quiet, but if anyone has a message to share with the group, he or she will. In the same complex is a K-12 school and community library. Email mfschool@racsa.co.cr if you're interested in **teaching.** Classes are in English with Spanish at every level; bilingual teachers preferred. Basic tenets of Quaker philosophy—pacifism, respect for nature—are incorporated into the curriculum. *(A little less than 1km southeast along the road from Stella's Bakery, past the cheese factory.)*

CAÑAS

Sweltering Cañas sits on the Interamerican Hwy. amid dusty Guanacaste farmland. It can be a transportation hub, particularly for those traveling between the Pacific coast and Volcán Arenal. The town is dull, but some use it as a base for Parque Nacional Palo Verde, 30km to the west, or for trips on the Río Corobicí.

▉ TRANSPORTATION

The bus station is five blocks north of the *parque*'s northwest corner behind the *mercado municipal*, a couple of blocks east of the Interamerican Hwy. **Buses** go to: **Abangares** (9:20am and 2:20pm); **Bebedero** (11am, 1, 3pm); **El Hotel** (5am, noon, 4pm); **Liberia** (1½hr., 12 per day 5:40am-5pm, ¢465); **Puntarenas** (2hr., 8 per day 6am-4:30pm, ¢450); **Tilarán** (45min., 7 per day 6am-5:30pm, ¢185); and **Upala** (6 per day 6am-5pm). Many buses between San José and Liberia (3hr., about every 30min., ¢1200) pass by on the Interamerican but do not stop at the station; to flag them down, head to a stop 200m west of the *parque*'s southeast corner.

▉ PRACTICAL INFORMATION

The **Banco Nacional** with **ATM** is on the northwest corner of the *parque*. (Open M-F 8:30am-3:45pm.) For basic groceries, try **Palí Supermarket,** two blocks north of the northwest corner of the *parque*. (Open M-Sa 8am-7pm, Su 8am-6pm.) The **police station** is north of the *parque* on the west side of the Interamerican. (☎ 669 0057, emergency 116.) In case you need any medicines, **Farmacia Cañas** lies 1½ blocks east of Banco Nacional. (☎ 669 0748. Open M-Sa 7:30am-9pm, Su 8am-noon.) You can receive medical care at **Dr. Juan Acón Chen's clinics,** one block north and one block west of the *parque*'s northwest corner. (☎ 669 0139, emergency ☎ 669 0471. Open M-F 8am-noon and 2-6pm, Sa 8am-noon.) There is also the public **Clínica de Cañas,** two blocks west of the *parque*. (☎ 669 0092.) Try **Ciberc@ñas** for **Internet** access, one block north and half a block east of the church's northeast corner. (1½hr. ¢250. Open M-Sa 8am-9pm, Su 2pm-9pm.) The **post office** is one block north and two blocks west of the *parque*, and has **fax** and **Internet.** (Open M-F 8am-noon and 1-5:30pm.)

▉ ▉ ACCOMMODATIONS AND FOOD

Hotel El Parque ❶, on the south side of the *parque*, has somewhat dingy cream-colored rooms, communal baths, and a breezy porch overlooking the *parque*. (☎ 669 2213.¢1300 per person. No credit cards.) **Cabinas Corobicí ❶,** is a good choice, three blocks east and two blocks south of the *parque*'s southeast corner—the rooms are cleaner and more spacious and have TVs and closet-like private baths. (☎ 669 0241. Singles ¢3500; doubles ¢7000; triples ¢10,500.) **Hotel Central ❶,** next door, is adequate but dark. (☎ 669 1101. Doubles with communal bath ¢2500, with private bath ¢3500. No credit cards.) **Nuevo Hotel Cañas ❸,** one block north and 1½ west of the *parque*'s northwest corner, is more expensive, but worth it if you put a premium on hot water. The hotel also has a pool, A/C, cable TV and private baths in every room.

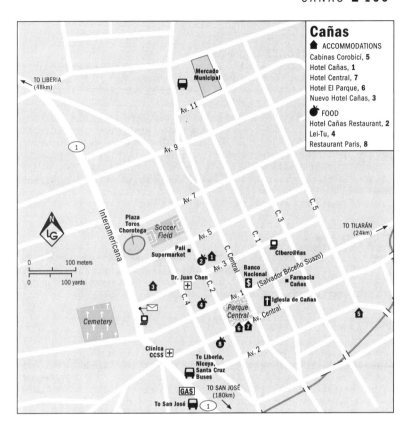

Cañas

🏠 ACCOMMODATIONS
Cabinas Corobicí, **5**
Hotel Cañas, **1**
Hotel Central, **7**
Hotel El Parque, **6**
Nuevo Hotel Cañas, **3**

🍴 FOOD
Hotel Cañas Restaurant, **2**
Lei-Tu, **4**
Restaurant Paris, **8**

(☎ 669 1294 or 669 5511. Singles US$26.40; doubles US$42; triples US$54.70. AmEx/MC/V.) **Hotel Cañas ❷,** one block north of the *parque's* northwest corner, is notable for its bright white rooms with frame beds and the option of A/C and cable TV. (☎ 669 5118. Doubles ¢7650, with cable and A/C ¢11,200.)

Hotel Cañas Restaurant ❷, which is part of Hotel Cañas, is by far the best in town. They brag of firewood cooking, the food is simple and fresh, and the interior is cool and classy. (Fish fajitas ¢2350; *casado* with chicken filet ¢1700. Open M-Sa 6am-10pm, Su 7am-2:30pm.) **Restaurant Paris ❷,** half a block west of the southwest corner of the *parque,* serves unremarkable Chinese food. (Open daily 10am-midnight.) **Lei-Tu ❷,** half a block west of the northwest corner of the *parque,* also serves Chinese food. (Open 10am-midnight.)

🔺 OUTDOOR ACTIVITIES

Safaris Corobicí, 4.5km north of Cañas on the Interamerican, runs class I and II **float trips** on the Río Corobicí. (☎/fax 669 6091; safaris@racsa.co.cr. 2hr. trips US$37 per person, 3hr. trips US$45, half-day trips with lunch included US$60. 2 person minimum. Rafts handicapped-equipped.)

N.W. COSTA RICA

NEAR CAÑAS

CENTRO DE RESCATE LAS PUMAS

Four and a half kilometers north of Cañas off the Interamerican. Buses running from Cañas to Bugaces and Liberia will drop you at the entrance if you ask the driver. Call ahead to arrange for a guided tour. ☎ 669 6044; fax 669 6091; safaris@sol.racsa.co.cr. Open daily 8am-4pm.

The residents of this modest shelter include white-tailed deer, parrots, parakeets and macaws, and stunning, sleepy ocelots, pumas, jaguars, and other wild cats. Lily Haghauer founded it in the 1960s to care for Guancastecan wildlife in danger, whether the animals had been poached for the pet trade or displaced by deforestation. Many are released into the wild when ready. Nowhere else gives you the chance to see these species up close. Today, MINAE and individuals brings in animals and drop them off; the center depends on visitor donations to keep them healthy. There is a souvenir shop at the entrance.

TILARÁN

About the only travelers who don't breeze in and right out of this gusty little town are windsurfers setting sail on **Laguna de Arenal,** 5km away. For everyone else, Tilarán's wide streets and reviving, fresh climate make it a convenient stopover when traveling from Fortuna to the Pacific coast.

⬛ TRANSPORTATION

The church is east of the *parque* and windmills sit on hills north of town. **Buses** leave half a block west from the *parque's* northwest corner (terminal ☎ 695 5611 for San José buses) to: **San José** (4hr., 5 per day 5am-4:55pm, ¢1200); **Puntarenas** (2½hr., 6am and 1pm, ¢700); **Monteverde** (3hr., 1 per day 12:30pm, ¢800); **Ciudad Quesada/San Carlos** (4½hr., 7am and 12:30pm, ¢700) via **Fortuna** and **Arenal; Guatuso** (3½hr., 1 per day noon, ¢500); **Arenal** (1½hr., 5 per day 5am-4:30pm, ¢280); and **Cañas** (1hr., 8 per day 5am-5pm, ¢200). Buses go from Cañas to **Liberia** all day. **Taxis** (☎ 696 5324) line the west side of the *parque* by the phones.

🛈 PRACTICAL INFORMATION

Tourist Office: For **tourist information** in English, visit **La Carreta** hotel and restaurant (see **Accommodations** below).

Bank: Banco Nacional lies across from the southwest corner of the *parque.* Open M-F 8:30am-3:45pm.

Police: (☎ 695 5001), half a block west of the bus station. Open 24hr.

Red Cross: (☎ 695 5256), 100m east of the *parque's* northeast corner.

Hospital: (☎ 695 5093), 200m west of the *parque's* southwest corner.

Internet Access: Cafe Internet lies diagonally across from the bus terminal. ¢800 per hr. Open M-F 9am-11pm, Sa-Su 10am-10pm.

Post office: One block north and 1½ blocks east of the *parque's* northeast corner. Open M-F 8am-noon and 1-5:30pm.

ACCOMMODATIONS

Hotel Mary (☎/fax 695 5479), on the south side of the *parque*, is homey and spacious with private bath, TV, and clean, wall-to-wall carpeting. The restaurant downstairs is recommended over other hotel restaurants and is reasonably priced. Singles ¢2000; singles and doubles with bath ¢3500. ❷

Cabinas El Sueño (☎695 5347), sits half a block north of the *parque*'s northwest corner. Luxurious rooms surround a sky-lit courtyard complete with mock-Egyptian fountain and garden, and guests can enjoy free self-service coffee on the broad balcony. The cheaper rooms with shared bath are considerably less comfortable but still decent. Singles US$8, with bath US$15; doubles US$15, with private bath and TV US$25. ❷

Hotel Naralit (☎695 5393), on the south side of the church, has 26 well-kept rooms with private baths, miniature tables, and cable TV, plus a tiled patio for a higher price. Singles ¢5000-8000; doubles ¢7000-8000; triples ¢10000. V. ❶

La Carreta (☎695 6593; fax 695 6654; pppiedra_z@yahoo.com), behind the church, is a very convenient all-in-one souvenir shop, hotel, and restaurant. However, bear in mind that convenience has it's price. Cable TV, private baths, skylights, and high ceiling fans in nice comfortable rooms that feel brand new. Singles US$35; doubles US$45; 2 matrimonial beds US$60. Prices almost 50% lower in low season. MC/V. ❹

Hotel Tilawa (☎695 5050; www.hoteltilawa.com), 10km north of Tilarán, is isolated and has spacious standard rooms with two queen beds looking out on Laguna Arenal. The hotel's architecture is grand, with imitation ancient murals, huge windows, and Etruscan-style columns framing the scenery. Trails, tennis courts, a pool, mountain bikes (US$25 per day), kayaks (US$15 per day), and horses (US$20 for a 2hr. tour) are available, along with a restaurant (meals US$5-10), a skateboarding bowl with a vertical wall (skateboards US$10 per day), and a windsurfing center. Singles US$48; doubles US$58; triples US$65; rooms US$10 higher in high season. ❹

FOOD

El Nilo, 100m north and 100m east of the *parque*, is a cheerful *soda* with a comfortable sofa chair, magazines, and TV. *Platos típicos* with *refresco* ¢1200. Open 7am-9pm. ❷

La Carreta, behind the church, has an extensive Italian and American menu that includes typical *tico* options under new management. Pizza ¢1400 small, ¢1950 large. Open daily 7am-10pm. ❷

Restaurante Nueva Fortuna (☎695 5069), 50m north of the northwest corner of the *parque*, across from Cabinas El Sueño, stirs up popular Chinese food. Entrees ¢1500-2900. Open daily 11am-11:30pm. ❷

OUTDOOR ACTIVITIES

Laguna de Arenal, a man-made lake 29km long, is one of the world's premier **windsurfing** spots, especially from December to May. April is the best month. The **Hotel Tilawa**, 10km north of Tilarán, rents boards and offers classes. (☎695 5050. Boards US$35 half day, US$45 full day. Classes US$55 for 3-4hr.) The windsurfing center is on the lake shore and does not take reservations for non-guests; call or drop by daily from 7am-5pm (☎695 5710). In town, **Tour Varela**, in a garage one block north and half a block west of the *parque's* northeast corner, offers **water skiing, fishing,** and a **boat tour** up to Volcán Arenal. (☎695 5292. Skiing ¢7000 per hr. Fishing 4hr., US$150. Boat tour $150.)

N.W. COSTA RICA

VOLCÁN TENORIO

Although this area was decreed a National Park in 1995, as part of the *Cordillera de Guancaste*, the infrastructure to make this grand volcano accessible to tourists and biologists was not developed until 1997. Tenorio, rising up to 1916m and extending 12 sq. km, is now being infiltrated due to the development of the nearby small town of **Bijagua,** which offers the easiest access to the volcano and has two beautiful mountain hotels. MINAE has been working hard at its new post in **Río Naranjo** and at **El Pilón,** researching the local flora and fauna of the volcano. Bridges through the cloud forest, hot and cold springs, craters, the impressive sapphire-blue **Río Celeste,** and its majestic waterfall are only some of the great sights to explore in this area. There is a 3.2km nature trail called *Misteriosos del Tenorio.*

⌐ TRANSPORTATION

The best way to get to Volcán Tenorio is to take the **bus** from **Upala** to **Bijagua.** (☎ 669 0216. 45min., 7 per day, ¢300.) If you are coming from San José, take the bus heading toward Upala through **Cañas,** from which Bijagua is a 15km ride by 4WD, motorcycle, or taxi up an unpaved road. Follow the road until you reach the *Pilón* or *Casona* of **San Miguel,** from which it is an 8- 9hr. hike up to the new crater. It is best to coordinate a ride in advance with **Albergue Heliconia** (see **Accommodations,** below) for ¢1500. Otherwise, you can seek the local *taxista* **Upaloco,** who will take you up to the *Pilón* (¢3000). The less popular entrance to Tenorio is the city of **La Paz,** where farm owner **Pedro Elbarado** can guide you to the *fumaroles.*

⚡ PRACTICAL INFORMATION

There is a small **Banco Nacional** 10m north of the pizzeria on the main road, at the corner of the unpaved street heading to Albergue Helconia. (☎ 466 8555. Open M-F 8am-noon and 1-4pm.) There are two **supermarkets** in Bijagua so you can stack up on snacks and water before your adventures. **Super Express Paika** is in front of Bar Tropical (☎ 466 8011; open M-Sa 7am-8pm, Su 7am-noon), and the **Centro Commerical El Pueblo** is next door (☎ 466 8021; open M-Sa 7am-8pm, Su 7:30-11:30am). For **medical assistance,** direct yourself to the **MINAE office** in Río Naranjo, 5km south of Bijagua, where the manager Julio Quiros will attend you. His new office has a small documentation center with may interesting books on the biodiversity and conservation of the region. The closest **hospital** is in Upala. Three **public phones** are at your service along the main street. **Internet** is available at Albergue Heliconia Nature Lodge (see **Accommodations,** below).

♦ ACCOMMODATIONS

There are two *cabinas* in the mountains of Bijagua. **Cabinas Samora ❶** offers two spacious, family-style rooms, which can sleep up to five people. (☎ 466 8826. ¢3500 per room.) **Cabinas Bijagua ❶,** on the main road in front of Distribuidora Bijagua, has five clean rooms with private baths (¢1500 per person).

The two hotels, which offer tours to the spectacle of Volcán Tenorio's nature are at a much higher altitude and hide deep in the mountain. **Albergue Heliconia Nature Lodge ❸** is the closest of the two to Bijagua, and offers six beautiful, rustic lodge-type rooms with bunkbeds for four people. (Breakfast included. **Internet** available. Singles US$25; doubles US$38; triples US$45.) The other upscale option for mountain lodging is **Carolina Lodge ❸,** 10km up a windy dirt road on the right, going 3km from Bijagua towards Upala in **Areno.** This simple, rustic, Costa Rican resort has great food, a few luxuries, and is perfect for the nature-lovers. The affordable

US$45 lodge package includes a guided horseback ride or tours to Caño Negro in addition to a one-night stay and one of three meals. Further options include: swimming, fishing, and birding. (☎ 380 1656; info@lacarolinalodge.com.)

🎭 🍴 FOOD AND ENTERTAINMENT

The restaurant at **Albergue Heliconia Nature Lodge ❷** has delicious food and incredible views of the Volcán Miravalles, the Guatuso Valley, and the Lago de Nicaragua on clear days. (Meals about US$6.) Apart from the excellent meals available at the hotels, **Pizzería El Barrigón ❸**, across from the Templo Bíblico Fuente de Vida, next to the gas station, is a must, if not for the rich, homemade pizzas, then for the original *artesanías*. (☎ 466 8602. Mexican pizza ¢2100-2600. Open T-Su noon-9pm.) **Bar Tropical,** in front of the *carnicería*, next to cabinas Bijagua, has two pool tables and traditional *bocas* (appetizers) for ¢200. (☎ 466 8144. Open daily noon-midnight.) **Juegos de Video,** in front of Paica Express, offers Playstation games on four TV sets. (☎ 466 8109. ¢300 per hr. Open daily 9am-10pm.)

🏔 OUTDOOR ACTIVITIES

The **Albergue Heliconia Nature Lodge,** founded by the Bijagua Community Association, has a 140 hectare private reserve and **trails** leading to **Laguna Danta** and the numerous **aerial bridges** (1-2 hr., US$10). At the **biological station** run by the Institute of National Biodiversity (INBio) lucky researchers who discover new bug species get the insects named after them. To further enjoy the natural wonders of the area, check out **Carolina Lodge**'s 170 acres of vast farmland, bordered by the Chimurio and Achiste rivers on the eastern slope of Tenorio. Within walking distance to **Río Celeste,** enjoy hot and cool springs and mineral mud baths (2hr. hike).

AROUND VOLCÁN MIRAVALLES

The area around Volcán Miravalles is now better known for the ambitious **Proyecto Geotérmico Miravalles**—a power plant that uses geothermic energy to generate electricity—than for its natural wonders. The eerie, silver alien pipes of the project wind unexpectedly through the landscape. Still, the volcanic activity that surfaces as *hornillas* around the bases of the volcano heats natural **hot springs** and beautifying bubbling mud that attract tourists and local vacationers. There are a couple of relaxing places to stay near Fortuna and Guayabo.

Buses leave Bagaces (p. 160) bound for **Fortuna** (30min.) and **Guayabo** (6 per day 6am-5:30pm). The last returning bus passes Centro Turístico Yokö, 5km from Fortuna and 6km from Guayabo, at 5pm. From Bagaces, the road forks left to Guayabo and right to Fortuna; these converge again before Aguas Claras. The curvy drive from Bagaces to Guayabo yields beautiful views of the gently rolling countryside and the tall volcano.

Centro Turístico Yokö ❷ is between Fortuna and Guayabo (obvious signs start on the Interamericana). Many visitors come at night to enjoy the three modern thermal pools (¢1000 for non-guests). There are seats for the bar in the water, and while this isn't a Tabacón resort, the natural water is just as enjoyable and perhaps of a higher quality. The minimalist design of the pools is classy and simple. Rooms are spacious with TV, phone, fans, and thermal-water showers. (☎ 673 0410. Restaurant, pool, and bar open 7am-10pm. Breakfast included. US$22 per person.) **Miravalles Volcano Lodge ❷,** 1km north of Guayabo on the way to Aguas Claras, is a remote hotel in the shadow of the volcano. It's not badly-kept, and it has short trails up the hills behind it and a comfortable restaurant. Some rooms have bathtubs, and all have A/C and hot water. (☎673 0823. Breakfast included. Doubles US$39; triples US$45.) For cheaper accommodations, **Cabinas Las Brisas ❶**, on the outskirts of Guayabo towards Aguas Claras, has rooms with mirrored ceilings and headboards and a restaurant/bar popular with locals. (☎673 0333. *Pargo rojo y tilapia* ¢1500-2000. Restaurant open daily 10am-2:30am. Rooms ¢3500-4000.)

Following the unpaved road to Thermo-Manía (see below), 3km slightly uphill, you will pass an ICE plant and some *hornillas* 100m off the road across the street from it. Follow your nose to delicious **Bar Restaurante Las Hornillas ❶**, farther up the hill. (☎673 1551. *Casados* ¢1100. Open Tu-Su 8am-10pm.)

Further down the Fortuna road from Centro Turístico Yokö towards Guayabo, you will see signs for **Thermo Manía,** a new water park whose best feature is probably its *aguas termales.* Here the pools are built to look natural, out of sight from the waterslide, Mickey-mouse shaped pool, mini-zoo, man-made fishing tank, and arcade. (US$3 entrance fee includes camping. Open Tu-Su 9am-10pm.)

BAGACES

At a certain heat, small temperature differences don't matter, however you might still want to know that Bagaces is even hotter than Cañas, 22km to the southeast. Nature lovers, however, will put up with this discomfort and the lack of things to do in town in anticipation of the annual rodeo held on Dec. 8th (as in other Guanacaste towns), the numerous fairs on the calendar for mid-July, and the daytrips to nearby Parque Nacional Palo Verde and the Reserva Biológica Lomas Barbudal.

▐ TRANSPORTATION

The bus station is just west of the *parque*, but **buses** heading south to San José (and stopping in Cañas) and north to Liberia pass every 30min. to an hour on the highway by the gas station. From the bus station (☎222 1650), buses go to: **San José** (4hr., 12 per day 5:25-8:30pm, ¢1300); **Liberia** (30min., 9 per day 6am-11:30pm, ¢250); **Puntarenas** (2-2½hr.; 5 per day 10am-3pm); **Fortuna** (not the big one); **Guayabo; Aguas Claras** (6 per day, 6am-4:15pm). **Taxis** also pull up near the bus station.

▐ PRACTICAL INFORMATION

The church is on the park's north side and the bus station on its west. To change money, go to **Banco Nacional** on the park's southwest corner. (Open M-F 8:30am-3:45pm.) The **medical clinic** is across from the gas station on the Interamerican Hwy. (☎671 1400, emergencies 671 1003. Open M-F 7am-10pm, Sa and Su 7am-7pm.) Otherwise, call the **Red Cross** (☎671 1186 or 128). The **police** are one block west and one block north of the gas station (☎671 1173 or 127), and the **post office** is next door. (Open M-F 8am-noon and 1-5:30pm.)

▐ ▐ ACCOMMODATIONS AND FOOD

The best hotel, **Albergue Bagaces ❷**, is on the east side of the gas station. The rooms are spacious with fans, desks, and private baths, and a large and quiet common room is filled with leather couches and chairs. (☎671 1267. Singles ¢4000; matrimonial double ¢6000.) Albergue Bagaces also has a **restaurant ❶** with trustworthy food open 24hr., although it might actually be closed if no one is dropping by. The menu is limited to a few dishes. (*Casados* with chicken or steak ¢700, garlic shrimp ¢3000.) **Restaurant Hambo ❷,** serves delicious Chinese food on the corner two blocks north of the northeast corner of the park. (Fried chicken with lemon and cilantro sauce ¢1500. Open daily 11:30-10:30pm. MC/V.) On the southwest corner of the park is **Soda La Puesta del Sol.** (*Plato del día* with *refresco* ¢950. Open daily 6am-9pm.)

PARQUE NACIONAL PALO VERDE

Parque Nacional Palo Verde is one of Central America's most important wetlands. The bird life is the allure: 278 species are in residence, including jabirus, egrets, ibis, and the only colony of scarlet macaws on the tropical dry Pacific. The park has an array of habitats, including lowland mangroves, riparian forest, and floodplain marsh, and is home to at least 1400 plant and animal species.

AT A GLANCE	
AREA: 20,000 hectares	**GATEWAYS:** Bagaces (p. 160)
CLIMATE: Average temp. 27°C; average rainfall 1500-2000mm per year.	**CAMPING:** Camping permit US$2 per night.
FEATURES: Mirador Guayacán, Isla de Pájaros, Puerto Chamorro, Cerro Pelón.	**FEES AND RESERVATIONS:** Entrance US$6
HIGHLIGHTS: Night tours; boat tours to Isla Pájaros; birding; hiking	

⌨ TRANSPORTATION

The park entrance is 30km southwest of the town of **Bagaces,** off the Interamerican Hwy., where **buses** running between Cañas and Liberia will drop you off. There is no public transportation between Bagaces and the park, but you can get a **taxi** (¢6000 each way). When school is in session (early Feb.-Dec. save the 1st two weeks of July) there is also a **student bus** that runs from Bagaces, outside the medical clinic, to **Bagatzi,** near the park entrance. (M-F 3pm, ¢500; return at 5:15am—you will have to spend the night or call a taxi to return.) The last bus from Bagaces to STET leaves the Bagaces station at 11:30pm, from Bagaces to San José via Cañas at around 8:30pm.

🧭 ORIENTATION

Parque Nacional Palo Verde lies on the northwest corner of the Gulf of Nicoya, about 30km west of Cañas. From the entrance, the main road traverses the park's length. After 6km, a road branches left from the main road, leading 5km down to **La Bocana,** a lake popular with birds, and 9km down to **Catalina,** the first ranger station. From here, a 2.5km trail ascends to lookouts on Cerro Pelón.

Back on the main road, 1km past the fork, a trail leads to **Mirador La Roca.** This 570m trail offers views of much of the park. Four hundred meters farther up sits the **biological station,** an independent research facility run by the renowned **Organization of Tropical Studies (OTS).** Although the biological station is officially for students and researchers, it's possible to negotiate for a bed when space is available. Near OTS, **Laguna Palo Verde** features hundreds of birds and ducks in December, January, and February. **Palo Verde,** the second ranger station, lies 1½km beyond the biological station.

⁊ PRACTICAL INFORMATION

The regional Ministerio del Ambiente y Energía (MINAE) office that oversees Parque Nacional Palo Verde is on the west side of the gas station on the Interamerican Hwy. They have information and can contact park rangers who can guide you inside the park. The park is open daily 6am-6pm. Boat tours: US$20 per person for 2½-3hr. ride. Call **Tempisque Conservation Area** (☎/fax 671 1290) or the **MINAE** office in Bagaces (☎671 1062) in advance. (Open M-F 8am-4pm.)

 WHEN TO GO. The best time is September through March, especially from December to February, when the birds flock together. Keep in mind that the park is most pleasant in the early morning and late afternoon, when the heat is less oppressive, and that the best viewing time for mammals is at dusk (after 5pm). Don't forget to bring comfortable shoes for hiking, light clothes, bug repellent, and an umbrella or light rain jacket (Jun.-Nov.).

⁊ ACCOMMODATIONS AND CAMPING

Six kilometers from the entrance, the road branches left from the main road, leading 9km down to **Catalina, a ranger station** with water and camping facilities. **Puesto Palo Verde,** the second ranger station, lies 1½km beyond the biological station and has potable water and bathrooms. A good place to camp, it is close to many of the park attractions. The station also offers dorm rooms with fans. It will cost more than a dorm room, but there is Internet access and interesting biological equipment. (US$13 per night, US$10 in low season), meals (breakfast US$3, lunch and dinner US$5 each), and horse rental (US$6 per hr.).

◈ HIKING

A 30min. hike from the Palo Verde station leads to **Mirador Guayacán,** the best viewpoint in the park. Crocodiles laze along the banks, and nearby is **La Isla de Pájaros,** the most important breeding ground for water birds in Central America. At the end of the main road, 2km beyond the ranger station, is **Puerto Chamorro,** the park's dock along the banks of Río Tempisque. From the Catalina station, a 2.5km trail ascends to lookouts on **Cerro Pelón.** The park rangers can also arrange a **boat tour** of the park; contact them in advance.

RESERVA BIOLÓGICA LOMAS BARBUDAL

Lomas Barbudal (Bearded Hills) is a 23 sq. km rare, tropical dry forest. It is still springing back from a 1994 fire and is well-know for its bee diversity. There are around 250 species of bees, 60 species of butterflies, and 130 species of birds. Some patches of the Lomas forest along the Río Cabuyo remain green year-round. The most eye-catching of these are the *cortezas amarillas* at the end of the dry season, when they burst into yellow bloom after the first rains. Other rare trees include mahogany and rosewood.

✻ ORIENTATION

The **Reserva Biológica Lomas Barbudal** is 15km southwest of Bagaces. A Visitors Center run by the neighborhood association of San Ramón lies 6km from the community of Pijije on the Interamerican north of Bagaces. Twenty kilometers later, this same road reaches Paloverde, south of Lomas.

AT A GLANCE

AREA: 2279 hectares; 23 sq. km.	**GATEWAYS:** Bagaces (p. 160).
CLIMATE: Tropical dry forest.	**CAMPING:** available for US$2.
FEATURES: La Poza el Eden de Cabuyo.	**FEES:** Entrance fee US$6.
HIGHLIGHTS: Hiking, birding, swimming.	

TRANSPORTATION

Take a **taxi** (¢3000 one-way) to the entrance, 6km off the Interamerican Hwy.; the turnoff is at the small community of Pijije. Many visitors hitch a ride here with drivers headed for San Ramón, although one should always consinder the risk. About 20km south of Lomas Barbudal lies Paloverde. Although the dirt road to get there is in fairly good condition, it may require 4WD in the rainy season.

PRACTICAL INFORMATION

WHEN TO GO. Although Lomas Barbudal is a tropical dry forest, it can be very wet. Hiking can be impossible during the rainy season. In addition, the many dirt roads in this area can become muddy. This makes the park most easily accessible during the dry season. (Dec.-Apr.).

The **Visitors Center,** 6km from the community of Pijije on the Interamerican, north of Bagaces, is open during the dry season and collects very necessary donations to continue running. There are also small exhibits on the wildlife. Although Lomas Barbudal is no longer managed by the government, the regional **Ministerio del Ambiente y Energía (MINAE)** office that oversees Parque Nacional Palo Verde, on the west side of the gas station on the Interamerican Hwy., has information and may put you in touch with **guardaparques** (park rangers) who give tours and can guide you through the park. (☎ 671 1062 or 671 1290 for Tempisque Conservation Area. Open M-F 8am-4pm.)

HIKING

Most visitors never enter the actual reserve, whose northern edge is across the Río Cabuyo from the Visitors Center. (The southern side of Lomas is accessible by the roads leading to Palo Verde from Bagaces.) The delightful, rarely-used **trail** runs along the river through dense riparian forest, which is rare in the actual reserve. **Birding** is excellent along this trail. It makes for a leisurely 1½hr. walk. Many locals take advantage of **La Poza el Eden de Cabuyo,** the swimming hole right behind the Visitors Center that feels like it's in the middle of the jungle.

LIBERIA

Inviting and spacious Liberia (pop. 50,000), the commercial center of Guanacaste, is the heart of this dusty cowboy region. The white-washed colonial houses lining the streets, the strutting *sabaneros* (cowboys) passing by, and the rustle of the Liberia flag above the *parque central* hint at the pride, history, and tradition that make Liberia unique. Although there's little else to see in Liberia, it is a pleasant place to spend a day or two and is a base for visits to national parks, including

N.W. COSTA RICA

Rincón de la Vieja, Santa Rosa, and Palo Verde. It's also a convenient stop en route to Pacific beaches or the Nicaraguan border. **Guanacaste Day** on July 25, the day the province left Nicaragua and annexed Costa Rica, is celebrated by a week of traditional festivities—costumed children perform on the steps of the church or march in parades; several bull ridings and runnings stun and entertain, and *fiestas* around the fairgrounds go on all night. Liberia is Costa Rica's birthplace of cattle ranchers, and the "Expo-feria Ganadera-Liberia", from July19-29, more than adequately displays the spirit of the town and its people. Come to experience the bullfights, games, dances, and traditions of the original city of *"libertad."*

▐ TRANSPORTATION

Flights: Sansa (50min.; high season 5:15 and 11:50am, return 6:20am and 12:50pm; low season 11:35am, return 12:25pm; US$66) and **Travelair** (50min.; high season 6, 8:30, 11:30am, return 7:30, 9:55am, 3:05pm; low season 5:30, 8, 11am, return 7:05, 9:35am, 12:35pm; US$73) fly from San José (see **p. 85**) to the airport 12km west of Liberia. The airport is accesible by taxi or any Nicoya/Playa del Coco bus, which pass by the entrance road 1.6km from the terminal.

Buses: Schedules change often; check beforehand. Unless otherwise noted, the following depart opposite the market, 5 blocks west and 3 blocks north of the *parque:* **Cañas** via **Bagaces** (1hr., 11 per day 5am-5pm, ¢460); **Managua, Nicaragua** (from Hotel Guanacaste; 5hr., 5 per day 8am-12:30pm, US$12.50); Nicaraguan border at **Peñas Blancas** via **La Cruz** (1hr., 10 per day 5:30am-8pm, ¢600); **Nicoya** via **Santa Cruz** and **Filadelfia** (2hr., every 30min. 4:30am-8:20pm, ¢450); **Playa del Coco** (1hr., 7 per day 5:30am-8:20pm, ¢500); **Playa Hermosa** and **Playa Panamá** (1hr., 6 per day 5am-5:30pm, ¢300); **Puntarenas** via **Cañas** (3hr., 7 per day 5am-3:20pm, ¢1000); **San José** (4½hr., 6 per day 5:30am-5pm, ¢1600; from the Pulmitán terminal a block south of the main terminal, every hr. 4-10am and every 2hr. 10am-8pm, ¢1410).

Taxis: Line up at the north side of the *parque.* (Taxi Liberia ☎666 1778 or 666 0073.)

Car Rental: Sol Rent-a-Car (☎666 2222; solcar@racsa.co.cr), on the Interamerican, 5 blocks west of the parque on the north side of Burger King. Open daily 7:30am-5pm. **Toyota Rent-a-Car** (☎666 0016), across the Hwy in front of Burger King. Open M-F 7:30am-5:30pm, Sa-Su 8am-noon. For a Hyundai 7-person *doble tracción* it should cost around US$68 per day.

✳ ▐ ORIENTATION AND PRACTICAL INFORMATION

The city is built on the regular grid, with **Avenida Central** (or Ave. 25 de Julio) acting as the southern border of the **parque central** (officially known as **Parque Ruiz**). **Calle Central**, or **Calle Real**, is halved by the *parque.* The oldest *barrios* of **Cerros, Los Angeles, Condega** and **La Victoria** give justice to the other name of Liberia, **Pueblo Blanco.** In front of the church in the main plaza sits the **Frondoso Arbol de Guanacaste**, a tree after which the whole province was named. The **Universidad de Costa Rica** is on the west side of town.

Tourist Information and Guided Tours: Tourist office (☎665 0135 or 665 1606), 3 blocks south and 1 block east of the *parque.* Tours to Rincón de La Vieja, Palo Verde, and Santa Rosa National Parks. (Round-trip US$40 for groups of 3; Santa Rosa guided tour US$18 per person, plus US$35 for transportation. Open M-Sa 8am-noon and 1:30-5pm). **Hotel Guanacaste** and **Hotel La Posada del Tope** also offer tours (see **Accomodations,** below) to Rincón for $36 alone and $18 in group. The bus leaves at 7am and 4pm and return at 8am and 5pm. **La Posada del Tope** hostel (see **Accomodations,** below) offers tourist info and makes cheap national park transfers (Rincón US$12,

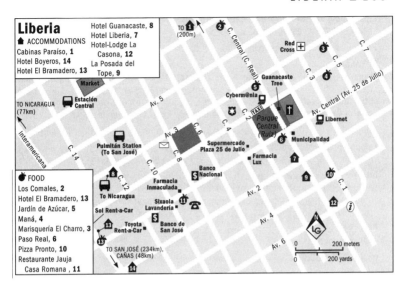

Liberia

♠ ACCOMMODATIONS
Cabinas Paraíso, **1**
Hotel Boyeros, **14**
Hotel El Bramadero, **13**

Hotel Guanacaste, **8**
Hotel Liberia, **7**
Hotel-Lodge La
    Casona, **12**
La Posada del
    Tope, **9**

♦ FOOD
Los Comales, **2**
Hotel El Bramadero, **13**
Jardín de Azúcar, **5**
Maná, **4**
Marisquería El Charro, **3**
Paso Real, **6**
Pizza Pronto, **10**
Restaurante Jauja
    Casa Romana , **11**

Santa Rosa US$17, for 6-8 people per *busesta*) and special hotel deals with vouchers. Ask about the canopy tours if interested too (US$30). **Acaturivie** in the mercado, cubicle 10, (☎691 8177 or 666 5257; www.acaturivie.com) is a **microempresario** group which makes reservations to nearby albergues in Rincón de la vieja and national/international flights. Ask them about the excellent new guide book produced by the UN developmental program for rural tourism, *Guia de Turismo Rural Comunitario*. Open M-Sa 8am-noon, 1pm-5pm. A very practical booklet to have if staying a while in the province of Guanacaste is the free **directorio comericial y profesional de Guanacaste** updated annually, with important phone numbers of institutions in each district. Should be available at the municipalidad, or at the house of the Colombian producers of **Linea Creativa.** (☎/fax 666 4995, 25m west of El Capulín bridge on the right side behind the Mamón bus stop).

Municipalidad (☎666 0169), M-F 8am-4pm, east side of police. **MINAE,** next to MAG after the bridge.

Banks: Banco Nacional (☎666 0259), 3 blocks west of the *parque.* Exchanges traveler's checks. Visa cash advances. Open M-F 8:30am-3:45pm. **Banco de San José** (☎666 2020), 4½ blocks west of the *parque.* Cirrus **ATM,** MC/V cash advances. Open M-F 8am-5pm, Sa 9am-1pm. **BCAC** (☎666 0611), 300m east of main traffic lights. Visa, cash exchange. Open M-F 8:30am-5pm. **Western Union** in bamboo mall 20m north of *municipalidad.*

Market: 5 blocks west and 3 blocks north of the *parque,* across from the central bus station. Open M-Sa 6am-7pm, Su 6am-noon.

Supermarket: Plaza 25 de Julio (☎666 7171), half a block west of the *parque*'s southwest corner. Green, yellow, and white building. Open M-Sa 8am-9pm, Su and holidays 8am-2pm. **Supermercado Palí** (☎666 2109), in front of the Palacio Municipal. Open M-Th 8am-7:30pm, F-Su 8am-8pm.

Laundry: Sixaola Dry Cleaning & Lavandería (☎666 333), 4 blocks west and 25m south of the *parque*'s southwest corner, behind Casa Romana. Open M-F 8am-noon and 1:30-5pm, Sa 8am-noon.

Emergency: Red Cross (☎666 0994, emergency 118), on the east side of town 100m north and 200m east of *parque*.

Police: (☎666 0213, emergency 911), on the *parque*.

Pharmacy: Farmacia Luz (☎666 0061), 100m west of the *parque*'s southwest corner. Open M-Sa 8am-10pm, Su 8am-noon. **Farmacia La Inmaculada,** Avenida 25 de Julio (☎666 7657), 50m west of Banco Nacional. Open M-F 8am-10pm, Sa 8:30am-9pm, Su 4pm-8pm. Doctor Jose Manuel and Lic. Raquel are considered very good. The **Health Center** is 100m west, 200m north, and 1km east of *municipalidad*.

Hospital: (☎666 0011, emergency ext. 325).

Telephones: Telecomunicaciones Internacionales (☎665 0403), 3 blocks west and half a block south of the *parque*. Open M-F 7:30am-5pm, Sa 8am-11:30am.

Internet: Ciberm@nía, on the northeast corner of the *parque* with A/C. Fast connection, A/C. ¢450 per hr. Open daily 8am-10pm. **Libernet** (☎666 9024), between calles 1 y 3 on ave Central, 150m east of *gobernación*. Offers cheaper connections in a modern space with 16 computers. ¢300 per hr.; ¢100 per 10min. Open M-Sa 8am-9pm.

Post Office: 3 blocks west and 1 block north of the *parque*. Open M-F 8am-5:30pm, Sa 7:30am-noon.

Postal Code: 5000.

🏠 ACCOMMODATIONS

Some rates may increase during the high season, between December and April.

▣ **Hotel Liberia** (☎666 0161), half a block south of the *parque*'s southeast corner. Rooms are separated from the street by a pleasant restaurant and sitting area. Breakfast served in nice, open patio inside in front of TV (buffet style, ¢800). The simplest have toilets, showers, and sinks, but rooms vary in size and style. Laundry ¢1500 per kg. Rooms ¢4500 per person; smaller rooms with private bath ¢3000; large rooms with private bath ¢5000. 10% discount for ISIC holders. ❷

Hotel-Lodge La Casona (☎666 2971), 3 blocks south of the *parque*'s southeast corner. Comfortable rooms, pleasant common baths, a living room with couches, cable TV, and a new restaurant especially for guests. Laundry and Internet. US$5 person; doubles with private bath US$15; triples US$21; quints US$25. ❶

La Posada del Tope (☎/fax 666 3876), 1½ blocks south of the *parque*, across the street from Casa Real, offers cable TV for ¢500 more. Staff keeps rooms neat and bright. The hotel's tourist information center offers transport to Rincón de la Vieja (US$12 round-trip per person), tours, and help with rental cars. ¢2000 per person. ❶

Cabinas Paraíso (☎666 3434), 500m north of the *parque*, with freshly painted white rooms, flowered sheets, and a balcony that catches the breeze. Plenty of common baths to go around; optional private bath and cable TV. Singles ¢2100, with TV ¢2800, with bath ¢3000; doubles ¢4200/¢4800/¢5300; triples ¢4600/¢5300/¢6300. ❶

Hotel Guanacaste (☎666 0085; fax 666 2287), 2 blocks south of the bus station. English-speaking owner Luis runs a tight and bustling ship. Liners ¢1100 per person. Dorms without towels and sheets US$10; singles US$17; doubles US$30; triples US$42; quads US$52; quints US$60. HI and ISIC discounts. AmEx/MC/V. ❷

Hotel El Bramadero (☎666 0371), on the Interamerican just north of the main road into Liberia, has an old-west, *sabanero* ambience and a pool basking in the sunlight. A/C, TV, and small private baths. Attached restaurant serves excellent meat entrees (see **Food,** below). Singles US$29; doubles US$37; triples US$43; quads US$50. ❸

Hotel Boyeros (☎ 666 0722; hboyeros@racsa.co.cr; www.hotelboyeros.com), on the Interamerican just south of the road into Liberia's center, comforts many a business-traveler with spacious rooms that have A/C, cable-TV, phone, terrace, and hot water bath. Adult and kiddy pools with a mosaic waterslide. 24hr. room service available. Singles ₡13,500; doubles ₡16,000; triples ₡18,000; quads ₡19,500. AmEx/MC/V. ❸

🍴 FOOD

Always ask before to see if the restaurant might serve some good traditional drinks, made out of **coyol** or the flower seed called **chan** (smells really strong).

Los Comales (☎ 665 0105), 2½ blocks north of the northeast corner of the *parque*, and a second, newer location three blocks west of the *parque*. Twenty-five women run the place, serving hearty Guanacaste *típico* for all the locals. *Arroz de maíz* ₡650; *carne* ₡800; *casados* ₡800-1000. Open M-F 7am-5:30pm. ❶

Paso Real, on the southeast corner of the *parque*, has a pleasant balcony and excellent seafood. Inside, loud pop stars on the big screen TV will be your extra guests. Risotto with shrimp ₡2000; Creole style fish fillet ₡1800. Open daily 11am-10pm. ❷

Maná (☎ 666 8468), 125m east of the church. A Christian family serves *típica* from heaven at this small and easy-to-miss restaurant with tree stump-style tables and stools. No sign in front. *Casados* ₡900; *sopa de albóndiga* (meatball soup) ₡600. Open M-Sa 7am-10pm. ❶

Marisquería El Charro (☎ 666 7321), 275m east of the *parque*. Big seafood menu. Hearty cut of fresh fish prepared in delicious sauces. Medium whole fish ₡1800; *pollo al ajillo* ₡2300. Open daily 11am-10pm. ❷

Casa Romana Jalija (☎ 666 0917), 4 blocks west of the *parque*. An indulgent Roman motif, replete with limestone columns and outdoor fountain help justify the decorators claim to classic Italian greatness. Pizzas and pastas attest. There are many locals as well as tourists. Artichoke pizza ₡2400; sea bass ₡2900. Open daily 7am-10pm. ❸

Hotel El Bramadero (☎ 666 0371; see **Accommodations**, above). Serves excellent meat entrees. Pepper steak ₡2950; *pollo al vino* ₡1900. Open 6am-10pm daily. ❸

Pizza Pronto (☎ 666 2098), 2 blocks south and 1 block east of the *parque*, cures rice-and-beans blues with adobe-baked pizzas. Delivery available. Vegetarian pizzas ₡1400-3800. Open daily noon-3pm and 6-11pm. ❷

Jardín de Azúcar (☎ 666 3563), 100m north of the *parque's* northeast corner. Cheap buffet with vegetarian dishes. Look for the coin-op kiddie rides in the front. Breakfast ₡400-950; *plato del día* with drink ₡750. Open daily 6:30am-8:30pm. ❶

Restaurante Jauja Casa Romane (☎ 666 0917), 500m west of parque on Av. 25 de Julio, diagonal from the Tribunal de Justicia. Once called Pizza Beppe, this joint is now fancier and very classy. Italian pizza and pasta ₡1500-2900. Open daily 7am-10pm. ❷

Restaurante Pan y Miel (☎ 666 3733), 25 m east of Instituto Nacional de Seguros (INS) on Av. 25 de Julio. With all sorts of bread (₡125-265), cheap but typical meals (₡475) and desserts (₡450). Open M-F 7am-6pm, Sa 7am-2pm). ❶

👁 SIGHTS

Iglesia de la Ermita, six blocks southeast of the *parque* along Av. Central, is the oldest church in town. (Open daily 2:30-3:30pm.) A small *sabanero* (cowboy) **museum**, now in the government building on the *parque*, displays various *sabanero* accessories and explores the historical evolution of the Guanacaste region. (Open M-F 8:30am-noon and 1:30-5pm. ₡100.) The **Camandancia Station,** north of Liberia, houses a makeshift museum for the Daniel Quiros collection, which has artifacts dating from 500BC to AD1500. (Open M-F 8am-noon and 1-4pm.)

N.W. COSTA RICA

🎵 ENTERTAINMENT

Apart from the wild annual celebrations organized by the town, Liberians love to go out dancing and sing karaoke. *Parranda*, the local dance, is popular in local dance halls (follow the crowd). On weekends, stop by the **Tsunami Bar and Grill**, on the road to Nicoya, 600m from center next to the Hotel Sitio, and best reached by cab. Weds. is Ladies Night. (☎666 1211). **Disco Kurú,** across the road, has kareoke and dancing. Kurú is one of the busiest late-night sposts in Liberia, with two bars and a dance floor surrounded by mirrors. Dancers sometimes overflow into the seating area and get down between the tables to mostly Latin Music. (☎666 0769. Karaoke M, Tu, W nights. Beer on tap ¢400. Open M-Sa 8pm-4am).

NORTH OF LIBERIA

PARQUE NACIONAL RINCÓN DE LA VIEJA

While the rest of Costa Rica parties to the *tico* groove and ocean breeze, head north of Liberia for seclusion and peace in the a park filled with waterfalls, raging rivers, and endless forests. The magical blend of colors, textures, and scents seeping through Rincón de la Vieja makes it one of the most enthralling national parks in Costa Rica. A gigantic active volcano demands much attention. Before going straight for the glowing magma, take a little time to explore the park's out-of-the-crater wonders. The park's sulfuric lagoons, boiling mud pits, *volcancitos*, inviting thermal waters, excellent trail network, and fine birding ensure quality bonding with Mother Nature and a lasting impression of natural beauty.

AT A GLANCE	
AREA: 141 sq. km. **CLIMATE:** Average 26°C. **FEATURES:** Colorado, Blanco, and Ahogados rivers; largest amount of *guaria moradas* (the national flower). **HIGHLIGHTS:** Hiking Sendero las Pailas, La Cangreja waterfall, Escondida waterfall, visiting hot springs, the crater, and swimming holes.	**GATEWAYS:** Although it is very close to Liberia (p. 163), there is no public transportation to the park. **CAMPING:** At ranger station; campgrounds with showers and pit toilets. **FESS AND RESERVATIONS:** Camping US$2; entrance fee US$6.

✳️ 🚌 ORIENTATION AND TRANSPORTATION

The park has two entrances, **Las Pailas** and **Santa María,** each with a ranger station. Although they are fairly close, the access roads are separate. Las Pailas, with trails leading past waterfalls and up the volcano, is more visited. The river next to it is perfect for swimming in the dry season.

The park is only 25km northeast of Liberia, but public transportation covers this distance. Coming by **private car,** a dirt road leads from Liberia's Barrio La Victoria to the Santa María entrance. Another dirt road starts 5km north of Liberia on the Interamerican Hwy. and heads 10km east to the town of Curabanda; from there it is another 10km east to the Las Pailas entrance (¢700 to drive on the road). Public **buses** go only as far as Curabanda. From there, some catch a ride with occasional traffic, although hitchhiking is never the safest idea.

More reliable **tourist shuttles** from Liberia are offered by Hotel Guanacaste (departs Liberia 6am and 4pm, returns 8am and 5pm; US$18 round trip per person for groups of 3 or more) and La Posada de Tope hotel (US$12 round trip, 3 person minimum). It's also possible to hire a 4WD **taxi** in Liberia (at least ¢10,000 each way). **Ranger station** ☎661 8139. (Park open daily 7am-4pm. US$6, camping US$2 per person per night.)

PRACTICAL INFORMATION

WHEN TO GO. Rincón de la Vieja's dry climate makes this park most beautiful during the rainy season (May-Nov.), when waterfalls spill through its forests and hot springs bubble over with water. To get to the hot springs, however, you must cross two rivers, which is not feasible if it has rained a lot the previous night. Fortunately, the park is accessible year-round.

ACCOMMODATIONS AND CAMPING

Both ranger stations have **campgrounds** with showers and pit toilets (US$2 per person per night). You can also arrange basic room and board at the stations; call the park in advance. Near the Las Pailas entrance sit a number of **lodges** that offer meals and activities. **Rincón de la Vieja Lodge ❸** is 2.5km before the entrance, with quiet woodsy cabins, some of which come with bunk beds, and hammocks on porches. The property is a 400-hectare *finca* with a canopy tour and horses. The restaurant serves a flavorful buffet and the bar occasionally has live music. There is no transportation to the park entrance, so some avoid an extended hike by hitching a ride on the main road. Hitchhiking always entails a risk. (☎/fax 661 8198; info@rincondelaviejalodge.com; www.rincondelaviejalodge.com. Canopy tour US$50; 3hr. horseback tour to hot springs US$30. Mountain bike rental US$5 per hr. Breakfast 6:30am-7:30am US$6.50, lunch 12:30-1:30pm US$10, dinner 6:30-7:30pm US$10. Singles US$35; doubles US$51; triples US$69; quads US$75. Larger cabins with balcony on riverbank, doubles US$75; triples US$90; quads US$110.) The **Hacienda Lodge Guachipelín ❸**, 5km before the entrance, is a 19th-century cattle ranch-turned-hotel. Activities (at a significant extra cost) include a ten-platform canopy tour and horseback tours of the park. Transportation from Liberia costs US$50 round-trip or US$10 to the park. (☎666 8075; info@guachipelin.com; www.guachipelin.com. Restaurant buffet: breakfast 7-9am, US$5 for non-guests; lunch noon-3pm US$10; dinner 7-9pm US$10. Breakfast included. Singles US$38; doubles US$30-45; triples US$74.)

HIKES

East of Las Pailas ranger station is a 3km **loop trail Sendero Las Pailas,** which passes turn-offs to a picturesque waterfall (only in the rainy season), a sulfuric lagoon, a *volcancito*, and boiling mud pits. A well-marked branch about halfway around this trail, leads another 6km east to the **Santa María station.** A trail to the west of the Las Pailas leads to the park's biggest waterfalls: **Cataratas Escondidas** (4.7km) and the awesome **Catarata La Cangreja** (5km). For a swim without the 2hr. hike, there's a crystal-clear **swimming hole** just 600m down the trail toward the waterfalls. It's 8km to the **crater** of Rincón de la Vieja; allow a day for the round-trip journey (about 7-8hr.) and register at the park office. It is required that solo hikers must be accompanied by a guide (check with the rangers or at one of the lodges). Access to the crater trail and the waterfalls is closed after 11am, as the area is prone to floods. From the Santa María station, a 3km trail leads west through thick, monkey-filled forests to the **aguas termales** (hot springs), 6km east of Las Pailas. Other points of interest accessible from the station are cold water pots, the enchanted forest waterfall, and a scenic outlook.

PARQUE NACIONAL SANTA ROSA

*Buses traveling along the Interamerican Hwy. between the Nicaraguan border and Liberia (such as the Liberia-Peñas Blancas bus, leaving Liberia every 2hr. 5:30am-7pm) drop off at the entrance station (La Casetilla). About 12 buses per day pass in each direction. No buses run the 7km to the administration center or along the dirt road to the beach, so those without wheels walk or hitch (try asking the rangers). Let's Go does not recommend hitchhiking. Hotel Guanacaste in Liberia sometimes runs a shuttle to and from the park. **Park open** daily 8am-4:30pm. US$6, US$2 extra for camping. Park information is available at the **Oficina de Ecoturismo** in the administration center. (☎666 5051, ext. 219; fax 666 5020; www.acguanacaste.ac.cr. Open daily 7:30am-4pm.)*

Established in 1971 as one of the first national parks in Costa Rica, Santa Rosa preserves the largest remaining tropical dry forest in Central America and is a UNESCO World Heritage Site. The park stretches over most of the Península Santa Rosa, at Costa Rica's northwest corner, and has isolated beaches famous for surfing and turtle-watching. The park is part of the **Area de Conservación Guanacaste (ACG),** almost 200,000 hectares of land and sea, and one of 11 conservation areas in Costa Rica. The unique flora such as the **Guanacaste tree, Pochote, Naked Indian,** and **Caoba,** as well as **115 species of mammals** (white-tail deer, howler monkeys, and white-faced monkeys), **250 species of birds,** and more than **30,000 species of insects.** There are many enchanting and accessible lookout points (*miradores*), or on the numerous natural and manmade trails (*senderos*).

The park also houses a famous historical sights, **Hacienda Santa Rosa (La Casona).** On March 20, 1856, a ragtag Costa Rican army defeated invading troops sent from Nicaragua by American imperialist William Walker in just 14 minutes of fighting. This brief moment of violence and national pride in a long history of peace has great significance for Costa Ricans. Invasions were also prevented in 1919 and 1955. Alas, La Casona did not withstand its most recent invasion, when, on May 20, 2001, two vindictive deer hunters, angered by hunting prohibitions, snuck into the park and set fire to the site, burning over half the fort to ash. The arsonists were caught and convicted, and Costa Ricans raised ₡200,350,000 in a united effort to rebuild the fort. La Casona now stands restored, with roof tiles from 1886 and, appropriately, a state-of-the-art fire alarm system. In front, you can view cattle being cleaned in immersion baths in preparation for their truck journey from the **embarcadero** to the **corrales de piedra.**

■ **ORIENTATION** The national park's entrance station is 35km north of Liberia and 24km south of La Cruz, on the west side of the Interamerican Hwy. From here, a dirt road leads 7km to the park's administration center, with MINAE offices and an information center. A bit farther to the left is the campground, and to the right, past the cabins, is the *comedor* (cafeteria). Beyond the administration center is a 4WD road (often closed to traffic during the rainy season) leading to the coast, 12km away. The road forks after 7km; the left branch leads 4km to **Playa Naranjo,** a popular campsite and famed surfing beach, and the right heads 8km to the turtle-hatching beach of **Playa Nancite.**

The park's **Sector Murciélago,** encompassing the isolated northern coastline of Península Santa Rosa, isn't accessible from the rest of the park; visits require starting from Cuajuniquil, a town 8km off the Interamerican and reachable by bus from La Cruz at the Nicaraguan border or from Liberia, then a 9km walk on a dirt road to the sector's ranger station. On the coast, you can swim at **Bahía El Hachal,**

Bahía Danta, Coquito, Santa Elena, or **Playa Blanca,** and hike on the 600m trail **(Poza del General).** You can **camp** in the area with sufficient notice (bring your passport).

▚▐ ACCOMMODATIONS AND FOOD. The park offers **lodging** near the main offices (US$15 per person, students US$10) and amazing meals (¢800-1300) in the *comedor.* Reserve lodging at least 1-2 weeks before (☎666 5051) and give a few hours' notice for food, which is always served at noon. There's also a snack bar. A campground near the administration center has drinking water, flush toilets, and cold-water showers. The campground at Playa Naranjo has toilets and non-potable water. Ask about **camping** overnight in Nancite and in the Sector Murciélago.

◪▐ SIGHTS AND TRAILS. La Casona, near the administration center (follow signs past the administration center to the left), is the main building of the historic Hacienda Santa Rosa where the battle of 1856 was fought. (Open daily 8am-4pm.) The **Monument to the Heroes of 1856 and 1955** lies beside La Casona, with a windy view of nearby volcanos Orosi, Cacao, and Rincón de la Vieja. The lookouts **Mirador Tierras Emergidas,** and **Mirador Yalle Naranjo** are about halfway to the administration center from the entrance on the way to the coast, and offer some stellar views. All **trails** and points of interest are marked on a useful map available at the entrance (US$2). The short (800m) **Sendero Indio Desnudo** (a.k.a. *Gringo Pelado,* "Peeling Gringo") begins near La Casona and is a revealing introduction to the plants of the region. **Sendero Los Patos,** 5km beyond the administration center on the road to the coast, is one of the best trails for wildlife viewing. The 2km **Sendero Palo Seco** lies near Playa Naranjo, as does the 4km **Sendero Carbonal** that leads to **Laguna el Lirubo,** a crocodile hotspot.

Right next to Laguna el Lirubo is the **Estacíon Experimental Forestal Horizontes,** (Experimental Forest Horizons Station), an investigation center, which is part of the ACG project. (Acessible only from the Interamerican Hwy. 12km south of the park's main entrance or 23km north of Liberia.) About that same distance from Liberia is a huge *finca* (farm) called **La Cueva,** belonging to 9 brothers (Juan is in the white house at the entrance and Elias works in the Libernet Internet store in Liberia). The *finca* is a great example of how Costa Rican national parks coordinate with their neighboring communities. The brothers should be ready to offer **river rafting** along the Río Tempisque by 2003. Very outgoing, they will tell you about their *finca,* as well as about local legends such as that of the glorious white bull statue that stands on another *finca* between La Cueva and the national park (on the west side of the Interamerican; great photo opportunities).

◣ BEACHES. There is outstanding surfing at **Playa Naranjo.** Try Piedra Bruja, 3km north of the campground, with 3m waves and, according to legend, *sirenas* (mermaids). The high waves make the beach a bit too dangerous for families with small children. **Playa Nancite** has the country's second-largest arrival of olive ridley sea turtles. The nesting season is July-Dec. and is best in Oct-Nov., during a vague 8-day, crescent moon period when 1000-6000 turtles arrive on the 800m of beach every night at around 9pm. Access to Playa Nancite is restricted, and you need permission at the administration center. (No charge; maximum 30 people per day. Call administration center, ext. 233, 20 days ahead to reserve camping near the beach; US$10 for up to 20 people.) If you arrive by at the car by park, it is forbidden to drive to Nancite. Drop it off at Playa Naranjo before going on to Nancite (a guard will watch it); don't you leave your car anywhere other than with the guard.

N.W. COSTA RICA

PARQUE NACIONAL GUANACASTE

Parque Nacional Guanacaste lies on the opposite side of Parque Nacional Santa Rosa, across the Interamericana. While the western reaches of Guanacaste share Santa Rosa's lowland habitats, the environment chages as the park rises toward the summits of Volcán Orosi (1487m) and Volcán Cacao (1659m). The park, created in 1991 in part from old ranch land, is open mainly to students and scientists in the dry season, and is difficult to visit without private transportation. However, there are three well-developed research stations scattered about the park: **Marzita, Cacao,** and **Pitilla.** Tourists are sometimes permitted to stay at the stations, which have dorm beds and cold-water baths. **Camping** by the stations is permitted. For information, contact the Santa Rosa headquarters (☎ 666 5051, fax 666 5020). Contact **Gisel Méndez,** who is in charge of the Guanacaste Parque's stations (extension 223 of Parque Santa Rosa's headquarters). About 100 groups visit the *Parque* annually, but individuals rarely visit; as such , it is best to find a group to go with.

The most modern of the three station, **Marzita Biological Station,** is 18km off the Interamerican Hwy., along an unpaved road. The turnoff is east at the Cuanjiniquil intersection, 8km north of the entrance to Santa Rosa. Marzita has lodging for up to 32 people, electricity, and food service (request in advance). At this station, research is focused on aquatic insects and there is a 2hr. trail hike called **Pedtroglifos El Pedregal** for its approximately 800 observable petrogypls. Observations of Volcán Orosi, La Fila del Cacao, the Pacific coast, and the transition of dry to moist forest make this trail a real treat if you are allowed entrance (you have a better chance in the dry season).

A 12km trail ascends to the **Cacao Biological Station.** It begins in Potrerillos, about 9km south of the Santa Rosa park entrance. From Potrerillos, head 7km east to Quebrada Grande (take the daily 3pm bus from Libreria), then 10km north along a 4WD road to the station. During the rainy season, you will have to park 5km before the station at Río Gangora. You can lodge in Mata de Caña in Quebrada Grande or directly explore the Cacao Biological Station grounds. There is a 900m trail called **Pedregal** which leads to an observatory for forest fires. You can also climb to the top of Volcán Cacao, a 3hr. hard climb into the cloud forest that starts on the east side of the lab. You will need a permission slip.

Pitilla Biological Station, which is the least likely to allow visitors, is 28km off the highway near the Nicaraguan border, around 10m south from the town of Santa Cecilia. There is a 7pm bus from Liberia to Santa Cecilia (there are cheap hostels if you need to stay the night). Buses also run from La Cruz (noon, 12:30, 1:15, 7pm). At Pitilla, you can delight in incredible birdwatching and catch a glimpse of Lago de Nicaragua from the top of mini-Volcán Orosilito. There is lodging for up to 20 people with advance reservation at the Santa Rosa headquarters, along with a study room, two-way radio, drinking water, parking, and a 6hr. trail.

Another lodging option is at the private **Volcán Cacao Base Camp,** affiliated with Hotel Guanacaste in Libreria (☎ 666 0085). It is 6km south of the park and offers bunk beds with common baths and camping. The camp also offers transport from Liberia (US$10 one way). Horse tours to Volcán Cacao are also available (US$45 from Liberia, not including park entrance fee).

✖ PEÑAS BLANCAS: BORDER WITH NICARAGUA

Liberia is only 1 hr. away from the border at Peñas Blancas which is not a town but a frontier. (1½hr., 10 daily 5:30am-7pm, ¢600). To reach Peñas Blancas from **San José,** catch a bus from Calle 14, between Av. 3 and 5 (6hr.; M-F 6 per day 5am-4:10pm, Sa-Su more frequent; ¢1860). To get to Peñas Blancas from **La Cruz,** catch the bus from Liberia (¢150) or take a taxi (¢500 per person if in a group).

Both Nicaraguan and Costa Rican immigration offices are "open" from 8am to 8pm, but it's wise to get there well before closing time (around noon is a good idea), as bureaucracy and transit from one to the other can take a surprisingly long time (up to 6hr.). The Costa Rica immigration office (☎677 0064) has two lines: one for entering Costa Rica (US$7) and the other for exiting Costa Rica (¢200 plus US$1.50). If you're leaving Costa Rica, buy the exit stamp from any *cambista* outside, or from the booth. For those entering Nicaragua and planning to stay more than 3 months, stamps are more expensive (US$35 for Costa Ricans and tourists and US$55 for Nicaraguan residents of Costa Rica). Entering Costa Rica for a stay of more than 3 months costs US$20.

Once you get your passport stamped, you can have a snack in **Restaurante de Frontera** inside, and change your money at the small **Banco Credito Agricole** (which has long lines). **Money changers** (*cambistas*) abound on both sides of the border, but the rates are better on the Nicaraguan side. Hotel Guanacaste in Liberia will also change money.**Buses** from the Nicaraguan border run to **Rivas** (1hr.; every 30min. 6am-5:30pm, 10C), and continue to **Managua.** For **San Juan del Sur,** take the Rivas bus, get off at La Virgen (30min., 4C), and change there for San Juan (30min., every 30min. 5am-6pm, 4C).

LA CRUZ

Only 20km south of the Nicaraguan border at Peñas Blancas, in the province of Guanacaste, the city of La Cruz is the area's only urban mix of *Nica* and *Tica*. Somewhere, between the sweeping views of Bahía Salinas is the legend of the namesake of La Cruz. Some say it commemorates a mule driver who died working his way up a cliff, and is now buried amidst the natural splendor with only the denotation of a cross. Others say that the town was named for the infamous *Cruz de Pierda*, in the nearby Parque Nacional de Santa Rosa. While the origin of its namesake is open to questioning, the lush, natural beauty of the area is not. The city is a surprisingly quiet and charming base for day-trips to the deserted and even more beautiful Playas Soley, Morro, Jobo, and La Rajada.

▐ TRANSPORTATION

The **bus** terminal is on the north side of the town, about three blocks north from the *parque*. All **Transporte Deldu** buses from **San José** to Peñas Blancas pass by La Cruz (6hr., 6 per day 5am-4:10pm, ¢2065). You can also catch a Deldu bus from **Liberia,** across from the new *mercado* to Peñas Blancas via La Cruz (1hr., 10 per day 5:30am-7pm, ¢500). A **taxi** from Peñas Blancas is ¢500 in a collective ride. From La Cruz, buses go to **San José** (6hr., 8 per day 4:30am-4pm, ¢1565) via **Liberia** (1hr., 5 per day 7am-5:30pm, ¢500). Buses to the local beaches of **Soley, Morro,** and **Jobo** leave at 5, 10:30am, and 3pm; and return at 7, 8am, noon, and 5pm from the main terminal. Red **taxis** line up on the north and south side of the *parque* (¢2000 to the beaches, ¢1000 to the border, ¢200 around town).

▐▐ ORIENTATION AND PRACTICAL INFORMATION

The town of La Cruz sits on a sharp cliff overlooking the glorious bays, beaches, *fincas*, and mountains of the region. A former restaurant 100m west of the north side of the *parque* is now a popular hangout. Continuing to the right 6km will lead you to Playa Soley; further along is Playa Moro (1km), Playa Jobo (15km), and Playa Rajada (19km).

N.W. COSTA RICA

Banks: Banco Nacional de Costa Rica (☎679 9296), 50m east of the *parque*. Open M-F 8am-noon and 1-4pm, Sa 8am-noon.

Supermarket: Supermercado el Unico, on the northeast side of the *parque*. **Mini Super and Licorera Jauga,** 20m east of the northeast side of the *parque*. Open daily 7am-10pm. The hotspot for tourists, the so-called "gringo supermarket" is on the main calle, 50m northeast of the *parque*.

Police: (☎679 9197), next to the Clinica de la Cruz. Open 24hr.

Red Cross: (☎679 9146), 200m east of the *parque*. Open M-F 7am-10pm.

Medical facilities: Clínica de la Cruz: (☎679 9116), 500m southeast of the *parque*, emergency 24hr. service. **Medical Center Jesus de Rescate:** (☎679 9318), 75m north of the *parque*.

Internet: Available at the **public library** (☎679 9718), next to the Post Office, 50m west of the south side of the *parque*. Free; max. 30min.; best to go in the morning before school lets out. Open M-F 8am-noon and 1-5pm. **The Radio Cultural de la Cruz** (☎679 9113), next to the police station, also has access. Open M-Sa during the day. Internet is available for guests at **Hotel Bella Vista** (see **Accommodations,** below).

Post Office: (☎/fax 679 9329), 50m west of the southwest corner of the *parque*. Open M-F 7:30am-noon and 1-5pm.

🛏 ACCOMMODATIONS

Camping is available on Playa Morro near the sand bridge. Bring your own equipment and potable water; pay ¢1000 per night at the local bar.

Cabinas Maryfel, across from the bus terminal, offers the cheapest lodging and the best local social scene, amidst the chirping and champing of animals on the grounds and churchgoers next door. Singles with fans and private baths ¢1500. ❶

Hotel Bella Vista (☎/fax 679 8060; keeskoen@racsa.co.cr), 50m west of the northwest corner of the *parque*, appropriately offers some of the best views in town. The adjoining bar/restaurant offers excellent national and international food (US$10; open daily 10am-10pm). Also offers Internet access, beaches and jungle tours, scuba diving, horseback riding, and fishing. Singles with private bath, fan, and breakfast US$15. Half-price for students or handicapped, children under 10 free. ❷

Cabinas Santa Rita (☎679 9062), 100m south of the southeast corner of the *parque* across from the children's playground, offers breathtaking views. Singles ¢2800; with bath, TV, A/C ¢6700. ❶

Amalia's Inn (☎679 9181), next to the Ministerio de Salud, 100m south of the *parque*. Has some of the highest prices in town, but its paintings adorning the walls and exquisite scenery make it worthwhile. Singles US$25, with hot-water private bath US$30. ❸

Hotel Cabinas del Norte (☎679 9132), 7km north toward the border, is where Cruzeños head for some luxurious vacationing and great parties in its new discotheque. Has a pool and an Italian restaurant. Offers horseback riding and mini golf amidst the tropical rainforest setting. US$40 per night. ❸

🏙🍴 FOOD AND NIGHTLIFE

The best restaurants in La Cruz are **Thelma** and **Orquideo** on both sides of the gas station. The *sodas* in La Cruz offer quality restaurant-type food. **Soda Candy** ❶, in front of the bus terminal, serves great family-style food and original fare cuisine. (Dinner ¢800. Open daily 6am-10pm.) **Soda Rascal** ❶, next to the AYA office 50m east of the *parque*, offers cheap fast food. (Chicken ¢600; rice ¢800; *casados* ¢700-¢1300. Open daily 10am-9pm.) **Soda la Marita ❶,** is smaller in size but not in quality (open M-Sa 6am-6pm, Su 6am-3pm).

In town, the local crowd flocks to **Bar Restaurante Dariri,** 300m south of the *parque,* which serves seafood and Italian food and has a full bar (open daily 1pm-2am). **Bar Salinas** is a pleasant bar right next to Playa Morro, where you can watch the sun set with a beer and *boca.* **Bar Pizote,** in front of Tienda La Pampa 100m north of the *parque,* pleases hungry crowds. Other options include **Bar Natani,** in front of Importadora Monge, and **Bar Mar de Plata,** in front of Banco Popular. Go dancing at **Disco Bahía Tropical,** 50m north of Banco Popular.

NORTHERN LOWLANDS

Costa Rica's sparsely populated northernmost region is, not surprisingly, one of its least visited. Culturally and geographically close to Nicaragua, the vegetation here was once mixed tropical forest but much of that has been replaced by pasture land. Some of this floods for much of the year, as in Refugio Nacional de Vida Silvestre Caño Negro, an aquatic wonderland teeming with birdlife.

CIUDAD QUESADA (SAN CARLOS)

Hovering amid the Cordillera Central's sloping green hills, Ciudad Quesada (San Carlos to its residents) marks the fusion of the *campo tico* with everyday small city life. *Campesinos* stroll along modern streets and vendors sell overflowing crates of ripe fruit. The agriculture and ranching center of the north, San Carlos pumps out much of the country's beef and milk. It also serves as a major saddlery center; locals make traditional, detailed leatherwork in the *talabarterías* around town. Northwest of San José (110km), the city is a transport hub within the Alajuela province. Travelers connect here to nearby Fortuna and Volcán Arenal (40km), as well as Los Chiles and Puerto Viejo de Sarapiquí.

■ TRANSPORTATION

The city's bus station (☎ 460 5064), referred to as *"parada nueva"* by most locals, is 500m north of town. A shuttle bus leaves from the *mercado*, 100m north of the northeast corner of the *parque*, to the terminal's side for ¢75. Here, catch **buses** to **San José** (3hr.; 11 per day M-Sa 5am-6:15pm; Su 6, 9:15, 10am, 4, 5, 5:30pm; ¢780); **Fortuna** (1½hr., 10 per day 6am-8pm, ¢375); **Los Chiles** (3hr., 14 daily 5am-7pm, ¢725); and **Puerto Viejo de Sarapiquí** (3hr., 9 per day 4:40am-5:30pm, ¢550).

■ ORIENTATION

Ciudad Quesada has the classic grid layout, in which Av. 0 and Calle 0 intersect on the northeast corner of the **parque central**—but of course, none of that really matters because locals go by units of 100m *(cuadras)* up, down, right, and left. A cream-colored **cathedral** borders the park to the east. **Limited tourist information**, mostly on other destinations, can be found at **Aeronort Agencia de Viajes,** 300m north and 50m west of the northeast corner of the *parque* (☎ 460 3711 or 460 3636; fax 460 7656; ecoservi@racsa.co.cr. Open M-F 8:30am-6pm, Sa 9am-1pm).

■ PRACTICAL INFORMATION

Banks: Banco Nacional, (☎ 460 0290) 50m east of the *parque's* northeast corner, will exchange currency and change traveler's checks. The 24hr. **ATM** at Cocique, behind the cathedral, accepts Cirrus. Open M-F 8:30am-3:45pm. **Western Union,** sharing a complex with Restaurant Coca Loca and another bank (tucked in the back), is on the west side of the park. Open M-F 8am-noon and 1-5pm.

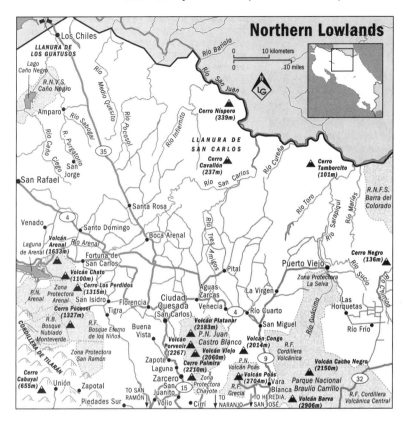

Northern Lowlands

Police: (☎460 0375), 1km east of the *parque*.

Hospital: (☎460 1176), 3km north of the northeast corner of the *parque*. **Red Cross** (☎460 0101), 150m north and 100m west of the northwest corner of the *parque*.

Internet: Internet Café, 100m north and 50m east of the northeast corner of the *parque*. ₡350 per hr. Open M-Sa 9am-8:30pm, Su 3-8pm.

Post office: Post office with fax, 300m north and 150m west of the northwest corner of the *parque*. Open M-F 7:30am-6pm, Sa 7:30am-noon.

ACCOMMODATIONS

Hotel del Norte, (☎460 1959 or 460 1758). 100m east and 150m north of the northeast corner of the *parque central*. Small rooms, comfy beds, fans, color TV. Check-out noon. Singles US$7, with bath US$11; doubles US$11/18. MC/V. ❶

Hotel del Valle, (☎460 0718; fax 460 7551). 200m north and 50m west of the *parque's* northeast corner, has some carpeted rooms with generous wardrobe space; all 11 have cable TV, fans and private baths. For all this and the price, it's slightly lackluster. Reception closed Sundays. Singles ₡3000; doubles ₡6000. ❶

IN RECENT NEWS

TROUBLE ON THE SAN JUAN

Nicaragua and Costa Rica are riding shaky waters on the controversial river separating the two countries. The San Juan is the subject of an over 3-year-long debate that flared when the Nicaraguan government prohibited armed Costa Rican police from patrolling the river, claiming that they posed a threat to their national security. The Costa Rican government officials argue that the same 1916 ruling by the Central American Court of Justice establishing the river as Nicaraguan property, however, also upheld the Costa Ricans' right to travel the river with standard issue arms and maintain that their police presence on the river curbs illegal drug trafficking.

Though Nicaragua has threatened to impose taxes on Costa Rican goods and tensions are rising, anything more aggressive that heated debate is out of the question. Perhaps the most significant factor in the way of solidly resolving the dispute, is both country's plan to mutually develop tourism near the border. Costa Rica has planned to invest in hotel development, and Nicaragua has promised US$20 million for the project.

More interesting than the legal and business issues on the San Juan, however, are the worried sentiments of citizens, who feel the severe poverty of Nicaraguans living on the river banks presents a much more serious dilemma than territorial disputes. In the face of so many social problems, Nicaraguans argue that patriotism isn't a likely priority yet wish their government was nationalist in fighting the country's real problems rather than harmless Costa Ricans on the river.

Hotel Central & Casino, (☎460 0301; fax 460 0391; hcentral@racsa.co.cr). A tan building that dominates the west side of the *parque* and hosts many business people and salesmen. For this reason, it is important to reserve these very comfortable and complete rooms (with cable TV, phone, fan, private bath, and end tables) weeks in advance. Singles ¢5000; doubles and matrimonial suites ¢9000. ❷

Conquistador S.A. lies 700m south of the *parque,* and this uphill position makes for second-story views of the town. The location of **La Casita Restaurant** (Open 6am-11pm) right next door softens its remoteness, and rooms come fully loaded with baths and TVs. Singles¢4600; doubles ¢7500. V. ❷

Hotel Cristal, 75m north of the northwest corner of the *parque,* is a cheap but still decent option. Clean, sky-blue rooms and some windows facing a concrete wall. Checkout noon. Singles ¢1200, with bath ¢2000; doubles ¢2300/3000. AmEx/MC/V. ❶

🍴 FOOD

Steak is what's for dinner in San Carlos. It is easy to miss the best steakhouse in town under its overhang, but **Restaurante Coca Loca ❸** sits directly on the west side of the parque, and the dark wood, swinging saloon doors and yellow curtains inside set the mood for a thick filet mignon (¢2550). Milanesa steak with cheese (¢1750) is finger-licking good. (☎460 32 08. Open daily 11am-11pm.) Lighter eaters can try the fancy-shmancy service at **La Terraza ❷,** 250m north from the northeast corner of the *parque.* The terrace may overlook a gas station, but the atmosphere is inviting. Besides steak, specialties include *fettuccine alfredo* (¢1000) and sea bass with an orange-citrus sauce (¢1300) is recommended by locals. (Open daily 11am-midnight.) For cheaper eats, head over to the surprisingly spotless *sodas* inside the *mercado* (see **Transportation** above), or try **Restaurant Cristal ❶,** on the north side of the *parque.* (*Casados* ¢950. *Gallo pinto* ¢700. Open daily 7am-11pm.)

👁 SIGHTS IN AND AROUND SAN CARLOS

Forty-four years ago a dairy farmer with a passion for wildlife started taking in abused, sick or otherwise endangered wild animals from individuals, the government, circuses, and other sources. His 'hobby' became public in 1989 because it was so expensive to run. Today, he and his family, the Rojas farmers, own **El Zoológico la Marina,** a fabulous zoo-park-preserve where jaguars, elastic-nosed tapirs, toucans, crocodiles, and remarkably human spider monkeys that swing from huge trees, are happier. In fact, fences are so minimal that you'll feel like you're inside their habitats. It is low-key and frequented by locals and if you need/want vet experience or just love animals, Mr. Rojas welcomes volunteers. To get to the zoo, take any bus heading north from the terminal (Puerto Viejo, Pital, Venecia, Río Frío, etc.; 35min.; ¢115) and ask to be let out at the Zoológico La Marina. (☎474 2100. Open daily 8am-4pm. Adults ¢1000, children ¢500).

Soak in the thermal-water luxury at **El Tucano Resort and Thermal Spa,** 2 km south of the zoo. The ritzy resort's only services to non-guests are its US$13-15 thermal bath and hydrothermal therapy. (☎460 6000. Open daily 8am-6pm). To marinate in warm water with a more local (or at least *tico*) set, head 1 km south to **Termales del Bosque,** where you can enjoy seven connected blue pools of different temperatures for ¢1500. Breakfast in the restaurant is included if you stay in one of the modest cabin-rooms on the hill above. (☎460 4740; fax 460 1356. Check-out noon. Receptionist leaves after 10pm. Guard 24hrs. Restaurant open daily 7am-9pm. Singles US$32 plus tax; doubles with bath, fan, and TV—but no cable, they like it quiet—US$45. AmEx/MC/V).

For some leather of the north, check out the **Mercados de Artesanía** on the northwest corner of the *parque.* (Open M-Sa 8:30am-6:30pm.)

PARQUE NACIONAL JUAN CASTRO BLANCO

Parque Nacional Juan Castro Blanco was established from a pre-existing conservation area in 1992. Since this park is still such a baby, it is still developing the proper infrastructure for eco-tourism. MINAE has only been able to acquire about 96 hectares of the 14258 total hectares of the park, the rest still in the hands of local *finceros.* However, it is still possible to visit the park, and you can be a pioneering tourist in the unexploited land. Discover the region's sulfur baths, the 100 yr. old abandoned mines, the numerous hydroelectric projects, and four volcanoes- Platanar, Porvenir, Viejo, and Cañón del Río Tor. There are also three mountain peaks which give birth to five major rivers. The lagoons of Pozo Verde and El Congo are impressive, as well as the cold-water, crystalline waterfalls of Catarata Río Toro, Claro, Agrio, and Quebrada Gata. Hidden in the park's cloud forest are 80% of the country's endemic species, including sloths, white-faced monkeys, pumas, linets, wild chickens, and ever elusive quetzales. Until MINAE technically owns all the land, there will be only one official pathway through the *parque* leading to the mines and sulfur basins, still nevertheless preponderant with the vegetation of the area (including oaks, magnolias, quinine, ferns, and orchids).

▐ TRANSPORTATION. From the capital of San José, the road going to the northern zone of the country, toward Ciudad Quesada, leads to the entrances of the *parque:* **Venecia, Aguas Zarcas, San José de las Montaña** (from Sucre), **Quebrada del Palo, Las Brisas, Alpes, San Vicente** (from Ciudad Quesada), **San Gerardo, Palmira** (from Zarcero) and **Bajos del Toro Amarillo** (from Sarchí). There are two entrances that are recommended to stay a night and get a feel for the *parque:* either **San José de la Montaña,** in the *canton* (small village) of San Carlos (don't mistake this for the San José de la Montaña of Heredia) or **Bajos del Toro** in the *canton* of Valverde Vega. For the first option, take a bus from the capital of **San José** heading to Ciudad Quesada (2½hr. daily, every hr. 5am-7:30pm, ¢600.), and ask the driver to let you off in **El Sucre,** in front of the MINAE office, after the Río Viejo bridge and the *Salon Comunal.* You will need to call the MINAE office (see **Practical Information,** below) or the Ecological Refuge Monterrey del Norte Lodge (see **Accommodations,** below) a few days in advance to arrange transportation from El Sucre to San José de la Montaña. The second option, Bajos del Toro, is via the public bus to **Sarchí.** (1¾hr. from San José, daily 3:15pm in front of the Sarchí Sur tourist office.)

⑦ PRACTICAL INFORMATION. The official **MINAE** office, administers the park from El Sucre (☎ 460 7600), is next to the police station in town, in front of the check point gate. The official **MINAE** pathway is only accessible from San José de la Montaña, in the *canton* of San Carlos. Also contact the regional headquarters of **Area de Conservacion Arenal Huetar Norte** (☎ 460 0055; achn@ns.minae.go.cr) to get more information about the *parque*. The closest **hospital** from El Sucre is in Ciudad Quesada, and from Bajos del Toro, Sarchí. There is a **health center** in Bajos del Toro in case of a local emergency (☎ 761 1399).

⑦⑤ ACCOMMODATIONS AND FOOD. In the rustic and tranquil **Ecological Refuge of Monterreal Del Norte ①,** you can stay in one of three furnished cabins equipped with electric lights and bathrooms with hot water. Call in advance and tell Bernardita how many people are going to stay, and they will also prepare meals. (Trout and salad ¢1500. ☎ 385 8696. US$10 per person.) You can also stay in the two-person cabins on the *finca* of the family **Bargas Varela ①** (US$25 for 2 people, breakfast included.)

In **Bajos del Toro Amarillo** there are more lodging and food options. Avilia's **Típico Toro Amarillo ④** is located in the center of town, 100m north of the church. There is a restaurant with excellent trout and good meals for ¢1000-1200. (☎ 761 1199. Cabins for 1-2 people ¢5000; for 3 people ¢7000.) Aldo Francesa's **Hotel de Montaña ②,** 7km north of the town center, has three rooms and includes breakfast and hot water. People come to this spot to see the *cantarus* (goldfinch) and experience the richness of biodiversity: 286 species of birds and 82 insect families. The forest here is under reconstruction, with two rivers on Aldo's private **Finca Catarata del Toro,** only 15m from the famous 120m high waterfall of el Toro. The restaurant here (M-F 8am-5pm, Sa-Su) serves rural food and *casados* with *refrescos* (soda) for around ¢1500. (☎ 463 3886; catarata@costarricense.cr. Triples and family size rooms ¢7500-12000 per night.) Freddy Salazar's **Nene ⑤** lodging, 300m east of the crossing at Palmira at the marked signs after the entrance gate of town, offers a cabin for two people with a private bathroom and a big house which fits up to 10 people. (☎ 454 1407. Cabins ¢7000; Rooms in the house ¢15000.

⑤ GUIDED TOURS. In San José de la Montaña, Bernardita of the Ecological Refuge has two sons who can take you on the official **MINAE trail,** which leads to the **mines** (3hr. hike, unfixed price., or the fossilized crater to see the **Pozo Verde** (45 min.) Guards are scheduled to be stationed sometime in the near future, and the entrance fee for the park will be US$6. In Bajas del Toro, Din Notor and Luis Guillermo Rodriguez are reputable tour guides; ask around. There is a private biologist on the property of Aldo Francesa willing to give tours on his daily investigation excursions (US$20 for 2hr. tours, maximum 8 people.) Freddy at Nene's gives free tours to his guests to the cheese factory, Catarata La Silomas, and Catarata el Toro (¢300). Sport fishing is also available here at Villa Nelly's, 150m east and 300m north of the sport field in the center. (☎ 463 3668. ¢800 for 1kg of caught trout.)

PUERTO VIEJO DE SARAPIQUÍ

Eighty-two km north of San José sits Puerto Viejo, a tiny community in a majestic valley surrounded by rainforests. Though most travelers pass through Sarapiquí en route to Volcán Arenal to the west or Tortuguero to the east, an increasing number of nature enthusiasts are lingering in this small jungle town to take advantage of some of Costa Rica's most diverse and dense wildlife and vegetation. No longer a major trade port to the Caribbean, Puerto Viejo's location on the banks of the Río Sarapiquí, the "river with two personalities," has made it a popular destination for those seeking adventurous white water rafting and much calmer river tours. Both provide excellent opportunities to observe the area's 500+ species of birds.

TRANSPORTATION

All **buses** leave from the spotless, white-tiled station opposite the southwest corner of the soccer field. A schedule is posted inside at the ticket counter, from which you must purchase your tickets before boarding. Buses go to **San Carlos** (5:30, 9am, 12:15, 2, 3:30, 7:30pm), **San José** direct (2hr., 8 per day 5:30am-9:20pm, ¢920), **San José** via **Vara Blanca** (5, 7:30, 11:30am, 4:30pm), **San José** via **Heredia** (3½hr.; 7:30, 11:30am, 4:30, 9:20pm; ¢770); **San José** via **El Tunel Zurquí** (7 per day 5:30am-5:30pm, ¢920), and **Guápiles** (1hr.; 5:30, 7, 9:30am, noon, 2:30, 4, 6pm; ¢480).

Many buses stop at **Bajo de Chillamate, La Virgen,** and **Río Frío** and make additional stops along the way; ask at the ticket counter for information. **Taxis** line up along the main street just north of the soccer field. A taxi to La Virgen costs about ¢1500.

ORIENTATION

Puerto Viejo extends along one main street for about 300m. A **soccer field** bordering this street marks the town center. The bus station is opposite a turquoise **church** that sits on the soccer field's east side. About 100m past the bus station, a small road to the right leads to the **Super Sarapiquí** supermarket. (Open daily 7am-4pm.) Another 100m down the main road, a second small road to the right leads to a few hostels and to the **port** along the Río Sarapiquí.

PRACTICAL INFORMATION

Tourist Information: For the most comprehensive tourist information, talk to Alex Martínez, owner of **Andrea Cristina Bed and Breakfast** (☎/fax 766 6265), 1km from the town center. Walk south (toward the soccer field) for 500m until you reach a major fork, turn right, and walk another half kilometer; the B&B is to your right. Closer to town, friendly, English-speaking Luis Alberto offers good information at **Souvenirs Río Sarapiquí** (☎ 766 6727), 100m north of the soccer field. Rafting tours US$45-55, river tours US$15 per hr. Open M-F 8:15am-5:30pm, Sa-Su 8:15am-6pm. **Comercial Rojas Guzmán** (☎ 766 6108), 50m north of the soccer field under a yellow awning marked "tourist information," is yet another good source. Open daily 7am-7pm.

Banks: Exchange traveler's checks and dollars at the **Banco Nacional** (☎ 766 6012), at the intersection of the main road and the road to the port. Open M-F 8:30am-3:45pm. There is also **Banco Popular,** 20m north of the soccer field. Open M-F 9am-3pm, Sa 8:30am-noon. Both have **24hr. ATMs.**

Police: (☎ 766 6575, emergencies ☎ 911), down the first small road off the main road, near the supermarket.

Medical Services: The **hospital** (☎ 766 6307) is 250m south of the soccer field on the left. The **pharmacy** (☎ 766 3134) is 100m past the taxi stand. Open M-Sa 7am-8pm, Su 7am-1pm.

Internet Access: Sarapiquí Internet is 300m south of the soccer field, just past the hospital. ¢300 for 30min., ¢500 per hr. Open daily 8am-10pm.

Post Office: The **post office** is across the street from Banco Nacional at the turn off to the port. Open M-F 7:30am-6pm, Sa 7:30am-noon.

⚑ ACCOMMODATIONS

Many travelers who come through Puerto Viejo stay at upscale nature lodges a few kilometers outside the village, but tiny Puerto Viejo offers a surprising number of decent budget options.

Mi Lindo Sarapiquí (☎/fax 766 6074), just south of the soccer field and opposite the bus station, has spacious, polished cabin-like rooms with TVs, fans, and private warm-water baths. Laundry is available. Singles ₡3500; doubles ₡7000; triples ₡10,000. ❷

Andrea Cristina Bed & Breakfast (☎/fax 766 6265) is 1km from the town center. Walk south (toward the soccer field) for 500m until you reach a major fork, turn right, and walk another half kilometer; the B&B is to your right. Six cozy, fan-cooled cabins, each with a private hot shower. Breakfast is included. US$23 per person. AmEx/MC/V. ❸

Cabinas Laura (☎ 766 6316), 100m down the road to the port, accommodates those on a tighter budget. The friendly owner will lead you through the large courtyard to your clean room with marble-tiled cold water bath, fan, one double bed, and one single bed; some rooms have TV. All rooms ₡3000. ❷

Cabinas Monteverde (☎ 766 6236), 100m north of the soccer field on the left, offers more basic rooms with private, cold-water showers. Singles ₡2500; doubles ₡3000.) ❷

Hotel El Bambú (☎ 766 6005; fax 766 6132; www.elbambu.com), next to Cabinas Monteverde, charming and comparatively fancy, is for the thick-walleted traveler. Bambu's 12 elegant and spacious rooms are fully-equipped with A/C or ceiling fan, private hot water bath, TV, telephone, and safe deposit box. Restaurant, pool, exercise equipment, room service, and tours are also available. Check-out 11am. Breakfast included. Singles US$40; doubles US$55; triples US$75. AmEx/MC/V. ❹

Hotel Gonar (☎ 766 6196), across the street from Cabinas Laura and above the *ferretería* (hardware store), is the cheapest place in town. Its grim, Spartan rooms with fans and shared, cold-water showers are a decent value. Singles ₡1500; doubles ₡2000. MC/V. ❶

🍴 FOOD

You musn't worry about finding a place to eat at Puerto Viejo either; *sodas* line the main road. Numerous locales also offer tasty, fresh baked goods.

Mr. Pizza (☎ 766 6138), just north of the soccer field next to the Clínica Santa Mónica, serves a variety of *comida rápida* (fast foods) as well as deliciously cheesy pizzas, from the Hawaiian to the vegetarian. Pizzas: small ₡950, medium ₡1500, large ₡2500, grande ₡2450. Tacos ₡350. Combo plates ₡500-900. Open daily 10am-9pm. ❷

Restaurante Mi Lindo Sarapiquí, attached to the hotel of the same name, provides a fine atmosphere for a slightly more upscale, sit-down meal. The large menu includes tasty rice dishes (₡800-1350), pastas (₡1500-2200), and seafood dishes (₡5000). Only ₡400 for delicious *frescos naturales*. Open daily 9am-10pm. ❸

🔎 SIGHTS

Stray from Puerto Viejo de Sarapiquí or La Virgen into the maze of cages of the **Snake Garden (Serpentario),** where a vast range of reptiles reside, from the deceptively tiny, yet venomous black and green dart frog to the 29 ft. long anaconda, and Costa Rica's largest venomous snake, the rainforest-dwelling bushmaster. Lucky visitors can watch the friendly owner feed live rabbits to the enormous snakes. English/Spanish explanations of the scaly animals make for a worthy visit en route to the *Centro Neotrópico Sarapiquís*. To get there from Puerto Viejo de Sarapiquí, take a bus headed toward La Virgen and ask the driver to let you off at the entrance to the *Centro Neotrópico SarapiquiS*. From the Center gates, walk 300m south along the highway until you see the large "Serpentario" sign. If coming from La Virgen, walk north along the highway (Rte. 4) 2km; the snake garden will be on your right. Otherwise, a taxi from Puerto Viejo costs ¢1500. (US$6, students US$3. Open daily 9am-5:30pm.)

⬛ DAYTRIPS FROM PUERTO VIEJO

CENTRO NEOTRÓPICO SARAPIQUIS

From Puerto Viejo de Sarapiquí, take a bus to La Virgen. Ask the driver to let you off at the entrance to Centro Neotrópico SarapiquiS. Otherwise, a taxi from Puerto Viejo costs ¢1500 or from La Virgen, walk north along the highway (Rte. 4) 2km; the entrance to the park is on the right, 300m past the snake garden. Reservations strongly recommended. ☎761 1418 or 761 1004 ext. 244; fax 766 6535; tirimbin@racsa.co.cr; www.tirimbina.org. 3hr. guided tours: adults US$12; students US$9; children ages 6-16 US$6. Self-guided tours: adults US$10; students US$8; children US$5. Open daily 7am-4pm.

Recently opened in 2000 by USA Wisconsin-based Tirimbina Rainforest Center, the non-profit, non-governmental ⬛**Centro Neotrópico SarapiquiS** is a preserve dedicated to interactive cultural, biological, and ecological awareness and conservation. Unlike other Costa Rican forest tours and national parks, its goal is to promote sustainable tourism and engage visitors in the culture and history of life in the tropical forest by making programs and trails accessible to people of almost all ages and abilities. Before entering the preserve, the 1000 sq. ft. **museum** includes an informative film presentation, rainforest ecology displays, and examples of pre-Columbian architecture, enlightening visitors about pre-Columbian forest lifestyles. Inside the park gates is the well-maintained **Alma Ata Archaeological Site,** where in Oct. 1999, 600 year old tombs and indigenous artifacts were found. The site features a reconstructed 15th-century pre-Columbian village, complete with informative Spanish/English explanations of each of the displays. The center also maintains a small **botanical garden,** where it grows an assortment of pre-Columbian, medicinal, spice, ornamental, fragrant, and edible plants.

The gem of the center, however, is the 350-hectare **Tirimbina Rainforest Preserve,** of which 150 hectares have been developed for public use. A number of easy, cement supported trails lead tour groups into the beautiful primary and secondary forest. One of Tirimbina's most unique features is its suspension bridges through the forest. The first bridge, **El Puente Colgante,** stretching 262m across the rushing Río Sarapiquí, is the largest bridge of its kind in Costa Rica. The smaller bridge, **El Puente Del Dosel,** hovers above the dense rain forest canopy. Both bridges were constructed with minimum damage to the surrounding forest and offer unparalleled views of rainforest life. A spiral staircase descending from El Puente Colgante leads to a small island formed by Río Sarapiquí. A few trails cross the island, and crystal-clear natural pools on the island's edge are ideal for swimming. Otters and kingfishers are often spotted on the riverbanks. Both day and night tours are available; morning tours are better for bird watching, while night tours often include bat identification, armadillo, and kinkajou sightings.

This center was built as a pre-Columbian village using ecologically sustainable technologies like solar power, local natural materials, and a waste-water treatment system. The on-site **lodge,** restaurant, and bar overlook the reserve and follow the *palenque* architectural style of indigenous people. Three large, round huts each house eight beautiful cabins with private hot water bath, two beds, fan, and phone. Safety deposit boxes and laundry services are also available. (Breakfast US$5, box lunch $6, lunch and dinner US$10 each. Rooms US$65-72 May 15-Nov.; US$77-85 Dec. 1-May. Additional US$15 each for up to 2 extra children ages 4-16.)

NORTHERN LOWLANDS

The center also maintains an extensive **education program** with over 2000 local children and hundreds of foreign volunteers, teachers, and ecologists. Student/volunteer lodgings are also provided on the center grounds. **Volunteer opportunities** are most frequently offered to groups of students, but individual opportunities can be arranged. Contact the center for more information. All profits are reinvested in conservation efforts, education, and scientific research.

ESTACIÓN BIOLÓGICA LA SELVA

From Puerto Viejo, take the 6:45am or 12:15pm bus headed to Río Frío to make the 8am or 1:30pm tours (15min., ¢120). Buses to Guápiles also pass this way. Ask the driver to let you off near La Selva. From this stop, follow the dirt road on your right 1km to the station's gates; signs mark the way. To get back to Puerto Viejo, have the station call you a cab (¢1000) or flag down one of the frequent buses down on the main road.

Only 6km south of Puerto Viejo, La Selva is one of the jewels of the **Organization for Tropical Studies (OTS)**, a non-profit consortium of universities and research institutions founded on the principles of investigation, education, and conservation. OTS maintains three biological stations in Costa Rica (the others are Wilson Botanical Gardens and a section of Parque Nacional Palo Verde). La Selva borders Parque Nacional Braulio Carrillo to the south and boasts 1560 hectares of primary and secondary rainforest. Hundreds of scientists and students come to La Selva each year to study over 450 species of birds, 70 species of bats, and 5 species of felines. The 57km of path, 8km of which are made of concrete, make La Selva accessible to casual nature lovers as well; just come prepared with proper hiking boots, insect repellent, and rain gear, as the station receives over 4m of rain annually. Unless you are staying in the station's upscale lodge (singles US$75; doubles US$65 per person; meals included), the trails can only be explored with a guide. Two tours leave each day (3hrs.; 8am, 1:30pm; US$25 per person). Bilingual guides can lead groups of up to 10 people (US$22.50 per person). It is important to reserve a spot three or four days in advance. Call the station to inquire about various volunteer opportunities. (☎766 6566; fax 766 6535.) For reservations call the San José office at ☎240 6696 and ask for Ana Carter. (Breakfast 6-8am US$6; lunch 11:30-1pm US$8; dinner 6-7pm, US$8. Office open M-Sa 7-11:30am and 12:30-5pm, Su 7:30am-noon and 12:30-4pm.)

RÍO SARAPIQUÍ AND RÍO SAN JUAN

*Guided tours offered by Alex Martínez (☎766 6265. 2-6 people US$150 per day), Yacaré Tours (☎238 3009; US$10 per person per hr.; 2 person min.), through Souvenirs Río Sarapiquí (see **Practical Information,** above), or Captain Mena (beeper ☎224 4000 or 225 2500; leave a message in Spanish; 2-4 people US$25 per hr.).*

The Río Sarapiquí, flowing calmly alongside Puerto Viejo's eastern boundary, continues north for 40km before meeting the Río San Juán, which forms the border between Costa Rica and Nicaragua. Flanked on one side by dense forest and to the other by banana plantations, the Río Sarapiquí demonstrates the constant battle between the goals of conservationists to protect the rain forest and the needs of farmers to use the land commercially. Most tours of the Sarapiquí consist of 2-3hr. rides in slow-moving, motorized boats. Guides stop periodically to observe the diverse river-dwelling wildlife; frequent sightings include alligators, crocodiles, turtles, howler monkeys, and a vast range of birds. Catch an early morning tour for the best chances to see wildlife, and don't forget to ask for a good bilingual guide if you need one. Travelers should take note that the Río Sarapiquí is not a zoo, and one should not expect to see throngs of animals. Nonetheless, the opportunity to observe rain forest wildlife in its natural habitat is a unique one, and, at the least, the boat ride is quiet and relaxing. Otherwise, boatmen offer day and overnight trips up to and along the Río San Juán (which is technically Nicaraguan territory), as well as to Oro Verde, Tortuguero, Barra del Colorado, and other locations along the river. Ask the boatmen at the port for more information or inquire at any of the above mentioned tour providers.

LA VIRGEN

The miniature community of **La Virgen** appears briefly before disappearing along Rt. 4, a highway connecting the larger towns of San Miguel and Puerto Viejo de Sarapiquí. Besides from its proximity to the Centro Neotrópico Sarapiquí, La Virgen offers little of interest and few accommodations. There is no official printed **bus** schedule, but several buses stop at La Virgen's two bus stops along the highway. From La Virgen, buses go to Guápiles, Heredia, Horquetas, Puerto Viejo de Sarapiquí, Río Frío, San José, and Vara Blanca. Ask locals in town or flag down a bus and ask for information.

La Virgen stretches about 300m along Rt. 4, before fading away to farms and banana plantations along the highway. Pick up basic foods and essentials at the **Super San Martín** supermarket. (Open daily 8am-9pm.) An **Internet** cafe, near the southern end of town, provides slow service for ¢500 per hr. (hours vary). Nearby, a **Banco Nacional** changes cash and travelers checks and has a **24hr. ATM.** (Open M-F 8am-3pm, Sa 8am-noon.) **Hotel Cabinas Claribel** ❸ (☎761 1190), at the north end of town, is the only decent budget option in town. Clean and basic cabins each have two beds, fan, and private cold-water showers. (Cabins ¢5000). A few standard *sodas* and bars dot the small main street. **Soda el Lobo** ❶ offers a good *plato del dia* (¢600-800). The slightly fancier **Restaurante Mar y Tierra** ❷ specializes in meat and seafood dishes (most dishes ¢1000-2500).

VARA BLANCA

The mountain village of Vara Blanca is a cold and misty environment, as mysterious and captivating as the neighboring cloud forest. Along the curves of the highway you will also encounter delicious *típico* restaurants, picturesque views, an impressive chain of waterfalls, the largest butterfly observatory in the world, *calas* flowers, cattle farms, hydroelectric industries, and strawberry cultivation fields. Nearby in the village of Cari Blanco are three impressive hidden lagoons: Laguna de Hule, Congo, and Bosque Alegre. Camp at amazing bird-watching sites and see first-hand Mother Nature's wonders on the road from Vara Blanco into Puerto Viejo de Sarapiquí.

▐ TRANSPORTATION

From the capital of **San José,** take a bus from El Gran Caribe (Calle 12 between 7/9. ☎257 6859.) heading toward **Puerto Viejo de Sarapiquí.** (1½hr., 9 daily 6:30am-6pm, ¢400.) getting off at the gas station in the destination town of Vara Blanca. From **Heredia** take a bus (in front of El Principe Restaurant of the market), heading towards **Carrizal** (on the road via Barva). From there, take another bus to **Poasito,** getting off 5km before also at the gas station. Or, take a bus to **Cartago,** where you will also have to make a change. It is easiest to catch the bus heading toward **Sarapiquí** from San José, to avoid these transfers. If you miss these buses, a **taxi ride** from **Heredia** should cost ¢6000. Since Vara Blanca village is spread along the highway, your only option for transport from the gas station is by foot (watch out for trucks), motorcycle (though risky when raining), or a 4WD car. Watch out for the curves; one is actually a 180° turn.

■◆ ▌ ORIENTATION AND PRACTICAL INFORMATION

On the road from **Vara Blanca** towards **Sarapiquí** you pass the village of **Chinchona** (after the famous **La Paz bridge** and **waterfall**) which has its own rather secret 120m **San Fernando Waterfall** (on the right side after **ICE** sign), then **Cari Blanco** (with its 3 secret, hidden lagoons, the biggest one, 100m north of the gas station and 7km east in from the highway, is only accessible by 4WD), then **San Miguel** and **La Virgen**. It's about 6km along the road from the gas station at the entrance of town to the **La Paz Waterfall Gardens** (see **Accommodations,** below) where the **butterfly garden**, magic **hummingbird garden** and numerous **trails** leading to the 5 waterfalls are located. Less than 1km north is **La Paz** waterfall observable from old wooden bridge.

Tour Information: Inquire at the reception of **La Paz Waterfall Gardens** (see Accommodations, below), or contact Aaron directly. (☎476 0315, in San Miguel of Sarapiquí, averica@racsa.co.cr; rates start at US$15). Offering tours for beginners, intermediates and professionals in English and Spanish. You'll see toucans, parrots, honeycreepers, taragers, quetzales, sooty robins, mountain Elaenias, black and yellow silky flycatchers Also, garden tours and lectures (in a private flower garden with 140 varieties of heliconias). At the **La Paz WaterFall Gardens** itself there are many tour options on their 3½km of paved tails (1-4hr.) with altitudes of 1310-1524 meters above sea level. The **Fern Trail** (600m), and **Río La Paz Trail** (685m) bring you up along banks of La Paz río with swimming. **Bernardo's Trail** (550m, through the hummingbird garden and the orchids up to the Magia Blanca Waterfall) and the **Trail of Falls** (350m on metal staircase and platforms along the 4 waterfalls of **Magia Blanca, Encantada, Escondida** and **La Paz**) are all worth hiking. Obtain a picture **map** at the reception; trails are well marked and most people opt to venture around the 70 acres of wildlife and forest without a guide, although one is at your service if you desire (additional US$25 with the normal entrance fee of US$25 for 13 years and above, US$12 kids under 12, US $12 for those with ISIC or student ID. This is included with a US$8 meal at the restaurant. Call or email in advance for the **guide** (☎482 2720; email wgardens@racsa.co.cr. Park open daily 8:30am-5pm, last admission at 4pm). Very helpful **Diego** can give you great info at the reception. If you are interested in learning about the cultivation of **strawberries** and speak Spanish, farmer and huge soccer fan **Juaquin** can take you to his farm on work days (☎482 2359, about 500m east on a dirt road off of highway). Also you can see whether you are allowed to visit the **Fabrica de Mermeladas y Leche El Angel,** a national jam and milk producing factory in Cariblanco, which would be really informative. Diego's father **Fernando** has 3 butterfly farms you can visit as well in Cariblanco (☎476 0305).

Supermarket in town: Super Vara Blanca (☎482 2650; right before police station on way to Sarapiquí on right side of road, daily 6am-8pm).

▌ ACCOMMODATIONS

On the way to Vara Blanca, turn toward the village of Poasito. A sign points you toward English-owned **Poas Volcano Lodge ❸,** an eco-tourist hotel in a working dairy farm at the foothills of Poas Volcano. Nine well-decorated homey rooms with incredible views and shared bathrooms. (☎482 2194; fax 482 2513; poasvl@racsa.co.cr; www.poasvolcanolodge.com. Budget rooms US$35 per person.) Another lodging option is one of **Maria's 5 cabins ❸,** 300m north from school on the highway, with views of the strawberry fields and a good option for a more isolated experience in Vara Blanca (☎482 2368. ¢3000 per night). In the Montañas Azul near the Laguna de Hule (see **Orientation,** above) is **Cabinas Bosque Alegre ❶,** with rustic cabins owned by Juan Carlos with great prices and a friendly environment. (open only on weekends). You can also **camp** for free around this huge lagoon surrounded by rubber trees.

FOOD

All along the road from **Vara Blanca** to Sarapiquí are charming and typical **sodas** and **food outlets** selling food of the region: apples, *cotoletas* (Spanish type of tortilla), *palmito* (heart of palm vegetable), *cajetas* (delicious sugared boiled milk nougat) and *natilla* (sour cream). All of these eats can be had in the famous 100-year-old restaurant next to the gas station, Geraldo Fonseca's **Restaurante Vera Blanca ❷**. Built with volcano stone, food bakes in a *leña* (firewood) oven, and the place is infused with the warmth and company of Geraldo and his crew. Put some money in the old juke box and peruse the personal sentiments of past visitors adorning the wooden walls. (☎ 482 2193. Trout, *picadillos*, and *carne de ternero*, ₡600-1200. Open daily 7am-8pm. Credit cards accepted).On weekends, **Restaurante El Bosque ❷**, next to Cabinas Bosque Alegre (see **Accomodations**, above) serves good rustic food, and **Soda y Abastecedor El Mirador ❷**, inside Chincona, is worth finding (ask around), as such views on Waterfall San Fernando are truly incomparable. Have a great buffet lunch at the panoramic restaurant of **La Paz Waterfall Gardens ❷**. The view of the Poas Volcano makes it feel like you're eating in the clouds. (Open daily 11:30am-4pm).

VOLCÁN ARENAL AND AROUND

On July 29, 1968, Volcán Arenal woke up from a 450-year dormancy and erupted, burying two villages and 87 people. It has been actively spewing orange lava and boulders ever since, gradually growing into the sky above the small town of Fortuna. Tourists flock to the hot springs at the base of the famous conical volcano, and hike through primary and secondary rainforest catching glimpses of lava. Rounding out the nature-lover's palette are the Volcán Arenal National Park, Catarata La Fortuna, and Las Cavernas de Venado.

FORTUNA

According to local legend, Fortuna got its name from the flotsam and jetsam that would drift down the nearby Río Fortuna during floods—*indígena* tools and relics were scooped up by villagers as signs of good fortune. The small town's luck hasn't run out yet. The lava of Arenal, 6km to the west, flows away from town yet is close enough to make the views spectacular and volcano visits easy. With good transportation connections and plenty of hotels and restaurants, Fortuna has quickly become one of the most frequented towns in the country.

TRANSPORTATION

The main street into Fortuna runs east-west; many businesses line this thoroughfare. Along its north side is Fortuna's simple central park, formerly a soccer field. The church sits on the field's west side. **Buses** pick up passengers on the south side of the field and head to: **Ciudad Quesada/San Carlos** (1½hr., 7 per day 5am-5:30pm, ₡380); **San José** (4½hr., 12:45 and 2:45pm, ₡950; or transfer in Ciudad Quesada); **Tilarán** (3hr., 8am and 5:30pm, ₡950) via **Arenal** (2hr., ₡750). **Taxis** line up on the east side of the park. **Alamo,** behind the church on the main drag, rents **cars** and **jeeps.** (☎/fax 479 9090. Open 7:30am-6pm.)

NORTHERN LOWLANDS

🛈 PRACTICAL INFORMATION

Bank: Banco Popular, on the main drag two blocks east of the park, has currency exchange and **ATM.** Open M-F 8:30am-3:30pm, Sa 8:15-11:45am. **Banco Nacional,** 1 block east of the northeast corner of the *parque.* Open M-F 8:30am-3:45pm.

Market: The **Super Christian** supermarket is across from the southeast corner of the *parque.* Open M-Sa 7am-10pm, Su 8am-noon.

Police: (☎479 9689), 1½ blocks east of the *parque.* Open 24hr.

Medical Services: Farmacia La Fortuna (☎479 9778), 25m east of the southeast corner of the field. Open M-Sa 8am-8pm, Su 8am-noon. The **medical clinic** (☎479 9142) is 100m east and 50m north of the northeast corner of the *parque.* Open M-F 7am-4pm by appointment, 4pm-10pm for emergencies; Sa-Su and holidays 8am-8pm.

Telephones: You can make **international phone calls** at **Sunset Tours** and **Pura Vida Tours,** both on the southeast corner of the *parque.* Open daily 7:30am-10pm.

Internet Access: Access is available 100m west of the northwest corner of the *parque,* inside the Eagle Tours office. ₡400 per hr. Open daily 8am-8pm.

Post Office: Post office with **fax** is opposite the northwest corner of the *parque,* next to Desafío. Open M-F 8am-noon and 1-4:30pm, Sa 8am-noon. New office opening just west of the northwest corner of the *parque.* **Postal code:** 4417.

🏠 ACCOMMODATIONS

Cabinas Sissy, (☎479 9256), 100m south and 200m west of the southwest corner of the park, facing the Río Burío, has fresh turquoise rooms with private baths, free laundry, a kitchen, and an inviting backyard with volcano view. US$6 per person. ❶

La Posada Inn (☎479 9793), 300m east of the park on the main street, is a backpacker magnet. Cheap, spotless rooms come with fans and communal hot showers; the front porch is open for lounging. Internet ₡600 per hr. Rooms US$5 per person; camping ₡500 per person. ❶

Hotel Fortuna (☎479 9197), 100m east and 100m south of the southeast corner of the *parque* offers pristine, undecorated 3-bed rooms with private baths. Includes breakfast in the restaurant. US$8 per person, high season US$10. ❶

Cabinas Iguana Keanda (☎479 9127), down the street from Sissy, only has two rooms, but both are nicely tiled and have big beds. Doors carved with iguanas open to private baths with hot water. US$5 per person. ❶

La Choza Inn (☎479 9361), 300m north of the northwest corner of the park before a dead end, is a structure of thin brown planks that promises a summer-camp-like experience in big, pine-fresh rooms with bunk beds. The shared bathroom has an airy shower with a tiled wall; private baths are also available in less rustic rooms. Solarenal@racsa.co.cr. US$5-10 per person. V. ❶

Sierra Arenal (☎479 9751) is a short hike west up the main road and looks like a big orange brick, but inside, the rooms have sliding glass doors, high ceilings, and A/C. Dorms US$10 per person; singles US$15; gigantic quad US$40. ❷

Hotel San Bosco, (☎479 9050; www.arenal-volcano.com), 100m north of the northwest corner of the park, has 34 comfortable rooms facing the tropical landscape. Singles US$30, with A/C US$35; doubles US$35/40; triples US$40/50. Prices a little lower during the off-season and with cash. V. ❸

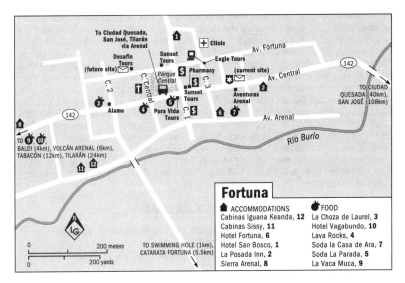

Fortuna

♠ ACCOMMODATIONS	🍅 FOOD
Cabinas Iguana Keanda, **12**	La Choza de Laurel, **3**
Cabinas Sissy, **11**	Hotel Vagabundo, **10**
Hotel Fortuna, **6**	Lava Rocks, **4**
Hotel San Bosco, **1**	Soda la Casa de Ara, **7**
La Posada Inn, **2**	Soda La Parada, **5**
Sierra Arenal, **8**	La Vaca Muca, **9**

🍴 FOOD

Lava Rocks, on the southwest corner of the park, is a great restaurant noted for its tasty breakfasts, milkshakes, and fish plates. Pancakes with fruit ¢750; grilled Chilean sea bass ¢1500. Open daily 7am-10pm. ❶

Hotel Vagabundo, 1.5km west of the church, serves pasta and wood-fired pizza (try Pizza Olga ¢3250). It also has a disco bar with pool (¢500 per hour) and darts. Both are worth the short taxi ride on weekends. The DJ plays a fun hit-or-miss mix of salsa, merengue, reggae, pop, and rock. Restaurant open daily noon-11pm; bar open daily 7pm-2am. No cover charge. Live music on Fridays. ❷

La Vaca Muca, the bar and restaurant next door to Hotel Vagabundo, is widely recognized for flavor and authenticity. There is a pool of lazy fish and minnows at the entrance, and a welcoming country atmosphere. Whole fried fish ¢2200 tax included, *churrasco* steak ¢3500. Open M-Sa 11am-11pm. ❸

Soda la Casa de Ara, 100m south and 150m east of the southeast corner of the park, satisfies locals with its *comida típica,* and offers penny-pinchers a buffet with hearty options. ¢100-600 per item; pork chop with onions ¢1100 Open daily 6am-10pm. ❶

La Choza de Laurel, under a sloping zinc roof 125m west of the *parque* on the main street, is a safe bet for *casados* (¢1450) or *pollo a la leña* (whole ¢3250, half ¢1750). Open daily 6:30am-10pm. ❷

Soda La Parada, directly across from the bus stop, is dirt cheap and the only 24hr. place in town. ❶

🎿 OUTDOOR ACTIVITIES

In Fortuna, everyone is a "guide." Innumerable hotels and companies offer the same general stock of activity options, with small and confusing variations. Avoid individuals who approach you on the street—quality is low. Reputable operators include **Sunset Tours** (☎ 479 9415), **Aventuras Arenal** (☎ 479 9133), and **Pura Vida Tours** (☎ 479 9045).

The most popular tour, of course, is to Volcán Arenal (see **Parque Nacional Volcán Arenal,** below), although none of the volcano tours gets close or guarantees a lava sighting; these either go through the national park or to private lookout points. Other tours head to the caves at Venado (see below) or to wildlife viewing at Caño Negro. The latter is quite popular, but currently only **Eagle Tours** (☎ 479 9091) takes tourists into the refuge proper (US$55), and waiting for views of incredible wildlife can be as tiresome as the long bus ride. **Horseback tours** travel to La Catarata de La Fortuna waterfall (see p. 187) and to Monteverde (4½hr., US$45-65); but the treatment of the animals varies. Pricey **fishing tours** on Laguna de Arenal are also available (half-day US$150 per person). Tircío Hidalgo (☎ 479 9310) comes recommended. Class III and IV **whitewater rafting** is available on rivers east of Fortuna; one of the most established operators is **Desafío Tours** (☎ 479 9464), opposite the field's northwest corner (full day on the Toro River US$65). Aguas Bravas rents out **mountain bikes** (☎ 479 9431; US$10 per half-day). Other options include **canopy tours** and **kayaking.**

◥ PARQUE NACIONAL VOLCÁN ARENAL

*You can reach the station by bike, private car, or taxi (¢4000 one day). It's easier to take one of the **guided tours (Sunset Tours** offers a US$24, 2½hr. walking tour through lava trails and secondary forest, which leaves Fortuna at 8am and 3pm). Station open daily 8am-4pm. Park admission US$6.*

The volcano is the obvious centerpiece of the park. Created in 1994, Parque Nacional Volcán Arenal covers 12,016 hectares including the towns of Tilarán, San Carlos, and San Ramón. The park's **ranger station** is 17km west of Fortuna (driving, head west for 15km and turn left at the sign). Just beyond the station is a lava and volcano **lookout point.** The park also has three short but pleasant trails. Since the 1968 eruption, plants have sprung up along the **Sendero Las Heliconias** (1km). **Sendero Las Coladas** (2.8km) crosses the 1993 lava flow trail. **Sendero Los Tucanes** runs through thick primary forest and delivers a stellar view of the volcano, Cerro Chato, and the Arenal dam. Hikers are forbidden to stray from the trail.

The road west of Fortuna has good but more distant views of the volcano; one of the best is from Montaña del Fuego Inn, 9km from town (round-trip taxi ¢2000). Be warned that climbing the volcano is dangerous and strongly discouraged.

◉ CATARATA FORTUNA

*To reach the falls, head south on the road that runs along the west side of the church. About 1km later, a dirt road branches off to the right. After about 1½-2hr. (4km) of uphill walking, you hit the waterfall parking lot. **Taxis** can take you as far as the parking lot (¢1500)—cabbing it there and then walking back to town downhill is a practical option. Pay a ¢1000 fee and follow trail to the falls.*

At Catarata Fortuna, 5.5km outside of Fortuna, the Río Fortuna tumbles down through 70m of rainforest canopy. Swimming is encouraged by the fall's overseers, but beware of the thumping cold water, it can hit you pretty hard. Guided **horseback tours** are also available (US$15). From the parking lot, there is a trail to **Cerro Chato,** the dormant sidekick of Volcán Arenal. It's steep and muddy, but there's an impressive crater lake at the top. The climb takes about 2½hr. one-way.

◥ HOT SPRINGS

*Three buses per day to **Tilarán** pass the springs (departing Fortuna 8am, 5pm; return around 3pm). Take a taxi (¢1500 each way) or bike it. It is possible to hitchhike, although it always entails some risk*

The famous hot springs of **Tabacón,** 12km west of Fortuna, are actually a single river of hot water. The **Tabacón Resort** has 10 hot and cool swimming pools, including one with a swim-up bar, a pricey restaurant, great views of the volcano, and a man-made waterfall behind which you can sit on conveniently shaped rocks. (☎460 2020. Open daily 10am-10pm. US$17.) **Las Fuentes Termales,** diagonally across from Tabacón, is a slightly cheaper extension of the resort's hot springs. More low-key and local, friendly Las Fuentes indulge all the same. (☎460 8050. Open M-F 10am-9pm, Sa-Su 8am-9pm. US$7.) People also hit many of the several unattended springs along the road. Continue past the resort for a few hundred meters and look for trails—there are no signs. Hot springs at **Baldi Termae,** 4km west of town, are closer by and, like Tabacón, feature a swim-up bar in the middle of one pool. (☎479 9652. US$10, with dinner US$15. Open daily 10am-10pm.)

CAVERNAS DE VENADO

In the *cantón* of San Carlos de Guatuso, in a pueblo named **La Tigre,** are the relatively unknown, family-owned Venado Caves. The caves were discovered in 1942 by Laël Herrera and Manuel Arrollo, two hunters chasing a *tepescuintle* (pig-like animal). On a farm now owned by the well-recognized **Solís-Jiménez family,** guides can take you in to discover the 10 galleries full of stalactites, stalagmites, *columnas* (called papayas because of their resemblance to the fruit), water passage-ways and fossils. During the rainy season, an 18m waterfall awaits you half-way through the 2hr. tour in *Río de La Muerte.* These caves are not the best for claustrophobes. If you visit during the summer time, gallery **Boca de la Serpiente** receives a magical stream of light from 11am to 1pm, but beware of the bats.

▐ TRANSPORTATION

From San Rafael de Guatuso, take any **bus** heading toward **Ciudad Quesada** (San Carlos) or **San José,** and ask the driver to drop you off in **Jicarito** (40min.) Buses from Ciudad Quesada (daily 7:20am and 2:30pm) pass by Jicarito to pick you up and drive the 7km unpaved road up to the small town of **El Venado,** passing through **Linda Vista.** From there, it is a 2.5km hike or hitchhike to the entrance of the caves, after the bridge in **La Tigre.** Buses leave from El Venado at 1:30pm and 6:20am (next day).

If planning public transportation is too complicated, you can take a **taxi** from San Rafael de Guatuso (¢1200 round-trip) or set up a tour with the many adventure companies, mostly all in **La Fortuna** (see p. 187). Renowned guide Guillermo, who speaks perfect English, gives 5hr. tours for US$35 with **Experience Arenal,** in front of Farmacia Fisher. (☎460 1788 or 479 9332. Open daily 7am-4pm.)

▊ ▐ ORIENTATION AND PRACTICAL INFORMATION

76km from Ciudad Quesada, the Venado Caves are close to the town of **El Venado,** which has a few accommodations for the weary adventurer. Contact **Yoleni Cuero** (pager 296 2626 #900566), the cave manager for information on group rates, the on-site restaurant, and 6 to 8hr. expert tours. Remember to bring a set of clothes to change into and a towel for the showers; chances are you will get drenched. A **waterproof camera** is best for pictures. Without a guide or tour group, the **entrance** to the caves is ¢2500 per person, which includes a local guide and all the necessary equipment (helmet, torch, boots).

ACCOMMODATIONS AND FOOD

If you bring your own tent, you may **camp** on-site for free. Otherwise **Hospedaje Las Brisas ❶** has two basic rooms to spend the night down in the town of Venado. It is in front of the Bar/Soda Venado and is your only option for lodging. (Rooms ¢2000 per person.) **Salón Odaneu ❶**, next to Soda Venado, serves *ceviches* and *bocas* from ¢200 to ¢600. (☎460 4077. Open daily 11am-midnight.) You can buy a huge block of cheese from **Productos Lacteos JJ Valenciáno,** across from the Salón Multiuso, where seven workers directly process the milk into cheese. Marita will show you around the factory if you are curious to learn more. (Open daily 6am.)

SAN RAFAEL DE GUATUSO

Part of the large tropical plains of the *cantón* (district) of Guatuso, called *llanuras de Guatuso*, the district of **San Rafael** (pop. 7000 people) covers 304 km of land. Two percent of the *cantón* is made up of the indigenous **Maleku** communities, descendants of the Guahisos, a Corobicí tribe that emigrated from the Central Valley to establish itself in the hillsides of the rivers Tonjibe, Venado, La Muerte, and Margarita. Three of their towns (Margarita, El Sol, and Tonhibe) can be visited. Otherwise, the Guatuso region is now known for its agriculture and for its many churches and religious denominations.

Although rural San Rafael is not frequented by many tourists, it has enough bars to entertain you for a few days and is an excellent base from which to explore the region's numerous natural wonders: Over a fifth of the *cantón* is part of **Refugio Nacional Caño Negro** (p. 197). Two enormous lakes join to bring thousands of birds to **Caño Ciego** (15km away), and the mysterious, heart-shaped **Laguna de Cote** in Volcán Tenorio boasts numerous UFO sightings! As if this weren't enough, the famous **Venado Caves** (p. 191) are only 18km away (1½hr.).

TRANSPORTATION

Although not many tourists have set foot in San Rafael, many *Guatuseños* travel here for work and the town has an efficient **bus** system. **Autotransporte San José-San Carlos** leaves from the *Antigua Parada de Puntarenas* in San José for San Rafael. (☎255 4318; 6hr.; daily 5, 8:30, 11:30am; ¢1400.) From Upala, **Transporte Upala** (☎470 0743; 2hr., 5 per day 5:30am-4:30pm, ¢600) and **La Cañera** (☎470 0197) all service San Rafael and drop off at the bus stop 10m east of Soda La Macha. Buses leave San Rafael right in front of **Restaurante El Turístico** on the main *calle* to: **San José** (6hr., 5 per day 8am-4:30pm, ¢1400) via **Ciudad Quesada** (2hr., 6:30am and 9am, ¢510) and also Naranjo, Sarchí, Zarcero and Alajuela. The easiest way to get to the **Venado Caves** is to take one of these buses, and ask to be dropped off at **Jicarito** (40min.). Buses to Upala (5 per day 8am-8pm) can drop you off in Colonia Puntarenas, where a bus to **Caño Negro** passes by (11am and 4pm.) Special buses can take you to **Río Celeste** (10, 11am, 3, 4pm; return 6am the following day; ¢400). Ask anyone in or in front of **Restaurante El Turístico** for more info and possible schedule changes. There are no licensed **taxis** in Guatuso. **Luís Alberto,** who has a pick-up truck fitting 12 people max is a popular and cheap option. He serves the whole community as well as passers-by. (Pager 224 2400, #110230; cell ☎355 1022. ¢1200 to and from the **Venado Caves,** including wait.) You may also be able to borrow someone's **bike** for a day.

■ 🛈 ORIENTATION AND PRACTICAL INFORMATION

San Rafael stretches along one main *calle*. The action runs from **Bar Restaurante Rancho Ukurin,** coming from Upala on the main *Calle Central* before the bridge (over Río Frío), to **Bar Restaurante El Rancho Guanacaste,** about 800m south.

Tourist Information: Enrique or **William,** at **Restaurante El Turístico,** offer the best tourist information. **Eunice Montiel Alvarez** (☎ 464 0065), is also helpful, at the *municipalidad,* 200m north of Banco Nacional and 100m east. Open M-F 7:30am-4pm. As of August 2002 **Henry's** (☎ 464 0131), tourism office at the gas station was closed, but plans to reopen at the **Tío Albergue Hotel** with a new **Chamber of Tourism.**

Banks: Banco Nacional (☎ 464 0024 or 464 0126) 200m south of Albergue Tío Henry, has **ATMs.** Open M-F 8:30-3:45pm. **Coocique R.L.** (☎ 464 0044), 100m south of Albergue Tío Henry, has **Western Union** Service. Open M-F 7am-4pm, Sa 8am-noon.

Market: Super Sinay (☎ 464 0052), 100m west and 50m north of the school. Open daily 7am-8pm. **Mega Super,** 50m west of the school. Open daily 7am-8pm. **Super Pague Menos** (☎ 464 0373), in front of Importadora Monge on the main *calle.* Open daily 7am-7pm.

Police: Fuerza Pública (☎ 464 0257), next to the post office. Open daily 24hr. You can also ask for assistance at the laid-back **"muni"** (as *guatuseños* call their *municipalidad;* ☎ 464 0065), 200m north of Banco Nacional and 100m east.

Red Cross: (☎ 464 0026), next to the Tribunales de Justicia (the court offices). Consult Fabio Rodríguez. Open daily 7am-6pm.

Medical Services: Clínica S.R. (☎ 464 0161), 500m south of Banco Nacional. Open daily 7am-10pm. **Farmacia Guatuso** (☎ 464 0017) is right next to Tio Henry's. Open M-Sa 6:30am-8:30pm, Su 6:30am-noon.

Phones: Well dispersed. You can use the one in **Restaurante El Turístico.**

Internet: Free access across from the *municipalidad,* although it is mostly for the local community.

Post Office: (☎ 464 0132), on the main *calle.* Open daily 7am-5pm.

📍 ACCOMMODATIONS

There are a number of clean accommodations, though some are a bit stuffier than others. The first one to your right coming in on the main road from Upala is **Cabinas El Gordo ❶,** on the south side of Super Sinay. It has 14 small rooms, TV, A/C, hot water and a 24hr. guarded parking lot. (☎ 464 0009 or 464 0166. Rooms sleeping up to four. ¢3000). **Cabinas Doña Chenta ❶,** in front of Super Sinay, behind the garden lot, is run by Gladys and Martín and has 10 clean family-style rooms. It includes private baths, A/C, TV, parking, Internet access, and free coffee in the morning. Gladys will gladly cook for ¢800, and Martín gives tours and transportation services. (☎ 464 0023; fax 464 0045. ¢1500 per person. Groups ¢1000 per person.) Francisco's **Hotel Las Bribao ❶** (☎ 464 0439 or 464 0352), 50m south of school above the jewelry store, is the cheapest option, with very clean shared bathrooms and a nice balcony. **Albergue Tío Henry ❶** offers 4 rooms with shared baths, A/C and TV. (¢2500 per person. Discounts for larger groups.) Although Tío Henry no longer works here, Ignacio still gives tours (US$40 to **Caño Negro**); ask in advance.

🍴 FOOD

Start off your day with a great pastry or some homemade bread from Noemi's **Panificadora del Norte ❶,** in front of Cabinas Gordo. (☎ 464 0351. Open daily 5:30am-

8:30pm). **Breddy ❶**, in front of Mega Super, is another good bread shop. A number of *sodas* decorate the main *calle*. The most popular is Elia Mora's **Soda La Macha ❶**, in front of Farmacía Guatuso, which sells all kinds of *típico* for under ¢1000. (☎464 0393. Open daily 6am-9pm.)

If you're looking for restaurants, **Jang Ma ❷** (☎464 0048), next to Cabinas el Gordo, sells the only Chinese food in town. **Restaurante Las Orquídeas ❷** is 6km south on the road toward Tilarán in Cabanga, in front of the *salón comunal*. Take a cab for ¢1500. (Open daily 7am-10pm.) There is also well-known **Restaurante El Turístico ❶**, in front of the bus stop on the main road, with great service and TV. Don't forget to taste the homemade, rich *menonita* cakes sold here. (☎464 1000. Meals ¢700-1200. Open daily 6am-10pm.) Of the many bars that serve food, definitely set foot into the family-run **Bar/Restaurante El Rancho Guanacaste ❶**, 200m south of the *colegio*, owned by friendly María Pineda Dávila. María's father, Juan, can teach you how to cook the best *arepas* (flat cornbread) and *empanadas* (turnovers). (☎464 1082. Simple food for ¢500; beer ¢375. Open daily 11am-2am.) The very popular **Bar/Restaurante Rancho Ukurin ❷**, 300m north of the Río Frío on the road toward Upala, has a restaurant serving pricier typical food under a straw hut roof. (☎/fax 464 0308. Cover ¢500. Open daily 10am-2:30am. Accepts credit cards.) **Bar Restaurante La Bomba ❶**, next to La Bomba gas station, serves *casados* (¢850), and rice with shrimp (¢1300), with a TV. (☎464 6104. Open M-Sa 6am-8pm.)

👁 SIGHTS

Guatuso is a great option for a rural experience. Its *fiesta patronal* (patron saint festival) to San Rafael is on October 24. If you have never seen a cattle auction, **Subasta Ganadero Maleco**, only 2km south of the center, is quite an experience, with typical auctioners zooming the weight and prices of the infinite cattle passing by every Wednesday. Ask **Luís Alberto** (see **Transportation**, above) to take you. Also ask about the *cabalgatas* that take place every month, where seemingly thousands of horse riders head off to a nearby pueblo on their beautiful horses for a daily festival to entertain the community.

🎭 NIGHTLIFE

Bars are open late. **Bar/Restaurante El Rancho Guanacaste** (see **Food**, above) has a very spacious cement "hut" with a dance floor that gets hopping. (☎464 1082. Beer ¢375. Open daily 11am-2am.) Popular **Bar/Restaurante Rancho Ukurin** (see **Food**, above), has karaoke and Friday night parties. (☎/fax 464 0308. Cover ¢500. Open daily 10am-2:30am.) A more laid back locale where young locals hang out is **Bar Los Ganaderos**, 150m east of Banco Nacional. It has a huge TV, only a few nude pictures, three pool tables (¢50 per game), and specializes in *bocas* (appetizers) with *cerveza* for ¢500. (☎464 0313. Open daily 11am-midnight).

UPALA

In the province of Alajuela, only nine kilometers from the border of Nicaragua and resting on the shores of the Río Zapote, Upala is the perfect base for excursions into Volcán Tenorio, Volcán Miravalles, Refugio Camelias, and even Caño Negro. This city has every modern comfort, but is relatively unfamiliar to the international tourist. Many of the proud Upaleños descend from Nicaragua, and will take you into their homes and hearts during your stay here.

▐ TRANSPORTATION

There are three offices inside the **bus** terminal to buy your tickets in advance. **Office Autotransporte Upala** (☎ 669 0261. Open daily 5:30am-1pm and 2:30pm-5:30pm) sells tickets for route 509 to **Cañas** (2hr. daily, 7 per day 5am-5:15pm, ¢530), via **Canalete** (¢150), **Areno** (¢280), **Bijagua** (45min., ¢300), and **Río Naranjo** (1hr., ¢370). There are two options to travel to **San José: Office Transnorte Upala** (☎ 470 0747. Direct M-F 5am, ¢1625; express M-F 5:15am and Sa-Su 9:30am), and **La Cañera** (5hr., M-F 2pm, Sa-Su 1:30pm; ¢1625). Ask at Soda Tapia for Don Rafa (☎ 470 0105) for information on buses to: **Ciudad Quesada** (3½hr., ¢1100), via **San Rafael de Guatusos** (2hr., 6 per day 5:30am-4:30pm, ¢600); **Aguas Claras** (2½hr., M-Sa 11:30am, 1, 4:30pm; ¢600); **San José de Upala** (1hr.; 10:30am, 1:30pm; ¢400); **Cuatro Bocas** (1½ hr.; daily 11am, 4:30pm; ¢400). **Taxis** cluster outside of the bus terminal and are recommended for travel around Upala.

◼▮ ORIENTATION AND PRACTICAL INFORMATION

The *parque principal* is divided into four parts, with a basketball court and three rectangles of grassy areas, surrounded by benches and pay phones. The bus terminal and Río Zapote are to the south, the road to Cañas faces north, the main white church is to the east, and to the west you'll see the *mariposario* (butterfly house) and hospital.

There is no **tourist office** in Upala, so the best place to find out information is at the **Municipalidad** (☎ 470 0157 or 470 0167; fax 470 0087). Other good sources of information include the bus terminal and local Antonio Salgado. For information about natural sites **MINAE** (☎ 470 0100) is 150m east of the *fiscalía* on the southeast side of the plaza, open M-F 8am-4pm. The **bank** in town, Banco Nacional, 500m east of the bus terminal, charges to change money and traveler's checks, and has one **ATM** (☎ 470 0134 or 470 0147. Open M-F 8:45am-3:45pm.) **Supermarket Upala** is on the west corner of the bus terminal. (☎ 470 0092. Open M-Sa 7:30am-8pm, Su 8am-noon.) The **police station** (☎ 470 0134) is 55m south of the northeast side of the plaza, open 24hr. daily. The **red cross** (☎/fax 470 0080; emergency ☎ 128 or 911), on the south side of the plaza. Open M-Sa 7am-4pm, daily 24hr. for emergencies. the **hospital** (☎ 470 0058), is 1km west of the Red Cross along the principal road to Cañas, open 24hr. There is one **pharmacy** in the bus terminal, and also Farmacía Amistad (☎ 470 0884.), 20m east on the main street south of the bus terminal, open M-Su 8am-8pm. The **post office** (☎ 470 0545; fax 470 0174), next to the police station, is open M-F 8am-noon and 1pm to 5:30pm. **Internet** access is available at Centro de Amigos Fresas Cafe Internet (☎/fax 470 0893; vindasmartin@hotmail.com). Open M-F noon-9pm, Sa-Su noon-10pm, 30min ¢400, 1hr. ¢600.

▐ ACCOMMODATIONS

Hotel Rosita (☎ 470 0198), 50m east of the metallic bridge, has a pink theme, and is probably one of the best deals in town. Well maintained rooms and a nice, tiled shared bathroom. ¢1500 per person. ❶

Cabinas Marita (☎ 470 0442), 175m east of the Palacio Municipal, offers very clean, orange rooms with private bathrooms. Single¢2500; matrimonial double ¢3500. ❷

Cabinas del Norte (☎ 470 0636), for a quick place to sleep, is right above the bus terminal. Surprisingly clean, fanned rooms and private bathroom. ¢2000 per person. ❷

Hotel Upala (☎ 470 0169), on the west side of the plaza, has good natural lighting and a breeze. Clean, private bathrooms. ¢2500 per person, ¢3000 with TV. ❷

Pensión Familiar, 7m east of the Palacio Municipal across from the cable TV store, has tiny rooms with thin mattresses and one dark, public bathroom. The poor conditions are compensated by the kind owners. ¢1000 per person. ❶

Cabinas Maleku (☎470 0142), in the square on the north side. Simple rooms ¢3000 per person, 10,000¢ with TV and A/C. ❹

Cabinas Buena Vista (☎470 0186), 150m south of the metallic bridge, with no vista and 17 luxurious, spacious rooms. ¢2000 per person. ❷

🍴 🎵 FOOD ENTERTAINMENT

Sodas abound around the bus terminal/market area. The most popular one is Don Rafa's Soda Tapia. **Restaurante Buena Vista ❶,** at the east corner of the metallic bridge. This Chinese restaurante serves great food and has an even better view of the Río Zapote. (☎477 0063. Open daily 10am-1am.) **Cafe Internet Fresas ❶** (see **Orientation and Practical Information,** above), serves cheap fast food, with great super tacos (¢325) and milkshakes.

Salón Marketable, located in front of the metallic bridge, is a good bet for a beer (¢400) or liquor. (Open daily 11am-midnight.) **Bar Tere** is next to the Librería Americana, 10m west of Cabinas Buena Vista. *Bocas* (appetizers) are served with any beer. As of August 2002 a *discoteca* is under construction. (☎470 0123. Open M-Sa 11am-midnight.) Most Upaleños go to the *bailes calientes* (hot dances) at **El Rodeo,** 1km away. (☎470 8057. Open daily 10am-3am. Taxi ¢1000.)

👁 SIGHTS

Beyond the nearby natural wonders, be sure to check out the spacious **mariposario** (butterfly house). Located 175m east of the metallic bridge, on the other side down an unpaved road along the river, peruse a butterfly collection from all over the world. Beautiful handicrafts are made and sold here too.

LOS CHILES

Los Chiles, a border town 101km north of Ciudad Quesada and 3km south of the Nicaragua border, radiates a sleepy, small-town feel. In the past, this area has been home to huge cacao plantations and the rubber industry. The town's namesake dates back to the days of the rubber extractors, who passed time telling each other *chiles,* or jokes. Those who come from Nicaragua usually have their sights set on the Refugio Nacional de Vida Silvestre Caño Negro, accessible via the Río Frío.

🚌 TRANSPORTATION

Buses leave from the station 300m east of the northeast corner of the *parque,* next to the municipal market, to: **San José** (6hr., 7 per day 5am-7:45pm, ¢1515); via **Ciudad Quesada** (3hr., 11 per day 4:30am-5:30pm, ¢750); **Caño Negro** (1½hr., M-F 5am-2pm, ¢450); **Upala** (3½hr., 850C). Buses also leave for **San José** from the bus terminal on Av.9, Calle 12/10 (5hr., daily 5:30am-3:30pm, ¢1450). Boats go to and leave from **San Carlos, Nicaragua** (45min., ¢80). There are **taxis** all over to get around the city, but beware of getting ripped off.

✈ 🛈 ORIENTATION AND PRACTICAL INFORMATION

The **Río Frío** and **docks** are 200m west of the southwest corner of the *parque.* A **soccer field** marks the center and **parque central** of Los Chiles. **Tourist information** can be found at **Servitur,** located in the Cabinas Jabiru (See **Accommodations,** below.

Open 7am-9pm), **Eco Directa,** 100m west of the southwest corner of the soccer field. (☎471 1414. Open M-Sa 8am-midnight, Su 8am-3pm.), and the **Municipalidad,** 50m west of the southwest corner of the *parque.* **Banco Nacional,** 50m east of the northeast corner of the *parque,* changes US dollars, Euros, and traveler's checks. (☎471 1150. Open M-F 8:30am-3:45pm.) The **green house** on the west side of Banco Nacional and the **little store-house** next to the Hotel Eco-Rancho, across from the immigration office, are the only places that change Colones into Córdobas and vice versa. Other services include: **supermarket,** 10m east of the immigration office (open daily 6am-10pm); **police** (☎471 1183 or 911 for emergencies), 300m east and 100m south of the southeast corner of the *parque* on the highway; **Red Cross,** on the northwest corner of the soccer field (☎471 1037; open 24hr.); **hospital,** 200m south of the police station (☎471 1045; open 24hr.); and **post office,** in front of the courthouse, 2½ blocks east of the northeast corner of the *parque.*

🏠 ACCOMMODATIONS

The cleanest and nicest rooms in town are at **Hotel Rancho Eco Directa ❸,** across from the immigration office. (☎/fax 471 1414; cocas34@hotmail.com. Breakfast is included. Singles US$25; doubles US$30; triples $US45) **Hotel Central ❶,** next to the store in front of the *casa cural* on the southeast corner of the *parque,* has 16 rooms around a dark but spacious *sala* where you can watch TV and hang out. (Singles ¢800 per person; doubles with private bath ¢2000.) **Hotel Cinco Estrella ❶,** on the south side of the soccer field, is far from a five-star hotel, but the price is right. A bright green, narrow hallway leads to 12 bare rooms with fans. Also serves *típico* food for ¢900 a plate. (☎471 1088. Singles ¢800; doubles ¢1500; quads with private bath ¢2000.) A bit farther away, uphill toward the hospital is **Hotel Cardina ❶,** 3 blocks east of the southeast corner of the *parque* and 100m south uphill, offers clean rooms and cabins. (☎471 1116; fax 471 1151. Doubles ¢2200; Cabins ¢3500-6000, some with TV and A/C.) **Cabinas Jabirú ❶,** 2 blocks east and ½ block north of the northeast side of the *parque,* offers 10 cabins. Reservations recommended. TV, hot water, and laundry are available. (☎471 1055; fax 471 1496; jabiru@hotmail.com. Singles US$8.50; doubles US$12; triples US$15. Prices don't include taxes or A/C.)

🍴 🎵 FOOD AND ENTERTAINMENT

Kick back with the tour bus crowd and dine at **Restaurante El Parque ❷** on the southwest corner of the soccer field. (*Arroz con pollo* ¢850. Open 7am-8pm.) Or, pull up a stool at the exceptionally friendly **Soda Pamela ❶,** 300m east of the northeast corner of the *parque.* (☎471 1454. *Casados* ¢800; Eggs, toast, and coffee ¢550. Open 6am-9pm.) Next door is hopping **Socalo Disco Club Los Rables,** the only bar/disco in town. (☎471 1198. Beer ¢275, on disco night 350¢. Open daily 10am-2:30am. No cover on dancing nights Th-Su with DJ Misterioso.) **Bar Los Parados,** 100m south of the church in the *parque,* has big screen cable TV, and great beers and appetizers. (Open T-Su 11am-midnight.) **Bar/Restaurante Sonia** is where the locals eat breakfast. (Meat ¢1000-1300; *casados* ¢800. Open M-Sa 6am-10pm, Su 9am-10pm.)

REFUGIO NACIONAL CAÑO NEGRO

Refugio Caño Negro is one of the wettest places in Costa Rica. The refuge is soaked by 3.5m of rain every year, and 85% of its 100 sq. km are flooded from May to December. In the heart of this aquatic wonderland is the enormous Laguna Caño Negro, a 9 sq. km lake that refills every May when the banks of the Río Frío and Río Caño Negro overflow. The swampy, canal-linked labyrinth of mangroves, rivers, and small lakes harbor one of the most important wildlife shelters in the country, with over 315 species of birds and 160 species of mammals. Reptiles abound, with crocodiles, iguanas, turtles, caimans, and snakes appearing most frequently. Rare species of fish swim the waters, including the tarpo, guapote, and the prehistoric gaspar. Caño Negro is part of the protected area of the Conservación Arenal Huetar Norte, and focuses on the betterment of the socioeconomic conditions of the community by developing sustainable development programs. Most of the year, guided boat tours are the only way to visit the refuge, but between February and April, you can also explore the refuge by foot over the dried-up lake, though there are no official trails. (Park open daily 7am-4pm. US$6.) On the edge of the refuge, 23km southwest of Los Chiles by dirt road, is the peaceful village of Caño Negro. There are few outside visitors and—thanks to unpaved roads—no tour buses. It's worth the extra effort to see the refuge from here.

🚌 **TRANSPORTATION.** The shortest road from **San José** by **car** is to head north on the road toward Los Chiles. The entrance to the Refugio is 1km after the Tanques Gas Zeta. Go toward "Jobo" until you reach the new bridge crossing Río Frío, turn left, and continue 12km until the Caño village. Although the unpaved road is very bumpy, the public **buses** do pass by Caño Negro; always ask and make sure you're on the right bus. Buses go from **Los Chiles** via **Caño Negro** (1½ hr.; daily 5am and 2pm, return 6:30am and 6:30pm; ¢400.) Buses from **Upala** also pass by the refuge (2hr.; daily 4:30, 11am, 4:30pm; return 6:30am, 1, 3:30pm; ¢400.) Wait for the bus on the northwest side of the *parque*, or anywhere in front of the hotels on the town's main entrance road.

🔳🔢 **ORIENTATION AND PRACTICAL INFORMATION.** The bus enters the village on the main road, ultimately reaching the northwest corner of the *parque*. There you'll find the only good mini-super in town, next to the church and across from the primary school. The **refuge** entrance, under the RAMSAR sign, is on the southeast corner of the *parque*. You can also enter from Albergue Caño Negro or Hotel Fishing Club, which are on the lagoon and have boats. The **MINAE** office, 200m west of the mini-super, provides solid **tourist information** (open M-F 8am-4pm, Sa-Su 8am-9am), as does the **information booth** in front of Albergue Caño Negro, 200m north of the northwest corner of the *parque* (open daily, no fixed hours). There is no bank and the nearest medical facility is the **Red Cross** in Los Chiles (☎471 1061, see **Los Chiles,** p. 196). There is a **health center** on the northwest side of the *parque*. The **police station** is on the southeast side of the *parque*, 50m from school, and can be reached by radio in an emergency (with the help of a local business). The town has three **public telephones:** one at the mini super (☎461 8466; open M-Sa 7am-8pm, Su 7am-noon), the second across from the information booth (☎461 8464; open M-Sa 7am-11am, noon-5pm, and 6-8pm; Su 7-11am), and the third 100m west of the church (☎461 8442. ¢10 per min.).

🛏 **ACCOMMODATIONS. Albergue Caño Negro ❶,** 200m north of the northwest corner of the park, sits on a field that directly borders the Lago Caño Negro, with charming cabins on stilts. Good mattresses and wall fans come with concrete, communal, cold-water bathrooms. There are three outdoor grills to cook your own food; be sure to turn lights on downstairs to attract the harmless but annoying beetles so they leave you alone. (☎/fax 461 8442, beeper ☎224 2400. US$7 per person; camping US$3 per person.) **Cabinas Martín Pescador ❷,** is 100m past the MINAE office in the field at the end of the road. Check in at the "reception" 100m north and 50m east of the park's northwest corner. The large, fanned rooms are in good shape and have tiled bathrooms and covered porches. (Beeper ☎233 3333. US$10 per person.) It is possible to **camp ❶** on the grounds of the Caño Negro

TOURS FROM LOS CHILES AND FORTUNA. Tour companies in Fortuna, Los Chiles, and Ciudad Quesada offer "Caño Negro Trips" along the Río Frío, though only some make it into the borders of the refuge. The Río Frío flows south from Los Chiles and into Refugio Caño Negro, where it eventually meets Lago Caño Negro. While much of the same wildlife that's in the refuge can be seen from the river, you may have bus loads of tourists for company. The advantage of large, pre-packaged tours from Fortuna or Ciudad Quesada is that single travelers can latch on from Los Chiles for US$20-25. One such company is **Aventuras Arenal** in Fortuna; call a day or two before and set the price. (☎479 9133; fax 479 9295; www.arenaladventures.com.) **Eco Directa** organizes trips from Los Chiles. (☎/fax 471 1414. US$60 for 1-8 people, US$70 for 8-12; US$10 per additional person. See **Los Chiles: Practical Information.**) **Servitur** offers similar trips for US$80 per person, 1-4 people with lunch and transportation included. (☎471 1055/fax 471 1055; see **Practical Information,** under Los Chiles.) **Restaurante El Parque** offers a 3hr. bilingual, guided trip to the first lagoon. (☎/fax 471 1090. Trip 9:30am, 1-10 people US$70, lunch US$7 per person. See **Food and Entertainment,** under Los Chiles.) Adventure **fishing** companies such as **Costa Rica Jungle Tours** in Fortuna can take you for a full week of action-packed fishing. (☎469 1400; maxtrost2001@yahoo.com; www.costaricanjungletours.com.) **Jungle River Big Game Fishing** leaves from Los Chiles. (☎239 4037; sanjuan@racsa.co.cr.; www.nicaraguafishing.com.) If you have time, it is more economical and enriching to take a bus to the village of Caño Negro and hire a local guide.

MINAE office, with access to cold-water showers and bathrooms (¢300 per person). The **Salón/Bar/Restaurante Danubio Azul ❹** has rooms in cabins along the river. Rooms have private bathrooms and fans (¢2500-3000). **Hotel Fishing Club ❻**, located at the entrance to the village of Caño Negro, has a nice restaurant and luxurious cabins with TV, private baths, hot water, and fans. (☎656 0071. Doubles US$70; US$14 per additional person.) **Natural Lodge Caño Negro ❺**, 300m north and 50m west of the mini-super, offers ten high-style rooms with double queen beds. Amenities include a pool, jacuzzi, bicycles, volleyball, and a restaurant. (Food ¢900-3800. Open daily 7am-10pm.) The hotel also sells two day tour packages (☎265 6370; fax 265 4561; www.canonegrolodge.com; natural@racsa.co.cr. Tours 2 people US$140. 1-4 person rooms US$56-86.)

◻ FOOD. There are not many places to eat in Caño Negro, but **Sodita la Palmera ❶**, on the southeast corner of the *parque*, should satisfy almost any appetite. (Breakfast ¢500; lunch and dinner ¢700-900. Open daily 7am-8pm.) **Salón/Bar/Restaurante Danubio Azul ❷**, on the southeast side of the *parque*, has a nice, spacious eating area, which transforms into a discotheque from M-W. With nightly games of *ruleta* (roulette) you can play (¢325) to win 7 beers. The house specialty is *guapote* fish (¢1500-2000), but meals start at ¢400. (Open daily 10am-2:30am.)

◧ ⚑ SIGHTS AND OUTDOOR ACTIVITIES BEYOND THE REFUGE. There are five *mariposarios* (butterfly farms) in Caño Negro. One farm, 100m west of the northwest corner of the *parque*, is the five-year-old project of *La Asociación de Mujeres de Caño Negro* (The Women's Association of Caño Negro, ASOMUCAN). Be sure to buy some of their fresh homemade bread on your way out. (Open daily, no set hours.) The other four are in homes like that of La Reinata, 10m east of the southeast side of the *parque*, and also sell crafts. (US$7 entrance fee.)

⚡ VISITING THE REFUGE. The park is most easily accessed from Caño Negro village and is best seen by boat, though it is possible to hike. **Colibrí Tours,** run by Dolores and Julia, runs tours of the refuge. (beeper ☎225 2500. 2½hr. tours for five people US$45.) Antonio at **Cabinas Martín Pescador** (see above) takes people out on his canopied *lancha* (3hr., 1-3 people US$40). Álvaro, at **Albergue Caño Negro,** also leads tours (3hr., 1-4 people, US$50; 4hr. US$100). Álvaro and Colibrí Tours offer **fishing** tours (1-3 people, US$80 per day). Those serious about fishing should bring their own gear. Other hotels also offer tour services such as the **Martín Pescador Hospedaje** (3hr., US$20 per hr.) and **Natural Lodge Caño Negro** (2½hr., US$25 per person; horses US$10 per hr.). **Hotel Fishing Club** specializes in sportfishing (8hr. full day US$300; 4hr. half day US$200. See **Accommodations,** above.)

Prices for wildlife and fishing trips do not include park entrance (US$6) or fishing license (license US$30). You can pay the fee to the ranger in the kiosk at the refuge entrance, on the southeast corner of the *parque.* Fishing is prohibited between Apr. 1-July 31. To arrange for a fishing license, make your US$30 deposit in any Banco Nacional in the country and pick it your package up at any national MINAE office, including the one 100m north and 200m west of the northwest corner of the *parque* in Caño Negro. Call the Area de Conservación Huetar Norte in Upala with any questions (☎470 0100).

⚑ TO NICARAGUA VIA RÍO SAN JUAN

The Río San Juan river-crossing into Nicaragua was a main route for Contras during the 1980s. Today, the cross-over is made mostly by locals and the border is accessible for all travelers. Those who have experienced the interminable lines at the Peñas Blancas frontier crossing might want to look into crossing on this side, as it is virtually hassle free. To leave Costa Rica, you must go through the **Oficina de Migración,** 1 block west of the southwest corner of the *parque.* (☎471 1233. Open daily 8am-6pm.) The municipality charges ₡200 for use of the dock. **Boats** leave frequently (9am-4pm) to **San Carlos, Nicaragua.** Contact the immigration office or police (☎471 1183) for more information.

NICOYA PENINSULA

While the roads can be difficult and the journeys hampered by backtracking, the seclusion of the Nicoya Peninsula will have you puzzling about where all those other bus passengers disappeared to. The inland is filled with rugged cowpokes ambling through dusty streets and *pueblos* where the people guard a proud history. Travelers are beginning to leave their mark along the beaches, but for the most part, they are still appreciated by the people whose homes line the shore. The locals share their beautiful environment with pride, and take care of it accordingly. Meander through the streets, pick a favorite beach and tell everyone you meet that it's the *"playa más bonita del mundo,"* and you'll fit right in.

PLAYA HERMOSA

Wealthy and budget-minded tourists alike enjoy the clean waters, warm sands, and tame tides of Playa Hermosa. Joggers run the beaches early in the morning, but crowds are never overwhelming, and because the beach remains the real attraction, the town itself is low-key. Whether you plan to stay a day or a decade, bring a towel and swimsuit for tranquil relaxation. Hermosa is one of the best **scuba diving** beaches in Costa Rica and **snorkelers** will befriend their fair share of tropical fish around rocky points.

TRANSPORTATION

Buses to **Hermosa** depart from San José on Av. 5/7, Calle 12, one block north of the Atlántica Norte Terminal (4½hr., 3:30pm, ¢1700) and from Liberia (1hr., 6 per day 5am-5:30pm, ¢300). **Taxis** are available from El Coco to Playa Hermosa (15min., ¢2000). Out of Playa Hermosa, buses leave from Playa Panamá and pass the second entrance to Playa Hermosa. Buses depart to **San José** (4½hr., 5am, ¢1700) and **Liberia** (1hr., 7 per day 8am-7pm, ¢300) via **Sardinal.**

ORIENTATION AND PRACTICAL INFORMATION

Playa Hermosa runs north-south; the beach is to the west. There are two entrances to the beach from the main road. **Playa Panamá** is about 3km farther along the main road to the north, 5km if you're looking for the Playa Panamá **pueblo.**

The **Aquatic Sports MiniSuper** is 500m west and 25m south of the second entrance to the beach. (☎672 0050. Open daily 6am-9pm. ¢200 to shower.) There are **public showers** and **toilets** at **Pescado Loco Bar y Restaurant.** A **public phone** can be found 150m east of the beach at the second entrance. International collect calls and credit card calls can be made from the phone outside Aquatic Sports. The only **Internet** is at the Villa Acacia resort, 350m east of the beach. (¢1000 per 30min., ¢1500 per hr. Open 6am-9pm daily.)

ACCOMMODATIONS

The town's budget selection is limited to a few relatively comfortable places.

NICOYA PENINSULA

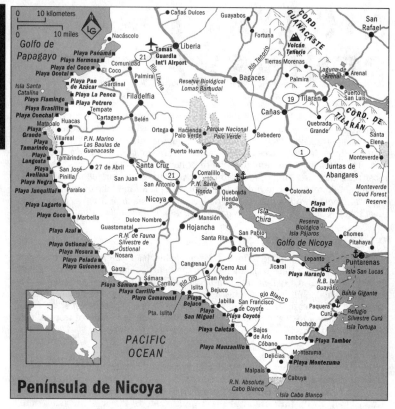

Península de Nicoya

 Ecotel (☎ 672 0175), is the most unique, set amongst the trees right on the sand. Walk 500m down the road from the second entrance, and turn left at the last road before the beach; the hotel is beyond Aquatic Sports. The French-Canadian owner, a long-time conservationist, will offer you a choice of a wood-paneled room with bunks (US$10-15 per person), a comfortable mattress in an indoor loft with a view of palm trees (US$10), or a mosquito net-draped bed on the balcony outdoors, made private by standing screens (US$10). He rents the whole floor (sleeps 10) with a complete kitchen, living room, porch, and bath for US$30-50 per night. You can also **camp** in the yard, with access to an outdoor kitchen and simple bathrooms ($10 per tent). ❶

Cabinas La Casona (☎ 672 0025), 500m west of the second entrance and to the right. The perks of a stove and refrigerator save the bright rooms from feeling like a random conglomeration of bunk beds. Doubles ¢7000-11,000; quads ¢10,000-17,000; quints ¢15,000-20,000. Discounts on longer stays. ❷

The Iguana Inn (☎/fax 672 0065; iguanainn@hotmail.com), has spacious, wooden rooms that fit up to six people. Private baths, a common kitchen, pool, laundry, and informal taxi service are additional incentives. 6-person room with kitchen ¢10,000-15,000; ¢30,000 per night in high season for house with kitchen, 2 double bedrooms, living room, TV. ❶

Cabinas Playa Hermosa (☎/fax 672 0046; visani@racsa.co.cr), down the road from the first entrance, is a big complex of pale pink cabins with blue trim, separated from the beach by a garden. Inside rooms are roomy and breezy (try to get one close to the water). Hot-water baths. Excellent and affordable Italian restaurant. Singles US$15-20; doubles US$25-40; triples US$40-50, depending on the season. ❷

Villa Huetares (☎672 0052), is a killer deal for groups of 6; the arrangement includes kitchen, two bedrooms with A/C, cable TV and bath. Basketball court and pool available. Doubles US$40, high season US$90; room for 3-6 people US$60/US$90. ❸

Hotel El Velero (☎672 0036 or 672 1017; elvelerocr@yahoo.com; www.costaricahotel.net), of the high-end hotels, has the most cohesive design, with cool whitewashed hallways, pool, a decorative fountain, and a common area on the second level with wicker rocking chairs, TV, and book exchange. Rooms have A/C and close to the water. Pricey but well-regarded restaurant. Sailboat tours are offered (5hr. tour on a 38 ft. boat with snorkeling, lunch, and drinks US$60 per person). Doubles and triples US$59-110 depending on season, fourth person US$10. ❹

Hotel Villa del Sueño (☎/fax 672 0026; delsueño@sol.racsa.co.cr; www.villadelsueno.com.), down the road from the first entrance, has friendly staff and big, cool, bare rooms. All rooms have A/C, private hot-water bath, and pool access. The restaurant hosts live music—think 60s, 70s, Beatles, and Van Morrison—several times a week during the high season, with a menu that changes nightly. Peppercorn steak US$16. Restaurant open 7am-10pm. Standard doubles US$54-59, superior US$74-89. ❹

Villa Acacia (☎672 1000; villacacia-guana@hotmail.com; www.villacacia.com), across from Villa Huetares, is fronted by a convenient round restaurant/*rancho* with Internet. The eight villas have rosy facades and are equipped with kitchen, A/C, hot-water baths, and cable TV. Standard rooms sleep 3. Pool. Cappuccino ¢700; *plato del día* ¢1800. Restaurant open 6am-9pm. Doubles US$53, in high season US$89; triples US$75/US$119; 2-person villas US$70/US$100, 3-person US$85/US$120, 4-person US$100/US$150. ❹

🔲🎵 FOOD AND ENTERTAINMENT

Restaurants are geared almost exclusively toward tourists: budget deals are rare, and *comida típica* is not common.

🔲 **Restaurante Puesta del Sol,** on the north end of the Pescado Loco road, is well worth the extra money for its delicious Spanish *paella* and tapas. *Paella* with seafood ¢3200 per person, minimum 2 persons; sangria ¢1100. Open daily noon-9pm. ❸

Pescado Loco Bar y Restaurant, 500m toward the beach from the second entrance and 50m to the right, has popular *tico* food at reasonable prices. The bar is often filled with jovial locals. *Casado* ¢1000; orange filet of fish ¢1950. Open daily 7am-midnight. ❶

Cabinas Playa Hermosa, 400m toward the beach on the first entrance (follow the road around the bend). An excellent Italian restaurant with the tempting odors of garlic and oregano. Grilled sea bass ¢2100; spaghetti and macaroni ¢1900. Open daily 7-9:30am and 6-9pm. Open for lunch (in high season only) noon-2pm. ❸

Sunset Restaurant (☎672 1042) doesn't have a sign. Known as "Los Turcos" for the Turkish owners, it is the only true beachside place. No fixed menu, but fresh fish is excellent, if pricey. Seafood soup ¢3500; fish ¢3500. Open daily 7 or 8pm-midnight. ❹

Restaurante Bahía (☎672 0061), on the highway between entrances, is under a new management and trying to change its former reputation as an ugly bar. Now offering a wide menu and fondue (steak, chicken, or pork fondue for two ¢10,000). On rainy nights, call for delivery service (free within 1km). Open Th-Tu 10am-11pm. ❹

Monkey Bar, between the two beach entrances, set back in the trees, is the only bar in Playa Hermosa that functions strictly as such. Sophisticated and fun. Shows sporting events on satellite TV. Tequila Bob plays guitar on Sunday nights in the high season. Beer ¢500. Pool ¢300. Fries ¢800. Hummus ¢1300. Open W-M 5pm-midnight. ❶

◪ WATERSPORTS

The calm, clear water is ideal for **snorkeling, kayaking,** or **waterskiing.** Following the signs from the second entrance to the beach, **Aqua Sport** runs waterskiing (US$60 per hr.), windsurfing (US$15 per hr.), not-to-be-missed banana-boat rides, kayak rentals, snorkeling tours, and boat trips. (☎672 0050. Boat trips ¢1000 per person, 5-person max. per boat. Open daily 6am-9:30pm; in low season until 8pm.) Another option for diving and snorkeling is **Diving Safaris,** 300m from the Villa Acacia complex. Morning dives daily from 8:30am-1pm. Several levels of training available. (☎672 0012 or 672 0147. 2-tank dives US$80 per person including equipment. Snorkeling US$30 for the same amount of time. Open daily 7am-4pm.) The owner of **Ecotel** (see **Accommodations,** above) offers a vast variety of guided tours to Rincón de la Vieja, Santa Rosa, Lao Verde, and the Caño Negra Wildlife Refuge, among other eco-sites. (☎672 0175. 2-person min.)

NEAR PLAYA HERMOSA

PLAYA PANAMÁ
*Buses run from Liberia and pass the second entrance of Hermosa at 8:30am, 12:30, 1:30, and 4:30pm. The last return bus from Panamá leaves the pueblo around 7pm. It's a pleasant **walk** to the beach along the highway, although the miniscule village of Playa Panamá is a few kilometers beyond the beach.*

A little less than 3km north of Playa Hermosa is Playa Panamá. The coastline wraps around in a long and impressive arc, and the water is perfect for swimming. The **Four Seasons Hotel** is staking its claim on the beaches across the Papagayo gulf—Virador and Blanca will be private come December 2003—and promises to drastically alter the view. Other resorts between Hermosa and Panamá have already changed the character of the land. The **"Papagayo Project,"** for example, includes the resorts Costa Esmeralda, Nakuti, Costa Blanca, Alegro, and Giardini di Papagayo (the latter overlooks Playa Panamá to the north). These hotels are well-connected to tour agencies in the US and offer a luxurious experience of Costa Rica with imported amenities. Back on humble Playa Panamá, however, many people **camp** on the shore—you'll recognize the area by the scattered garbage. There are no services like bathrooms or potable water to be found, but if you want a quiet spot, it'll do. Please be responsible with your trash.

PLAYA DEL COCO
The dark and dingy Coco shore gives no indication of the treasures that lie beyond—divers have known for years that the nearby waters hold all sorts of delightful surprises. The public culture of the town revolves around the snorkel, the scuba, and the boats, which can take you out to the more wondrous nature at Playas Huevo, Blanca, and Nacazcolo, and the Bat and Catalinas Islands. Local merchants have, of course, capitalized on the heavy traffic—streets are lined with souvenir shops and stands. Though you might not be able to avoid the tourists on the street, you can certainly escape them in the water.

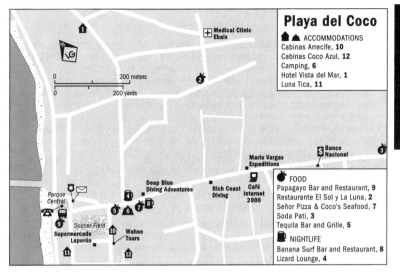

Playa del Coco

ACCOMMODATIONS
Cabinas Arrecife, **10**
Cabinas Coco Azul, **12**
Camping, **6**
Hotel Vista del Mar, **1**
Luna Tica, **11**

FOOD
Papagayo Bar and Restaurant, **9**
Restaurante El Sol y La Luna, **2**
Señor Pizza & Coco's Seafood, **7**
Soda Pati, **3**
Tequila Bar and Grille, **5**

NIGHTLIFE
Banana Surf Bar and Restaurant, **8**
Lizard Lounge, **4**

▟ TRANSPORTATION

Buses head to **San José** (5hr.; 4, 8am, 2pm; ¢1775) and **Liberia** (1hr., 8 per day 5:30am-6pm, ¢250) via **Sardinal** (5min., ¢120).

✚ ❼ ORIENTATION AND PRACTICAL INFORMATION

The main road runs from the **highway** to the **beach,** where you will find the not-very-obvious **parque central** with public phones at its center. Buses stop on the *parque's* south side. When facing the beach, the **soccer field** is about a block to the left.

Bank: Banco Nacional, 750m inland from the beach on the main road, exchanges US dollars and traveler's checks and provides cash advances on Visa. Open M-F 8:30am-3:45pm. You can also exchange currency at **Supermercado Luperón** on the west side of the soccer field. Open M-Sa 7am-8pm, Su 7am-1pm.

Market: Supermercado Luperón (see above).

Medical Services: Medical clinic Ebais (☎670 0987). Walk 150m east on the road north of Lizard Lounge (see **Nightlife,** below), turn right after the bridge and left after Hotel la Puerta del Sol. Open M-Th 7am-4pm, F 7am-3pm. **Farmacia Cocos** (☎670 1186), 200m north of the Banco Nacional. Open M-Sa 8:30am-8pm, Su 9am-1pm.

Red Cross: (☎697 0471), the nearest is in Sardinal.

Emergency: ☎911.

Police: The **police station** (☎670 0258) is across from the bus stop. Open 24hr.

Internet Access: Café Internet 2000 (☎670 0948), 400m south of the *parque.* US$4.50 for 30min., US$6 per hr. Open M-F 9am-7pm, Sa 9am-5pm. **Cabinas Catarino** is 150m south of the *parque.* ¢500 per 30min., ¢900 per hr.

Post Office: In the same building as the police. Open M-F 8am-noon and 1-5:30pm.

Postal code: 5019.

◪ ACCOMMODATIONS

▨ **Hotel Vista del Mar** (☎670 0753; hvistamar@racsa.co.cr; www.beach-hotels-in-costa-rica.com), 1km east on the road that runs north of the Lizard Lounge, is an old-fashioned ranch-style hacienda directly on the beach that puts on no airs. A smattering of chatty scarlet macaws greets you from the shaded courtyard, which has a pool and BBQ grill. The Canadian owner is affectionate to her guests and fixes tremendous breakfasts. Air-conditioned rooms are comfortably antique—the most expensive has a TV and huge bath, while the most rustic is perfect for backpackers, who can also share the TV in the living room and the beach garden at sunset. Breakfast included. Doubles US$40, high season US$55; backpacker room US$10 per night. US$15 per additional person. ❸

Cabinas Arrecife is perfect for those feeling a twinge of homesickness; you will be delighted to meet your parent-like, gracious hosts. Lovely wood-paneled rooms have comfortable beds and balconies. New rooms have TV and private bath. Laundry service and breakfast available. US$10 per person, with private bath US$20; doubles US$23. More basic rooms out back US$6 per person. ❶

Cabinas Coco Azul (☎670 0431), 100m west and 50m south of the soccer field, has big rooms for up to 6 people and is more homey than the price suggests. Big windows, private baths, one room has a kitchen. ¢2500 per person, high season ¢3000. ❶

Luna Tica (☎670 0127), 10m north and 20m west of the *supermercado*, is like two hotels, with a completely different building on each side of the street—rooms are brighter on the beach side. All rooms have private baths. Try for a room with ocean views. Singles ¢4000, in high season ¢5000; doubles ¢7000/¢9000; triples ¢12,000/¢14,000; quads ¢14,000/¢18,000. ❶

Camping (☎670 0151), 200m inland of the *parque* (look for the "camping" sign amongst the souvenir kiosks on the right). Well-shaded site with bathrooms, showers, grills, laundry facilities, and a guard in high season. ¢1000 per person, ¢800 for extended periods. ❶

◪ FOOD

Marisquería La Guajira, right on the beach, has great sunset views. The menu is filled with mouth-watering descriptions that dare you to try everything on the menu. Fried red snapper ¢1700. Coconut *flan* ¢300. Open daily 10am-10pm. ❶

Marisquería Islas Catalina, catch a taxi for the 4km drive from Playa del Coco. Getting here requires a bit of effort, but the fresh, cheap seafood certainly merits the ¢1200 round-trip cost. *Ceviches* ¢1500-1800. Open daily noon-10 or 11pm. ❷

Soda Pati, next to Rich Coast Diving, 300m south of the *parque*, is the best-kept secret in town. The *soda* has no sign, but locals know what it hides: *casados* at unbeatable prices (¢850-900) and other tasty *típico* to match. Open M-F 7am-2pm. ❶

Tequila Bar and Grille, 150m south of the *parque*, serves up a wide variety of Mexican favorites on Mexican crockery. Try the smooth "Howler Tequila" with marinated hot peppers and chaser for ¢900. Fajitas ¢3000. Open Th-Tu 11am-10pm. ❸

Coco's Seafood teams up with **Señor Pizza** (☎670 0532 or 670 0113) in a popular combination of surf and slice. Delivery available. Small cheese ¢1356; *filet de dorado* ¢2350. Open daily 11am-11pm. ❷

Restaurante El Sol y La Luna is the place where Coco Italians bring their native flavors to the table. Handmade pasta and nightly specials are out of this world. *Arrabiata* ¢2000; mushroom lasagna ¢3300. Open 1pm-2:30pm and 5-10pm. ❸

Papagayo Bar and Restaurant (☎ 670 0272), on the beach, on the west side of the *parque,* is more expensive but dependably delicious. Specializes in seafood. *Casados* ¢1750; shrimp kebab ¢4500. Open daily 11am-2am depending on crowd. Kitchen closes at 11pm. ❸

🍷 NIGHTLIFE

Lizard Lounge, 150m south of the *parque,* is mellow, has the snazziest decorations, and draws mostly a tourist crowd with its soundtrack of American music. Pool ¢300. Beer ¢500. Open M-Sa 3pm-2am.

Banana Surf Bar and Restaurant, 300m inland, is the hot spot in town, luring in locals from other beach towns. The dancing gets hot and sweaty under the black lights to the beats of techno, reggae, disco, and the ubiquitous *salsa* and *merengue.* Pool (¢1000 per hr.) and darts are additional diversions. Beer ¢500. Open daily 5pm-3am.

🌊 WATERSPORTS

Prime dive season is Apr.-Sept. The best scuba and snorkeling are reached by boat. The nearby Catalinas and Bat Islands are hot sites for turtles, sharks, and octopus. The warm water and abundance of fish make up for mediocre visibility.

Rich Coast Diving (☎/fax 670 0176, in the US and Canada 1-800-4-DIVING; dive@rich-coastdiving.com), 300m south of the *parque,* offers diving, including a 3-day trip to the Bat Islands (US$495 per person), training for a variety of levels, and equipment rentals. Open daily 8am-5pm.

Mario Vargas Expeditions (☎/fax 670 0351; mvexped@racsa.co.cr; www.divexpeditions.com), 400m south of the *parque,* across from Café Internet 2000, is the cheapest place to rent equipment. Dive trips to the Catalinas and Murciélagos Islands are a bit more expensive. Ex-President Figueres dives exclusively with Mario. 2-tank dive around Catalina US$75 per person. Wet suits US$6 per day, mask and snorkel US$4 per day. Open daily 8am-6:30pm.

Wahoo Tours (☎ 670 0413; cell 374 4326; wahootours@hotmail.com), runs out of Cabinas Arrecife, 100m west of the southwest corner of the soccer field. Offers sportfishing trips (full day to Bat Islands US$500), tours to the islands and Santa Rosa National Park, snorkeling trips (1hr. at each of 3 beaches US$25 per person for a minimum of 3 people), and transportation to renowned surf spots like Witch's Rock and Ollie's Point (US$80 per person). Discounts for Arrecife guests. Open daily 8am-5pm.

Deep Blue Diving Adventures (☎ 670 1004, deepblue@sol.racsa.co.cr; www.scuba-diving-in-costa-rica.com), run out of the Best Western, has competitive rates on snorkeling and scuba trips and equipment. They also offer PADI certification courses. 2-tank morning dive US$35. Open water certification US$225. Open daily 8am-5pm.

OCOTAL

From the stacked hills that wrap around the small bay of **Playa Ocotal,** the view of expansive water and verdant islands is breathtaking. Ocotal is undoubtedly a wealthy enclave, and although walking up the road you may hear solitary hammers working on dream homes, for now it retains an untouched tranquility that similar beaches have lost. Boats are moored in the bay for diving and sportfishing and swimmers and sunbathers have no interference from rough surf or sudden tides. Save the Ocotal Resort's employee shuttle, no buses run to Ocotal from Playa del Coco (3km away). A taxi costs ¢1500.

The few places to stay at in Ocotal can be quite pricey. The relatively comfortable rooms at **Ocotal Inn Bed and Breakfast ❸**, on the road to Ocotal, are the cheapest, with hot-water private baths and a second-floor lounging balcony. For good eats, make a reservation to dine at its Peruvian restaurant in the courtyard. Breakfast is included. (☎ 670 0835; info@ocotalinn.com; www.ocotalinn.com. Mahi mahi in beer with ginger, onion, garlic, tomato on pasta US$5.35. Singles $25-30; doubles $35-45; triples $45-60; quads $55-70. Prices vary by season. Student, group, and extended stay discounts.) **Hotel Villa Casa Blanca ❹** has ten richly-decorated Spanish colonial rooms and two intimate honeymoon suites. It also offers a condo with a separate entrance, protected terrace, kitchen, TV, king-size bed, and sofa. Buffet breakfast is included and open to the public. There is also a pool with a bridge and a jacuzzi in the garden. (☎ 670 0518; fax 670 0448; vcblanca@racsa.co.cr. Breakfast 7:30-9am ¢2000. Standard suite double US$70; family suite US$95; condo US$110; honeymoon prices US$20-30 lower in low season; US$10 per additional person.) Don't pass by **Villa Vista Mar ❸**, farther uphill along the same road as Hotel Villa Casa Blanca, thinking it's just a house. The three homey apartments Ed and Laurie rent out are distinct, self-contained, and comfortable. The big one has a fully stocked kitchen, TV, two matrimonial beds, and a breakfast bar, while the medium room that shares the terrace has beds arranged on two levels and a slightly more limited kitchen. All have generous windows overlooking the pool. Hammock and *ranchito* (thatched hut) with BBQ outside. (☎ 368 0240; elscanlan@hotmail.com. Big room US$60-80, medium US$50-70, small US$35-50.)

Fusión Natural Spa offers 25 spa treatments (think muds, manicures, massages) and **aerobics, yoga,** and **powerwalks** around Ocotal. Call about "destination packages" that include lodging and a specially designed menu of food. (☎ 670 0914; www.fusionnaturalspa.com. Pura Vida massage US$50; volcanic mud wrap US$55; sports adventure package US$95. Open M-Sa 9am-5pm in the high season, by appointment in low season.)

POTRERO

The beaches of Playa Potrero, Playa Penca (a deserted white-sand beach), Playa Prieta, and Playa Pan de Azúcar spread out from the village of Potrero, and the ancient islands off the coast seem lifted from a Japanese landscape. Potrero itself is so small, you could shout across it. Life is unhurried. This is the end of the bus line and traffic goes one way—out. Down on the shore, Flamingo is visible across the bay and provides a nice-and-distant contrast to the quiet rocky cove where fishermen stand in the water, culling food from the sea.

▐▀ ▄▌ **TRANSPORTATION AND ORIENTATION.** The bus from Brasilito departs Potrero for **Flamigo** and **Santa Cruz** (5 per day 6am-4:30pm). Catch it on the south side of the field by **Supermercado Ceimy,** on the southeast corner. The unobtrusive **church** is on the west side of the field.

▐▘ **ACCOMMODATIONS.** Walk just north of the northwest corner of the field and turn left to reach **Restaurante and Cabinas La Penca ❸**, which is *the* place to eat in Potrero, and to find a clean, roomy place to sleep. Behind the restaurant, air-conditioned rooms with private baths have good matrimonial beds with refrigerators, as well as a two-room apartment with kitchen. (☎ 654 4535. Doubles ¢12,000-15,000 in high season, ¢2000 per additional person; apartment US$50 per night, US$200 per week. V.) Many foreign students stay at **Bahía Esmeralda ❷**, south of the southeast corner of the *parque* as you enter Potrero center, for its discounted prices. It is a comfortable hotel with a pool and restaurant. In addition to four simple rooms with bunk beds and individual beds,

There's only one way to max out your travel experience and make the most of your time on the road: The International Student Identity Card.

 Packed with travel discounts, benefits and services, this card will keep your travel days and your wallet full. Get it before you hit it!

Visit **ISICUS.com** to get the full story on the benefits of carrying the ISIC.

90 minutes, wash & dry (one sock missing).
5 minutes to book online (Detroit to Mom's)

Save money & time on student and faculty
travel at **StudentUniverse.com**

there are four 2-bedroom apartments with kitchens and living rooms, and four villas with 2 matrimonial beds, a trundle in the dining area, and A/C and microwave. (Rooms US$18 for students. Doubles US$26; triples US$31; 2-person apartments US$35; 4-person US$65; villas US$55.) **Cabinas Isolina Beach ❸** is a longer walk toward Brasilito from Potrero's center, but is only 100m from Playa Potrero beach. Recent renovations installed A/C and refrigerators in every room, and some 2-room setups have a kitchen and microwave. Rooms are bright and surround a garden with a pool and *rancho* (thatched hut), where breakfast (included) is served. (☎654 4333; admin@isolinabeach.com; www.isolinabeach.com. Doubles US$30; triples US$35; quads US$45. Additional US$10 for rooms with kitchen.) About 3km northeast of Potrero is **Hotel Sugar Beach ❺**, a sweet 4-star getaway spot honeymooners may swoon over. In addition to standard rooms and deluxe duplexes with adjoining decks, there are three suites. One has a kitchen, living room, and panoramic ocean view. Another is a beach house with its own private entrance, luxurious bath, and hammock deck. Families or groups as big as eight often occupy the lower level. A cascade pool can't quite compete with the secluded Sugar Beach, where the hotel launches its 25ft. outrigger canoes on snorkeling tours to Playa de Amor. (☎654 4242; sugarb@sol.racsa.co.cr; www.sugar-beach.com. Standard doubles low season US$65, high season US$110; deluxe doubles US$85/US$138. 2-bedroom Catalina suite US$150/190; honeymoon suite US$95/US$165.)

◘ **FOOD. Restaurante and Cabinas La Penca ❸** is *the* place to eat in Potrero. The restaurant is cheery and welcoming, and the antique jukebox will make you want to stay a while if the juicy *típico* fare doesn't. (☎654 4535. Appetizers ¢500-1000; *casados* ¢1200; onion steak ¢1600. Open daily 7am-10pm. V.) Another friendly place to have a drink or a heavy snack is **Bar Las Brisas ❷**, a walk toward the beach from the southwest corner of the field. US license plates, mixed flags, and mini-disco balls are suspended from the roof. A pool table draws friends into one corner, and half-price rum, vodka, and *guaro* draw the ladies on Wednesday nights. There is also occasional dancing. (☎654 4047. Nachos ¢900; chicken caesar salad ¢1600; tequila sunrise ¢1200. Open daily noon-midnight.) The **Paraíso ❸** restaurant, by Bahía Esmeralda, specializes in Italian and Argentine food. (Coconut shrimp ¢4400; coconut *flan* with *dulce de leche* ¢850. Open daily 6am-9am and 6pm-9:30pm, lunch served to guests on request.)

PLAYA FLAMINGO

The only pink things on this beautiful beach are the massive resort hotels, the private villas, and the sunburned guests who pay for them. Wealthy vacationers come for the sportfishing, the pampering, or both. Everything is expensive on the hill at the end of the bay, but the beach, with its calm dark-blue water, is ideal for swimming, and draws in plenty of *ticos* too.

▐ **TRANSPORTATION**

Buses run to Flamingo from **San José** and **Santa Cruz.** To get to Flamingo from **Tamarindo,** take a San José or Santa Cruz bus as far as **Huacas,** where buses to Flamingo via Brasilito pass frequently. TRALAPA buses go from the Flamingo marina to **San José** (5½hr.; M-Sa 3am and 2pm, Su and holidays 8:45 and 10am; ¢2130). Reserve in advance by calling the marina (☎654 4536). Buses depart for **Santa Cruz** (1hr., 8 per day 5:45am-10pm, ¢560) and **Liberia** (2hr., 5:30am and 2:30pm, ¢500).

🔃 PRACTICAL INFORMATION

The **Banco de Costa Rica,** on the hill across from Flamingo Marina Resort, has a Visa/PLUS **ATM,** changes traveler's checks, and gives Visa advances with passport. (Open M-F 8:30am-3pm.) The **medical clinic** (☎ 654 4141) and **pharmacy** are at the Flamingo Marina Resort. There is **Internet** access at the **Flamingo Marina Resort** bar. (¢500 per 30min.)

🏠 ACCOMMODATIONS

Soda-Restaurante Pleamar (☎ 654 4521), on the way from Flamingo to Brasilito, is the last peek at cheap you'll get. Behind the restaurant (see **Food,** below) there are 3 clean *cabinas* with fan, dresser, and private bath. Triples US$20, high-season US$24. ❶

Mariner Inn (☎ 654 4081), about 1km farther along the shore beyond a bridge, is right by the **marina** and has A/C rooms with matrimonial beds and TV. It also features a nice breezy restaurant (see **Food,** below). Doubles US$33.75; triples with fridge US$45; suite with kitchen and balcony US$68. Discounts for longer stays. ❸

Flamingo Beach Resort, (☎ 654 4444; toll free reservations ☎ 1-888-500-9090; www.cardelhotels.com; gamboawilberth@hotmail.com), on the beach, left from the Mariner Inn, has a giant pool as its centerpiece and a bar in one corner. It also features a gym, pharmacy, casino, tennis courts, and two **restaurants.** Rooms have mountain or beach views, cable TV, A/C, phone, and assorted kitchen and bathroom appliances; the suites also have two terraces. At sunset, the blinding reflection of the water gilds the outdoor hallways in golden light. Standard rooms US$80, high season US$120; poolside rooms US$110/US$140; surf side suites US$160/US$225. ❺

Flamingo Marina Resort, (☎ 654 4141; tickledpink@flamingomarina.com), just up the steep hill from the Mariner Inn, has 4 pools, activities, a tour center, and a tennis court. Rooms are either standard doubles, "sportsman's suites" with jacuzzi, kitchen, and patio bar/sitting area, or sprawling 2-bedroom beachfront apartments with great views. Doubles US$85, high season US$110; "sportsman's suites" US$115/US$145; 2-bedroom apartments for 4 people US$190/US$250. Each additional person US$15. ❺

🔄 FOOD

Soda-Restaurante Pleamar (see **Accommodations,** above). Fresh fish served right on the beach under thatched umbrellas. Cheeseburger ¢500, fish *casado* ¢1200. Open daily 10am-10pm, M 10am-5pm in low-season. ❶

Marie's, (☎ 654 4136) is the best restaurant in town. Friendly waiters and good-sized hot and cold appetizers. Papaya pancakes ¢1500; shrimp-stuffed avocado ¢3000; snapper filet ¢3400. Open daily 6:30am-9:30pm. ❸

Mariner Inn (see **Accommodations,** above), has a breezy restaurant; its casual Spreader Bar draws a chummy group of sport fishermen who pull the guitars off the walls for an impromptu jig when they're not watching TV. Open daily 6am-9:30pm. ❸

The Monkey Bar, Flamingo Marina Resort's popular restaurant, features American theme nights (think "NFL pizza") and all-you-can-eat BBQ Saturdays for US$17. Lunch US$8; dinner US$12.95. Happy Hour 5:30-6:30pm. Restaurant open daily 7-10am, 11am-4pm, and 5-10pm. Bar open 8am-11pm. ❷

Amberes (☎ 654 4367), up the hill from the Mariner Inn. This Belgian bar-casino-restaurant promises a pricey international vacation club atmosphere into the wee hours, with a big dance floor, pool table, and minimum casino wager of US$20. The menu changes daily. Open daily 6pm-3 or 4am. Food served all night. ❷

🔰 🔋 ACTIVITIES AND GUIDED TOURS

The Edge Adventure Company, just before the bridge and the marina, has a user-friendly menu of daytime activities, including diving, snorkeling, kayaking, surf trips to **Witch's Rock** and **Ollie's Point,** and sportfishing. Many of these take place, in part, on a 47 ft. yacht. (☎654 4946; theedge@racsa.co.cr. 1 tank US$45, 2 tanks US$60, PADI certification course US$375 for 3 days. Snorkeling 4hr. US$35. Kayaks 2½hr. US$25. Surf trips US$75 per person full day with lunch, 10 person minimum. Sportfishing half day US$900, full day US$1400. Open daily 7am-4:30pm.) Inquire at the **Marina Flamingo** about the plethora of sportfishing opportunities, although they do charge commission. (☎654 4537. Open M-F 6am-5pm, Su 6am-2pm.) **Shannon Sailing Charters,** also based there, offers a sunset cruise to Playa de Amor and other beaches. (☎654 4537; marflam@marflam.com; www.marflam.com. US$45 per person.)

Two dive shops are **Costa Rica Diving,** on the hill next to Marie's Restaurant (☎654 4148; open M-F 7am-6:30pm, Sa-Su 8am-6pm), and **Flamingo Dive Shop** (☎654 4403), next to the Mariner Inn. Both offer a variety of tour packages, many unrelated to diving, and charge about US$75 for a 2-tank dive. Costa Rica Diving also has **Internet** access (¢570 for 30min.) and 5 simple guest rooms with private baths designed for divers. (Breakfast included. Singles US$15; doubles US$35.)

BRASILITO

The proximity of the water makes tiny Brasilito a pleasant place. Without the beach the town would be uninspiringly dull, but refreshing storms and beautiful sunsets ceaselessly crowd the skies. Visitors can also experience the slow pulse of small town *tico* life, since there are fewer foreigners than in surrounding towns. Use Brasilito for its economical lodgings and convenient transportation to nearby Playa Flamingo or Playa Conchal (a walk along the shore).

🚍 TRANSPORTATION

The TRALAPA station is just north of the northwest corner of the soccer field. **Buses** coming from Flamingo stop in Brasilito on their way to **San José** (5½hr.; M-Sa 3:10, 8:55am, 2:10pm; Su 8:55, 10:10am, 2:10pm; ¢2130) about 10min. after they depart from Flamingo. Reserve tickets in advance. (☎357 0698. Office open 7:30-11:30am and 12:30-5:30pm.) Buses going as far as **Liberia** pass at 5:40am and 2:40pm. Buses also pass on their way to **Santa Cruz** (8 per day 5:55am-10:10pm).

🔅 🔢 ORIENTATION AND PRACTICAL INFORMATION

The nearest **bank** is **Banco de Costa Rica** in Flamingo. **Mini-Super Brasilito** is on the southwest corner of the soccer field. (Open M-Sa 7am-9pm, Su 7am-5pm.) The **police station** is on the southwest corner of the soccer field (☎654 4425 or 654 4117 for emergencies). The ocean is to the east.

🔥 ACCOMMODATIONS

Hotel Brasilito (☎/fax 654 4237), on the beach at the southeast corner of the soccer field. Although the classy and clean rooms don't have views, they are snug and of high quality. Guests get a 10% discount in the restaurant **Las Playas.** Restaurant open 7am-10pm. Singles US$15-20; doubles US$20-25. ❷

Cabinas Olga (☎654 4013), set back from the police station, has comfortable and basic rooms with fans. Rooms ₡2500. ❶

Cabinas Ojos Azules, (☎/fax 654 4346), on the main road south of the soccer field, has the nicest, most spacious rooms with high roofs, lined windows, and mirrored headboards. A great budget option. Simpler rooms on a lower level hold up to 8 people. All have private baths (hot water optional) and access to a communal kitchen. There is a little pool and hammocks in the garden. Rustic rooms as low as ₡2000 per person for groups. Doubles US$20, high season US$35; US$5 per additional person. ❶

Cabinas La Gloria (☎654 4878), is a few doors down and offers brighter, newer rooms with high ceilings, fridges and A/C. Comfortable and quiet with private baths. Doubles ₡8000, with A/C ₡12,000; triples ₡12,000/₡16,000. ❶

Apartotel Nany (☎/fax 654 4320), succeeds in creating a cheerful vacation atmosphere with ten rooms whose identical cylinder windows look out onto a small rocky pool. Common kitchen area with appliances, two rooms, and cable TV. Most have A/C. Doubles US$30-50; US$10-15 per additional person. ❷

Brasilito Lodge (☎654 4552; brasilito@racsa.co.cr; www.brasilito_conchal.com), 100m along the beach towards Playa Conchal from Hotel Brasilito. Eight spacious rooms are equipped with mosquito canopies, cable TV and ceiling fans. Camping and a common kitchen available. **Internet** ₡1000 per hr. **Camping** ₡1000 per person; tent rental ₡500 per day. Rooms ₡3000 per person. ❶

🍴 FOOD

Restaurante Camarón Dorado, according to Brasiliteños, is the best restaurant in town and has excellent fish. The waiters bring floral water for a pre-meal hand wash and flowers for women's hair. The tables are out on the beach. Fish *casado* ₡1200; lobster ₡7000. Open daily 11am-10pm. ❶

Soda La Casita del Pescado, next to Hotel Brasilito on the beach, is a hole-in-the-sand *soda* with tasty *mariscos* (seafood). Fish filet with tomato sauce ₡1500; calamari in its ink ₡2500. Open W-M 9am-9:30pm. ❷

Il Forno, next to Cabinas La Gloria, has delicious pizza and pasta al dente. Tagliatelle with mushrooms ₡2200; Hawaiian pizza ₡1900. Open Tu-Su 12:30-10pm. ❶

🏄 ACTIVITIES

Hotel Brasilito Excursions is located in the hotel's restaurant. Offers horseback rides, diving, kayaking, hydro discs, and motorbike rentals, to name a few. (☎654 4236. Horseback tours 1hr. on the beach US$25, 2hr. on monkey trail US$35. Motorbike rentals half day US$30, full day US$45. Open M-F 8am-4pm.) **Brasilito Sport Adventures,** on the main road about 500m south of the soccer field, specializes in ATV tours and rents scooters. (☎654 4087 or 394 8876. ATV tours US$45 per 2hr., US$55 per 3hr., full day including canopy tour US$90. Scooters US$10 per hr., full day US$45 with US$50 deposit.)

NEAR BRASILITO

PLAYA CONCHAL

Playa Conchal is an easy 2km walk south along the beach. The shore is blanketed in the pink-white sand of crushed *conchitas* (shells), and it is an ideal place to snorkel. A huge resort called **Meliá Playa Conchal,** soon to be called Paradisos Playa Conchal and still expanding, hovers above most of the beach. The biggest pool in

Central America, a golf course, a disco, and a convention center are the tip of this iceberg. The main entrance, on the highway from Brasilito, is far from the beach and the reception area. It is controlled like a presidential palace, but with legitimate business you can drive through, visiting one of the five restaurants on the **Cocodrilo Sports and Adventure Center,** open to the public and located by the beach gate. They rent ATVs, bikes, kayaks, snorkel equipment, boogie boards, waverunners, and scooters, and offer horseback riding, sportfishing, and diving tours and trips with a certification program. (☎ 654 4123, ext. 8813 or 8913.)

FILADELFIA

Mexicans used to visit the Chorotegan Indians who lived in this town, near the mouth of the Río Tempisque, to trade and vacation during pre-colonial times. The cacique Zapandí, who often wears a lizard headdress in his iconography, presided over this fruitful cultural exchange with Aztecs and Spaniards, and Filadelfia's annual December *fiestas* are thrown in his honor. But the modern-day town is neither a tourist spot nor a commercial center, even though it's the official county seat and serves as a transportation hub for tourists. There's no real action to get off the bus for, but Filadelfia is a pleasant place to escape other tourists.

▐▀ TRANSPORTATION

Buses pass through the station on the northwest corner of the *parque central* about every hour (5am-9pm; the last bus to Liberia departs around 8:45pm) and go to **Liberia** (45min., ¢210); **Nicoya** (1hr., ¢300) via **Santa Cruz** (40min., ¢175); and **Playa del Coco** (1hr.; 10:30am, 12:30, 3:15pm). **Alfaro,** located in the same station, has service to **San José** (4½hr., 5 per day 5:45am-3:15pm, ¢1860), as does **Tralapa,** 50km east (8 per day 3:30am-5:30pm with a 3am bus on M).

▚ ▟ ORIENTATION AND PRACTICAL INFORMATION

Exchange money at **Banco Nacional,** 100m west of the northwest corner of the *parque.* (Open M-F 8:30am-3:45pm.) **Supermercado Filadelfia** is on the south side of the *parque.* (Open M-Sa 8am-noon and 1:30-6:30pm, Su 8am-noon.) The **Seguro Social,** one of two **medical clinics,** is 100m north and 200m west of the northwst corner of the *parque.* (☎ 688 8276. Open M-Th 7am-4pm, 4-10pm for emergencies, Sa-Su 7am-7pm for emergencies.) Otherwise, call the **Red Cross,** 100m west and 50m north of the northwest corner of the *parque.* (☎ 688 8224, emergency 128.) The **police station** is 250m north of the Red Cross. (☎ 688 7168, 688 8229 or 911 in emergencies.) The **post office** is 100m south and 25m west of the *parque's* southwest corner. (Open 8:30am-noon and 1-5:30pm.)

▐ ▐ ACCOMMODATIONS AND FOOD

There are only two places to stay in Filadelfia. **Cabinas Amelia ❷,** 100m west and 150m north of the *parque's* northwest corner, has a pool, a *soda,* and a popular bar, in addition to clean if slightly cramped rooms. (☎ 688 8087. Singles ¢5000; doubles ¢9000 triples with A/C and TV ¢11,000.) **Cabinas Tita ❷** also has rooms with private bath. (☎ 688 8073. ¢5000 per person.)

Good and fast *típico* fare can be found at **Soda Gaby ❶** on the *parque's* northwest side, where cheap *casados* come with *refresco* and ice cream included. (Chicken or beef casados ¢1050; fish or pork ¢1200. Open daily 5am-6:30pm.) Another good option is surprisingly cheerful **Soda Gasatica ❶,** in the shadow of the gas station across the highway, 500m west and 200m north of the *parque.*

(*Casados* ¢800. Open daily 6am-10pm.) Other options are limited to the three *tico*-Chinese places. **Restaurant Helen ❷,** on the south side of the *parque* is the biggest. (Chicken curry ¢2500. Open M-Sa 11:30am-3pm and 5:30-9:30pm, Su hours irregular). The other two, **Nuevo Mundo ❶** and **Ginette ❶,** are side-by-side 50m north of the *parque's* northwest corner. (Seabass filet in tomato sauce ¢1350; arroz cantonés ¢1000. Nuevo Mundo open daily 11am-10pm. Ginette open daily 5pm-11pm.)

◎ SIGHTS

Visit **La Casa de la Cultura** next to the bus station to see traditional musical instruments, pottery and old photographs of young Filadelfian musicians, among other things. (Open daily 7am-noon and 1-6pm.)

◎ NIGHTLIFE

Bars outnumber restaurants. The one definitely worth visiting is locally famous **Bar Arenas,** over 1km southeast of the center; take a taxi (¢500). The food is good any time of day in the thatched *rancho*, but on crowded nights some of the tables are cleared for karaoke or dancing. Once in a while the industrial space next door fills with Latin music. (☎688 8614. Appetizers from ¢150; *casados* ¢1200. Open 10am-12am.) **Bar La Casona,** in Cabinas Amelia, is probably the most popular, small and inviting. (Open 4-11pm.) **Bar Mariah** is located under a second floor disco 100m west of the *parque.* (Beer ¢325. Open daily 11am-2am, disco Th-Su.) Pool hall **Julis Billares** is just off the *parque's* southwest corner. (¢500 per game. Open M-F 3-10pm, Sa-Su 10am-10pm.)

SANTA CRUZ

Santa Cruz is officially *La Ciudad Folclórica de Costa Rica*, steeped in history and traditions revived every January during *Las Fiestas Patronales de Santo Cristo de Esquipulas*. The rest of the year, the statues that stand on the four corners of Parque Bernabela Ramos (the town's new center since 1993, when Plaza de los Mangos was ravaged by a fire) serve as reminders of Santa Cruz's legacy. On the northwest corner, a stoic Bernabela wearing a *campesina* apron holds a scroll in her hand, representing the land donation that gave birth to the city. She was a wealthy Catholic Spaniard who hung the "sacred cross" on her porch and held mass for both Spanish and indigenous worshippers. A statue of Chorotega cacique Diriá guards the southwest corner of the *parque;* an action statue of a *montador* (bull-rider) with his *vaquetero* (assistant) a tortilla-making scene complete the display. The new park is pleasant year-round, and Santa Cruz is en route to the most popular beaches on the peninsula.

◪ TRANSPORTATION

From the TRALAPA bus station, on the north side of Plaza de los Mangos, **buses** depart to **San José** (4½hr., 9 buses mostly in the morning 3am-5pm, ¢1860); **Nicoya** (30min.; M-Sa 24 buses 6am-9:30pm, Su 13 buses 6:20am-9:20pm; ¢150); **Liberia** (1½hr.; M-Sa 24 buses 4:30am-7:30pm, with a 10:30pm bus to Filadelfia; Su 12 buses 5:35am-10:30pm; ¢350); **Filadelfia** (daily every 30min. and every hr. on Su). The **Tamarindo** (8:30pm) and **Flamingo-Conchal-Brasilito** (3:30pm) buses also leave from this terminal, but most beach buses leave from a second station behind the Mercado Municipal, 200m south and 300m east of TRALAPA, to **Tamarindo** (1hr., 5 per day

8:30am-5pm, ¢250); **Flamingo** (4 and 10:30am; ¢250); **Puerto Potrero** (2pm); **Junquillal** (10:30am and 5:30pm); **Marbella Ostional** (12:30 and 2:30pm).

⚓ 🄻 ORIENTATION AND PRACTICAL INFORMATION

Standing in Parque Bernabela Ramos, **Restaurante Jardín de Luna** is north and the church, with a visible, weathered pink church tower, is east. **La Plaza de los Mangos** (basically a bare field) and the bus station where you will probably arrive are 400m north of this *parque;* some directions are given from "Mangos."

Bank: Banco de Costa Rica, 200m north of Mangos' northwest corner, exchanges dollars and traveler's checks. It also has a **24hr. ATM** for Visa and Visa Plus.

Market: One of several is **Super Santa Cruz,** 200m south of Mangos' southwest corner. Open M-Sa 7:30am-8pm, Su 8am-noon.

Police: (☎680 0136 or 911), 100m south and 300m east of Mangos' southeast corner, across from the Mercado Municipal and bus station. Open 24hr.

Red Cross: (☎680 0330), on the west side of Parque Bernabela.

Medical Services: The **medical clinic** (☎680 0436) is 100m south of Parque Bernabela's southeast corner. Open M-F 7am-4pm, 24hr. for emergencies.

Telephones: Phones can be found in the *parque* and the plaza.

Internet Access: Access at **Ciberm@nía,** 100m north and 50m west of the church. ¢600 per hr. Open M-Sa 8:30am-9:30pm, Su 1-8pm.

Post Office: 200m north and 50m east of Parque Bernabela's northeast corner. Fax available. Open M-F 7am-5:30pm, Sa 7:30-noon.

Postal Code: 5150.

🄵 ACCOMMODATIONS

▩ **Hotel Diriá** (☎680 0080 or 680 0402; www.nieuveld.nl; hoteldiria@hotmail.com), four or five blocks north of Mangos' northwest corner, across from Banco Nacional, is the biggest and best hotel. Soft quilted beds, TVs, tile baths, kiddy and adult pools, wicker rockers in a patio, and a restaurant that turns into a disco on Sa nights. Singles with fan US$25, with A/C US$30; doubles US$40/US$45; triples US$50/US$55. ❸

Hotel Anatolia (☎680 0333), 100m north of Parque Bernabela's northwest corner, is brighter on the outside than the inside. The soda-style restaurant and big front room with TV, however, compensate for the dim rooms and shared baths. Singles ¢2200; doubles ¢3500; triples ¢4000. ❶

Pensión Isabel (☎680 0173), just east of the northeast corner of the church, has small, white rooms. ¢2000 per person. ❶

Hotel La Pampa (☎680 0586), just west of Mangos' southwest corner, is much nicer. Comfort, however, jumps up with prices. This hotel attracts business travelers with bright rooms that have A/C, cable TV, and good bathrooms. One huge room has a queen-size bed and 3 singles. Singles with fan US$18, with A/C US$23; doubles US$25/US$35; triples US$30/US$40. ❷

La Estancia (☎680 0476), 100m west of Mangos' northwest corner, is faded inside, but comfortable and spacious. Singles ¢6500; doubles ¢9000; triples ¢10,500. MC/V. ❷

Hotel la Calle de Alcalá (☎680 0000), east of Mangos' northeast corner, is extremely comfortable. All rooms have TV and A/C, and there's a pool and restaurant. It's a 3-star hotel by international standards. Singles US$25; doubles US$40; triples US$50. ❸

🗒 FOOD

🍴 **Coopetortillas,** west of the old church, gives new meaning to "slaving over a hot stove"; huge industrial pots simmer over firewood cooking-pits in a barn-like structure with family-style tables. You will feel like you just came in from the fields, eating basic traditional foods like *arroz con maíz* (corn rice), *empanadas* (turnovers), *sopa de albóndigas* (meatball soup), and of course, piping corn tortillas made before your eyes by the factory's cheerful, uniformed women. *Casados* ¢900-1000. Open daily 4am-6:30pm. ❶

El Portoncito, a welcoming, homey *soda* on the east side of Plaza de los Mangos, has embroidered curtains, chatty ladies, and hearty food. *Casados* ¢900. Hamburgers ¢400. Open daily 6am-9pm. ❶

El Jardín de Luna, on the north side of parque Bernabela, is one of the three best and coziest Chinese bar-restaurants in town. Cashew shrimp ¢2350; sweet and sour chicken ¢1980. Open daily 10am-3pm, 5:30-11pm. ❸

Restaurante Pampero, the Chinese eatery on the south side of Mangos, has a giant TV. Grilled fish with mushrooms ¢1860. Open daily 10am-midnight. ❷

Restaurante El Milenio, 100m west of Mangos' southwest corner, has bad acoustics but great Chinese seafood. Calamari with vegetables and sauce ¢1100. Open M-F 10am-midnight, Sa 10am-1am, Su 10am-12:30am. ❶

👁 🎵 SIGHTS AND ENTERTAINMENT

Santa Cruz's history and traditions are revived every January during *Las Fiestas Patronales de Santo Cristo de Esquipulas*. On the 15th, a huge crowd performs indigenous and folk dances and bull riders mount rowdy bulls to the tune of a folkloric band. Late in July, the *sabaneros* (cowboys) also show off their horses in *Las Fiestas de Santiago*.

Not far from Santa Cruz, around Guaitil's soccer field, is the **Pottery Village of Guaitil,** where you will find family pottery stands selling the earthen pots on which the whole village depends. You can spy on hive-like kilns in people's yards, and some artisans decorate jugs, vases, and bowls for tourists to watch. The art is based on Chorotegan indigenous crafts passed down through generations, and currently, about 100 families are engaged in ceramics. They don't use pottery wheels, and the paint is made of a clay and sand mixture that yields rich grays, browns, and reds. Intricate animal motifs are often scraped out. If you want to learn how to make the pottery, there are ways of staying in the village for a while. (Call ☎ 681 1099 and ask for Silma Villafuerte Cortés.) *Guaitil is a 15min. bus ride, or a ¢1500 cab ride, from Santa Cruz.* **Buses** *leave the mercado station (7am, 1:30, 3pm). You will have to take a cab to return to Santa Cruz.*

PARQUE NACIONAL MARINO LAS BAULAS

Parque Nacional Marino Las Baulas was officially founded in 1995 and covers 4.2 sq. km, one of which is beach. The remainder of the park is tropical dry forest and swamp. It is best known as the nesting site of *las baulas*, the endangered **leatherback turtles**, which emerge from the ocean, pick a spot on **Playa Grande**, and deposit their eggs before covering them and returning to the water. These beautiful reptiles can be longer than 1.5m. They are easily disoriented by light and noise, so photography is forbidden. Playa Grande is national parkland, but is used casually for surfing and sunbathing.

AT A GLANCE

AREA: 4.2 sq. km total, 1 sq. km of beach.

CLIMATE: Semi-arid.

FEATURES: Playa Grande; Las Baulas estuary.

HIGHLIGHTS: Nesting leatherback turtles; Las Baulas estuary; surf; birdwatching; museum El Mundo de la Tortuga.

GATEWAYS: Tamarindo (p. 218); Playa Grande.

FEES & RESERVATIONS: Park entrance fee US$6. Turtle watching tours Oct. 20-Feb. 15 US$13 including park fee. Reservations ☎ 653 0470. Office open daily 8am-4pm.

ORIENTATION

The Tamarindo estuary marks the park's southern border, on the northeast corner of Tamarindo village. The **leatherback turtles** come from mid-October to March to lay their eggs on **Playa Grande.**

TRANSPORTATION

Buses going from Tamarindo to San José stop at Huacas. From there, it's 12km to the entrance station on **Playa Grande.** A **taxi** from Huacas is about ¢3000; all the way from Tamarindo to the park is US$25-30. Alternatively, you can hop on a **boat** across the Tamarindo estuary at the north end of Playa Tamarindo. (Boats ¢200 per crossing; leave the estuary around 4pm.) From the far shore, it's about a 3km, 45min. walk along the broad beach to the **entrance station,** up the road from Hotel Las Tortugas. Start walking early during nesting season, and take a taxi back (the beach is closed 6pm-6am during nesting season).

PRACTICAL INFORMATION

 WHEN TO GO. If you're going to the park especially to see the turtles, you must go during the **nesting season** (Oct. 20 - Feb. 15). During this time, **Playa Grande** is closed to surfers and all casual visitors 6pm-6am every night; only official tours are allowed on the beach. If you are visiting between March and September, you can still enjoy the park by taking a **kayak** or **boat tour** into the estuary. There are 174 species of water and land birds, not to mention 5 species of swamp trees. Also of interest is the small gem of a museum **El Mundo de la Tortuga,** down the road from the park office. Museum ☎ 653 0471. Open Oct. to mid-March 6pm to late.

Entrance station: From the far shore of the Tamarindo estuary, it's a 3km, a 45min. walk along the broad beach to the entrance station, up the road from Hotel Las Tortugas.

Fees and Reservations: Park entrance fee US$6. Guides registered with **MINAE** bring groups of 15 people to watch the turtles. Reserve at ☎ 653 0470. Office open daily 8am-4pm all year.

Tours: Adventure specialists in Tamarindo offer many varieties of package tours and include the US$6 entrance fee in their prices (generally in the US$30 range). Ask about available **kayak** and **boat tours** into the estuary. MINAE guides bring groups of 15 people to watch the **turtles,** using radios and numbered signposts to track them down. No more than 120 people are allowed on the beach in one night. Tours run every night during the nesting season. Tour US$13, including US$6 park entrance fee.

Post office: Up the road north from Tamarindo to Huacas.

ACCOMMODATIONS

Centro Vacacional Playa Grande (☎/fax 653 0834), a 5min. walk up the road and to the right from Hotel Las Tortugas, is the area's cheapest option. Rooms have matrimonial beds and bunks, plus kitchen supplies. The bar-restaurant is also the cheapest around. ¢2000 per person in low-season; ¢12,000 per 6-person room in high-season. Camping ¢700 per person with bathrooms. V. ❶

Jammin' Surf Camp (☎653 0469; www.jamminsurfcamp.com), inland from beach marker 29, offers friendly bargains for surfer types. Four cozy cabins have tent-like slanted walls, reading lamps, shared kitchen and bath; or you can camp in a real two-room tent for US$3 per person. Cabins US$13 per person, including breakfast; doubles with private bath US$35; 2-bedroom house for 5 people US$90. ❷

Villa Baula (☎653 0493; fax 653 0459; www.hotelvillabaula.com; hotelvb@sol.racsa.co.cr), on Playa Grande, 200m north of the estuary (or a 20min. taxi ride from Tamarindo). The 20 airy rooms have lots of windows; the slight dampness suits a true beach lodge. Five bungalows on stilts have porch kitchens and two rooms. Hot water available in high season. There's a pool and restaurant, and the hotel offers horse and estuary tours, as well as bike and surfboard rental. Doubles US$52, high season US$70; bungalows US$93/$117. AmEx/MC/V. ❸

Hotel Las Tortugas (☎653 0423; www.cool.co.cr/usr/turtles; surfegg@cool.co.cr), a 45min. walk down the beach by the park entrance, feels less private, but is more luxurious, with stone floors, tile showers, A/C, and hot water. Escape the heat in the pool or shaded bar/restaurant. Doubles US$50, high season US$90-100; 5-person suite US$60/US$90-100. V. ❸

Hotel El Bucanero (☎/fax 653 0480; www.elbucanero.com; jandrews@elbucanero.com), also near the beach (follow the signs). Built 6 years ago by the English architect owner and still well-tended, with simple rooms and hot-water baths in nice layouts, plus a raised, open-air hexagonal restaurant. Doubles US$30, high season US$50, with A/C extra US$5. Each additional person US $5-10. ❷

Hotel-Restaurant Cantarana (☎653 0486; cantarana@hotmail.com), off the dirt road next to the estuary, is more luxurious, with a pool, restaurant, and rooms with A/C, hot-water bath, and laundry. Beach bungalows can be rented for three or more nights only. Doubles US$70 with breakfast; 4-person bungalows US$700 per week. V. ❹

PLAYA TAMARINDO

While the long, white shore has some rocky patches, Tamarindo is perhaps Costa Rica's most cosmopolitan beach. Few places have so much entertainment by day—scenery, sunbathing, snorkeling, surfing, and shopping—*and* such a lively nightlife. Although the town is not nearly as crowded as other Pacific coast beaches like Jacó, tourists and expats make their presence abundantly clear. Here you'll find more resort-hoppers than backpackers and just as many Thai restaurants and French bakeries as *sodas*. The crowd on the beach is composed of people from all walks of life: *tico* families on vacation, retired gringos, surfers from the north and south, and backpackers seeking a break from their diet of rice and beans. Socialites can find plenty of people to schmooze with, and those preferring peace can wander out to the rocky points at either end of the beach and take in a stunning sunset, reflected on the endless silvery waters. If standard after-hours activities don't suit your taste, take advantage of fantastic natural splendors, like watching a leatherback turtle lay her eggs at nearby Parque Nacional Las Baulas. Tamarindo is a good place to think about Costa Rica's many contradictions, but also an easy place to forget about them.

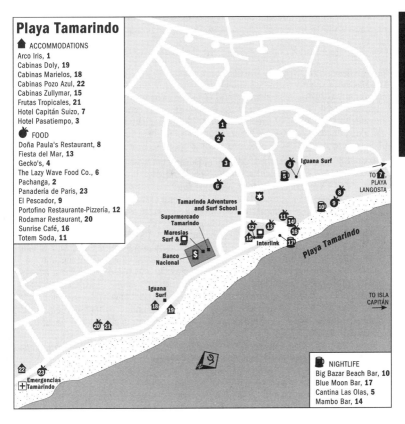

Playa Tamarindo

🏠 **ACCOMMODATIONS**
Arco Iris, **1**
Cabinas Doly, **19**
Cabinas Marielos, **18**
Cabinas Pozo Azul, **22**
Cabinas Zullymar, **15**
Frutas Tropicales, **21**
Hotel Capitán Suizo, **7**
Hotel Pasatiempo, **3**

🍴 **FOOD**
Doña Paula's Restaurant, **8**
Fiesta del Mar, **13**
Gecko's, **4**
The Lazy Wave Food Co., **6**
Pachanga, **2**
Panadería de Paris, **23**
El Pescador, **9**
Portofino Restaurante-Pizzería, **12**
Rodamar Restaurant, **20**
Sunrise Café, **16**
Totem Soda, **11**

Iguana Surf

TO **7**,
PLAYA
LANGOSTA

Tamarindo Adventures
and Surf School
Supermercado
Tamarindo

Maresías
Surf &

Banco
Nacional

Playa Tamarindo

Interlink

Iguana
Surf

TO ISLA
CAPITÁN

Emergencias
Tamarindo

🍸 **NIGHTLIFE**
Big Bazar Beach Bar, **10**
Blue Moon Bar, **17**
Cantina Las Olas, **5**
Mambo Bar, **14**

▐ TRANSPORTATION

Flights: Sansa (50min.; high season 6 daily 5:15am-3:50pm, return 6 daily 6:20am-4:55pm; low season 4 daily 5:15am-1:30pm, return 4 daily 6:20am-2:35pm; US$66) and **Travelair** (50min.; high season 4 daily 6am-3pm, return 4 daily 7:10am-4:10pm; low season 3 daily 5:30-11am, return 3 daily 6:40am-12:10pm; US$73) depart from San José (see **p. 85**) and arrive at the airstrip 3km north of Tamarindo.

Buses from Tamarindo to **San José** leave from the Alfaro office in the Tamarindo Resort driveway, 200m east down the road 200m north of the semi-circle (5½hr.; 3:30am and 5:45am, Su 12:30pm; ¢1950). Reserve tickets 3 days in advance. From the semi-circle, buses go to **Santa Cruz** (1½hr., 6 per day 6am-10pm, ¢350) and **Liberia** (9am and 4:45pm); they can also be flagged from anywhere along the main road. Coming to Tamarindo from **Nicoya,** first take the bus to **Santa Cruz** (45min., 14 buses 3:50am-6:15pm, ¢125), then walk to the *mercado* bus station, 300m south and 300m west of where the bus drops you off. Buses leave from there to **Tamarindo** (1½hr., 5 per day 4:30am-3:30pm, ¢250).

Car rental: Elegante Rent A Car (☎653 0015), in the Hotel Pueblo Dorado, north of the Best Western. Open daily 8am-5pm. US$1000 deposit; must be 25+. Or try **Budget** (☎653 0829), in the Best Western. Rents to under 21. Open daily 9am-6pm.

Bike rental: Robert August Surf Shop (☎653 0114), in the Best Western complex. Bikes US$10 per day, US$ 50 per week. Open daily 7am-6pm.

ORIENTATION AND PRACTICAL INFORMATION

The main road in the village of Tamarindo extends 2.4km from Parque Nacional Las Baulas at the far northeast down to the main bus stop, in a semi-circle of shops and restaurants on the southwest end. The Best Western, on the northeast end, is a key landmark. There are two main beach entrances—one off the semi-circle, and another in the middle of the strip. Everything along the main street is geared to travelers' needs. Centro Comercial Aster is a small strip of white shops 200m north of the circle. A road south of it leads east to more restaurants and tour agencies.

Tourist office: 500m north of the circle. Doesn't have much information, sells a few maps and has a **book exchange.** Open M-F 9am-noon.

Tours and surfing equipment: Iguana Surf Tours (☎653 0148 or 653 0613; iguanasurf@aol.com), has two locations, one 800m north of the circle, and the other up the street immediately south of the Centro Comercial Aster and to the right. They offer a wide variety of tours, including **snorkeling** and **kayaking** trips, as well as surf lessons, boards, kayaks, and snorkel equipment. Surf lessons US$35 for 2hr. Open daily 8am-6pm, until 8pm at location south of Aster. **Tamarindo Adventures and Surf School** (☎653 0108), up the street south of Centro Comercial Aster, offers ATV tours and rents ATVs and motorcycles to licensed drivers. Impressive selection of old and new boards. Surf lessons US$25 per person. Open M-F 8am-12:30pm and 1:30-6pm, Su 3-6pm.

Bank: Banco Nacional, 375m north of the circle. Changes traveler's checks and gives advances on Visa. Lines are long, so get there early. Open M-F 8:30am-3:45pm.

Supermarkets: Supermercado Tamarindo, just south of the bank. Open M-Sa 7:30am-9pm, Su 9am-8:30pm.

Police: (☎653 0238, emergency 911), 200m east on the road and 200m north of the circle, in a bungalow in the Tamarindo Resort driveway.

Hospital: Tamarindo lacks a proper hospital or clinic, but **Emergencias Tamarindo** is across from Cabinas Pozo Azul, north of the Best Western.

Internet access: InterLink, on the circle. ¢350 per 30min., ¢800 per hr. Open daily 8am-10pm. Also on the 2nd floor of **Maresía's Surf Shop,** 375m north of the circle. ¢500 per 30min. Open M-Sa 9am-7pm.

ACCOMMODATIONS

▨ **Arco Iris** (☎653 0330; www.hotelarcoiris.com; cabinasarcoiris@yahoo.it), hidden up the hill behind Pachanga (see **Food,** below), about 500m south of the Centro Comercial Aster. Guests may feel like babies whose parents have gone all out decorating the nursery in these eye-popping cabin rooms. Each has a unique color scheme, theme, and mood: the "romantic room" has a butterfly mobile and Mona Lisa print, the oriental room is decked out with gorgeous fans, and the Mexican *casita* bursts with colors. Cabins have cozy hammocks, porches, private baths, radios, and books. The imaginative Italian owners serve breakfast on request (US$7 for 2) and offer yoga classes. Doubles US$25 low-season, US$40 high-season; US$10-15 per additional person; 2-room apartment with kitchen US$50. ❸

Cabinas Marielos (☎/fax 653 0141), across from Cabinas Doly and next to Iguana Surf. On the high end of budget deals, but worth a splurge. Super-clean, cool *cabinas* are set far back from the main road. Rooms have sparkling private baths, powerful fans or A/C, safes, and access to a fully-stocked kitchen. Some rooms have balconies. Surf and boogie boards for rent from helpful staff. Singles US$20-30; doubles US$30-40, with A/C US$35-45; triples US$40-50. AmEx/MC/V. ❸

Cabinas Pozo Azul (☎/fax 653 0280), just north of the Best Western. An excellent deal—each clean, spacious room has a private bath, fridge and stove. There is also a pool and long porch. ₡3500 per person; July ₡5000. ❷

Cabinas Coral Reef (☎ 653 0291), 50m up the road from the Centro Comercial Aster. A good budget option, with clean dark wood-paneled rooms. Communal fridge, surf lessons, and massage available. ₡2000 per person. ❶

Cabinas Doly (☎ 653 0017), about 800m north of the circle on the beach side. A few of the rooms face the ocean, and there is a narrow 2nd-story terrace overlooking the water. Shared baths in courtyard. US$8 per person low-season, US$10 high-season. US$17-28 for 3 person room with private bath. ❶

Frutas Tropicales (☎/fax 653 0041), 900m north of the circle, about 100m south of the Best Western. Behind the popular fast-food restaurant, 3 tile floor rooms with TV and hot baths. Doubles US$20; triples US$28. AmEx/MC/V. ❷

Cabinas Zullymar (☎ 653 0140; www.tr506.com/zullymar; zullymar@sol.racsa.co.cr), visible from the main drag by its pool and white boulders. Carved Mesoamerican-design doors open onto 40 spacious, relatively plain rooms with private bath (and with balconies above the ground floor). Doubles US$30, with balcony US$40, with A/C US$45; triples US$46/US$54/US$60. Prices US$10 higher in high season. AmEx/MC/V. ❷

Hotel Pasatiempo (☎ 653 0096; www.hotelpasatiempo.com; passtime@racsa.co.cr), 300m east on the road south of the Centro Comercial Aster. The guest book is filled with gushing compliments about the cheerful service and bright rooms, which are decorated with hand-painted tropical fish. All rooms have A/C, luxurious beds, and tiled baths; suites have hammocks and sitting rooms with throw-pillow window seats. Doubles US$49 low-season, US$59 high-season; US$10 per additional person; 5-person suites US$69/US$79. AmEx/MC/V. ❸

Hotel Capitán Suizo (☎ 653 0075; capsuizo@sol.racsa.co.cr), about 1km south on the road parallel to the main drag, 200m east of the Centro Comercial Aster. This top-of-the-line hotel has grand, balconied rooms with sleeping and sitting areas on different levels, sliding glass doors, and giant bathrooms with fancy tubs. Pool, restaurant, and beach. Many activities offered, including horse tours, kayaking, snorkeling, badminton, and massages. Breakfast included. Doubles US$95-125, with A/C US$110-145; bungalows US$130-175; US$20 per additional person. AmEx/MC/V. ❺

FOOD

Whether you're seeking variety or a bargain, Tamarindo's bounty of restaurants is sure to fit the bill.

◪ **Pachanga** (☎ 653 0404), about 400m east on the road south of the Centro Comercial Aster. The imaginative menu changes nightly. Elegantly dim lighting makes you feel like you're eating in New York or Chicago. Entrees ₡3000-5000. Rich desserts come garnered with flowers. Open Tu-Sa 6-10pm. ❸

◪ **The Lazy Wave Food Company,** on the same road as Pachanga, across from the mini-super inside a building with other establishments. The chefs of Pachanga and The Lazy Wave were partners; both incorporate Asian elements into their jazzy gourmet menus. Watch from the counter seats as the gregarious chefs artistically arrange heaping plates from an ever-changing menu. "Swinging" lounge with wooden swings in the outdoor courtyard. Entrees US$10-15. Open M-Sa 11am-11pm, Su 6-11pm. ❸

El Pescador (☎ 653 0109), on the beach 100m south of the circle; turn right (west) on the road beyond Iguana Surf. Tasty fresh fish right on the beach, where the locals outnumber the tourists. Every entree comes with a sample of *ceviche*. Filet *a la plancha* ₡1800. Open daily 6am-10pm. ❷

Doña Paula's Restaurant, behind El Pescador, has meals that can satisfy even raven-ous ones who have been out in the waves since the sun came up, at a price that anyone can afford. *Casados* ¢800. Open daily for breakfast, lunch, and dinner. ❶

Totem Soda (☎653 0081), on the northeast corner of the circle, offers many varieties of hamburgers, as well as sandwiches and simple breakfast. Honey-mustard chicken ¢1800; fruit pancakes ¢750. Open daily 8:30am-10:30pm. ❷

Panadería de Paris (☎653 0255), across from Hotel Pueblo Dorado, just north of the Best Western. Delicate and delicious pastries, cookies, and other baked treats. Choco-late croissants ¢250; sandwiches ¢900. Breakfast with baguette, juice, and coffee or hot chocolate ¢900. Open daily 6am-7pm. ❶

Rodamar Restaurant, a bargain option hidden in the back of Frutas Tropicales cabins, serves hearty *típica* food with large mugs of juice (¢300). Open daily 7am-8:30pm. ❶

Portofino Restaurante-Pizzería (☎653 0020), on the circle. Handmade pasta and authentic thin-crust pizza are the draw. Vegetarian pizza ¢2300, carbonara ¢1900. Open daily noon-11pm. V. ❷

Fiesta del Mar, on the circle. The only 24hr. place in town, open 7 days a week. Serves fine *comidas típicas.* Buffet options after 11pm (small portions ¢200). Whole snapper *asado* ¢2850, tortilla *rellena especial* ¢950. AmEx/MC/V. ❷

Gecko's (☎653 0334), next to Iguana Surf. Called Gil's by day, the restaurant adds can-dles at night, and the night chef endows meat with creative flavors. Teriyaki tuna ¢3300. Open from 5:30pm until the last guest leaves. ❹

Sunrise Café (☎653 0029), at the end of the circle on the beach. Popular yet quiet breakfast spot. Vegetarian omelet ¢1945; tall cup of yogurt with fruit and granola ¢975. Open daily 6-11:30am, 11am-5pm, and 6-9:30pm. AmEx/MC/V. ❸

🏔 🏄 OUTDOOR ACTIVITIES AND GUIDED TOURS

Surfers craving bigger waves than those in Tamarindo have a number of options: head 10km south to **Playa Avellana,** home of the reef-break "Little Hawaii," 15km south to **Playa Negra,** or just north to **Playa Grande,** another good beach break.

Other nature-seekers can also head to Playa Grande, now part of the 420-hectare **Parque Nacional Las Baulas,** on the northeast end of Tamarindo village. From mid-October to mid-February, the park is a nesting site for the *baula,* the **leatherback turtle.** Sportfishing is another great option; contact **Warren Sellers Sportfishing,** diag-onally across from Frutas Tropicales. (☎653 0186; fax 653 0248.) **Agua Rica Diving Center,** by the bank, is the most professionally equipped when it comes to diving. Certification is available; half a day with 2 dives is US$85, equipment rental US$20. (☎653 0094. Open M-Sa 9:30am-6:30pm, Su 3-6:30pm.)

💃 NIGHTLIFE

Although high-season nightlife gets thumpin', low season generally consists of relaxing at beach-side bars with a beer and some music. The Best Western hotel often throws huge poolside parties reminiscent of high school days (you wish!).

Big Bazar Beach Bar (☎653 0307), next to El Pescador. This beachside bar-restaurant, with seats on the sand, a dance floor, and huge bonfire, heats up on Sa nights. Music runs the gamut from hip-hop to salsa. The salads are named after surf spots. Beer ¢500, shots ¢600. Open Su-F 11am-4pm, Sa 11am-4am. Dancing starts at 11pm.

Cantina Las Olas, next to Iguana Surf, east of the main drag. Walk up the street next to the Centro Comercial Aster, take your first right, and follow the beat. A good Mexican restaurant, often extremely crowded with pulsing music and dancing. W ladies' night (women drink free 9-11pm). Open M-Sa 6pm-2:30am.

Mambo Bar, on the circle. Some nights happening, some not so much. Pool, techno music, and striking up new friends. Guaro-ginger-fresca ₡500. Open Th-Su from 8pm.

Blue Moon Bar, on the circle and the beach, attracts a crowd just about any night of the year. Especially popular are Tu and Th nights, when the live blues music gets feet tapping. Try your skills at karaoke any other night. Spectacles of all sorts dazzle the eyes every night. Beer ₡400. Open daily 7:30pm-12:30am.

Bar y Restaurant El Delfín, 500m north of the circle, is a great place to finish off the night. Open 24hr. to satisfy late-night munchies. The tasty desserts are sure to provide pleasant dreams (₡900-1500).

PLAYA JUNQUILLAL

The people who vacation in Playa Junquillal consider it a well-kept secret, and would like it to remain so. Anyone seeking typical tropical beach action, such as music and dancing, should look elsewhere. Junquillal's seclusion makes it an ideal place to unwind if you have an appreciation for quiet relaxation and the wallet for comfortable lodgings. There are a few good surfing spots, a swampy estuary that is fun to explore, and activities such as horseback riding, fishing, and snorkeling. The waves are strong, so swimming is difficult.

☎ ? TRANSPORTATION AND PRACTICAL INFORMATION

Buses go back and forth between **Santa Cruz** and **Junquillal,** leaving the beach from Hotel Playa Junquillal (5 and 11:30am). The town of **Paraíso** is 4km inland (about a 45min. walk), with a few restaurants and a **police station.** The nearest **medical clinic** is **27 de Abril,** and the nearest **post office** is in Santa Cruz.

☛ ACCOMMODATIONS

Guacamaya Lodge (☎658 8431; www.guacamayalodge.com; alibern@racsa.co.cr.), on a hill near the beach (follow the signs from the main road), has hexagonal cabins circling the pool, a few simple budget singles hidden in the back, and a 2-bedroom house for rent. The gentle view of the ocean and surrounding hills is best seen from inside the restaurant. The lawn features a beach volleyball court. Simple singles US$15; cabins US$50; house US$120. ❷

Hospedaje El Malinche (☎658 8114), located behind the *pulpería* of the same name, 200m from the beach, has spacious rooms. Doubles ₡2500, high-season ₡4000, with private bath and kitchen ₡6000/₡10,000. Camping in the yard ₡1500 per person. ❷

El Castillo Divertido (☎/fax 658 8428; castillodivertido@hotmail.com). Small, but truly delightful. Behind the pastel rooftop battlements is a funky circular bar with a good view and stereo system. Rooms (especially inside the tower) have lots of windows and sparkling private baths. German owner Paulo, a musician whose drum sets crowd the lobby, cooks breakfast and dinner in the restaurant. Breakfast US$4; dinner US$8-10. Doubles US$32, in high-season US$39. ❷

Iguanazul Hotel (☎658 8124; www.iguanazul.com; iguanazul@ticonet.co.cr), about 1km down an entrance road signed from the main road into Junquillal. High-ceilinged turquoise rooms face the ocean or a garden. The service is friendly, the resort atmosphere relaxing, and the location perfect. There's also an impressive pool and a bar-restaurant. Kayaks US$25 per person. Ocean-facing doubles US$64, with A/C US$72; garden-facing doubles US$55. Prices somewhat flexible. ❹

El Lugarcito B&B and Dive and Tour Center (☎/fax 658 8436; ellugar-cito@racsa.co.cr), up the hill from Hotel Tatanka, is run by Martin and Miki, a friendly Dutch couple. Those who enjoy the intimacy of B&Bs will love the 3 stone-floor rooms—a honeymoon suite with private hot water bath, and two rooms that share a bath. Cozy bar and dining room, with dinner on request. Diving (including certification courses) available. Martin runs jungle tours. Doubles US$50; honeymoon suite US$60 with breakfast. Prices US$25-30 lower in low-season. ❹

Hotel Villa Serena (☎/fax 658 8430; serenaho@racsa.co.cr), on the beach just past Hotel Playa Junquillal, has tastefully decorated rooms with quiet floral designs, sitting terraces, and big showers. The energetic manager, Xinia, runs free 2hr. aerobics sessions in the main building, where the second-story terrace restaurant yields a calm ocean view. There is also a pool, tennis court, and spa with massage and facials by the owner, who hails from Cape Cod, MA. Doubles US$70; each additional person US$15; about US$25 less in low-season. Breakfast US$6.50. AmEx/MC/V. ❹

◨ FOOD

LaKampu is a proudly Peruvian restaurant overlooking one of Junquillal's few surf spots. Enjoy a delicious *ceviche* (raw fish cocktail ₡2150) in the comfortable space filled by music. Open daily noon-9pm. ❸

Hotel Villa Serena's balcony (see **Accommodations,** above) is perfect for dinner. Cool and classy, with fancy *casados*. ❸

Guacamaya Lodge has wonderful food with a view hard to leave (see **Accommodations,** above). Open daily 8am-10pm. ❷

La Puesta del Sol (☎658 8442) is a genuinely Italian restaurant. Your host-couple takes their expensive but authentic menu very seriously, making sure your special occasion tastes that way. Handmade ravioli and spaghetti *alla puttanesca* around ₡5000. Open after 6:30pm. Reservations required. ❺

◪ ACTIVITIES

Most hotels have tour information and can refer you to the appropriate specialists, such as **local fisherman** Ovidio (☎396 1330) and Erika at **Paradise Riding,** who offers 12 different horseback tours (☎658 8162; www.paradiseriding.com; prerikal@racsa.co.cr. 2½hr. tours to Playa Negra, Paraíso, and through the mangroves US$25 per person. Longer trips also available). The **Iguanazul Hotel** offers **kayak** tours in the Junquillal estuary. (2hr., 4-person max.; US$25 per person.) Earn scuba certification at **El Lugarcito B&B** (US$350 for 4 days), or if already certified, go **diving** and experience Junquillal's underwater volcanic rock. (1 tank US$40, 2 tanks US$00.) A good surfing spot is near the Peruvian restaurant LaKampu.

PLAYA NEGRA

Playa Negra is arguably Costa Rica's second-best surf spot. In surfer language, it's a right-hand point-break beach, where strong tubular waves break over a lava rock reef. There are several surfer-style budget crash pads in the area, but accommodations are not limited to them. If you don't surf, you can rent a horse or go snorkeling, and there's always sun to be had. Once the sun goes down, though, there's very little to do in the town of **Pargos,** which isn't even marked by a sign.

🗲 🔃 TRANSPORTATION AND PRACTICAL INFORMATION

Playa Negra is about 4km north of the village of **Paraíso,** where **buses** running from **Santa Cruz** to **Junquillal** stop. The dirt road may require 4WD in the rainy months. Travelers report safe hitchhiking along the road, but *Let's Go* does not recommend hitchhiking. Walking from the bus stop takes about an hour, and it's also possible to walk along the beach from Junquillal (4km south of Paraíso) if you time your journey to coincide with low tide. **Playa Avellana** (4km) and **Tamarindo** are farther north. Major services can be found in Paraíso, 27 de Abril, and Santa Cruz.

🗲 ACCOMMODATIONS

🔲 **Mono Congo Lodge** (☎/fax 658 8261) nearby, is soothing and elegant: invitingly dark and cool. All wooden, with tall, solid white beds, a shared hot-water tiled bathroom, and hammocks lining a wraparound terrace. The living room, community kitchen, BBQ, and restaurant are well-integrated. Tennis courts available. Horseback tours US$15 per hr. Surfboard rental US$10 per day. Doubles US$30 including breakfast, US$45 in high-season. Guesthouse with 2 rooms, kitchen, and bath US$85 for up to 12 people. ❸

Aloha Amigos (☎658 8023), a 15min. walk down the main road (do not go left at the first fork) beyond the soccer field. Owned by friendly Hawaiians, this hotel offers a few airy, clean rooms with shared or private bath, kitchenette, and loft, plus washing machine and hammock on the back porch. The complex centers around an inviting *rancho* with open kitchen and restaurant meals. US$10 per person with shared bath; 2-person cabins US$30 per day, US$50 for up to 6 people. ❶

Hotel Playa Negra (☎658 8034; fax 658 8035; www.playanegra.com; playanegra@racsa.co.cr), take a left (coming from Paraíso) at the first fork in Pargos. Comfortable beachfront bungalows perfect for the surfer dude/dudette. Bungalows have 3 beds and private tiled baths with hot water. The restaurant features a wide-ranging menu. Spaghetti ¢2700. Surf lessons US$20 per hr. Board rental US$20 per day. Horse rental US$12 per hr. Doubles US$50, high-season US$60; triples US$55/US$70; quads US$60/US$80. AmEx/MC/V. ❹

Juanito's Ranchitos (☎658 8038), next door to Aloha Amigos, offers lots of free extras including bikes, snorkels, surfboards, and Happy Hour. Renovations in progress. Call for availability. US$25 per person; US$10 per person for groups of 3-4. ❶

Kon-Tiki (☎658 8117), on the main road just past the turnoff to Aloha and Juanito's, is a cheap tree house-like place with good group rates. Rooms sleep up to 6 people. Shared baths are dark but not cramped, and there's space for hammock-lounging and surfboard-storing. Breakfast ¢1000; lunch or dinner plate ¢1800; there's also a kitchen. US$10 per person; US$8 per person for groups larger than 4. ❶

Pasta Mike's Hotel, (☎658 8270) the first place you come to on the road from Paraíso, is another good budget option with three basic, buggy rooms and a vegetarian restaurant with tantalizing meals. Surfboard rental US$5 per day. Singles US$10; doubles US$15; quads with private bath US$25, with A/C US$40. ❶

Pablo Picasso's (☎658 8151), is close to the waves. Take a left (coming from Paraíso) at the first fork in Pargos (there are signs). Ten spacious but run-down rooms in a big house filled with mostly male guests. The A/C room with kitchen (used by groups) has a private hot-water bath; the rest have communal sinks and showers. There's also a bar, restaurant, and pool table. Dorms US$10; room with fan and fridge US$15 per person, with A/C and fridge US$22.50 per person, with A/C and kitchen US$25 per person. Prices flexible for long stays. ❷

FOOD

Secret Spot Bakery and Restaurant (☎658 8083), across from Pasta Mike's Hotel, has scrumptious fresh muffins (¢400), pizza (¢1750), and many vegetarian options such as soy burgers (¢18*

PLAYA AVELLANA

Playa Avellana, 4km north of Playa Negra, is a surfing beach that requires less experience and skill. The waves are kinder, yet still significant; surfers are only rarely disappointed. Algae-carpeted tide pools emerge at low tide. There's no real town, and no **buses** stop at Avellana; the nearest stop is **Paraíso**, about 10km south. Many people hitchhike, though *Let's Go* does not recommend it. You can also take a **taxi** from Paraíso to Avellana. (☎680 0706. ¢7000.)

Camping is right on the beach at **Eureka**, with toilets and showers. (¢1000 per tent.) The best lodging is farther north on the dirt road. Committed Italians keep **Cabinas El León Bed and Breakfast ❷** immaculately clean and serve US$3 breakfasts with rich, black coffee. The three spacious rooms have hot-water baths and effective fans. There's satellite TV in the dining area, and laundry on request. (☎658 8318. US$12 per person, US$15 in high-season.) Just behind El León, **Cabinas Las Olas ❸** is the best hotel in the area. Cabins have tiled floors, inviting reading tables, power fans, long mirrors, glass doors, and hot-water baths. A long boardwalk meanders through the swamp straight to the beach. There is also a restaurant. (☎658 8315. Doubles US$50, in high-season US$60; triples US$70/US$80; quads US$80/US$90. AmEx/MC/V.) Back in the center of town, one of the first buildings you hit coming from Playa Negra is the **Iguana Verde ❷**. Budget rooms have small triangular baths and up to 6 beds. The restaurant is open daily. (☎658 8310. ¢2000 per person.) A few doors closer to the beach is **Gregorio's ❶**, with five slightly darker, somewhat less clean rooms, and shared baths. The restaurant serves good, massive fish *casados* for ¢1500. (☎658 8319. ¢1500 per person, ¢2000 with private bath.) **Restaurante Yoruba ❷**, about 300m north of the Eureka campground, is so stylish that it's out of place. It serves vegetarian pizzas on flour tortillas (8-slice margarita pizza ¢2860) in a funky setting of sleek, wooden furniture under umbrellas. (☎658 8097. Open Tu-Su noon-5pm.)

NICOYA

Nicoya, 78km south of Liberia, is the main settlement on the peninsula. The town was named after Chorotegan Indian Chief Nicoya, who ruled the region and welcomed the Spaniards when they arrived in 1523. It has more tourist services and better transportation than nearby towns, yet lacks the personality to be an attraction in and of itself.

▐ TRANSPORTATION

From the main bus stop, 200m east and 200m south of the *parque*, **buses** leave for **San José** (4½hr. via ferry, 6 per day 3:45am-5:20pm; 5-5½hr. via Liberia, 5 per day 5am-2:30pm; ¢1860); **Playa Sámara** (1¼hr., 5 per day 5am-6:30pm, ¢400); and **Nosara** (3½hr.; 5, 10am, 2pm; ¢560). Buy tickets at the window in advance. (Open daily 7am-5pm.) From another stop, 100m north and 150m east of the *parque*, across from Hotel las Tinajas, buses run to **Liberia** (2hr.; M-Sa 26 per day 3:50am-10pm, Su and holidays 12 per day 5am-7pm; ¢450) via **Santa Cruz** (45min., ¢140); **Filadelfia** (1¼hr., additional bus Su and holidays 10pm, ¢300). A 10pm departure that goes to Filadelfia on Sundays and holidays. Nicoya's **taxis** don't have meters; the standard fare is ¢100 per km.

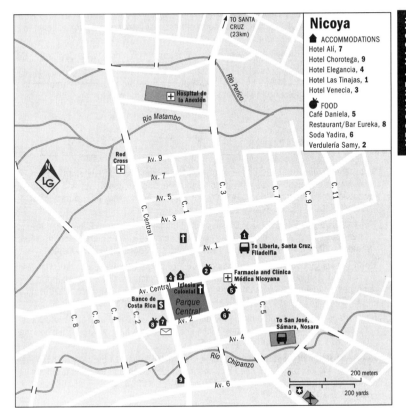

Nicoya

NICOYA PENINSULA

⌂ ACCOMMODATIONS
Hotel Alí, **7**
Hotel Chorotega, **9**
Hotel Elegancia, **4**
Hotel Las Tinajas, **1**
Hotel Venecia, **3**

🍴 FOOD
Café Daniela, **5**
Restaurant/Bar Eureka, **8**
Soda Yadira, **6**
Verdulería Samy, **2**

✴ 🔰 ORIENTATION AND PRACTICAL INFORMATION

The two landmarks in the city center are the **parque central** and the main road, **Calle 3,** which runs north-south one block east of the *parque*. The bus drops you off at various locations, so your best bet is to ask to be directed to the *parque central*. Once in the *parque*, Hotel Venecia is north, the *municipalidad* is south, Banco de Costa Rica is west, and Soda el Parque is east.

Bank: Banco de Costa Rica (☎685 5010), on the west side of the *parque* with Visa/Plus **ATM,** cashes traveler's checks and gives Visa cash advances. Open M-F 8:30am-3pm. There's also an ATM next door to Western Union that accepts Cirrus.

Red Cross: (☎685 5458, emergency 128), 500m north and 50m west of the *parque*.

Medical Services: Farmacia and Clínica Médica Nicoyana (☎685 5138), 100m east and 10m south of the northeast corner of the *parque*. Open M-F 8am-8pm, Sa 8am-6pm. Clínica open M-F 8:30am-12:30pm and 2-5:30pm, Su 8am-noon. **Hospital de la Anexión** (☎685 5066), 100m east and 600m north of the *parque*.

Police: (☎685 5516, emergency 117), 150m south of the bus station, next to the airport.

Telephones: Phones for international calls can be found at the **Instituto Costarricense de Electricidad (ICE)** offices, 125m north of northeast corner of the *parque*. Open M-F 7:30am-5pm, Sa 8am-noon.

Internet Access: **Nicoy@ Netc@fe,** next to Western Union. Open M-Sa 7am-9pm, Su 1pm-9pm.

Post office: (☎685 5088, fax 685 5004),across from the southwest corner of the *parque*. Fax available. Open M-F 8am-5:30pm, Sa 7:30am-noon.

Postal code: 5200.

⌂ ACCOMMODATIONS

Hotel Elegancia (☎685 5159), next to Hotel Venecia on the north side of the *parque*, has spacious, bright rooms with good ventilation. The common bath is a bit small. Meals on request. 4-bed dorms ₡1500 per person. Singles with private bath ₡3000; doubles ₡4000; triples ₡5100. ❶

Hotel Chorotega (☎685 5245), 150m south of the post office, has old but clean rooms looking out on a garden, most with very clean private baths. The single rooms are small and dark. Singles ₡1500, with bath ₡3000; doubles ₡3500; triples ₡5500. ❶

Hotel Venecia (☎685 5325), on the north side of the *parque*, has some dim, viewless rooms and stall-like common bathrooms. Windowed rooms with bath are comfortable and has a redeeming TV common area. Singles ₡1300-1500, with bath ₡3000; doubles ₡3000/₡4000; triples ₡3200/₡4100; quads with private bath ₡5100. ❶

Hotel Alí (☎685 5148, although phone may not be working), just west of the southwest corner of the *parque*, is the cheapest place in town. Rooms have private baths; try for a room with a window. ₡1000 per person. ❶

Hotel Las Tinajas (☎685 5081), 100m north and 150m east of the *parque*, has large windows, the option of A/C, and one room that fits seven people in three adjoining suites. Clean private baths. Singles ₡3700, with A/C ₡6000; doubles ₡5100/₡8000; triples ₡5775/₡10,000. ❷

⬚ FOOD

Café Daniela, 100m east and 50m south of the northeast corner of the *parque*, offers the biggest selection of *comida típica*, which is prepared with great care. *Casados* ₡1000. Open M-Sa 7am-9:30pm and Su 5-9:30pm. ❶

Soda Yadira, 75m east of the *parque's* southeast corner, is known for its desserts and midday snacks. Ice cream ₡250; cake ₡175 per slice. Open M-Sa 6:45am-8:30pm. ❶

Restaurant/Bar Eureka, on the southwest corner of the *parque*, across from the post office, is another good *típico* option. *Casados* ₡900-1000. Open daily 8am-10pm. ❶

Verdulería Samy, the vegetable store on the *parque*, offers fresh produce. ❶

⊙ SIGHTS

Iglesia Colonial, on the northeast corner of the *parque*, is one of the oldest churches in Costa Rica, constructed in 1644 of stone, brick, and *cal*, a sand unique to the area and stronger than cement. The church was damaged by earthquakes in 1822 and rebuilt in 1831. The restoration process is stop-and-go; the floors have recently been touched up. Several religious artifacts—a baptismal font, statues, and paintings—are worth a look as well. If you have extra time and the heat isn't too oppressive, the folks at **Ciclo Mireya #2,** 400m north of the northwest corner of the *parque,* can rent you a bike to explore the surrounding countryside. (☎685 5391. Bikes ¢1500 per day.)

NEAR NICOYA

PARQUE NACIONAL BARRA HONDA

*Buses leave for **Santa Ana** from the main bus stop in Nicoya, 200m east and 200m south of the* parque, *and drop you off 2km from the park entrance. (M-Sa 1 per day 12:30pm, early Feb.-June and mid-July-Dec. 2 per day 12:30 and 5pm; ¢200). To visit the park as a daytrip, you can hire a **taxi** (30min., ¢3000). Buses returning to Nicoya stop at the sign 2km from the entrance 1-1:30pm. To ensure that there will be enough guides available, call Nicoya's branch of the Ministerio del Ambiente y Energía (MINAE) or drop in (on the northeast corner of the* parque) *the day before your visit. One guide speaks English. Children under 12 are not permitted in the Terciopelo cave, although a children's cave is open to educational groups. MINAE ☎685 5667, fax 686 6760. Open M-F 8am-4pm. Park ranger station open daily 24hr. Park entrance open daily 7am-4pm; if going into the cave, you must begin by 1pm. Admission US$6. Trail guides ¢2500; cave guides ¢7000 for group of 1-4, ¢1500 for each additional person. Spelunking equipment rental US$12.*

Hidden beneath the Parque Nacional Barra Honda, 22km northeast of Nicoya, are a series of limestone caves dating back 70 million years. Only one cave, **Terciopelo,** is open to the public. With three guides, harnesses, and repelling gear, you can descend 62m underground to an amazing stalactite and stalagmite forest. The descent is not for the timid, but the amazing works of nature that lurk below are worth the effort. In several distinct caverns, you'll have the chance to make music on the long, hollow spikes of calcium, and see "fried eggs" in the beginning stages of growth. The cave is about a 1½hr. hike from the park entrance—the first half is a bit of a climb, but then it levels out. Be sure to take the short **trail** to a spectacular **mirador** (lookout spot), from which you can see a large portion of the verdant Nicoya peninsula, 825m above sea level.

For many visitors, the hike and final view are reason enough to visit Barra Honda. On the walk through the deciduous tropical dry forest (all green during the wet season, with many mosquitoes in June; and dry with high fire danger in the dry season) one may come upon deer, anteaters, armadillos, white-faced monkeys, howler monkeys, and multiple lizards, iguanas, and butterflies. Also, if you should visit the park in August or September when its rainy, take the 2hr. **Las Cascadas** hike to a swimmable spring with water falling down high calcified steps.

If you use public transportation, you'll have to spend the night. There are two options. You can **camp** in a small grassy area (¢300 per person with toilets and showers nearby), or stay in dusty cabins (one bath for 8 people; ¢1500 per person). Basic meals are available through MINAE if you call ahead (breakfast ¢500, lunch and dinner ¢1000). You can call MINAE for **volunteer opportunities** as a cave guide, for which you will receive room, board, and a small salary. Ask for Maynor Díaz, the park's administrator, or Gerardo Martínez Muñoz, chief of MINAE.

PLAYA NOSARA

The town of Nosara is sleepy and quiet, spread out over about 6km of dirt roads, which are often mud roads come rainy season. Rent a bike and go exploring: it's hard to get lost and easy to spot wildlife ambling around. All of the beaches are at least 5km from the town center, where the pace of everyday life is slower and more settled than down by the water. Lodging is cheaper, although die-hard beach bums can find good seaside deals.

⌸ TRANSPORTATION

Sansa (1hr.; high season 11:50am, return 12:55pm; low season 7:30am, return 8:20am; US$66) and **Travelair** (1hr.; high season 1pm, return 2pm; low season 11:45am, return 12:55pm; US$73) fly out of San José (see **p. 85**) and arrive at the airstrip 3km northeast of town. **Buses** to Nosara leave from Sámara, Nicoya, and Liberia. Leaving Nosara, buses go to **San José** (6hr., 12:45pm, ¢2800) from Soda Vanessa, 150m west of the soccer field. Buses to **Nicoya** (3½hr., 6am and 12:15pm, ¢600) leave from the northeast side of the soccer field, outside Bambú Bar.

▰▰ ❼ ORIENTATION AND PRACTICAL INFORMATION

The main road into Nosara from Nicoya and Sámara runs north to south. All directions are in relation to the **soccer field** in the town's center, which doubles as horse grazing grounds. Renting a **bike** or **all-terrain vehicle (ATV)** is a necessity if you plan to explore Nosara. Beaches are far from the center and buses are rare. Clemente, at **Cabinas Agnnel,** has a **taxi** service; try to arrange ahead (☎682 0058 or 682 0142).

Tourist Office: Tuanis (☎ 682 0249), Nosara's unofficial tourist information center, is on the northeast corner. They have maps, postcards, a book exchange, beach wear, the cheapest **Internet** around by far (¢1000 per hr.) and offers horseback tours and referrals to other tour-type activities. (See **Guided Tours,** below.)

Financial Services: The town has no bank or ATM, but **Supermercado Nosara,** 300m west and 400m south of the soccer field, changes US dollars and traveler's checks. Open M-Sa 8am-7pm, Su 8am-3pm.

Police: The **police station** (☎ 682 0317), on the southeast corner of the soccer field, is consistently staffed.

Red Cross: Next door to the police station.

Medical Services: Ebais Clinic (☎ 682 0266) is 300m south of the southeast corner of the soccer field.

Telephones: Public phones are outside the police station and just west of the soccer field.

Post office: 50m south of the southeast corner of the soccer field. Open M-F 7:30am-noon and 1-6pm. **Postal code:** 5233.

⌂ ACCOMMODATIONS

The hotels in Nosara's center are much cheaper than those near the beach.

Cabinas Agnnel (☎ 682 0142), 200m west of the southwest corner of the soccer field, has blue rooms with private baths and fans. ¢2088 per person; low season ¢1750. ❶

Cabinas Chorotega (☎ 682 0105), 200m west and 300m south of the soccer field, a few doors down from Super Nosara, has its own restaurant, sturdy beds, and the option of a private bath. The host family is welcoming and rooms are bright and comfortable. ¢2500 per person, low season ¢2000; triples with private bath ¢6000/¢5000. ❶

Hotel Chorotega (☎ 682 0129), 200m west and 300m south of the soccer field, has its own restaurant, comfortable rooms with sturdy beds, and communal baths. Restaurant open 7am-10pm. Doubles ¢3000; quads ¢6000. ❶

Casa Río Nosara (☎ 682 0117), about 2km out of town, offers spacious cabins, each with private bath and a hammock on the porch. US$10 per person. ❶

Hotel Ángel (☎ 682 0142), 200m west of the southwest corner of the soccer field, is the cheapest option in the area. Front rooms are spacious and all have private baths and fans. ¢2000 per person; low season ¢1500. ❶

FOOD

Rancho Tico has a large selection and reasonable prices, and its open and welcoming atmosphere makes it a favorite among locals and visitors. The *pollo a la campesina* (¢1695) is especially flavorful. *Casados* ¢1590; filet mignon ¢2650. Open daily 5-10pm; bar open until midnight. ❸

La Casona (☎ 682 0442), a 7min. walk south of central Nosara on the main road toward the beaches, has even lower prices and a quiet ambience occasionally broken by huge Sa night dance parties, at which delicious pizza is served. *Casados* ¢900-1300; chicken with mushrooms ¢1200. Open daily 9am-9pm. ❸

Soda Vanessa, 110m west of the soccer field, is small, simple, and the most reliable place for quick, good food. *Casados* ¢1200. Open daily 6:30am-4:30pm; high season 6:30am-4pm and 6pm-9pm. ❷

ENTERTAINMENT AND NIGHTLIFE.

For those looking to bump and grind, **Tropicana Disco Bar,** by the soccer field, is the most exciting option, perhaps more than ever since its renovation. Be prepared for a wide range of music. (☎ 682 0140. Open F-Sa 9pm-3am.) If all that dancing just gets in the way, try **Bambú Bar,** where you can sip extra-cold *Pilsens* and *Imperiales* in bamboo chairs at the bar, sometimes to live marimba music. They also have a full Chinese menu. (Appetizers free with drinks. Open daily 10am-2pm.) At sunset, stop in at **Lagarta Lodge,** 4km south of central Nosara with a spectacular vista of Playa Nosara and the Nicoya coast. While meals are pricey, a few drinks won't break the bank. **Las Iguanas Locas,** nearby, also often maintains a rather jovial crowd long after the sun has set.

GUIDED TOURS

Tuanis (☎ 682 0249), on the northeast corner of the soccer field, organizes horseback riding tours, bike rentals, fishing trips, and trips to see turtles in **Ostional**. Horseback tours US$24. Bikes US$8 per day, US$40 per week. Open daily 7am-6pm, but hours are rather flexible.

Ciclo Nosara (☎ 682 0249), on the northwest corner of the soccer field, also rents bikes. ¢2000 per day. Open M-Sa 7am-5pm, Su 7am-noon.

Gunter's Quads (☎ 682 0574; gunquad@infoweb.co.cr) rents ATVs. US$45 per day, US$250 per week.

Casa Río Nosara (☎ 682 0117 or 682 1082; www.rionosara.com; infor@rion-osara.com), also runs horseback tours and rents canoes, bikes, and kayaks. 2hr. horseback tour US$25, 5hr. tour to Pilas Blancas waterfalls US$45. Kayaks US$15.

NEARBY BEACHES

PLAYA PELADA AND PLAYA GUIONES

Playa Pelada, a short, inset crescent of beach with a rocky point and some stony out-croppings breaking up the waves, is the most easily accessible of the three sister beaches (**Nosara, Pelada,** and **Guiones** from north to south) and welcomes swimmers and campers to its white-sand shores. Signs for specific establishments abound on the main road from grittier-sanded Nosara, which first branches west toward Pelada and then, a few kilometers later, toward Guiones. The area is a magnet for repeat vacationers and foreign retirees. Generally, Pelada is less crowded and more private than Guiones, which is crawling with surfers in the summertime (Dec.-Apr.). White-sanded **Guiones** offers the longest uninterrupted coastline of these beaches and a forging break that all surfing novices appreciate.

Many hotels with their own restaurants back the beaches, are spread out over circuitous roads, and nestled in trees. Most are pricey, yet have negotiable rates depending on the season, group size, and length of stay. Important **services** (buses, post office, police) are in Nosara's center, except for supermarket **Las Delicias** and a makeshift **bank** at **Café de Paris** that changes US dollars and traveler's checks.

ACCOMMODATIONS AND FOOD NEAR PELADA. Almost Paradise ❷, about 350m from the beach, is an aptly named beach house with a communal terrace that catches the breeze up on a hill. The five rooms have dark wooden floors and private baths. Although the building feels old, it's filled with young guests and a relaxed ocean vibe. Snorkeling, sportfishing on a 23ft boat, and kayak trips are easily arranged. (☎682 0173. Snorkeling US$10 for gear, US$200 for tour; fishing US$550-600 for full day. Breakfast included. Doubles US$35, in high season US$45; quads US$45/US$55. Prices negotiable.) **Hotel Playas de Nosara ❸,** crowned by a dramatic tower whose spiral stairs lead to a panoramic view of Playas Guiones and Pelada, will transport you to Europe with its Greek-Mediterranean architecture—smooth white arches frame blue water everywhere you turn. It also has a restaurant and a pool. Rooms are less splendid, but offer incredible terrace views, lots of light, tiled floors, and comfortable beds. (☎682 0121; fax 682 0123; www.nosarabeachhotel.com.) There are two comfortable rooms at **Rancho Congo ❷,** where howler monkeys will wake you in the mornings. It is more removed from the beach, but the place feels very private. Breakfast is included. (☎/fax 682 0078. Doubles US$35 in high season; triples US$45.)

Panadería La Mariposa ❷, a pink-orange landmark in the Pelada vicinity, hits a sweet spot with Swiss cookies, chocolate croissants (¢300), and cakes as well as fresh salads (¢1600), tuna (¢2500 with salad), and quiches. (☎682 0545. Open Sa-Th 6:30am-7pm; high season 6am-7pm.) **Olga's Bar Restaurant ❷,** by the beach on Pelada, is a cool place to rest from sunbathing. (Whole fish ¢2000. Beer ¢400. Open daily 7:30am-9pm.) The small restaurant and bar **El Nuevo Milenio ❶,** off the main road to Pelada, a stone's throw from the beach, has super-cheap, super-*típico* food and is most popular and wild on Karaoke Sunday nights. (*Casados* ¢800; grilled fish filet ¢1500. Open daily 9am-9pm. Bar open until 10:30pm.)

ACCOMMODATIONS AND FOOD NEAR GUIONES. Alan's Surf House ❷ has clean, spacious rooms with solid bunk beds and shared baths. Friendly owners serve up huge power-breakfasts and give Swedish and Hawaiian massages on the side. (☎682 0251. "Surfer's special" board rental US$20 per day. Breakfast ¢1500-2000. Singles US$20; doubles US$30. Discounts for longer stays.) **Blew Dog's Surf Club ❷,** 100m from the beach, oozes youth and reggae, with colorful wall murals, a restaurant-bar, a pool, pool table and TV. Brighter and more crowded than most, it also offers one hexagonal bungalow with four beds for US$10 per person. (☎682 0080; www.blewdogs.com. Double with fridge US$35, US$150 per week. Two-room suite with kitchen US$45/US$200. Flexible prices.) **Hotel Café de Paris ❸,** has a poolside restaurant and wood-paneled rooms. In the high season, a small **theater** shows movies on F and there's live music on Su. (☎682 0087. **Internet** US$5 per 30min. Breakfast included. Rooms US$29 for first person, US$10 per additional person;

US$39 with A/C; US$49 with A/C and kitchen.) **Giardino Tropicale ❶** has some of the cheaper rooms in Playa Guiones. They are simple and clean, with private baths and ceiling fans. (☎ 682 0258. Rooms US$15 per person; US$25 in high season; US$7/US$10 with shared bath. Prices are negotiable.) Cartoon iguanas dot the exterior of **The Gilded Iguana ❸.** Its six rooms near the beach are airy and spacious. It is perfect for splurging surfers, with fans, sinks, and fridges in every room, and an excellent, casual restaurant with live music on Tu nights. (☎/fax 682 0259. US$25-45 depending on room size, additional US$15 in high season. V.) At sunset, stop in at **Lagarta Lodge ❺,** 4km south of central Nosara, to enjoy the spectacular *vista* of Playa Nosara and the Nicoya coast. While the rooms here might break a bank, a few drinks at the restaurant won't. (☎ 682 0035; www.lagarta.com.)

If you find yourself craving something sweet, fresh, and European, the bakery at **Hotel Café de Paris ❸,** will satisfy you with goodies and breads. The chef is Swiss-French and bakes it all himself. The pool-side restaurant serves a wide range of food. (☎ 682 0087. Fruit crepe ¢1000; pizza margherita ¢1600; chicken sandwich ¢2000). For breakfast, go to **Alan's Surf House ❸** and fuel up for surfing. (¢1500-2000. Open 7-11am.) **The Gilded Iguana ❷** serves fresh lunches at reasonable prices. (☎/fax 682 0259. Breakfast 7-9:30am, lunch 11am-2pm, dinner 5-10pm. Bar open 10am-10pm.) The Italian food at **Giardino Tropicale ❶** garners praise. (☎ 682 0258. Make your own pizza ¢1750, toppings ¢200 each.)

NEARBY ACTIVITIES. Many hotels offer various tours and rentals. Several surf shops and surf schools in Guiones offer **board rentals** and **surf lessons.** The **Nosara Surf Shop** (☎ 682 0186) and **Coconut Harry's,** across from Café de Paris, rent boards for US$20 per day, give lessons, and rent all-terrain vehicles **(ATVs). Casa Río Nosara,** along the road between Nosara and Pelada, runs **horseback riding** tours and also rents **canoes** and **kayaks.** (☎ 682 0117 or 682 1082; info@rionosara.com. US$25 for 2hr.) **Snorkeling** tends to be best and safest at nearby San Juanillo beach—ask about rentals and tours at hotels. There are some natural **waterfalls** with many swimmable holes (the falling water makes for a hearty massage) during the rainy season in the hills behind Nosara; ask for a **guide** to take you there at Cabinas Chorotega, in Nosara, or at The Gilded Iguana, near Guiones. If you have a free day and just want to get away to a secluded spot, take a 2hr. hike past Playa Guiones to the pink beach of **Playa Rosada.** Ask for directions at a hotel on your way south. Finally, to stretch, relax, and meditate, try the **Nosara Yoga Institute,** which offers public classes. To get there by foot, take the path marked with the blue frog behind Café de Paris, turn left and immediately right on the road, and follow the white gravel. (☎ 682 0071; www.nosarayoga.com. US$10 for a 1½hr. class.)

OSTIONAL

This gritty strip of black-sand beach is Costa Rica's most important breeding ground for olive ridley turtles, and every month, at the start of a new quarter moon (usually at the end of the month), females flock by the thousands to lay their eggs. During that time, the tiny town of **Ostional** (p. 207) comes to life (relatively speaking): the two modest hotels fill to the brim and the fires at the two *sodas* never die down. Luckily, Ostional is an easy daytrip from Nosara and Sámara, and many tourist agencies in these two towns can get you there and back before bedtime.

The arrival of the turtles is termed *arribada*, and on these special days, most turtles arrive between 3 and 8pm, though a trickle continues through most of the night. The hordes travel in from as far away as Peru and Baja California to give their progeny a chance to begin life in the same place they themselves were born. During the process, the sand is barely visible, as hundreds to thousands of turtles scramble over each other and dig up each other's eggs in order to find a cozy hole for their own. To make sure you don't miss this event, contact biologist

Rodrigo Morera (☎/fax 682 0470; adioturt@sal.racsa.co.cr) at La Asociación de Desarollo Integral de Ostional, 100m north of Soda La Plaza (see below), or check in with the tourist agencies in Nosara or Sámara. Surfing is prohibited during the *arribada*.

To get to Ostional from Nosara, contact Clemente at Cabinas Agnnel for a **taxi**. (☎682 0058 or 682 0142. 20min., ¢3000.) The trip between Nosara and Ostional (8km) also makes for a pleasant 1½hr. bike ride over dirt roads lined with cow pastures. Or, hop on one of the many **buses** from the bigger hotels in the surrounding towns. One bus makes the bumpy 3hr. ride between Santa Cruz and Ostional, stopping at small towns along the way. (Cabinas Guacamayas in Ostional 5am, Santa Cruz noon.) The bus can't make the trip during heavy rains.

The central **Soda La Plaza ❶** has a mini-market stocking snacks and a menu of all the *típico* basics for bargain prices. (*Casados* ¢900-1000. Open daily 7am-9pm.) **Cabinas Ostional ❶**, across from Soda La Plaza, has simple triples and quads with private baths and nice balconies. (☎682 0428. ¢1500 per person.) **Hospedaje Guacamayas ❶**, 125m left of Soda La Plaza if you're facing the beach, has darker, but clean rooms. (☎682 0430. ¢1500 per person.) For a beautiful view of Guiones, Nosara, and Ostional, and all the way to Punta India, buy a meal or have a beer at the round outdoor **Restaurante Las Loras ❷**, up a hill about 400m south of Soda La Plaza (the restaurant has a sign at the turnoff); it is especially romantic at sunset. (Pancake-like crepes ¢700-900; vegetarian plate ¢1500. Open daily 7am-10pm.) Hungarian-owned **Rancho Hotel Brovilla ❸**, 3km north of the town of Ostional, organizes horseback trips, fishing trips, snorkeling tours, and ATV rentals. Rooms are extremely pricey, but it has a pool, sauna, restaurant, and a rustic "surfer house" that is a great deal. (☎380 5639. Surfer house US$10 per person, with two trips to the beach and back for US$5.) **Camping** is allowed next to the beach behind Soda La Plaza. (Portable toilet outside. US$3 per person, 3 meals a day ¢2800. Camping fee waived for student groups who pay for meals.)

PLAYA SÁMARA

Not too long ago, Sámara was a tiny fishing and farming community where the soccer field was the hub of activity and development was limited to a few *cabinas*, *sodas*, and the simple houses of easy-going locals. But with one of Costa Rica's cleanest, prettiest, and most swimmable beaches, this little village was eventually discovered by vacationing foreigners and *ticos*, who now come in droves to let the warm, powdery white sand and pristine blue waters take away all their worries. Luckily, Sámara isn't nearly as busy and commercial as many of Costa Rica's hot spots, so when the waves wash away all footprints, everyone can feel like they're discovering this national treasure for the very first time.

▐ TRANSPORTATION

Since the roads along the southwestern Nicoya Peninsula are in such poor shape, getting to Sámara via public transportation from places like Montezuma and Mal País in the southern Nicoya Peninsula involves going back to Paquera, catching the ferry to Puntarenas, taking a bus to the town of Nicoya, and then taking one final bus to Sámara. Even if you take the first bus to Paquera in the morning, you'll likely have to spend the night in the town of Nicoya and catch a bus to Sámara the next morning. You'll be better off taking a private transfer to Sámara in a 4WD vehicle or coming via bus from San José (6hr.; M-Sa 12:30pm, return 4am, Su 1pm.), Liberia, or other points in northwestern Costa Rica.

NICOYA PENINSULA

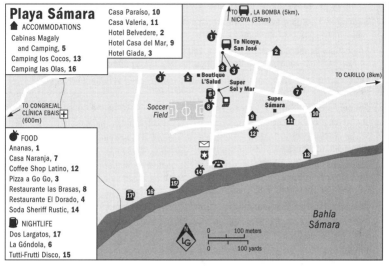

Playa Sámara

♠ ACCOMMODATIONS
Cabinas Magaly
and Camping, **5**
Camping los Cocos, **13**
Camping las Olas, **16**

Casa Paraíso, **10**
Casa Valeria, **11**
Hotel Belvedere, **2**
Hotel Casa del Mar, **9**
Hotel Giada, **3**

TO CONGREJAL,
CLÍNICA EBAIS
(600m)

🍎 FOOD
Ananas, **1**
Casa Naranja, **7**
Coffee Shop Latino, **12**
Pizza a Go Go, **3**
Restaurante las Brasas, **8**
Restaurante El Dorado, **4**
Soda Sheriff Rustic, **14**

🎵 NIGHTLIFE
Dos Largatos, **17**
La Góndola, **6**
Tutti-Frutti Disco, **15**

TO 🚌, LA BOMBA (5km),
NICOYA (35km)

To Nicoya,
San José

Boutique
L'Salud   Super
Sol y Mar

Super
Sámara

TO CARILLO (8km)

Soccer
Field

Bahía
Sámara

0   100 meters
0   100 yards

Buses: Complete schedule posted in **Super Sol y Mar,** on the main drag. Buses drive in along the main drag to the beach and drop passengers off in front of Hotel Giada or at the end of the road, just past the soccer field, before continuing to the tiny village of Congregal, 1km west, or Playa Carillo, 8km east. Buses leave from in front of Hotel Giada for: **Carillo** (25min.; 11am, 1, 4:30, 6:30pm; return 11:20am, 1:30, 5pm; ¢200); **Nicoya** (1hr.; M-Sa 6 per day 5:30am-4:30pm, Su 7am, 12:45, 4:30pm; return M-Sa 7 per day 6am-5pm, Su 8am and 3pm; ¢400); **San José** (5½hr.; M, F, Sa 4:30 and 8:45am; Tu and Th 4:30am; Su 8:30am and 1pm; ¢1780). Purchase San José tickets in advance from Super Sol y Mar. Buses leave for San José more frequently from Nicoya (5hr., 6 per day 5am-5pm, ¢1680). Buses to **Nósara** leave from La Bomba, a gas station 5km from the town center (1hr., between 10:30 and 11am, ¢365).

Taxi: No local number, but call Super Sámara at ☎ 656 0256 and ask for Rafael. To Carillo ¢1500, to La Bomba ¢600.

Rentals: Hotel Giada (see **Accommodations,** below) has a Budget Rent-a-Car service and also rents ATVs for ¢6000 per hr. **Flying Crocodile** (see **Outdoor Activities and Guided Tours,** below) rents cars (US$55 per day), motorbikes (US$35 per day), and mountain bikes (US$5 per day). **Hotel Belvedere** (see **Accommodations,** below) rents bicycles for US$6 per half day, US$8 per day. **Tio Tigre** (see **Outdoor Activities and Guided Tours,** below) rents bikes for US$9 per half day, US$14 per day.

⚒ 🛈 ORIENTATION AND PRACTICAL INFORMATION

Playa Sámara is on the west coast of the southern Nicoya Peninsula, 8km east of Playa Carillo and 35km southwest of Nicoya. The main drag runs south into town and ends just before the beach; orient yourself by remembering that the beach is south. Two main side roads branch off the main drag to the east; many hotels are in this area. Another road branches off the main drag to the west; this road leads to the tiny village of Congrejal.

Tourist Information Office: No official office, but Hotel Giada and the family that runs Super Sol y Mar (see **Transportation,** above) can help you out with basic information.

Currency Exchange: Closest banks are in Nicoya, so stock up on colones beforehand.

Supermarket: Super Sámara, 200m east down the side road closest to the beach. Open M-Sa 7am-8pm, Su 7am-6pm.

English-Language Bookstore: Koss Art Gallery, a 500m walk east along the beach, has a few English-language paperbacks for exchange. Usually open M-Sa 9am-5pm.

Laundry: No self service in town, but several hotels (see **Accommodations,** below) will wash your load for you.

Police: (☎656 0436), at the far south end of the main drag, on the beach.

Hospitals: For serious medical emergencies, go directly to the hospital in Nicoya. **Clínica Ebais** (☎656 0166), 1km west of Sámara in Congrejal, can help with minor injuries and illness.

Pharmacy: Boutique L'Salud (☎656 0727), just west of the main drag on the side street farthest from the beach, has basic over-the-counter medicines and cosmetics. Open M-Sa 8am-5pm. AmEx/MC/V.

Internet: At **Super Sámara.** ¢400 per 15min. Open M-Sa 7am-8pm, Su 7am-6pm.

Public Phones: Near the beach on the main drag. Hotel Giada has a **credit card phone** for calls to the US and Canada.

Post Office: Next to the police station at the far south end of the main drag. Open M-F 8-noon and 1-5pm, but hours change often.

Postal Code: 5235.

ACCOMMODATIONS AND CAMPING

Because of its popularity with nearly every kind of traveler, from the thrifty back-packer to vacationing North American and *tico* families, Sámara has accommodations suiting every budget and comfort level. Many of the nicer places are owned by friendly Europeans, while the cheaper ones tend to be locally run. Especially popular with nearby locals and youth are the several **campsites** along the beach.

Casa Valeria (☎656 0316), 50m east of Super Sámara on the side street closest to the beach. Anyone looking for tranquil, private accommodations should check out Valeria. The best rooms are the *casitas,* little houses set off from the others. However, even the simpler rooms with their pink walls, ceiling fans, shell decorations, patios, and hot-water baths are cozy. The included breakfast is served in the pleasant beachfront dining area. Fully stocked communal kitchen available. Laundry ¢3000. Check-out noon. Doubles US$20, high season US$30; triples US$25/US$35; *casitas* US$40/US$60. ❶

Casa Paraíso (☎656 0749), down the street and around the corner from Super Sámara, is a good option for groups of 2 or 3. The spotless rooms look brand new and have bright white walls, private hot-water baths, fans, comfortable beds, and patios. Laundry available. Check-out noon. Singles US$15, high season US$25; doubles US$20/US$25; triples US$30/US$35. Major credit cards accepted. ❷

Hotel Belvedere (☎656 0213; www.samara-costarica.com), just off the main drag on the side street farthest north of the beach. One of Sámara's more luxurious options is actually quite affordable as a splurge option. The German owners keep the 10 bright and comfortable rooms with enormous private solar-powered hot-water baths, canopy beds, nice decor, and the option of fan or A/C, TV, and fridge. Parking, large pool, jacuzzi, laundry (US$8 per kilo), included breakfast, and good views of the entire bay. Singles US$20, high season US$22; doubles US$35/US$38; triples US$40/US$45; quads US$45/US$50. Additional US$5 for A/C. 2 apartments US$50 per night, high season US$55; US$300/US$400 per month. AmEx/MC/V. ❷

Hotel Giada (☎ 656 0132; www.hotelgiada.net), 300m north of the beach on the main drag, is one of Sámara's nicer options and is often filled with international students enrolled in nearby language schools. The 13 spacious rooms have fresh, yellow walls, comfortable beds, bamboo furniture, ceiling fan, private balcony, and private hot-water baths. Tour and laundry service, pool, restaurant/bar, and an extremely professional multilingual staff will spoil you to your heart's content. Breakfast included. Check-out noon. Singles US$26; doubles US$38; triples US$45. AmEx/MC/V. ❸

Hotel Casa del Mar (☎ 656 0564), 100m east down the first side street off the main drag, has extremely helpful and friendly French owners and 17 comfortable rooms for just about every budget. Rooms upstairs have fans and share a clean, hot-water bath, while the more luxurious nooks downstairs open up to the beautiful jacuzzi and pool and have private baths, fans, tasteful accessories, and A/C on request. Continental breakfast included. Laundry US$10. Check-out 11am. Singles US$20, with private bath US$30; doubles US$25/US$35; triples US$30/US$45; quads US$55; quints US$65; rooms sleeping six US$75. Discounts in low season and for long stays. AmEx/MC/V. ❷

Camping los Cocos (☎ 656 0496), 300m west of the main drag on the beach, is the best campsite, with large, shady palms and sandy floors. Plenty of showers. Electricity until 10pm. ¢800 per person. ❶

Camping las Olas (☎ 656 0187), 300m east of the main drag on the beach, is another good and large campground with tight, hard-packed sand floors, large leafy trees, hammocks, a pool table, showers, and an attached restaurant/bar. ¢1000 per person. ❶

Cabinas Magaly and Camping (☎ 656 0052), 25m west down a side street off the main drag, 100m east of the beach. Sámara's cheapest and most basic. It's a family-run place with 10 clean but dark rooms, fans, and cold showers. Campers can pitch tents in the small grassy area outside. Rooms with shared bath ¢1500 per person, with private bath ¢2000 per person. ❶

FOOD

Sámara's increasing population of foreign residents means that you'll find just as many Italian and French restaurants as simple *típico sodas*. Not surprisingly, everything is a bit pricier, but the food is generally high quality, and the beachfront cafes have soothing, tropical atmospheres.

Soda Sheriff Rustic, at the south end of the main drag on the beach. Families and friends still dressed in bathing suits and dripping with salty ocean water take a seat at the tree stump tables and chairs for some tasty and simple *gallo pinto* (¢600-700), burgers (¢500), and rice and fish dishes (¢1000-1300). Their ice-cold papaya-pineapple-mango smoothies (¢350) are super refreshing. Open daily 8am-7pm. ❶

Pizza a Go Go, inside Hotel Giada. Real Italian ingredients and creativity go into each spicy and sumptuous pizza and pasta dish. Treat your tummy to classy dishes like ravioli in vodka sauce (¢2500), shrimp with avocado (¢2300), or special steamed mackerel (¢2500). The wood oven-baked pizzas (¢1200-2300) are enormous and topped with tasty ingredients like fresh basil and portobello mushrooms. Beer ¢500. Open daily noon-11pm. Closed Tu in low season. AmEx/MC/V. ❷

Casa Naranja, 100m north and 150m east of the beach on a side street off the main drag. This sweet and honeyed B&B doubles as a romantic spot where you can dine on homemade Caribbean and international dishes. The cozy backyard dining area is lit by twinkling Christmas lights and candles, and shady and tropical plants strategically placed between tables provide more intimacy. Vegetarians will love the veggie avocado sandwich (¢800) and rice and beans cooked in coconut milk (¢1500). Seafood lovers will enjoy the shrimp in garlic curry (¢2600), and the sweet tooth will savor the pineapple and rum flambé crepes (¢1200). Open daily for lunch and dinner; exact hours vary. ❷

Ananas, 350m north of the beach on the main drag. Any local will direct you to peaceful Ananas for a midday snack or light dinner. Enjoy a veggie burger (¢600), fruit pancake (¢900), heart of palm salad (¢950), or delicious fresh fruit milk shake (¢600) in the open-air hut with a nice view of the town. Open W-M 7am-7pm. ❶

Restaurante El Dorado, 50m west of Cabinas Magaly on a side street off the main drag. The adorable Italian owner serves tasty pastas (¢1500-2000), cheesy pizzas (¢1800-3000), and fresh fish starters (¢1800-3000) under a small and cozy thatched roof. Open daily noon-10pm. V. ❷

Restaurante las Brasas, 150m north of the beach on the main drag, is a classier place with Spanish and international cuisine, exceptional service, and upbeat Spanish music. Sit in the 2nd-story open-air balcony to fully enjoy a platter of *paella* (¢3500 per person, 2-person minimum), *tortilla española* (¢1750), BBQ meats (¢8000 for 2 people), or T-bone steak (¢3200). If the dinner entrees are too steep for you, maybe the ¢700 flan with chocolate and fruit will be easier to rationalize. Open daily noon-10pm. V. ❸

Coffee Shop Latino, opposite Hotel Casa del Mar, on a side street off the main drag. Travelers ambling along the beach wander into this cute, open-air, Euro-style cafe, where they can simultaneously dig their toes into the sand and sink their teeth into the specialty crepes. Breakfast and lunch entrees ¢800-1600. Sweet crepe ¢500, with ice cream ¢750, with chocolate ¢800, with mushroom and tomato ¢1100, with ham, cheese, and egg ¢1200. Open daily 7am-6pm. ❶

OUTDOOR ACTIVITIES AND GUIDED TOURS

If you somehow tire of the beach, several hotels and tour operators can offer you tours and trips for just about every interest and activity. Most center around water, as several areas nearby have excellent **fishing, snorkeling,** and **surfing** opportunities. Also popular is **dolphin watching,** as the magnificent mammals migrate along the coast and get quite close to the shore before realizing the waters are too shallow.

Hotel Giada (see **Accommodations,** above), has a good variety of well-organized tours. Their most popular is the dolphin trip, a relaxing 4hr. boat ride with snorkeling, sportfishing, and drinks (US$35 per person). They also offer kayak trips, diving, and horse rental (US$6 per hr.). Three days a month, the hotel arranges 5-6hr. jeep rides to Playa Ostional to watch nesting sea turtles.

Hotel el Ancla (☎656 0716), next door to Casa Valeria, on the beach, offers dolphin tours leaving at 7:30am (US$30 per person including drinks and fruit), sunset boat rides leaving at 5pm (US$10 per person), and snorkel trips (US$15 per person).

Wingnuts Canopy Tours (☎656 0153; canopytours@samarabeach.com), 1.5km east of Hotel Belvedere. A family-run canopy tour operator that prefers small groups. Two 2hr. trips leave daily from Sámara. US$39 per person, children under 18 US$30.

Alexis y Marco Boat Tours (☎656 0468; boattours@samarabeach.com), 500m west of the main drag on the beach. A friendly Italian duo offers fun and laid-back boat trips, perfect to laze some time away. Dolphin and snorkel trips US$120 per 4hr., US$200 per 8hr. Fishing trips US$120 per 4hr., US$200 per 8hr. 4-person max. per trip.

Jesse's Gym and Surf (☎656 0055), 500m east of the main drag next to Koss Art Gallery, on the beach. Friendly American Jesse has free weights and machines if you need to work out (US$3 per day), rents a few surf boards (US$6 per hr.), and offers surf instruction (US$25 per hr.). Open M-Sa 9am-8pm.

Tío Tigre (☎656 0098 or 656 0336), usually set up 1km east of the main drag on the beach, offers good prices for groups of 4 or 5. Kayak or boat snorkeling trips (US$35 per person), dolphin tours (US$50 per person), and sportfishing (US$60 per person). The larger the group, the lower the price. Boogie boards (US$2 per hr., full day US$7), kayaks (US$3 per hr.) Snorkel equipment (half day US$8, full day US$13).

Flying Crocodile (☎ 383 0471; www.flying-crocodile.com), 4km northeast of town. Walk east along the beach about 500m until you see a gravel road on your left; walk north along this road 3-4km until you see the lodge and flying center. Finally, you can experience Costa Rica's forest tree tops in something other than a canopy tour. One of Flying Crocodile's licensed and trained commercial pilots will fly you in an ultra-light glider over the peninsula's forests, beaches, and seas, and if you'd like, he'll teach you how to fly the ultra-light yourself. Ultra-light tours US$50; ultra-light charters US$45-70; ultra-light instruction US$80-90 per hr. Checks and traveler's checks accepted. V.

🔊 NIGHTLIFE

Sámara's nightlife is lively and crowded in the high season and during school holidays, when locals and youngsters from nearby Nicoya and the metropolitan area pack the beachfront bars and discos. In the low season, count on fewer crowds and a much more laid-back atmosphere.

Dos Largatos, about 250m west of the main drag on the beach, where you can enjoy a casual beer with a game of pool and popular Latin and rock music, is a good place to start. Beer ¢400. Open 7pm until the crowds leave.

La Góndola, 175m north of the beach on the main road, is the place for games and revelry of all sorts. Ping pong, pool, darts, and a mix of reggae and Latin music are sure to delight anyone. Beer ¢400. W 2-for-1 drinks. Pool ¢1500 per hr. Darts or Ping Pong ¢500. Open daily 8pm-2:30am.

Tutti-Frutti Disco, on the beach, is darker and louder, and attracts a younger *tico* crowd. Come after 11pm for the best crowds and atmosphere. Beer ¢400. Cover ¢500 in high season. Open daily 8pm-2:30am; low season F-Su 8pm-2:30am.

PLAYA CARRILLO

Anyone seeking an archetypical palm-lined beach with chalky white sand, few crowds, and calm waves will find Carrillo euphoric. Significantly less developed than its budding neighbor Sámara to the west, Carrillo is unique in that the beach remains naked of any hotels and restaurants, giving the small, crescent-shaped bay an unforgettably secluded, tropical feel. Sunworshippers share the beach with sailors and fishermen who like to anchor their boats in the bay's shallow waters, but you'll almost always be able to find a little patch of shore to call your own. If you can't spend much time here, at least swing by in the evening to witness one of Costa Rica's most famed sunsets from atop the hills of Carillo village.

🚍 TRANSPORTATION

The easiest way to get to Carillo from San José is by air. **Sansa** (75min.; high season 8:10 and 11:50, return 9:15am and 12:55pm; low season 7:30am, return 8:40am; US$66) and **Travelair** (75min.; high season 8:30am and 1pm, return 9:55am and 2:20pm; low season 11:45am, return 12:55pm; US$73) depart from San José (see p. 85) and arrive at the small airstrip just outside town. Transportation between Carillo and Sámara (see p. 234) has improved drastically over the past year following the construction of a well-paved road that winds between the two towns. **Buses** from **Sámara** to Carillo (25min.; 11am, 1, 4:30, 6:30pm; ¢200) leave from outside Hotel Giada and drive east into Carillo, stopping first near the beach before ascending a steep hill and dropping passengers off on the main street. To get back to Sámara, flag one down near the intersection of the beach road and the main drag (11:20am, 1:30, 5pm). Schedules change often, so check for the most up-to-date times. If you find you need a **taxi,** have a hotel call one for you.

✦ ⑦ ORIENTATION AND PRACTICAL INFORMATION

Playa Carillo is tucked in a small, protected bay about 8km southeast of Sámara. The village of Carillo stretches about 500m along an uphill road that starts about 200m from the beach. Walking along the main street away from the beach, you'll be facing north. Most services are in Sámara, so take care of essentials before coming. Carillo Tours (see **Outdoor Activities and Guided Tours,** below) has sporadic **Internet** access, can arrange **car rentals,** and can book Travelair **airline tickets.** Cabinas el Tucán (see **Accommodations,** below) has some books for exchange.

⌂ ACCOMMODATIONS

Staying in Carrillo is much quieter and more relaxed than Sámara but can be expensive for single travelers.

■ **Casa Pericos** (☎656 0611 or 656 0194). From the intersection of the main drag and the beach road, walk 200m west toward Sámara. From the sign on the right side of the road, follow the gravel path up another 300m, and you'll find the house on your left. Little-known, but the best place in town. German owners converted this small, secluded home into a cozy guesthouse with a full kitchen, common cold bath, and immaculate wood-paneled A-frame bedrooms. A fabulous outdoor patio sits at least 20m above sea level and 5m above the forest canopy, affording perfect views of the bay and greenery below. Laundry service, bike shed, and outdoor shower available. Call ahead. Prices vary from ¢3000-4000 per person. ❶

Cabinas el Tucán (☎656 0305). Walk 300m north along the main drag and turn right at the side street; you'll see inexpensive El Tucán 100m down the side street on the left. The rooms are a bit cramped but have comfy beds, private hot baths, and fans, and guests can enjoy the peaceful garden and restaurant out back and the TV room in the lobby. Breakfast included. Singles US$15; doubles US$25. ❷

Hotel Esperanza (☎656 0564; www.hotelesperanza.com), 300m north on the main drag, is kept in tip-top shape by French-Canadian owners Guy and Marisa. The fresh, airy rooms with balconies, private hot-water showers, fans, and tasteful artwork, are good mid-range options. Lounge in the well-manicured garden with hammocks and comfy chairs. Gourmet breakfasts (included) and an elegant selection of French and international cuisine (full meals about US$8). Laundry US$6 per load. Free Internet for guests. Singles and doubles US$35; triples US$43; quads US$51. ❸

Cabinas El Colibrí (☎656 0656). Turn left on the side street past Hotel Esperanza, walk 10m, and turn the corner; you'll see it on the left. A good option for larger groups, the large rooms are private and clean with shiny new hot-water baths. Doubles ¢8000, with breakfast ¢9000, with breakfast and fridge ¢10,000; triples ¢11,000. ❷

Hotel Guanamar (☎656 0054), a modern hotel with enormous rooms with A/C, TV, huge hot-water baths with tubs, and wall-to-wall carpeting. Carrillo's most upscale place. Laundry available. Breakfast included. Check-out noon. Poolside doubles US$75, with ocean view US$85. Low season discounts available. AmEx/MC/V. ❹

◖◗ ▨ FOOD AND NIGHTLIFE

Restaurante Mirador el Yate del Marisco, a simple restaurant at the top of the hill at the far south end of the main drag, has the best view in town. Come for dinner to enjoy some of the area's freshest seafood with a spectacular view of the bay and sunset. Lobster with garlic and butter ¢4300; jumbo shrimp ¢3800; rice dishes ¢1100-1500; *casado* ¢950. Beer ¢400; cuban cigars US$10. Open daily 11am-10pm. ❶

Cafe and Pizzería El Tucán, inside Cabinas el Tucán (see **Accommodations,** above), has a secluded atmosphere and good Italian food. Their pizzas (small ¢1000) and pastas (¢1000-2200) will satisfy any carbo craving. Open M-Sa noon-9pm. ❷

Fandango Discotheque and American Bar (☎656 0644), 800m north of Hotel Guanamar on the main road, is the place where locals and tourists jam to popular America beats as soon as the sun sets. Happy Hour daily 8-9pm. Open Tu-Su 6pm-2:30am. ❷

⚠ 🐟 OUTDOOR ACTIVITIES AND GUIDED TOURS

Popo's (☎656 0086; www.poposcostarica.com), on the side street just north of Hotel Esperanza, is the most personable and well-organized tour operator. Popo, one of the town's best sources of information, offers single and multi-day kayak trips (US$65-85 per day), float trips with inflatable kayaks on the Río Ora followed by an ox-cart ride (US$55 per person including lunch), kayaking and snorkeling at Isla Chora (US$75 per person with lunch), whitewater kayaking (US$85 per person with lunch), and surfing packages (US$150 per group of 3-4).

Carillo Tours (☎656 0543; www.carillotours.com), 100m up the main drag, offers the most tours in and around Carillo as well as to other major Costa Rican destinations. Tours include: Monteverde Cloud Forest (US$110-170 per person); kayaking in Playa Camaronal (p. 242) and Río Ora (US$40 per person); Playa Ostional turtle nesting excursion (US$35 per person); Palo Verde National Park and crocodile tour (US$85 per person); Rincón de la Vieja (US$80 per person); Nicoya city tour, forest canopy, and Monkey Park (US$90 per person); and horseback riding to a waterfall (US$40 per person). Open daily 8am-7pm.

Watersport Center (☎656 0497 or 656 0209; kuhnrica@sol.racsa.co.cr), offers a wide selection of trips and rentals. Tours include: amateur sportfishing (half day US$170, full day US$290); dolphin tours (US$105 per 4 people); snorkeling excursions (US$25 per person); combined snorkeling, fishing, and dolphin tours (US$140 per 4 people); surf trip to Playa Camaronal and Playa Coyote (US$210 per 4 people); waterskiing (US$35 per 30min., US$60 per hr.). Sea kayak and boogie board rentals.

Kitty Cat (☎656 0170), 200m north up the main drag, is the place where sportsfishers should head to find Captain Rob Gordon, a truly passionate fisher who will take you out on this custom-built aluminum 78 ft. sportfisher. Half-day fishing tours with lunch run US$500 for 5-6hr. for 5-6 people and US$700 for a full day. Captain Gordon also takes non-fishers out on his boat for dolphin tours (US$100 per hr. for 4-6 people).

Cabinas el Tucán rents kayaks (US$5 per hr.) and arranges US$25 horseback rides to Playa Camaronal. See **Accommodations,** above.

Hotel Esperanza will take you on an amazing waterfall hike (US$15 with lunch) and rents horses for US$6 per hr. See **Accommodations,** above.

SOUTH OF PLAYA CARILLO TO MAL PAÍS

The 30km stretch of coastline extending south of Playa Carillo to the southern tip of the Nicoya Peninsula is one of Costa Rica's least traversed areas. The road here is almost non-existent, and no public transporation covers this route. Those attempting the drive should prepare with a sturdy 4WD vehicle. At the road's best, you'll be bouncing along a gravel path; at its worse, expect to be window-deep in rivers in the rainy season. Make sure to speak with locals for current river and road conditions before starting the trek. Be sure to fuel up on gasoline beforehand and bring all supplies you'll need with you. That said, the drive up is a spectacular and adventurous ride in itself and makes for a great story to tell when you get back home. The coast hides some of Costa Rica's most picture-perfect beaches and decent surf spots, and the area's inaccessibility means you'll have absolutely no trouble escaping the crowds. The following beaches are described as they appear as you travel southwest from Playa Carillo to Mal País.

◪ **PLAYA CAMARONAL.** About 8km south of Playa Carillo is Playa Camaronal, a 3km-long rock-engulfed beach stretching from the mouth of the Río Ora from the west to the cliffs of Point Camaronal to the southeast. Local surfers from Sámara and Carillo rave about this place for its strong and consistent left and right beach breaks, but it remains almost completely unknown by travelers who opt for the more touristed and accessible surf spots along the coasts. Yet even non-surfers can revel in the seclusion and scenery that is Playa Camaronal; the beach is surrounded by volcanic hills covered with all types of exotic vegetation like spiny cedar, stinking toe (a Carribean fruit), and balsa wood. In addition, leatherback and Pacific Ridley sea turtles use the beach to lay their eggs in the rainy season. Camaronal has no facilities, but **camping** is possible near **Playa Vuelta del Sur,** on the other side of the river, and the **Camaronal Quebrada estuary,** from which you can bottle up some fresh water. Those without their own wheels can take a boat ride here from a tour operator in Playa Carillo (p. 239) or Playa Sámara (p. 234).

◪ **PUNTA ISLITA AND PLAYA COROZALITO.** These two little beaches are just 5km farther down the coast from Camaronal and 13km southeast of Carrillo. Cattle ranching is the area's primary activity, and the sparse population of those involved in the industry are scattered in tiny hamlets at the foot of the hills. Islita and Corozalito are separated by volcanic rocks more than 80 million years old. Islita, with a barely 1km-long shore in a protected bay, is fed by two clean streams ideal for swimming. Neighboring Corozalito is a swampier 1.5km-long area with an estuary, mangroves, and fresh water. Both sections of coastline have rough cliffs and tide pools which harbor an exotic collection of brilliantly colored fish and sea urchins. Leatherback and hawksbill turtles sometimes nest here, mostly during October. Driving between Islita and Corozalito, you'll pass Barranquilla Ranch; just north of here is a 5km mule track that ascends over 500m to **Potal Peak,** from where you can enjoy a fantastic view of over 20km of Nicoya coastline.

The only real service in the area is **Hotel Punta Islita** ❺, a posh luxury hotel frequented by honeymooners and resort hoppers in search of ultimate peace and quiet. Rooms start at US$150 and climb to an astonishing US$700 in the high season and come with about every amenity and luxury you could imagine. (☎231 6122; www.hotelpuntaislita.com.) Islita also has an **airstrip;** book flights through Travelair or Sansa from San José (p. 85).

◪ **PLAYA BEJUCO.** Nine kilometers farther southeast from Camaronal and 17km southeast of Carrillo is Playa Bejuco, an infrequently visited 3.5km-long beach surrounded by large mangroves and estuaries. The bay is completely protected, facilitating the anchorage of boats.

◪ **PLAYA SAN MIGUEL.** The gray sands of little-known San Miguel are 4km from Bejuco and 21km southeast of Carillo. In addition to its secluded natural bay banked by an imposing coastal mountain range, San Miguel has a 1 sq. km lagoon with calm waters and a soft, sandy bottom, perfect for wading. Deer, parrots, and armadillos are among the most commonly sighted animals in the area. Small *sodas* are sporadically open for the handful of locals who live in the area.

PLAYA COYOTE. Of the beaches along this stretch of coastline, Playa Coyote is among the most frequently visited, although you'll still find very few people who have made the trek out. The large horseshoe bay and small village, **San Francisco de Coyote,** are about 5km down the coast from San Miguel and 26km from Carillo, almost exactly halfway between Sámara and Mal País. The beach is picture-perfect, with clean, soft sands, a wide bay fringed by coconut trees, and water so shallow you can sometimes walk 200m into the sea and still stand on your feet. Just past the beach near **Punta Coyote,** a 20min. walk along the rocky beach formations, is an excellent **surf spot** often overlooked because it is not visible from the beach. The right and left beach breaks are best when the swells pick up from the south.

Slightly more developed than its more virginal neighbors, Coyote has a few small bars and simple restaurants on the beach as well as some basic *cabinas*, **Muco Rey** and **Lomo Clara,** in the village 5km north of the beach.

PLAYA MANZANILLO. About 42km southeast of Carillo, Manzanillo is the last spot along the Nicoya coast before Mal País, about 5km south. Mal País locals can't stop praising Manzanillo for its absolutely idyllic and picturesque beach, draped by stout palms and twisty almond trees. Though low tide brings with it some risky rocks in the ocean, you can wade, swim, and snorkel in the tide pools. Most visitors, however, just come for a day of relaxation and solitude, to have a picnic on the beach or stop for lunch at one of the two small restaurants on the beach. Most people come from Mal País either by car, driving through river estuaries, or by bike, 1hr. past Santa Teresa. The roads are often impassable in the rainy season, however, so ask locals about conditions before heading off.

CARMONA (NANDAYURE)

Situated about 45km southeast of Nicoya near the mouth of the Río Ora, the tiny, steamy village of Carmona, almost exclusively referred to as Nandayure by locals, has never been a stop on the standard tourist itinerary. Activities here are limited to picnicking in the pleasant *parque central* and exploring the surrounding green hills, but the town is otherwise little more than a stop in the lush and uninhabited central Nicoya Peninsula. Those driving from Playa Naranjo to beaches in the northwest might want to stop here to refuel on gasoline or grab a bite for the road.

Nandayure has a structure similar to most other Costa Rican towns, with the *parque central* and *iglesia* functioning as the town center. **Buses** to **Nicoya** (1hr., 6 per day 6am-5:30pm, ¢300) and **San José** (4½hr.; 4:30, 6:30am, 2:30pm; ¢1480) leave from the bus station 100m south of the *parque.* Other local services include: **Banco Nacional,** 50m west of the bus station (open M-F 8:30am-3:45pm); **Super San Marcos** supermarket, 50m east and 50m north of the bus station (open M-Sa 8am-7pm); **police** (☎657 7074), 150m east and 300m north of the bus station; and the **post office,** adjacent to the police (open M-F 8am-noon and 1-5:30pm).

If you do happen to be driving through and need a place to stay, **Cabinas Anny ❶,** has five inexpensive, clean, and comfortable rooms for a night's stay. Each room has private cold-water bath and fan, and guests get free parking and access to a TV room in the lobby. (☎656 7030. Doubles and triples ¢2000 per person.) **Cabinas Palma Real ❶,** across the street from the post office, is the only other place in town. Most rooms have two single beds, private cold-water bath, fan, and a small TV and are clean but can get a bit stuffy. (☎657 7053 or 657 7325; ask for Porfirio Quesada. Singles ¢2000; doubles ¢3500, with A/C and TV ¢5500.) There aren't many places to eat around town, but a handful of simple *sodas* surround the *parque central.* **Soda Mary ❶,** on the north side of the *parque,* is the cheeriest place around. Munch on fried *plátanos* with cheese or sour cream (¢300), a bowl of *gallo pinto* (¢400-600), or a *casado* (¢900), or sip a refreshing *fresco* (¢200) while people-watching in the *parque.* (Open daily 7:30am-8pm.)

THE BIG SPLURGE

HOTEL THE PLACE

This tropical paradise proves that elegance and style do not have to come at prohibitive costs. Upon walking through the hotel's main entrance and into to the delicately manicured bamboo garden, you'll realize that you've entered a unique romantic getaway. The Swiss owners built and decorated the place, adding a special touch to everything from the courtyard's playful sandbox to the comfortable cushions placed strategically near shady palms and inviting hammocks. Beyond the soothing garden are relaxing private bungalows, each with its own theme; choose from Mediterranean Breeze, Spicy Colors, Out of Africa, Beach House, or *El Nido de Amor* (The Love Nest). Each is cool and secluded with Venetian wall paneling, tasteful furniture, large and luxurious baths, and marshmallow-soft sheer-canopy beds.

Waking up to leave your haven of comfort will be made easy only by the delicious breakfasts the Belgian manager whips up himself. In the evening, enjoy a sensuous candlelit dinner of sushi or creative Mediterranean and Mexican entrees, accompanied by a tantalizing *maracuyá* margarita from the classy Mandela Bar. Other services include car and bike rental, tours, laundry, babysitting, Internet, room service, and massages. Regardless of whether you came to surf or to escape the country's swarms of tourists, Hotel the Place will rejuvenate and spoil any traveler. (☎ 640 0001; theplace@caramail.com; www.hoteltheplace.com. 150m down the road to Mal País. Bungalows US$40-70, US$10 per additional guest.)

MAL PAÍS AND SANTA TERESA

Don't be fooled by the literal translation of this quiet, remote surfing village near the southern tip of the Nicoya Peninsula; with long, empty beaches, dramatic rock formations, and scenic coves, Mal País could hardly be called a "bad land." Settled by a small community of locals nearly 30 years ago and more recently inhabited by a growing contingent of hippieish foreigners, the Mal País area remains relatively undeveloped and inaccessible, meaning that only true peace worshippers and wave riders make the effort to trek all the way out here to the sticks. But those who do come usually stay for weeks, magnetically attracted to the wide variety of breaks and utterly relaxed small town atmosphere.

◼ TRANSPORTATION

Buses: Most travelers take the **ferry** from Puntarenas to **Paquera** and either drive directly to Mal País or head first to Montezuma and then take **buses** to Mal País. From Montezuma, take the bus to **Cóbano** (15min., 6 per day 5:30am-4pm, ¢200) and catch a connecting bus from the same stop to **Santa Teresa** via **Mal País** (1hr., 10:30am and 2:30pm, ¢500). Return buses start in Santa Teresa and pick passengers up at the main crossroad by Frank's Place before heading back to **Cóbano** (7 and 11:30am).

Taxis: Almost no taxis drive around town, but the service in Cóbano can send a 4WD car to shuttle you to Mal País (¢5000).

Private Transportation: Bad roads and infrequent public transportation make moving on from Mal País time-consuming and complicated, so transfer services, though expensive, may prove well worth it for the convenience. **Montezuma Expeditions** (☎ 642 0919 or 440 8078) and **Collective Taxi Transfer Service** (☎ 642 0084) arrange private transportation to just about anywhere in the country (US$120-US$150 for 4 people), and **Bernadino Samora** (☎ 640 0151) can take you on his boat to Montezuma, Sámara, Cabo Blanco, or Tortuga (US$25 per hr.).

Rentals: Getting around Mal País is easiest with a bike or 4WD vehicle. Several places rent **mountain bikes;** try the **surf shop** 200m down the road to Santa Teresa (bikes US$8 per 5hr., US$10 per day; open daily 7-11am and 1:30-7pm) or **Pacific Divers,** 1km down the road to Mal País (bikes US$8 per day). The friendly couple who lives next door to Richard (see **Practical Information,** below) rents **motorcycles** (US$35-50 per day, US$300 per week), **jeeps** (US$40-60 per day,

US$350 per week), **landrovers** (US$50-70 per day, US$410 per week), and mountain bikes (US$2 per hr.).

✈ 🛈 ORIENTATION AND PRACTICAL INFORMATION

What most surfers and locals refer to as Mal País is actually three separate beaches stretching a total of about 6km on the southwest corner of the Nicoya Peninsula, 11km southwest of Cóbano. Buses from Cóbano stop first at the **crossroad**, which marks the center of the bumpy **dirt road** that spans the length of the area. All accommodations and services are off this main drag. From the crossroad, **Mal País** stretches 3km south (to the left facing the beach), and **Santa Teresa** stretches 3km north (to the right). **Playa Carmen** is 100m west down a gravel road directly in front of the bus stop.

Tourist Office: No official tourist information center, but **Richard** at **Las Olas** (see **Laundry,** below) is an excellent source of information and services. Open daily 9am-5:30pm.

Currency Exchange: The nearest bank is the **Banco Nacional** in Cóbano (open M-F 8:30am-3:45pm), but **Super Santa Teresa**, 350m down the road to Santa Teresa, will cash traveler's checks with a purchase of ¢4000 or more. Open M-Sa 8am-8pm, Su 8am-noon and 5-8pm.

English Language Bookstore: Bambú, 1km down the road to Mal País, has newspaper and magazines for sale and books to exchange. Open daily 8am-1pm.

Supermarket: Super Tierra Mar, 100m down the road to Santa Teresa. Open M-Sa 7:30am-8pm, Su 7:30am-5pm.

Laundry: Many hotels (see **Accommodations,** below) can wash your clothes. For quick turn-around, drop by the house marked by the *"lavandería"* sign 150m down the road to Santa Teresa (¢800 per kilo). **Las Olas,** 200m down the road to Santa Teresa, charges ¢700 per kilo with 10% off loads over 5 kilos and 15% off loads over 10 kilos.

Gas Station: Tano Gas, about 3km down the road to Santa Teresa. Open M-Sa 7am-6pm.

Medical Services: None in the area; for emergencies, call the clinic in Cóbano (☎642 0630, emergency ☎380 4125). Open M-Sa 8am-6pm.

Police: ☎117.

Phones: Several along the main drag; at the crossroad and Super Santa Teresa are the most centrally located. Buy **phone cards** at the Super Tierra Mar supermarket.

Internet: Las Olas (see **Laundry,** above) charges ¢1400 per hr. Open daily 9am-5:30pm. **Cyber Surf,** at the crossroad, charges ¢1500 per hr. Open M-Sa 8:30am-6pm.

Post Office: Closest full-service office in Cóbano, but **Cabinas las Higuerones,** next door to Santa Teresa Surf School, sells stamps.

⌂ ACCOMMODATIONS

Santa Teresa is where most of the budget places are, while Mal País has several new, cozy, and more luxurious options. Many rooms come equipped with full kitchens to accommodate surfers, who come for weeks at a time. Several **camping areas** provide sandy grounds for the bare-bones traveler: **Zeneida's Cabinas y Camping ❶**, 3km down the road to Santa Teresa (☎640 0118; ¢1000 per person); **Iguana Camping ❶**, 1.5km down the road to Mal País (☎661 2392; ¢800 per person); and the **campsite ❶** just north of Cabinas Playa Carmen, about 150m down the road to Santa Teresa (¢1000 per person, ¢1500 per person to rent a tent), are the best beachfront locations with showers and bath.

MAL PAÍS

Mal País Surf Camp and Resort (☎640 0061; www.malpaissurfcamp.com), 500m down the road to Mal País. Owned and operated by surfers, the "surf camp," as it's more commonly referred to by locals, prides itself on fostering a true surfer atmosphere and a variety of accommodations for all budgets. Their 10 acres of land are a bit of a walk from any good surf spots but feature a restaurant/bar, 17m pool, gym, pool tables, satellite TV, and a mechanical bull that, not surprisingly, gets a lot of use on wilder nights. Surf lessons, board rental, tours, laundry, and babysitting also available. Check-out noon. Surfer package with 3 meals, board rental, and basic accommodations US$50 per day. Open-air rancho-style cabins with sand floors, fan, and shared bath sleeping up to 5 people US$35 per night. Open-air dorms US$10; rustic doubles with shared bath and fan US$25; 5-person poolside villas and houses with private hot bath US$65 per double, US$10 for each additional person. AmEx/D/MC/V. ●

Cabinas Bosque Mar (☎640 0074), about 2.3km down the road to Mal País. One of the few cheaper options in Mal País, Bosque Mar is ideal for larger groups or families. Individual cabins are cozy and have fridge, kitchen, spotless bath, and dining table. Quads US$30, high season US$35. AmEx/MC/V. ●

SANTA TERESA

Cabinas Charlie (☎640 0066), 130m down the road to Santa Teresa, has 4 plain and clean fan-cooled rooms. The 2 shared cold baths have a bit more privacy than some other budget places. ¢2000 per person. ●

Cabinas Playa Santa Teresa (☎640 0137), 3km down the road to Santa Teresa. Close to the good breaks, this place is a deal for groups of 4. The spacious rooms are clean and comfy with fan, kitchen, bath, and tiled floors. Quads US$20, with kitchen US$25; in high season US$25/US$30. ●

Cabinas los Tres Pinedras, just north of the crossroads on the road to Santa Teresa, has clean and simple rooms with tile floors, fan, and shared cold showers in the large outdoor courtyard. ¢2000 per person. ●

Frank's Place (☎640 0096 or 640 0071; www.frankplace.com), at the crossroad, has plenty of rather overpriced rooms that are nonetheless popular, since it's the first place people see when they get off the bus. The friendly staff of mostly local surfers keep the rooms, restaurant, and 17m pool in tip-top condition. Tours, transfer service, domestic airline ticketing, phone, fax, and email also available to guests. Small singles US$10, with private bath US$13; doubles US$20/US$25; larger triples with balcony, fridge, and private bath US$35; US$8 per additional guest. Cabins with 2rooms, kitchen, and private bath US$60 per quad; US$5 per additional guest. MC/V. ●

Trópico Latino Lodge (☎640 0062), 800m down the road to Santa Teresa. 6 lovely bungalows built with local materials and set in a garden shaded by a grove of Pochote trees. Cool and fresh with tiled floors, huge fans, luxurious ho-water baths, and private porches with hammocks. Roll out of bed and onto the beach or into the pool and jacuzzi. Poolside restaurant/bar. Boat excursions to fish or dolphin-watch US$15 per boat per hr. Singles US$45, high season US$55; doubles US$55/US$65; triples US$65/US$75. Children under 12 free. All rates add a 15% tax. AmEx/D/MC/V. ●

Cabinas el Bosque (☎640 0104), just north of Santa Teresa Surf School. A good place for travelers planning on staying a while. Thatched roof cabins with 2 bedrooms share an equipped open-air kitchen. Quads ¢10,000. Discounts for singles and doubles. ●

Cabinas Playa Carmen (☎640 0179), 120m down the road to Santa Teresa, next to the supermarket. Small simple rooms with bright green walls, fan, and decent cold baths ¢2000 per person. Larger cabins with kitchen sleeping up to 4 people ¢5000. ●

🔲 🔳 FOOD AND NIGHTLIFE

The long road running through Mal País and Santa Teresa is sprinkled with several good cafes, restaurants, and *sodas*, but despite their "official" schedules, many have unpredictable hours.

▨ **Mary's,** 3km down the road to Mal País. Locals rave about this place and surfers crowd around the clustered tables evening after evening to enjoy the filling and creative entrees. Baked macarel ₡2100; medium spicy shrimp pizza ₡3100; fresh dorado filet with white wine sauce ₡2100. The rum raisin ice cream (₡800) is just one of the many delicious flavors available for dessert. Open daily 5:30-10pm. ❷

▨ **Soda Piedra Mar,** 2km down the road to Mal País and then 200m down a dirt path toward the beach. Because it's set back from the main road, this quiet little *soda* between huge jetting rocks and powerful crashing waves remains a secret among most travelers. The standard *típico* entrees are as delicious as they are affordable, and the friendly owner will let you sit in the open dining area and watch the white-washing waves for hours. *Gallo pinto* ₡600; *casados* ₡850-950; rice dishes ₡1250; shrimp in sauce ₡3500. Open M-Sa 7am-8:30pm. ❶

Ristorante Italiano La Bella Napoli, 2km down the road to Mal País. The huge mural of Napoli, Naples Italy, sets the mood at this hearty Italian restaurant. Homemade pasta, cannelloni, lasagna, pizza, and seafood are a tasty and fresh finish to a long day on the waves. Most entrees ₡1500-3000. Open Tu-Su noon-9pm; bar open 11am-11pm. ❷

Restaurante La Fonda, about 3km down the road to Santa Teresa, past the soccer field. The Costa Rican and international dishes are good and filling, but the best part is the flicks they show every Tu and Th at 8pm and the surf and skate videos on Su. English-language books for exchange as well. Open daily 8-11:30am and 6-9:30pm. ❶

Frank's Place, at the crossroad. The large, open-air dining area is a popular breakfast place serving mostly Costa Rican dishes. Lunch and dinner are good, with surprisingly tasty pastas, filets, and casados. Most entrees ₡1000-₡2200. Open daily 8am-9pm. ❶

Restaurante Playa Boa, inside the Trópico Latino Lodge, 1km down the road to Santa Teresa. The large, palm-woven thatched-roof restaurant, just meters from the beach, serves classy north Italian and international meals in a swanky, upscale atmosphere. Chips and salsa ₡875; spaghetti al pomodoro ₡1750; penne primavera ₡1950; fish filet with garlic in coconut milk ₡2800. Open daily 8am-midnight. ❷

Las Olas, 300m down the road to Santa Teresa. Fabulous Richard whips up delicious, fresh fruit smoothies the size of two full beers. Choose from mango, papaya, blackberry, and other tropical potions. Open daily 9am-5:30pm. ❶

🔳 BEACHES AND SURFING

The Mal País area is supposedly one of the world's best surf spots, not because the waves are extraordinary, but rather because of the consistent swells and crowds. Its location between the central Pacific and Guanacaste lends it big southern swells in the rainy season and good offshore breaks in the dry season. The currents are strong, however, so swimming is dangerous. There are actually several isolated surf spots along the coast with slightly different conditions. South of the crossroad to **Playa Mal País** is actually poor for surfing and better for tide pool exploration. **Playa El Carmen,** directly ahead of the crossroad, has a long right wall and a shorter left breaking on a soft sandy bottom. The best spot on **Playa Santa Teresa** is 3km north of the crossroad behind Cabinas Santa Teresa. It's a more powerful, consistent break than El Carmen and holds a better wave at low tide. **Playa Hermosa,** the next beach north of Santa Teresa, has almost no crowds and fast peaks rising along the beach. Four kilometers north of the crossroads is **Playa de Los Suecos.** The best place here has good lefts with frequent hollow tubes to glide through. The beach farthest north in the area is **Playa Manzanillo** (see p. 243), an idyllic spot 8km from the crossroads with an offshore reef and waves much less reliable and less surfable than its neighbors'. It's only accessible by 4WD vehicle or a 1-1½hr. bike ride over rough roads and through shallow rivers, but it's worth a daytrip for a picnic and the amazing unspoiled scenery. Several surf shops in Mal País and Santa Teresa rent boards and provide instruction. Look for:

Santa Teresa Surf School, 2.2km down the road to Santa Teresa, is one the most comprehensive and well-run surf shops around. Plenty of boards and gear to pick from and a knowledgeable and friendly staff. The newly opened organic juice bar and cafe in the back of the store serve healthy and refreshing snacks. Check out the large collection of videos for rent. Snorkel gear rental US$7-10 per day. Surf board rental US$10-15 per day. 2-3hr. surf lessons plus half-day board rental US$30. Open M-F 9am-5pm.

La Cavana de Surf, 200m down the road to Santa Teresa, buys, sells, and trades surf boards. Board and bike rental US$8 per 5hr., US$10 per day. Also sells hammocks and a small selection of beach wear. Open daily 7-11am and 1:30-7pm.

Corduroy to the Horizon, 100m west of the crossroad down the path to Playa El Carmen. The closest rental place to the El Carmen break, Corduroy's gives surf lessons, designs custom boards and repairs and rents boards. Open M-Sa 7:30am-7pm, but hours vary.

◤ GUIDED ACTIVITIES AND TOURS

Southern swells and cascading waves aside, the Mal País area offers many fun outdoor activities for the non-surfer or for days when the swells aren't picking up. The truly adventurous and bus-weary can walk 2.5km along the road to Mal País until they reach the fork in the road. Turn left and continue 6.5km to the **Reserva Natural Absoluta Cabo Blanco;** call ahead to make sure these gates will be open. Otherwise, rent a snorkel and explore the **tide pools** just behind Sunset Reef Hotel. To get there, walk 2.5km down the road to Mal País, turn right at the fork, and continue another 500m until you see the hotel at the end of the road. Those with a bit more cash can take one of the **package tours** or organized trips offered by many people around town.

Las Olas (☎ 640 0239), 300m down the road to Santa Teresa. The chill and friendly owner Richard offers many activities at reasonable prices. With over 10 years knowledge of the area, he's about as good a guide as you'll get. Horseback and snorkel tour to Isla Cabuya US$110 per 12hr. with breakfast, lunch, and snacks. Horseback ride US$30 per 3hr. Sportfishing with fisherman Camillo, who boasts over 40 years experience, US$30 per hr. Water boat ride to Jacó US$35. Open daily 9am-5:30pm.

Pacific Divers (☎ 640 0169; wingnut@sol.racsa.co.cr; www.pacificdivers_costarica.com), 1km down the road to Mal País; ask for Toby. Mal País's nutrient-rich waters, good visibility, and several rock and reef formation offer some of Costa Rica's best diving opportunities. PADI-certified Pacific Divers has opportunities for beginner and experienced divers to see the diverse marine life. Toby reports that sail fish, sharks, dolphins, and sea turtles are among the most commonly seen. Beginner "Discover SCUBA" courses halfday US$30, full-day US$65; open-water certification US$300; advanced open-water US$275. Specialty dives, equipment rental, and underwater photography also available. Best diving months are from mid Dec.to May and mid. June to Aug. Call at least 24hr. in advance. Traveler's checks accepted. V.

Paraíso Adventure Tours (☎ 683 0383; paraisoadventuretours@hotmail.com). Gary and Cynthia Versijl Aguial offer a number of tours and trips. All prices listed are for 4 people unless otherwise noted. Boat trip and snorkeling at Isla Tortuga US$120; snorkeling around a sunken ship US$120. Coastal fishing US$225 per 4hr. Rafting US$160 per 5hr. Spelunking at Barra Honda caves with a stop at Quatil for souvenir shopping US$90 per person for 8hr. Bungee jumping US$130 per person.

Horse Tours (☎640 0007), 30m down the road to Santa Teresa, in a house set back from the road on the left. Beach, mountain, and full moon ride on well-kept horses.

NIGHTLIFE

Nightlife here is pretty scant, and those with cars sometimes head to **Montezuma** for a livelier scene. Otherwise, join the hordes of people on the beach for the beautiful **sunsets,** and head to **Tropicana Bar,** on the path to Playa El Carmen, for drinks, Latin, pop, and reggae music, and plenty of seats where you can share stories of the day's waves. Tropicana gets packed with crowds spilling out of the bar in the high season. (Beer ¢400. Open for breakfast 8-11am and dinner 6-9pm; bar open until the crowds leave.) **Mal País Surf Camp's** open mic night is *the* place to be on Wednesday nights, when surfer dudes express their artistic talent jamming on guitars and drums. All of the Surf Camp's equipment is available for use. Crowds arrive around 9pm and sometimes stay until early in the morning.

MONTEZUMA

The tiny beach haven of Montezuma is stuck in somewhat of a trippy time warp. An almost exclusively foreign regimen of batik-clad flower girls and starry-eyed, dread-locked *rasta* boys are the town's most frequent inhabitants, echoing the image of a fun-loving 60s town that never grew up. Considering that Montezuma was barely discovered 25 years ago by a group of North Americans, it's no wonder that it's still in its first stages of development. But perhaps that's what keeps hordes of tourists returning year after year. Montezuma's sparse dirt roads and immaculate, endless beaches lead to some of the peninsula's most spectacular waterfalls, wildlife, and waves. Sure, English-speaking Montezuma may feel like it's not part of Costa Rica, but it's a long way from selling its soul and giving up its native charm.

TRANSPORTATION

If you're coming from other towns on the north or northwest peninsula, note that backtracking to Puntarenas and taking the ferry to Paquera is the fastest way to reach Montezuma, even though other routes

THE BIG SPLURGE

LUZ DE MONO

Perfect for the environmentally conscious traveler who wants guilt-free indulgence for a night or two, eco-resort Luz de Mono offers luxurious accommodations in an amazing setting while actively encouraging environmental awareness and conservation. The Italian-American owners were among the first to arrive in Montezuma 30 years ago and have dedicated themselves to maintaining the area's natural beauty and local culture. Two wooden monkey sculptures guard the entrance to the reception area and the Bar of the Blue Congo, the hotel's restaurant, which is surrounded by 300 hectares of primary forest replanted with endangered and tropical plant species. The restaurant doubles as a concert hall on weekends and as an art gallery featuring works by local artists. Creative tropical dishes like papaya mustard pork tenderloin (¢2900) and fried yucca (¢800) are served in this rustic gazebo.

Just beyond the restaurant are a few short trails that lead through a tropical garden to the main hotel complex. Perfect for groups of two are the 12 rooms in the main building, with ceramic floors, a queen bed or two singles, fan, mini-bar, fridge, coffee maker, security box, and CD player, creating an amazingly cozy get-away-from-it-all forest respite. (☎642 0010, fax 642 0090; luzdmono@racsa.co.cr; www.luzdemono.com. 100m down the road to the right of Chico's, on the left. Standard rooms high season US$100, low season US$75. AmEx/D/MC/V.)

THE HIDDEN DEAL

COCOLORES

If it weren't for the small sign and flickering Christmas lights just barely visible from the main road, you'd be sure to overlook this sumptuous and charming restaurant. Tree-stump tables are set with conch shell napkin holders, and colorful paper lanterns and fishing nets hang from the thatched roof, creating a delicate and cozy tropical ambience. The waitstaff is friendly and laid-back, frequently chatting with the customers or some of the local folk who drop by for a casual drink. Though the decor and atmosphere are light-hearted and fun, the broad selection of international dishes is nothing short of elegant. Even the simple dishes like the vegetarian pasta in white sauce (¢1400) and spicy fajitas (¢1700-2300) are prepared with fresh vegetables, homemade sauces, and unique flavors like mint, sweet chili, and cumin, and every entree is preceded by warm, fresh-from-the-oven sweet bread. If you fancy something a bit more exotic, the *pollo al curry con banano* (¢1900) is a customer favorite, and locals say the fish and shrimp dishes (¢1600-4900) are Montezuma's best. *(100m down the street left of Chico's, opposite Bakery Cafe. Open M-Sa 5-9pm. V.)*

look shorter on a map (those roads are tediously slow, not much public transportation goes that way).

Buses go to **Paquera** (1½hr.; 5 per day 5:30am-4pm, return 6 per day 6:15am-6:15pm; ¢700) and **Cabo Blanco** (30min.; 8, 9:50am, 2:10, 6:30pm, return 7:10, 9:10am, 1:10, 4:10pm; ¢400) via **Cabuya** (25min., ¢380). To go to **Santa Teresa** via **Mal País**, take the 10am or 2pm bus to Cóbano, where the Mal País bus to Santa Teresa will be waiting (1½hr.; 10:30am and 2:30pm, return 6:45 and 11am; ¢500).

ORIENTATION AND PRACTICAL INFORMATION

Near the southern tip of the Nicoya Peninsula, Montezuma is 41km southwest of Paquera and 8km south of the town of **Cóbano**. Most services are in Cóbano. Montezuma consists almost entirely of accommodations, restaurants, and souvenir shops. **Chico's Bar,** where the bus stops, is on the main drag and functions as the center of town. All directions here are given in terms of right and left as you stand with your back to Chico's and the ocean. The road intersecting the main drag at Chico's points directly west and leads to a fork about 100m up. Turning right at the fork heads to Cóbano. Turning left leads to a number of restaurants, accommodations, and **Reserva Absoluta Natural Cabo Blanco,** 1km away. The road to **Cabo Blanco** can be found by walking up the hill from Chico's and turning left at the fork.

Tourist Information: There is no official tourist information office. A number of tour agencies offer a variety of trips (see **Montezuma: Outdoor Activities and Guided Tours,** below). For good, unbiased information, talk to Shelena at La Creperie (see **Montezuma: Food and Nightlife,** below).

Rentals: Montezuma Eco-Tours (☎642 0467) rents mountain bikes (US$15 per day), motorcycles (US$45 per day), and ATVs (US$65 per day).

Private Transportation: Montezuma Eco-Tours (☎642 0467) arranges transfers in an air-conditioned vehicle for up to 4 people to: **Arenal** (US$150), **Manuel Antonio** (US$130), **Monteverde** (US$130), **Sámara** (US$120), **San José** (US$130), and **Tamarindo** (US$140).

Banks: Montezuma has no banks, but there is a **Banco Nacional** in Cóbano. Open M-F 8:30am-3:45pm. Be forewarned that this is the only bank along the coast between Playa Naranjo and Montezuma, so expect long lines, especially around mid-day M and F. If you're in dire need of colones, try the tour agencies in town or the supermarkets. The **tourist services center,**

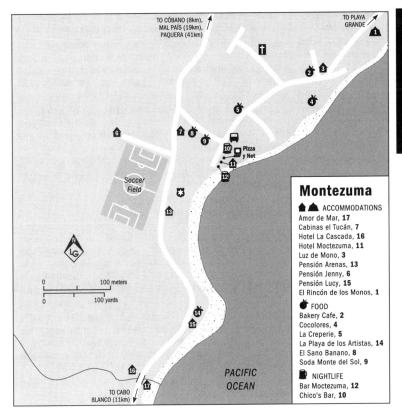

TO CÓBANO (8km),
MAL PAÍS (19km),
PAQUERA (41km)

TO PLAYA
GRANDE

Soccer
Field

N

0   100 meters
0   100 yards

TO CABO
BLANCO (11km)

Pizza
y Net

PACIFIC
OCEAN

Montezuma

■ ▲ ACCOMMODATIONS
Amor de Mar, **17**
Cabinas el Tucán, **7**
Hotel La Cascada, **16**
Hotel Moctezuma, **11**
Luz de Mono, **3**
Pensión Arenas, **13**
Pensión Jenny, **6**
Pensión Lucy, **15**
El Rincón de los Monos, **1**

● FOOD
Bakery Cafe, **2**
Cocolores, **4**
La Creperie, **5**
La Playa de los Artistas, **14**
El Sano Banano, **8**
Soda Monte del Sol, **9**

■ NIGHTLIFE
Bar Moctezuma, **12**
Chico's Bar, **10**

at Aventuras en Montezuma, near Soda Monte del Sol on the road leading west from Chico's, will exchange traveler's checks and US dollars. Open daily 8am-8pm in high season, 8am-2pm and 4-8pm in low season. The closest **Western Union** is in Cóbano (see **Cóbano: Practical Information**).

Supermarket: Mamatea Delicatessen, next to Chico's. Open daily 7am-9pm.

Bookstore: Librería Topsy, 100m to the right of Chico's. A huge selection of fiction, magazines, and travel books in several different languages. Look out for their annual book blow-out sale in July. Book rental ₡500 for 2 weeks, plus ₡1000-3000 deposit. Open M-F 8am-4pm, Sa 8am-noon. Hours are flexible.

Laundry: Hotels have the cheapest prices. **Pensión Jenny, Pensión Arenas,** and **Hotel la Cascada** (see **Accommodations,** below) all charge ₡600 per kilo. **Express Laundry Montezuma,** by El Sano Banano on the road leading west of Chico's, has a 3hr. turnaround. ₡700 per kilo. Open M-Sa 9am-1pm and 3-6pm.

Police: (☎ 117), on the beach near Restaurante El Parque. Little English spoken. Cóbano police: ☎ 642 0517.

Pharmacy: Nearest in Cóbano (☎ 642 0508), 100m south of Banco Nacional on the road to Montezuma. Open M-F 8am-3:30pm. AmEx/MC/V.

Medical Services: Clínica de Cóbano (☎642 0950 or 380 4125), next to the pharmacy on the road to Montezuma. Open M-Sa 8am-6pm, 24hr. for emergencies. AmEx/MC/V.

Telephones: Public phones near Chico's and next to the supermarket. **Phone cards** sold at the supermarket. The tourist services office at **Aventuras en Montezuma,** near Soda del Monte del Sol on the road heading west of Chico's, does international calls. US$1 per min. to Central America; US$1.50 per min. to US, Puerto Rico, and Mexico; US$2 per min. to the rest of the world.

Internet: Cheapest rates at the refreshing A/C room in **Pizza y Net,** next to Chico's. ₡20 per min., ₡1200 per hr. Open daily 9am-9pm. The folks at **El Sano Banano** (see **Food,** below) and **Aventuras en Montezuma** (☎642 0050; see **Outdoor Activities and Guided Tours,** below) charge ₡1500 per hr.

Post Office: The closest full-service post office is in **Cóbano,** 300m west of Banco Nacional on the road to Paquera (open M-F 8am-noon and 1-5:30pm. **Librería Topsy** (see above) sells stamps and mails letters.

ACCOMMODATIONS AND CAMPING

Catering to the young and the budget-oriented crowd that makes up the bulk of its visitors, Montezuma is packed with good, inexpensive rooms, many in the ₡2000-3000 range. The most quiet and scenic spots are just a short walk along the road to Cabo Blanco; however if you stay near Chico's, you'll definitely need earplugs to drown out the music. **Camping** on the beach is free, relatively safe, and popular, especially in the high season (Dec.-Apr.).

▧ **Amor de Mar** (☎/fax 642 0262), a 10min. walk down the road to Cabo Blanco. If you're going to splurge, do it here. A river runs alongside, the ocean crashes at the edge of the lush lawn, and they're never short on hammocks. Killer Su brunch ₡2500. Laundry service available, priced by item. All but 2 rooms have beautiful private baths, and most have hot water. High season (Nov.-Apr.) US$30-75; low-season US$20-65. ❷

▧ **Hotel La Cascada** (☎642 0057), just before the river on the road to Cabo Blanco. Excellent value for those who want a step up from Montezuma's standard. Big, sparkling, private baths with hot water, and new, wood-paneled rooms to match. The spacious upstairs balcony has plenty of hammocks, and the attached restaurant serves delicious crepes (₡800). US$10 per person; prices increase during school holidays. ❶

Pensión Lucy (☎642 0273), about 400m from the road to Cabo Blanco. Its prime beachfront locations, family ambience and clean rooms with shared, cold-water showers make Lucy the nest of the truly budget options. Ask for a room upstairs for nice views and refreshing breezes, and don't miss the delicious homemade *gallo pinto* in their cozy restaurant. Laundry ₡600 per kilo. ₡2000 per person. ❶

Pensión Jenny (☎642 0306). Walk 75m down the road to Cabo Blanco and then 50m right up the road just before the soccer field. The quiet rooms get lots of light and fresh air, and the shared, cold-water baths are clean. Communal bathrooms are a bit inconvenient. Laundry ₡600 per kilo. Ask about the *cabina* with a full kitchen for longer stays. ₡2000 per person. ❶

Cabinas el Tucán (☎642 0284), at the fork just down the road to Cabo Blanco. The location is convenient, the small wood-paneled cabins are spotless, and the shared bathrooms are clean. Singles, doubles, and triples ₡2000 per person. ❶

Pensión Arenas (☎642 0308), 150m down the road to Cabo Blanco on the left. Rooms are a bit small, but with the waves crashing on the beach in the front lawn, you won't find much reason to stay locked in your room. ₡2000 per person. ❶

Hotel Moctezuma (☎/fax 642 0058). Facing Chico's, it's 2 buildings to the right, between two bars. As the first hotel people see upon getting off the bus, Moctezuma is the place almost everyone crashed for their first night before realizing that there are much higher-quality budget options close by. High traffic keeps the bathrooms sandy, and you'll think you never left Chico's with the music thumping until the wee hours. ¢2500 per person. ❶

El Rincón de los Monos, 300m down the beach toward Playa Grande. Hammocks, showers, and luggage storage (¢150 per bag per day) make this a comfortable camping spot. Check-out 11am. Reception open daily 8-10am and 5-7:30pm. ¢800 per day. ❶

🍴 FOOD

🍽 **La Playa de los Artistas,** on the beach 400m down the road to Cabo Blanco, on the left. For a romantic setting with class and style, this is a fantastic choice. Moon-lit waves reflect the light of ambient dim lanterns hanging from the dried palm leaf roof. Fresh, delectable, and authentic Mediterranean dishes and seafood. The menu is always changing, but there are always at least a few veggie options. Entrees US$8-15. Open M, W-Sa 5-10pm, but hours are subject to change, especially in the low season. ❸

🍽 **La Creperie,** 50m down the street to the right of Chico's, opposite Hotel El Capitán. French and Canadian chefs Stefan and Shelena have perfected their recipe for these light and heavenly crepes: soft, buttery, and warm on the outside, filled with fresh fruits, vegetables, yogurt, or chocolate inside. The laid-back street-front tables are the best spot for dessert and people watching. Original sweet or savory crepe ¢350, toppings ¢150 each. Open daily 7am-11pm. ❶

Soda Monte del Sol, just down the street leading west from Chico's, on the left. A welcome change from the rest of Montezuma's more extensive, touristy menus. Delicious and filling *casados* come with fresh avocado (¢1100). Open daily 8am-10pm. ❶

El Sano Banano, 50m up the road leading west from Chico's. A good spot for families and vegetarians. Good service and nightly English movies (free with min. ¢1500 order) draw almost an exclusively gringo crowd. The chocochiller is a bit pricey (¢900) but worth every sweet, mocha sip. Most entrees ¢1400-2800. Open daily 7am-10pm. AmEx/MC/V. ❷

Bakery Cafe, 100m down the road to the right of Chico's, opposite Librería Topsy. No place in town does breakfast better. The portions are generous and everything is incredibly fresh—just be sure the monkeys that inhabit the shady trees nearby don't snatch away your food. *Gallo pinto* ¢680, with guacamole ¢1050; banana and chocolate pancakes ¢1000; veggie sandwich ¢900. Open daily 7am-2pm. ❶

🏊 BEACHES

The main beach at Montezuma, just to the left of Chico's, is tightly bordered by imposing rock formations and has a strong **rip tide,** so take precautions when swimming. In the low tide, it's possible to continue farther south along the beach by walking on the rocky headlands. Here you'll find several safe, shallow tide pools teeming with interesting fish and aquatic plants; rent a snorkel from any tour agency (see **Outdoor Activities and Guided Tours,** below) for the best view.

A hundred meters down the road to the right of Chico's is an entrance to the vast expanse of beach north of Montezuma. These beaches, the largest of them **Playa Grande,** are usually less crowded and better for swimming and long walks along the soft sand or over the large rocks. Also popular is **Playa Cedros,** 2km south along the road to Cabo Blanco.

⚠ 🏊 OUTDOOR ACTIVITIES AND GUIDED TOURS

Montezuma's most rewarding and inexpensive activity is hiking to the several **waterfalls** near town. The best one is also the closest, about a 7min. walk along the road to Cabo Blanco; a sign just past Hotel La Cascada marks the entrance. From there, take the short trail through the woods to the river and hike about 20min., climbing over rocks or treading through cool water until you see the 80 ft. waterfall to your left. Past these falls is another trail that climbs through steep and dangerously loose banking and to a flatter trail that eventually leads to a smaller waterfall; you can jump off the edge and swim around in a large natural pool. It takes at least 1hr. to reach these falls. The trail then climbs into the forest canopy, where it's common to see howler and white-faced monkeys swinging about the trees. Be aware that although many people complete this trail, it is extremely dangerous in some places and should only be attempted by experienced climbers comfortable with the terrain. **Do not jump off the first large waterfall**—the pool is small, and many people have died. Be sure to wear sturdy, waterproof footwear and be careful climbing the slippery river rocks.

A smaller and less spectacular **waterfall** with good swimming is a 2hr. walk north along the coast. A trail that is sometimes hard to follow alternates between the beach and a flat path behind the rock formations; if you're unsure of where to go, just follow the horse tracks. On the way, you'll pass seven beaches (including Playa Grande) and several private nature preserves. Many people opt to visit these falls on a **horseback tour.** Paraíso Natural (see below) and the Bakery Cafe (see **Food,** above) have the best rates (US$20 including breakfast).

Several tour agencies in Montezuma offer organized packages to nearby sights and activities. **Montezuma Eco-Tours,** across from Chico's Bar, offers trips to Isla Tortuga, including breakfast, snorkeling and a barbecue, kayak tours with snorkeling gear, fishing tours, scuba diving, horseback tours, and mountain bike rides to a waterfall. (☎ 642 0467; ecotoursmontezuma@hotmail.com. Isla Tortuga US$35; kayak tours US$25; fishing US$150 per 3hr.; 2 scuba dives US$75; horseback tours US$75. Open daily 8am-8pm; hours shortened in the low season.) **El Sano Banano** (see **Food,** above) and **Paraíso Natural** (☎ 642 0733), down the street to the right of Chico's, near La Creperie, provide similar tours. **Aventuras en Montezuma** offers comparable prices in addition to a bird watching tour (US$15) and whitewater rafting. They also function as a travel agency and can make flight reservations and arrange Spanish or dance lessons. (☎ 642 0050. Open daily low season 8am-noon and 4-8pm, high season 8am-9pm.) For the ambitious amateur, **Restaurante y Bar Moctezuma,** next door to Hotel Moctezuma, offers **surf lessons** (US$30 per 2h.).

🎵 NIGHTLIFE

The masses congregate at the **Tucán Movie House** in El Sano Banano to take in English-language movies. (Movies daily 7:30pm. Free with minimum ¢1500 order.) From there, everyone trickles out to either **Chico's Bar** or **Bar Moctezuma,** underneath Hotel Moctezuma, to meet up with the locals and sip on Imperiales. Music ranges from reggae to salsa to old US rap, and expect as many stray dogs on the dance floor as hip-shaking merengue experts. If you tire of the local beer, Chico's mixes hot *cucarachas* (¢1000), a spicy tequila and coffee concoction lit on fire and slurped through chilled straws. (Beer ¢450. Chico's Bar open daily 11am-2:30am. Bar Moctezuma open daily 8am-2:30am.) The beach is another popular hang-out, with frequent bonfires and many communal bottles of rum. For **live music concerts** usually free of charge, inquire at **Luz de Mono.**

CABUYA

Nine kilometers south along the bumpy road from Montezuma, the sleepy village of Cabuya can be hard to miss. Consisting mostly of farms and a scattering of infrequently patronized restaurants and hotels, Cabuya was settled by farmers around the same time as Montezuma but never reached anywhere near its neighbor's level of development. Today the town is home to an exceptionally tranquil *tico* population and a growing contingent of retired North Americans who idle away in the hills. There isn't much to do in Cabuya, but it makes for a pleasant escape from touristed Montezuma and a convenient base to visit **Reserva Absoluta Cabo Blanco**, just 2km south.

TRANSPORTATION. From Montezuma, a **minibus** departs from in front of Chico's bar and drops passengers off at El Delfín de la Luna restaurant in Cabuya, before continuing to **Cabo Blanco** (30min.; to Montezuma 7:20, 9:20am, 1:20, 4:20pm; to Cabuya 8, 9:50am, 2:10, 6:30pm; ¢380). Keep in mind that very little traffic comes through this way, so it is almost impossible to hitch or find a taxi. *Let's Go* does not recommend hitchhiking. In an emergency, call ☎642 0241 for a taxi ride to Montezuma (US$10), Cóbano (US$15), or Mal País (US$25).

ORIENTATION AND PRACTICAL INFORMATION. The area around the bus stop functions as the only thing remotely resembling the town center. The main drag continues 2km south from here to Cabo Blanco, while a small, dirt road leads 130m to Playa Cabuya, and a larger, gravel road leads west to Mal País. Cabuya is essentially devoid of services, save for **Pulpería David**, a small food store 300m south along the main road to Cabo Blanco. (Open daily 6am-9pm.) **EcoLodge Sunshine** (see **Accommodations**, below) may provide **laundry** service (¢600 per load) and **Internet** access (¢1000 per hr.). A **public phone** is near the bus stop. In the high season, **Tienda Artesanía**, on the main drag 200m north of El Delfín, rents **mountain bikes** (US$15 per day), offers **horseback tours** to Mal País (US$27) and along Playa Cabuya (US$10 per hr.), and also provides Internet access (¢30 per min.).

ACCOMMODATIONS. If your idea of relaxation is unwinding on deserted coastline and ambling along gravel paths with rolling green hills in the distance, you'll likely benefit from a night or two in Cabuya. Note that many of Cabuya's hotels won't be open in the low season (May-Nov.) and close sporadically even in the high season (Dec.-Apr.), so be sure to call in advance. For complete quiet and isolation, **camp** on the beach. If you opt for a sturdy roof overhead, **Villas el Yugo ❶** has five decent bungalow-type *casitas* 20m from the beach. Walk 100m down the road leading east of El Delfín and another 100m down the dirt path to the right; El Yugo is the pink complex on the left. The duplex A-frames sleep up to four people and have fans and private cold-water baths. Guests also have access to the pool and communal family kitchen. The owners will also arrange snorkeling and horseback tours and allow **camping** for ¢800, with access to the pool and bathrooms. (☎642 0303. Singles ¢4000; doubles ¢7000.) **El Ancla de Oro Hotel and Restaurant ❷**, on the main drag, 200m north of El Delfín, has rustic tree house-like cabins and nicer rooms with kitchens (☎642 0369). Between August and May, you can also try **EcoLodge Sunshine ❷**, on the main drag 500m south of El Delfín. The friendly old man who runs it rents out three basic rooms with fan, private cold bath, and fridge. The sitting area outside has plenty of hammocks and reading material. (☎642 0328. Singles US$15-20; doubles US$25.)

FOOD. For excellent seafood, locals recommend **El Ancla de Oro Hotel and Restaurant ❸.** Unfortunately, it's usually only open in the high season, when lobster in garlic (¢3600) is their specialty. **El Delfín de la Luna ❶** serves excellent and filling breakfast with *gallo pinto* (¢600) and huge plates of fruit, as well as *casados* (¢1000), fish (¢2200), and shrimp (¢2000), among other hearty lunch and dinner options. (Open daily 6:30am-9pm.) Specializing in fresh and homemade entrees is **Café El Coyote ❷,** 250m down the road leading west to Mal País. Fresh-from-the-oven bread or a creamy milkshake (¢400) is a perfect accompaniment to pancakes (¢650) or a veggie plate (¢1400). Come around 6:30pm to take advantage of their nightly pizza specials. (Open daily 7:30am-10pm.)

SIGHTS. Just a few hundred meters east of Playa Cabuya is **Isla Cabuya,** visible from the shore and accessible by foot during the low tide. The island has a tiny cemetery with a handful of disorganized gravestones and a large, rather old, distinct archway. If you're waiting for the bus back to Montezuma from Cabo Blanco, it's not a bad way to pass the time, but otherwise there is not much to see.

NEAR CABUYA

RESERVA NATURAL ABSOLUTA CABO BLANCO

From Montezuma, take the Cabuya/Cabo Blanco minibus from outside Chico's Bar (30min.; 8, 9:45am, 2:10, 6:30pm; return 7:10, 9:10am, 1:10, 4:10pm; ¢400). Park ranger station ☎ 642 0093. Open W-Su 8am-4pm. Entrance fee US$8.

A bumpy dirt road runs the 8km from Montezuma to the Reserva Natural Absoluta Cabo Blanco, Costa Rica's first protected tract of land and the cornerstone of the country's reserve system. It was founded in 1963 by European couple Karen Mogensen and Nils Olaf Wessberg, who, with the help of the Costa Rican government, succeeded in purchasing and protecting the 5 sq. km of primary and secondary forest. The reserve extends 1km from the shore to help protect marine life. Cabo Blanco is one of the few sea-level reserves and contains plant species from both the humid Pacific region and the dry northern forests. Cabo Blanco is home to the Nicoya Peninsula's most important population of pelicans and Central America's largest number of brown booby birds find their homes high in the reserve's trees, which are an exemplary result of forest regeneration. Since foliage here is less dense than in many other national parks, animals are easier to spot.

The bus from Montezuma will drop you off at the park's entrance, about a 1km walk from the **ranger station.** Here you can view the small exhibition about the park's history and flora and fauna, use the clean bathrooms, purchase a map and plant guide (¢200), and fill up on potable water. From the station, there are two trails. The 4.5km **Danish Loop** *(Sendero Danés)* leads into the reserve. It's a hilly and tiring hike, but the trails are well-maintained, wildlife is aplenty, and the views are fantastic. A second trail, the **Swedish Loop** *(Sendero Sueco),* begins about 800m from the ranger station, making a 1km loop that crosses the Danish Loop and winds over a few streams. Most people take the Danish loop all the way to the beach and detour to the Swedish Loop on the way back.

The trip to and from the beach should take about 4hr. at a moderate pace, leaving you just enough time to catch the 1:10pm bus back to Montezuma if you arrive on the 8am bus. Nap on the beach or veer off the main trail to the 15min. path to the *mirador;* however, you're better off catching the 4:10pm bus back. Be sure to bring insect repellent and closed-toe shoes. Camping is not permitted.

CÓBANO

With some of the only medical services and the only bank on the southern Nicoya Peninsula, hot and dusty Cóbano, 8km inland of Montezuma, is an important local hub. Regardless, it remains little more than a stop-and-go point for most travelers. A rough 4WD-only road leads westward to Mal País, and a much better road continues north along the coast to Paquera.

TRANSPORTATION. From Cóbano, **buses** leave from the stop 100m east of the Banco Nacional for **Santa Teresa** via **Mal País** (1hr.; 10:30am and 2:30pm; ¢500); **Montezuma** (15min.; 7:15, 8:45, 11:15am, 12:30, 4:50, 6:15pm; ¢200); and **Paquera** via **Pochote** and **Tambor** (1hr., 7 per day 4:30am-4:30pm, ¢500). Taxis (☎642 0241) line up on the main drag near the station. (Ride to Montezuma ¢2000, to Mal País ¢5000.)

ORIENTATION AND PRACTICAL INFORMATION. Buses from Montezuma drive north into Cóbano and turn east onto the main drag. The **Banco Nacional** is just west of the bus stop at the intersection of the two roads. Lines start early and are the longest on M, F, and at midday. **24hr. ATM** and cash advances. (☎642 0210. Open M-F 8:30am-3:45pm.) A **Western Union** service is available at the pharmacy (see below). Other local services include: **police**, 300m east of Banco Nacional (☎642 0570, emergency 117); **pharmacy,** 100m south of Banco Nacional (☎642 0508; open M-F 8am-3:30pm; AmEx/MC/V); and a **medical clinic** next to the pharmacy (☎642 0630, emergency 380 4125; open M-Sa 8am-6pm; AmEx/MC/V). **El Mundo Café,** 100m east of the bus stop on the main drag, is both a travel agency and **Internet** cafe (¢25 per min.), and also sells international magazines. (☎642 0652. Open daily 8am-7pm.) The **post office** is 300m east of Banco Nacional by the police. (Open M-F 8am-noon and 1-5:30pm.) Postal code: 5361.

ACCOMMODATIONS AND FOOD. Few travelers stay in Cóbano, but if you happen to miss the last bus out of Cóbano, **Hotel Cóbano ❶**, across from Banco Nacional is a good choice and conveniently located by the bus stop. Ascend the pink staircase to the pleasant balcony, where you'll find neat and tidy rooms with wood paneling, ceiling fans, and private cold-water baths. (☎642 0219. Singles ¢3000; doubles ¢6000; triples ¢9000.) The attached **Restaurante Caoba ❶** is a good place to sit down for a snack before jumping on the bus. (*Gallo pinto* ¢600-800; *casados* 900-1200; pastas ¢1400-1800. Open daily 6am-5pm.) Popular with *tico* families for Sunday breakfast is a nameless **soda ❶** 50m west of Banco Nacional on the road to Mal País. The friendly women serve tasty *típico* dishes. (*Gallo pinto* ¢700; huge *casados* ¢800-1000. Open daily 7am-8pm.) For a break from the standard rice and beans, follow the garlic aroma to **Pizzería Mamma Rose ❷,** across from the pharmacy. Tasty gnocchi (¢2100-2800), pastas (¢1400-3000), and pizzas (¢1100-2200), are all well complemented by a glass of Italian wine. (Open M-F 11am until the dinner crowd leaves, Sa and Su for dinner only.)

TAMBOR

Looking at Tambor *pueblo*'s gravel roads and dark, volcanic silvery-gray beach, you'd never guess it has such an extravagant past. Temporarily abandoning its humble beginnings as a quiet little fishing village, Tambor became somewhat of a mecca for resort-hoppers with the construction of several luxury hotels just outside the center in the early 90s. A few years later, Tambor gained international fame as the site of the popular American reality program *Temptation Island 2*. These days, however, the long crescent-shaped bay retains enough of its small-town charm, palm tree-enhanced tropical atmosphere, and luxurious resorts to attract dozens of *ticos*, off-the-beaten-track budget travelers, retired foreigners, and even a few whales that swim by during their migration along the coast.

⌐ TRANSPORTATION

The quickest way to arrive in Tambor is by plane. **Sansa** (35min.; high season 10:25am and 4:25pm, return 11:05am and 6:05pm; low season 7am and noon, return 8:10am and 12:40pm; US$55) and **Travelair** (35min.; high season 8:30am and 1pm, return 9:10am and 1:40pm; low season 9:15am, return 9:55am; US$60) leave from San José (see p. 85) and arrive at the airstrip by Playa Barcelo Hotel Tambor, about 5km north of Tambor.

The Paquera-Montezuma **bus** passes Tambor about 1hr. after departing from Montezuma and 30min. after departing from Paquera. When arriving, be sure to tell the driver to let you off at *Tambor pueblo*, not the airstrip; when leaving, flag the bus down on the correct side of the road at the bus stop on the southern end of town. Buses drive in along the main drag beside the beach, which lies east.

✦ 🛈 ORIENTATION AND PRACTICAL INFORMATION

Tambor is located on the southern end of **Bahía Ballena** (Whale Bay), 27km north of Montezuma and 14km south of Paquera. The town has little in the way of services, so you'll have to head to Cóbano, 19km south, for a bank, post office, medical services, and Internet. **Super Lapa,** 25m down the side street heading east just past the bus stop, has basic food and toiletries. (Open M-Sa 8-11am and 1-8pm.) **Dos Lagartos** (see **Accommodations,** below) has a small English-language **book exchange.** You can do your **laundry** (¢1500) at **Cabinas El Bosque** (see **Accommodations and Food,** below). The **police station** (☎117) is next door to the supermarket on the street heading east just past the bus stop.

🛏 ACCOMMODATIONS

All of Tambor's budget places are along the main drag or on the beach in the heart of town, with a few luxury places sprinkled on the outskirts.

Dos Lagartos (☎683 0236) has the best value and is on the beach. Walk 100m down the street heading east just past the bus stop, turn left at the beach; Dos Lagartos is 50m down on the left. Rooms are a bit small, but spotless and comfortable, and the gorgeous, fenced-off garden area with tall palm trees, hammocks, and a raised cement walkway more than compensates. The friendly American owners serve breakfast from 7-10am, organize tours, and provide laundry and towel service. Tours include: Isla Tortuga (US$30), Refugio Nacional de Vida Silvestre Curú (US$30), Montezuma waterfall (US$30), Islas del Golfo (US$70), sportfishing (US$180 for 4hr. and 4 people). Singles US$13; doubles US$17; triples US$30. ❶

Cabinas el Bosque (☎683 0039), on the main drag 100m north of the bus stop, is better for larger groups. Warm owners offer sparkling rooms with wood-paneled ceilings, private baths, and patios that sleep up to 4. Larger rooms sleeping 6 have two separate bedrooms and fully equipped kitchen. A shaded, covered area outside has plenty of hammocks and tables. Laundry ¢7000. Singles ¢4000; doubles ¢6000; triples ¢7000; quads ¢8000; family room ¢1600; ¢1500 per additional person. ❶

Cabinas Cabita (☎683 00691), on the main drag, 50m north of the bus stop, is another good option for folks planning on staying a while. Big rooms sleep 4-5 people, with kitchen, fridge, ceiling fans, closet, and private bath. Rooms ¢8600. ❶

Cabinas Christina, next door to the supermarket on the street heading east past the bus stop, has a cozy, family feel with a pretty balcony and restaurant and 10 large, clean rooms with fans and soft beds. They also arrange tours to: Isla Tortuga, Refugio Nacional de Vida Silveste Curú, and Montezuma US$35 each; US$85 for all three. Singles and doubles ₡5000, with private bath ₡7000. ❷

Tambor Beach Restaurant and Hotel (☎683 0057), near the end of the strip, has ten simple rooms sleeping four with cement floors and sufficiently clean baths. Larger rooms sleeping eight have a kitchen and two bedrooms. Quads ₡6000, high season ₡8000; larger cabin sleeping 8 ₡25,000. ❶

☎ 🎵 FOOD AND ENTERTAINMENT

Tambor's nightlife consists of one whopping bar, the large and casual **Los Gitanos,** on the beach straight east of the bus stop. (Beer ₡400, cocktails ₡800-1000. Open daily 11am-11pm.) Just outside the center of town is a young and hip scene at **Los Delfines Discoteca,** part of the Barceló Hotel Playa Tambor. (☎683 0317. Cover ₡1000 for non-hotel guests. Beer ₡400. Open F-Sa 10pm-2am.)

Tambor Beach Restaurant and Hotel offers delicious, reasonably-priced food and a pleasant view. A charming patio with tree stump tables overlooks a garden and some mangroves. *Gallo pinto* ₡600-900; *casados* ₡1100; rice dishes ₡1600-2100; lobster ₡5800. Open daily 6:30am-9:30pm. ❶

Restaurante Costa Coral, on the 2nd floor of the Hotel Costa Coral on the main drag, 200m north of the bus stop, serves fancier meals in a brightly colored dining area with yellow and orange tables and chairs and adobe walls. Seafood and *típico* dishes ₡1500-3000. Beer ₡400; margarita ₡1000. Open daily 11am-11pm. MC/V. ❷

POCHOTE

Nestled in an estuary on the northern side of Bahía Ballena, 8km from Tambor, is the remote ghost town of Pochote. Zinc sheet-roofed houses line the two dirt roads, and barefoot children playing soccer is almost all the activity this tiny village sees until a few avid anglers swing by to sportfish in the high season. The beach is long, gray, and deserted, and rivers flowing from the mountains deliver forest trash (dead leaves and driftwood) to the ocean during the rainy season.

The Paquera-Montezuma **bus** can drop you off at the entrance to Pochote on the highway, a 1km walk from town. There's a handful of *pulperías* and a few public phones, but you'll have to go to Tambor, Paquera, or Cóbano for more services. **Camping** on the beach is safe and reportedly popular with *tico* summer visitors who visit Tambor during the day. Pochote's only hotel is **Estrellas de la Playa ❹,** a large, family-friendly fishing lodge on the beach. To get there, walk east 500m along the road from the highway and turn right at the first dirt path with a sign. The hotel is another 300m down. The most luxurious rooms are country-style wood cabins with full kitchen, microwave, TV, VCR, A/C, hot-water bath with tub, and other amenities that make you feel like royalty. There are also smaller, but very comfortable doubles with A/C, and four triple cabins with wooden floors, fans, and private hot-water baths. There is also a breezy beach-front restaurant with TV, pool table, and pricey entrees. (☎683 0169. Lobster ₡5500-9100; filet mignon ₡5500. Doubles US$60; triple cabins US$90; luxury quads US$125.)

The only other decent and consistently open restaurant is **Cevichería Lila ❶,** just off the main entrance road on the way to Estella de la Playa. Photos of naked women don't exactly set the most comfortable mood, but the fresh fish and shrimp will appease your hunger. (Open daily 1pm-midnight.) After dinner, a mostly local male group grabs a beer or two at **Salón Maracuyá** or **Momo's Bar,** both near the dock at the end of the main entrance road from the highway.

PAQUERA

Most travelers arrive in Paquera on the ferry from Puntarenas and immediately jump on the connecting bus south to Montezuma or Tambor. For those hoping to pack the most action into the fewest days, skipping Paquera is a good idea, as the small and bustling town offers little to do or see. Just a short boat or car ride away, however, are unspoiled beaches and a wildlife refuge that make for incredibly laid-back and relaxing daytrips. If you've got some time to spare, take the bus to Paquera *pueblo*, spend a night or two hanging with the locals, and explore the fantastic sights nearby.

▐ TRANSPORTATION. From Paquera, **buses** connect with the ferry and head south from the ferry terminal to **Montezuma**, via **Paquera, Pochote, Tambor,** and **Cóbano** (1½hr., 6 per day 6:15am-6:15pm, ₡700). The road north to Naranjo is in poor condition and can only be traveled with a 4WD car or **taxi** (☎641 0784). The **bus stop** is near the center of the main strip across from El Gallo Más Gallo.

▐▐ ORIENTATION AND PRACTICAL INFORMATION. Paquera *pueblo* is about 4km west of the **ferry terminal**, 8km northeast of **Refugio Nacional de Vida Silvestre Curú**, and 41km northeast of Montezuma. The town center stretches about 500m along the highway, marked at its southern end by a bridge. A side street heading west starts about 100m north of the bridge.

A **tourist information center** (☎641 0673) is 300m north of the bridge on the main road opposite the gas station. It runs tours to Isla Tortuga and Refugio Nacional de Vida Silvestre Curú for US$20 and rents kayaks and snorkel gear. **Banco Popular,** 300m from the side street, has an **ATM.** (Open M-F 8:15am-4:30pm, Sa 8:15-11:30am.) Other services include: **Mega Super Supermarket,** 100m north of the bridge (open M-Th 8am-7pm, F-Sa 8am-8pm, Su 8am-1pm); **police** (☎641 1017), 50m north of the bridge; **public phones,** near the police, at the bus stop, and at the **Instituto Costarricense de Electricidad (ICE) office,** 200m down the side street (open M-F 8am-5pm, Sa 8am-noon); and **Internet** at the tourist information center and on the side street, across from Cabinas Ginana.

▐▐ ACCOMMODATIONS AND FOOD. You won't have any trouble finding good, cheap places to stay in Paquera. A comfortable option is **Cabinas El Paraíso ❶,** opposite the police, 50m north of the bridge. The 15 rooms are small but very clean with wooden floors, fans, private cold-water bath, and DirecTV. A few larger cabins that sleep six are available. A private guard and laundry service will make your stay even more comfortable. (☎641 0340. ₡1500 per person.) **Cabinas Ginana ❶,** 200m down the side street, has the added luxury of A/C in a few of its 24 rooms with private cold-water bath, TV, fan, and parking. (☎641 0119. Singles with fan ₡2500, with A/C ₡6000; doubles ₡4500/₡7000; triples ₡6000/₡9000; quads ₡8000/₡10,000.) A large, shaded, grassy **campground ❶** with bathrooms and showers is 400m north of the bus stop, just past the cemetery. (₡800 per person.)

The large open-air *soda* at Cabinas El Paraíso, called **Soda los Ranchos ❶,** is very popular with local *tico* families especially on Su after church. They serve a standard menu of *gallo pinto, casados*, rice dishes, fried chicken, and burgers at very reasonable prices. Another good place is **Restaurante Guaraní ❶,** a large, friendly bar 20m north of the police station. Evenings and nights invite a fun-loving crowd with up-beat *salsa* and *merengue* music in a lively atmosphere. (*Casados* ₡700-800. 2-for-1 Heineken every night. Open daily 11am-11pm.) **Restaurante Ginana ❶,** attached to Cabinas Ginana, dresses up in fancy tablecloths, has marble-tiled floors, and a big-screen TV. However, the food remains simple and inexpensive *típico* fare. (Beef with vegetables and rice ₡1200; chop suey in garlic ₡1000; *gallo pinto* ₡650-750. Beer ₡350. Open daily 5am-10pm.)

NEAR PAQUERA

REFUGIO NACIONAL DE VIDA SILVESTRE CURÚ

*Curú is privately owned by **Sra. Schultz,** so you'll have to call her at least a week in advance to make sure the gate will be open (☎ 661 2392). Once you've confirmed your arrival, take any of the Paquera-Montezuma buses and tell the driver to let you off at the entrance. The park is open to 30 visitors at a time, with priority given to students, so it might be booked solid for months straight, especially during the high season. Many **tour agencies** in Montezuma and Tambor run package trips to Curú (US$20-30), which may be easier and more convenient than visiting on your own. If you go on your own, guides are available for about US$15; ask Sra. Schultz to have one ready for you. Camping is not allowed. Entrance fee US$6.*

Unique in Costa Rica's national park system, Curú is a privately owned farm that experiments in sustainable agriculture. Until 1974, the farm and enclosed *hacienda* were settled by squatters, and it eventually achieved "Protected Forest" status as a National Wildlife Refuge in 1983. Most of the 12 sq. km remain dedicated to primary and secondary forest, though a good portion of it (20%) has been set aside for agriculture and cattle. Seventeen diverse trails, ranging from very easy to difficult, give the public access to 232 species of birds, including hawks, *motmots*, and woodpeckers, and to the successfully reintroduced spider monkeys, scarlet macaws, and white-nosed *coatis*. But the park's most spectacular features are its fascinating mangrove wildlife and pristine, forest-lined beaches that give it the feel of a less-touristed and quieter version of Manuel Antonio (p. 290). Be sure to bring your bathing suit and towel if you want to take a refreshing dip in the ocean.

CENTRAL
PACIFIC COAST

The central Pacific is Costa Rica's perfectionist poster child; snapshots of sunsets over its rocky coastline grace the covers of travel brochures, people-sized marlin and snapper lure sportfishermen from all over the world, rugged rain forests sprawl just meters from soft sandy beaches, and the surf breaks high and low for waveriders of all abilities. The area sees tons of traffic in just a few spots, but the visitors vary from vacationing *tico* families and foreign backpackers to resort-hopping honeymooners, all of whose every whim and tropical fantasy is satisfied by the well-developed tourist infrastructure and convenient public transportation. Popularity, however, comes at an unavoidable price; the major beach towns of Jacó, Quepos, and Manuel Antonio are invariably more crowded and a bit pricier than Costa Rica's more remote Caribbean side. Diehard peace-seekers, however, need only move on to less-visited Playa Hermosa, Playa Esterillos Oeste, or Dominical for more remote, unspoiled scenery and long stretches of empty beach. Dry or wet season, the central Pacific delivers—be prepared to be pampered.

OROTINA

Though it boasts lively streets and an extremely friendly, laid-back population, Orotina has never been a major stop on tourists' itinerary. However, the town is a regular stop for locals buying cheap and tasty typical eats on their way to the beach. The *parque central* is clean and relaxing, and the town makes a decent base from which to explore Iguana Park, 14km away. Most travelers pass by Orotina en route to Jacó to the south or Puntarenas for the beautiful Nicoya beaches.

▐ TRANSPORTATION

The main local **bus terminal** is 100m north of the northeast corner of the *parque*. Buses for **Puntarenas** leave from a stop 150m west of the northwest corner of the *parque* (1hr.; direct 5am, 12:30, 5:30pm; indirect 5 per day 6am-5:30pm; ¢270). Buses to **San José** via **San Mateo** leave from the stop opposite the gas station, 250m north of the northwest corner of the *parque* (1¼hr., 9 per day 5am-6pm, ¢480). Buses to the **Iguana Park** leave from the main bus terminal (30min.; 5:30am, noon, 4:30pm; ¢220). Buses to **Jacó** leave from the stop 150m north of the northwest corner of the *parque* (1¾hr., 6 per day 5:30am-4:30pm, ¢500). Schedules change often, so check with locals for up-to-date times. **Taxis** wait at the main bus terminal.

❈ ⚑ ORIENTATION AND PRACTICAL INFORMATION

Orotina is located 66km west of San José and 42km northeast of Jacó. The center of activity is the **parque central.** Orient yourself by remembering that the **church** is on the east side of the *parque*.

Banks: Banco de Costa Rica, on the southwest corner of the *parque*. Open M-F 8:30am-3pm. **Coope Orotina** (☎ 483 8045), on the north side of the *parque*, also changes US dollars and has a **Western Union.** Open M-F 8am-3:45pm, Sa 8-11:30am.

Central Pacific Coast

Market: Super Mercado Laurente, bordering the *parque*. Open M-Sa 7am-8pm, Su 7am-1pm.

Police: (☎428 8010), 150m south of the southeast corner of the *parque*. Open daily M-F 7:30am-6pm, Sa 7:30am-noon. Open 24hr. for emergencies.

Medical Services: Farmacia Kalina (☎428 7997), 100m north and 50m east of the northeast corner of the *parque*. Open M 8am-9pm, Tu-Su 8am-10pm. V.

Red Cross: (☎428 8304 or 428 5051, emergency 128), 100m east of the northeast corner of the *parque*.

Telephones: ICE office (☎428 8123), 100m south of southwest corner of the *parque*. Open M-F 7:30am-5pm, Sa 8am-noon.

Internet Access: Oronot Cafe Internet, 100m north of the northwest corner of the *parque*, on the 2nd fl. ¢200 per 30min. Open M-Sa 9:30am-9pm.

Post office: 150m south of the southeast corner of the *parque*, next to the police station. Open M-Sa 8:30am-5pm.

ACCOMMODATIONS

Not usually a tourist destination, Orotina has few hotels and a limited restaurant selection. However, you'll find lots of *sodas* and vendors.

Hotel Yadi (☎428 8329), opposite Servicentro La Pista on the highway, just before the entrance to Orotina coming from San José. Simple rooms have two single beds with cement floors, private hot-water baths, and fans. A few nicer rooms come with ceramic tiled floors and A/C. Check-out 1pm. Doubles with fan ¢5800, with A/C ¢7000. ❷

Cabinas Kalina (☎428 8082), 100m north and 100m east of the northeast corner of the *parque*, is closer to the town center. The 11 rooms are simple and clean with tile floors, double or single beds, and fans. Singles ¢2500; doubles ¢3500. ❶

Rancho Oropendola (☎428 8600), about 5km from Orotina, in the tiny ghost town of San Mateo. One of the nicest and most relaxing places in the area. Extremely friendly owner Alvaro keeps the place in wonderful condition. Guests stay in private cabins nestled between ripe mango and avocado trees and crystalline creeks that flow through the surrounding forest area. A-frame cabins with tile floors, tasteful artwork, and big, clean, hot-water bathrooms. The hotel grounds have trails, a volleyball court, badminton net, boche ball area, pool table, and a huge open gazebo with a fantastic forest view. Check out Alvaro's rad '58 Cadillac in the garage. Breakfast included. Doubles ¢10,000; quads ¢14,000; 7-person rooms ¢18,000. ❷

FOOD

The cheapest places to get a bite to eat are the *soda* stalls just behind the main bus station. You can snag a good *plato del día* or *casado* for just ¢600.

Soda El Parque, at the northwest corner of the *parque*, is a popular lunch spot with the local police and provides more comfort. Zone out watching the TV with a plate of *gallo pinto* (¢700), a *casado* (¢900), or a chocolate milk shake (¢300), or just enjoy the view of the pleasant *parque*. Open daily 7am-10pm. ❶

Bar y Restaurante Tropical, 300m north of the northeast corner of the *parque*, is a good casual spot for dinner with tables and picnic chairs. The menu is standard tasty *típico* fare and the atmosphere calming. *Casado* ¢900; burrito ¢1000; rice dishes ¢1000-2400; ice cream ¢350; beer ¢500. Open W-M 11am-midnight. ❶

Heladería Danny, at the northwest corner of the *parque,* has fruity soft serve ice cream refreshing at anytime of day. There are only a couple of flavors at a time, but they're all creamy and sweet. Scoops ₡200. Open daily 8am-7pm. ❶

🔺 OUTDOOR ACTIVITIES

Formerly located in the Iguana Park, **The Original Canopy Tour** has recently been moved to **Mahogony Park,** a private reserve located 12km from both Orotina and Esparza on the Interamerican highway connecting San José and Puntarenas. The 2½hr. tour is a 10-15min. hike from the park entrance and consists of 10 safe platforms, seven traversals, and a rappel, from which it's common to see a few monkey species and many birds. Though walk-ins are accepted, it's best to make a reservation if you'd like to do the tour, especially in the low season. (☎ 257 5149. US$45, students US$35, children US$25. Package with lunch and round-trip transportation from San José, Jacó, or Puntarenas US$75/US$65/US$55.)

NEAR OROTINA

IGUANA PARK

*From Orotina, take a **bus** from the main bus terminal to Iguana Park (30min.; 5:30am, noon, 4:30pm; ₡220). Schedules change often, so check with locals for up-to-date times. A **taxi** from Orotina to the park should cost ₡2000-2500. Park ☎ 240 6712. Open daily 8am-4pm, but call in advance to ensure the gates are open, as the park is sporadically closed. Admission US$15; guided tour US$10.*

Located 14km from Orotina, the Iguana Park is founder Dr. Dagmar Werner's living experiment on economically feasible and sustainable forest management and preservation of the endangered green iguana. Necessary to the iguanas' survival are habitats that combine open spaces and trees, areas that humans have historically been known to destroy for development and agriculture. Werner's project aims to encourage the preservation of these natural habitats and thereby increase specific types of wildlife and fauna and also teach farmers to be self-sufficient producers and more environmentally sensitive. In its first five years, the park released more than 80,000 iguanas into the wild, and continues to educate the local communities in the farming and hunting of iguanas. The park restaurant and souvenir shop, oddly enough, sell leather products and the world's only legal iguana meat. Although a strange way to promote iguana preservation, both are effective and practical methods to regulate poaching and over hunting.

The park's second major effort is to restore the scarlet macaw population, which has drastically declined due to habitat destruction and uncontrollable poaching—macaws sometimes sell for up to US$1000 in the black market. Werner and her workers encourage farmers to breed and raise the birds for sale in legal markets, which not only protect the existing populations from poaching, but also provide farmers with a stable and sustainable source of income.

Until early 2002, the Iguana Park was popular as a major site for the **The Original Canopy Tour,** which has since re-located to **Mahogony Park,** a private reserve located 12km from both Orotina and Esparza. The activities in the Iguana Park now include learning about the interesting conservation projects and traversing the 4km of well-maintained trails, transiting through zones of dry tropical lowland forest, humid tropical rainforest, and mountain cloud forest. It's a good ideas to bring rain gear, proper hiking shoes, and insect repellent.

PUNTARENAS

Once a bustling port town and major spot on tourist itineraries, Puntarenas is now a shadow of its former self. Fish are fresh, but otherwise the city feels stale. Many headed for Puntarenas detour to one of the friendlier, quieter, and more pleasant towns or beaches just south, skipping the city altogether. Come to catch the ferry to the beautiful beaches of the Nicoya Peninsula, but don't plan on staying long.

TRANSPORTATION

Buses: From Av. 1, Calle Central/1, just east of the Palí Supermarket, buses run to the Barrio Carmen **ferry terminal** (10min., every 10min. 6am-9:30pm, ¢65); **Orotina** (1hr., 8 per day 6am-8pm, ¢345.); **El Roble** (25min., every 15min. 5:30am-8pm, ¢2000.) From the stop on Calle 2, Av. 1/3, just south of the *mercado central* and in front of the ZumZum shop, buses leave for **Caldera** (40min., 6 per day 7:30am-5:30pm, ¢220). The main **intercity terminal** is at the corner of Calle 2 and the beach front road, Paseo de los Turistas, on the northeast side of town. From inside the terminal, buses leave for **San José** (2hr., about every 40min. 4:15am-9pm, ¢620). From the stop just across the street from the terminal, buses run to: **Filadelfia/Nicoya/Santa Cruz** (3hr., 6am and 3:45pm, ¢720); **Las Juntas** via **Monteverde** and **Santa Elena** (3hr., 8 per day 4:40am-3:30pm, ¢940); **Miramar** (45min., about every 40min. 6am-9:40pm, ¢180); **Quepos** via the entrance to **Jacó** (3hr., 4 per day 5am-4:30pm, ¢1050); **Tilarán/Cañas** via **Arenal** (2½hr., 11:45am and 4:30pm, ¢680).

Boats: Ferries leave from the Contramar Terminal near Av. 3, Calle 31/33 on the far northwest side of the peninsula (☎661 1444). Ferries to **Paquera** (1½hr.; 6 per day 5am-8:15pm, return 6 per day 6am-8:30pm; ¢620, children under 5 ¢300, cars ¢4000). An additional *lancha* runs to Paquera from behind the *mercado central* (6, 11am, 3:15pm; return 7:30am, 12:30, 5pm; ¢700). From Paquera, buses connect with ferries to **Montezuma** via **Tambor, Pochote,** and **Cóbano.** Ferries (☎661 1069) also leave for **Puerto Naranjo** (1hr.; 5 per day 3:15am-7pm, return 5 per day 5:10am-9pm; ¢620, children under 12 ¢280, cars ¢4400). From Puerto Naranjo, buses connect to **Nicoya,** where you can take a bus to **Playa Sámara, Playa Nosara,** or **Santa Cruz,** for connections heading to beaches on the southern peninsula.

Taxis: (☎663 5050 or 663 2020) line the streets near the *mercado central* on the northeast side of the peninsula. A taxi from the San José bus terminal to the ferry dock costs ¢500.

ORIENTATION AND PRACTICAL INFORMATION

Puntarenas is a long, skinny peninsula 10km from San José. Nearly 60km northwest, *calles* stretch across the town's entire width, while only five east-west *avenidas* span its length. The center of town is marked by the *parque central*, bordered by Av. Central to the south, Av. 1 to the north, and Calles 7 and 3 to the west and east. The main **bus terminal** is on the southeast edge of town on Calle 2, and *ferries* arrive and depart from the dock at the northwest end near Av. 3, Calle 31/33. Along the peninsula's southern border runs the Av. 4, more commonly referred to as **Paseo de los Turistas** because it holds the more upscale restaurants and hotels once popular with wealthier tourists. Travelers should note that no part of Puntarenas is safe past dark, especially around the *mercado central*. If you must go somewhere, it's best to take a cab.

Tourist Office: The main tourist office (☎661 9011), just opposite the main ferry terminal, has a post office, **Internet** service, sells phone cards, and changes dollars. Internet ¢250 per 30min., ¢500 per hr. Open daily 8am-6pm.

Puntarenas

▲ ACCOMMODATIONS

Hotel Ayicon, 2
Hotel Cabezas, 4
Hotel Chorotega, 1
Hotel Helen, 7
Pensión Chinchilla, 6

● FOOD

Pizzería, 3
Restaurante Aloha, 8
Restaurante Kahite Blanco, 5
Rincón de Surf, 9

Map labels:

To HOSPITAL MONSEÑOR SANABRIA (8km), PLAYA DE DOÑA ANA & BOCA BARRANCA (14km), ESPARZA (20km), OROTINA (35km), JACÓ (40km), SAN JOSÉ (110km)

Paquera Lancha
Mercado Central
To Caldera
Av. 2
To San José
To other destinations

C. 6
C. 4
C. 2

Banco de Costa Rica
Banco Nacional
BCAC
Pali Supermarket
To El Roble, Orotina
Farmacia Szustor

Av. 3
C. Central
C. 1
C. 3
C. 5
C. 7
C. 9
C. 11
C. 13
C. 15
C. 17
C. 19
C. 21
C. 23
C. 25
C. 27
C. 29
C. 31
C. 33
C. 35
C. 37

Museo Histórico Marino
Parque Central
Av. 1
Av. Central

Río Naranjo Estuary

Red Cross

Millenium Cybercafe
Av. 2
Laundry

Av. 4 Bis

Paseo de los Turistas

Golfo de Nicoya

Contramar ferries to Paquera, Puerto Naranjo

Av. 3
Av. 1
Av. Central
Av. 2

Municipal Pool

0 200 meters
0 200 yards

Banks: The peninsula's banks cluster along Av. 3 between Calles 1 and Central. **BCAC** (open M-F 8:30am-5pm), **Banco Nacional** (open M-F 8:30am-3:45pm), and **Banco de Costa Rica** (open M-F 8:30am-3pm) all have **24hr. ATMs.**

Police: The **police station** (☎661 0640; emergency 911) is on the northeast edge of town behind Banco Nacional, one block north of the post office.

Medical Services: Farmacia Szuster (☎661 0580), 200m east of the *parque central,* 100m south of Banco Nacional, is well-stocked. Open M-Sa 7am-9pm, Su 8am-noon. **Hospital Monseñor Sanabria** (☎663 0033), is 8km east of town; take any bus for Esparza, Miramar, Barranca, El Roble, or Caldera. The **Red Cross** (☎661 0184) is located 250m west of the northwest corner of the *parque.* Open 24hr.

Internet Access: Millenium Cybercafe, on Paseo de los Turistas at Calle 17. ¢400 per 30min.; ¢600 per hr. Open daily 10am-10pm. **Internet Cafe Puntarenas** lies east of the church in the *parque central.* ¢350 per 30min.; ¢500 per hr. Open daily 9am-7pm.

Post Office: Av. 3, Calles Central/1, 100m north and 120m west of the *parque.* Open M-F 7:30am-6pm, Sa 7:30am-noon.

Postal code: 5400.

🏠 ACCOMMODATIONS

Camping on the beach is unsafe, unsanitary, and not recommended. Good, safe budget accommodations are available. Be careful of where you plan to stay, especially around the round *mercado central* area, since crime rates have risen.

Hotel Cabezas, Av. 1, Calles 2/4 (☎661 1045), is a friendly and secure option. The rooms are small, but clean, all with fans and common cold water baths. You'll probably find yourself watching hours of Spanish programs on the large TV in the sitting area with the extremely friendly and helpful owners. ¢2000 per person. ❶

Hotel Chorotega, Av. 3, Calle 1 (☎661 0998), diagonally across from Banco Nacional, offers more privacy and comfort. Clean rooms with fans. Singles ¢3300, with bath 5600; doubles ¢4500/¢7900; triples ¢5700/¢10,000. ❶

Hotel Ayicon, Calle 2, Av. 1/3 (☎661 0164), near the *mercado central,* has basic, dim rooms for a variety of budgets. Singles ¢2500, with private bath ¢3400, with A/C ¢5250; doubles ¢4400/¢6800/¢9700. ❶

Pensión Chinchilla, Calle 1, Av. Central/2 (☎661 1047), 100m east and 50m south of the *parque,* has thin mattresses and dark rooms with shared cold-water baths, but the hotel is safe, clean, and friendly. Singles ¢1500; doubles ¢2500; triples ¢3500. ❶

Hotel Helen, Calle 2, Av. Central/2 (☎661 2159), is overpriced for its basic rooms, but the manager is friendly, and the place is safe and well-kept. Singles and doubles ¢4500, with bath ¢5000; triples ¢5000/¢6000. ❷

🍴 FOOD

Several decent, mid-priced restaurants serving seafood and *típico* fare line Paseo de los Turistas. Otherwise, try the *mercado central* for quick and cheap eats. A small strip of *sodas* calls to those waiting for a ferry. Most are open M-Sa 5am-6pm and some are open on Su.

🏆 **Restaurante Kahite Blanco,** Av. 1, Calle 15/17, 100m northwest of the stadium, is very popular with the better-dressed locals. All seating is on a breezy patio. Rice with shrimp ¢2200; *ceviche* ¢1050. Open daily 10am-11pm. ❷

Restaurante Aloha, on the Paseo de los Turistas at Calle 19, also has good seafood. Enjoy your lobster (¢5300-5600), pizza (¢2300), or rice (¢1400-2700) in an open dining area with good views of the beach. Open daily 11am-midnight. ❸

Pizzería, on Av. 1, Calle 3, has hot cheesy pizzas (¢1250-2350) and a large selection of pastas (¢1500-2200). Open daily noon-10pm. AmEx/DC/MC/V. ❷

Rincón de Surf, on the Paseo de los Turistas near Calle 15, will ease your worries with its casual atmosphere, jammin' reggae beats, and beach-front location. Surprise your taste buds with octopus *ceviche* (¢2300) or the less daring black bean soup (¢830). ❶

 ## SIGHTS

The **Museo Histórico Marino de la Ciudad de Puntarenas** (☎661 5036), in the *parque central*, highlights the history of Puntarenas and its inhabitants through exhibits on archaeology, customs, and trade relations and a brief display on the region's natural resources. Housed in a building that was once the city prison, the museum is worth a glance if you have a couple hours between buses or ferries.

If you prefer your water chlorinated, there's an Olympic-sized **municipal pool** at the western tip of the peninsula. Take a Barrio Carmen bus from Av. Central, Calle 1/Central to get there (¢65). The pool is 5m from the ocean and surrounded by water on three sides. (Open Tu-Su 9am-4:30pm, but closed sporadically. ¢400, children ages 2-10 ¢200.)

 ## BEACHES

PLAYA PUNTARENTAS. Along the south side of the peninsula is **Playa Puntarenas,** a long, powdery beach of which only the westernmost kilometer or so is clean enough for swimming. Just a 15min. bus ride away is a cleaner and calmer beach behind Cabinas de San Isidro, 7km from Puntarenas. *(Take a bus toward Esparza, Miramar, Barranca, or El Roble from the stop on Av. 1, Calle Central/1, and ask the driver to let you off. 15min., every 15min. 5:30am-8pm, ¢120.)*

PLAYA DE DOÑA ANA AND PLAYA BOCA BARRANCA. Playa de Doña Ana, 14km from Puntarenas and 2km from the port of **Caldera,** is the only beach in the area even moderately developed for tourism; here, you'll find toilets, showers, and a basic restaurant. A large road sign on the highway points the way to a ticket booth and short forest trail that winds to the small, cup-shaped shore with a decent left beach break . Just a 200m walk north along Doña Ana leads to rocky **Boca Barranca,** enticing surfers and boogie boarders with its long left-hand run that rises out of a river mouth. Nearby to both beaches are two moderately-priced hotels that make a good base for anyone craving peace and quiet. From the entrance to Doña Ana, head north (left) along the highway and over the bridge about 0.5km until you see **Hotel Río Mar ❷** on the right. Popular with local surfers, rooms are large and basic with tiles, fans, and private cold baths. Their location slightly below street level might subdue some of the highway noise, but the roosters are guaranteed to wake you up for morning high tide. (☎661 0158. Singles ¢6000, with A/C ¢8700; doubles ¢8700/¢11,200; triples ¢10,400/¢13,000. AmEx/MC/V.) Just up the highway on the left is **Cabinas Oasis ❷,** a small establishment with clean rooms, bunk beds, cable TV, and A/C. Titi, the pet monkey in the courtyard, can entertain for hours. (☎663 7934. Singles ¢5000; doubles ¢6000; triples ¢6300; quads ¢8000.) The beach at **Puerto Caldera,** 2km south, is not noteworthy except for its good left. (*Doña Ana open daily 8am-4pm. Beach admission ¢500. Both Doña Ana and Barranca are accessible via the Caldera bus, leaving from Puntarenas at Calle 2, Av. 1/3 in front of the ZumZum shop. 40 min., about ever 2hr. 7:30am-5:30pm, ¢220.)*

CENTRAL PAC. COAST

SOUTH OF PUNTARENAS TO JACÓ. Further south of Caldera and before Jacó are numerous less-developed beaches primarily of interest to **surfers.** They are most easily accessible by car along the **Costanera Sur** highway, although any Puntarenas-Jacó bus will drop you off near the turnoffs, where you may have to walk a kilometer or two. Just south of Caldera, about 17km from Puntarenas, are **Playa Tivives** and **Playa Valor**, with reliable beach breaks off a river mouth. **Playa Escondida**, 10km north of Jacó, is an excellent point break with slow-forming lefts that crash after building to a solid peak.

ESPARZA

You'd never guess that the adorable hamlet of Esparza, some 20km inland of Puntarenas, was an important trading post frequently raided by greedy pirates over 300 years ago. The town's clean streets and smiling, laid-back residents now live in anything but a hotbed of activity. Neighbors escape the sweltering mid-day heat chit-chatting for hours on front porches, while their school-uniformed children sip Fantas after class in the *parque central*. Though there isn't much to see in town, anyone in Puntarenas would benefit from taking the 40min. bus ride over and taking advantage of Esparza's suburban coziness and quality accommodations.

E TRANSPORTATION. Buses to Esparza from Puntarenas leave from Av. Central/Calle Central and drop off passengers on the south side of the *parque central*, where they return to Puntarenas (every 20min., 5:30am-8pm, ¢180).

■☑ ORIENTATION AND PRACTICAL INFORMATION. Getting off the bus and facing the *parque*, the church is east, and the **Comprebien** supermarket is west. (Open M 8:30am-7:30pm, Tu-Th 8:30am-7pm, F-Sa 8:30am-8pm, Su 8am-1pm. AmEx/MC/V.) The **mercado central** is 50m north of the supermarket. (Open most days 7am-6pm.) At the northeast corner of the *parque* is **Banco Nacional.** (Open M-F 8:30am-3:45pm.) Across from the *mercado*, 50m north of the northwest corner of the *parque*, is **Farmacia Szuster**. (☎636 6366. Open daily 7am-10pm. AmEx/MC/V.) Just a few doors north is the **ICE Office.** (Open M-F 7:30am-5pm, Sa 8am-noon.)

☞☒ ACCOMMODATIONS AND FOOD. Esparza's best and highest concentration of budget mid-range rooms are along the street east of the Church. From the Banco Nacional, walk east 100m and north 250m to get to **Cabinas Cristal ❶**, a small row of sparkling clean, splurge quality rooms with A/C, private cold-water bath, and cable TV. (☎635 5235. Singles ¢4000; doubles ¢5000.) The most modern and comfortable place in town is **Hotel Castañuelas ❷**, on the highway, 600m north of the northeast corner of the *parque*. A convenient option for visitors speeding by the highway and looking for a quick one-night stay, Castañuelas has spacious rooms, comfy beds, private cold-water baths, and parking space. (☎635 5105. Singles ¢4500, with A/C ¢5000; doubles ¢5500/¢7500; triples ¢6800/¢9000.)

For cheap *gallo pinto* and a refreshing *fresco natural*, the few friendly *sodas* in the *mercado central* are your best bet, as long as you can tolerate the strong smells of raw meat and seafood from the surrounding vendors. If you want a little more fresh air and a prime location for people watching, pull up a chair at the **Soda Torrejas ❶**, 50m west of the northwest corner of the *parque*. The motherly owners will serve you delicious *gallos* (¢200-350) and hearty *casados* (¢550-800) just the way you like them. (Open daily 6am-4pm.) A favorite of *tico* families on weekend evenings is **Pizza Espartacus ❷**, 250m north of the northwest corner of the parque, just past Cabinas Cristal. Espartacus himself whips up delicious, melt-in-your-mouth cheesy pizzas (personal ¢500-700, medium ¢1500-2000). Larger groups can take advantage of their combo values. (Two medium pizzas, 2 garlic breads, 2 2-liter bottles of soda ¢3600. Open M-F 11am-10pm, Sa 11am-11pm).

PARQUE NACIONAL CARARA

Although this park only encompasses 4700 hectares, its unique location includes three life zones, the tropical humid forest, premontane tropical rainforest, and montane rainforest. Several rare and endangered species reside in these zones, including the great anteater, fiery-billed aracari, spider monkey, American crocodile, black-and-green poison arrow frog, and phantom scarlet macaw. More easy to spot are the park's species of hardwoods and softwoods, which are identified by informative signs along the trails. Some of the highlights in the greenery are the *kapok* (silk cotton) trees, water hyacinth, and purple heart trees.

AT A GLANCE	
AREA: 4700 hectares.	**FEATURES:** Río Tárcoles.
CLIMATE: Mean annual temperature 27°C. Annual rainfall 2.8m.	**GATEWAYS:** Jacó (p. 272).
	CAMPING: Not allowed in the park.
HIGHLIGHTS: Rare and endangered species; 3 life zones; Precolumbian archaeological site; crocodile bridge.	**FEES:** US$8 admission.

▐ TRANSPORTATION

Few **buses** pass by the reserve. From **Jacó** or **Playa Hermosa,** take any Puntarenas- or San José-bound bus (see **Transportation** sections) and ask the driver to let you off at the park entrance. If you don't see a large parking lot and the **ranger station** when you get off, chances are the driver dropped you off at the park's volunteer lodging station, 300m north (to the left with your back to the road) up the highway. To return, you'll have to rely on the few buses that pass along the highway from San José or Puntarenas to Jacó or Quepos. Ask the park ranger about what time the buses usually pass by the park, but as the schedule is not fixed, you may have to wait anywhere between 10min. and 2hr. for a bus. If you're en route to San José or Puntarenas from Jacó, you can take an early morning bus to the park, have the ranger watch your bags while you're hiking, and then flag down a bus. Park open daily 7am-4:30pm dry season; open daily 8am-4pm rainy season. US$8.)

▐ ORIENTATION

Parque Nacional Carara, 17km northeast of Jacó and 90km west of San José, was created in a transition zone where the wet tropical jungle of the south meets the dry forest of the north. Originally created to facilitate scientific studies and investigations in 1978, the park's three shaded, level, and easy-to-traverse trails are good for a quick glance at the diverse flora and fauna.

▐ PRACTICAL INFORMATION

  WHEN TO GO. Carara is best visited as a short day trip, as there is not a full day's worth to see, there is no inexpensive nearby lodging, and camping is not permitted in the park. Get an early start to beat some of the heat and humidity, and don't forget insect repellent and drinking water. The ranger station has bathrooms and a picnic area but sells only drinks (no food), so bring a snack.

⚡ HIKING

The first two trails form a figure eight and leave from the ranger station. **Las Ará-ceas,** the first loop, is 1.2km and takes about 45min. if you just walk through. **Quebrada Bonita,** the second loop, is 1.5km, takes about 50min., and involves a shallow river crossing. The trails consists of primary forest and are very similar, but you have a greater chance of seeing wildlife on the Bonita trail. The third trail, **Laguna Meándrica,** is 4km each way and takes about 2½hr. to complete. This trail starts about 1km north of the ranger station and follows the Río Grande de Tárcoles. A murky lagoon about halfway along is a good place to spot birds, water-borne plants, and crocodiles. This trail is closed in Sept. when the lake floods.

◉ SIGHTS

Hidden under Carara's thick foliage are 15 uninteresting pre-Columbian archaeological sights, some dating back to 300 A.D. One worth checking out is **Lomas de Entierro,** an ancient village with housing and funeral remains at the top of the hill facing the Río Grande de Tárcoles. A guide can be helpful in identifying the interesting features of the ruins.

About 3km north of Parque Nacional Carara, on the highway to Puntarenas and San José, is the **Río Tárcoles Bridge,** more commonly called the **Crocodile Bridge** for the dozens of crocodiles that reside in the muddy river and doze by the trail. Guides claim that the crocs often prey on the farm animals that roam the surrounding pastures, and there have been at least a few reports of people being eaten alive or having had their limbs chewed off. If you're lucky, you might see a live feeding in action, but more likely is a view of 10 to 30 of the immobile reptiles lounging on the banks of the river. Though the bridge is hardly worth a visit in its own right, many private bus and transfer companies stop here for a quick peak; public buses to and from San José and Puntarenas speed right by. If you do happen to want a closer look, however, call **Jungle Crocodile Safari** (☎ 236 6473 or 637 0338) for a 2hr. tour down the Tárcoles River (don't worry, the boats are safe), complete with a bilingual guide that will do some daring crocodile tricks. (US$25.)

JACÓ

A swimmer might be intimidated by the waves that ravage the cinnamon-colored sands of Jacó, but surfers from around the world heard the call and brought a subculture with them which locals have now embraced. Almost every establishment offers a discount for *surfeadores,* and with good reason—those muscular bodies are what keep the economy going in this simple, tourist-trap strip of a town. Such a young, active crowd also lures quite a number of surfers, swimmers, and partiers from San José on the weekends, when the music never stops thumping and the beer never stops flowing. Of course, all this activity comes with a price—restaurants charge just a little more, budget accommodations aren't quite as cheap, the streets are littered with tour agencies and all sorts of trash, and crime and prostitution become more common with each passing year. Nonetheless, there is a peace to be found on the ink-black sand and crashing waves of paradise-worthy getaway Playa Hermosa, just a few kilometers south.

▮ TRANSPORTATION

Buses to **San José** (3hr.; 5, 7:30, 11am, 3, 5pm; ¢935) arrive and leave from Plaza Jacó, opposite the Best Western, 1km north of the town center on the main drag.

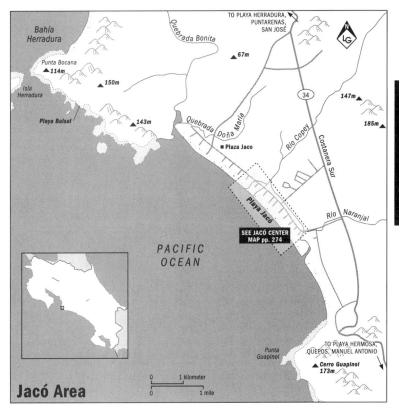

Jacó Area

Buy tickets from the office on the southeast corner of the plaza. Other buses stop along the main drag; a good place to catch them is from the stop in front of the Más X Menos. To: **Orotina** (1½hr.; 5, 7, 9am, 12:30, 2, 4, 5pm; ¢400); **Puntarenas** (1½hr.; 6, 9am, noon, 4:30pm; ¢520); **Quepos** (1½hr. 6:30am, 12:30, 4, 6pm; ¢480). **Taxis** (☎663 5050 or 663 2020) line up in front of Más X Menos. To **Playa Herradura** ¢1500-2000, **Playa Hermosa** ¢1000. Buses stopping in Jacó drop off passengers along the main road toward the center of town. Otherwise, buses passing near Jacó along the **Costanera Sur** highway will drop off pasengers at the far south end of town, from where it's about a 1km walk to Jacó center.

ORIENTATION AND PRACTICAL INFORMATION

Jacó center stretches for about 1km along its **main road,** which runs northwest to southwest parallel to the beach. For simplicity's sake, here it will be described as north-south, the far north end of town marked by the **Best Western.** Several side roads branch west off the main road and lead to the beach. **Playa Herradura** is 6.5km north of Jacó, **Playa Hermosa** about 5km south.

Tourist Information: Jacó has no official tourist office, but many tour operators and shop owners speak English and are more than willing to help. A few particularly helpful folks are Eric of **Mexican Joe's Internet Cafe** (see **Internet**, below), George of **Chatty Cathy's Family Kitchen** (see **Food**, below), and Paula of **Cabinas White House** (see **Accommodations,** below).

Banks: Banco Nacional, in the center of town, across from Chatty Cathy's Family Kitchen. Open M-F 8:30am-3:45pm. **Banco Popular,** 100m south of Banco Nacional. Open M-F 10:45am-5pm, Sa 8am-noon. Both have **24hr. ATMs.**

Western Union: (☎ 643 1102), in the north side of town near La Hacienda, inside Happy Video. Open M-F 9am-12:30pm and 1-3pm, Sa 9am-noon.

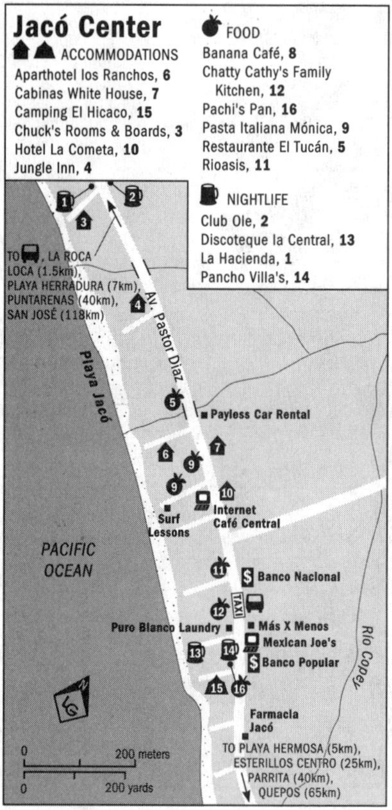

Car Rental: Payless Car Rental (☎ 643 3224), formerly Elegante Rent-a-Car, 325m north of Banco Nacional, across from Restaurante La Ostra. Min. age 23. US$1000 credit card deposit. High season free mileage with minimum 3 day rental; low season no minimum. Cheapest rentals US$42-55 per day. AmEx/DC/MC/V. **Zuma Rent-a-Car** (☎ 643 3207), 150m north of

Jacó Center

🏠 ▲ ACCOMMODATIONS
Aparthotel los Ranchos, **6**
Cabinas White House, **7**
Camping El Hicaco, **15**
Chuck's Rooms & Boards, **3**
Hotel La Cometa, **10**
Jungle Inn, **4**

🍴 FOOD
Banana Café, **8**
Chatty Cathy's Family Kitchen, **12**
Pachi's Pan, **16**
Pasta Italiana Mónica, **9**
Restaurante El Tucán, **5**
Rioasis, **11**

🍸 NIGHTLIFE
Club Ole, **2**
Discoteque la Central, **13**
La Hacienda, **1**
Pancho Villa's, **14**

[Map of Jacó Center showing Pacific Ocean, Playa Jacó, Av. Pastor Díaz, Río Copey, and numbered locations. Directions note: TO LA ROCA LOCA (1.5km), PLAYA HERRADURA (7km), PUNTARENAS (40km), SAN JOSÉ (118km); Payless Car Rental; Surf Lessons; Internet Café Central; Banco Nacional; Puro Blanco Laundry; TAXI; Más X Menos; Mexican Joe's; Banco Popular; Farmacia Jacó; TO PLAYA HERMOSA (5km), ESTERILLOS CENTRO (25km), PARRITA (40km), QUEPOS (65km). Scale: 0 - 200 meters; 0 - 200 yards.]

Banco Nacional inside Centro Comercial el Paso. Drivers 23+. Cars US$215 per week; Jeeps US$309; insurance included. Daily rates available on demand. Open M-Sa 7am-noon and 1-5:30pm. AmEx/D/MC/V. **National Rent-a-Car** (☎ 643 1152), 100m south of Banco Nacional, next to Guacamole. Drivers 23+, but 18-21 year olds can rent by paying double the deposit (US$800-1500). Rates from US$36 per day or US$230 per week. AmEx/D/MC/V.

Supermarket: Más X Menos, just south of Banco Nacional. Open M-Th 8am-9pm, F-Sa 8am-10pm, Su 8am-8pm. AmEx/MC/V.

Laundry: Puro Blanco Laundry, across from Más X Menos. ¢2000 per 5kg. Ironing ¢150 per item. Open daily 8am-6pm. **Aquamatic Lavandería,** 50m south of Banco Nacional. ¢1700 per load. Open M-Sa 7am-noon and 1-5pm. AmEx/MC/V.

Police: (☎ 643 3011 or emergency 117). Walk south along the main road for about 500m past Banco Nacional and turn right when the road forks. The police station is 200m down on a side road to the right.

Red Cross: (☎ 643 3090) 50m south of Banco Popular. Open 24hr.

Pharmacy: Farmacia Jacó (☎ 643 3205), 200m south of Banco Nacional. Open M-Sa 8:30am-9pm, Su 8:30am-7pm.

Medical Services: Clínica de Jacó (☎ 643 1767), a 5min. walk south of town along the main road, near the post office. English spoken. Open M-Th 7am-4pm, F 7am-3pm, Sa and Su emergencies only.

Telephone: Public coin and card phones are all along the main drag; **phone cards** are sold at Más X Menos. **Mexican Joe's Internet Café** (see **Internet,** below) allows international calls (US$1 per 5min. to US, Mexico, Central America, and Canada. US$0.50 per min. to Europe, South America and the Caribbean.

Internet: Mexican Joe's Internet Café, about 125m south of Banco Nacional, is one of the cheapest in town. ¢350 per hr. Open daily 8am-10pm. **Internet Café Central,** in the Centro Comercial El Paso, about 150m north of Banco Nacional. ¢200 per 15min., ¢300 per 30min. Open M-Sa 8am-noon and 1-8pm, Su 8am-noon.

Post Office: Way out on the south side of town, near Hotel Jacó Fiesta. Follow the main road south and make a right in front of the *municipalidad;* turn right on Calle Cocodrilos before the *clínica.* Open M-F 7:30am-6pm, Sa 7:30am-noon.

Postal code: 4023.

ACCOMMODATIONS AND CAMPING

Jacó's main drag is lined with small *cabinas,* the majority with clean and reliable budget to mid-range rooms. A few nicer, more luxurious places cluster at the south end of town. High season rooms fill up quickly, so it's not a bad idea to reserve a few days in advance. In the low season, bargain down the prices for groups and extended stays.

Camping El Hicaco (☎ 643 3070), on the side street 100m south of Banco Nacional, across from Discotheque La Central (see **Nightlife,** below). Surrounded by a fence and guarded during busy times. A shaded yard with showers, toilets, laundry basins, and rickety grills. ¢1000 per person. ❶

Chuck's Rooms and Boards (☎ 643 3328), 700m north of the bridge; turn toward the beach at La Hacienda Restaurant; Chuck's will be on your left. The hundreds of surf-slang bumper stickers are proof that almost all surfers crash here for a night after a rough day on the waves. Relax in the courtyard or rest in the hostel-style rooms. Dorms ¢2700; doubles with private cold bath ¢6000; 1 triple with A/C and private hot-water bath US$30; 1 cabin with full kitchen, A/C, private hot bath, and TV US$50. ❶

Aparthotel los Ranchos (☎ 643 3070), 100m down the first side street south of the bridge, near the beach. A beautiful beachfront complex with private patios, lazy day hammocks, and a fantastic pool attracts a crowd of surfers planning on staying a while. Spacious, apartment style rooms with kitchen, private hot-water bath, and comfy beds. Check-in 2pm. Check-out noon. Laundry ¢50 per item. Discounts available for long stays and low season. Doubles US$40; triples US$45; rooms for 6-7 US$70. MC/V. ❹

Hotel La Cometa (☎ 643 3615), 150m north of Banco Nacional, across from Centro Comercial El Paso. Simple, clean, quiet rooms with fans and hot water in shared or private baths. All rooms share an airy courtyard with hammocks and a kitchen. Singles ¢4500, with private bath ¢7000; doubles ¢5000/¢8000; triples ¢6500/¢9500. ❷

Jungle Inn (☎ 643 1631), 100m south of the bridge on the first street leading west. Colorful jungle murals, a well-kept pool, and Jane/Tarzan themed bathrooms in the courtyard spice up the simple, but spotless, rooms with private hot-water showers. Safe deposit box, night guard, and jacuzzi. Singles/doubles US$25-40. ❸

Cabinas White House (☎ 643 1140), 100m south of the bridge, has enormous rooms with private cold water bath, 2 double beds, couch, fan, and a small fridge. The rooms can get a bit stuffy even with the fans, but the sweet Italian owner Paula will try to make your stay as comfortable as possible. Guests get discounts at a few nearby restaurants for breakfast and lunch. Laundry US$4. Rooms for 1-4 people US$10 per person; larger, fully-equipped apartment for 4 people US$50. ❶

FOOD

A dash of surfer and a pinch of *gringo* (American) flavor most of Jacó's restaurants. That doesn't mean the food is not good, though—just expect to pay a bit more to break away from the staple rice and beans.

🍽 **Pasta Italiana Mónica,** 50m down the second side street south of the bridge. Delicious food made by native Italians. Lasagna night draws a crowd. Classic Italian pastas ¢1300-1700. Open M-Sa noon-2pm and 6-9pm. ❶

🍽 **Chatty Cathy's Family Kitchen,** across the street from Más X Menos, upstairs. Ex-proprietors Rainy and Cathy have passed the torch to friendly owner George, but the sugary, fresh cinnamon buns (¢600) and home style breakfasts (¢1250-2200) haven't lost any of the mouth-watering flavor. Expanding lunch menu. Open M-Th 7am-2pm, although hours may shorten in rainy season and include weekends in high season. ❷

Rioasis, still known by some as its former title Killer Munchies, 25m down the side street just north of Banco Nacional. Whoever dreamed up the toppings on these wood-oven baked pizzas (¢1900 for a medium) was a creative genius. The menu of pastas (¢2000-2500) and Mexican dishes (¢1200-2000) come in huge, well-priced portions. M-Th lunch special (noon-7pm) of salad, ice tea, and personal pizza, pasta, or burrito for ¢1300. M 2-for-1 pizzas, Th 2-for-1 pastas, M-Th 3-for-2 burritos. Open daily noon-11pm; bar open until midnight. ❷

Banana Café, about 80m south of the bridge on the right, serves unique tropical- and Caribbean-influenced rice, seafood, and meat dishes in addition to their famous "natural" American and *típico* breakfasts (¢800-1200). Seafood with *yuca* ¢1200; beef tenderloin in teriyaki garlic sauce ¢3000. Open M-W and F-Su 7am-3pm. ❷

Pachí's Pan, across from Banco Popular, bakes fresh bread and delicious pastries (¢200-300) for breakfast, and satisfying sandwiches (¢500-750) and rich cakes (¢400-600) for lunch or dessert. Open M-Sa 6am-6pm, Su 6am-5pm. ❶

Restaurante El Tucán, just north of the bridge, is a simple *soda* great for filling up on inexpensive and hearty *casados* (¢1000), *gallo pinto* (¢600-800), and rice dishes (¢1500-2000). Open daily 8am-10pm. ❶

OUTDOOR ACTIVITIES AND GUIDED TOURS

Intense Sunset Tours (☎643 1555, fax 643 1222), next to Banco Nacional, has English, Spanish, German, and French guides. Special prices for students and groups. Horseback riding (US$30), canopy tours (US$45), class IV rafting (US$80), Manuel Antonio visits (US$45), and more. Ask for Morris. Open daily 7am-11pm. V.

Green Tours (☎643 2773, 24hr. 643 1936), 50m south of Restaurante Colonial, has a friendly staff and an extensive selection of tours and services. Tours include: horseback riding, canopy tours, kayaking, rafting, sportfishing, and trips to Isla Tortuga, Manuel Antonio, Parque Nacional Carara, and Volcán Arenal. Open daily 7am-8pm.

King Tours (☎643 2441 or 388-7810 24hr.), 150m north of Banco Nacional, arranges well-organized tours that satisfy every wildlife, relaxation or adventure craze. Snorkeling by kayak, Isla Tortuga, rafting, and the waterfall canopy tours, among others. Also rents scooters (US$25 per day) and motorbikes (US$45 per day). Discounts available for groups and those who sign up for more than one tour. Open daily 8am-8pm. V.

Jacó Equestrian Center (☎643 1569), near Payless Rent-a-Car, 325m north of Banco Nacional; follow the signs. Excellent horseback tours to their mountain farm. Fixed morning and afternoon tours available for US$55-65, or design your own. AmEx/MC/V.

Ricaventura (☎/fax 643 1981), just north of Banco Nacional, rents scooters (US$30 per day with US$100 deposit) and motorbikes (US$50 per day with US$300 deposit). Also arranges dirt bike tours (US$80). Open daily 10am-6pm. V.

Cocobolo Souvenirs (☎643 3486), 150m north of Banco Nacional, has the best deals on bike rentals (¢600 per hr., ¢2000 per day), and good prices on surf boards too. Boards ¢3000 per day with ¢10,000 deposit. Open daily 8am-8pm. V.

Pac Moto Rentals (☎643 1310), 200m north of Banco Nacional near Planet Food, fulfills your land and water transportation needs. Bikes ¢2000 per day; scooters US$50 per day; motorbikes US$65 per day; surfboards ¢3000 per day. Open daily 8am-8pm.

▶ BEACHES AND SURFING

Long renowned as one of Costa Rica's most famous surf spots, the waters at and around Jacó have some of the country's most diverse and consistent waves and breaks. Jacó's main beach has gentler waves that break on dark sand, ideal conditions for beginners and intermediates. Experts craving more challenging surf head to the point break in front of the Best Western and **La Roca Loca,** a rocky point with good rights that break over submerged rocks, about 1.5km south of Jacó. La Roca Loca is easily accessible by foot—head south along the beach on the rocks. Just 5km away, **Playa Hermosa** (p. 279) has a challenging beach break also popular with advanced surfers. Farther south of Jacó are **Esterillos Oeste** (see p. 282), **Esterillos Centro** (p. 283), **Esterillos Este** (p. 284), and **Playas Plama, Bandera,** and **Bejuco** (p. 284). North of Jacó is **Boca Barranca** (p. 269). Most of these have good, isolated surf spots where you won't have to wait behind dozens of others to catch a wave.

Dozens of surf shops and surf outfitters line Jacó's main drag, and many report Jacó as one of the cheapest places in Costa Rica to buy new or used **boards.** Some recommended shops are: **Chuck's Chosita del Surf,** next door to La Hacienda Restaurant (☎643 1308; open daily 7:30am-8pm), and **Walter Surf Shop,** across from Cabinas White House (☎643 4080; open daily 8am-8pm). Surfboard virgins aching to ride a wave can take a brief introductory **lesson** from one of many private or group instructors in Jacó. Most lessons include board rental, land and water practice, and a guarantee that you'll stand up at least once on your first day out. Locals recommend **Chuck** from Chuck's Chosita del Surf, and **Gustavo Castillo,** a surfer with 18 years of experience and 4 years on the Costa Rican national team (☎643 3579 or 643 1894). Find Gustavo at the surf shop on the beach 100m down the second side street south of the bridge, near Pasta Italiana Monica. Most lessons run US$35 for 2½-3hr., although individual instructors can adjust the length of the class to your preference.

▶ NIGHTLIFE

Jacó's high season nightlife is serious business, with locals and foreigners packing the clubs and bars from dusk till dawn all week long. Come low season, however, most of the town's hotspots remain relatively empty, save for a handful of surfers and some *ticos* on vacation. Be aware that Jacó has had recent drug problems, and prostitutes linger in many bars.

La Hacienda (☎643 3460), is located 50m north of the bridge, just past the first side street, above the restaurant of the same name. A young trendy crowd meets for pre-salsa drinks and games. You'll find a friendly mix of locals and foreigners playing darts or trying to chat over the blasting rock and reggae. Cover ¢1500. Beer ¢500; 2-for-1 beers M-F till 9pm. Open daily 4pm-2:30am.

Club Ole, across the street from La Hacienda Bar. Classy *salsa* and *merengue* beats draw in both skilled tico dancers and tourists with two left feet. If you fit into the second category, you can always watch from the larch bar and couches surrounding the huge cow in the middle of the club. Cover ¢110. Beer ¢550. Open F-Sa 6:30pm-4am.

Discotheque la Central (☎ 643 3076), 100m down the side street 100m south of Banco Nacional. After 11pm people head to this classic disco/bar. Popular Latin and pop music attract so many people to the spacious hall in the high season that it's best to show up by 10 or 10:30pm. Cover Th-Su ¢800. Open daily 8:30pm-2:30am.

Pancho Villa's, toward the southern end of town, across the street from Mexican Joe's. After the other bars and discos close, a largely male crowd stumbles here for pricey grub and gambling or to use the Internet Café. The late-night/early-morning scene is as packed as it is rough. Appetizers ¢1000-1500; entrees ¢1000-4000; hamburgers ¢738. Open daily 10am-5am.

PLAYA HERRADURA

Not long ago, Playa Herradura, 7km north of Jacó, was little more than a quiet fishing village. Now that it is home to one of Costa Rica's largest and most luxurious resorts, the beach's local feel is showing slight sighs of corporatism. Nevertheless, the secluded beach remains charming in a rural sort of way that is becoming increasingly rare in the country. The easiest way to get to Playa Herradura is to take a **taxi** from Jacó (¢1500). **Buses** running to San José, Puntarenas, or Orotina can drop you off at the turn off to the beach; it's a 3km walk along a paved road. When you're ready to come back, call a taxi.

Anyone seeking a drastic contrast from gringo-filled Jacó will enjoy a quiet daytrip here or a night **camping** on the calm, palm-lined, black sand shore. You can set up your tent for free along the beach or use the campground 100m past the entrance to the beach. (¢1500 per tent. Bathrooms, lights, and electric outlets available.) During the day, keep busy exploring the abandoned crescent-shaped bay, or, during low tide, wade out to nearby **Isla Herradura,** an uninhabited patch of land just a few hundred meters off shore, and take a nap under the shady trees.

Those with more money to spend can splurge on a night at the luxurious **Los Sueños Marriott Ocean and Golf Resort ❺,** or at least participate in some of their activities. Rates in the high season can climb to as much as US$250 for a quad, but during the low season, when standard rooms drop to as little as US$109 including breakfast, spending a night here isn't nearly as impractical. (☎ 630 9000.) For those just visiting Herradura as a day trip and unable to resist the urge to jump into Los Sueños' gleaming 1-acre **pool,** be prepared to pay. The hotel charges US$35 per person for use of the facilities and allows US$20 of that fee to go toward dinner at their classy La Vista restaurant. Other activities include: sportfishing, wave runners, parasailing, banana boat rides, kayaking, boogie boarding, water raft rental, snorkeling, water bike rental, canopy tours, a mangrove and crocodile adventure, horseback riding, tennis courts, golf, and a casino. For cheaper sportfishing you can contact English-speaking **Andrea José,** who leads 4hr. trips with beverages and snacks. (☎ 643 2773. US$250 for 4 people).

A few beachfront restaurants make quiet and pleasant lunch stops. **La Puesta del Sol ❷,** the first place off the road to the beach, serves simple local dishes and always seems to have some *tico* fishermen hanging around for a drink. (*Ensalada de palmito* ¢1200; spaghetti ¢1800-2000. Open daily 11am-midnight.) Just a few meters down the shore is **El Pelícano ❷,** a fancier Mexican joint with killer homemade guacamole and great lunch specials. (Entrees ¢1500-2000. Open daily 10am-10pm.) For the unlucky fisherman who returned to the shore empty-handed, **Marisquería Juanito ❷** is the place to pretend you reeled in the fresh fish and lobster on your plate. (Seafood entrees ¢1400-2500; lobster ¢4900. Open daily 9am-10pm.)

PLAYA HERMOSA

Surfers at Hermosa who never leave will tell you to skip Jacó entirely and head directly to this idyllic miniature surf community. A stark contrast from the upscale beach of the same name in the Nicoya Peninsula, Hermosa is virtual paradise for those seeking long, quiet days, lazing away in hammocks on beachside patios or catching the near-perfect waves that roll onto the long, black-sand beach. After high tide drags back a piece of the shore for the last time each day, the town's sprinkling of locals and a handful of mostly American visitors meet at one of the charming beachfront restaurants or bars to enjoy the evening. Life here is as laid back as the surfers who live in it.

⊫ TRANSPORTATION

Any Quepos-bound **bus** from San José, Puntarenas, Orotina, or Jacó will drop you off in town. (See each town's **Transportation** for bus schedules.) You can also rent a **bike** in Jacó to make the trip (a hilly 30min. ride). Follow the main road to the south end of Jacó and turn right in front of the *municipalidad*. Keep straight for 1km until you reach a fork in the road, where you will turn left. At the next fork shortly after that, turn right away from the gas station. The road will lead you directly there. A slightly more expensive option is to take a **taxi** from Jacó. (☎643 2000, cell 367 9363. ₡1000.) Arrange a time to return or ask a hotel to call one when you're ready. From Hermosa, buses depart in front of Abastecedor La Perla del Mar for **Puntarenas** (2½hr.; 6:30am, noon, 4:30pm; ₡740); **Quepos** (2hr., 8 per day 6:30am-7pm, ₡560); **San José** (3hr., 5 per day 6:30am-5pm, ₡800). Give or take 20min. on all bus departures, and check with locals and hotels for most up-to-date times, as schedules change often.

◆❓ ORIENTATION AND PRACTICAL INFORMATION

Playa Hermosa is 5km south of Jacó and 85km north of Quepos, stretching about 1km along the **Costanera Sur** highway. The main road actually runs northeast-southwest, but all directions here are simplified to north and south. From Jacó, you will ride south into town, passing **Hotel La Terraza del Pacífico** and **Rancho Grande** (at the north end of town). The **supermarket** Abastecedor La Perla del Mar is near the center of town (open M-Sa 7am-8pm, Su 7am-7pm), and **The Backyard Bar** marks the southern end of town. The nearest **banks, pharmacies, clinics, Internet,** and **laundry** are in Jacó. (See **Jacó: Orientation and Practical Information**, p. 273.)

⋔ ACCOMMODATIONS

All accommodations are along the main road facing the beach. Catering to an audience of mostly surfers who often stay for several weeks, most of Hermosa's hotels and cabinas are at the high end of budget to mid-range, and are accordingly more comfortable and equipped than the usual basic places. Nearly all offer discounts in the low season and for extended stays.

▨ **Rancho Grande** (☎643 3529), made of upright wooden logs, is cozy and uniquely decorated like a tree house. Cool rooms are large and have private hot-water bath, but most guests spend their time enjoying the view from the large patio or playing with the friendly owners' adorable children. Communal kitchen available. US$10 per person. ❶

Cabinas Las Olas (☎643 3687), near the center of town, is an amazing value for larger groups planning on staying a while. Wooden ladders grant access to second-floor private bungalows; 3 smaller cabins sleep up to 6 and have small patios and A-frame upstairs lofts. For a real treat, the skybox suite is a luxurious third-story bungalow with a breathtaking view. All rooms have tile floors, private hot-water baths, fans, fridge, and kitchen. A small pool and beach front sitting are perfect for breaks between the tides. Reservations recommended. Singles US$25; doubles US$40; triples US$60; 6 people US$110; large rooms in main building sleeping 4-6 people US$80-90. Significant discounts in low season and for long stays. ❸

Costa Nera Bed and Breakfast (☎ 643 1942), just north of Cabinas Las Olas, has fresh, new rooms with private hot-water bath and a beachfront terrace. Singles US$20; doubles US$30-40; large room with kitchen US$45-55. Discounts for long stays. ❷

Cabinas Vista Hermosa (☎ 643 3422), near the south end of town, offers large, apartment-style suites for two, four, or eight, with a fully equipped kitchen, private bath, and two swimming pools. Singles US$15-20; doubles US$20-25; quads US$35-40; 8 people US$50-60. Good discounts for surfers. ❷

◧ ◪ FOOD AND NIGHTLIFE

As in Jacó, most food at Playa Hermosa is geared towards American visitors.

▨ **Costa Nera,** two doors north of Cabinas Las Olas in the Costa Nera Bed and Breakfast, has a limited menu of authentic, tasty pastas in filling portions. Chef and owner Nada prepares creative bruscetta appetizers with veggies and cheese, all included with every entree. Pastas ¢1800-2300. Open daily 6:45-9pm. ❷

Soda Choy-lin, next to the supermarket, offers simple fare at the cheapest prices. *Gallo pinto* with eggs ¢500; *casado* ¢700. Open daily 7:30am-8:30pm. ❶

Hard Chargers Café, behind Cabinas las Olas, is the big gazebo with a dried palm-leaf roof serving beach bums on a breezy, open porch graced with beautiful ocean views. Delicious American and *tico* breakfasts and Asian-inspired dinners. Banana pancakes ¢1000; dinner plates ¢1500-3400. Open daily 7-9:30am and 7-9:30pm. ❷

The Backyard Bar, restaurant by day, bar and pool hall by night, is the place where surfers and most of the locals congregate when the sun begins to set. Continuously running surf videos and dozens of bronzed, tattooed surfer dudes and bikini-top-clad girls create a scene straight out of southern California. Pizzas ¢1800-3000; beer ¢500. W and F ladies drink free 10pm-midnight. Open bar Sa 9:30-10:30pm. Open daily noon-2am. ❷

◉ ◪ SIGHTS AND GUIDED TOURS

Hermosa's waves might be where most of the action is, but the surrounding forests and tame waters nearby have enough pricey activities to keep non-surfers busy for at least a day or two. However, budget travelers don't have to break the bank to hike the easy **Monkey Trail,** which begins across from Bar Palmeras, past the Jungle Surf Café at the north end of town. And if you're around anytime between July and December, you have a good chance to see the 3000-4000 **Olive Ridley turtles** that emerge from the water to lay their eggs.

▨ **Diana's Trail Rides** (☎ 643 3838), in the stables located on a dirt road 100m past Hotel la Terraza, offers horseback tours on "fat and happy horses." Riders have the option of going to a private waterfall (US$45), the turtle hatchery on the beach (US$45), or the mountain top (US$25), and can also purchase full-day (US$120-200) or week-long packages (US$1200, all included).

Hotel La Terraza del Pacífico (☎ 643 3222 or 643 2441) has a variety of activities for those with a bit more cash to spend. Ask for Randall. Canopy tour US$55, kayak tour with snorkeling US$50, Isla Tortuga tour with snorkeling US$90-100. Surf lessons with Costa Rica national champ US$45. AmEx/D/MC/V.

SURFING

Intermediate and expert surfers swear by Hermosa's perfectly cascading waves, regularly reaching heights of 8-13ft. and breaking powerfully onto the endless black-sand beaches. High tide translates into dozens of skilled surfers in and out of the white wash, but save for a few busy weeks in the high season, you won't have to dodge boards to catch a wave. For a memorable moon-lit ride, inquire at Hotel La Terraza about when they plan to flood-light the waves after dark. The truly expert flock to Hermosa for the annual **surf competition** held by Hotel La Terraza, usually from the first week to the end of May. Those still learning can sign up for a week-long to several-week surfing programs at **Loma del Mar Surf Camp** (☎ 643 1423 or 643 3908), off the road to the left past the restaurants and hotels.

PARRITA

Tiny Parrita bustles with the air of a larger city crammed into barely a 1km stretch of highway. Once dependent on banana production, Parrita has since shifted its economic focus to harvesting the rich oil of the towering African palms that dominate much of the Central Pacific coast. Most travelers just catch a blurred glance of the town's dusty streets and handful of cheap accommodations en route to **Jacó,** 40km north, or **Quepos,** 22km south.

▐ TRANSPORTATION. To get to Parrita from Quepos (45min. ¢155), take any **bus** bound for **Jacó** (4:30, 10:30am, 3pm); **Parrita** (7 per day 5am-4pm); or **San José** indirect (5, 8am, 2, 4pm). From Jacó, take a bus to **Quepos** and have the driver let you off in Parrita (1hr.; 6am, noon, 4, 6pm; ¢200). From Parrita, buses pass through on their way to **Puntarenas** (3hr.; 5:30, 8:30, 11:30am, 4pm; ¢460). **Taxis** in and around Parrita can be reached at ☎ 779 9023.

▐ PRACTICAL INFORMATION. You can stock up on groceries at **Palí Supermarket.** (Open M-Th 8:30am-7pm, F-Sa 8am-8pm, Su 8:30am-6pm.) Exchange dollars and travelers checks at **Banco Nacional** near the south end of town. (Open M-F 8:30am-3:45pm.)

▐▐ ACCOMMODATIONS AND FOOD. When it comes to lodging, the best value in town is the **Hotel Río Lindo ❶,** 100m north of the Musmanni Bakery on the main road. The simple rooms have bright pink walls, clean, cold-water baths, and fans. Some have fridge and cable TV at no extra cost. Guests also have access to a communal kitchen. (☎ 799 8306. ¢2000 per person.) **Cabinas Parrita ❷,** near Banco Nacional at the south end of town, charges a bit more for blue-tiled rooms with comfy beds, private cold water bath, cable TV, A/C, and fan. (☎ 799 8346. Singles ¢4000, doubles ¢5000.) **Bar y Restaurante Parrita ❶,** attached to Cabinas Parrita, serves cheap *casados* (¢950-1100) and beer (¢450) to a friendly local contingent. If you're not in the mood for another *casado*, head to **Pizza Gabriel ❶,** near the center of the strip, for steamy cheese pies. They'll even deliver to your *cabina*. (☎ 777 1085. Burgers ¢500-1100; pastas ¢850-1850; personal pizzas start at ¢1350. Open M-F 2-10pm, Sa and Su 10am-10pm.)

▐ BEACHES. From Parrita, a 5km taxi ride (¢500-800) heading south along a bumpy road and passing more African palm plantations leads to **Isla Palo Seco,** (locally called **Playa Mar y Sol**), a 14km black sand beach lined by sparse palms. The often strong **rip tide** is more ideal for surfing or body boarding than swimming, so the few local *tico* families that visit spend most of their time picnicking on the beach or exploring the tangled mangrove swamps just beyond the sandy shores. Isla Palo Seco remains an extremely quiet, secluded beach with a distinctive jungle feel and would be enjoyed most by nature enthusiasts who have cars, since there are no bus stops or facilities (save for a sporadically open restaurant with bathrooms, ¢100). **Beso del Viento ❸**, a luxury French-run villa just 100m east of the road to the beach, accommodates road-weary travelers who want to get away from it all. Cabins are spacious, classy, and private, with access to the hotel's pool and kayak rental service. Some have full kitchens. (☎779 9674. Singles and doubles US$50; triples US$60.) Travelers can **camp** for free on the beach.

SOUTH OF JACÓ TO QUEPOS

The well-paved Costanera Sur Hwy. curves along the Central Pacific Coast, south of Jacó to Quepos, passing many quiet, deserted beaches short turn-offs from the highway. The tiny beach communities can barely be called towns, as almost none have services, and feel fantastically remote and relaxing as a result. The beaches draw vacationing *tico* families and some local surfers during the Christmas holidays and Semana Santa, but otherwise the long, pristine beaches and their powerful waves are yours to discover. Surfing is good at several of these beaches, especially Esterillos Oeste and Playa Bejuco, where big waves break on soft, white sand. Conditions are generally similar to those at Playa Heremosa. The following beaches are listed in the order they appear from Jacó to Quepos.

◪ PLAYA ESTERILLOS OESTE

The first major beach south of Jacó is Esterillos Oeste, 22km south along the Costanera and 47km north of Quepos. The beach here is long and crisp with perfect waves and a wide shore; it recently earned a "blue flag" for meeting rigid ecological standards. Life here is incredibly laid-back. Plenty of accommodations provide lodging for a variety of budgets. Camping is not allowed on the beach.

▦ ORIENTATION. Esterillos is actually split into two small communities; one sits at the end of the first entrance, while the other is at the end of a second entrance separated by a 500m walk south along the beach. Esterillos Oeste is the most developed of the beaches between Jacó and Quepos.

▮ ACCOMMODATIONS. One of the best values in town is **Bar/Restaurante/ Cabinas Las Brisas ❶**, just north of the second entrance on the beach. The rooms are simple, private huts with cement floors and cold-water showers. A few cabins are cleaner with tile floors and full kitchens. (☎778 8059. Quads ¢6000; equipped 6-person cabins ¢15,000.) The nicest place to stay is **La Sirena ❷**, about 400m north of the first entrance, on the beach; look for the large siren statue in the ocean in front of the hotel. The rooms are large and cheery with sun-orange exteriors and wood panelled interiors. TV, private hot-water bath, and plenty of fans. Guests also have access to the large pool (¢1000 for non-guests), foosball and pool tables, and a breezy, open-air bar/restaurant. (☎778 8020. Quads with A/C ¢17,400; 8-person rooms with kitchen ¢23,200.) Another popular option is **Cabinas Don José ❶**, 100m north of the bus stop. The owner maintains strict rules about visitation, and the grounds resembles somewhat of a weathered cement park, but the simple rooms are nice enough and extremely inexpensive for large groups. All have private cold-water bath, cement floors, fridge, kitchen, and fan. (Doubles ¢4000; 6-person rooms ¢6000; 8-person rooms ¢16,000; 10-person rooms ¢20,000.) One of the newest places in town is **Walt-Paraiso ❸**, 350m down the second entrance to Esterillos. Rooms are modern and massive, with tile floors, huge closets, private hot-water baths, and a couple of fans. (☎778 8060. Quads or quints US$60.) Anyone planning a long stay should check out **Cabinas Don Joaquín ❸,** which rents out eight fully-equipped rooms sleeping up to four or eight people. Rooms have private cold-water bath, kitchen, and fans. Two simpler rooms are available for shorter stays. (☎887 7230. Simple rooms ¢1500 per person; equipped quads ¢35,000 per month; equipped 8-person rooms ¢45,000 per month.)

⬛⬛ FOOD AND ENTERTAINMENT. Several good *sodas*, restaurants, and bars are near the beach. **Bar y Restaurante Las Brisas ❶,** at the *cabinas* of the same name, has standard *típico* fare at low prices. (*Gallo pinto* ¢550; *casados* ¢800; rice dishes ¢800-1500; omelets ¢1000. Open daily 7am-7pm.) **Bar y Restaurante Oleaje ❷,** 150m before the beach on the first entrance, has a flavorful atmosphere with ox-cart tables, a colorful bar, and delicious *típico*, Mexican, and American food with lots of vegetarian options. (Burgers ¢800-1100; heart of palm salad ¢1800; filet mignon ¢3000. Open daily 10am-11pm or when the crowds leave.) **Bar y Restaurante Barilito ❶,** at the end of the second entrance, on the beach, is a popular nighttime hangout with outdoor seating and simple food. When the crowds pick up, music blasts from the speakers inside, locals and visitors belt out karaoke (F-Su), and everyone gets their toes tapping and hips shaking. (*Casados* ¢900; fish entrees ¢1000-1300; rice dishes ¢1100-1200. Open daily in high season 7am-11pm; in low season 11am-11pm.) Once Barilito dies down, people usually head to **Costa Brava,** at the end of the first entrance, where dancing and karaoke continue late into the night. (Beer ¢350. Open 7pm until the crowds leave; mostly open on weekends in high season, sometimes in low season.) A slightly classier haunt is **Shake ❷,** about 500m north of the first entrance, on the beach. The bar sits one story above beach level and has a pleasant outdoor sitting area that hosts an older crowd. (*Ceviche* ¢1200; burgers ¢1300; spaghetti ¢1300; shrimp ¢3800; beer ¢500. W karaoke; Th romantic music and cocktails; F Mexican night with half-priced tequila; Sa Happy Hour with live music and girl dancers; Su tropical music and drinks. Open daily 10am-midnight or 1am.)

◤ PLAYA ESTERILLOS CENTRO

This is perhaps the most deserted of the Esterillos trio, located 3km south of Oeste and 25km south of Jacó. Any Jacó-Quepos **bus** will drop you off at the entrance to the tiny neighborhood, a 200m walk from the beach. The beach here is pretty and calm, but not good for surfing, and the sprinkling of visitors here are mostly vacationing *tico* families that come for at least a week at a time. Consequently, accommodations are rather pricey for single travelers and couples.

The nicest place to stay is French-Canadian-run **Auberge la Felicidad ❸,** on the beach. From the main entrance, follow the gravel path into town 200m, turn right and go another 200m. Turn left to the beach; the hotel is 100m down on your left. Homey, clean rooms have nicely painted walls, hard wood floors, private hot-water baths, and decorative touches like fruit baskets. Restaurant, laundry, and international telephone available. (☎778 8123. Breakfast US$3; lunch and dinner US$5; beer ¢450. Restaurant open daily 8am-8pm. Doubles with kitchen US$32, in high season US$40. Doubles without kitchen US$20/US$25. US$5 per additional person.) Another nice place near the beach is **Villarce ❶,** with three fully-equipped duplex rooms. Private cold-water baths, kitchens, tile floors, and plenty of hammocks and little pools to relax outside. (☎446 5052; ask for Martín García. 8-person rooms ¢16,000, in high season ¢20,000). **Cabinas Isabel ❷,** just off the main entrance, is cheapest for smaller groups. The two *cabinas* are fully equipped with kitchen, fan, two bedrooms with beds for up to five people, and private cold-water baths. (☎778 8207. Rooms ¢8000.)

◪ PLAYA ESTERILLOS ESTE

Another 5km south of Esterillos Centro is Esterillos Este, a charming but equally small beach village with few accommodations, no services, and a boundless white-sand beach prime for exploring and napping. Be careful in the water, however, as the tides are often extremely strong and the waves large and powerful. The southern end of the beach experienced significant erosion in 2000, but as of February 2001, strong ocean currents were beginning to restore the sand. **Buses** drop passengers off at the entrance to the village.

Travelers seeking luxury and indulgent services can't miss charming ◪**Auberge du Pelican ❸**, a perfect country style inn. To get there, walk down the gravel path from the main entrance of the beach and turn left at the dead end near the airstrip. The hotel is another 500m down on your right. The two-story building has screens instead of walls, granting perfect views of the beach, just 50m away. Ten rooms, two with wheelchair access, are classically decorated with calming blue walls, fan, and comfortable beds with romantic sheer canopies. Upstairs is a pleasant sitting area to read or just watch the waves, while downstairs in the dining area, the French-Canadian owners whip up elegant and tasty meals. Outside is a pool, plenty of beach chairs, a relaxing swing, and a pretty garden. (☎778 8105. Singles with shared hot water-bath US$25; doubles US$35, with private bath US$45. Fully-furnished 4-person apartment US$350 per month.) Another option is **Caiman Inn ❷**, 200m south of Auberge du Pelican, with three large but simple carpeted and air conditioned rooms with clean hot-water bath and fridge. The owner can arrange a private taxi on request. (☎778 8125. Rooms sleeps 5 or 6 people US$40.)

◪ PLAYAS PALMA, BANDERA, AND BEJUCO

Further south of Jacó and inching toward Quepos are three, even more unfrequented beaches. The sand darkens and coconut palms and *almendro* trees thicken the vegetation. Fishing and swimming are popular with *tico* families that have beach houses here and foreigners, who are making a significant presence in the small village life. All have decent **surfing** conditions when the swells pick up. At **Playa Bejuco**, stay at **Hotel El Delfin ❹**, an elegant but cozy place whose 14 rooms have private hot-water baths, a private balcony, A/C, and all the little extra touches to make your stay luxurious. (☎770 8308 or 771 1640. Doubles US$50.) **Playa Palma,** a 7km shady beach which ends at Playa Bandera, is a bit more popular with surfers and has more of a small town atmosphere than the other two. **Cabinas Maldonado ❶** is good for groups planning to stay a while. The six huge cabins sleep six to ten people and have full kitchen, private bath, and fan. Guests can also use the pool, jacuzzi, and outside grill. (☎286 1116. Cabins US$50.) **Las Brisas ❶**, at **Playa Bandera,** is the cheapest, most basic option. (☎779 9238. ₡2000 per person.)

QUEPOS

Three and a half hours south of San José, the city of Quepos is one of the Central Pacific's most well-trodden destinations, not so much because it has anything of real interest to see, but rather for its proximity to tourist-magnet Parque Nacional Manual Antonio and the dozens of tour operators who run adventure trips into the raging rivers and wild mountain terrain just outside town. Tourism has definitely jump-started the economy here; sportfishing easily rakes in more money than the banana crops on which the town once depended, and the zig-zagging rows of African palms along the coast are quickly forgotten en route to raftable rivers and canopy tours. The streets are often deserted during the day when travelers are out

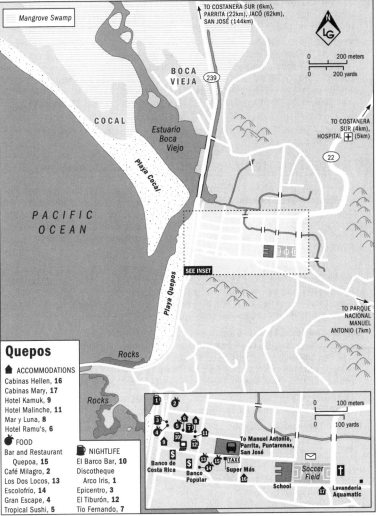

Quepos

🛏 ACCOMMODATIONS
Cabinas Hellen, **16**
Cabinas Mary, **17**
Hotel Kamuk, **9**
Hotel Malinche, **11**
Mar y Luna, **8**
Hotel Ramu's, **6**

🍴 FOOD
Bar and Restaurant
  Quepoa, **15**
Café Milagro, **2**
Los Dos Locos, **13**
Escolofrío, **14**
Gran Escape, **4**
Tropical Sushi, **5**

🍸 NIGHTLIFE
El Barco Bar, **10**
Discotheque
  Arco Iris, **1**
Epicentro, **3**
El Tiburón, **12**
Tío Fernando, **7**

exploring, but come sunset, doors and windows open up everywhere, and the chatter of an upbeat population mixes with the relaxing beat of music: the perfect accompaniment to a nice cold beer. If adventure tours don't fit in your budget, Manuel Antonio is a relaxing escape, and Quepos is a convenient base with more budget accommodations.

▧ TRANSPORTATION

Flights: Sansa (30min.; high season 6 per day 7:45am-4:25pm, return 6 per day 8:30am-5:10pm; low season 4 per day 7:40am-1pm, return 4 per day 8:20am-1:40pm;

US$44) and **Travelair** (30min.; high season 6 per day 6am-4pm, return 6 per day 6:35am-4:40pm; low season 4-5 per day 6am-2pm, return 4-5 per day 6:35am-2:35pm; US$45) fly out of San José (see p. 85) and arrive at the airstrip 5km northwest of town.

Buses: From **San José,** buses depart from Calle 16, Av. 1/3. (Direct 3½ hr.; daily 6am, noon, 6, 7:30pm. Indirect 5hr., M-F 5 per day 7am-5pm, ¢1230.) Only direct buses continue to **Manuel Antonio.** From the main bus station in Quepos, buses go to **Manuel Antonio** (25min, about every 30min. 5:30am-9:30pm, ¢80); **Parrita** (45min., 7 per day 5am-4pm, ¢155); **Puntarenas** (4hr.; 4:30, 7:30, 10:30am, 3pm; ¢800); via **Jacó** (2hr.; 4:30, 10:30am, 3pm; ¢660); **San José** (direct; 6:15, 9:30am, noon, 5pm; ¢1665; indirect; 5, 8am, 2, 4pm; ¢1300).

Taxis (☎ 777 1207) line up across the street from the bus station. A taxi to Manuel Antonio should cost ¢1000.

◼◼ ❼ ORIENTATION AND PRACTICAL INFORMATION

Quepos is 144km southeast of San José, 65km south of Jacó, and 7km north of **Parque Nacional Manuel Antonio.** No one knows or uses the street names here, but most hotels, restaurants, and services cluster around the few main streets. The bus station marks the center of town; with your back to it, facing the supermarket, the beach is to your right (west), and the soccer field and road to Manuel Antonio are two and three blocks to your left (east).

Banks: Banco Popular, 100m south of the southwest corner of the bus terminal. Open M-F 8:15am-3:30pm, Sa 8:15-11:30am. For shorter lines, try **Banco de Costa Rica,** 100m east of the bus station. Open M-F 8am-5pm, Sa 9am-1pm. Both have Plus/V ATMs. **Lynch Travel** (☎ 777 1170), near Restaurante El Pueblo, west of the bus station, exchanges US dollars and traveler's checks. Open daily 7am-6pm.

English Bookstore: La Buena Nota (☎ 777 1002), in Manuel Antonio, 750m northeast of Restaurante Mar y Sombra near Cabinas Piscis. Large selection of American magazines and English-language used books. Open daily 9am-6pm. A small but conveniently located used book selection is at **Café Botánico,** 100m west of the southwest corner of the bus station, across from Hotel Kamuk. Open M-Sa 8:30am-6:30pm.

Supermarkets: Head across the street from the bus station to **Super Más** for groceries. Open M-Sa 7:30am-8pm, Su 7am-noon. AmEx/MC/V.

Laundry: Lavandería Aquamatic (☎ 777 0972), 100m west of the southwest corner of the soccer field. Self-service wash (¢750) and dry (¢750), or have it done for you (¢900). Open M-Sa 8am-5pm. AmEx/MC/V.

Car Rental: Elegante/Payless Rent-a-Car (☎ 777 0015), 150m west of the southwest corner of the soccer field, just past the lavandería. Drivers 23+. US$1500-2000 credit card deposit required. Open M-Sa 7:30am-5:30pm. AmEx/D/DC/MC/V. **Alamo** (☎ 777 3344), on the east side of the soccer field. Rents to 21 year olds with a min. US$1000 credit card deposit, and to 18-20 year olds for at least double the deposit. Open daily 7:30am-6pm.

Police: Organización de Investigación Judicial (OIJ; ☎ 777 0511), 100m behind the bus station. Open 24hr.

Pharmacy: Farmacia Catedral (☎ 777 0527), across from the bus station. Open daily 8am-8pm. AmEx/D/MC/V.

Medical Services: Red Cross (☎ 777 0116, emergency 128), 25m east of the bus station. Open 24hr. The **hospital** (☎ 777 0922), about 4km northeast of town on the Costanera Sur Hwy., is reachable by buses to Silencio and Londres (5-10min., M-F 5am-10pm, ¢60). Taxi ¢1000.

Public Phones: across from the bus terminal. The supermarket and pharmacy sell phone cards.

Internet: Quepos Diner, 75km west of the southwest corner of the soccer field, has the best deals. ¢300 per 20min., ¢600 per hr. Open daily 10am-10pm. **Internet Café,** 50m west and 50m north of the southwest corner of the bus station, across from Hotel Pueblo, has similar prices. ¢10 per min., ¢600 per hr. Open M-Sa 9am-11pm.

Post Office: Facing the soccer field on the north side. **Fax** available. Open M-F 7:30am-6pm, Sa 7:30am-noon.

Postal Code: 6350.

ACCOMMODATIONS

Budget accommodations are more plentiful and less touristy in Quepos than in Manuel Antonio, making it a nice, albeit less scenic base, for visits to the park and beaches. The basic places are pretty similar—simple, with cold water—but some offer more appealing common areas. Location is key: Mar y Luna, Ramus, and Malinche are closer to a bar, while Cabinas Helen and Cabinas Mary are in quieter parts of town, so decide if you want to make noise or avoid it.

Mar y Luna (☎ 777 0394). With your back to the bus station, walk right to the end of the block, turn right, and then left at the next corner; Mar y Luna is a few meters down to the right. Friendly and helpful owner Alvaro maintains plain fan-cooled rooms in cheerily painted hallways with super clean bathrooms. The best features are the common area with TV, the upstairs balcony, and the small courtyard where breakfast is served. Laundry ¢650 per kilo. Singles ¢2000; doubles with private bath ¢4500; triples ¢6000. ❶

Hotel Malinche (☎ 777 0093), across from Mar y Luna. Larger, modern rooms have efficient fans, furniture, and big clean, cold-water private baths. Credit card phone available in lobby. The Barco Bar next door can be a bit noisy. Singles ¢3500; doubles ¢7000; triples ¢10,300; quads and quints ¢13,500. ❶

Hotel Ramu's (☎ 777 0245), a few doors down from Mar y Luna, across from Barco Bar. The hallways are a bit dark, but the small bedrooms are clean and have two fans. ¢2000 per person. ❶

Cabinas Mary (☎ 777 0128), on the main road across from the soccer field, is for those who prefer to be away from the noisy bars. Clean rooms have powerful fans and private cold-water baths. Parking available. ¢2000 per person in rooms for up to 4 people. ❶

Cabinas Hellen (☎ 777 0504), 150m west of the soccer field on the main drag. Clean rooms with fridge and private cold-water baths in the yard of a friendly family. Chat up the parrots in the courtyard. Singles ¢5000; doubles ¢6500. ❷

Hotel Kamuk (☎ 777 0811), 150m west of the bus station. Part of the Best Western chain, Kamuk lacks flair, but is a good option for those seeking a cushier stay. All rooms come with A/C, cable TV, wall-to-wall carpeting, and some of the hottest, most powerful showers around. A nice pool, two small restaurants, casino, and sitting area to boot. Breakfast included. Laundry ¢700/kg. Check-out noon. Doubles US$30, high season US$60; quads US$80-90. 17% tax not included. AmEx/D/MC/V. ❷

FOOD

Not surprisingly, restaurants in Quepos specialize in Tex-Mex, American-style breakfasts, and seafood and are subsequently pricier than the standard *típico* fare. You can find cheaper meals at the *sodas* near the bus station.

Escalofrío, on the street just west of the bus station, next door to Los Dos Locos. Fabulously tasty and authentic Italian cuisine seem strangely out of place in this casual, gringoized restaurant twinkling with Christmas lights, but who cares. Five types of bruchetta (¢600-900); pasta (¢1400-1800); gnocchi (¢1800); huge pizzas (¢1300-1800). Save room for the light and creamy *gelato* dessert (¢400). Open Tu-Su 2:30-10:30pm. ❶

Tropical Sushi, right by Hotel Ramu's and across from El Barco Bar, serves Costa Rica's freshest seafood in some way other than ceviche or filet. An English menu carefully describing every dish makes choosing and ordering especially easy for non-Spanish speaking sushi virgins. Veggie tempura ¢1200; California rolls ¢1300-1800; sushi box ¢2750-3500; sashimi dinner ¢4500. Open M and W-Su 5pm-1am. AmEx/D/MC/V. ❸

Gran Escape, 100m north and 100m west of the southwest corner of the bus station. Travelers congregate at this legendary seafood restaurant to swap fishing stories before or after getting on the boat. The fresh fish is fantastic, and the burgers are as creative as they are filling (jurassic park burger ¢2500). Also serves a good variety of Mexican dishes (fajitas ¢2000-3750) and tasty cocktails in yard glasses (margaritas ¢3000-4000). Kitchen open 7am-10pm; bar open until midnight. AmEx/MC/V. ❸

Los Dos Locos, 50m west of the southwest corner of the bus station. High-priced Mexican favorites. They'll cook your catch. Sip a margarita (¢950 per glass, ¢3750 per pitcher) and people-watch from the open-air dining area. Live *tico* music W 7pm and F 5pm. Banana pancakes ¢1150; burrito ¢1900; taco plate ¢2500; fajitas ¢3100. Open M-Sa 7am-11pm, Su 11am-9pm. 6% surcharge with V. ❸

Bar Restaurante Quepoa, across the street form the bus station. One of the few places in town that serves good, authentic *típico* fare. Locals gather here for filling rice dishes (¢1350-2400) and chicken platters (¢1150-2000) before belting out tunes at karaoke (W and F 9pm-1am). Beer ¢400. Open daily 8am-1am. ❶

Café Milagro, 100m west and 100m north of the northwest corner of the soccer field. When the rainstorms hit, take shelter with a cup o' joe at Milagro. Cappuccino ¢500. Tasty, over-priced pastries (muffins ¢500). They sell US newspapers and magazines and feature a CD listening station. Open daily 6am-10pm; in low season 6pm. ❷

⚠ 🏊 OUTDOOR ACTIVITIES AND GUIDED TOURS

The only reason tourists spend an afternoon in Quepos is to make plans for an outing—the surrounding environs offer numerous tempting options, including rafting, canopy tours, mangrove exploration, and some of Costa Rica's best sportfishing. Plan ahead and bring your checkbook—most of them will make a pretty sizable dent in any budget traveler's wallet.

Iguana Tours (☎ 777 1262 or 777 2052; iguana@sol.racsa.co.cr), at the southeast corner of the soccer field. Arranges hiking and horseback tours of Parque Nacional Manuel Antonio (US$37), boat trips to Damas Island (US$60), and kayaking tours (US$65). Experienced guides specialize in rafting trips on Ríos Naranjo, Parrita, and Savegre (US$65-90). Prices for full-day trips include a rescue kayaker paddling alongside you at all times. Second location at Manuel Antonio (☎ 777 2746). Open daily 7am-7pm.

High Tec Sportfishing and Tours (Business hours ☎777 3465, 24hr. 388 6617), on the east side of the street that passes the bus station, across from the soccer field. Eight different boats, so you're almost guaranteed one that fits your budget. Generally has the cheapest trips. Also offers other water-oriented excursions. Half-day in-shore fishing US$296, half-day off-shore fishing US$345. Student and senior discounts.

Blue Water Sportfishing (☎ 777 1596 or 390 6759; www.sportfishingcostarica.com). Experienced captains will welcome you aboard one of two fully equipped, custom-crafted boats to catch yellowfish tuna, snook, snapper, and more. Half-day US$550-650 for up to 4 people. Fees do not include US$15 per person fishing license.

Bluefin Sportfishing Charter and Tours (☎ 777 2222 or 398 2222; www.bluefinsport-fishing.com). Three high-tech boats from 26 ft. to 33 ft. leave on 4, 6, and 8hr. trips at 7, 7:30am, and 1pm. Inshore starts at US$360 for 4hr. for 5-6 people. Fees do not include US$15 fishing license. Open M-Sa 7am-6pm, Su 7am-noon.

Costa Rican Dreams (☎ 777 0593), next to Café Milagro, offers rafting (US$65), canopy safaris ($65), boat trips (US$450), massages (US$60), horseback tours to a waterfall (US$55), mangrove tours (US$60), sailboat trips (US$69), and diving. Group and low season discounts. Reserve in advance in high season. Open daily 7am-6pm.

Estrella Tour, (☎/fax 777 1286; estrellatour@hotmail.com), facing Hotel El Pueblo on the street west of the bus station, specializes in mountain biking with highly skilled guides and good equipment. Trips range from half-day (US$39) and full day (US$89) rides to hardcore 5-day adventures (US$520, food and lodging included), with varied difficulty levels. Open M-Sa 8:30am-12:30pm and 3-7pm, high season 8:30am-8pm.

Mar Alva Sportfishing Charters (☎ 777 2522, 24hr. 777 2423; maralva2000@hotmail.com). Two fully equipped boats. Reel in sailfish, mahi-mahi, mackerel, hammer jack, and much more. Starting at US$450 for half-day. Open daily 7am-5pm.

Lynch Travel (☎ 777 1170 or 777 0161; fax 777 1571; lyntur@racsa.co.cr). Airport transfers, sportsfishing US$350, rafting US$75, kayaking US$65, and more. Also books airline tickets. Open daily 7am-6pm.

Fourtrax Adventure (☎ 777 1829), near the southeast corner of the soccer field, 50m past the lavandería. Offers exhilarating full-day ATV tours (US$95) to the town of Londres in the mountains. Open daily 7am-9pm.

Pacific EcoTours Corporation S.A (☎ 777 3030 or 777 1924; www.canyoning-tours.com/dreamforest). Excellent canopy tours on steel cables hovering over 100ft. above the forest floor and extending up to 600m between trees (US$60). The more daring should try their canyoning tour (US$60), a thrilling experience descending and ascending rushing cascades with safety lines and belts. Includes breakfast, lunch, drinks, and transportation.

Amigos del Río (☎ 777 0082; www.amigosdelrio.com), 2km from Quepos along the road to Manuel Antonio. This reputable company specializes in ocean kayaking (half-day US$65) and rafting trips (half-day US$65, full day US$90) on the Class III-IV Río Naranjo. Price include meals, snacks, and transport to and from hotel.

Rainmaker Conservation Project (☎ 777 3565 or 777 3566; www.rainmakercostarica.com). Quepos office located on the street just north of the bus station near the small Iguana Tours office. The Project is 22km from Quepos in the Fila Chonta Mountain Range. This reserve is one of the last bits of primary rainforest in the Central Pacific area. Its 1530 acres are home to 70% of all the flora and fauna species in Costa Rica. The project's primary focus is a series of five **canopy bridges,** one of which is Central America's highest (250 ft.) and longest (270 ft.). Built with minimum damage to the forest, the bridge system affords unparalleled views of the surrounding tree tops, as picturesque streams and waterfalls rush below. After descending the hundreds of stairs back to the forest floor, you can explore several **trails** of varying lengths and difficulties, all with informative postings about the different plants and animals. One trail winds along the Río Seco, ending at a sparkling river-fed pool where you can jump in and cool off. The reserve can only be visited on an organized tour (4½hr., US$65 per person), which includes transportation to and from Quepos or Manuel Antonio, light refreshments, lunch, and a bilingual naturalist guide. Call the office or stop by to make a reservation.

NIGHTLIFE

For a fairly small city, Quepos has quite a few bars and clubs, which get packed with locals and tourists in the high season. In the rainy months, however, most places remain relatively mellow, ideal for a quiet drink or an audible conversation.

El Barco Bar, 100m west of the bus station. Sports fans flock to watch any sporting event in this chill bar and restaurant. The stereo lets loose with jazz, reggae, and country on the weeknights, while local bands perform on most weekends in the high season. They'll cook your catch for ¢2000. Tex-Mex, burgers, seafood, and steak. Beer ¢450. Open W-F 4pm-2am, Sa-Su noon-2am.

Discotheque Arco Iris, 100m west and 300m north of the northwest corner of the bus station, one block after the bridge out of Quepos. *Salsa, merengue,* and reggae beats get bodies moving. Beer ¢450; F cover ¢300, Sa ¢500. Open W-Su 10pm-2:30am.

El Tiburón, on the street just west of the bus station, is marked by a shark sign on a second story. The upstairs balcony overlooking the street is the perfect place to get away from the crowds and people-watch over a nutella crepe (¢350) or the popular blue margarita (¢1400). Open daily 6pm-1am.

Epicentro, 100m north and 100m west of the southwest corner of the soccer field, next to Gran Escape. Where the younger crowd gathers to share adventure stories. Their foam parties attract locals and travelers that revel in suds and techno. Happy Hour 5-7pm. Beer ¢300. Ladies' night W. Open bar F 9-11pm. Open daily 4pm until late.

Tío Fernando, between Hotels Ramu's and Mar y Luna. A neighborhood bar particularly popular with older male *ticos,* but suiting for those who like a quieter atmosphere. Beer ¢350. Open M-Sa 11am-midnight, Su 3pm-midnight.

PARQUE NACIONAL MANUEL ANTONIO

Parque Nacional Manuel Antonio offers the perfect combination of Costa Rica's best terrains: warm, jade-green waves lap at the roots of a lush tropical forest. *Ticos* treasure it, and almost all tourists stop here. Despite government efforts to regulate hotel development and pollution, litter, traffic, and car exhaust are threatening the once pristine park. With families toting beach chairs and picnic coolers along the trails and souvenir shops lining the streets, the national park is gaining a somewhat family-vacation feel, but that doesn't make the setting any less incredible: birds fill the trees with color, iguanas and spider squirrels dodge your feet, and armadillos and agoutis amble along in the underbrush. An encounter with the park's most outgoing inhabitants, the white-faced monkeys, is virtually guaranteed. They have neither fear nor shame: they'll snag your snacks, ham it up for your camera, and toss mangoes at your head all in the span of a minute. Their favorite hang-out is on the sands of the park's four spectacular beaches, all of which are easily accessible by path (or tree branch). As a result of tourists carelessly feeding the wildlife (and consequently disrupting their natural behaviors and instincts), the monkeys are especially responsive to gloating humans. Please refrain from feeding any of the animals.

ORIENTATION AND TRANSPORATION

Parque Nacional Manuel Antonio is located 7km south of Quepos and is surrounded by its own little town. From Quepos, the **bus** (25min., every 30min. 5:30am-9:30pm, ¢80) will drop you off at the stop at a T intersection. From here, you'll see a street leading east, marked by the Restaurante Merlin on the left; many budget and mid-range accommodations are on this street. The direct buses from San José to **Quepos** also continue to Manuel Antonio (3½hr.; 6am, noon, 7:30pm). A **taxi** from Quepos should cost ¢1000.

AT A GLANCE

AREA: 683 hectares on land, 55 on water.

CLIMATE: Tropical humid.

FEATURES: Punta Catedral Peninsula, Playa Espadilla, Playa Espadilla Sur, Playa Manuel Antonio, Playa Escondida.

HIGHLIGHTS: Hiking the numerous trails, canopy tours, parasailing, kayaking, diving, snorkeling.

GATEWAYS: Quepos (p. 284).

FEES AND RESERVATIONS: US$7.

PRACTICAL INFORMATION

WHEN TO GO. Manuel Antonio is one of Costa Rica's most visited national parks, so if you want the beaches and trails to yourself and don't mind overcast skies, come during the rainy (read low) season, when not as many people are on vacation. Bring light clothes, comfortable shoes, sunscreen, and water.

The **park entrance** and **ranger station** are about 1km down the road in front of the bus stop. English-speaking **guides** are available at the ranger station and can help you spot the more elusive wildlife; however, they are definitely not necessary to see the animals or enjoy short hikes. (US$15 for 2hr. Park open Tu-Su 7am-4pm. Entrance fee US$7. Park map ¢300.) In an emergency, call the **police station** (☎777 0196). Other services and conveniences can be found in **Quepos.**

ACCOMMODATIONS

Staying in Quepos is cheaper than in the small and touristy town of Manuel Antonio, but isn't as convenient or scenic. **Camping** is not allowed.

Albergue y Travotel Costa Linda (☎777 0304), on a side road a couple hundred meters up the road to the ranger station, is an inviting backpacker crash pad. Basic rooms are bright and clean with double beds and fans. The common area is great for lounging and meeting other travelers, and the owner is knowledgeable about the area. Situated in an open courtyard, the common cold-water baths are plentiful but lack privacy. Laundry ¢200 per item. The attached restaurant serves good breakfasts of *gallo pinto* and fruit pancakes. Singles US$8; doubles US$14; triples US$18; quads US$20. ❶

Cabinas Ramírez (☎777 5044), a short walk back in the direction of Quepos just 80m from the beach, past Restaurant Mar y Sombra. Three basic rooms with private cold-water baths surround a flowery garden. Singles and doubles ¢8000; triples ¢9500. ❶

Cabinas Irarosa (☎777 5084), all the way up the main road near the park entrance and ranger station, is another good budget option. Basic rooms with shared cold-water bath. TV and private hot-water shower also available. Basic rooms US$8 per person; singles with TV and hot shower US$18; doubles US$20; triples US$25. AmEx/MC/V. ❷

Hotel Vela (☎777 0413), just past the turn off Costa Linda on the main road to the park entrance, is a cushier stay closer to the park. Rooms equipped with a fridge and spacious hot-water baths open up to beautiful gardens and furnished patios. Treat yourself to a few drinks during their daily Happy Hour (2 for 1 drinks, 5-7pm) and relax some more in the hammocks scattered around the courtyard. Check-out noon. Laundry ¢100 per piece. Smaller singles and doubles with fan US$30-35; bigger rooms with A/C US$35-40. Discounts available with cash in low season. AmEx/MC/V. ❸

CENTRAL PAC. COAST

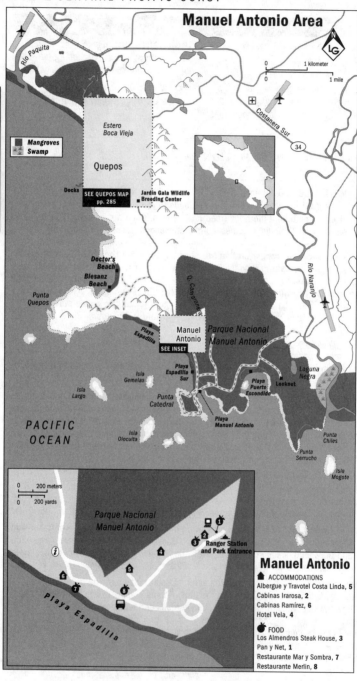

Manuel Antonio Area

N

0   1 kilometer
0   1 mile

**Mangroves
Swamp**

Río Paquita

Costanera Sur

34

Estero
Boca Vieja

Quepos

Docks

SEE QUEPOS MAP
pp. 285

Jardín Gala Wildlife
Breeding Center

Doctor's
Beach

Blesanz
Beach

Punta
Quepos

Río Naranjo

Q. Camaronera

Manuel
Antonio

SEE INSET

Parque Nacional
Manuel Antonio

Playa
Espadilla

Playa
Espadilla
Sur

Playa
Puerto
Escondido

Lookout

Laguna
Negra

Isla
Gemelas

Isla
Largo

Punta
Catedral

Playa
Manuel Antonio

Isla
Olocuita

PACIFIC
OCEAN

Punta
Serrucho

Punta
Chiles

Isla
Mogote

0   200 meters
0   200 yards

Parque Nacional
Manuel Antonio

Ranger Station
and Park Entrance

Playa Espadilla

Manuel Antonio

ACCOMMODATIONS
Albergue y Travotel Costa Linda, **5**
Cabinas Irarosa, **2**
Cabinas Ramírez, **6**
Hotel Vela, **4**

FOOD
Los Almendros Steak House, **3**
Pan y Net, **1**
Restaurante Mar y Sombra, **7**
Restaurante Merlin, **8**

FOOD

▨ Restaurante Mar y Sombra (☎ 777 0003) sits where the road from Quepos meets the beach. Feast your eyes on the waves and your stomach on a T-bone steak (¢2500). Spaghetti ¢850; *casados* ¢1000. If the crowd is big enough, the restaurant pumps out techno and *salsa* at night. Open daily 7:30am-11pm, until 2am on dance nights. ❶

Pan y Net, 700m up the road to the ranger station, serves all-you-can eat pizza for the ravenous backpacker (every Su ¢1500). Or come for breakfast and feast on banana, pineapple, or papaya pancakes (¢680). Internet ¢1000 per hr. Patrons get 20% off **Internet** use. Closed M in May, June, and Sept.-Nov. Otherwise, open daily 7am-11pm. Live music every Th and Sa night. ❶

Los Almendros Steak House, just 50m down the road, is a slightly classier joint where you can dine on breaded steak (¢1400) or delicious desserts like pancakes with sweet cream (¢800) over a game of chess. **Internet** service also available (¢500 per 30min.). Open daily 7am-10pm. ❶

Restaurante Merlin, directly across from the bus stop, has higher prices, but the lights are bright, the tiles cool, and the food is definitely worth the splurge. Go for the filling burger with fries (¢1800) or indulge in the rich seafood and beef dishes (¢14,000). Happy Hour daily 4:30-6:30pm. Margarita ¢1000. Open daily 7am-10pm. ❷

◤▨ BEACHES AND TRAILS

As the smallest of Costa Rica's national parks (just over 680 hectares), Manuel Antonio is easily explored in a leisurely 2hr. jaunt through the park's several inter-connecting trails, including stops to ogle the wildlife. Be lured into the warm waters of the fine, white-sand shores of any of the four beaches, though, and you can easily watch the entire afternoon slide by. To exit the park, follow the trails back to Playa Espadilla Sur, continuing south along the beach. Pass the gates, and cross a shallow estuary to Playa Espadilla. The water can get up to waist- or chest-high, so be prepared to get wet.

PLAYA ESPADILLA. Playa Espadilla is a relatively large, crowded, public beach flanked by mangroves and estuaries just outside the park. The waters are nice for wading, though the strong **rip tide** makes deep swimming risky. Get here by heading right (south) dwon the road when you get off the bus from Quepos.

PLAYA ESPADILLA SUR. Playa Espadilla Sur, popular with both visitors and monkeys, stretches from the northern limit of the park to the **Punta Catedral Penin-sula,** which is an easy 1.5km hike from the park entrance. The sand is white, and the slender shore stretches over a long, curved bay.

PLAYA MANUEL ANTONIO. The same path leading to the peninsula returns to the southern tip of Playa Espadilla Sur. There, it reconnects with the main trail and leads to Playa Manuel Antonio (also called Playa Tres), the third beach, with pic-nic areas, bathrooms, showers, and a refreshment stand. As the park's most pro-tected beach, Playa Manuel Antonio has calm surf and narrow shores, making it enjoyable for sunbathers and swimmers of all abilities.

PLAYA ESCONDIDA. The next big stop along the trail leads to Playa Escondida (1.6km), only accessible during certain times of the year. The rain and tides often render the path impassable, so check with the rangers before attempting it.

ONDIDO TRAIL. This 40min. up-and-down trail is full of red crabs. n **Playa Espadilla Sur** and circles **Punta Catedral,** once a large island the years, become linked to the land by sediment build-up to form a etween the fertile terrains. The trail onto the peninsula promises ews of the islands off the coast. It then returns to the southern tip of la Sur and leads to **Playa Manuel Antonio** and **Playa Escondida.**

SLOTH TRAIL (SENDERO PEREZOSO). This 1.3km trail originates at the same place as the Puerto Escondido trail and leads to the spectacular **mirador.** It's a 30min. hike through butterflies and hanging vines up a slippery ramp. A gorgeous ocean view awaits at the top. Although it's a road for official vehicles, it is nicknamed the *perezoso* (sloth) trail because of the many sightings from the path.

SENDERO CATARATAS. Sendero Cataratas breaks off the Sloth Trail's gravel road and leads to a **waterfall.** Walk 15min. up to a sign on your right (before the cement bridge), which marks the **Sendero Cataratas.** This trail winds 700m through the forest and over a stream to a small, pretty waterfall where you can take a dip.

DOMINICAL

With chocolate brown rocky beaches and reliable waves year-round, tiny Dominical (pop. 300), 50km south of San Isidro on the Pacific coast, is a surfer's paradise. Though it attracts a constant trickle of surfers, the dry season (Dec.-Apr.) attracts crowds, and quiet evenings give way to thumping dance parties. However, the three-road town is more than just a stop on a surfer's checklist; it is a close-knit community of people who came down for vacation and never left. Travelers will be pleased by a tree-canopied shore, mountainous back-drop, and expansive beach, but the overwhelming American influence might make Dominical a less than ideal vacation stop for those more interested in discovering the *tico* culture.

◤ TRANSPORTATION

Bus: The official station is a covered bench across the street from San Clemente, in the northern part of town, but you can catch a bus anywhere along the main road. Buses head to **San Isidro** (1½hr.; 6:45, 7am, 2:45, 3:30pm; ¢440); **Uvita** (45min.; 5:45, 10:30am, 5:30, 9pm; additional buses Dec.-Feb. daily 11:30am; ¢200); **Quepos** (2½hr.; 5:45, 8:15am, 1, 3pm; additional buses May-Nov. Sa-Su 1:50pm; Dec.-Apr. daily 1:50pm; ¢400). Buses to **San José** speed down the Costanera Sur (6hr.; May-Nov. Sa-Su 5:45am, 1:30, 2pm, Dec.-Apr. daily; ¢1500). Buses don't always run on schedule, so come 30min. early. The only taxi service available with TAXI Dominical (☎296 2626). You can also hire **taxis** or check bus schedules at the **San Clemente Bar and Grill** (see below).

⚙ 🛈 ORIENTATION AND PRACTICAL INFORMATION

Dominical spreads out over a 1km stretch of the main road, which connects the **Costanera Sur** highway to the beach road. A side street that forks off the main road, forming a well-trodden shortcut to the beach. Orient yourself be remembering that the ocean is always west.

Banks: None, but **San Clemente Bar & Grill** will exchange dollars and traveler's checks. Come to Dominical with enough cash—prices are high, and the nearest **ATM** is in San Isidro.

Laundry: Many services in town. The cheapest is **Lavandería Las Olas** (☎787 0105) in the town center; ask for Señora Miriam. ¢600 per kg. Open 7am-9pm.

Police: Emergency ☎ 117. On the main road, south of the side-street.

Hospital: Clínica de Primeros Auxilios (☎ 787 0310 or 787 0024), next to Diu Wok.

Telephones: At the southern end of the main road in front of Cabinas San Clemente.

Internet: Internet Río (☎ 787 0156), at the north end of town. Internet ¢1000 per hr. Also has fax. Open M-Sa 8:30am-7pm, Su 12-8pm.

Post Office: None in town, but **San Clemente Bar & Grill** can send and receive mail.

ACCOMMODATIONS

Dominical's *cabinas* range from bed-in-a-box rooms to nicer beachfront cabins. Reservations are necessary, and prices rise during the high season (Dec.-Apr.). Generally, you won't get as much bed for your buck as in other places in this over-priced surfer town. **Camping** on the beach is possible, although belongings and equipment should not be left unattended. Check with the police for up-to-date security information. Campers can use showers at Cabinas El Co-Co for ¢200.

Camping Antorchas (☎ 787 0307), 25m from the beach road at a turn-off beside Tortilla Flats (see below). Cheerful rooms with high ceilings or camping under low roofs outside. All guests can use cooking utensils, sink, and food storage space in the small kitchen. Rent a gas tank (¢1000) from owner Luis García to use the stove. Basketball court, hammocks, river tubes. Common outdoor bath located. Camping ¢700 per person; ¢1000 to rent a tent. Dorms ¢1500 May-Nov. per person, Dec.-Apr. ¢2000. ❶

Cabinas El Co-Co (☎ 787 0239), at the south end of the main road. Run by Luis García, it has the cheapest *cabinas* near the beach. Rooms are basic but comfortable. ¢2000 per person; Dec.-Apr. ¢3000. Nice rooms facing the beach with private baths for ¢7000. AmEx/MC/V. ❶

Cabinas San Clemente (☎ 787 0026), toward the northern end of the beach road, is wrapped in outdoor jungle decor. Luxurious rooms, spacious tiled floors, and small tables. Rent snorkel (US$10 per day), boogie (US$7 per day), and surf equipment (US$18 per day), or take surf lessons (US$35 per day, board included). You can also exchange US dollara and traveler's checks. Laundry service ¢800 per kg. Doubles with fans and cold water US$20, with hot water and A/C US$40; Dec.-Apr. additional US$10. ❷

Posada del Sol (☎ 787 0085 or 787 0067), 30m south of the Dominical School, just before the fork in the road. Quiet and clean with private baths and firm beds. The owners, Leticia Porras and Mariela Badilla, want to create a family atmosphere in this small place. Their garden is closed for all but guests and features a beautiful array of flowers and porch side hammocks. Singles US$15-20; doubles US$17-35; triples US$22-40. Apartment with kitchen US$500 per month. ❷

Tortilla Flats (☎ 787 0033), north of the side street on the beach road. Its newly redone, spotless rooms and tiled bathrooms with hot water make it one of the most popular places among those with money to spend. Rooms facing the beach have balconies. Others include a private outdoor hammock. Rooms with double beds and fan ¢8500 per person, with A/C ¢10,000; triples ¢10,000/13,000. Credit cards accepted. ❹

FOOD

Locals bemoan the lack of restaurants in Dominical; everyone is awaiting the opening of new locales to enjoy good food. For **groceries** go to **Diu Wok,** where the side street splits off the main road (☎787 0087; open daily 5am-10pm) or to the *abastecedor* across from Cabinas San Clemente. (Open daily 8am-6pm.)

San Clemente Bar & Grille. TV, beer, and large Tex-Mex menu in the town's center. This place dominates Dominical and has wait staff that speaks English to you before you even open your mouth. Watch NBA games with local expats or play pool (¢300). Breakfast at 7:30am (super french toast ¢1250). The restaurant continues to buzz through lunch (grilled chicken salad ¢1600) and into the evening. Bargain Taco Tuesdays has tacos for ¢250. Open daily 7am-10pm. ❷

Jazzy's River House (☎787 0310), through the white gate to the right of the *abastecedor*, has live music. On W nights before the show, catch a full-course veggie meal (¢1800-2000, dessert ¢700). Reservations required. The kitchen closes and shows begin at 7pm on W and 8pm on Sa . ❸

Thrusters Bar & Grill (☎787 0127), at the intersection of the main road and the beach road. Su fish and chips special. Pizzas and burritos ¢1500 and up. Open 4pm-late. ❸

Restaurante Su Raza, next to the *Aabastecedor,* has locals purring about the big portions of *típico* and gringo cuisine. Four-category menu: tropical, American, Continental, and *tico*. Toast, fruit, yogurt, and coffee ¢800. Open daily 7am-9pm. ❶

Tortilla Flats (☎787 0033), has a restaurant on the beach attached to its *cabinas*. It's the uncontested favorite hangout for surfers. Open 7am-9pm. ❷

NIGHTLIFE

San Clemente Bar & Grille. (See **Food,** above.) This restaurant buzzes through dinner and into the evening. Tacos ¢250 and half-price margaritas and tequila shots on Bargain Taco Tuesdays. Shake it to *salsa, merengue,* and funk F 10pm-2am. No cover. Bar open daily until 11pm. ❷

Jazzy's River House (☎787 0310; see **Food,** above) has live music from Irish folk to rock to classical. On W nights before the show, catch a full-course meal. The house serves cinnamon rolls (¢400) to accompany the sweet music on Sa. Shows start 7pm on W and 8pm on Sa. ❸

Thrusters Bar & Grill (☎787 0127; see **Food,** above). One of the trendiest hangouts among the young and sun-bleached. Open 4pm-late. ❸

Tortilla Flats (☎787 0033; see **Food,** above). Beach-front bar open till around midnight. Th ladies' night. ❷

Roca Verde, 1km south of Dominical along the shore. The place where the disco scene picks up on Sa nights. The bar opens onto the beach, the perfect location for a *salsa* and *merengue* bash. Cover ¢600. ❶

La Rosa Blanca (☎743 8145), shows a movie on Th 8pm. Follow the sign at the north end of the town and ask for Uli. US$2. ❶

OUTDOOR ACTIVITIES

Check out **Don Lolu's Nawyaca Waterfalls** for tours that include a horseback ride to the waterfalls and breakfast. (☎787 0198 or 771 3187; navyacacr@ns1.bruncanet.com; www.ecotourism.co.cr/navyacawaterfalls/index.html. Tours US$40.) **Posada del Sol** has information about renting **horses** for ¢2000 per hour. For those bored of surfing, Kim at Jazzy's River House offers lessons in everything from basket weaving to yoga (see **Food** above). The **Surf Shack,** next to San Clemente, rents boards and bikes and offers surf lessons. (Surf boards US$7-15 per day; boogie boards US$5; surf lessons 1-2hr. US$35; bikes US$15 per day, more than two days US$10. Open 7am-2pm.) **Tortilla Flats** will take you on a **mountain bike tour** around the surrounding area. They also rent boards and **bikes** with safety equipment. (Tours US$40 full day with lunch, US$25 half day with snack. Boards

US$10 per day; bikes US$10 per day). Treat yourself to a massage at **OM Massage and Meditation** or take a meditation workshop on a rainy afternoon (☎ 787 0101. Massage US$35 per hr.; meditation 4hrs., US$150).

 ## DAYTRIP FROM DOMINICAL

HACIENDA BARÚ

From Dominical, take a left on the Costanera Sur out of town; walk 3km past the road to San Isidro, taking the 1st left after the gas station. From Dominical or San Isidro, any Quepos-bound bus will drop you off at the same gas station. ☎ 787 0003; fax 787 0004. Admission US$3 including guide. Breakfast included. Cabins for 2, US$40 in low season, US$60 in high season; each additional person US$10.

Climb high into the rainforest canopy with a guide at your side or spend a night camping amidst monkeys and tree sloths at the Hacienda Barú, 3km north of Dominical. Visit for the day and sign up for guided hikes or get a monkey's eye view from the canopy platform (US$35 per person). Also, not to be missed is the beautiful butterfly garden, which includes most of Costa Rica's colorful species. There are also over six kilometers of carefully marked trails, which allow for observation of nature during either season. The 1km **Strangler Trail** features the Strangler Fig and the 2km **Teak and Canal Trail** provides incredible sights. Six **cabins** are available for overnight stays. The rooms are light, bright, and extremely pleasant, with hot water, fans, living rooms, and kitchenettes. Friendly conversation is never lacking here, as Diane and Jack are happy to shoot the breeze.

UVITA

The little-used highway from Dominical to Uvita, 15km to the south, has recently been paved, but the coastal village's previous isolation is still evident. The pebble and sand beach, lapped by gentle waves (no surfers here) looks like it has never seen a tourist's beach towel. If you are looking for an isolated tropical paradise, Uvita is the place. Although the town has many available *cabinas*, most residents are Costa Rican families who derive much of their livelihood from small farming plots. A wooden sign on the beach indicates the northern boundary of **Parque National Marino Ballena,** where tortoises, whales, and coral reefs provide a few intrepid visitors with uncensored views of Costa Rica's marine life.

TRANSPORTATION

Buses go to **San José** (7hr.; M-F 5am, Sa-Su 1pm; Dec.-Apr. 1pm daily; ¢1500); **San Isidro** (2½hr; 6am, 2pm); **Ciudad Cortés** (1½hr.; 5, 11am, 3pm; ¢450). An Ciudad Cortés you can connect to **Neily**—leave from the fork in Bahía, 50m north of the public phone. Also at this fork, the family with the white pickup truck gives rides. (☎ 743 8084; ¢1000 to Uvita.)

ORIENTATION AND PRACTICAL INFORMATION

Uvita, is 1km west of Bahía along the highway (past Río Uvita), on the strip of road heading north. Uvita is split into two distinct sections: the village up on the highway, called **Uvita,** and Playa Bahía Uvita, or **Bahía,** which lies along the beach 2.5km to the northeast and borders the national park. A gravel road off the highway leads south to Bahía. Uvita boasts a couple of decent hotels that are at least a 45min. walk from the beach, but closer to the mountains and waterfalls. Some buses to Uvita continue into Bahía; the others will let you off at the start of the main gravel road.

The **public phone** is on the west side of Bahía's main road, 50m south of the fork. (Open daily 7am-noon and 1-8pm.) Local businesses and hotels have radio contact with the **police station**, 3km from Bahía. Small supermarkets in the area are **Abastecedor Tatiana,** 600m up from the fork in Bahía (☎743 8080; open daily 7am-6:30pm), and **Abastecedor Cocotico**, next door to Los Laureles, on Uvita's main strip. (Open M-Sa 6:30am-8pm, Su 6:30am-1pm.)

🏠🍴 ACCOMMODATIONS AND FOOD

There is a spattering of *cabinas* in **Bahía,** none of which are luxurious.

▧ **Villa Hegalva** (☎743 8016) occupies an acre of grassy land 25m before the fork on the right and is the smoothest operation in town near the beach. Screened and curtained rooms have wooden floors, sturdy beds, huge fans, and colorful private baths. Separate huts have nice thatched roofs. Toilets and showers outside. Owners are very helpful and will gladly make connections with tour companies for their lodgers. The hotel's *soda* cooks for individual tastes. The extensive menu offers simple but savory green salads (¢500), french toast (¢150), *casados* (¢900-1000), and surprisingly good pastas. Restaurant open daily 7am-8pm. Rooms US$7 per person, US$10 in high season; huts ¢1500/2000 per person. **Camp** in the leafy backyard for ¢750 per person. ❶

Cabinas Las Gemelas (☎743 8009), 200m from the Minisuper Peri, take your 2nd left with the school on the right side of the road. Three separate spruced-up buildings in the backyard of a family home have polished, private bathrooms and large ceiling fans that provide cool, relaxing nights. The *cabinas* are at the end of the street on the right. Owner don Giovanni also drives most of the buses to and from Uvita so if you're coming in by bus, he'll show you the way. Laundry ¢1500 per load. Triples with TV ¢2000 per person; ¢3000 in high season. ❶

Cabinas Punta Uvita (☎743 8015), across from the public phone, has rooms with bamboo doors, fans, and outdoor hammocks. The owner also has some fame as a jewelry maker and sells earrings (¢1000) and necklaces (¢1500) made from fish bones and bamboo to interested guests. Singles ¢2000; doubles ¢3000, with bath ¢4000. ❶

Los Laureles (☎743 8235 or 743 8008), in mountainside Uvita, offers spotless rooms in private cabins. The office is off of Uvita's main road, but cabins in the mountains are large and spacious. 2-person cabins ¢3000; 3-person ¢7000; 5-person ¢10,000. ❶

Cascada Verde (cascadaverde@hotmail.com; www.cascadaverde.org), is a self-sufficient organic permaculture farm, self-styled as a holistic utopia in the middle of the jungle, and is mostly frequented by foreigners. Head north on Uvita's main drag for 600m, turn left after the graveyard and follow the sign 400m away. A three-day visit provides a private room and three delicious raw vegetarian meals per day. Any longer stay includes a work exchange in the garden of at least 4hr. per day. Longer stays include Spanish classes, yoga, and an intro. course in permaculture. US$50; US$100 for 1 week. ❷

Soda y Frutería Marel next door to Cabinas Punta Uvita, sells fruit, sodas, and ice cream sundaes. Open during high season M-Th 7am-9pm, F-Su 7am-noon. ❶

🏊 GUIDED TOURS

There are some professional tour companies in Uvita, but hotels and individuals also arrange horseback riding and snorkeling excursions upon request. **Villa Hegalva** will set you up with Saúl, who will take you on a 7hr. **horseback ride** into the mountains inland of Bahía, past lakes and a waterfall perfect for swimming. Saúl rents gentle horses for other excursions at ¢1000 per hr. He can take you on snorkeling trips by boat to Isla Ballena and Tres Hermanas in the national park or will even take you as far as Parque Nacional Isla del Caño, off the Osa Peninsula.

(☎743 8016. Horseback tour US$20 per person, including lunch. Snorkeling 2hr., US$20 per person. Isla del Caño US$200-300 per trip.) Mario of **Cabinas Punta Uvita** will also take you on horseback tours to nearby waterfalls, Punta Uvita, or the mountains. (☎743 8015. US$30, US$15, and US$55 for 2 people.) **Delfín Tour** offers a 2hr. tour of the marine park for a minimum of two people. (US$25 per person, US$35 for a more comprehensive tour of the entire park.) **Juliana Tour** offers similar tour of the park. (☎743 8069. US$15 per person.) Jonathan Dunam of **Ballena Adventure,** next to Soda Marel, offers snorkeling, fishing, and boat tours in English. (☎370 9482; ballenavent@hotmail.com. AmEx/MC/V.)

🔊 DAYTRIP FROM UVITA

PARQUE NACIONAL MARINO BALLENA

Ranger offices ☎786 7161; fax 771 8841. One ranger office is 200m west of the park entrance on the beach in Bahía; the other is 8km south of Uvita on Playa Ballena, which can be reached by buses heading to Ciudad Cortés. If you catch a ranger in Playa Ballena (the beach owned by the government), they will request ¢600 from nationals and US$7 from foreigners plus ¢1000 for each vehicle.

The Parque Nacional Marino Ballena was founded in 1989 as the first (and only) national aquatic park in Costa Rica. Of its seven beaches, only one is owned and maintained by the government. The rest are cared for by dedicated members of the community. If you enter past one of the two **ranger offices,** they will request a donation of ¢300. The money goes exclusively to help preserve Marino Ballena. In general though, the park is very loosely run, with no hours and stray chickens wandering its grounds.

The park consists of 110 terrestrial hectares and 5375 marine hectares, including 5 types of coral in its extensive reef. **Snorkeling** is possible off **Punta Uvita** when the tide is right (check the tide chart at Villa Hegalva or ask the ranger, if you can find him), or from a boat off the rock islands of **Piedra Ballena** and **Tres Hermanas.** (See **Guided Tours,** below.) If you need gear, ask at Villa Hegalva (see **Accommodations** above). From January to March, you may spot *ballenas* (whales) migrating from Southern California with their newborns. From September to November, whales migrate from the south through the park. Baby tortoises hatch in a sand pit next to the ranger station from June to September. It is possible to camp in the park with permission from the rangers, but they may encourage you to stay in Bahía hotels to promote local economic development.

SOUTHERN COSTA RICA

Costa Rica's "untouched nature" has been so intently sought after you'd think it'd all be "touched" by now. While that is true for much of the country, southern Costa Rica is a commendable exception. The area from San Isidro and Parque Nacional Chirripó to the vast wilderness of Parque Internacional La Amistad retains the thrills that originally drew travelers, such as hiking through mystical cloud forests and climbing Olympian peaks. Few locations cater to tourists, but the extra effort needed to explore these isolated areas is well worth it. The warm populace makes this part of Costa Rica even more memorable for those who stop and chat.

SAN ISIDRO

About 136km southeast of San José, the small, modern city of San Isidro de El General, also known as Perez Zeledón, links several surrounding farming villages to the rest of the world. Its location makes San Isidro a springboard for trips into southern Costa Rica, particularly for its proximity to the unreal splendor of Parque Nacional Chirripó, whose main entrance stands in nearby San Gerardo de Rivas. Don't bounce away too hastily. Take advantage of San Isidro's urban conveniences, enjoy its small town charm, and explore the numerous plant nurseries, coffee farms, and cattle farms that are sprinkled on its slopes.

◪ TRANSPORTATION

Finding the right **bus** out of San Isidro may seem a bit overwhelming at first—there are 6 different bus companies. The city is small, so everything within the city is within walking distance. TUASUR (☎771 0418) has service to **San José** (3½hr.; 6:30, 9:30am, 12:30, 2:30, 3:30pm; ¢870). MUSOC (☎771 0414) buses leave for **San José** from the terminal next to Vargas Rojas on the Interamerican Hwy. between Calles 2/4 (5am, every 1-2hr. 5:30am-4:30pm; ¢870). Transportes Blancos (☎771 2550) buses head to: **Dominical** (1½hr.; 7, 9am, 1:30, 4pm; ¢415); **Puerto Jiménez** (6hr.; 6:30am, noon, 3pm; ¢1330); **Quepos** (3hr.; 7am, 1:30pm; ¢655); **Uvita** (2½hr.; 9am, 4pm; ¢505) via **Playa Hermosa** (2hr.; ¢480). From the west side of the *parque* buses go to **San Gerardo de Rivas** (1½hr.; 5am; ¢400). Another bus to San Gerardo leaves at 2pm from the main terminal. TRACOPA (☎771 0486) buses go to **San Vito** (3hr.; 5:30am, 2pm; ¢925); **Golfito** (3hr.; 7am, 2pm; ¢850); the **Panamanian border** at **Paso Canoas** (2½hrs.; 7am, 1pm; ¢850). GAFESO (☎771 1523) buses leave for **Buenos Aires** (1¼hrs.; 11 per day 5:15am-5pm; ¢400). Many buses to other villages leave from the terminal on the *mercado's* south side. **Taxis** line the west side of the park. A ride to San Gerardo will cost about ¢6000.

◪ ◪ ORIENTATION AND PRACTICAL INFORMATION

A fair number of streets are marked, but addresses in San Isidro, as in most of Costa Rica, do not include street names. **Avenida Central** and **Calle Central** meet at the northwest corner of the **parque central.** The modern **cathedral** borders the *parque* to the east.

Southern Costa Rica

Tourist Information:

Ciprotur, Av. 1/3, Calle 4 (☎ 771 6096; fax 771 2003; www.ecotourism.co.cr; www.costarica-sur.co.cr.), can answer questions about San Isidro and offers information about tours and activities in the surrounding area. **Internet** services available for ¢600 per hr. Open M-F 7:30am-5pm.

Selva Mar, Av. 12, Calle Central (☎ 771 4582; fax 771 8841; www.exploringcostarica.com; selvamar@racsa.co.cr.), 50m south of the southwest corner of the *parque*, has information on tours to Bahía Drake, Delfines, Isla del Caño, Parque Nacional Corcovado, Tortuguero, Golfo Dulce, and Parque Nacional Chirripó. It also has hotel information and makes reservations throughout Costa Rica. Open M-F 8am-noon and 1:30-6pm, Sa 8am-noon. AmEx/MC/V.

Ministerio de Ambiente y Energía (MINAE), Av. 2/4, Calle 2 (☎ 771 4836 or 771 3155; fax 771 3297), has national park and reservation information. Open M-F 8am-4pm.

Bank: Banco Nacional de Costa Rica, Av. Central, Calle 1 (☎ 771 3287), on the northeast corner of the *parque*. Changes traveler's checks, gives cash advances on Visa, and has 24hr. **ATM** service for Visa and Visa Plus holders. Open M-F 8:30am-3:45pm. **Banco Crédito Agrícola de Cartago,** Av. 4, Calle 7 (☎ 551 0061 or 550 0202; fax 552 0364), offers cash advances on Visa. Changes cash until 4pm. Open M-F 8:30am-5pm.

Market: From chicks to machetes to backpacks, you can get it all at the **Mercado Municipal,** between Av. 4/6, Calles Central/2. Public bathrooms available for ¢50. Open M-Sa 6am-5pm, Su 6am-noon.

Supermarket: Supermercado La Corona, on Av. 2 between Calle 3 and the Interamerican Hwy. Open M-Sa 7:30am-8pm, Su 8am-4pm. AmEx/MC/V.

Laundry: (☎ 771 4042), Av. Central/2, Calle 4, across from Hotel Jerusalem. ¢400 per kg. Open M-F 8am-5:30pm, Sa 8am-3pm.

Police: The station (☎ 117) is 10km outside of San Isidro, near Río San Isidro.

Red Cross: Emergency ☎ 911. Toll-free ☎ 128. Ambulance service ☎ 771 0481.

Pharmacy: Farmacia San Isidro, (☎ 771 1567) on Av. Central across from the *parque.* Open M-Sa 7am-8:30pm, Su 8am-1pm. AmEx/MC/V.

Hospital: Hospital El Labrador (☎ 771 0318 or 771 0874), the blue and yellow building 5 blocks south of the cathedral on Calle 1 facing the stadium.

Internet: BTC Internet, on the south side of the *parque* next to Taquería México Lindo. Connections ¢600 per hr. Open M-Sa 8am-8pm. **Brunca Café Internet** (☎ 771 3235), on Av. Central on the north side of the *parque* next to Hotel Astoria. ¢150 per 15min. Scanning ¢100 per image. Fax US$2.35 per min. M-Sa 8am-8pm, Su and holidays 9am-5pm.

Post Office: Calle 1, Av. 6/8, on the way to the hospital, offers fax service. Open M-F 8am-5:30pm, Sa 7am-noon.

Postal Code: 8000.

"BLACK AND YELLOW KILL A FELLOW, RED AND BLACK, FRIEND OF JACK" So goes the popular rhyme among English-speaking tourists to help distinguish the venomous coral snakes from their non-venomous brothers. If the two stoplight warning colors, black and yellow, are touching, the snake is probably venomous. If its red *only* touches black, it's definitely harmless. However, you shouldn't always be shocked when you encounter a snake that is black, yellow, and red. These colors make up only two more of the numerous species located in southern Costa Rica; and to make you feel even better, coral snakes are known to be quite docile. They have tiny teeth, rarely bite, and their venom is almost never fatal. These snakes dwell mostly in the lowland rainforests but may appear at over 1000 meters of elevation.

However, the best way to tell apart the dangerous coral snakes from *"corales falsos,"* their mimics, is by their eyes. Non-venomous snakes have large eyes with clearly visible pupils, while their venomous counterparts have tiny black eyes you can barely see. An even better rule of thumb: don't get close enough to notice this detail. Coral snakes are a pretty part of the landscape, but a closer look is not worth the risk.

SOUTHERN C.R.

ACCOMMODATIONS

Hotel Chirripó (☎771 0529). Well-kept rooms, clean showers, a convenient café, free parking, and a helpful staff. Nice courtyard area, perfect for relaxing after a long hike. Singles with bath ¢2500; doubles ¢4500; triples ¢6500; quads ¢8500. ❶

Hotel Astoria (☎771 0914). The incredibly friendly hostess will take you through airy, mint green hallways, which lead to tight singles and good-sized doubles/triples. Clean rooms, tiled bathrooms. Singles ¢1500, with bath ¢2500; doubles ¢2800/¢4000. ❶

Hotel El Valle, Calle 2, Av. Central/2 (☎771 0246; fax 771 0220), 100m west and 25m south of the *parque's* northwest corner. Spacious rooms, fan, TV, and lawn chair. Parking until 11pm. Singles ¢2000, with bath ¢3100; doubles ¢3700/¢5500. ❶

FOOD

Soda Chirripó, Av. 2, Calle 1 (☎771 8287), on the southeast corner of the park. A solid, popular *soda,* with heaping plates of *casados* (¢500-1200). Also has a fast food menu that includes tacos (¢600), hot dogs (¢375) and fruit juice (¢350). Open M-Sa 6:30am-6pm. Tu open until 7pm. AmEx/D/V. ❶

La Cascada, Av. 2, Calle 2 (☎771 6479), serves fairly expensive but delicious meals in an open-air locale perched on the second floor. Here, you may also enjoy three large televisions and cushioned seats. Meals ¢800-2950, desserts ¢350-450, and beers (¢350-750). Open daily 11am-11pm. ❸

Marisquería Marea Baja, Calle 1, Av. 4/6. (☎771 4325 or 771 4882). The best seafood in San Isidro. Try the *filete con salsa de hongos,* (fish with mushroom sauce ¢1660) or the *arroz con camarones* (rice with shrimp ¢1414). The *sopa de mariscos* (seafood soup ¢1353) is the most popular appetizer. ❷

Pizza La Piccolina, Calle Central, Av. 8/10 (☎771 8692), Caters to those who have had their fill of *gallo pinto.* Aside from pizzas (small cheese ¢1000; large tomato, shrimp, onion ¢3150), this little restaurant also serves rice dishes (¢1150-1350), pasta (¢1200-1500), and milkshakes (¢300). Delivery available. Open F-W 11am-10pm. ❷

⊙ SIGHTS

Museo Regional del Sur, Calle 2, Av. Central/1, hosts three exhibits per year featuring art from southern Costa Rica. (☎771 5274. Open M-F 9am-5pm. Often closed in between exhibits. Free.)

The **Fundación para el Desarrollo del Centro Biológico Las Quebradas (FUDEBIOL)** is a reserve in the mountains above the Quebradas River Basin, 7km from downtown San Isidro. Managed by a group of devoted volunteers, FUDEBIOL is open to the public, providing visitors with a chance to learn about conservation at Las Quebradas, hike through bird-filled trails, visit the reserve's butterfly garden, and enjoy the streams and lagoon. Its isolated mountainside location makes the reserve as relaxing as it is educational. Students can stay for ₡5000 per night, including breakfast, although overnight guests usually come in groups to study the reserve. Most casual observers stick to a daytrip. To get to the reserve, take the bus to Quebradas that leaves from the main bus station (by the market) or in front of Hotel Astoria and get off at the last stop (₡75). Walk 2.5km up to the dirt road, turning right at the FUDEBIOL sign and continuing until the end of the road. (☎771 6096 or 383 7794. Admission ₡5000 for foreigners. Open M-F 7am-3pm, Sa-Su 8am-3pm.)

CHIRRIPÓ AND SAN GERARDO DE RIVAS

A high point of many Costa Rican vacations, Parque Nacional Chirripó is home to the tallest peak in Costa Rica (3820m). From the rocky summit, you can see both the Atlantic and Pacific Oceans, if the weather cooperates (read: high season). Other days, you may not be able to see farther than the cloud 2ft. in front of you. But it almost doesn't matter; the hike up the mountain is just as beautiful as what awaits at the top. The rushing rivers and otherworldly primary forest are sure to make even the most jaded cynic wax poetic. Spectacular glacial forms, from moraines to terraces to U-shaped valleys to lakes and circles, all date back some 25,000 years. The world on top of Chirripó is sure to induce chilling goose bumps and awed stares. Of course, you'll need the distraction—the trek up the peak is 20km with some 2400m-elevation gain. The route is very well marked, however, and quite accessible to the average outdoor enthusiast. And for the extremist, there's always the annual Chirripó marathon. Here, hundreds of daring runners come to challenge the mountain in fearless, fast-paced stride; the record to beat stands at 3hr. and 15min. round-trip. The race takes place every March 25th.

SAN GERARDO DE RIVAS

Peaceful San Gerardo de Rivas is the gateway to Parque Nacional Chirripó. It's a place to rest up, eat up, and relax your sore muscles at the nearby hot springs.

▐ TRANSPORTATION

The bus from San Isidro will drop you off at the edge of town in front of the ranger station (2km from the trail), or uphill in the center of town. Catch the return bus at the ranger station (1½hr.; 7am, 4pm; ₡1000) or in front of the church 15min. earlier.

◨ ▐ ORIENTATION AND PRACTICAL INFORMATION

The town stretches along a 1km uphill section of road. A **pulpería** (little food store) across from the soccer field at town center, has the town's only public **phone**—call it to reach anyone in San Gerardo. (☎771 1866. *Pulpería* open daily 6:30am-8pm.) Some travelers get dropped off at the station, check in, and then find a nearby hotel while most others prefer to find a hotel closer to the trail (i.e., in town), stash their gear, and then walk down to check in. Reservations are recommended for those planning to stay at the hotel closer to the trail during the high/dry season (Dec.-Apr.); call the town phone (☎ 771 1866).

ACCOMMODATIONS

Albergue Urán (☎ 388 2333 or 771 1669; ciprotur@racsa.co.cr; www.hoteluran.com), has the good fortune of being 100m downhill from the trail entrance, with free pick-up available from the ranger station. Attached *soda/restaurante* offers cheap, hearty food. Small rooms line a hallway leading to clean, collective bathrooms. ¢2000 per person; triple with bath US$8 per person. ❶

Albergue Vista a El Cerro (☎ 373 3365), the 2nd closest hotel to the trail (1km from Urán), has spotless collective rooms. A shared bath has hot water and the bright sky-light-filled hallway adds a sunny charm. Owner Eneída makes great vegetarian food for cheap prices anytime you need it. ¢2000 per person. ❶

Cabinas el Bosque (☎ 386 2133 or 771 4129 from San Isidro), across from the ranger station, caters to the hiker's needs: free luggage storage, breakfast as early as you need it, hammocks, and complimentary rides to the trail in the morning in the owner's car. Although a tad bit pricier, rooms delight with sturdy beds and warm blankets. There's an attached bar/restaurant open from 10am-midnight; during the wet season until 10pm. Rooms US$7 per person, with bath US$12. ❶

Cabinas El Descanso (☎ 771 7962 or 771 1866; eldescanso@ecoturism.co.cr). Descanso provides rides to the trail entrance after 5am. Camping on owner Francisco Elizondo's nearby farm, Finca Mirador, is ¢2000. The attached **restaurant** invites indulgence in fresh vegetarian dishes from homegrown produce. Restaurant open daily 5am-9pm. Tight, spotless rooms share baths. US$7 per person, US$8 in the high season; triples with bath US$12. ❶

Hotel Roca Dura (☎ 355 3466; jurena@costarricense.com) was built upon a big, tough rock and named accordingly. The rock greets you at the entrance, makes up one of the walls downstairs, and even makes a guest appearance in the lower level bedroom. The rock is halfway between the ranger station and the trail entrance, and is the last stop of the bus. Look out for monthly karaoke at the *soda* upstairs. The owner also offers a small cabin for rent in the mountains (US$200 per month). Open 7am-10pm. Singles ¢2000, with bath ¢5000; shared quads in the high season ¢8000. ❶

OUTDOOR ACTIVITIES

PARQUE NACIONAL CHIRRIPÓ

*Hikers to the summit almost always stay at Base Crestones. Reservations required, but no-shows are frequent, and you may be able to nab a spot from the San Gerardo rangers. Reservations can be made up to a month in advance from the **MINAE** office in San Isidro. ☎ 771 4836 or 771 3155. Open 8am-4pm. Note that you may be required to pay by wire transfer to secure your reservation. Reservation or not, your first stop in the area should be the **ranger station** in San Gerardo, where the buses drop you off. There's an admission fee, and the rangers can update you on the latest conditions. Ranger station open daily 6am-5:30pm. Park admission US$15 per person for the first two days, not including the day you hike out, then US$10 for additional days. Camping in designated areas US$5 per person per night, 5 days max. Hostel lodging 4-day max. stay US$10 per person per night.*

The hike up Chirripó leaves from San Gerardo de Rivas, with signs pointing to the trailhead beginning at the ranger station 2km below. Once on the trail, it's easy to follow. The climb passes through many altitudes and vegetation zones,

HYDROELECTRIC POWER: PROJECT BORUCA

Like many other countries, Costa Rica is struggling with an increased demand for electricity and few possible sources. Currently, officials at the Instituto Costarricense de Electricidad (ICE) are considering a very controversial project to place a hydroelectric plant on the *Río Térraba* in the Boruca Indigenous Reserve. ICE has devoted much time and effort to defending its goals from the wrath of the general public, who are proving themselves to be quite defensive of the rights of the tiny native population. The organizers have declared their intention to include the tribes (Brunka, Teribe, Cabécar, and Bribrí) in the decision making. ICE has professed their profound respect for the native culture, laws, and identity, though still claiming that they must be most concerned with the greater good. however, as the Brunka people have pointed out, their voice might be "respected," but it has certainly not been obeyed. Meanwhile, the native villagers divide the limited water supply among their homes as they wait for officials to come repair a broken water pipe.

from farmland and rainforest to moss-covered cloud forest, to the unique, high-altitude *páramo* ecosystem. Here, trees grow no more than 4 ft. tall and the land is barren and black, the result of a 1992 forest fire.

It is not possible to climb Chirripó in a day. It is a 16km uphill climb to the rugged yet well-equipped **hostel** at the base of the peak; this could take anywhere from 7-16hr., depending on your fitness level. The hostel, officially named Centro Ambientalista el Páramo but more commonly known as **Base Crestones,** is a top-of-the-line facility 400m vertical below the summit. It offers beds with mattresses, a phone, limited solar power, and (very cold) showers. The hostel has two hours of electrical light per day from 6-8pm. One thing it doesn't have is heat—the temperature at the base can drop to 7°C at night from May to December and as low as 6°C from January to April—plan accordingly. (☎770 8040. Sleeping bags ¢500 per night. Stoves ¢300. Blankets ¢300. Shirts ¢3000. Drinks ¢500.)

From Base Crestones it is another 6km with over 500m of altitude to climb to the summit—allow at least 2hr. even if you're fit. You'll need 2-3 days to make it all the way, climbing to the hostel on the first day, ascending the peak, and (possibly) returning to San Gerardo on the second. The last **bus** leaves San Gerardo at 4pm.

Besides Crestones, the only other shelter in the park is **Llano Bonito** (8km within the park), which has a roof, sink with potable water, flush toilet, and shower. This is a good mid-way point for lunch and water, but spending the night here is only possible with a guide hired from the ranger (US$30). Note that in the dry season, Llano Bonito may be the only **water source** until the hostel.

It's possible to do a day hike in the park and return to San Gerardo. The official park entrance is actually about 4km from the start of the trail in San Gerardo. The Llano Bonito shelter is the recommended turnaround point.

During the dry season you can rent **horses** from the **Asociación de Arrieros** to carry you or your equipment up. During the rainy season, you can hire porters. (☎771 1866; call ahead. Horses ¢7500 for 35kg. Porters ¢7500 for 14kg.)

🏃 DAYHIKES FROM BASE CRESTONES. The unmistakable trail to the peak of Chirripó is not the only hike you can take once you're at the Base Crestones hostel. The second most popular trail (some say even more impressive than Chirripó itself), is **Sendero Crestones** (2.5km one way), which crosses the Río Talari in front of the base and ends at **Cerro Terbi**

(3760m). Some valiant hikers attempt to climb the barefaced rocks along the way, while other groups arrive to make pilgrimages and offerings to the empowering peaks. An incredibly surreal trail runs through the **Valle de Los Lagos** (Valley of the Lakes), where crystal lagoons reflect the mountains above. Other trails include **Valle de Los Conejos** (Valley of the Rabbits), **Sabana del Los Leones** (The Lion's Savannah), and **Valle de Las Morrenas** (Valley of the Moraines). **Sendero Ventisqueros** (6km) leads to the *cerro* of the same name. The hike is harder than the one to Chirripó, but it follows an exciting ridge route and offers a stellar view. All the trails are well marked and take roughly 5-6hr. Rangers at the base can answer specific questions about hiking conditions.

■ **AN ALTERNATIVE ROUTE.** If climbing to Cerro Chirripó the direct way isn't tantalizing enough, another option is to take the considerably more challenging two-day hike along a newer trail and tackle the mountain from the opposite side. The trail, **Ruta Herradura,** leaves from the village of Herradura, 3km uphill from the San Gerardo ranger station. It's a two-day trek via several peaks before reaching Chirripó. Camping is permitted in designated areas. The path can be difficult to follow, so local guides are necessary for this trip. They can be found through the rangers in San Gerardo (plan on about US$25 per day, US$20 more if you would like the guide to cook or carry your pack). José Mora (☎771 1199), an English-speaking guide who helped build the park's facilities, will cook you hot meals of *gallo pinto* and keep you on the right trail.

BEYOND CHIRRIPÓ

Everyone comes here to trek up the mountain, but a few other diversions may interest you before or after the climb. One opportunity is the soothing hot springs, **aguas termales,** tucked in the nearby forest. The water comes from a natural spring, but is funneled into two stone pools. Take the path to the left of the white bridge 50m uphill from the ranger station. Proceed uphill about 600m, follow the trail to the right marked with a painted red tree. Cross the suspension bridge and follow the red marks uphill for 10-15min. Señora Vitalia rents a couple of nice **cabinas.** (☎770 6785; ciprotur@racsa.co.cr; www.ecotourism.co.cr. Baths ¢650 per day; pay at the *soda* on top of the hill. Open 7am-6pm. *Cabinas* US$7 per person with shower.) Not enough relaxation? Certified **massage therapist** Francene can be found in the conveniently located A-frame cottage right next to Albergue Urán near the trailhead (1hr. full-body massage US$25).

Francisco Elizondo of Cabinas El Descanso (see **Accommodations,** above) and his family offer guided treks in English through their **Finca El Mirador,** with views of the entire valley and a lesson on coffee harvesting and production (4hr., US$5 per person). Francisco will also take you on a trout fishing tour to catch your own dinner or serve as a guide to Chirripó for a group of no more than 5 people (US$30). Marcos Romero Valverde, of Albergue Urán, will take you on **horseback rides** to nearby **waterfalls** or **caves** (¢3500 per person). You can also rent horses from Marcos or Cabinas El Descanso.

BUENOS AIRES

A close-knit community in the center of a major pineapple-producing region, Buenos Aires is quite a contrast to bustling San Isidro, 64km northwest. The town has few attractions, though tourists often find it a necessary layover on a southern-bound bus route. The sleepy town also serves as a base for exploring nearby **Reserva Indígena Boruca** and the underappreciated **Parque Internacional La Amistad.**

THE LOCAL STORY

NEW ROYALTY, NEW LOYALTY

Costa Rica's dwindling indigenous population continues to face pressures by global development and may have to give up their land and culture as a result. One of the most persistent outside groups is **Global Country of World Peace,** a Holland-based organization associated with Indian Guru Maharishi Mahesh Yogi, which has offered up to US$44 million in development capital to the Talamanca Bribrí community in exchange for land use and cooperation. While the Bribrí Reserve development (ADITBRI) is staunchly opposed to accepting the monetary aid, there is no doubt that many members, estimated at anywhere between 5 and 25% of the community, are tempted by the prospect of such huge sums of money. ADITBRI claims that Global Country has already made US$4 million available to Bribrí Shaman Epe Apawa Lissandro, who expressed interest in Global Country's offer, and crowned him king despite his being of the wrong lineage and receiving little support form the Bribrí community. Luckily for those opposed to development, the Bribrí collectively and privately own their 17,000 hectare reserve, and it will take far more action than Lissandro's hasty move to implement real changes in the community. According to their website, Global Country's intent is to "awaken the Cosmic potential of every human being as the unbounded ocean of peace, harmony, and unity, and organize groups of peace-creating professionals to create an integrated,

E TRANSPORTATION. The TRACOPA terminal is inside the market, while the Vargas Rojas terminal is right outside the corner of the market. From the TRACOPA terminal, **buses** leave for **San José** (5½hr.; M-Sa 5 per day 6:30am-3:30pm; Su 9:30am, 1:45, 2:45pm; ¢1450). Additional buses leave daily from the Vargas Rojas terminal. (☎771 0418; 6:30, 9:30am, 12:30, 3:30pm; ¢870.) Buses leave for **San Isidro** from TRACOPA and GAFESO about every hr. (1¼hr., ¢400). Call a **taxi** (☎730 0700 or 730 0800) or hail one from the side of the market.

⚡🚻 ORIENTATION AND PRACTICAL INFORMATION. Both of the bus companies in Buenos Aires, TRACOPA and Vargas Rojas, drop off passengers by the market square. From here, the *parque central* Montero and the church sit next to one another, with streets stretching out from the town's center.
If you need to get cash, you'll find a **24hr. ATM** for Visa inside the marketplace. The **Banco Popular** faces the marketplace. (Open M-F 9am-3pm, Sa 8:30-noon.) **Supermercado el Sol** is also near the market. (Open M-Sa 7am-8pm, Su 7:00am-noon.) Facing the church, the **police station** lies 50m down the road heading left (☎730 0103). The **Red Cross** sits in back of the market square, on the same block (☎730 0068). The **hospital** is about 2km out of town walking uphill from the church. (☎730 0029.) Every corner of the **market** has public **phones.** (Open daily 6am-6pm, Su 6am-noon.) The **post office** is next door to the police station. (Open M-F 7:30am-6pm and Su 7:30am-12pm.)

🛏🍴 ACCOMMODATIONS AND FOOD. There are few places to stay here. The best option in town is **Cabinas Violeta ❶,** next to the fire station. The motel-style, rainbow-colored *cabinas* have cheerful rooms with small tables, chairs, and bathrooms. Lots of available parking space. (Singles ¢2000; doubles and triples ¢3000.) Farther from the town's center and with slightly musty rooms, **Cabinas Mary ❶** has the basics: fan, bath, and cold water. There's a *soda* attached to the *cabinas.* (☎730 0187. Rooms ¢2000 per person.)
Rancho Azteca ❷ must be reached by taxi (¢300), but is the center of the town's entertainment, and has a varied menu, disco, karaoke, roller skating rink, bar, and super-relaxed wait staff. A large thatched hut attached to an enormous newly built building, this impressive restaurant also offers delivery to any place in town for ¢250 extra. (☎730 0162 or 730 0212. *Comida típica.* ¢1000-2000, seafood ¢1200-1400.) With bamboo furniture and wooden stands, small **Soda El Dorado ❶** stands on the corner of the marketplace closest to the Vargas Rojas terminal. It has a friendly staff and good *comida típica.* (*Casados* ¢700. Filet ¢700. *Bistec* ¢700).

NEAR BUENOS AIRES

RESERVA INDÍGENA BORUCA

Buses leave Buenos Aires from the TRACOPA station (2hr., 2 per day 11am and 3:30pm, ¢500). Schedules are subject to change.

Twenty kilometers into the mountains south of Buenos Aires lies a welcoming and culturally rich community of indigenous people. Although the Boruca people have long since adopted modern dress and the Spanish language, some traditional customs persist. Women still use pre-Columbian back-strap looms to weave cotton textiles. Men still craft balsa wood carvings and masks, which are used every year in the famous Boruca festival, *Fiesta de los Diablitos* (Festival of the Little Devils) from December 30 through January 2. The celebration represents the indigenous struggle against the Spanish. Men wear carved devil masks and burlap costumes and fight a man dressed up as a bull, which symbolizes the Spanish. The representative fight/dance ends when the "bull" takes off his "face" and throws it on the ground, marking his defeat. This *fiesta* is one of the few indigenous festivals in Costa Rica, since the *indígenas* make up only about 1% of the population.

The one-room museum, **Museo de la Comunidad Indígena,** is in a thatch hut and is open for perusal at any time. If staff is given prior notice, the museum will feature many examples of crafts (both for purchase and display). Normally, it contains photographs of the *Fiesta* and historical facts about the Boruca people. The crafts available include handmade cotton belts, bags, money purses, small blankets, and tablecloths. Doña Marina Lásaro Morales lives next door to the museum and is in charge of the village's group of artisans. She will demonstrate the processes, sell the products, and direct you to the other families with goods for sale.

The Boruca people are eager to share their artwork with tourists, but highly value the relative isolation of their village. In fact, there is an emerging trend towards preservation of their original history, as children a few years ago began receiving intensive language instruction in the Boruca's native tongue. If you're not traveling in a group, you may make friends with the immensely kind villagers on the bus to Boruca and easily receive an invite to go home with one of the families. (If staying with a family, it is expected that a guest leave about ¢2000.) Villagers ask that tourists in groups call at least two days ahead to the village's phone so that they may prepare the museum and the *cabinas.* (☎730 1673; 7am-5pm. Rooms ¢2000 per person; ask for Luis.)

harmonious collective consciousness in every country and the world as a whole." Now they have brought this mission to Costa Rica. Claiming to have "helped" indigenous people in 30 different countries, the organization hopes to use the Bribrí reserve as the site of a Maharishi University and farm for organic produce and plants to sell under the Maharishi brand. Furthermore, the company wants the Bribrí to change their name and recognize Lissandro as their king.

PALMAR NORTE

Though mostly a transportation hub for tourists, Palmar Norte (pop. 10,800) is home to a colorful community of Costa Ricans. The town is in the center of a major banana-growing region. Complicated bus schedules to the Osa Peninsula may force you to spend more than a few hours in this town. Though not a haven of biological splendor, Palmar Norte can certainly show you a good time. Music from stores fills the streets and when the air is clear, the views of the surrounding forested mountains provide a hint of the great hiking the region has to offer.

TRANSPORTATION. Most likely, the bus connections in Palmar Norte will be the focus of your stay. Fortunately, all transportation options are located in the town center and are clearly marked. TRACOPA **buses** (☎786 6511) will take you to: **San Isidro** (3hr.; 8:30, 11:30am, 2:30, 4:30pm; ¢1300); **San José** (5hr., M-Sa 7 per day 5:25am-4:45pm, ¢1900); **Paso Canoas** (1hr.; 10:30am and 6:30pm; ¢600); **Golfito** (45min.; 12:30 and 8:30pm; ¢535). Térraba buses (☎786 7627) will take you to **Ciudad Neily** (1hr., 6 per day 6am-4:50pm, ¢330) or to **Ciudad Cortés** (45min., every hr. 6:30am-6:30pm, ¢135). From Supermercado Térraba, a bus will take you to **Sierpe** (30min.; 7, 11:30am, 2:30, 5pm; ¢300). **Taxis** depart from the TRACOPA station, but the pricey trip to Sierpe costs at least ¢10,000.

PRACTICAL INFORMATION. In the small **shopping center** across the Interamerican Hwy., you can check **email**, get **money**, or talk to **Osa Tours**, which can reserve hotels and provide information on the area. They also offer tours for larger groups; call ahead. (☎786 7825 or 369 9107; luis@centeno.as.) **Banco Popular** has a **24hr. ATM** and cashes **traveler's checks.** (☎786 7033. Open M-F 8:45am-3pm, Sa 8:15am-noon.) The largest **supermarket** in town, **Megastore,** has everything a hungry traveler could desire. (☎786 6541. Open Th-Tu 7am-8pm.) Other services include: **police** (☎786 7652); **pharmacy** (☎786 6282; M-F 6am-7pm, Sa 6am-6pm, Su 6-11am); **public phones** on most corners, and at the ICE office (see map); fast **Internet** connections in the shopping center (☎786 7749; ¢500 per 30 min., ¢800 per hr.; open M-F 8am-5pm, Sa 8am-1pm); and the **post office** (☎786 6290; M-F 8am-noon and 1-5:30pm).

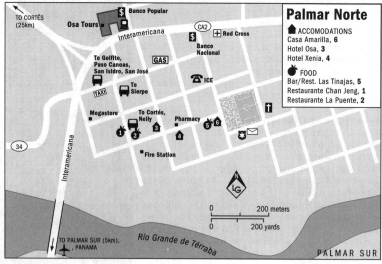

⌐☐ ACCOMMODATIONS AND FOOD. You can find several cheap hotels in the area that don't require reservations. **Hotel Xenia ❶,** offers basic rooms with a stool, bed, fan, and communal bathrooms. (☎ 786 6129. ¢1000 per person.) Another possibility is the basic **Hotel Osa ❶.** (☎ 786 6584. No-frills singles ¢1300; matrimonial rooms ¢2500. Payment upfront.) Down the street from Xenia, in a big yellow house are the more expensive *cabinas* at **Casa Amarilla ❶.** (☎ 786 6251. Singles with hallway bathrooms ¢1200; rooms with private baths ¢2500; special single with A/C ¢6000.) Next door, the hotel owns the airy and pleasant **Bar/Restaurante Las Tinajas ❶,** with cheap food and a large TV. (☎ 786 6251. Open daily 6am-10pm.) Palmar is home to some Chinese immigrants and offers several good Chinese restaurants. One local favorite is **Restaurante Chan Jeng ❶,** with many varieties of chop suey (¢850-1650), meat (¢1550), and seafood (¢1500-2500) specialties. (☎ 786 6195. Open daily 10am-11pm.) Sporting a cheesy tropical decor but a great selection of authentic *tico* food and drink is the **Bar/Restaurante La Puente ❶.** (☎ 786 7265. *Gallo pinto* ¢550-650. Steak/rice ¢950-1400. Mixed drinks ¢450-1000. Open M-Sa 8:30am-10:30pm, Su 1-10pm.)

CIUDAD CORTÉS

Travelers may also find themselves stopping in Ciudad Cortés (pop. 6900) on their way south. Although this fairly isolated town has no amenities for tourists, have no fear—the bus will drop you off in front of the *parque central*, where your speedy connection to **Palmar Norte** and beyond will arrive. Ask the bus driver for more details, including the exact arrival time of your connecting bus.

SAN VITO

Set in the heart of the breathtaking Coto Brus Valley, refreshing San Vito stands 980m above sea level, providing a bit of a break from the oppressively hot jungles of southern Costa Rica. Marked by warm days and crisp nights, this small, sloping village fuses culture, climate, and breathtaking views. Italians founded the town in the early 1950s, arriving in WWII jeeps and setting up some of the coffee plantations for which the valley is known. San Vito is still home to Italian-speaking families, and Italian restaurants are the highlight of the town. It is also a useful base for exploring the Wilson Botanical Gardens or Parque Internacional La Amistad.

⌐ TRANSPORTATION

Buses to **San José** (8hr.; 7:30, 10am, 3pm; direct 5am) via San Isidro (4hr., ¢1000) leave from the TRACOPA terminal (☎ 773 3410), 400m north of the park on the main street. There are additional buses to San Isidro at 6:45am and 1:30pm. To reach **Neily,** take a bus (2hr.; 5:30, 7, 7:30, 9, 11am, 2, 5pm; ¢330) from the Santa Elena/Cepul terminal (☎ 773 3848), reachable by walking down the main street from the *parque,* taking your first left, and continuing up the hill 250m. Before leaving town, buses stop on the corner across from the museum to pick up passengers—look for the sign.

⬛ ⓘ ORIENTATION AND PRACTICAL INFORMATION

The **parque central** lies in the town's center, where a charming statue of two children under an umbrella stands. The main street is **Calle Dante Alighieri.** Uphill from the park along the main street is the **Centro Cultural** and the road to the Wilson Botanical Gardens and Neily. Downhill, the main street leads to the TRACOPA bus station and post office. San Vito is surrounded by forest, and the main street continues to extend uphill out of the northern edge of town to great views.

Banco Nacional has two ATMs and will exchange traveler's checks. (☎ 773 3601. Open M-F 8:30am-3:45pm.) **Banco de Costa Rica** offers similar services. (☎ 773 3901. Open M-F 8:30am-3pm.) The **Coto Brus** pharmacy has a decent selection. (☎ 773 3077. Open M-Sa 7:30am-7pm, Su 8am-noon.) The **hospital** (☎ 773 4125 or 773 4103) is 1km from the park past the Banco de Costa Rica. The **Red Cross** (☎ 773 3191) is just past the Cepul bus station. Slow **Internet** (by satellite) is available at **Éxitos Video.** (☎ 773 5029. Open M-Sa 8am-8pm; ¢600 per hour.) The **police** (☎ 773 3225 or 911 for emergencies) are on the main street next to the **post office** (☎ 773 3830), with fax. (Open M-F 8am-5:30pm, Sa 7:30am-noon.) **Postal code:** 80257.

🏠🍴 ACCOMMODATIONS AND FOOD

The cheerily managed **Hotel Rino ❷**, 200m north of the park on the main street, has spacious rooms around a second-floor balcony. It's more expensive than other locations but definitely worth it. Rooms come with cable TV, carved bedposts, tiled bathrooms with hot water, and towels. (☎ 773 4030 or 374 1214. Singles ¢3500, with A/C and king size bed

San Vito

🏠 ACCOMMODATIONS
Hotel Colono, 5
Hotel El Ceibo, 6
Hotel Rino, 2

🍴 FOOD
La Gamba, 1
Hotel El Ceibo, 6
Pizzería Liliana, 4
Soda Familiar, 3

¢4775; double suite ¢6000. AmEx/MC/V.) **Hotel Colono ❶**, facing the park across from the *centro cultural*, has third floor cabinas that offer bright rooms and blankets for chilly nights. With ripped nets above the doors, you might hear more of your neighbors than you wish. (☎ 773 5110. ¢2000 per person; room for 4 with private bath ¢4000.) **Hotel El Ceibo ❸**, on a quiet dead end street, has 40 luxurious rooms with TVs, private baths with warm water, and fans. All rooms on the 2nd floor have balconies over the hotel's landscaped front. (☎ 773 3025; fax 773 5025. Singles ¢6300; doubles ¢11500; triples ¢14700; quads ¢18400. V.)

San Vito doesn't have as many Italian restaurants as you would suspect. **Pizzería Liliana ❶**, up the taxi-lined street on the left, was the first Italian restaurant established in town and remains the local favorite. You can sit on the breezy terrace and choose from two dozen Italian favorites. (☎ 773 3080. Small cheese pizza ¢1300, medium ¢1500, large ¢1700, meat pizza ¢1600-2900. Pastas ¢1300-1700. Open daily 10am-10pm. V.) For some (relatively) swanky service and *al dente* pasta (¢1000-1300), try the restaurant in **Hotel El Ceibo ❷**, located down a driveway to the left of the main street with your back to the park. (Open daily 6:30-10pm.) In case you're missing *tico* food, or want to save a few *colones* on a more modest dinner, there are plenty of tasty *sodas* in San Vito. **La Gamba ❶** has quite possibly the best selection of standard Costa Rican fare and fast food. (☎ 773 3072. Tasty *batidos*

WHAT'S LOVE GOT TO DO WITH IT

The story of San Vito began long before the first colonists settled there in 1952. Thirteen years prior to WWII, an Italian sailor named Vito Sansonetti met a Costa Rican girl named Olivia Tinoco at a party in a Panamanian port town. The two promptly fell in love, and although Vito was called home for war shortly thereafter, the lovers kept in touch. For seven years, they sent letters through a friend in Spain (Costa Rica sided with the Allies and direct mail to fascist Italy was forbidden). In 1946, Olivia traveled to Europe and married Vito in Rome. Vito, longing for a fresh start and a peaceful existence, and eager to know his wife's homeland, came up with the idea of founding a town for Italian farmers in Costa Rica. He contacted the Costa Rican government, eventually signing a contract in 1952 proclaiming the new settlement of Ciudad de San Vito (guess who picked the name), in a remote part of southern Costa Rica. In the following years, 120 Italian families tamed the tropical forest for farming and eventually saw the growth of a prosperous town. Vito and Olivia, thus able to enjoy both pizza and *casado*, became local heroes, and of course, lived happily ever after.

(shakes) ¢250 and *gallo pinto* ¢550-600. Open M-Sa 7am to 8 or 9pm.) In the morning, you can buy delicious fresh bread and baked treats at the nameless Italian-owned bread shop ❶. (☎ 773 3174. Open M-Sa 5am-8pm, Su 5am-noon.) **Soda Familiar** ❶ is a cheap, reliable *soda* on the main street. (*Casados* ¢600. *Gallo pinto* ¢400-500. Rice dishes ¢850-950. Open M-F 6am-8pm, Su 6am-7pm.)

SIGHTS

The **Centro Cultural Dante Alighieri** is an enjoyable little museum sharing the town's Italian heritage. Black-and-white photos line the walls, and a small room off to the side houses Italian periodicals and reference books that have been sent to San Vito over the years. The center also has a sizable collection of Italian videos and gives beginner, intermediate, and advanced classes in Italian to locals and interested visitors. (Open M-F 1-7pm.) **Finca Cántaros**, 2km outside town, has a landscaped park, children's library, and crafts store. The park is 6 hectares of beautiful trails encircling a bird-filled lagoon. Picnic tables are available for family outings. The *finca* also has a splendid view of red-roofed San Vito. The store sells handiwork, mostly jewelry and ceramics, made by the **Guaymi** (an indigenous tribe 2hr. away). The *finca* can be reached by taxi (¢500) or by any bus headed to the Wilson Botanical Gardens. (☎ 773 3760. Library and crafts store free. Park ¢300, children ¢150. Open Tu-Sa 9:30am-4pm, Su 9:30am-1pm. AmEx/MC/V.)

NEAR SAN VITO

▨ WILSON BOTANICAL GARDENS

The gardens are 6km from San Vito. Only buses headed to Neily via Agua Buena head to the gardens; let the driver know you want to stop. The buses leave San Vito's Cepul terminal (10min.; 7, 9am, 2, 5pm; ¢105). Outside the park entrance, buses head back to **San Vito** *(10 buses 6:30am-5:15pm). Some people walk or take a taxi (¢900). ☎ 773 4004; fax 773 36 65; lcruces@hortus.ots.ac.cr; www.ots.ac.cr. Reservations ☎ 240 6696; fax 240 6783; reservas@ots.ac.cr. US$6. Open daily 8am-4pm.*

Founded in 1963 by tropical plant-lovers Robert and Catherine Wilson, the botanical gardens' 25 acres overflow with a mind-boggling diversity of plant and bird life. The gardens hold more than 1000 genera in some 200 plant families, along with 320 bird species and 800 species of butterflies. There are over 700 species of palms alone, the second largest collection worldwide. International biologists and botanists spend months studying here, but the park is very accessible to the casual visitor, with a series of well-done self-guided trails. The **Natural History Trail** is a 2hr. highlight tour featuring violet-colored bananas, colossal bamboo shoots, and the delightful "marimba palm." Rub a stick along its spines and watch it boogie away. Or specialize by following such trails as the **Palm Tour** (the park's most famous), the **Orchid Tour,** the **Hummingbird Tour,** and the **Anthurium Trail,** designed by the famous Brazilian landscaper Roberto Burle Marx, a disciple of Pablo Picasso. The spectacular **Río Java Trail** (1.1km) runs through the adjacent secondary rainforest, which is richly populated by mammals. The river is often flooded, so the park strictly forbids all overnight guests but those with tour guides from taking this hike. The garden provides overnight guests with walking sticks and rubber boots.

Tour books are available at the entrance shop; the most broad-based is the *Self-guided Tour of the Wilson Botanical Garden* (¢490). For a more in-depth look, call in advance to arrange a guided tour with a resident biologist. (☎773 4004. Half-day US$15; full day US$25; children US$10/15.) Free maps of the hikes are available with the entrance fee. You may also arrange for the more expensive overnight lodging or eat in the garden's dining room with the resident scientists and students. For the family meal, reserve a spot before 10am the same day.

CIUDAD NEILY

Although this town is the main center for African oil-palm and banana plantations in the southern Valle Coto Colorado, it doesn't have much to offer in the way of tourist attractions. However, it is an important transport hub for southern Costa Rica, so at some point you will probably have to switch buses here or spend the night before a morning connection. Locals are accustomed to travelers breezing through on the way to the border, and will make sure you enjoy your stay.

▐▀ **TRANSPORTATION.** Ciudad Neily endears itself with its user-friendly bus terminal. As always, there are several bus companies, but all list their schedules on clearly marked signs. **Buses** are frequent and reliable. The bus to **Golfito** also picks up passengers next door to the gas station downtown, and drops people off in front of the *Hotel Musuco* (1½-2hr., 13 buses 6am-6pm, ¢200.) Hop on a bus to **Zancudo** at 2:15pm (change buses at 4:30 in Conte, ¢500). *Fronbus* takes you to the border at **Paso Canoas** (½-1hr., 17 buses 6am-5:30pm, ¢220). *Tracopa* (☎783 3227) takes you to **San José** (7-8hr.; 4:30, 5, 8:30, 11:30am, 3:30pm; ¢2420). *Térraba* (☎783 4293) runs buses to **Palmar Norte** and **Ciudad Cortés** (1-2hr., 7 buses 11am-5:45pm, ¢330-345), **Puerto Jiménez** (6-7hr., 7am and 2pm, ¢1740), and **Dominical** (3hr., 1 per day 6am, ¢1145). *CEPUL* runs buses solely to San Vito (2hr., 7 per day 6am-5:30pm, ¢370).

▐▐ **ORIENTATION AND PRACTICAL INFORMATION.** The most commercial part of town lies between the plaza and the Interamerican highway to the south. Streets vary in length and do not follow the typical small city pattern. However, locals don't use street names to give directions. The gas station downtown is an important landmark. The **Banco de Costa Rica,** across from the gas station, has two 24hr. Visa ATMs. (Open M-F 8:30-3pm.) The two ATMs of **Banco Nacional** accept all other cards. The **Red Cross** (☎783 3757) and **police** (☎783 3151) are located in the north end of town. The **hospital** (☎783 4011) is 2km from town along the Interamerican highway. **Internet** is available at air-conditioned **NeuroTec,** next door to Hotel Andrea. (☎783 4455; neurotecer@racsa.co.cr. Open M-Sa 8am-8pm. ¢500 per hour. AmEx/MC/V.) The **Santa Lucía** pharmacy, in the center of town, is well stocked. (☎783 3600. Open M-Sa 8am-8pm.) **MegaSuper** offers basic groceries at cheap prices. (☎783 3015 or 783 4044. Open M-Sa 7am-9pm, Su 8am-8pm.)

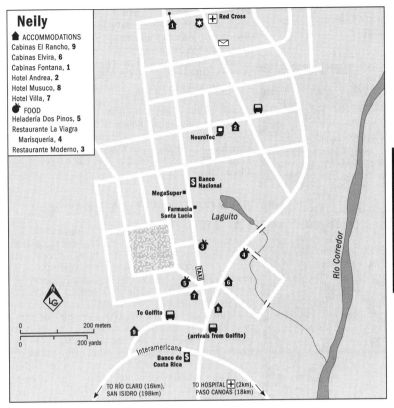

Neily

🏠 ACCOMMODATIONS
Cabinas El Rancho, 9
Cabinas Elvira, 6
Cabinas Fontana, 1
Hotel Andrea, 2
Hotel Musuco, 8
Hotel Villa, 7
🍎 FOOD
Heladería Dos Pinos, 5
Restaurante La Viagra
  Marísquería, 4
Restaurante Moderno, 3

Red Cross

NeuroTec

Banco Nacional

MegaSuper ■

Farmacia Santa Lucía ■

Laguito

Río Corredor

TAXI

To Golfito

(arrivals from Golfito)

Interamericana

Banco de Costa Rica

0   200 meters
0   200 yards

TO RÍO CLARO (16km),
SAN ISIDRO (198km)

TO HOSPITAL ✚ (2km),
PASO CANOAS (18km)

SOUTHERN C.R.

▌ ACCOMMODATIONS. The city is full of cheap sleeps. Most cluster around the gas station. **Cabinas Elvira ❶** has a large private courtyard with a common TV with cable. Basic rooms all have bathrooms and small fans. (☎ 783 3057. Singles ¢2000; doubles ¢3000.) **Hotel Villa ❶** is even cheaper, but lies in a row of bars that may keep you up all night. Basic rooms have dusty ceilings, but reliable fans and clean sheets. (☎ 783 5120. ¢1300 per person with shared bath.) **Cabinas Fontana ❶** is 600m from the bus stop and the bustling part of town, but is more spacious and quiet, with simple rooms. (☎ 783 3076 or 783 3078. ¢2000 per person with bath.) A slightly more expensive option with a convenient location for catching a bus to Golfito is **Cabinas El Rancho ❷**. The tiny, separate *cabinas* are well-organized and well-kept. All rooms have tiled floors, private bath, and a movable wardrobe. (☎ 783 3063. ¢2800 with fan, ¢6000 with cable TV and A/C. V.) Another option is **Hotel Musuco ❶**, 50m from the bus drop from Golfito, which has a balcony onto the street, thin sheets, and small rooms. (☎ 783 3048. ¢1500 per person, ¢1700 with bath.) **Hotel Andrea ❷**, the most luxurious hotel in Neily, with a beautiful courtyard, wooden benches and doors, and a welcoming tiled staircase, is located in the north of town and has handsome, well-furnished rooms with huge private bathrooms and TVs. Parking available. (☎ 783 3715 or 783 3784. ¢7400 for 1-2 people; ¢9500 with A/C.)

FROM THE ROAD

THE WOMEN OF BORUCA RESERVE

From personal experience, I know that women are wholly capable of independent management of the home. However, I have also grown to understand that preserving one's culture and heritage can mean sacrificing the advanced position that women have achieved in today's society.

The Indigenous Reserves in Costa Rica make up a very small portion of the population, and, therefore, feel even more pressure to preserve the disappearing culture of their ancestors. Along with improved opportunities for education on these reserves, children now learn the native tongue of their respective tribes. Like always, though, the process of recovering one's past in the present is full of compromises (and inconveniences). Although still practicing crafts using pre-Columbian techniques and cooking with smoldering logs under thatched roofs, the Boruca people have refused to give up one modern advancement: the emancipation of women. The Boruca woman with whom I stayed during my visit to the reserve is a single mother of five. Proud of her family and happy with her position in the close-knit community, every Tuesday, she leaves the village with female friends to attend a class in Buenos Aires that teaches women about their rights. When I mentioned the conflict between the advancement of women and the preservation of past culture, she laughed and commented, "my right to be an independent woman is more basic to me than plumbing or electricity!"

— **Natalia Truszkowska**

🚩 **FOOD.** Fortunately, not a single street in Neily lacks a splattering of hearty *sodas*. For a better selection, try **Restaurante Moderno ❸**, the favorite of local families. Many enjoy the generously portioned pizzas (¢1300-2500) and soups. (☎783 3097. Open daily 6am-10pm. AmEx/MC/V.) **Restaurante La Viagra Marisquería ❷** is a tiny but delicious open-air locale, with TV and a good stereo, that serves a large variety of fish. (☎783 3544. Fish ¢1000-2000, mixed drinks ¢200. M-Sa 7am-10pm.) **Heladería Dos Pinos ❶** has little personality but fantastic ice cream and a nice play area for kids. (☎783 3245. Cones ¢250. Milkshakes ¢750. Banana splits ¢750. Sundaes ¢600. Open daily 10am-10pm.)

PARQUE INTERNACIONAL LA AMISTAD

Parque Internacional La Amistad, founded in 1983, offers a breathtaking array of plants, animals, and gorgeous vistas, but due to its remote location and a lack of publicity, it remains the best-kept secret of Costa Rican ecotourism. The park, which encloses the southern part of Cordillera de Talamanca, stretches across the border well into Panama. This crossing of frontiers accounts for the park's name, La Amistad, a natural boundary marking the friendship between Costa Rica and Panama. Together with the adjacent Parque Nacional Chirripó and Parque Nacional Tapantí, La Amistad forms the largest protected area in Central America. The park's huge size (194.2 hectares) and mountainous terrain make the vast majority of the area fairly inaccessible. However, the wide range of altitudes found in the park is partly why the terrain is the most biologically diverse area in the country. Recently, the park was designated a World Heritage site by UNESCO. Sensitive to the peaceful atmosphere of the park, the small communities of coffee farms surrounding it, and aware of the danger of increased popularity, the government hopes, above all else, to protect La Amistad.

◼ ORIENTATION

The easiest place to begin exploring Parque Internacional La Amistad is the **Estación Altamira** entrance point. It's accessible by bus from San Isidro or San Vito. Transportation is complicated, however, and Altamira Station is not a feasible daytrip—it is best to plan on camping overnight. Park admission US$5.

AT A GLANCE

AREA: 1939 sq. km

CLIMATE: Tropical humid. Average temp.: 25°C near sea level; -8°C on highest peaks.

FEATURES: The town of Biolley, Cerro Kámuk (3549m, the park's highest peak), Cerro Dúrika (3280m).

HIGHLIGHTS: Hiking Sendero Valle del Silencio.

GATEWAYS: San Vito (p. 311), Buenos Aires (p. 318).

CAMPING: US$2 per person at Estación Altamira.

FEES AND RESERVATIONS: Call MINAE to alert them of your arrival. ☎ 730 0846. Open M-F 8am-4pm. Reservations not required.

▄ TRANSPORTATION

Unlike more touristed parks, Amistad has no *colectivos* running to its ranger stations. You must rely on infrequent, slow **buses** that run as far as the town of Carmen (6km from Altamira), and then get to Altamira on your own. Road conditions are extremely poor and officials are waiting for repairs before extending any public transportation to Altamira. Calling MINAE in Buenos Aires will help you obtain up-to-date transportation details. Departing from San Vito, head to the TRACOPA station and take the Autotransportes Saenz 10:00am bus to **San José,** getting off at **Las Tablas** (45min., ¢500). A bus runs from Las Tablas to **Carmen** (1hr., 2 per day 1 and 5pm, ¢350). There is also a return bus from Carmen to **Las Tablas** (1hr., 2 per day 5am and 2pm, ¢350.) Another option is to take the GAFESO bus from San Isidro to **Buenos Aires** and then switch to a bus for **Las Tablas.** There is a direct bus to **Las Tablas** from the TRACOPA station in San Isidro (1 per day, 5:30am).

From Carmen, the walk is 4km up a winding, narrow road to the town of Altamira. Then turn right at the fork in the road after the church (marked by a MINAE sign) and walk 2km up an even steeper incline to the ranger station and camping site. The walk is intense, but the views of the nearby valleys are breathtaking.

▚ PRACTICAL INFORMATION

WHEN TO GO. Because there are fewer tourists during the rainy season, you may have **Estación Altamira,** the park station, entirely to yourself; however, it is best to call the **MINAE** office in Buenos Aires to alert them of your arrival. (☎ 730 0846. Open M-F 8am-4pm.) If you need more information and can't get a hold of the Buenos Aires MINAE office, try the one in San Isidro. (☎ 771 4836 or 771 5116. Open M-F 8am-4pm.) Estación Altamira does not have a phone of its own, but is in close radio contact with the Buenos Aires office.

▐ ACCOMMODATIONS AND CAMPING

In Carmen, you can stay at **Soda y Cabinas Carmen de Biolley ❶** and buy limited groceries. (*Casados* ¢950, rice dishes ¢800. *Soda* open daily 6am-9pm. Rooms ¢1500 per person.) **Estación Altamira ❶** is well-equipped for camping, with bathing facilities, potable water, electric outlets, and a picnic area. There is also an exhibition room, an amphitheater, and a biodiversity lab. All facilities are in excellent condition. You'll have to bring your own food and camping equipment, though you can restock in the nearby town of Altamira, 2km down the hill.

(Camping US$2 per person.) At any time, reservations are not generally necessary, but be sure to call ahead to the **MINAE** office in Buenos Aires to alert them of your arrival. (☎730 0846. Open M-F 8am-4pm.)

⬛ HIKING FROM ESTACIÓN ALTAMIRA

The views from the station itself are gorgeous, but several trails beckon you to explore further. Be sure to check with the rangers; they'll let you know the latest conditions and offer more suggestions. Some trails are more difficult to follow than others, so a guide is both advisable and often required. (Guides ¢5000 per day; can be arranged in advance through the ranger station or MINAE office.) Most guides are local farmers, so another option is simply to ask around in Carmen. Most groups are capped at 10 people. You can also hire a local to carry your stuff along the trails for the same amount.

SENDERO GIGANTES DEL BOSQUE

The **Sendero Gigantes del Bosque** is a 3hr., 3km hike through secondary and primary forest, named after the trees that tower up to 40m. The trail mostly hovers around 1300m, but inclines up to 1500m. There is a bird watching observatory at the border of the primary forest along the trail. Along the way, you'll certainly see strangler figs and numerous species of birds and butterflies, and maybe even a toucan or a quetzal. Wear long pants; the grass is hip-deep on the second half of the route, but can be avoided by turning around at the abandoned house.

SENDERO VALLE DEL SILENCIO

This 20hr. round-trip journey through the poetically named Valley of Silence is the best known and the most highly recommended. Hikers claim that a magical, awe-inspiring tranquility haunts the trail; even the rivers are silent. The hike travels more than 20km each way through cloud forest and unique natural *páramo* gardens up to an altitude of 2700m. The trail has a camping area, and 15km from Altamira along the trail is a newly built *albergue*, with 4 rooms and a bath.

⬛ HIKING FROM NEARBY RANGER STATIONS

SENDERO ALTAMURA-SABANAS ESPERANZAS

This trail takes you to natural savannas 1808m above sea level, leads past an indigenous cemetery, and provides excellent views of the small towns below. Keep an eye out for the many birds, including quetzales, which live in the oak and cedar trees. To reach this trail, take a left instead of a right at the fork in the road next to the church in Altamira. This dirt road will lead to the town of **Biolley,** which has its own small ranger station and the entrance to this beautiful hike. Another option to get to Biolley (during the dry season only) is to take a left onto the dirt trail running by Comercio Tuca, 300m up the road from Soda Carmen. Elsewhere in the park, the very adventurous can take five to six days and hike to La Amistad's highest mountain, **Cerro Kámuk** (3580m). A guide is an absolute requirement for this trek. The closest ranger station is Potrero Grande, which is 10km from Paso Real. Twenty kilometers into the hike, there is another ranger station, **Tres Colinas.**

✖ PASO CANOAS: BORDER WITH PANAMA

Paso Canoas, the site of immigration offices at the Panamanian and Costa Rican border, is not scenic. It is easy to accidentally wander from one country to another while shopping, but the (fairly) painless passport and tourist card process is absolutely necessary for those advancing further into either country. Although immigration offices may have you jump through a few hoops, visitors with proper papers rarely encounter more serious troubles.

▐ TRANSPORTATION. To get to the border from the Costa Rican side, take a **bus** to Ciudad Neily, where you can transfer to a bus for Paso Canoas. **Taxis** travel one way between the towns for US$5. Paso Canoas is 50km west of David, with buses linking the two every 10min. Leave comfortably on **LaFron.** (☎ 727 6511. US$1.50.) On either side, TRACOPA (100m west and east of the intersection) sells tickets to David and San José. (☎ 732 2119 or 727 6581. David 7-8hr.; 4, 8am, 3pm; ¢2545. San José 6½hr., 9am, ¢2625.) Even if you have no intention of visiting either city, you have to fork over the cash for this ticket. A plane ticket out of Panama is the only other accepted proof of exit. TRACOPA restaurant next door to the terminal will hold your bags while you sort things out. (¢300 per suitcase/backpack, ¢500 overnight.)

◪ ▐ ORIENTATION AND PRACTICAL INFORMATION. The main street, **Calle Central,** runs north-south, with perpendicular **Av. Central** neatly dividing Costa Rica on the west and Panama on the east. Stores on one side of the street use *colones* (¢), while those on the other use *balboas* (i.e. US$). The **Interamericana** from Neily and San José cuts straight through town towards David and Panama City.

To leave, go to the Costa Rican **General de Migración,** 175m west of the main intersection. Fill out a worksheet at the *salida* counter and buy a ¢200 passpoolrt stamp. (☎ 732 2150. Open daily 7am-8pm.) **Customs** is next door. (Open M-Sa 6am-11pm, Su 6-11am and 1-5pm.) Entering Panama, travelers need a passport, a tourist card (available at the border checkpoint; US$5, lasts 30 days), and a return ticket. Entering Costa Rica has the same requirements. Tourist cards are sold at Instituto Panameño de Turismo on both sides. (Open 6-11am and 1-5pm, but schedule varies.) Both sides have additional checkpoints 1km down the Interamericana. **Money changers** abound. *Bolsijeros* on the Panamanian side, identifiable by the fanny packs slung across their chests, give the best exchange rate, but check the rate before you approach them to avoid getting hustled. The **police** are 50m from either border. (Costa Rica ☎ 732 3402 or 911 for emergencies; Panama ☎ 727 6521.) In Panama, the **Banco Nacional de Panamá** is 25m from the crossing and has a 24hr. ATM for US dollars. (☎ 727 6522. Open M-F 8am-3pm, Sa 9am-noon. MC/V.) Buses drop off in front of the **post office** in Costa Rica. (☎ 732 2029. Open M-F 8am-noon and 1-5:30pm.) There is another post office in Panama. (Open M-F 8-11am and 2-5pm, Sa 8am-noon.) You can find telephones at almost every corner.

▐ ▐ ACCOMMODATIONS AND FOOD. Though lacking major points of interest, Paso Canoas will not leave you hungry, and the town's hotels serve hapless travelers who get their feet stuck in bureaucratic mud. In Costa Rica, **Cabinas/Restaurante/Bar Antares ❶,** across the street from TRACOPA, fulfills all basic needs. Some mirrors are broken, but baths are clean and private. (☎ 732 21 23. Singles ¢2000; doubles ¢3000. Bar/restaurant open daily 8am-1am.) **Cabinas El Hogar ❶,** next door, has brightly painted walls and a friendly host family. All rooms have baths and face a courtyard garden. (☎ 732 2653. ¢2000 or US$5 per person.) A good option is **Cabinas/Bar/Restaurante Interamericana ❷,** 200km east of the Interamericana, which has an excellent restaurant and basic beds. (☎ 732 2041 or 732 2478. Seafood up to ¢4500, rice dishes ¢1200-1500, appetizers ¢300-900. Restaurant open Tu-Su 11am-11pm. Rooms ¢2000 per person; ¢500 less for groups. V.) **Cabinas Hilda ❶,** next door to Cabinas Interamericana, has a welcoming 24hr. reception, clean flowered curtains, and garden areas. (☎ 732 2873. ¢2000 per person with bath.) On the Panamanian side of the shopping strip, try **Hotel Mamy ❶** for good management and the cheapest beds in town. (☎732 1506. ¢1000 per person.) **Cabinas Zapatería Andrea ❶,** also on the strip amidst the street's commotion, has cheap beds with private baths. (☎732 1766. Parking available. US$5 per person.)

Expect good, quick meals at the border—but nothing too authentic. In Costa Rica, next to the post office, **Tico Pollo ❶** has clean tables and fast food. (☎732 1075. Combo meals ¢995-2850. Open daily 9am-11pm.) The Panamanian equivalent is **Café Raul ❶,** 50m east of the crossing. (☎727 6311. *Comidas corrientes* US$1.50. Open 24hr.) Across from the Costa Rican immigration office, **Restaurante Brunca Steakhouse** actually houses **Restaurante Don Julio ❷,** with a large selection of more complete meals and Chinese food. (☎732 2117. *Casados* ¢1100, rice dishes ¢1320-1650. Open 5am-10pm.) **Supermercado San Isidro** is well-stocked and on the shopping strip. (☎732 1616. Open daily 7am-7pm. AmEx/MC/V.)

PENÍNSULA DE OSA & GOLFO DULCE

If what you seek is pristine rainforest teeming with monkeys, macaws, and mysterious beasts, the Peninsula de Osa in the southwest is the place to go. From the wetlands around rural Sierpe and secluded Bahía Drake, to Parque Nacional Corcovado, nowhere else in Costa Rica will you find such intense and diverse tropical flora and fauna. Bounded only by long, empty beaches, the wilderness seems endless. Puerto Jiménez is the only sizeable city on the peninsula, and the most convenient base for explorations of Corcovado. If you want to escape other travelers, try the virgin nature reserves around Golfito on the mainland just across the Golfo Dulce. If the jungle isn't challenge enough, test your surfing skills on one of the world's longest lefts in Pavones, or sip the milk of a freshly cut coconut and enjoy the sunset on the area's secluded beaches.

SIERPE

Founded about 60 years ago, tiny Sierpe was originally a community of banana plantation farmers. The gravel road leading to this town still cuts through 10km of banana plantations. However, the residents of the village now make their livelihoods through fishing, cattle-ranching, and ecotourism. Locals are welcoming and tourist-savvy in this slow-paced, small town. In addition to providing indispensable transit to Bahía Drake, Sierpe boat owners provide many tours to the nearby lagoons and the adjoining river.

TRANSPORTATION. The trip to Sierpe and ultimately, Bahía Drake, is fairly complicated. To get to Sierpe from anywhere in Costa Rica, you must first travel to Palmar Norte (for transportation details see **Palmar Norte,** p. 310). **Buses** leaving Sierpe to Palmar depart across the street from Sonia's Abastecedor (every 2-3hr. 5:30am-5:30pm, ¢200). **Taxis** can be negotiated from the same spot (US$10).

ORIENTATION AND PRACTICAL INFORMATION. The **parque central** and **Bar/Restaurante Las Vegas** on the *parque*'s corner comprise the heart of the tiny village. Doña **Sonia's Abastecedor** (grocery) across from the *parque central* can also help you with bus questions and give advice for travelers to Bahía Drake. (☎/fax 786 7366; elfenix@sol.co.cr. Open M-Sa 6am-6pm, Su 6am-5pm.) The **police** station (☎786 7539) is located across the street from Las Vegas. **Phone** calls can be made from a pay phone outside Las Vegas or in the Pulpería Fenix (fax available). **Internet** is available at **El Fenix Dos,** the all-purpose store next to Sonia's grocery. (US$5 per 30min., US$9 per hr. Open M-Sa 6am-5pm, Su 6am-4pm.)

ACCOMMODATIONS AND FOOD. If you do spend the night here, **Hotel Margarita ❶,** 200m inland from the left side of the *parque central* past the soccer field, offers the best rates in the area, is clean, and has friendly hosts. Its tiled

IN RECENT NEWS

X MARKS THE SPOT...

Isla del Coco, an island 532km from Cabo Blanco (the southernmost tip of the Osa Peninsula), has long been considered a prime location for the study of evolutionary biology and ecology. No one supposed, however, that astronomy would be the science to cause the most recent stir about the island.

Using satellite technology, the Russians discovered high concentrations of precious metal on the island. Now, the Costa Rican and Russian embassies are busy trying to negotiate and engage in further studies. Some suspect that the gold may be the buried treasures of the infamous pirate Henry Morgan (1635-1688).

After the discovery of the island in 1526 by Spanish explorer Juan Cabezas, the island, with its thick jungle, torrential downpours, and misty atmosphere, became a favorite hiding spot for the fortunes of pirates of the Pacific. According to legend, Morgan used the island to bury the treasures he stole from Lima, Peru. Later reforming himself from pirate to colonial tyrant (appointed governor of the Jamaican Island), Morgan was said to have forgotten about his stash.

Far advanced from yellowed treasure maps and wooden ships, the Russian discovery belongs among modern day fairy tales. As of August 2002, the quest for the treasures of Isla del Coco remains as mysterious as the cloud-covered mountain jungles of the island—the Costa Rican government has not even issued a statement acknowledging a possible search.

floors and baths, hot water showers, and furnished patio will provide a welcome respite for a reasonable price. (☎786 7574. Singles with shared bath US$7; doubles with private bath US$12.) More upscale is **Hotel Oleaje Sereno ❸**, down the street from Las Vegas as you walk away from the park. The hotel was recently renovated and has an open air **soda ❶**. All rooms have large private baths and hot water. (☎786 7580; fax 786 7111; oloeajesereno@racsa.co.cr; www.oleajesereno.com. *Soda* open 6am-7pm. Laundry service ¢100 per piece of clothing. Singles US$20-25; doubles US$30-35; A/C US$5 extra. Prices vary by demand. V.) To spend a few pleasant hours in a social atmosphere, ▧**Bar/Restaurante Las Vegas ❶**, is *the* place to be in the crowded tourist months of the dry season. They serve everything from salad (¢500-800) to American fast food (¢400-700) to quell the gringo appetite. The *tico* food here is far better, but more pricey (rice dishes ¢900-1500; fish dishes ¢1500-1800; *batidos* ¢300-350). At night, neon beer signs light up and local families come out. (Karaoke Sa and every other F 7pm. Open daily 10am-11pm.)

▨ **OUTDOOR ACTIVITIES.** You can also hire tours from Sierpe. **Hotel Oleaje Sereno**'s (see above) English speaking **guide**, Carlos Gonzáles, offers the most possibilities in town. You can go **hiking** with him in the nearby Mangrove Forest (US$25), in Parque Nacional Corcovado (US$75), or in the nearby **bird-watching** regions (US$10). He will take you **horseback riding** at Violín Island (US$35) or **scuba diving** off Isla Caño (2 dives US$150). If you do not want to stray too far, Carlos will take you on a tour of the Sierpe Lagoon (US$40) or rent you a **kayak** or **canoe** to discover the area on your own terms (US$5 per hr.). The more extensive trips include lunch and park tours include the entrance fee.

Tours Marítimo, next door to Las Vegas, also offers to take you around the area. Featured tours are **bird-watching** at dawn (2hr., US$70 per boat) and a **night trip** to see crocodiles, snakes, and night birds (US$70 per boat). These boats fit five people, so try to find others to split the cost. They also rent **snorkeling** equipment for US$15 per person per day. (☎786 7591; cell 397 3166; fax 786 7579. M-Sa 7am-5pm.)

BAHÍA DRAKE

As the legend goes, Sir Frances Drake buried a treasure somewhere along this luscious coast in the 1570s. Gold, however, is not the priceless treasure you are going to find on a trip here. Bahía Drake's magic is found in its intense natural beauty, where monkeys drip off mango trees and waves crash on jungle coasts.

Península de Osa and Golfo Dulce

OSA PENINSULA

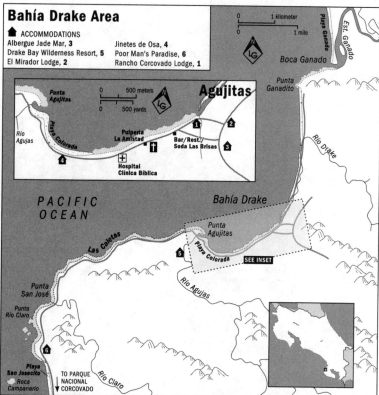

Bahía Drake Area

🔺 ACCOMMODATIONS

Albergue Jade Mar, **3**
Drake Bay Wilderness Resort, **5**
El Mirador Lodge, **2**

Jinetes de Osa, **4**
Poor Man's Paradise, **6**
Rancho Corcovado Lodge, **1**

Bahía Drake (pronounced DRAH-kay by locals) is not conducive to budget traveling, but few who travel here regret the expense. The area's wide, bending river, beaches, and extensive mangrove swamps also serve as a gateway to Parque Nacional Corcovado's teeming wildlife. The isolation of this town, with no telephone wires and almost exclusively boat access, is another huge draw. Bahía Drake may be one of the few places in Costa Rica where you can not only visit an undisturbed tropical paradise, but also (comfortably) live amidst the breathtaking nature.

▐ TRANSPORTATION

From Sierpe's *parque central*, the dock beside Bar/Restaurante Las Vegas sends a motor-boat down the Río Sierpe to Bahía Drake. (1hr.; US$15 if arranged through a hotel, US$80 if arranged through the lounging captains.) Even if you don't have a reservation, make sure to ask several captains and negotiate the price. With some effort, you can often wiggle your way onto another hotel's boat for US$15. Another option if you do not have a pre-arranged ride is to consult Sonia at the **Pulpería Fenix** (☎ 786 7311. See **Sierpe,** p. 321). She will know who is taking a boat out and at what times. Enjoy the ride as the boat winds past the legendary **Isla Violines,** where Sir Frances Drake's treasure is said to be buried. The mouth of the river becomes turbulent in the rainy season, so try to get on the earliest boat possible. The better captains will require passengers to put on life vests, while the less experienced ones will probably inspire even the fearless to wear the added security.

❄ ORIENTATION AND PRACTICAL INFORMATION

All hotels are along the bay's coast, with farms and uninhabited jungles lying farther inland. **Agujitas,** the main *pueblecito* on Bahía Drake, lies approximately in the center of the bay. Cutting through the town is a small river of the same name. The beach serves as a thoroughfare. **Bar/Restaurant/Soda Las Brisas** lies on the ocean front in Agujitas. To its right along the beach, facing inland, is the church, the *pulpería* **La Amistad** with a radio **phone** for national calls, and the medical clinic **Hospital Clínica Bíblica.**

🏠 ACCOMMODATIONS AND FOOD

The following hotels are the least expensive in town, though the average resort cost is three times as much—Bahía Drake's seclusion has its price. All supplies must be brought in by boat from Sierpe and all electricity is either solar- or generator-driven. Nearly all hotels offer activities; the larger resorts have more extensive offerings than others. Those listed can arrange for the boat ride from Sierpe (1hr., US$15). It's a good idea to make reservations in advance, particularly from November to April. Food options are mostly limited to hotels and usually included in prices; the **restaurant** in the village is sporadically open and rarely frequented.

▨ **El Mirador Lodge** (☎ 387 9138; fax 786 7292; info@mirador.co.cr; www.mirador.co.cr). A 10min. walk from Las Brisas. Facing inland, walk to the left along the beach. At the sign for the lodge, climb up onto the road and walk right where another sign will direct you left and 35m uphill. Mirador offers cheerful, simple rooms, a panoramic view, and many tour options. Home-cooking available is out of this world. Rooms have mosquito netting, private baths, and porches to enjoy the sunsets and brilliant starlight. US$35 per person, includes 3 meals and laundry. Camping US$5 per person with bathroom and water service. AmEx/MC/V. ❸

Poor Man's Paradise (☎ 786 6150 or 771 4582; poormans@cheqnet.net). A 2hr. walk south along the shore past the beautiful beach Playa San Josecito. This resort is heavily entrenched in rainforest thicket and offers one of the most nature-intensive properties in the area. Cabins with private baths and shower US$55 per person; with shared bath US$49 per person; tents with mattresses and outdoor bath US$39 per person. Camping US$7 per person. ❸

Albergue Jade Mar (☎ 786 7591 or 384 6681; pager 233 3333). Walk past the *pulpería* and then walk 5min. up the winding road. The five spacious, well-kept rooms have private baths and afford a central base where the locals live. Rooms are US$45 per person, cooking for yourself including pots and pans US$20 per person; US$35 for students; meals included. V. ❸

Rancho Corcovado Lodge (☎ 786 7903), 200m east of Albergue Jade Mar. The González family offers two sets of cabins, one in the shade of the rainforest and the other a stone's throw away from the beach. On their nearby *finca*, the family grows papaya and pineapple for your delicious meals. All newly remodeled rooms have private baths with showers. High season US$40; low season US$35; without meals US$20; camping in family's backyard US$10. ❸

Drake Bay Wilderness Resort (☎ 770 8012; fax 221 4948 in San José). Cross over the Agujitas River and head inland 300m. By far the most popular resort for large groups of students and families with children, this 5-acre resort maintains the utmost of order and class. Natural whirlpool, salt water swimming pool, and 24hr. hot-water showers. Buffet-style food included. Canoes for the nearby river are free. Triples US$95. Cash only. ❹

IN RECENT NEWS

A JUNGLE ADVENTURER'S DREAM COME TRUE...

A flawless map! As much as we all appreciate untouched wilderness, tourists and hikers in Costa Rica have been looking forward to a definite map to chart the areas of their adventures. Often, trails are less accessible and guides more imperative than in other countries. For the average traveler on too tight of a budget for a personal guide, the vast wilderness may be disappointingly difficult to explore. However, the professional cartographers of *National Geographic* and the Costa Rican *Instituto Geográfico Nacional* have been hard at work over the past year solving this very problem. Costa Rica, increasingly recognized as one of the most amazing adventure sites in the world, is the second country in the world after the United States to receive the honor of this effort. The map is 30% larger than usual (65 x 95cm), and waterproof for the wading rainforest trekker. The main map shows all of Costa Rica and the border regions of Panama and Nicaragua. In addition there is an inset showing all of Central America and another displaying street details of San José. The map also has indices to make it easier to find protected areas and towns, and a section with informative text on the region. The map's legend is in English and Spanish. (Available in 30 countries including Costa Rica, ¢4800).

Jinetes de Osa (☎371 1598; crventur@costaricadiving.com; www.costaricadiving.com). Facing inland, walk to the right up the beach and over the rocks (2min.) past the medical center. This American-run hotel isn't budget, but it is the only PADI-certified facility in the area (US$185 for a 2-tank dive off Isla del Caño, US$300-400 for courses), and also offers fullbody massages (US$40) and attractive rooms. On a hill, with views of the bay, each room includes a much-enjoyed porch. The staff will deliver a complimentary coffee to your door in the morning and point out the almond trees on their estate. All meals included. Rooms US$25 cheaper without food. Dec. 15-May 31 singles US$70; doubles US$60 per person; triples US$50 per person. June 1-Dec 14 singles US$60/US$50/US$40. Prices negotiable for students and longer stays. MC/V. ❹

⚑ OUTDOOR ACTIVITIES

Hotels arrange **horseback riding** (US$40-60), **kayaking** (US$15-40), or trips to the stunning **Isla del Caño National Preserve** (US$70-100), an ancient burial site for the indigenous people of the region. The island also holds a local archaeological mystery—several ancient, near-perfect round stones crowd the land. However, it is best known for outstanding **snorkeling** and **diving** and increasingly for its pristine kayaking through hidden lagoons and waterfalls. Hotels can also arrange guides into the depths of nearby **Parque Nacional Corcovado.** The cost of guides varies widely but runs at around US$70 per guide and day. It is recommended to enter Corcovado only with a guide from Bahía Drake. The park is more easily accessible from the southern part of the peninsula around Puerto Jiménez (p. 335).

GOLFITO

Golfito (pop. 18,000), home of the former headquarters of the United Fruit Company, sits on the northeast coast of the Golfo Dulce. Drastic regional cutbacks of banana production in 1984 led officials to save the town's economy by establishing a duty-free zone in the northern end of the city. Now, the famous shopping area draws *ticos* year-round and fills hotels on the weekends. The industrial ships that harbor here import fertilizer and export palm oil. Likewise, Golfito is a haven of spare machine parts, leftover from the banana company. For most tourists, it serves as a stopover to more exciting locales—the beaches of Pavones, Zancudo, and Cacao are nearby, as are the Golfito Nature Reserve and Puerto Jiménez.

FLORA, FAUNA, AND...POTTERY?

As adventurers to the Caño Island will discover, this biological reserve was not always so isolated from civilization. Caño Island is located 15km off the shore of Playa San Pedrillo, and every guide worth his binoculars offers a tour to its secluded shore. The main attraction? Engraved artifacts from the indigenous Agua Buenas (AD220-800) and Chiriquí (AD800-1500) civilizations. Archaeological research has proved that pre-Columbian Caño was a hub of commercial activity. The most astounding pieces are the human-sized, almost perfectly spherical *Diquis* stones, which can also be found in Pacific southern mainland Costa Rica. "Theories" about the stones' origin include that they were produced in "Poseidon," the capital of the mythical lost civilization of "Atlantis," which was, of course, located in what is now Costa Rica.

🗩 TRANSPORTATION

Flights: Sansa (1hr.; high season 6, 10:30am, 2:15pm, return 7:10, 11:40am, 3:25pm; low season 6, 9:30am, 12:30pm, return 7:10, 10:40am, 1:40pm; US$66) and **Travelair** (1hr.; high season 6, 8:30am, 2:30pm, return 7:20, 10am; low season 6, 8:30am, return 7:30, 10am; US$76) fly daily from San José (see **p. 85**) to the airport 4km north of Golfito. The Sansa office is 100m north of the docks.

Buses: Depart from the **TRACOPA** bus terminal (☎ 789 9037 or 789 9013) to **San Isidro** (4hr., 5am and 1:05pm, ¢1645) and **San José** (6-8hr., 5am and 1pm, ¢2920). Down the main street 100m north of TRACOPA, buses run to **Neily** (1½hr, about every hr. 5:30am-6pm) and the **Panamanian border** at **Paso Canoas**, 17km beyond Neily.

Boats and Ferries: For connections in the high season, plan to arrive early to secure a seat. From the *muellecito* (between Hotel Golfito and Hotel Uno in the *pueblo civil*) a **ferry** runs to **Puerto Jiménez** (1-2hr.; 11:30am; ¢1000 high season, ¢800 low season). Nearby, a **water boat** service, run by Froilan Lopez (☎ 775 2166), heads to **Playa Zancudo** (¢5000-7000) and other destinations like **Cacao, Casa Orquídeas, Pavones,** and **Playa Azul.** Similar service and prices can be found about 1km north from the gigantic *muello bananero*. For both water boat services, gathering up a group reduces individual fares. If you are traveling alone, some small talk with the customers at Dave's (see **Accommodations and Food,** below) will probably help you accomplish this.

Taxis: (☎ 775 0061). Terminal next to the gas station.

🔁 🔃 ORIENTATION AND PRACTICAL INFORMATION

Golfito runs along a 5km north-south stretch of beach road, with the gulf to the west. The city is physically and economically divided into two sections. The swankier **Zona Americana** lies near the duty-free zone and airport and takes up everything north of the hospital. It's home to a mix of US retirees and better-off *ticos*. The bus terminal and the Puerto Jiménez ferry dock, called **muellecito** (little dock), along with smaller businesses and *sodas* occupy the shabbier **Pueblo Civil** to the south. Two roads run south from the *muellecito:* one forks uphill, the other stays straight. White buses (¢100) and taxis (¢300) run up and down the length of Golfito between to two areas.

Tourist Office: There is no official tourist office in Golfito, but Dave Corella at **Coconut Café** (see **Food and Entertainment,** below) is a great source of information. **Club Centro** (see **Internet,** below) is another good source of information, even if only from the other tourists that flock here.

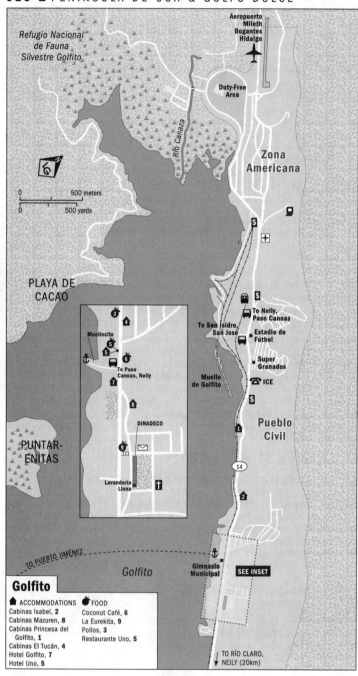

Refugio Nacional
de Fauna
Silvestre Golfito

Aeropuerto
Mileth
Bogantes
Hidalgo

Duty-Free
Area

Río Canaza

Zona
Americana

0   500 meters
0   500 yards

PLAYA DE
CACAO

PUNTAR-
ENITAS

Muellecito

To Paso
Canoas, Nelly

DINADECO

Lavandería
Llona

To Nelly,
Paso Canoas

To San Isidro,
San José

Estadio de
Fútbol

Super
Granados

ICE

Muelle
de Golfito

Pueblo
Civil

14

TO PUERTO JIMÉNEZ

Golfito

Gimnasio
Municipal

SEE INSET

TO RÍO CLARO,
NEILY (20km)

Golfito

🏠 ACCOMMODATIONS
Cabinas Isabel, **2**
Cabinas Mazuren, **8**
Cabinas Princesa del
  Golfito, **1**
Cabinas El Tucán, **4**
Hotel Golfito, **7**
Hotel Uno, **5**

🍴 FOOD
Coconut Café, **6**
La Eurekita, **9**
Pollos, **3**
Restaurante Uno, **5**

Tours: There are no tour offices in Golfito. It is most convenient to hire a tour guide in Puerto Jiménez (p. 335), but if you want to stay in Golfito, adventure day trips are available. Check out the bulletin board at **Coconut Café** and make a few phone calls. **Dolfin Quest** (☎775 1742 or 775 0373) offers a horseback riding tour that includes a 2hr. ride through the nearby rain forest and a tour of a butterfly farm, lunch, and kayaking. US$65. A less ambitious option is the sunset tour in the owner's boat US$25.

Bank: Banco Nacional (☎775 1101), 100m north of the bus terminal, changes traveler's checks and gives cash advances. Open M-F 8:30am-3:45pm. **Banco Coopealianza** (☎775 0025) has an **ATM** and sells phone cards. Open M-F 8am-5pm, Sa 8am-noon.

Market: Super Granados (☎775 1580), 300m south of the Banco Nacional. Huge grocery store with a large liquor selection. Open M-Sa 7am-7:30pm. AmEx/DC/MC/V.

Laundromat: Lavandería Ilona, near Hotel Delfina on the flat road south of the gas station. ¢600 per kg. Open M-F 8am-5pm, Sa 8am-noon.

Emergency: ☎911.

Police: ☎775 1022, emergency 117.

Hospital: ☎775 1001.

Internet: Club Centro, north of the *pueblo civil,* on the east side of the road just past the green hospital and university, has Internet access. ¢650 per hr., ¢550 for students; ¢1200/¢1000 for 2hr. Open Tu-Su 1:30-8:30pm. **Coconut Café** (see **Food and Entertainment,** below) also offers Internet access (¢1000 per hr.).

Post Office: (☎775 1911, fax 775 0373), uphill from the dock. Offers **fax.** Open M-F 8am-noon and 1-4:30pm, Sa 8am-noon.

OSA PENINSULA

ACCOMMODATIONS

There are cheap, simple accommodations in and around *pueblo civil.* In the quieter north end, many families take in guests.

Hotel Golfito (☎775 0047), south of the *muellecito,* offers some of the nicest rooms in town. Bright rooms have waterfront views, soft beds, and A/C. ¢3000 per person with fan; doubles with A/C ¢4000; triples with A/C ¢6000. ❶

Cabinas Mazuren (☎775 0058), 50m north of the soccer field on the high road. Offers a hodge-podge of rooms—all with bath—ranging from singles to family-style, two-room quads. A balcony overlooks the sea. Laundry service ¢500 per kg. Rooms ¢2000 per person; doubles ¢3000. Rooms must be paid in advance. ❶

Cabinas El Tucán (☎735 0553), 50m north of the *muellecito* on the right. Doña Desy offers basic rooms with private baths and fans. Parking available. ¢2000 per person. ❶

Cabinas Isabel (☎775 1774), farther up the road, offers slightly musty rooms with private baths and fans in a breezy house. Large balcony looks over the town's main drag. Parking available. Singles ¢1500; doubles ¢3000. ❶

Hotel Uno (☎775 0061), to the right of the *muellecito.* One of the cheapest places in town. Communal bath. A guard keeps things quiet at night. ¢580 per person. ❶

Cabinas Princesa del Golfito (☎775 0442), across from the Banco Nacional. Comfortable and sweetly decorated. Attached mini-*soda* open M-Sa 7am-9pm, Su 3-9pm. Rooms ¢2000 per person. ❶

OSA PENINSULA

◖ FOOD AND ENTERTAINMENT

You can grab a meal anywhere along the road between the Banco Nacional and the *muellecito*. There are more *sodas* than anything else, though prices hover consistently between ¢900 and ¢1500 for a full meal. Alternatively, go to **Super Granados,** a large grocery store (see **Orientation and Practical Information,** above).

▨ **Coconut Café** (☎ 775 0518; coconut@racsa.co.cr), in the pink building across the street from the dock. Personable American owner Dave will cook you up his homemade whole-wheat pancakes (¢1220), homemade chocolate cake (¢350), or a fresh milkshake (¢400). It's a good place to gather info from the bulletin boards and chat with other travelers, use the **Internet** (¢1000 per hr.), or park your gear for a few hours. Dave can also provide information on **volunteer jobs** and **available paid positions.** Open M-Sa 6:30am-10pm, low season M-Th 6:30am-8pm, F-Sa 6:30am-10pm. ❶

La Eurekita (☎ 775 1524), across from Cabinas Mazuren. Serves large plates of traditional fare in a breezy locale. Delivery available. Fish filet ¢1200. Open 6am-10pm. ❶

Pollos (☎ 775 2212), across the street from Cabinas Tucán. For a good dinner and some free entertainment to boot, try Th and Sa nights—a live band will play bolero, salsa, and other Latin music for an excited local crowd in the huge open air beachside place. Open daily 11am-whenever. ❶

Restaurante Uno (☎ 775 0061). If you crave Chinese food, this is the place for affordable chop suey (¢1000-1500). Open 10am-midnight. ❶

◣ OUTDOOR ACTIVITIES

For guided tours, see **Orientation and Practical Information,** above.

PLAYA DE CACAO. Although Playa de Cacao is easily accessible from Golfito, this beach is hardly ever crowded. The nearby rainforests and calm waters provide a refreshing afternoon respite before more ambitious trips. *(6km north around the bay from Golfito or a 1½hr. walk. Taxis cost about ¢1200. A taxi boat from the muelle bananero can also take you there.)*

REFUGIO NACIONAL DE FAUNA SILVESTRE GOLFITO. Besides nearby beaches, Golfito lies close to lesser-known hiking areas. Refugio Nacional de Fauna Silvestre Golfito (RNFSG) protects the steep, lush hills above Golfito. This forest area, with 125 species of trees, is visible from the entire town, and covers 13 sq. km, starting where the residential areas stop, 500m inland. The reserve has the advantage of remaining fairly dry even during the rainy season, and makes a pleasant alternative to more demanding routes in Parque Nacional Corcovado (see p. 339).

The park has several entrances. The main entrance lies just north of the Golfito airport and feeds into the Sendero Naranjal trail. A more popular path begins across from the Samoa Hotel, north of the *muellecito*. Walk inland past the school and the residential area; the main road uphill will become a trail and end at the radio towers at the top of the hill (1½hr.). A gravel road downhill will lead you back to Golfito and help you avoid a tricky descent (30min). A third access point starts from a gravel road 2km south of the town center, past the soccer fields but before Las Gaviotas Hotel, and heads to the radio towers 7km away. From the fourth access point, which starts behind the university, it may be possible to hike up with students that use the refugio for research, though this isn't very common for tourists. Other trails in the RNFSG include the Sendero Lechería and one leading from Playa Cacao. As of now, there is no fee to enter the *refugio* and services in the area are limited. Few people **camp** in the *refugio*, but it can be arranged. For more information and reservations, contact the MINAE office in Río Claro. (☎ 789 9092; fax 789 9292; rioclaro@ns.minae.go.cr.)

⚡ DAYTRIPS FROM GOLFITO

PARQUE NACIONAL PIEDRAS BLANCAS. Bordered by the Río Esquinas, the Río Bonito, the Golfo Dulce, and the Refugio de Vida Sivestre Golfito, the recently founded Parque Nacional Piedras Blancas radiates intense jungle beauty. Originally, the park was considered a section of the more famous Parque Nacional Corcovado, but in 1991, Piedras Blancas (144 sq. km) was declared independent, and its treasures now await exploration. Piedras Blancas teems with wildlife, from screeching monkeys to fierce jaguars. The park's astonishing contents have been acknowledged by MINAE, and the conservationists are currently developing projects to tame the wilderness and create greater accessibility for guideless tourists. Meanwhile, adventurous travelers can enter the park for free and surely find themselves alone on a breathtaking route.

Because the park is so new, the area has yet to develop a tourist infrastructure. Trails are marked, but not well-trodden. Most accommodations serving the area are overpriced private beach resorts that lead individual trips into the jungle. Though not isolated from surrounding towns, the park can be quite a challenge to reach with public transportation. There are many options to reach Piedras Blancas. If staying in Golfito, the best mode of transportation is to take a **taxi** (about ¢2000) north past the airport to the park's limits at **Río Bonito,** where five different short trails (1½-3hr.) start and end at the station. You can also catch a southbound **bus** in Golfito (anything heading to Ciudad Neily or Paso Canoas) to the small town **Río Claro** (35min., ¢150). In Río Claro, cross to the bus stop across the street to catch a bus northbound along the Interamerican Hwy. (every 30min, heading to San Isidro or San José). Ask to be dropped off at **Treinta y Siete** ("37"), the nickname for the small town of Villa Briceño (¢100). From here, head 3km west to La Gamba, then 13km south to Nueva Zelandia, and then 2km along the Río Bonito to the **ranger station.** Alternatively, you can ask your northbound bus driver from Río Claro to drop you off at **Chacarita** (¢300). Here, the Chacarita **MINAE office,** in a trailer across the street from the bus stop has more information. (☎ 741 1173. Open M-F 8am-4pm.) Turn left down the paved road to the peninsula off the Hwy. and take a left after 4km at the tiny town of **Riyito.** Here, crossing the tiny Río Esquinas will lead you to the jungle thicket. Beware: This river has no bridge, and may be impassable during the rainy season. Beginning here will be **full-day loops. Boats** from Golfito will also take you to the coastal properties (mostly hotels) at the westernmost edge of the park. Guides are not available, but the rangers will gladly accompany groups. It is best to call ahead to MINAE in Río Claro. (☎ 789 9092; fax 789 9292; rioclaro@ns.minae.go.cr.) If you are stuck without a place to stay, MINAE can give you a cot in El Bonito, but bring your own food. Another option is to stay at the pricey **Esquinas Rainforest Lodge ❹,** which specializes in hiking and horseback riding tours of the park. (☎ 382 5798; fax 775 0631; esquinas@sol.racsa.co.cr; www.esquinaslodge.com. Meals included. Singles US$100; doubles US$150.)

BEACHES SOUTH OF GOLFITO

PAVONES

Home to one of the longest lefts in the world (the wave goes on and on and on), Pavones is an essential stop on any true surfer's itinerary. When a swell is about to hit, the town itself swells with tourists. On these occasions, it is nearly impossible

THE BIG SPLURGE

PARROT BAY VILLAGE

Sitting on the waterfront of Golfo Dulce, Parrot Bay Village has eight *cabinas*, each named after a locally occurring animal that is carved into the door. If you are traveling in a large group, you may arrange an astoundingly spacious and beautiful suite in another two-story building in this small resort. Newly remodeled and eager for business, the owners are willing to negotiate discounts for students. In general, though, the luxurious wood floors and the spotless, enormous bathrooms look like they have never seen a backpacker's sullied boot. A Colombian native, arguably the best chef in town, prepares the meals in the resort's own restaurant and bar, so you can indulge yourself completely while gazing at the surrounding rainforest and Golfo Dulce. The beach is a mere 1min. walk away. Parrot Bay Village also offers guided tours, wildlife watching, and sportfishing trips. *(250m past the yacht club on the beach.* ☎ *735 5180; fax 735 5568; mail@parrotbayvillage.com; www.parrotbayvillage.com. High season US$90 for 1; US$110 for 2; US$130 for 3; US$150 for 4. Low season US$70/US$80/US$90/US$100. Year-round US$125 for private suite with cooking sink and private bath that sleeps 8 if you share double beds. MC/V.)* ❸

to find an inexpensive place to stay. Nearly everyone here is blond, bronzed, and in board shorts. Surfers come here for months at a time (especially during the wet season, when the swells are best), and the absence of anything but a spattering of *cabinas* here is a testament to their passion. However, with powerful waves smashing into the black jagged shore, Pavones is an aesthetic treat for the occasional nonsurfer who wanders into town. More sand and fewer surfers can be found on the beach of **Punta Banco,** 5km southeast. Follow the dirt road along the coast until the beach becomes less rocky (1km), and then continue your trek on the dark sands.

■■ **TRANSPORTATION AND PRACTICAL INFORMATION.** All **buses** pick up in front of the school along the shore. Two buses per day run from Pavones to **Golfito** (2hr.; 5:30am and 12:30pm, return 10am and 3pm; ¢550 for the bus, ¢30 for a ferry ride en route). The bus heading to Golfito stops in **Conte,** where you may catch a daily 4:30pm bus to **Playa Zancudo** (¢300). On the weekends, an 11:30am bus also runs from Conte to Zancudo.

The biggest **grocery store** in town, **SuperMares,** is 400m north of Esquinas, inland past the school. (Open M-Sa 6am-6:30pm.) **Public phones** are at Esquinas (¢100 per minute for all calls) and at Soda La Plaza. Across the street from Esquinas is the "Arte Nativo" shop with earrings, hats, posters, and, most importantly, the only **email access** (no Internet) in town from an American's cell phone. (☎ 383 6939; tamello@sol.racsa.co.cr. M-Sa 8am-8pm, ¢500 per 10 min.)

■■ **ACCOMMODATIONS AND FOOD.** Oceanside **Cabinas Esquina del Mar** ❶ in Pavones is a true surfer hangout with a popular *cantina.* This bar is open irregularly, and is always blaring music in the daytime. Nightlife in this town is lacking, as tourists wake up early to surf straight through the day. Rooms here have dying mattresses and boxy but clean communal bathrooms. Bring a mosquito net, as there are no screens on windows. Ask laid-back surfer owner Billy for room #1, the most popular suite. (☎ 383 6737. ¢2000-3000 per person, negotiable for students and longer stays.) Directly across the road is **Hotel Maureen** ❶, with high, varnished-wood ceilings, fans, and spacious floors. Communal baths are in mediocre condition, but are not unpleasant. (Singles ¢2000, negotiable for longer stays.) The restaurant downstairs offers a limited selection (*Casado* ¢1100; open daily 5am-10pm), but the attached store offers lots of packaged food. (Open daily 3pm-7pm.) **Cabinas Cazolas** ❶, a block from Hotel Maureen on the road perpendicular to the soccer field, offers neat, homey rooms. (Laundry ¢100 per piece. Check-out 11:30am. No noise after 10pm. Access to family's kitchen. Surfboard rentals US$10 per day. Rooms US$8; with sparkling, tiled bath US$10.) **Cabinas Willy Willis ❷,** next door to Maureen, is one of the cleanest, most newly-renovated hostels in town. Each room has a private bath and has two wooden beds. (US$20 per room, no discounts.) **Cabinas Celeste ❷,** up the street from Esquina La Plaza, has huge beds, spacious tiled floors, and communal bathrooms. (Shared double US$8 per person, negotiable for longer stays.)

Fresh thin-crust pizza and pasta made by resident Italians make **🖾Alerl ❶,** up the street from Esquina La Plaza, a local hot spot. Stay in their brightly painted cabinas, share an enormous pizza with friends or stop by early for delicious morning bread. (Pasta ¢1500-2000; 2-3 person pizza ¢3000-4000. Restaurant open daily 6pm-whenever. shared room ¢2500 per person; single with bath ¢3000.) Beat the surfers searching for munchies by visiting Doña Dora's popular **Soda La Plaza ❶,** up the soccer field from Maureen, for quick service of the best *tico* food in town. (Public phone inside. Open 6am-9pm.) **Puesta del Sol ❶,** 200m past the soccer field (follow the signs) is the tourist favorite. (Homemade tortellini ¢1600. Open 10am-10pm.)

ZANCUDO

With five kilometers of spotless black-sand beach, top-notch ocean swimming, and world-record sportfishing, Zancudo feels like it should be filled with tourists and have correspondingly high tourist prices—but that's not the case. There is a small ex-pat community cruising the main road in golf-carts, but in general, this beach town yet to be discovered by foreign travelers. During Christmas and Easter weeks the town swells under an influx of hundreds of *tico* families camping on the beach. The rest of the year, though, Zancudo remains one of the most quiet, relaxing and beautiful beaches in Costa Rica.

▐ TRANSPORTATION. From Golfito, boats are easiest; a **ferry** leaves from Golfito's *muellecito* to Zancudo (45min., noon, ¢700). It returns from the town pier, on the estuary side of the school, at 6am. A local boat captain, **Miguel Macarela,** usually departs Golfito at 5am and returns at 1pm (US$2). Macarela's competitors have newer boats and charge a few dollars extra for this luxury. These schedules are variable—check at the dock ahead of time.

During the dry season only, an afternoon **bus** runs between Golfito and Zancudo. Year-round, there's usually a bus from **Neily** and the Panamanian border—in **Conte** just look for it around 4:30pm along the Golfito-Pavones bus route.

▐ ORIENTATION AND PRACTICAL INFORMATION. Located on a peninsula jutting out into the Golfo Dulce, Zancudo is 15km south of Golfito and 10km north of Pavones. The town runs along a 3km beach road; the gulf is to the west and the estuary to the east. On the southern end of the beach, the waves are right for some gentle surfing. Farther north, however, the beaches attract only bathers. Mangrove forests surround the Río Sabalo, which runs inland from the middle of town. The dock is located on the estuary, 500m before the northern tip of the peninsula. Most businesses have handmade signs, and may be difficult to recognize.

During the dry season, a good source of **tourist information** is the gift shop and juice bar **Shangri-La** owned by an American, Sharon. (Open dry season Th-Su 10am-4pm.) For sports **fishing** information, contact **Roy's Zancudo Lodge** (☎776 008) or **Arena Altar** (☎776 0115), but expect high prices. The main *pulpería*, **Bella Vista,** lies in the center of town. (Open daily 7am-1:30pm and 2:30-7pm, but will extend hours during high season.) The **police station** (☎911 or 776 0166) is 100m from the deck, past the school on the road bearing right. One of the town's few **public phones** is located in front.

FROM THE ROAD

RAIN, RAIN COME BACK AGAIN

As a resident of Boston, a city grayed by clouds and rain year-round, I developed an embittered reaction to any sign of a shower, and I am always ready to shoot my umbrella open at the slightest provocation.

My experiences researching in Costa Rica, however, have completely changed my perspective on the ominous graying of skies. At the first stop in my itinerary, the fairly bustling San Isidro, I faithfully carried my umbrella during my 6hr. researching trek through the city streets. I shielded myself against the rain over the duration of the day, only to realize that I still got soaked, by my own sweat. By shying away from the rain, I not only revealed myself as the *gringa* I truly am, but also I missed the only possible respite from the grueling heat.

And after a while, however, it became more than a cure for the heat. The rain here is what every child dreams of. The huge drops really get you soaked in minutes. Yet since it's still warm, it's perfect to go out, uncovered, and just extend your arms and turn your face to the gray skies, as the rain hits your face and refreshingly crawls down, cooling your body. Not to mention the fresh smell of wet earth that inspires your journey.

Now, I have learned to look forward to the afternoon showers in this tropical paradise. My lips curl into a contented smile when I feel the familiar breeze that announces a storm. (Needless to say, "dry" is no longer in my vocabulary.) Forget sun worshipping—long live the rain!

— Natalia Truszkowska

Coloso del Mar, 2km south of the docks, offers the only **Internet** service in town. (☎ 776 0050, minimum ¢400 plus ¢30 per min. or ¢1700 per hr.)

ACCOMMODATIONS AND FOOD. Accommodations are generally divided into two categories: backpacker dives and luxurious, fully equipped cabins. If traveling in a large group, sharing a cabin with a kitchen might actually turn out to be an affordable option—and more comfortable. The best backpacker deals are usually attached to a *soda* or bar, and are a few meters from the beach. **Cabinas, Bar y Restaurante Tío Froilan ❶,** in the center of town, offers basic budget rooms with bath and fan to a mostly *tico* clientele. (☎ 776 0101. ¢2000 per person.) Other backpacker rooms are found in a light blue house with pleasant garden next door to the popular dive **Bar Sussy ❶.** (☎ 776 0107. US$5 per person with fan and private bath.) **Soda Katherine ❶** (see below) has clean and comfortable budget rooms with private bath, TV, and fan, but you have to cross the street to get to the beach. (☎ 776 0124. Doubles ¢5000; triples ¢7000.) **Bar/Restaurante Tranquilo ❶,** 2km south of the dock offers modest but well-kept *cabinas.* (☎ 776 0131. *Casados* ¢1100; Imperial ¢400. Restaurant open daily 6am-10pm. *Cabina* with collective bath ¢2000.) Although somewhat pricier, the beachfront **Cabinas Los Cocos ❸** are definitely worth it. Artists/owners Susan and Andrew offer beautifully designed, fully equipped cabins with palm frond roofs, private desks, hammocks, fans, kitchenettes, fridges, coffee makers, blenders, mosquito nets, European-tiled bathrooms, hot water, boogie boards, and bikes. (☎/fax 776 0012; loscocos@loscocos.com; www.loscocos.com. Restaurant open daily 7am-8:30pm. Family offers water boat service to Golfito for US$12.50 per person. Laundry included. 3- to 4-person cabin US$50-55; less if you stay a while.) You can fit even more (5-6 with shared beds) into a less luxurious cabin with fridge, bath, and full kitchen at **Cabinas BM ❸,** in the center of town on the beach. (☎ 776 0045. ¢12,000-18,000 per cabin.)

Alberto makes large brick oven pizza at **La Puerta Negra ❷,** as well as pasta topped with fresh basil from his herb garden; dishes burst with flavor. This is a favorite spot of locals and tourists. (*La Totale* pizza with everything ¢2400. Open Tu-Su 6pm until the last customer leaves.) If this isn't enough Italian food for you, try another favorite, **Maconda ❶,** snug behind a garden decor, following the stone walkway across from Tío Froilan. (☎ 776 0157. Fettuccini ¢1500; fish varies with size and seasons ¢1500-2500. Open roughly from 3pm until last customer leaves.) Next door, **Bar/Restaurante Los Ranchitos ❶** has a thatched roof and open air seating, with cheerful music playing as you enjoy your *tico* food. (*Casado* ¢1500-2000; juice ¢300; beer ¢400. Open daily noon-midnight.) One more house down the road is **Soda Katherine ❶,** a less expensive but equally delicious *tico* option. **Restaurante Mar y Sol ❶,** not to be confused with "Sol y Mar" a kilometer south, has cute seating and good local food. Su nights during dry season come alive with karaoke at 7pm. (☎776 0042. *Casados* ¢1000. Fresh fish ¢1300. Open daily 6am-7pm.)

PUERTO JIMÉNEZ

The backpacker alternative to Bahía Drake, Puerto Jiménez offers far lower prices and more options for collective transportation and tours into the nearby **Parque Nacional Corcovado.** Puerto Jiménez is undeniably convenient, but the high concentration of passing tourists has stripped the town of its individual character. The beach is unimpressive, and the town center is well-populated with confused foreigners and numerous stores that cater to them. It's best to stay in Puerto Jiménez as a base for exploring the nearby natural wonders.

TRANSPORTATION

Flights: Sansa (☎735 5017), 300m south and 25m west of the soccer field, and **Travelair** (☎735 5062), 450m south of the southwest corner of the soccer field on Calle Comercial fly daily from San José (see p. 85). Sansa (55min.; high season 6am and 2:05pm, return 7:05am and 3:05pm; low season 6am and 12:30pm, return 7:10am and 1:40pm; US$66). Travelair (55min.; high season 6, 8:30, 11am, 2:30pm, return 7, 9:40am, 12:25, 3:40pm; low season 6, 8:30, 11am, return 7:10, 9:40am, 12:30pm; US$76). Reservations are necessary for both airlines, as flights typically sell out well in advance in the high season. In the low season, it's fairly easy to get tickets a few days in advance. Both airlines also arrange **rental cars** and other transportation.

Bus: Departures 100m south of arrival stop. One daily bus to **San José** (9hr., 5am, ¢1950) via **San Isidro** (6hr., ¢1400). 2 buses depart daily for **Neily** (4hr.; 5:30am, 2pm; ¢1000). Getting to Golfito is easiest by ferry, but it's possible to take a Neily bus and transfer at Río Claro.

Boat: 1 ferry daily to **Golfito** (1-2hr.; 6am; ¢1000 high season, ¢800 low season).

Taxi: Osa Natural Tours (see **Guided Tours,** below) offers their own taxi service to various sites in the peninsula. Taxis (trucks or cars) must be arranged ahead of time and hold a maximum of 5 people. Destinations are **Carate** (US$60), **Matapolo** (US$25), **Los Patos** (US$60), **La Palma** (US$40), **Puntarenita** (US$15), **Playa Preciosa** (US$7). All prices per taxi. Accessibility based on season—be sure to call and check.

ORIENTATION AND PRACTICAL INFORMATION

The **Calle Comercial** (main road) runs from the **soccer field** in the north to a **gas station** in the south. Buses arrive 100m west of the soccer field. The beach road runs just north of the soccer field and heads east to the ferry pier and airstrip. The area around the airstrip is residential and is surrounded by a scattering of small farms.

Tourist Information and **Internet: CafeNet El Sol** (☎735 5718), 200m south of the soccer field on Calle Comercial. Although not a formal tourist office, this connection to the world wide web also connects visitors to good general information about area adventures. Have a bottomless cup of coffee here (¢100) and use the maps on the walls to figure out your hiking itinerary. Internet ¢500 per 20min., ¢1500 per hr., Open daily 7am-10pm. For more specific tour information, see **Guided Tours** below.

Bank: Banco Nacional de Costa Rica (☎ 735 5155), 400m south of the soccer field. Cashes traveler's checks and has an **ATM** for MC/V. The nearest source of cash for any other cardholder is Golfito. Open M-F 8:30am-3:45pm.

Supermarket: Super 96 (☎ 735 5168 or 735 5496), 200m south of the soccer field on Calle Comercial. Open M-Sa 6am-noon and 1-7pm, Su 6am-1pm. For mosquito nets or other essentials, try **Tienda el Record,** just south. Open M-Sa 7am-7pm, Su 7am-5pm.

Laundry: Lavandería Kandy (☎ 735 5347), on the northwest corner of the soccer field. Enter in the space between the buildings. Same day service if requested. ¢400 per kilo. Open M-Sa 8am-6pm.

Red Cross: (☎ 735 5109), across from the clinic.

Medical Clinic: (☎ 735 5061). 10m west of the southwest corner of the soccer field. Open 24hr.

Police: (☎ 735 5114, emergency 911). A few steps south of the soccer field on the main street.

Telephones: International Communications (☎ 735 5011; fax 735 5480), 200m south of the soccer field on Calle Comercial. International calls ¢1500 per min. **Fax.** Open M-Sa 8am-1pm and 2-8pm.

Post office: on the west side of the soccer field. Open M-F 7:30am-6pm; Sa 7:30am-noon.

Postal code: 8203.

ACCOMMODATIONS

Camping: Puerto Jiménez Yacht Club (☎ 735 5051), near the water at the eastern end of the beach road (and nary a yacht in sight). This place has it all: well water, bathrooms, showers, and immediate access to the beach. The grassy camping area is slightly elevated, so you can keep a bit drier than on the beach. ¢1000 per person; a few tents available to rent. Camping on the beach is free. ❶

Cabinas Puerto Jiménez (☎ 735 5090), 50m north of the northwest corner of the soccer field. The story around town is that Oscar, the owner, is so obsessively clean that he picks the brown leaves off the garden's trees before they fall to the ground. It pays off in the delightfully fresh rooms, which offer fans, private baths, small tables, and a spot on the gulf's edge. Singles ¢3000; doubles ¢4000. ❶

Cabinas Marcelina (☎ 735 5007; osanatur@sol.racsa.co.cr), 3 blocks south of the soccer field on Calle Comercial on the left, is run by the Franceschi family, one of the oldest families in town. The newly remodeled rooms are clean, luxurious, and comfortably sized. All rooms have night tables, bedside lamps, private baths, and fans. Singles and doubles US$12 per person; triples US$30. Student discounts may be negotiable in the low season. ❷

Cabinas Thompson, (☎ 735 7148), 100m south and 100m west of the soccer field, behind Soda Marilys. Plain, spacious rooms with fans and private baths. Popular with backpackers, cheap, and close to the bus station. ¢1500 per person with student discount. ❶

Oro Verde (☎ 735 5241; fax 735 56814), 200m south and 50m east of the soccer field. White, spacious rooms, oak dressers, private baths, a balcony, and a central location make this a solid place to stay. Owners provide a plethora of tourist information, from schedules to recommended tours. Singles ¢2500; ¢2000 each for groups sharing a room. Traveler's checks accepted. ❶

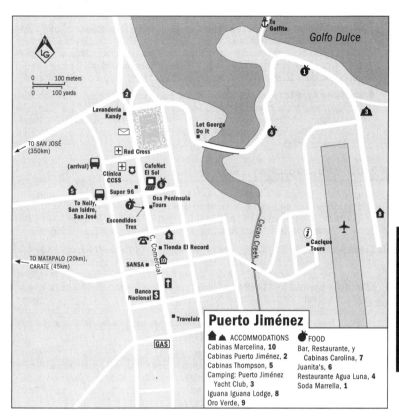

Puerto Jiménez

🏠▲ ACCOMMODATIONS
Cabinas Marcelina, **10**
Cabinas Puerto Jiménez, **2**
Cabinas Thompson, **5**
Camping: Puerto Jiménez
  Yacht Club, **3**
Iguana Iguana Lodge, **8**
Oro Verde, **9**

🍴FOOD
Bar, Restaurante, y
  Cabinas Carolina, **7**
Juanita's, **6**
Restaurante Agua Luna, **4**
Soda Marrella, **1**

Iguana Iguana Lodge (☎ 735 5261), along the airstrip. This site is the farthest out of town but offers more spacious grounds that include a pool. The patio is gorgeous, and the rooms are well-kept. A bar/restaurant serves guests from 3pm until whenever. ¢2500 per person; ¢2000 per person for groups or students. V. ❶

🍴 FOOD

Although the town has a wealth of tourist offerings, there are surprisingly few options for a hungry traveler. Most *sodas* in town serve slightly overpriced and bland food. Restaurants seem to be frequented according to trendiness (as deemed by the population of young beach bums).

Bar, Restaurante, y Cabinas Carolina (☎ 735 5185), on the Calle Comercial, consistently packs in tourists. A great place to chat with other travelers, people-watch on the Calle Comercial, and plan your next trip under the breeze of adjustable fans. *Tico* and American food at slightly inflated prices. Open daily 7am-10pm. ❶

Soda Marrella (735 5482), 100m down from the dock, is a reliable beachfront soda. Locals enjoy this place for its generous portions and convenient location. Fried fish ¢1200, rice dishes ¢1100, casados ¢900, tacos ¢350. Open daily 11am-8pm. ❶

Juanita's (☎ 735 5056), next to CafeNet El Sol (see **Orientation and Practical Information,** above), is the trendiest place in town for semi-authentic Mexican food. Locals and tourists flock here for specials, such as Taco Tuesday (₡200), half price entree Sundays (excluding fish dinners), free chips and salsa Saturday, and daily special on tap beer during Happy Hour (5-6pm, ₡250). Only a few vegetarian options. Most entrees ₡800-1500. Open daily 10:30am-11pm, bar may stay open longer depending on crowd. ❶

Restaurante Agua Luna (☎ 735 5033), on the beach road between the town and the ferry dock. Tourists flock here for the tropical Tiki bar decor and view of the mangrove-fringed lagoon and Chinese food. Classy, spacious seating, but still reasonably priced. Chop suey ₡700-1250, meat dishes ₡1370-1670, fish specialties ₡1270-1500. Open daily 10am-11pm. ❶

🐾 GUIDED TOURS

Puerto Jiménez serves as a launching point for the Osa Peninsula, and a number of tour operators have sprung up to cater to this need. Tours are not exactly "budget," but they provide access to places difficult to reach on your own. Also, the tours are heavily geared toward *gringos*, so most guides speak fluent English.

▓ **Escondidos Trex** (☎ 735 5210; osatrex@sol.racsa.co.cr), inside Restaurante Carolina about 150m south of the soccer field on Calle Comercial. Offers student and group discounts, and generally has fairly flexible prices if you call ahead. They offer everything "from super budget to super deluxe." Run by a fun-loving group of Americans, it's the oldest and most varied operation in town. Options include dolphin watching, mangrove kayaking, tree-climbing, waterfall rappelling, and multi-day hikes through Corcovado and the surrounding reserves. Best tourist information source in town. One of the only tourist organizations that rent tents. Open daily 8am-8pm.

Cacique Tours (☎ 735 5530; cocotero_tico@yahoo.com), next door to the MINAE office. Run by Oscar, an amiable local specialist on flora and fauna, who leads tours of Parque Nacional Corcovado and the surrounding area. These hikes are far more focused on biological identification and ecosystem education. Approximately $35 per person for 8hr. Student and group discounts. Open 8am-8pm.

Let George Do It (☎ 735 5313, 735 5062 to make reservations) is *the* place for marine adventures. Run by the entertaining George, who lives behind the Puerto Jiménez Yacht Club, 200m east of the dock on the beach road. He'll take you on dolphin tours, which include a dip with the dolphins as he swings you behind the boat on a boogie board, and whale watching tours. Open pretty much all the time, since he lives there.

Osa Natural Tourist Info (☎/fax 735 5440; osanatur@sol.racsa.co.cr; www.osanatural.com), facing the soccer field on the west side, is an umbrella organization for a number of local businesses. It offers guided tours of Corcovado, horseback riding, gulf tours, and air/ground/sea transportation. The website has links to many of the local tourist companies, and its bulletin board is packed with tourist possibilities. Here you can make reservations to fly to Sirena (10min., 5 people, US$200 per plane one-way). You will need to book through them in order to stay in Corcovado overnight, even if you are going on your own (see below). The staff is knowledgeable, friendly, and speaks English. 8hr. tours US$50-60; 3hr. kayaking tours US$25. Internet US$3 per hr. Get 2hr. for the price of 1 from 11am-3pm every day. Open daily 8am-8pm. V.

MINAE (☎ 736 5036 or 736 5580; fax 735 5276; corcovado@ns.minae.go.cr). Follow the beach road east until it curves inland. Take the 2nd left after the yacht club, and the busy MINAE office is 300m farther on the right. No tours, but some information available. Exhibits or Corcovado shells. Open M-F 8am-4pm.

Osa Pensinsula Tours (☎ 735 5107 or 735 5135; osapentours@racsa.co.cr), offers reasonably priced tours to Corcovado National Park (full day, 6am, US$50 per person), Matapalo (½ day, 6am, US$40 per person), kayaking (½ day, US$30 per person), bird watching (½ day, 5:30am, US$40 per person), waterfall tours (½ day, 7pm, US$50 per person) and tree climbing (½ day, 7am, US$50 per person). Flexible discounts for student groups. Open daily 7am-10pm.

Osa Aventura (☎/fax 735 5670; info@osaaventura.com; www.osaaventura.com), is the best option for longer (6- to 10-day) adventure tours. Mike Boston, the owner and sole guide, also operates an education program for students on rainforest ecology. Flexible pricing for students. Call for information.

PARQUE NACIONAL CORCOVADO

Sprawling along almost the entire western coast of the Osa Peninsula, Parque Nacional Corcovado is a virtual garden of Eden. The Peninsula, 57km in length and 25km in width, comprises only 4% of the land mass of Costa Rica, yet, it offers 50% of the biodiversity. Home to sloths, monkeys, anteaters, and almost 400 species of birds (including the magnificent scarlet macaw and the harpy eagle), it has earned the title from National Geographic as "the most biologically intense place on Earth." Furthermore, the primary and secondary rainforest in the region are comprised of hundreds of species of trees. Despite its popularity in the last few years, wild Corcovado still waits to be explored; some of the park's vegetation has yet to be even identified.

AT A GLANCE	
AREA: 440 sq. km land, 24 sq. km sea.	**CAMPING:** Camping only permitted in designated areas of ranger stations.
CLIMATE: tropical rainforest; dry (high) season Dec.-Apr., rainy (low) season May-Nov.	**FEES & RESERVATIONS:** Entrance fee US$8 for 1 day, US$17 for 2-3 days, US$26 for 4-6 days. Reservations strongly recommended, especially for longer trips. Reservation fee US$2.
HIGHLIGHTS: contains 50% of Costa Rica's biodiversity, including unidentified vegetation.	
GATEWAYS: Puerto Jiménez (p. 335), Bahía Drake (p. 322).	

OSA PENINSULA

⛏ ORIENTATION

There are four **ranger stations** inside the park boundaries, each of which has water, bathrooms, dining facilities, and campgrounds. Three of these form a triangle connected by year-round trails—**Sirena** on the southwest tip, **La Leona** on the southeast tip, and **Los Patos** to the north between them. Sirena and La Leona are the only stations with beds. **San Pedrillo,** on the northwest tip of the park, is accessible along the beach from Sirena only from December 1 to April 31. Seldom used by through-hikers, **El Tigre** is the 5th station, located outside of and detached from the park boundaries. **Los Planes,** a station in the northwest of the park, has been closed. Los Patos and La Leona are best reached from Puerto Jiménez; San Pedrillo is accessible from Bahía Drake.

⬛ TRANSPORTATION

Puerto Jiménez (p. 335) is the town on the peninsula that offers the most affordable and accessible transportation into the thickets of the national park. Most independent hikers choose this town as their base for exploring the park. To get to the ranger station at **La Leona,** take the *colectivo* truck or **minibus** from Puerto Jiménez to **Carate** (2hr.; M-Sa 6am and 1:30pm, return 8am and 4pm; ¢2000), which leaves in front of Mercado El Tigre on Calle Comercial, south of the soccer field. From Carate, turn right onto the beach and walk about an hour to the park entrance at La Leona. To get from Puerto Jiménez to **Los Patos** (1hr., 6 per day 5am-2pm, ¢500), first take a bus from Soda Marilys, 100m south and 100m west of the soccer field in Puerto Jiménez, and ask to be let off at **La Palma**. From there, hike to **Guadalupe** (2km, 30min-1hr.). From Guadalupe, it is a 1km **hike** to **Río Rincón** (1hr.), but it may be water-logged in the rainy season. Finally, from Río Rincón, **hike** 3km (1hr.) to the ranger station at Los Patos, along a path clearly defined by wooden markers. In the dry season it may be possible to take a **taxi** from Puerto Jiménez (2hr., US$60) or a taxi tractor from La Palma to Los Patos (2½hr., US$50-70), while in the rainy season this probably won't be an option.

From **Bahía Drake** (p. 322), the only way to get to the eastern and southern parts of the peninsula is by car or boat. Roads are very rough and often require passing through creeks. Boats, on the other hand, are very expensive. To reach the ranger station at **San Pedrillo** from Bahía Drake, either hike 18km (8-9hr.) along a shaded trail that hugs the beach, or hire a boat from one of the Drake hotels for US$60-80 per trip. (See **Bahía Drake: Outdoor Activities,** p. 326.) It may be necessary to take a boat when water levels are high; contact MINAE for more information. Osa Natural runs a *colectivo* on Tu during the dry season to Bahía Drake from Puerto Jiménez; call in advance to make reservations (US$20 per person).

🛈 PRACTICAL INFORMATION

 WHEN TO GO. Corcovado is tropical year round, with a rainy season from May to November, and a dry season from December to April. Some trails are only accessible during the dry season. Tidal changes make parts of some trails impassable at certain times of day. Although Corcovado is a lush rainforest, protection from the sun and proper hydration are absolutely essential, as hikes are long and in some stretches offer little or no protection from the sun. (See **Essentials,** p. 21 and p. 28.)

The park has an entrance fee. (US$8 for 1 day, US$17 for 2-3 days, US$26 for 4-6 days.) Because there are restrictions on the number of people in the park at a time, **Proyecto Osa Natural,** which handles the tourist traffic, strongly recommends making reservations one to two weeks in advance. Making a reservation involves planning and faxing an itinerary to Osa Natural; call them directly for instructions and information (US$2 reservation fee). The MINAE office in Puerto Jiménez answers specific questions on the park. (For Osa Natural and MINAE contact info see **Puerto Jiménez: Guided Tours,** p. 338)

If you plan on walking along the coast, pick up a **tide chart** from the ranger station, Osa Natural, or MINAE; water levels are often too high to cross. The heaviest rain falls from March to August, with nearly daily rain lasting until December. Stop at MINAE and ask for a helpful printout with safety information entitled *"Información Básica Importante para Visitantes"* before you head off to the park.

🏕 ACCOMMODATIONS & CAMPING

Most overnight trekkers hike between La Leona and Los Patos, spending the night at Sirena en route, or some other combination within that triangle. Rangers arrange lodging options and meals. (Breakfast ¢1500. Lunch and dinner ¢2500. Dorm beds US$8 high season, US$6 low season; bring sheets and mosquito net.

WHAT IS THE LARGEST LAND MAMMAL IN CENTRAL AND SOUTH AMERICA?

Believe it or not, it's the tapir. In Costa Rica, this animal, weighing up to 800lbs., is referred to as the *moli*, while Belizeans use the creative name "mountain cow." An ancient relative of the horse and the rhinoceros, the tapir can be a surprisingly strong and ferocious animal. In fact, its only natural predator in the southern rainforests is the jaguar (and bears in South America). The purely plant-eating tapir has somehow escaped human affection (and protection)—only now that the species is severely endangered is it getting some of the attention it deserves.

Camping US$4 per person; only allowed inside the station.) However, at the time of writing, the ranger station at La Leona was being remodeled and fumigated and didn't offer food or lodging; check in advance whether they have reopened.

There are two other inexpensive options along the beach before the ranger station La Leona. **La Leona Lodge Camping ❷** has 12 tents with small air mattresses, sheets, and towels at no extra cost. Newly built, the site has a kind staff and clean facilities. (☎735 5705; www.laleonalodge.com. High season breakfast US$8, lunch US$10, dinner US$12; low season US$8/US$13/US$14. High season US$15 per person, low US$10; US$5 with own tent, US$2.50 if meals bought at lodge.) A slightly more upscale camping experience is offered by **Corcovado Lodge ❸.** You can stay in large tents with real bed frames and mattresses and luxuriate in the hammock seating of the bar. (☎257 0766 office in San José; col@expeditions.co.cr. US$30 per double tent, US$60 with food.) Both camping areas are along the beach on the route to La Leona ranger station and are well marked.

HIKING

In addition to a tide chart, guides are recommended for attempting the three major long-distance hikes inside the park. The first trail, from **La Leona** to **Sirena** (20km; 6-7hr.) is along a sandy beach, with several parallel forest trails that are fairly well-marked. Three sections (Salsipuedes, Punta La Chancha, and Río Claro) are impassable at high tide. The second hike, from **Los Patos** to **Sirena** (20km; 6-8hr.), cuts right through the middle of the rainforest. This trail is especially difficult in the rainy season, particularly the crossing of the Río Pavo. The third trail, from **Sirena** to **San Pedrillo,** is only open from Dec. 1 to May 1. It hugs the beach and ends in the forest. (25km; 8-10hr.) This is one of the most dangerous hikes because it offers little shelter from the sun. **Use proper caution and hydration.**

Shorter **day hikes** are possible from Sirena, Los Patos, La Leona, and San Pedrillo. Behind the San Pedrillo station, the short **Sendero Catarata,** on the right with your back to the sea, loops near a waterfall. **Sendero Río Pargo** begins across the Río San Pedrillo, which runs along the station. This trail through the woods leads to Río Pargo ("Snapper River"), where you can swim while watching the fresh water run straight into the sea (1½-2hr. loop). **Sendero Playa Llorona** is a 6hr. round-trip, and much of it runs along the coast. Retrace your steps to return. From La Leona, a 3hr. hike (each way) takes you through the crocodile-populated Río Machigal and up the adjoining creek through caverns and rock formations. In the rainy season, this trail is only accessible if you are willing to wade up to your knees in water for the duration of the hike. Return to the beach via the same creek and then the river. This is an unmarked hike; find a guide and inquire whether it is safe and environmentally responsible to go on this hike.

CARIBBEAN LOWLANDS

The boggy coastal lowlands along Costa Rica's Caribbean shore contrast drastically with the terrain and culture of the Pacific seaboard. Here, there are no volcanoes, jagged peninsulas, or cool cloud forests. Instead, coconut palms, unbroken sandy beaches, and inland tidal marshes—all kept unfathomably muggy by constant precipitation—line the relatively deserted and remote Caribbean coast. Limón, or Puerto Limón, Costa Rica's decaying major Atlantic port, serves as a hub for tourists traveling to the fantastic Tortuguero breeding grounds, Parque Nacional Cahuita's spectacular coral reefs, and the placid beaches of Puerto Viejo de Talamanca. With fewer upscale resort hotels and a younger, more laidback feel, the southern Caribbean is a particularly popular alternative destination for young, international backpackers, while the difficult-to-reach northern corners invite dozens of turtle conservation volunteers and nature enthusiasts.

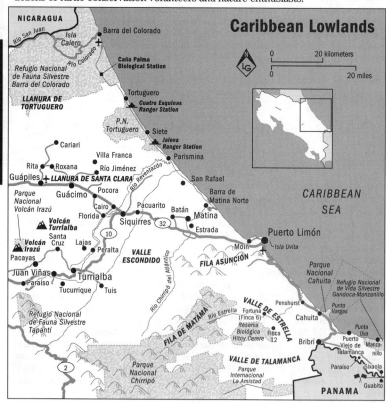

Caribbean Lowlands

Passing through, you'll encounter the region's ethnic and cultural diversity in a Spanglish mix spoken with a slight Caribbean accent, in which "okay" is a casual goodbye and "alright" a laid-back greeting. The region's minorities include Afro-Caribs and Chinese, who immigrated in the late 1800s to work on banana plantations and railroads, and the Cabécar and Bribrí indigenous groups in the South. The area's large minority population has long been overlooked and maltreated by the Costa Rican government. Although discrimination was outlawed in 1949 (when blacks were finally allowed to travel beyond the Caribbean Lowlands into the Central Valley), racism still persists, and black Limonenses are unwelcome by some people in the country. This discrimination greatly holds back development in the Limón Province. The Caribbean lowlands have a reputation for theft and casual drug use, and women travelers may feel less comfortable here. However, visitors with their wits about them should encounter few problems on this wonderfully slow-paced, reggae-loving coast.

GUÁPILES

In the days when the banana train hauled the valuable golden fruits for export to the Caribbean coast, Guápiles, 62km northeast of San José, was a city of cardinal importance on the San José-Limon banana highway. Now that roads have replaced the railways, however, Guápiles is used less as a trade hub than as a place where banana-hauling trucks can fill up on gas and get their breaks and tires repaired. Few travelers stop in this large, dusty city, as there is little to see or do in the immediate vicinity. Those with some money to spare can use Guápiles as a base for taking the unique Rainforest Aerial Tram, just 20km away.

▐ TRANSPORTATION

A few local **buses** shuttle passengers in and around town; ask anyone at a bus stop where the bus is headed. **Taxis** abound, although they tend to overcharge. A taxi from the bus station to the town center runs about ¢300. All intercity buses arrive and depart from the large **Guapileños Bus Station** at the south end of town. Buses depart from specific terminals, where up-to-date schedules of bus departures are posted. Many buses stop in smaller towns en route to those listed below; call ☎710 0808 or 710 6075 for additional information about schedules. Buses go to: **Puerto Limón** via **Guácimo, Pocora,** and **Siquirres** (2hr.; every hr. 6am-7pm); **Calle Vieja** via **Guácimo** (90min., 5 per day 6am-4pm); **Cariari** (direct about every 30-40min., 7:15am-7:15pm; indirect about every 30-40min., 6am-10:20pm) **Río Frío** via **La Finca** (5 per day 6am-4:25pm); **Río Frío** via **La Victoria** (5, 8:30am, 2, 3:30, 6pm); **Puerto Viejo de Sarapiquí** (7 per day 5:30am-5pm); and **San José** (every 30min. 5am-9pm).

▐▐ ORIENTATION AND PRACTICAL INFORMATION

Although streets are neither named nor labeled, Guápiles is not difficult to navigate. The **bus station** marks the southern boundary of town. The road alongside the bus station extends for about 250m before intersecting one of Guápiles' main arteries. At this intersection sits a **Más X Menos** supermarket. (Open M-F 9am-9pm, Sa-Su 9am-7pm.) Turning left at this intersection (coming from the bus station) and continuing about 400m brings you to another intersection marked by a large **church.** Turning right at this intersection and continuing 100m leads to yet another intersection; turn left and continue 50m to get to the **post office,** which will be on the left side of the street. (Open M-F 8am-noon and 1-4:30pm, Sa 7:30am-noon.) A busy fruit and vegetable **market** sets up next to the post office. Continuing another 200m down the road alongside the church leads to Guápiles' final main road.

IN RECENT NEWS

DRUGS IN CARIBBEAN PARADISE

The Province of Limón and Jamaica share many cultural and social similarities. Natives of both regions often speak a dialect derived partially from Jamaican English accents with an added inflection of the Spanish language. Likewise, Limonenses share many cooking styles and musical tastes with their (often) Jamaican ancestors. One commonality that is not so attractive, however, is the prevalence of drug production, trade, and use in both of these areas. While some protest that this is as much a part of the culture as Bob Marley and coconuts, the governments of Jamaica and Costa Rica firmly disagree.

Recently, officials in both countries have reaffirmed their commitment to the eradication of drug activity in Caribbean towns, as well as to international cooperation to achieve this goal. A Costa Rican-Jamaican committee specifically aiming to join forces between the sister cultures has now been established to purge these regions of their drug influence. Measures include increasing social awareness, instituting drug use prevention education programs, and organizing projects that emphasize community involvement, as well as detoxication and rehabilitation for those people who already suffer from drug addiction. Together with these programs, much is being done to clean up the reputation of these tropical paradises.

Turning left at the Musmanni Bakery and continuing 150m leads to several clinics and pharmacies. **Clínica del Caribe** handles emergencies 24hr. (☎710 1445 or 710 2164.) Turning right at the bakery and heading down the main road leads to a **Banco Popular** with a 24hr. ATM. (☎7100259. Open M-F 8am-5pm, Sa 8am-11:30am.) A **Palí** supermarket is another 150m down the road. (Open M-Th 8:30am-7pm, F-Sa 8am-8pm, Su 8:30-6pm.) Fifty meters later, a small road veers off the left. Just past this turnoff are the **Farmacia Santa María** (open 7am-8pm) and **Farmacia San Martín** (open M-F 7am-9pm, Su 8am-5pm). **Café Internet** sits another 100m down the road (¢500 per hr., open daily 7:30am-1am), and the **Banco de San José** is 30m further and has a 24hr. ATM. (☎7107484. Open M-F 8am-5pm, Sa 9am-1pm.) This road eventually dead ends at an intersection about 100m from the bank; turn left for the **Lavandería.** (¢700 per kilo, ¢150 per piece to iron. Open M-Sa 8am-6pm.)

ACCOMMODATIONS

Although Guápiles is not especially touristed, a few budget accommodations are available. However, don't expect any of them to be exceptionally charming or a good spot to meet other travelers.

Cabinas Car (☎710 1869), 20m from the church on the main road, right next to Happy's Pizza and Pops. Professional-looking lobby opens up to cozy hallways and clean, mid-sized rooms with private hot-water baths and large closets. Singles ¢4500; doubles ¢6000; triples ¢9000. ❷

Hotel el Tunel (☎710 6293), just before the turnoff to the post office, near the church. Basic and cheap. After ascending the funky aluminum staircase and passing through a "tunnel" decorated with colorful animal paintings, box-like rooms with fans and spotless shared cold showers await the shoestring traveler. Singles ¢1300; doubles ¢2400. ❶

La Reina/San Carlos Cabinas (☎710 5157), 300m from the church on the main road to Más X Menos. Set in a large, covered, dumpy courtyard, La Reina's rooms are a surprisingly good value. Large rooms with fans, TVs, and spotless private cold-water showers. Singles and doubles ¢3500. ❶

Hotel y Cabinas Wilson (☎710 2217), 100m from the church on the main road to Más X Menos. A pretty wood-paneled lobby and large balcony. Spotless and comfy singles and doubles with A/C, cable TV, and private hot baths are a decent value at ¢6000. Smaller basic rooms with TV and shared cold showers ¢3500. ❶

Cabinas Orquideas (☎710 7271), on a side road across the street from the Palí super-market. Rooms are basic and a bit dark. The owner's roosters may keep you from sleep-ing in. TVs, fan, and private showers. Singles and doubles ¢3000; triples ¢5000. ❶

Hotel Suerre (☎710 7511), 150m past the Lavandería. Situated outside the smog and bustle of the city center, this country club/resort caters to package-tours and Latino businessmen. Comfortable, A/C rooms have private hot showers, cable TV, two double beds, and phone. Included breakfast buffet, Olympic-size pool, gym, tennis courts, and restaurant round out this upscale hotel. Singles and doubles start at US$65. ❹

FOOD

Like most Costa Rican cities, Guápiles is filled with small, family-run *sodas* and bars that serve standard burgers, *casados*, and *gallo pinto;* there are few, if any, nicer, sit-down restaurants.

Happy's Pizza (☎710 2434), just past the church along the main road, near Cabinas Car. Shares a dining area with a local chicken chain, a Pops ice cream parlor, and a children's play area. Delicious pizzas of every variety, from *Mexicana* to *vegetariana*. Small ¢1600, medium ¢2550, large ¢3600. Limited selection of pastas ¢750-2500. Call for delivery (¢200) to your hostel. Open daily 10am-10pm. ❷

Hotel Suerre Restaurant and Bar (☎710 7511), in the hotel of the same name. A large, open dining area with perfectly set tables surrounded by attractive foliage pro-vides a peaceful and elegant atmosphere for the worn-out budget traveler. Standard menu of *casados*, seafood, and pastas (¢1600-4000). Open daily 7:30am-11pm. ❷

NEAR GUÁPILES

RAINFOREST AERIAL TRAM

*From Guápiles, take any **bus** to San José from the main bus terminal (every 30min., 5am-9pm). Though the tram is only 20km from Guápiles, most people visit from San José. From San José, take a bus to Guápiles from Terminal Caribe, Av. 13, Calle Central (every 30min. 5am-9pm) and have the driver let you off at the turn off to the **tram** (50min.); from there, it's a 1.5km walk to the entrance. Travelers on less of a budget will find that arrang-ing a tour through the tram office in San José is a much more convenient option (US$79, students US$54). Tours include transportation to and from your hotel, guided trips on the tram line, a 45min. nature trail hike, and breakfast or lunch. The office can also arrange late-night rides and offers combined packages with La Guácima Butterfly farm and the Café Britt coffee farm. Tram office in San José, Calle 7, Av. 7. ☎257 5961; www.rain-foresttram.com. Reservations recommended. Tram open Tu-Su 7am-4pm, M 9am-4pm. US$50, students US$25.*

Located at the edge of the Braulio Carillo National Park, the Rainforest Aerial Tram was completed in 1994 following the vision of naturalist mastermind Don Perry. After spending years exploring the rain forest canopy on ropes suspended high atop the trees, Perry designed a simple pulley system with 22 ski lift-like tram cars suspended along a 1.7km aerial track. Surprisingly, the construction of the tram network involved minimal damage to the surrounding rainforest, thanks to the help of the Nicaraguan Sandinistas, who loaned fighter helicopters to deliver the large steel poles to the site. The tram ride takes 45min. each way, affording a one-of-a-kind experience of rainforest life between tree branches and above birds' nests. Since life here is plenty distant from human life and the roar of cars, the resulting quiet means wildlife sightings will be much more likely, though visitors should remember that vegetation is dense, and many ani-mals remain identifiable only by their unique calls. The best way to see wildlife is to go early in the morning or with a guide. The 400 hectare area reserve around the tram also has a few nature trails that are open to visitors. Ten comfortable cabins with private hot-water shower, wooden floors, and balconies are available just outside the reserve. Reserve with the tram office. (Singles US$95; doubles US$160, three meals a day included.)

GUÁCIMO

Another small town with a quiet, simple feel, Guácimo lies 12km east of Guápiles along the banana highway. There is even less to do here than in the busier neighboring banana towns, but if you're driving through on your way to Limón or Moín on the Caribbean, it might be worth a stop for a relaxing lunch in the *parque* or to visit EARTH, an interesting university just a few kilometers west on the highway.

▐ TRANSPORTATION. From the main bus station, **buses** leave for: **Guápiles** (25min, 28 per day 5:20am-8pm, ¢180); **Limón** (2¼hr., 22 per day 5:50am-7:20pm, ¢745); **San José** (1½hr., about 7 per day 5:45am-6:30pm, ¢645); **Siquirres** (40min., 12 per day 6:30am-6:30pm, ¢235). To get to **EARTH,** take any Siquirres- or Pocora-bound bus (¢140). **Taxis** line up outside the bus station.

▐▊ ORIENTATION AND PRACTICAL INFORMATION. The bus station and the *parque central*, directly west of it, function as the center of town. Local services include: **Banco Nacional,** 100m west of the bus station (open M-F 8:30am-3:45pm); **Super Guácimo** supermarket, at the intersection just north of the bus station (open M-Sa 7am-6pm, Su 7am-noon); **Farmacia,** 50m north and 100m west of the bus station (☎716 6727; open M-Sa 8am-8pm, Su 8:30am-3pm); the **Red Cross,** 50m north and 50m west of the bus station (☎716 5171); **Internet,** across the street from the Red Cross (¢400 per hr. from 9am-noon, ¢500 per hr. after; open M-Sa 9am-9pm, Su 9am-6pm).

▐▐ ACCOMMODATIONS AND FOOD. The only real place to stay in town is **Cabinas Geminis ❶,** a 5-7min. walk from town. From the bus station, walk 100m west past the *parque*, turn left, walk another 300m, and turn right at the gas station. The hotel will be 50m down on your right. The 24 rooms are simple with clean tiled floors, fans, and private cold-water baths. (☎716 7476. Singles and doubles ¢3000, with TV ¢3500, with A/C ¢6000.) **Soda Tessty ❶,** opposite Banco Nacional, with childish decor, is a friendly and relaxing place for a quick bite to eat. (Fruit shakes ¢250; *gallo pinto* ¢550-¢750; *casados* ¢850; rice dishes ¢800-1200. Open M-F 7:30am-9pm, Sa 4-9pm.) Next door is a simple **pizzería ❶** with just two tables. (Personal pizza ¢1000 and up. Open daily 11am-9pm.)

NEAR GUÁCIMO

ESCUELA DE AGRICULTURA DE LA REGIÓN TROPICAL HÚMEDA
*From Guácimo, take any bus to Siquirres or Pocora (20 per day 6:30am-6:30pm) or from Siquirres, take any bus to Guápiles (21 per day 4:50am-7:20am) or San José (about 14 per day 5:30am-7pm) and have the driver let you off at the front entrance to **EARTH.** (☎ 713 0000; www.earth.ac.cr. 5- to 10-person groups preferred. Call in advance to arrange a tour.)*

Created in 1990, **EARTH** is a private, international, non-profit university that educates students from the Americas, Spain, and Uganda in agriculture, environmental conservation, and sustainable management of resources in tropical regions. The campus is massive, spanning nearly 1.3 sq. km with an additional 31 sq. km of private land.

The university's on-campus educational farm functions as a lab for hands-on projects, while the commercial farm, which includes forestry, agricultural, and cattle activities, generates profits to support the academic programs. Currently, projects funded by the European Community and the Program for the Establishment of Demonstration and Training Styles for the Reforestation of Abandoned Pasture and Natural Forest Systems in Humid Tropics (PROFORCE) are expanding the existing farms and forested areas from six to 10 sq. km. The University is open for tours, but arrangements should be made in advance.

SIQUIRRES

During the first half of the 1900s, Costa Rica's famous banana train rattled through bustling Siquirres, a stopping point for black train conductors and workers to trade places with their white or *mestizo* counterparts, who continued the journey to the Central Highlands, where blacks were not welcome to travel until 1949. These days, though trucks still haul bananas through Siquirres, the dry and dusty town serves mostly as a transport hub and stopping point on the way to Parque Nacional Tortuguero, 44km to the northeast.

TRANSPORTATION. Siquirres has two **bus** terminals clustered around the soccer field. From **Gran Terminal Siquirres,** at the southeast corner of the soccer field, buses leave for: **Guápiles** (1hr., 21 per day 4:50am-7:20pm, ¢300) via **Guácimo** (¢235); **Limón** (3½hr.; M 9 and 9:30am, Tu-Sa 19 per day 4:50am-8pm, Su 15 per day 5:30am-8pm; ¢400); **San José** (4hr., about 12 per day 5:30am-7pm, ¢680). From the station on the north side of the soccer field, buses leave for **Caño Blanco/Maryland** from where you can take the Parismina boat (2hr.; M-F 4am and noon, Sa-Su 6am and 2pm; ¢380) and **Turrialba** (2hr.; F-M 5:40, 6am, every hr. 7am-5pm; Tu-Th 8 per day 5:40am-6:30pm; ¢470) via **Pavones** (¢400). **Taxis** (☎768 8530 or 768 9333) line up along the roads east of the northeast corner of the soccer field.

ORIENTATION AND PRACTICAL INFORMATION. The soccer field is in the center of town; all directions will be given relative to the field. Orient yourself by remembering that the church is on the west side of the soccer field. The bus station for Turrialba sits on the field's north side and the main bus station is at the southeast corner. Be forewarned that the area around the mercado central, called the **"zona roja,"** 300m north and 200m east of the northeast corner of the soccer field, is considered dangerous, and should be avoided after dark.

The **Banco de Costa Rica** is located 100m north and 25m west of the northwest corner of the soccer field. (Open M-F 8:30am-3pm.) **Banco Popular** stands 50m north of the northwest corner of the soccer field. (Open M-F 8:45am-3pm, Sa 8:30am-noon.) Stock up at the **Palí supermarket,** 100m north and 100m west of the northwest corner of the soccer field. (Open M-Sa 8am-7pm, Su 8am-6pm. MC/V.) The **police station** is 100m south of the southeast corner of the soccer field (☎768 8797). For medical services you can visit **Farmacia Santa Lucía,** 50m east of the northeast corner of the soccer field (☎768 9304; open M-F 7am-8pm, Sa-Su 9am-noon; AmEx/MC/V), or **Farmacia Siquirres,** 50m north of the northwest corner of the soccer field (open M-F 7am-9pm, Sa-Su 8am-5pm. AmEx/MC/V). You can find **telephones** at the **Instituto Costarricense de Electricidad (ICE) office,** on the northwest corner of the soccer field. (☎428 8123. Open M-F 7:30am-5pm and 8am-noon.) For **Internet** access, try **Internet Cafe,** 100m south of the southeast corner of the soccer field (¢300 per 30min.; ¢500 per hr.; open M-Sa 8am-10pm), and **Café Internet Caribe,** 100m north of the northwest corner of the soccer field. (¢500 per hr. Open M-F 8am-9pm, Su 9am-3pm.) The **post office** is 100m south of the southeast corner of the soccer field, next to the police station. (Open M-F 8:30am-5pm.)

⚅⚄ ACCOMMODATIONS AND FOOD. Most travelers do not stay overnight in Siquirres, and, consequently, there are few safe, clean places that cater to them. Many locals advise to be especially cautious around the mercado central. A safe option is the **Centro Turístico Pacuare ❷,** about 1km southeast of town. From the main bus station, walk south 500m, turn left at the stop sign, and walk another 500m; the hotel will be on your left. A taxi costs ¢400. Pacuare's modern facilities, including restaurant/bar with big screen TV, pool tables, swimming pool, conference hall, and simple but comfortable rooms with fan, cable TV, and private hot-water baths, cater mostly to a business crowd. (☎ 768 6482. Singles ¢5000, with A/C ¢11,600; doubles ¢7000/¢15,000.)

If you need a place to eat before catching your bus, try **Soda Lorena ❶,** 50m south of the southeast corner of the soccer field, a pleasant *soda* with cheery teal walls and fake flower centerpieces. The friendly family that runs it serves satisfying *gallo pinto* (¢650), *casados* (¢950), and other *típico* fare. (Open M-Sa 5am-6pm.) **Tovir Pizza ❷,** on the south side of the soccer field, is popular with the locals for big, cheese pies. (Small ¢1150, medium ¢2550, large ¢3500. Open daily 9am-10:30pm.)

👁 SIGHTS

The only real sight in Siquirres is the dark, completely round **church** that sits on the west side of the soccer field. It was built as a replica of an indigenous hut and shelters simple wooden decor. Many tour groups make a stop at **La Esperanza Banana Plantation,** a Dole (formerly Standard Fruit Company) plantation that prefers large groups for tours. Guides demonstrate agricultural practices, such as bagging, harvesting, and packing. (☎ 768 8683 or 383 4596; banatour@sol.racsa.co.cr; www.sarapiquirainforest.com/bananatours. Walk-ins may be welcome during the high season; call in advance to check. US$10 per person.)

PUERTO LIMÓN

Though this Caribbean city is vital for transportation and financial services, it also offers a great selection for shoppers. Surprisingly perfect rows of towering palms line the beautiful Parque Vargas. The impressive shore is visible from most of the town center, and there are lookout areas throughout the eastern part of town. Limón is also a convenient launching point for vacations to **Tortuguero, Playa Bonita** (4km northwest), and other Caribbean towns. Although the pedestrian boulevards are pleasant and wide, the city can be busy and difficult to navigate. At night, taxis are advisable; the city has a bad reputation (many feel undeserved) for crime. The annual October 12 carnival celebrating Día de la Raza (Columbus Day), now officially named *Día de las Culturas*, especially calls for attention, as music, dancing, and drinking spill out into the streets for almost a week.

◰ TRANSPORTATION

Travelair (☎ 232 7883) and Sansa (☎ 666 0306) have **flights** to San José. The airstrip, reachable by taxi, is 4km south of town. Auto Transport Caribeños and Prosersa **buses** (☎ 222 0610 in San José, 758 0385 or 758 2575 in Limón) leave from the new spic-and-span station **Gran Terminal del Caribe,** Calle 7, Ave 1/2, and go to **San José** (2½-3hr.; 16 per day 6am-7pm, Su 8pm; ¢1095); **Moín,** the departure point for Tortuguero (1½hr., every hr. 6am-7pm, ¢80); **Siquirres** (1hr., every hr. 6am-7pm, ¢400); **Guápiles** (100min., every hr. 6am-6pm, ¢745). The smaller Coope Limón (☎ 798 0825), across the street from the Gran Terminal, south of the market, has 10 buses that leave for **San José** (2½-3hr., daily 5:30am-4pm, ¢890). Buses depart from the

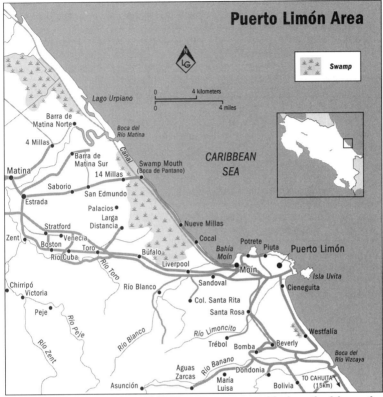

Puerto Limón Area

Swamp

Lago Urpiano

Barra de
Matina Norte

*Boca del
Río Matina*

4 Millas

Barra de
Matina Sur

Canal

Swamp Mouth
(Boca de Pantano)

Matina

14 Millas

CARIBBEAN
SEA

Saborio

San Edmundo

Estrada

Palacios

Larga
Distancia

Nueve Millas

Stratford

Cocal

Potrete

Zent

Venecia

Piuta

Puerto Limón

Boston

Toro

Búfalo

*Bahía
Moín*

Río Cuba

Río Toro

Liverpool

Moín

Isla Uvita

Chirripó
Victoria

Río Blanco

Sandoval

Cieneguita

Peje

Río Peje

Col. Santa Rita

Santa Rosa

Río Zent

Río Blanco

Río Limoncito

Westfalía

Trébol

Bomba

Beverly

*Boca del
Río Vizcaya*

Aguas
Zarcas

Río Banano

Dondonia

Asunción

María
Luisa

Bolivia

TO CAHUITA
(15km)

0   4 kilometers
0   4 miles

CARIBBEAN LOWLANDS

MEPE station (☎ 758 1572 or 758 3522) on the corner, one block north of the northeast side of the market, to **Manzanillo** (2½hr.; 6am, 2:30, 6pm; ¢680); **Puerto Viejo de Talamanca** (1½hr., 7 per day 5am-6pm, ¢500) via **Cahuita** (45min., ¢335); and **Panamanian Border at Sixaola** (3hr., 9 per day 5am-6pm, ¢500). All the Sixaola buses pass through **Bribrí** (additional buses at 9, 10am, 1pm; ¢610). **Taxis** line Av. 2 and patrol the city. A taxi to **Moín** costs ¢1000.

✳🛈 ORIENTATION AND PRACTICAL INFORMATION

Finding street signs in Limón is nearly impossible. Orient yourself by the Mercado Municipal, Av. 2/3, Calle 3/4, where buses drop off their passengers. All hotels and restaurants are within a few blocks of the *mercado*, which serves as the center for Limón's business and social activities.

Tourist Services: Caribbean Tour Center and Store (☎ 798 0816 or 798 1792), in the Gran Terminal. Open daily 7:30am-7:30pm. AmEx/MC/V.

Banks: Banco Nacional (☎ 758 0094), at the southeast corner of the market, exchanges US dollars and traveler's checks (1% commission) and offers cash advances for Visa holders. Open M-F 8:30am-3:45pm. The **ATM** at **Banco San José** (☎ 798 0155 or 798 0167), on the north side of the market, serves Cirrus holders. Open M-F 8am-5pm, Sa 7am-1pm. MC/V.

Market: Mercado Municipal, in the center of town 300m west of the beach; supermarket **Más X Menos** (☎798 1792), on the northeast corner of the market. Open M-Sa 8am-9pm, Su 8am-8pm. AmEx/MC/V.

Police: (☎758 0365, emergency 911), 100m east of the northeast corner of the market.

Red Cross: ☎758 0125 or 911. One block south of the southeast corner of the market. English spoken. Open 24hr.

Pharmacy: Farmacia Buenos Aires (☎798 4732), 25m east of the southeast corner of the market. Open M-Sa 8am-7pm.

Hospital: Hospital Tony Facio (☎758 2222), 300m north along the boardwalk.

Phones: On the northern side of the *mercado municipal*.

Internet Access: Cyber Cafe Interurbano, on the 2nd floor across from the northern side of the market. US$1 per hr. Open daily 24hr. Also try **NetCoffee,** Av. 4, Calle 5/6 (☎758 3424). ¢500 per hr. Open M-Sa 8am-10pm, Su 10am-7pm.

Post office: Southwest of the market. Open M-F 8am-5:30pm, Sa 8am-noon.

Postal code: 7300.

ACCOMMODATIONS

Be cautious of ultra-cheap places; they usually don't have strong locks. Most hotels have electronic locks for their entrances, so you have to wait a minute to be buzzed in. Accommodations in general are well priced and comfortable.

Hotel Continental (☎798 0532) and **Hotel Internacional** (☎758 0434), on the right 2 blocks north of the northeast corner of the *mercado*. Both are 25m from the beach, share the same owner, prices, and cleanliness. Rooms have fans and baths. Singles ¢2500, with A/C ¢3000; doubles ¢3600/¢4600; triples without A/C ¢4700. ❶

Hotel Miami (☎758 0490 or 758 4888), ½ block west of the southwest corner of the market. This fresh, pink-tiled hotel offers large, clean rooms with fans, hot-water baths, and lots of light. More expensive rooms come with A/C, telephone, and TV. Singles ¢5200-6800; doubles ¢5200-8700; triples ¢6000. AmEx/MC/V. ❷

Hotel Tete (☎758 1122; fax 798 0470), 25m west of the northwest corner of the *mercado*. Somewhat noisy but has everything you need—a lounge on the breezy balcony, couches, daily paper, and a big color TV. Comfortable beds with comforters; sparkling private baths with hot water. Singles ¢4000; doubles ¢7500; add ¢700 for A/C. ❷

FOOD AND ENTERTAINMENT. Limón's usual grub combines standard fare with a Caribbean twist. One of the best places in town, however, is the delightful Italian restaurant **Pizzería Roma ❶,** on Av. 4 Calles 1/3, which has it all: breezy ocean views, a brick-oven kitchen, and mouthwatering pizza and pasta. The friendly service is a pleasant bonus and take-home is always an option. (☎798 4305. Pizzas ¢1000-3800; pastas from ¢800; lasagna ¢1200-1700. Open Tu-Su 11:30am-midnight.) **Restaurante Mares ❷,** across the street from the south side of the *mercado*, has potted palm trees, cushioned wicker chairs, and a ship's wheel. The posh atmosphere, catering to foreigners, feels somewhat out of place in low-key Limón. The seafood is great, but a little pricey. (☎758 4713. Vegetable and peanut shrimp ¢3200; rice dishes ¢1000-1500. Open daily 8am-2am. MC/V.) **Restaurante Doña Toda ❶,** on the east side of the *mercado*, is one of the friendliest. Spend only ¢800 for a full meal of fantastic *casado* or ¢550 for a sandwich. (Open M-Sa 6:30am-7pm.) For good eats at any hour, try the airy and relaxed **Soda La Estrella ❶,** 100m west of the northwest corner of the *mercado*. (Cheap and quick *casados* ¢900; *gallo pinto* ¢600; sandwiches ¢600.)

Women traveling alone at night should be cautious. **Bar Acuarius ❶**, a dance club in the Hotel Acón, across the street from the northeast corner of the market, pounds reggae and *salsa* rhythms late into the night. (☎758 1010. Th-Sa cover ¢500; women free and 2x1 drinks Sa 8pm-midnight. Open daily 7pm-4 or 5am.)

◙ **SIGHTS.** While the **mercado municipal** seems calmer and more organized than most central *mercados*, it's still pickpocket territory. Vendors proudly display typical Caribbean fare: fresh coconuts, bananas, fish, and lobster. The market is open from dawn to dusk, though numerous *sodas* within often stay open later. **Parque Vargas**, in the southeast corner of town, is a gorgeous refuge from the town's bustling center. Waves lap nearby, and you might even see the occasional sloth bumbling in the treetops. To get to the *parque*, head two blocks east from the southeastern corner of the *mercado* toward the dense, towering coconut palms. Make sure to check out the impressive **seaside mural** by artist Guadalupe Alvarea. Though the paint is chipping, the work remains a powerful depiction of Limón's rich and tangled history. On a clear day, the **Isla de Uvita**, 1km away, is visible from a *mirador* in the southwest edge of the park. The tiny **Museo Etnohistórico de Limón**, on the second floor of the post office, provides a perfect, quick introduction to the region's diverse cultural heritage. (Open M-F 9am-noon and 1-4pm. Free.)

A young crowd looking for waves and rays usually heads over to **Playa Bonita**, 4km northwest of Limón. On one side, the water is calm and perfect for wading; on the other, powerful waves crash on the beach. As a result, surfers and swimmers live their afternoons in perfect harmony, and later relax with beers to the never-ending reggae beat from the beachside bar and restaurant **Reggae Mansion**. To get to Playa Bonita, take the Moín bus from the Gran Terminal del Caribe (every hr. 6am-7pm, ¢50). Buy a ticket at the window and get off at one of the first stops (just ask the driver). You can also take a taxi (¢600-800).

PARISMINA

The tiny hamlet of Parismina is sandwiched between the Río Parismina and the strong, salty Caribbean waves that lap at the small, deserted beach. Most travelers cruise right by the 150 sq. km island in boats from Moín on their way to Tortuguero, 50km north. Parismina boasts a less touristed and superior environment to observe the hundreds of leatherback, green, and hawksbill turtles that nest on its beaches. Though Parismina's eco-tourism turtle industry is much less developed than Tortuguero's, volunteer groups and sportfishermen are frequent visitors, immediately becoming a part of the small town and its quiet, simple appeal.

▐ **TRANSPORTATION**

Parismina has no roads and is accessible only by **boat**. The most inexpensive way to arrive from San José is to take a **bus** from Terminal Caribe at Av. 13, Calle Central, to **Siquirres** (1½hr.; 6:30, 8:30am, then every 2hr. until 6pm). From the Gran Terminal Siquirres, where the bus drops off, walk to the old bus station on the north side of the soccer field and catch a bus to **Caño Blanco** (2hr.; M-F 4am and noon, Sa-Su 6am and 2pm; ¢380). From Caño Blanco, a **public boat** meets the bus and shuttles passengers to Parismina (15min., ¢500). If you arrive at Caño Blanco from Siquirres by **taxi** (US$25-30) or private car, you can hire a **private boat** from the Caño Blanco dock to Parismina (¢1000). Just be sure to arrive at Caño Blanco long before 6pm as boats leave the dock early and there are no overnight facilities. Travelers continuing to **Tortuguero** can safely park their cars in Caño Blanco and hire a boat to the national park (US$30-50). Coming from further south in the Caribbean, jump on a boat from Moín to Tortuguero and tell the captain you only need to go to Parismina (see **Tortuguero: Transportation**, p. 355). The ride should cost no more than US$10-$20.

SAVING PARISMINA'S TURTLES

SAVING PARISMINA'S TURTLES Long overlooked by travelers who favor Tortuguero for turtle-watching, Parismina offers significantly less crowded and less expensive observation alternatives. Until recently, little action was taken at Parismina to monitor the hundreds of leatherback, green, and hawksbill turtles that come ashore to lay their eggs every year. As a result, poaching and egg theft increased to astonishing rates of 80%. Local awareness and concern for the endangered sea turtles, in addition to assistance from the Costa Rican Coast Guard, led to the creation of **La Comisión Salvemos Las Tortugas de Parismina** in April 2001. The organization was founded by Jason Taylor and his mother Doña Vicky, Americans who now live in Parismina and coordinate the turtle conservation activities. It started with just 10 eager and dedicated members and has now grown to include hundreds of volunteers from around the world who visit for anywhere from a few days to a few weeks to assist in the patrolling of the beaches and carry out turtle rescuing activities.

The association's primary efforts go into managing their own turtle hatchery. One of the country's only organizations with legal permission to handle turtle eggs, it takes the eggs soon after their mothers abandon the nest and relocates them to the hatchery, where they are placed in environments suitable for hatching and protected from poachers and egg thieves. When the palm-sized *tortuguitas* hatch, volunteers return them to the ocean. In the association's first year, over 10,000 hatchlings were safely returned to the water. Travelers interested in assisting with the volunteer efforts should see **Alternatives to Tourism,** p. 83.

From Parismina, it's possible to continue to **Tortuguero** by catching one of the boats passing by the docks from Moín on its way to the national park. It's often difficult to flag a boat, though, so try arranging in advance to be picked up with one of the captains in Moín. **Thomas McGinnis** (☎385 2266 or 280 0243) and **Modesto Watson** (☎226 0986) are good captains to call. To return to **Siquirres,** take the boat from Parismina to Caño Blanco (M-F 5:30am and 2:30pm, Sa-Su 8:30am and 4:30pm) and catch the bus back to Siquirres (M-F 6am and 3pm, Sa-Su 10am and 5pm).

ORIENTATION AND PRACTICAL INFORMATION

Parismina is tiny, and it shouldn't take you much time to find your way around. From the main dock where you'll be dropped off, a dirt path leads 200m to the town center, just a few meters away from the church and soccer field. There are few services here, so take care of essentials before hand. María Ester at the **Cariblanco Lodge** (see **Accommodations,** below) is the best source of information on the town and turtle watching activities. Pick up basic supplies and snacks at the **pulpería,** about 350m up the main path from the docks. For **medical assistance,** a doctor visits the village twice a week, usually on Tuesdays and Fridays; check with the locals. A **telephone** is available opposite from Soda Eduardo, about 250m up the main path from the docks. (Local calls ¢20 per min. Calls to US ¢800 per min. Open daily 6am-8pm.)

ACCOMMODATIONS

Budget accommodations are available in Parismina. Sportfishermen with more cash to spend usually stay at one of the sportfishing lodges just outside the village. Note that these lodges require private boat transportation from Parismina village.

Cariblanco Lodge (☎393 5481), from the main dock, walk about 400m to the end of the main path, turn right for 100m, turn right again for another 100m; the lodge will be on your right. Offers one of the best values for groups. The extremely well-kept *cabinas* have shiny tile floors, ceiling fans, and private cold-water baths. Triples ¢5000. ●

The Thorny Rose Inn (☎390 9963), from the dock, walk 200m up the dirt path, take the first right. The Thorny Rose will be on your right. A better value for solo travelers. Friendly owner Elizabeth Parker keeps the eight rooms cute and comfortable, with high ceilings, colorful headboards on the beds, private hot-water baths, fans, a pleasant balcony, and a charming restaurant with family style meals. ¢3000 per person. ❶

Cabinas Newball, in the center of town past Soda Eduardo, is a little bit cheaper and a lot more basic. Fifteen stuffy rooms have cement floors, thin mattresses, and private cold-water baths. No phone. ¢2500 per person. ❶

Río Parismina Lodge (☎800 338 5668; www.riop.com), directly across the river from Parismina, is famous among sportfishermen and specializes in tarpon fishing. Rustic, luxurious rooms have wood-paneled interiors, comfortable double beds, private hot-water baths, and TVs. The lodge, situated in 50 acres of riverside forest, has a gorgeous pool and jacuzzi, a restaurant/bar, and activities ranging from horseback riding to boat cruises. Most prices cater to all-inclusive sportfishing packages. The cheapest rate for fishermen is US$3250 for singles; US$6000 for doubles for 7 full days of fishing, meals, boat, guide, and activities. Non-fishermen can stay 3 days for US$1250. ❺

Jungle Tarpon Lodge (☎800 544 2261; www.jungletarpon.com), 2km north of Parismina, is another good place for sportfishermen. There are only 4 rooms, all spacious and luxurious, catering to small groups of 6-10 people. Rates start US$2400 per person for seven days of fishing and lodging, all-inclusive; US$1600 per person for six days of eco-tourism activities. ❺

FOOD AND NIGHTLIFE

Soda Eduardo, about 250m up the main path from the docks, is one of the friendliest places to eat in town. Pull up a seat in chef Amelia's kitchen and dine on *empanadas* (¢200), fried chicken (¢700), and *casados* (¢900). Open daily 8am-8pm. ❶

Restaurante Cariblanco, in the Cariblanco Lodge, offers fancier meals with Caribbean influences. Friendly María Ester and staff helper serve delicious combinations of rice and beans, *casados, gallo pinto*, and creative seafood dishes. Most entrees ¢1100-¢2500. Open for breakfast, lunch, and dinner, but no set hours. ❷

Salon Naomi, in the center of town, is a large bar/disco that usually picks up on Saturday nights with loud salsa, merengue, reggae, and rock music. A good crowd of locals and visitors dance and mingle the night away.

TURTLE WATCHING AND ORGANIZED TOURS

With the help of the National Coast Guard, Parismina has only recently taken an active step in patrolling the beaches and guarding turtles' nests to curb poaching and revive the turtle population. Green turtles primarily nest between June and October, leatherbacks from February to June, and hawksbills sporadically throughout the year. Aside from turtle watching, visitors can explore the wildlife-teeming canals around Parismina village.

La Comisión Salvemos Las Tortugas de Parismina, (public phone ☎798 1246) Parismina's own turtle association, organizes most turtle-watching tours and volunteer activities. Though it is legally permitted to observe the turtles on the beach without a guide, the association does not recommend it for safety reasons, because guides deter poachers, and because money generated from turtle tourism can be fed back into the system for further conservation efforts. The association can arrange guides. Turtle tour ¢500-1000. Call and ask for Jason, Miguel, Jenny, Rick, or Vicky. Otherwise, just arrive in town and ask any of the locals for Doña Vicky.

La Asociación de Boteros de Parismina is a small private group of boat captains that offer tours of the river canals from Caño Blanco. Most captains are bilingual and excellent at spotting the wide variety of wildlife lurking on the river banks. Prices range from US$3 for the short ride to Parismina to US$150 for a round trip ride to Tortuguero. Look for the boat captains at the Caño Blanco docks; be sure to get there well before 6pm.

Betania Tours (pager ☎ 296 5452 or 296 2626, ext. 158-895) offers bilingual eco-tours, fishing trips, transportation from Caño Blanco, and tours to Tortuguero and the Río Pacuare.

Rainforest World (☎ 556 2678; www.rforestw.com) runs 2-3 day all-inclusive tours that include visits to Jalova ranger station, crocodile tours, a visit to an animal rehab station, sea kayaking, fishing, and more.

PARQUE NACIONAL TORTUGUERO

Sheltering the most important nesting site for marine turtles in the entire Western Hemisphere, Parque Nacional Tortuguero, 84km north of Limón, encompasses 261.5 sq. km of coastal territory and 501 sq. km of marine territory and is almost exclusively accessible and navigable by boat. What has brought the park international fame and thousands of visitors year after year is its 35km beach, where thousands of turtles return every year to lay their eggs. Not content to surrender the show, howler monkeys echo in the treetops, rainbow-beaked toucans coast overhead, and leathery caimans glide stealthily through the canals intermingling with the park's swampy land areas.

The tiny village of Tortuguero, is the gateway to the park's entrance at the Cuatro Esquinas ranger station. With restaurants, lodging, basic services, and park information, it offers easy access to the park's attractions. Despite the thousands of visitors, however, touristed Tortuguero village (pop. 700) surprisingly retains an unspoiled and refreshing small-town flavor. Those who make the long and rather complicated journey to this remote section of Costa Rica's precious, northern Caribbean coast will be rewarded by laid-back living and a one-of-a-kind opportunity to learn about and observe some of the world's most fascinating animals.

TORTUGUERO VILLAGE

The village of Tortuguero has only around 700 residents, is drenched by an average yearly rainfall of 5-6m, and is accessible only by boat, yet it remains one of Costa Rica's most popular destinations. Flanked to the west by wide, glistening canals and to the east by foamy, copper-tinted Caribbean waves, the slender strip of land on which this village lies is just a few meters north of beautiful Parque Nacional Tortuguero. And if the fantastic scenery and wildlife aren't enough to hold your interest, Tortuguero's diverse population of native *ticos*, Nicaraguans, Afro-Caribs, and foreigners from all over the world mix to create a remarkably unified and unique culture anchored around the town's singular business of eco-tourism. Conservation awareness is especially encouraged here, and everyone you meet will be eager to share with you anything they can to make your stay and experience as ideal as possible. Tortuguero may be one of the few places in Costa Rica where you'll truly be an eco-tourist, learning about serious environmental problems while simultaneously actively helping to solve them.

Tortuguero village was founded in the 1930s by Colombians who made a living from exporting sea turtles and coconuts. The 40s saw exploitation of forest resources by lumber companies, and the increased work opportunities drew many immigrants, mostly from Nicaragua. In the 60s and 70s, man-made canals were connected to the existing river system as a more efficient way to transport

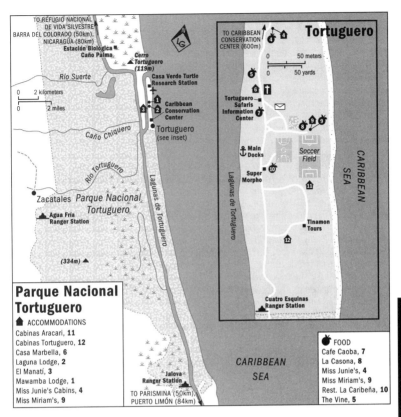

Parque Nacional Tortuguero

🏠 ACCOMMODATIONS
Cabinas Aracari, **11**
Cabinas Tortuguero, **12**
Casa Marbella, **6**
Laguna Lodge, **2**
El Manatí, **3**
Mawamba Lodge, **1**
Miss Junie's Cabins, **4**
Miss Miriam's, **9**

🍴 FOOD
Cafe Caoba, **7**
La Casona, **8**
Miss Junie's, **4**
Miss Miriam's, **9**
Rest. La Caribeña, **10**
The Vine, **5**

the lumber to Limón. After the 70s, however, lumber companies left for economic reasons, dragging with them many families that lived in Tortuguero. Today, the community remains sparsely inhabited and has experienced a new wave of immigration by foreigners and people of Afro-Caribbean descent.

▣ TRANSPORTATION

BY PLANE
Flying from San José to the airstrip, a few kilometers north of Tortuguero village, is hours faster and much more convenient than taking a lengthy bus-boat combo, but it's also more expensive. **Sansa** departs from Juan Santa María International Airport in Alajuela (☎221 9414; www.flysansa.com; 35min., 1 per day 6am, US$55; see **San José: Flights** p. 85); **Travelair** departs from Tobías Bolaños Airport in Pavas (☎220 3054 or 888-535-8832 in US for reservation; www.centralamerica.com/cr/tran/travlair.htm; 35min., 1 per day 6:15am, US$60; see **San José: Flights** p. 85).

VIA MOÍN
If you're traveling independently, the best-known route—from the Southern Caribbean coast via the port town of Moín—is the most scenic, but not the cheapest.

THE PRINCE OF THE RAINFOREST With bright red eyes and dazzling green back, the Agalychnis Calidryas (commonly known as the red-eyed tree frog) has become a poster child for the natural beauty of Costa Rica. Although its domain ranges from northern Colombia to southern Mexico, Costa Rica's advanced conservation efforts have helped secure a large population in the Tortuguero and Corcovado National Parks. Unfortunately, despite its unofficial status as a mascot of Costa Rican ecotourism it is actually a very elusive amphibian. You will find it in every tourist shop, on posters and postcards, but only rarely in the wild, for it hides, camouflaged, amidst the jungle's bright green foliage.

Some backpackers prefer this route in spite of its cost because it practically guarantees crocodile, bird, and monkey spottings. Visitors get a good taste of the park before they even arrive, with the relaxed trip through the Tortuguero canals.

From **San José,** take a **bus** from Terminal Caribe to **Limón** (2½hr., every hr. 5:30am-7pm, ¢1005) and from Limón, catch a bus to **Moín** (30min., every 30min. 6am-6pm, ¢75). *Lanchas* (small boats) depart early in the morning (8-10am, but try to arrive no later than 8:30am) for Tortuguero from Moín's small dock, behind Restaurante Papa Manuel. The *lancha* trip is 3-5hr. through canals teeming with wildlife (US$30 one-way, US$50 round-trip); it's best to arrange in advance. Large groups make for cheaper rides; if you're traveling alone, a tour guide might request up to US$180 for the trip. Arrive early to buddy up with other travelers.

Hang out at the main docks in Tortuguero and talk to the boat captains there; if they can't help you yourselves, they'll tell you where to find captains who might. **Harlan Hodgson** (☎ 798 4145) is a fantastic captain and guide and speaks English pretty well. **Captain Willis Rankin** (☎ 798 1556) and **Captain Ariel Nuñez** (☎ 795 1478 by night, 795 2611 by day) are also recommended. If you need help arranging transportation, call **Daryl Loth** or **Bárbara Tinamon** in Tortuguero (see **Orientation and Practical Information,** below); they will probably be able to help you out. Return trips can be arranged with your captain; get a phone number in case plans change. A more formal option is **Tortuguero Odysseys Tours,** which sells packages of *lancha* trips and lunch (US$50); or a *lancha* trip, food for two days, and lodging with shared bath (US$75) or private hot water bath (US$85). The owner, **Alfred Brown Robinson,** can best be contacted by cellular phone, but also spends afternoons in the Limón offices. (☎ 758 0824; beeper 233 3030; cell 369 8907.)

If you arrive in Moín too late and must spend the night, try **Cabinas Chitas ❶.** Stay on the bus coming from Limón, past the docks over a bridge, until you see the sign on the right side of the road. Every room comes with a private bath, comfy double beds, and a porch with lounging chairs. (☎798 3116. Doubles ¢2500.)

VIA CARIARI

A much cheaper route from **San José** to Tortuguero is to head to El Caribe Bus Terminal (☎221 2596) and take a direct **bus** to **Cariari** (2hr., 6:30 and 9am, ¢720). The cheapest route from Cariari is to catch the bus to **Pavona** (2pm, ¢1000) from the old bus station. From Pavona, Captain Juan Castro runs a **boat** to **Tortuguero** (4pm, ¢1000). The more traditional route from Cariari is to catch the bus to La Geest-Casa Verde (noon, ¢500), staying on until the end of the line in La Geest. A *lancha* to Tortuguero meets the bus at the river's edge at 1:30pm; most locals pay ¢1500, though tourists are charged US$8 or US$10 (2hr.). Two different captains make the trip from La Geest to Tortuguero: **Rubén Bananero** (☎382 6941 or 363 1681) and **Juan Torres** (pager ☎233 3030, #5489), who offers great tours at lower prices.

Three **boats** leave daily from the main docks for **La Geest.** Bananero's boats leave at 7 and 11am, and Juan Torres' boat leaves at 7am. Juan Castro's boat leaves for **Pavona** at 6am daily. It's recommended to make reservations for all traveling arrangements the day before at Restaurante El Muellecito (opposite the dock) or with Juan Torres himself for the cheaper ticket. The connecting **bus** leaves for **Cariari** from La Geest at 9:30am (ask for hours from Pavona), and buses to **San José** leave Cariari at 11am and 1pm.

There are a few days every year when water levels are too high or too low to make the journey. To confirm times or check on info, call **Daryl Loth** (☎392 3201; safari@racsa.co.cr) or **Bárbara Tinamon** (☎pager 223 3030, #3761; tinamon@racsa.co.cr), both of whom are guides in Tortuguero.

VIA GUIDED TOURS

Ecole Travel (☎223 2240; www.travelcostarica.net; see **San José: Practical Information** p. 90), offers two-day/one-night tours (US$95) and three-day/two-night tours (US$125) including transport from Moín, tours, and lodging at El Manatí Lodge. Operators in Cahuita (see **Guided Tours,** p. 368), and Puerto Viejo (see **Guided Tours,** p. 373) offer similar tours. **Fran** and **Modesto Watson**'s well-organized tours on their riverboat Francesca are highly recommended. Most include round-trip transportation from San José to Moín in a van and from Moín to Tortuguero in the Watsons' boat. They also include two-day/one-night lodging at the Laguna Lodge, five hearty meals, a canal boat tour, a guided turtle tour, a visit to Caribbean Conservation Center, and park entrance fees. (US$175-190 per person.) The Watsons can also arrange customized tours for cheaper budgets and for travelers who chose to arrive in Tortuguero on their own. (☎226 0986; www.tortuguerocanals.com.)

◼◼ ORIENTATION AND PRACTICAL INFORMATION

The main village of Tortuguero is only about 500m long, with sandy gravel paths winding their way to the building scattered all about. The **airstrip** is a few kilometers north of town and is accessible only by boat. Most travelers arrive at the *lancha* dock, in the center of town. From the docks, with your back to the water, north is to your left, and south is to your right. The **main path** runs from the Caribbean Conservation Center at the far north end of the village, past the docks, all the way to the **ranger station** at the park entrance, at the far south end of town. Frequent blackouts in the rainy season make bringing a flashlight a must.

Tourist Information Offices: Check out the **kiosk,** north of the soccer field, which offers information on park activities and the turtle history. The humble guru of information in Tortuguero is **Daryl Loth** (☎392 3201; fax 710 0547; http://tortuguero_s.tripod.com; safari@racsa.co.cr), a Canadian naturalist who runs ◼**Tortuguero Safaris Information Center,** 100m north of the docks, opposite the church. If the small center is not open, knock on the yellow house next door, which is the site of his new bed and breakfast. **Barbara** (pager ☎223 3030, #3761), a multi-lingual German biologist in the purple house 100m past Cabinas Tortuguero, is another great guide and source of information. At **The Jungle Shop** (☎391 3483), 100m north of the docks across from Tortuguero Safaris, Antoinette Gutiérrez, an American-turned Costa Rican citizen, and Elvin, her *tico* husband, sell souvenirs and give advice. (Open daily 9am-6pm.)

Banks: None in Tortuguero Village, but **Souvenirs Paraíso Tropical,** 200m north of the docks, exchanges traveler's checks *if* they have the cash. Try to stock up on colones before you arrive. Open daily 8am-9pm.

Supermarkets: Super Morpho, directly opposite the docks. Open daily 7am-10pm. **La Riveriana,** 200m north of the docks. Open daily 6am-8pm.

Police: Emergency ☎117. In the blue building 75m north of the dock.

Medical Services: A **doctor** can be reached at the south end of town in the central headquarters of the park service (Administración de Tortuguero). For a serious **medical emergency,** The Jungle Shop (☎ 391 3483) can call a doctor in Limón.

Phones: At Miss Junie's (see **Accommodations,** below); at the Super Morpho in front of the docks; and behind Souvenirs Paraíso Tropical. Local calls ¢20 per min. International calls with calling card only. ¢200 flat rate for connection.

Post Office: A few meters up a side path south of Daryl's house. Open M-F 8:30am-noon and 1-5pm.

▮ ACCOMMODATIONS

All the ritzy, expensive hotels, catering mostly to organized tours, are across the canal and accessible almost exclusively by boat. In Tortuguero Village, lodging is strictly budget and minutes from the park entrance, beach, and restaurants. Camping is not allowed on the beach, but backpackers can pitch tents for US$2 at the ranger station at the southern end of town.

TORTUGUERO VILLAGE

Cabinas Aracari, from the docks, head south on the main path and turn left on the path just past the Centro Turístico La Culebra; Aracari is the very last house 150m down the path. The owner is hospitable, and the clean rooms have tile floors with good screens, private cold-water showers, fans, droopy beds, and porches. Singles, doubles, and triples ¢2000 per person. ❶

Casa Marbella (☎ 392 3201), the yellow house next door to Daryl's place. Newly opened and named after Daryl's three-year-old daughter, Casa Marbella has four fresh, comfortable cabins with high ceilings, soft beds, good lighting, and solar-powered hot water. The best part is your interaction with Daryl, who will tell you everything you need to know about Tortuguero, and the fantastic breakfasts his wife cooks every morning. Singles US$25; doubles US$35. ❸

Cabinas Tortuguero (beeper ☎ 223 3030, dial 3771). From the main docks, head south along the main path and turn left at the small path 100m past La Culebra; the *cabinas* will be about 20m down on your right. The 5 clean rooms are extremely well-kept with wooden floors, fans, cheery pink walls, and private hot-water showers. Singles US$15; doubles and triples US$10 per person. ❷

Miss Junie's Cabins (☎ 710 0523), 200m north of the docks on the right, has fresh-smelling rooms decked with pretty wicker furniture, hot-water baths, fans, and shuttered windows. Groups often reserve the whole place in advance, so you may want to call ahead. US$17 per person plus 16% tax. ❷

Miss Miriam's (beeper ☎ 223 3030, #5757), on the soccer field. Right above Miss Miriam's delicious Caribbean restaurant are six second-story cabins that get refreshingly cool breezes from the beach. The cozy rooms have tile floors, spotless private cold-water baths, and high ceilings. Doubles US$15; triples US$20. ❶

ON THE CANALS

El Manatí (☎ 373 0330) is the most budget of the canal lodges. Eight simple *cabinas* with fans, private hot-water baths, and a relaxing, laid-back atmosphere. The hotel often fills up with visitors on package Ecole Tours trips, so call ahead and make sure there's room. Singles US$30 (but often not available); doubles US$40; triples US$50. ❸

Mawamba Lodge (☎ 710 7280 or 223 7490; www.grupomawamba.com). The closest to the village of the more expensive lodges, Mawamba is right on the beach and has over 50 quiet *ranchos* with ceiling fan, private hot-water bath, and a small balcony with views of the hotel's lush tropical garden and large pool. The restaurant serves a wide variety of Costa Rican and international entrees (usually included in room rates). All-inclusive 3-day/2-night packages start at US$295 during peak turtle nesting season. ❺

Laguna Lodge (☎ 225 3750 or 280 7843; www.lagunalodgetortuguero.com). Secluded in its 14 acres of gardens with the Caribbean on one side and the Tortuguero lagoons on the other, the lodge has 52 spacious rooms made of wood from *almendro* (almond) trees, private hot-water baths, comfortable beds, and ceiling fans. The lodge grounds also feature a 40m swimming pool, restaurant, and plenty of hammocks. 2-day/1-night packages, including lodging, meals, tours, and transport from San José, start at US$187 per person for double occupancy. ❺

FOOD

For such a small village, Tortuguero has a number of good places to eat and a variety of cuisines from which to choose. Though most places are pretty affordable, prices tend to be a bit higher than they might be elsewhere simply because of the difficulty in transporting food to such a remote area.

- ▨ **La Casona,** on the soccer field. One look at this rustic, hand-built restaurant with wooden bench tables, a tree stump patterned floor, and thatched roof with paper lanterns, and you won't want to sit down for a meal anywhere else in town. And just wait till you taste the delicious banana pancakes (₡1000), heart of palm lasagna (₡1500), and shrimp with chicken (₡1500)—you'll think you're in heaven. Ask to take a look at the guest book that visitors from all over the world have signed. Open daily 6am-10pm. ❷

- ▨ **Miss Junie's,** 200m north of the docks on the main path. She'll cook whatever is caught or bought that day and add her special flavorful Caribbean touch; it's a surprise sure to be scrumptious. Tell her in the morning or the day before what you'd like to eat. Breakfast ₡1000; lunch and dinner ₡2700. Open daily 7am-9pm. ❷

- **Miss Miriam's,** on the soccer field, is another Caribbean wonder. Miss Miriam and her daughters prepare delicious and uniquely flavored meals. Breakfasts (₡1000); Caribbean-flavored chicken with rice and beans (US$5); whole fish (US$5); *casados* with rice and beans cooked in coconut milk (₡1100). Open daily 6am-9pm. ❶

- **Cafe Caoba,** just south of the police on the main path, has a charming atmosphere with banana paper menus, a bright interior, and screened windows overlooking the lagoon. It's especially popular for its dessert crepes (try the Caribbean crepe with granola, ice cream, and coconut sauce ₡800). If you'd rather have a meal, go for the full breakfast (₡1200), tasty sandwiches (₡1300), or pizzas (₡1300-1500 per person). Open daily 9am-10pm, though it may close early if there are no customers. ❶

- **Restaurante La Caribeña,** the bright yellow house facing the docks next to Super Morpho. One of the simpler places in town with just a few tables and quick, homemade meals. *Gallo pinto* ₡500; *casados* ₡1000. Open daily 6am-7pm. ❶

- **The Vine,** a coffee shop, 100m north of the docks, offers made-to-order pizza (₡1000) and real New York cheesecake (₡500). Open Tu-Sa 11am-6pm, but often closed in the low season. ❶

SIGHTS

Before going on a run to see the turtles, check out the non-profit ▨**Caribbean Conservation Corporation Natural History Visitors Center (CCC)** at the north end of town. Follow the small dirt path that jets beach-side, toward the right, for about 1km past the docks. The Center is a must-see for anyone wishing to learn about the difficult plight of the severely endangered marine turtles. A 16min. video in Spanish or English documents the history of the pressures on the sea turtle population caused by habitat destruction and poaching and tells the story of CCC founder Archie Carr's efforts to monitor the Tortuguero turtles, starting in the 1950s. Over 50 years later, the CCC has continued Carr's work and has tagged nearly 50,000 turtles, making it the world's largest green turtle tagging program of its kind. Visitors can "adopt" a turtle giving a donation of US$25 and, in turn, receive an adoption certificate, photograph, turtle fact sheet, and promise of receipt of information about the tagged turtle when it is found. (☎710 0547, in US 352-373-6441; www.cccturtle.org. Open M-Sa 10am-noon and 2-5:30pm, Su 2-5pm. ¢350.)

PARQUE NACIONAL TORTUGUERO

*The area that can be seen without a guide or a boat is limited. The park headquarters is at the **Cuatro Esquinas Ranger Station**, at the park's north end. To reach the station from the village, follow the main path to the south, walking through locals' yards and over a makeshift bridge, where you'll see a sign indicating that you have reached the park. The ranger station has maps (¢200), information on the park's wildlife and vegetation, and preserved turtles and turtle eggs on display. It is possible to **camp** at Cuatro Esquinas, but expect very squishy grounds. (US$2 per person, includes access to cold-water baths.) The less-frequented and less-accessible **Jalova Ranger Station** sits on the canal at the park's south end. Both park entrances open daily 6am-6pm. US$7, combination 3-day ticket for Tortuguero and Parque Nacional Barra del Colorado US$10.*

The park's claim to fame is its incredible knack for attracting multitudes of hard-shelled marine reptiles, which outdate the prehistoric dinosaurs. Tortuguero is the largest and most important turtle nesting site in the western hemisphere. Indigenous peoples thought the turtles were drawn to the black sand Caribbean beaches by nearby Tortuguero Mountain. Scientists now believe the chemical qualities of the sand and sea may contribute to some kind of imprinting. The most famous turtles are the *tortugas verdes*, which nest from the end of June through September. Three other species also nest in the park—leatherbacks (Mar.-July), hawksbills (May-Sept.), and loggerheads (June-Oct.). They now face extinction due to the oceanic jetsam that suffocates their nests, the increased beachfront development which hinders the hatchlings' return to the sea, and the poachers who steal the newly-laid eggs. In 1954, Dr. Archie Carr founded the **Caribbean Conservation Corporation** (see **Sights**, above), based 1km north of Tortuguero village, to help bring the sea turtles into the international limelight. In 1970, the Costa Rican government declared this 35km strip a national park. Today, researchers tag turtles and use satellite tracking to determine patterns of birth dates, routes, travel tendencies, in an attempt to uncover once and for all the mystery behind the tenacity of those forever-returning females. Tagging turtles has revealed absolutely amazing information about their migratory and mating habits; one turtle tagged near Tortuguero was found just one month later on the coast of Senegal, Africa, and several reports show that female turtles, after visiting hundreds of beaches around the world, return to their exact same birth site to nest 30 years later.

 TOUR SMART. Concern in the area is rising over certain guides and tour companies with regards to other local business. Some companies have been known to tell unaware travelers that they can only patronize certain hotels and restaurants (from which they receive a fat commission). As a result, some locales see incredibly good business, while others lose money due to the unfair practices of the guides. Other guides have been known to sub-contract out to dirt-cheap guides with little naturalist training that speak poor English. *Let's Go* encourages you to use your own judgment in choosing your guides, accommodations, and restaurants. Compare establishments before making your choices and try to visit several different businesses during your stay in Tortuguero.

ECO-FRIENDLY TOURS. Regardless of which guide you chose to journey through Tortuguero's steely canals, remember to respect the wildlife. Official park rules require boats to switch from gas to electric motors, which are quieter and do not disturb the animals nearly as much as the roar from the loud gas engines. Tour boats should also glide along the canals extremely slowly to avoid causing wakes, which disrupt animal and insect life on the shores. Most tour guides observe these rules, but, for economical reasons, some ignore them. As an informed and eco-sensitive tourist, it's your duty to ask non-rule-abiding guides to slow down and shut up.

ACTIVITIES IN THE PARK. Starting from the **Cuatro Esquinas ranger station,** at the park's entrance, **Sendero El Gavilán** (1hr., 2km) is not a difficult hike but can be very muddy. The trail winds through the forest and ends on the beach, where you can wash off and then take a left and walk back to town. Another pleasant trail, but one that is tricky to reach, is **Sendero Tucán** (1.4km), which runs alongside the Caño Negro Waterway. The trail starts at the **Jalova ranger station,** about 15min. from the village of Parismina by motor boat. Parismina itself is 1hr. away by canal. You will have to hire a guide to take you there (see below), but most guides and locals say that the price of the boat ride is not worth the dearth of activities at Jalova. Quiet hikers may spot monkeys, toucans, and tiny, red poison dart frogs along the trails. The frogs make venom in their sweat, so as long as you don't lick them and get their sticky coating in your blood stream, they are completely harmless. Sorry girls, this is one frog that won't transform into a prince after a kiss. Two other very simple mini-trails (600m) are also quite enjoyable. **La Ranita Roja** makes a semicircle around Caño Harol, while **Tragón** follows a straight, short path. Daryl also rents out **kayaks** that you can use to explore the canals yourself (US$10 for half-day; proceeds benefit Tortuguero high school).

TURTLE WATCHING. The park's feature presentation is the nightly *deshove,* the time when turtles come to lay their eggs. The female turtle emerges from the sea, makes her way up the sand, constantly pausing to check for danger, until she finds the perfect spot, where she uses her flippers to dig a one-foot deep body pit. She finally lays her eggs, carefully buries them in the sand, and leaves them, never to see the final product. The intriguing process takes about two hours.

From July to October, visitors *must* be with a guide certified by the national park (ask to see a license). Even at other times, don't try to watch the *deshove* unguided; the beaches are dangerous at night due to unexpected waves and vast quantities of driftwood. There's a strategy to watching the great *deshove:* if you've already paid park admission for the day, it's best to go back to the park at night instead of the public beach. Here, there are fewer crowds (there can be as many as 100 people on the public beach) and more turtles. Turtle tours leave nightly at 8 and 10pm (US$10 per person).

Talk to any of the guides mentioned below to set up a tour. Otherwise, show up (daily 5-6pm) at the Cuatro Esquinas Ranger Station, where local guides await, and obtain the necessary permission slips. Wear good walking shoes and dark clothing. Don't bring a flashlight or camera—bright lights blind the turtles and hinder their return to the sea. Official park rules state that once a tour group has seen the egg-laying process, they must get off the beach, regardless of whether or not the two hours have elapsed..

⏷ GUIDED TOURS. Entirely enveloped by water, Tortuguero is best explored by canoe or motorboat. Although it's possible to go alone, hiring a guide is much more informative and fun. Keep in mind, however, that guides abound in Tortuguero and the competition is cut-throat. Many guides harass people on the street and can be very annoying. If you want a particular guide, stick with it, even when competitors try to mislead you

Daryl from **Tortuguero Safaris Information Center** is a fantastic guide, and his boat has an electric motor that is ecologically friendly and quiet. (US$5 per hr. per person; you can design your own tour.) **Bárbara** (beeper ☎ 223 3030, dial 3761; tinamon@racsa.co.cr; www.tinamontours.de), in the purple house 100m past Cabinas Tortuguero, is a German biologist who owns **Tinamon Tours** and leads canoe, hiking, and village tours in English, Spanish, French, and German. She prefers small groups (4-5 people) and rents her canoes from older villagers who have few sources of income (all tours US$5 per hr. per person).

CERRO TORTUGUERO AND CAÑO PALMA BIOLOGICAL STATION. The flora-and fauna-filled thrills of Tortuguero can be matched at the Caño Palma Biological Station and its surrounding canals in the Barra del Colorado Wildlife Refuge.

Though the **La Palma** ranger station and the surrounding **Caño Palma** area of the refuge, managed by the non-profit **Canadian Organization for Tropical Education and Rainforest Conservation (COTERC),** sit inside Parque Nacional Barra del Colorado (see below), they're most easily accessed from Tortuguero. Just south of the La Palma station, **Cerro Tortuguero** offers hikers a climb that is about 6km from Tortuguero village. Though rising only 390m, the summit affords a spectacular panoramic view of the lowlands and park. You will need a guide with a boat to reach the station and refuge. (US$5 per hr. per person.) There are also **volunteer** opportunities available that include research, trail maintenance, and tour guiding. (☎ 381 4116; canopalm@sol.racsa.co.cr. Admission to station US$2.)

BARRA DEL COLORADO

Even more remote than Parque Nacional Tortuguero is Barra del Colorado, a swampy neighbor 50km north that conspicuously rubs up against the Nicaraguan border. At first glance, Barra could be Tortuguero's long lost twin; both national parks are almost ecologically identical, accessible only by boat or plane, and traversed on quiet boats along lagoons that meander through the dense vegetation. It's obvious that Barra lacks Tortuguero's tourist appeal. Barra's tiny community lives in shabby houses sinking into the incessantly damp ground and manages a handful of lodges devoted to sportfishing, Barra's claim to fame. Though just as much wildlife can be seen here, and the snook and tarpon are even bigger than in Tortuguero, Barra's seclusion and lack of activities for anyone other than thick-walleted sportfishermen makes it an infrequent stop on most visitors' itineraries.

◪ ORIENTATION

Barra is located 99km northeast of San José and 50km north of Tortuguero, and is actually two separate small slivers of land, Barra Sur and Barra del Norte, which sit directly opposite each other at the mouth of the Río Colorado.

▤ TRANSPORTATION

Getting to Barra is more expensive and complex than getting to Tortuguero. The cheapest way to get here from **San José** is to head to El Caribe Bus Terminal (☎ 221 2596) in San José and take a direct **bus** to **Cariari** (2hr.; 6:30, 9am; ¢720).

AT A GLANCE

AREA: 920 sq. km, 50km of coastline.

CLIMATE: Hot and humid; avg. temp. 26°C (79F).

FEATURES: Remote and jungle-like Refugio Nacional de Vida Silvestre Barra del Colorado.

HIGHLIGHTS: Some of Costa Rica's best game fish sportfishing, turtle nesting, wildife sighting opportunities similar to Parque Nacional Tortuguero.

GATEWAYS: Cariari, Parque Nacional Tortuguero (**P. 354**).

CAMPING: Not allowed in the park.

FEES AND RESERVATIONS: Park admission US$7, combined 3-day pass to Tortuguero and Barra del Colorado US$10, fishing license US$30.

From Cariari there is daily public transportation to **Barra** (2pm; return 5pm). The first leg of the journey is by bus to **Puerto Lindo** (2hr.), where a **boat** picks up passengers and takes them to **Barra** (45min.) You can also get to Cariari from Guápiles.

The cheapest route from **Tortuguero** is a bit more complicated. Take the 6am **boat** to **Pavona** and wait there until 2pm (¢1000) when another boat leaves for **Barra** (2hr.; ¢1500). Otherwise, from Tortuguero, private boats can be hired for US$40-50

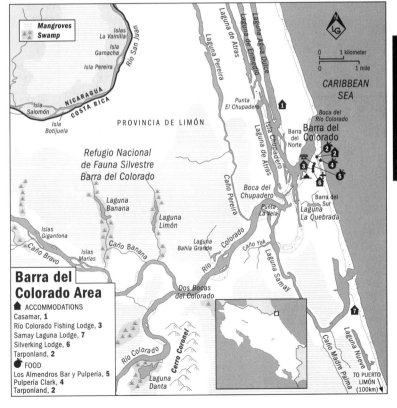

Barra del Colorado Area

🏠 ACCOMMODATIONS
Casamar, **1**
Río Colorado Fishing Lodge, **3**
Samay Laguna Lodge, **7**
Silverking Lodge, **6**
Tarponland, **2**

🍴 FOOD
Los Almendros Bar y Pulpería, **5**
Pulpería Clark, **4**
Tarponland, **2**

CARIBBEAN LOWLANDS

FROM THE ROAD

for 4-5 people for the 1hr. trip. From **Moín,** there are Tortuguero boats that continue to **Barra;** service is irregular. You can hire a boat for about US$70 one-way.

It is also possible to arrive in Barra from **Puerto Viejo de Sarapiquí,** but again, service is irregular; the **public boat** makes the trip about once every three to eight days (US$50). **Private charters** from Sarapiquí cost US$300. If you travel through Sarapiquí, be sure to bring your passport. The easiest way to get to Barra is by **flying** into the local airstrip on one of the daily flights offered by **Sansa** (30min.; 6am, return 6:45am; US$55) or **Travelair** (30min.; 6:15am, return 7am; US$60)

🛈 PRACTICAL INFORMATION

Barra Sur is almost completely residential, while Barra del Norte is home to the **main dock, airstrip,** and the area's few accommodations and services. Most non-fishers visit on daytrips from Tortuguero, so there are very few real services. In case of a **medical** or **police emergency,** have the guards near the main dock contact doctors and authorities in Limón on their radio. **A public phone** is available at CYD Souvenir, 100m down the airstrip from the docks and to the right. (☎710 6592. Local calls ¢15 per min., calls to US ¢450 per min. Open daily 6am-8pm.) **Los Almendros Bar y Pulpería,** a few meters down from CYD Souvenir, has another public phone (local calls ¢10 per min.; ¢60 per min to US, Mexico, and Canada; ¢80 per min. to Europe), a **Sansa ticket office,** and basic snacks and supplies. (Open daily 7am-noon and 3-7pm.) **Pulpería Clark,** on the left side of the air strip, sells basic snacks, fruits, vegetables, and supplies. (Open daily 6am-9pm.)

🏠🍴 ACCOMMODATIONS AND FOOD

Almost every lodge in Barra accommodates anglers on expensive sportfishing packages, making visiting for a night or two a rather expensive trip for non-fishers. The cheapest place in Barra is **Tarponland ❹** (☎710 2141 or 710 1271), about 50m down from the dock by the airstrip. It's a large, salon-like place with a worn light-blue exterior, a rusty red roof, and no sign. The 12 rooms are large but basic with small beds, wood-paneled walls, fans, and private cold-water baths. There's also a large, leafy pool outside and a **bar/restaurant ❷** that serves a variety of meats, fish, seafood, and Costa Rican standards. Owner Guillermo Cunningham can also arrange tours. (Restaurant entrees ¢1300-1500. 4-person round-trip to Tortuguero US$100. 2-8 person 4hr. whale watching tour ¢25,000. Sportfishing packages US$200 per double per night;

WHEN TO GO. Barra del Colorado is hot and humid year-round, with an average yearly rainfall of 6m. The rainy season is officially from June to Oct., but expect it to rain a lot year-round. The driest months are Feb.-May. Different from most of Costa Rica's national parks, Barra del Colorado has no hikeable trails, since the area is almost exclusively covered with swamps, muddy wetlands, and lagoons. Leatherback and green sea turtles nest on Barra's beach from July-Sept., and the snook and tarpon fishing season reaches its peak Jan.-May and Sept.-Oct. Be sure to bring good, waterproof footwear (rubber boots work well), rain gear, sun block, insect repellent, a hat, cash, and any medical supplies you might need since not many supplies are available in Barra.

US$250 per triple per night, including food, lodging, and fishing tours.) The rest of Barra's accommodations are prohibitively expensive for anyone but the thick-walleted avid sportfisherman. The following is a list of some of the nearby lodges and per person double occupancy rates for all-inclusive sportfishing packages: **Casamar** ⑤, across the river from Barra (in the US ☎ 800-543-0282 or 714-578-1881; www.casamar.com; 3-day/3-night packages starting at US$1325); **Río Colorado Fishing Lodge** ⑤, in Barra Sur (☎ 232 4063, in the US 800-243-9777; www.sportsmanweb.com/riocolorado; 6-day/5-night packages start at US$1430); **Samay Laguna Lodge** ⑤, 8km south of Barra Sur (☎ 384 7047; www.samay.com; 2-day/1-night package starting at US$445); **Silverking Lodge** ⑤, on Barra Sur just north of the ranger station (☎ 888 6TARPON; www.silverking.com; US$140 per night, US$450 with fishing).

◩ REFUGIO NACIONAL DE VIDA SILVESTRE BARRA DEL COLORADO

The Barra del Colorado Wildlife Refuge is one of Costa Rica's largest protected areas, covering almost 920 sq. km of swampy and hot humid tropical forest and canals teeming with wildlife. It gets drenched with 6m of rain yearly, and the average temperature hovers around 26°C (79°F). Created in the mid-1980s, the area remains relatively untouched and unexplored, save for quite a bit of illegal logging in the depths of the park. The park's **ranger station** is 1km south of Barra del Norte on the Río Colorado. (Open daily 6am-6pm. Admission US$7, combination 3-day pass for Tortuguero and Barra US$10. Fishing license US$30.)

Extremely little of Barra is accessible by foot, since the grounds are so swampy (especially in the rainy season), so the most popular activity remains sportfishing. Locals make much of their living fishing for spiny lobsters and exporting them throughout the country, while most tourism business centers on the enormous fighting fishes known to lurk in the murky Barra waters. Tarpon and snook season is best from January to May and September to October, but locals will tell you that fishing is pretty good year-round. Guillermo Cunningham of Tarponland (see **Accommodations,** above) offers the best rates on sportfishing trips. Most travelers, however, come with packages from pricier lodges a few kilometers from Barra.

An alternative to sportfishing is to take wildlife tours, which can also be arranged with any of the lodges in Barra. The wetland areas, navigable by silent motor boats, are home to jaguars, three-toed sloths, spider and white-faced monkeys, manatees, and a huge variety of birds, such as laughing falcons, keel-bird toucans, and green macaws. Green, leatherback, and hawksbill turtles also nest on Barra's beaches, but not nearly as many numbers as on Tortuguero. Samay Lodge (see **Accommodations,** above) offers all-inclusive 3-day/2-night jungle safari packages from San José with tours through the Barra canals for US$275 per person.

CAHUITA

Warm, turquoise waves lap up on black- and white-sand beaches. Howler monkeys in the treetops of the coastal rainforest cry out broken rhapsodies. Parque Nacional Cahuita, southeast of the village, is home to the largest coral reef on Costa Rica's Caribbean coast, and the other side of the village is a comparative paradise—there, sun-worshippers bask in paradise on Playa Negra. Some warn that not all of Cahuita is idyllic, so take precautions, especially at night. (Travelers are warned to avoid drug deals; the police close in with almost supernatural omniscience.) You can relax your grip on that can of mace, however; a vast majority of Cahuita's visitors feel the town's reputation as unsafe is exaggerated, and back their claims by the noticeable increased police presence.

▐▀ TRANSPORTATION

Buses: The MEPE bus company serves Cahuita (☎257 8129 in San José, ☎758 1572 in Limón). Buses depart from the front of the park to: **Limón** (1hr., 9 per day 6:15am-6:45pm, ¢350); **Puerto Viejo** (30min., 8 per day 6am-7pm, ¢165); **Manzanillo** (1½hr.; 7am, 3:30, 5:30pm via Puerto Viejo; ¢340); **San José** (3½hr.; 7:30, 9:30, 11:30am, 4:30pm; ¢1975).

Taxis: Mr. **Big J** (☎755 0328), one block southeast of the bus stop, is the most comprehensive source of info and tours in town. He has a list of taxi drivers, including Wayne (☎755 0078), Enrique (☎755 0017), and René (☎755 0243). Open daily 9am-noon and 3-6pm.

✱ ❓ ORIENTATION AND PRACTICAL INFORMATION

A road branching off the Limón-Puerto Viejo highway travels for 1km before intersecting with Cahuita's main road in the middle of town, in front of a small municipal park. The town's main road passes through Cahuita from northwest to southeast. Facing the bus stop (with the park in front of you), northwest is to your left and southeast is to your right. **Playa Negra** is on the northwest end of town; **Playa Blanca** lies in Cahuita National park over the bridge to the southeast.

Tourist information: Your best bet is **Mr. Big J** (see above). The **MINAE** office (☎755 0060; fax 755 0455), two blocks northwest of the bus stop, can answer questions about parks, but isn't designed to dispense other tourist info. If you're hitting the beach for the day, store your valuables in a steel case at **Mr. Big J.** ¢1000 per day.

Banks: The closest banks are in Limón. The **Cabinas Safari** hotel, however, exchanges traveler's checks (3% commission) and over a dozen currencies (3.2% commission). Open daily 7am-4pm. **Western Union** is inside Cahuita Tours, 2½ blocks northwest of the bus stop.

Laundry: Mr. **Big J** will wash, dry, and fold clothes. ¢1500 per load. Takes 2½hr. Open M-F 8am-4pm.

Police: (☎755 0217), at the northwest end of the main road, 3 blocks from the bus stop right next to the post office. Open 24hr.

Pharmacy: (☎750 0136), 10min. walk out of town on the main road, or hop on a bus headed for Puerto Viejo and ask to get off at the clinic on the right. Call ahead if possible. Open M-F 7am-4pm.

Medical Services: For medical care, contact the **Red Cross** in Limón (☎758 0125, **emergencies** 911). English spoken. Available 24hr.

Telephones: Next to the bus stop, at **Cahuita Tours,** in Hotel Cahuita, 2 blocks northwest of the bus stop, and in front of the police station. **Fax** service at Cahuita Tours and Cabina Vaz (about ¢100 per page).

Internet: Palmer CyberNet, across from Cabinas Safari. ¢1000 per hr. Open M-Sa 7:30am-10pm, Su 6-10pm. **Spencer Sea-Side Lodge** has similar prices and is open as requested.

Post Office: (☎ 755 0096), at the northwest end of the main road, 3 blocks from the bus stop. Open M-F 8am-noon and 1-5:30pm.

Postal Code: 7302.

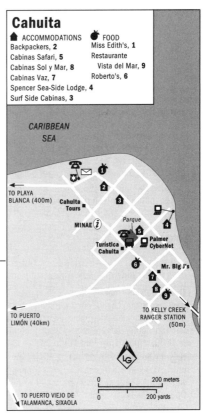

Cahuita

⌂ ACCOMMODATIONS
Backpackers, **2**
Cabinas Safari, **5**
Cabinas Sol y Mar, **8**
Cabinas Vaz, **7**
Spencer Sea-Side Lodge, **4**
Surf Side Cabinas, **3**

🍎 FOOD
Miss Edith's, **1**
Restaurante
  Vista del Mar, **9**
Roberto's, **6**

▐ ACCOMMODATIONS

There are more *cabinas* than anything in Cahuita. Competition, unfortunately, has not created more budget options. It is only easier to get cheap rooms in groups. Most *cabinas* are very clean and comfortable.

Spencer Sea-Side Lodge (☎ 755 0027). Walk 2 blocks down the crossroads from the bus stop and turn right at the beach. Sea-Side's location can't be beat and the grounds are full of hammocks. Simple rooms with iguana murals have worn private baths with cold water and comfortable beds. Daily reef tours US$15 per person. Internet access available ¢1000 per hr. Basic rooms US$8 per person; doubles with fridge and hot water US$25; each extra person US$5. Traveler's checks. ❶

Cabinas Sol y Mar (☎ 755 0237 or 755 0418; cabsolymar@hotmail.com), 1½ blocks southeast of the bus stop, near the entrance to the national park. Spacious, homey rooms are gracefully furnished. Immaculate private bathrooms have warm water, and there's an upstairs balcony overlooking the street and beach with comfortable rocking chairs. Singles US$10; doubles US$14-16; quads US$20-25. AmEx/MC/V. ❶

Cabinas Safari (☎ 755 0020), a block down the crossroads from the bus stop, past the park. Rooms are cheerfully decorated and baths are pristine. Beds are very comfortable with very clean sheets. Singles US$10-15; doubles US$15-20; triples US$20-25; quads US$25-30; 1 double with kitchen and refrigerator US$25-30. V. ❷

Backpackers (☎ 755 0174), a half block southeast of Edith's (see **Food,** below). Catering to those who need to stretch their budget, Backpackers offers tidy, unexciting rooms with ceiling fans and a cold-water, concrete communal shower. Owner offers a banana pancake and coffee breakfast for ¢300. Singles US$6; doubles US$10. ❶

LENDING A HELPING HAND Cahuita is a town founded as an historic act of kindness. In the mid-18th century, the area was only seasonally populated by Afro-Caribbean turtle hunters, who set up camps here on their way to Tortuguero or Bocas del Toro. However, the President of the Republic Alfredo González Flores (1914-1917) had a sailing accident in the nearby waters when returning from a diplomatic meeting in Sixaola. The hunters helped the sailors with provisions and saved their lives. President González Flores bought a block of land for the settlers and allowed them to officially found the town of Cahuita.

Cabinas Vaz (☎ 755 02138, fax 755 0283), across from Big J, is not as charming as the others, but offers good prices for spacious, clean rooms. Each room is a separate small concrete building, and offers more privacy than most. Singles US$10; doubles US$15; triples US$15; sextuplet ₡2500 per person. Student discounts. MC/V. ❶

Surf Side Cabinas (☎ 755 0246), a block down from the bus stop and 150m northwest, in front of the school. It may not be surf-side, but it still offers simple, recently renovated rooms with fans and hot water baths. US$10 per person. ❶

🍴 FOOD

Most restaurants in town are pricey, but gourmet. A couple groceries line the main road on either side of the bus stop, so you can stock up on the way to the park.

Miss Edith's, 3 blocks northwest from the bus stop, then right at the end of the side road past the police. Legendary Caribbean food served at a Caribbean pace. High prices, but locals swear by her cooking. Feast on incredible vegetable soup (₡1300), fish with coconut, curry, and yucca (₡2300), *rondon* stew with chicken (₡2600), or lobster (₡4800). Open daily 7am-10pm. ❸

Triple Cahuita (☎ 755 0244), 2 blocks up from the cross road bus stop, is one of the only places in town that will serve a cheap *casado* (₡1000) to budget travelers. Ask what the budget specials are when ordering—occasionally they are posted outside. Open 11am-10pm. AmEx/MC/V. ❶

Roberto's, 1½ blocks southeast of the bus stop, serves up Caribbean seafood dishes from shrimp to octopus (₡2500) from Roberto tours (see **Guided Tours,** below), and the restaurant will cook you a dinner made from your day's catch. Open daily noon-10pm in the low season; high season 6am-10pm. ❸

Restaurant Vista Del Mar (☎ 755 0008), 2 blocks southeast of the bus stop, overlooking the entrance to the park. Spacious and open-aired. Cooks up a wide variety of Chinese food with large portions and delicious spices like chow mein (₡750-4050), a half-dozen styles of scrumptious shrimp (₡1600-4150), and lobster (₡4150). Open daily 11am-10pm. AmEx/MC/V. ❸

🗺 GUIDED TOURS

Mr. Big J (see **Practical Information,** above) is run by a helpful Italian named Mañuela and the amiable Mr. Big J himself (a.k.a. Joseph). In addition to seemingly endless services at the office, these two can set you up with 3hr. **snorkeling** trips in the national park with boat, equipment, and guide (gear rental US$6, guided trips US$20 per person), **horseback riding** tours on the beach or through forest waterfalls (beach 3hr., US$30 per person; waterfalls 5hr., US$40 per person with lunch), fishing trips ideal for catching red snappers, mackerel, and kingfish (US$40 per person), as well as trips to **Tortuguero** (US$95 per person for 2 days).

Roberto Tours (☎/fax 755 0117), a block southeast of the bus stop. Run by sweet-man-nered Roberto. His family has been fishing in Cahuita for 40 years and he guarantees fresh catch on his **fishing trips** (day trips for mackerel and jack 4hr., US$50; deep-sea fishing night trips for tuna and red snapper US$100; equipment included). Cook up your catch in Roberto's Caribbean-style seafood restaurant next door. He also offers early-morning **dolphin tours, snorkeling trips,** and visits to Roberto's organic farm, exotic fruit orchard, and cacao plantation. (Dolphin tour 3hr., US$15. Snorkeling 3hr., US$15. Farm tour 3hr., US$15. **Bike** rental ¢350 per hr., ¢2000 per day.) Open M-F 7am-3pm in low season, daily 7am-8pm in high season. AmEx/MC/V.

Cahuita Tours (☎ 755 0232; fax 755-0082; cahuitat@racso.co.cr), 2½ blocks northwest of the bus stop. Offers similar services to the other two and visits Reserva Biológica Hitoy Cerere (US$85 per person). **Whitewater rafting** (US$95) and **night tours** (US$10). Rents **snorkeling** gear (¢2000 per day) and **binoculars** (¢1500 per day). Sells daily papers. Open daily 7:30am-noon and 1:30-7pm. AmEx/MC/V.

Turística Cahuita (☎/fax 755 0071; dltacb@racsa.co.cr), run by an American, offers a variety of tours in English. Rents boogie and surf boards. Boogies ¢3000 per day, ¢5000 deposit; surfboards ¢5000 per day, ¢10,000 deposit. Open daily 8am-6pm.

PARQUE NACIONAL CAHUITA

Parque Nacional Cahuita's claim to fame is its spectacular 600 hectare coral reef. Though 22,400 hectares of the park are marine, the very accessible 1067 hectare coastal rainforest is well worth a visit. The expansive **Playa Blanca** (named for its warm white sand) stretches south of the station, where less active park visitors laze on towels and take dips in the refreshing Caribbean waves.

AT A GLANCE	
AREA: 23,000 hectares of ocean, 1067 hectares of land.	**GATEWAYS:** Cahuita (p. 366).
CLIMATE: Hot and humid. Average 29°C.	**CAMPING:** Permitted near the Puerto Viejo side. 50 sites available with facilities at the ranger station.
FEATURES: Punta Vargas on the 600 hectare coral reef, Playa Blanca, hiking the rainforest trails, surfing, snorkeling.	**FEES AND RESERVATIONS:** US$7 park entrance fee if you enter from the Puerto Viejo station. There is no fee at the Kelly Creek staion, but donations are welcome.

TRANSPORTATION

Cahuita is the gateway town for the Parque Nacional Cahuita. See **Transportation** (p. 366) for transportation to and from Cahuita. To enter the park through the Puerto Vargas ranger station, take the Puerto Viejo de Talamanca bus in Cahuita and ask to be let off at the entrance to Puerto Vargas.

ORIENTATION

Parque Nacional Cahuita lies on the south end of the Atlantic Coast, in the province of Limón. The park has two ranger stations, both accessible from Cahuita. The **Kelly Creek ranger station** is three blocks southeast of the bus stop just over the small bridge at the edge of town. **Puerto Vargas,** the second station, is off the main highway between Puerto Viejo and Limón. To enter, take the Puerto Viejo de Talamanca bus in Cahuita. Ask to be let off at the entrance road to Puerto Vargas.

PRACTICAL INFORMATION

> **WHEN TO GO** The Cahuita area is very hot and humid year round, and is especially wet during the rainy season. For this reason, most people visit during the dry season (Dec.-Apr.). Bring a bathing suit to enjoy the ocean and light clothing so that you can enjoy the weather. When you hike, bring water, insect repellent, comfortable shoes you can get wet, and bottled water. The only trail is 5km to the tip, and 7km from there to Puerto Vargas. It is very important to keep hydrated throughout the hike. Muggings have occurred; however, during station hours (M-F 8am-4pm, Sa-Su 7am-5pm) there are frequent patrols. Still, people hiking alone should be cautious.

If you enter through the **Kelly Creek ranger station,** you must register in their logbook before entering. They gratefully accept donations to enter the park (open daily 6am to 5pm). A standard US$7 national park admission fee is required if you enter from the **Puerto Vargas station** (☎ 755 0302 or 755 0060; aclac@ns.minae.go.cr; open M-F 8am-4pm, Sa-Su 7am-5pm).

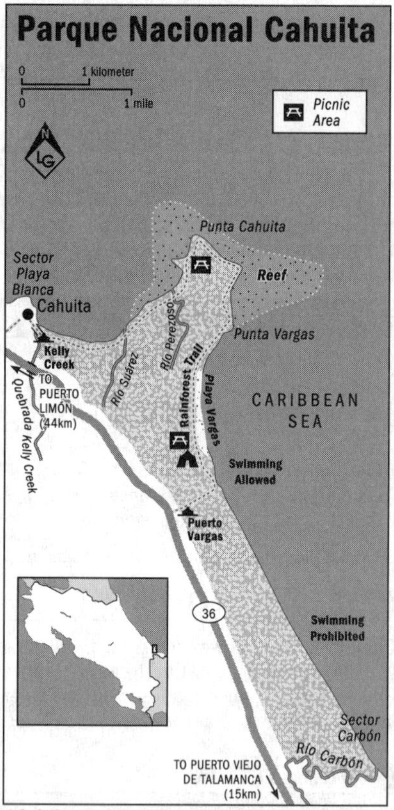

Parque Nacional Cahuita

Map showing the park with labels: Picnic Area, Punta Cahuita, Reef, Sector Playa Blanca, Cahuita, Punta Vargas, Kelly Creek, TO PUERTO LIMÓN (44km), Río Suárez, Quebrada Kelly Creek, Río Perezoso, Rainforest Trail, Playa Vargas, CARIBBEAN SEA, Swimming Allowed, Puerto Vargas, Swimming Prohibited, 36, Sector Carbón, Río Carbón, TO PUERTO VIEJO DE TALAMANCA (15km)

CAMPING

Camping is permitted near the Puerto Vargas side of the park (US$2 per person). The 50 camping sites are set back from the hiking path and include an ocean vista with access to showers, sinks, and toilets at the ranger station. Places where swimming is permitted are clearly marked and strictly enforced. Surfing, as well as volleyball and soccer, are allowed in certain areas.

RAINFOREST TRAIL

An easy 9km (2½hr.) trail leads from the Kelly Creek Station in Cahuita for 4km to Punta Cahuita, and continues for an additional 3km until it reaches Puerto Vargas. The hike finishes 2km past the station. The trail seems more like a narrow road than a path, with bikers riding through and local mothers pushing babies in carriages. Sometimes the tide is so high that the mini-road floods, soaking hikers and bikers alike. A little further on the path, crosses Río Suarez, which, during high tide, reaches chest-high. But all in all, the hike is worth it. On one side the rolling waves of the Caribbean drum against secluded white-sand **Playa Vargas;** on the other, there's a swampy forest with brush and towering coconut palms.

CARIBBEAN LOWLANDS

The treetops of Cahuita are among the best in the country for spotting congo and white-faced monkeys; at sunrise and sunset, the playful primates often come down from their perches to frolic on the beach.

FLORA AND FAUNA

The region's smaller flora and fauna are remarkable; be sure to look down and watch your step! Orange hermit crabs and white ghost crabs scurry across the path. Observe the backs of the brightly striped lizards carefully—if there are spines running down to the tail, it's an iguana; if not, then it's probably a **Jesucristo (Jesus Christ) lizard** (named for its ability to walk on water, not for any physical resemblance). The medicinal *sangrillo*'s tree trunk has thick folds that bunch up and out, making it look as though it's resting on a wrinkled pyramidal base. Look for the flaking white trees locals call *"gringo pelado"* under their breath: the trees peel from the sun like pale, blond gringos. And watch out for the deadly fluorescent **snakes** that slither in the nearby forest. The venom takes only about 20min. to kill an average-sized person, so wandering off the trail probably isn't a great idea. Other animals you will probably come across are sloths, howler monkeys, and dozens of species of birds, including green ibis, kingfishers, and toucans.

THE CORAL REEF

Fish of all shapes, sizes, and colors of the rainbow inhabit Cahuita's 600 hectare coral reef with 35 different species, and elkhorn and brain corals line the ocean floor. In the past few years, the reef has shrunk, due in part to the accumulation of eroded soil from banana plantations; the nasty chemicals sprayed on the bananas have drained into the water, contaminating the reef. Earthquakes have also heaved the coral upwards towards the sun; now, there's too much dead coral floating around for snorkelers to find good sites on their own. It's better to check with the rangers or go on a guided tour (see Cahuita **Guided Tours,** above). It's also a bad idea to go out the day after a heavy night storm has stirred up debris and dead coral in the water. The most popular spot to visit is **Punta Vargas.**

BRIBRÍ

This small town is often visited for its bank, but offers almost no tourist amenities. The town has a relaxed Caribbean feel mixed with deep pride in the indigenous heritage of the surrounding area. Although it has no beachfront, Bribrí could be a nice spot to relax for a few hours before further trips onward.

TRANSPORTATION. All streets in Bribrí stem from the main bus stop in front of Restaurante Bribrí. Many **buses** pass through Bribrí where buses sometimes stop for lunch. From here, buses go to: **Sixaola** (1½hr.; 10:30am, 2:30, 6, 8pm; ¢285); **San José** (4½hr.; 6:30, 8:30am, 1:30, 3:30pm; ¢2410); **Cahuita** (1hr., ¢275); **Puerto Viejo** (30min., ¢200). A couple of 4WD **taxis** usually patrol the center.

ORIENTATION AND PRACTICAL INFORMATION. Streets in Bribrí originate from the main bus stop. East leads to Puerto Viejo (10km), while the road west crosses the Carbón river and forks out to Volio (2km) and Bambú (9km). Banco Nacional gives Visa advances and has long lines. (☎751 0068. Open M-F 8:30am-3:45pm.) Ambulances can be reached at ☎751 0008. The Cruz Roja, 200m down the road from Restaurante Bribrí, offers medical services and simple bedrooms (☎751 0141). There is no post office or Internet service in town. There are coin-operated phones in front of the bus stop (¢200).

🛏️🍴 ACCOMMODATIONS AND FOOD. The **Cruz Roja ❶**, 200m down the road from Restaurante Bribrí, offers simple bedrooms with sparkling clean bathrooms. (☎751 0141. Reception 24hr. Triples ¢3500-4000; quads ¢6000; 5-7 people ¢7000. Make reservations as rooms fill up fast.) **Cabinas El Piculuna ❶**, down the street from the Cruz Roja, on the left, is a light blue building with a pleasant garden, airy rooms, and an attached *soda*. (☎751 0130. Huge *casados* with drink ¢1200. Singles ¢3000, with A/C ¢5000; doubles ¢4000/7000; triples ¢6000/10000. Restaurant open 6am-10pm.) **Bar/Restaurant Mango ❶**, 400 miles east of the main intersection on the left hand side, has bright decorations and ceiling fans. (☎751 0054. Singles ¢2600; doubles ¢3600.)

Soda El Banco ❶, next to the bank, is actually far more charming than the name suggests with comfortable reclined seating, large cable TV, and a creative, pleasant cook. (☎751 0045. *Casado* with drink ¢900; sandwich ¢300. Open daily 6:30am-3:30pm.) **Restaurante Bribrí ❶**, in the heart of town, has the sign "Ye Due Bliwa," which means "I am hungry" in indigenous dialect. Though this restaurant serves only standard *tico* food, it is a great place to get tourist information. (☎751 0044. *Gallo pinto* ¢600-900; *casados* ¢700-1500; chicken ¢700-1500. Variable hours.) **Abastecedor Sandí ❷**, across the street from Cabinas El Peculuna, has groceries. (☎751 0087. Open 6am-9pm.)

▲ RESERVA BIOLÓGICA HITOY-CERERE

*Sixty-seven kilometers from Limón, this reserve is most easily accessible from Cahuita. Take any bus heading north from Cahuita, and ask to be let off in the tiny town of **Penhurst** (20min., ¢150). Cross the street to the road heading inland (west) and wait at the gas station for the hourly bus to **Finca 6**. Ask to be let off at **Finca 12** (30min., ¢200). From there, it is a 1½km uphill hike along a dirt road winding through local farms. There are no signs until you arrive, but it is the only road in the area. It is virtually impossible to get lost. Arriving at the Reserva Biológica Hitoy-Cerere, rangers charge US$6 admittance and offer a variety of facilities. The **ranger station** has a large common area with TV, cook, sheetless beds (US$6), outdoor and indoor bathrooms, and a friendly staff. Camping not permitted. You can usually catch a ride back to civilization with one of the rangers, who descend daily in their 4WD vehicles.*

The ▓Reserva Biológica Hitoy-Cerere is cradled between the Talamanca Mountain Range and the Estrella Valley, as well as by the three major indigenous reservations of Tayni, Telire, and Talamanca. It receives approximately 3500mm of rainfall every year. As its isolated location suggests, this area is a gem of undiscovered beauty. Tourists rarely visit; biologists stay for years. Adventurous nature-lovers will appreciate this remote reserve. One famous resident here is the **luminous blue butterfly.** The rangers are eager to educate and will teach you all about the (dead, of course) collection of poisonous snakes and insects at the station. It is not customary to be guided by a ranger, but they will gladly help arrange a local guide. These guides are generally cheaper (¢5000-10000 per day) than any arranged in Cahuita or Limón, and have lifelong experience in the area. Except for the two described trails, the rangers request that visitors travel with a guide.

SENDERO CATARATA

This trail begins with a 10min. jungle path that starts in the station and intersects with Río Cerere. Build a cairn, or small pile of stones, to help you recognize the jungle exit when returning. The rest of the trip is not a trail, but rather an effort to follow the river along stone mounds on either side. Depending on recent rainfall, you could end up crossing the river about 7-15 times to reach more manageable, dry paths. Never wander far from the river and follow for 2km until you reach the first waterfall. The trail isn't marked but it is nearly impossible to get lost. Wear

CAUTION. A common anecdote about the Reserve is that the name in the indigenous language Cabécar means "fuzzy rocks" (Hitoy) and "clear water" (Cerere). Most of the hikes involve crossing the rivers over moss-covered (i.e. fuzzy) rocks. However, this beautiful feature can also be a major safety hazard since moss makes for slippery crossings. Normally, the first segment of the river reaches to one's knees, but common thunderstorms can fill the river to neck level. Be sure to ask the rangers about recent rainfall. Always cross the river by crab-walking and facing against the current. Swimming against the current is impossible. Bring a machete for trail underbrush and a bamboo stick your height to measure the depth of waters before crossing. The Sendero Catarata also requires significant sun protection, since the nearby forest offers little shade.

clothes you don't mind getting completely soaked. The waterfall at the end is astoundingly beautiful and provides luxurious bathing. There is a second waterfall 1km further on the trail, but is off limits without a guide.

SENDERO TEPEZCUINTLE
This is a tiny loop (1km, 45min.) through the woods near the ranger station. This trail offers the best views of Hitoy-Cerere flora and fauna. It is a light, safe, and well-marked path, but watch out for tiny bright, red frogs—they are poisonous.

PUERTO VIEJO DE TALAMANCA

Puerto Viejo, 61km southeast of Puerto Limón, is all about unwinding and forgetting life's worries for a while... or forever, as the growing population of resident Europeans and gringos can attest. These recent immigrants have further added to the eclectic mix of Afro-Caribbean, Spanish, and indigenous cultures here. Though there are plenty of opportunities for surfing, snorkeling, and other outdoor activities, life here is slow, and if you're considering anything beyond catching the perfect wave or the perfect tan, you're being far too ambitious. Puerto Viejo is also the most commercially active of the Caribbean towns. Check out the open market on the main street for local crafts and the many shops for handmade souvenirs.

CARIBBEAN LOWLANDS

⌐ TRANSPORTATION

Buses: Leave for: **San José** (4½hr.; 7, 9, 11am, 4pm, additional bus at 1:30pm on F and Su; ¢2300); **Limón** (1½hr., 7 per day 5:30am-5:30pm, ¢500) via **Cahuita** (45min., ¢145); **Manzanillo** (45min.; 7:20am, 4, 7:30pm; ¢4180) via **Punta Uva** (30min., ¢150); **Panamanian border** at **Bribrí/Sixaola** (Bribrí 30min., ¢200; Sixaola 1½hr., 7 per day 6:15am-7:30pm, ¢475; buses leave Bribrí at 12:30pm).

Taxis: Walk a half-block west of ATEC and you'll see a sign on the south side street for **"Charlie's Taxi Service."** Everyone knows Charlie as "Bull" (☎ 750 0112). If Bull's red minivan isn't there, ask at ATEC. Also try Sergio (☎ 750 0525) or Bruno (☎ 750 0426).

✱ ⟩ ORIENTATION AND PRACTICAL INFORMATION

The main road comes in from the west, crosses the bridge near an abandoned barge, and cuts through town before heading east to Manzanillo 13km later. To get to the center of town from the bus stop (marked by sheltered benches), head south away from the beach one block to the main road, and turn left. The ATEC office is 1½ blocks east.

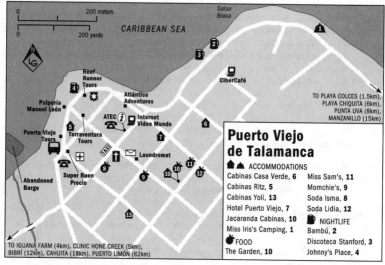

Puerto Viejo de Talamanca

▲ **ACCOMMODATIONS**

Cabinas Casa Verde, **6**
Cabinas Ritz, **5**
Cabinas Yoli, **13**
Hotel Puerto Viejo, **7**
Jacaranda Cabinas, **10**
Miss Iris's Camping, **1**

Miss Sam's, **11**
Momchie's, **9**
Soda Isma, **8**
Soda Lidia, **12**

NIGHTLIFE
Bambú, **2**
Discoteca Stanford, **3**
Johnny's Place, **4**

🍴 **FOOD**
The Garden, **10**

Tourist Information: Take your questions to **Talamanca Association for Ecotourism and Conservation** (ATEC ☎ 750 0398, fax 750 0191; atecmail@sol.racsa.co.cr) in the center of town. This grass-roots organization was founded to promote local tourism while preserving the region's heritage and ecology. Open M, Tu, Th, and F 7am-9pm, W 7am-noon and 2-9pm, Sa 8am-noon and 1-9pm, Su 8am-noon and 4-8pm. Access to **Internet** (¢900 per hr.). Photocopying (¢20 per page). **Puerto Viejo Tours** (☎ 750 0411; fax 755 0082), across from the bus stop, also gives advice. Many tour offices overstress the necessity of a guide; a more neutral source may be your hotel owner.

Financial Services: Pulpería Manuel León (☎ 750 0422; fax 750 0246), on the beach half-block west and 2 blocks north of ATEC, exchanges US dollars (1% commission) and cashes traveler's checks (1.5% commission). The owner, known as "El Chino," can help with directions. Open M-Sa 7am-6pm, Su 7:30am-2pm. **Banco Nacional** (☎ 751 0068), the nearest bank, is 30min. away in Bribrí. Visa cash advances with passport. Open M-F 8:30am-3:45pm.

Laundry: (☎ 750 0360), 30m south of the post office. ¢2500 per load. ¢500 extra for whites washed separately. Delivery service included. Locals or extended-stay tourists often negotiate special rates. Open daily 10am-6pm.

Police: (☎ 750 0230 or 911 for emergency) a half-block east and 1½ blocks north of ATEC facing the beach. Open 24hr.

Pharmacy: Clinic Hone Creek (☎ 750 0136), 5km out of town on the main road; hop on the bus headed for Bribrí. Call ahead if possible. Open M-F 7am-4pm.

Medical Services: (☎ 750 0303), a half-block block west and 1 block north of ATEC, Dr. Rodríguez and Dr. Ríos have a small office. Open M-F 4:30-8pm, Sa 8am-noon. The **dentist** is next door and shares the same phone line. For medical emergencies, contact the **Red Cross** (☎ 758 0125 or 911) in Limón. English spoken. Open 24hr.

Telephones: ATEC (see **Tourist Information,** above) offers international phone service. ¢274 per min. to US, ¢375 per min. to Europe and the rest of the world, ¢190 per min. in Central America. **Video Mundo** (☎ 750 0651), next door, has international phone service for approximately the same rates. Open daily 7am-9pm. There are payphones right outside, and a few around town.

Internet: Video Mundo (see above) has comfortable, quick connections. ₡1000 per hr.

Post Office: (☎750 0404), a half-block west and 25m south of ATEC. Open M-F 8am-noon, 1-5:30pm.

ACCOMMODATIONS

There are several extremely cheap options, but the superior conditions of the mid-range hotels are worth the extra money. US$12-16 here will get you a luxurious room with private bath and, usually, a private balcony with hammock.

Cabinas Casa Verde (☎750 0015; fax 750 0047; cabinascasaverde@hotmail.com; www.cabinascasaverde.com). From ATEC, continue half a block east on the main road and turn right, then turn left at the first street, and you'll see the green signs. With mosaic sinks, wind-chimes, and a patio, this is the perfect place to kick back and hide from the world for a while. Rooms have fans, mosquito nets, and porches for relaxing. Grounds have a frog farm, and the extensive tropical garden has bilingual labels. The Swiss-Costa Rican management is very amiable and flexible. Baths, some private, have hot water. Singles US$16-28; doubles US$18-34; triples US$28-38; quads US$40-48. Prices decrease in low season. AmEx/MC/V. ❷

Jacaranda Cabinas (☎750 0069), a half-block west and 2 blocks south of ATEC. Beautiful individual cabins have slanted ceilings, nice decorations, and protective, kind owner. Rooms are creative and varied, but make sure you get one with a fan *and* a mosquito net. A pleasant restaurant is attached. Singles US$10, with bath and porch US$15; doubles US$20/US$30; triples and quads US$25 and up. MC/V. ❶

Hotel Puerto Viejo, 1 block east and 1 block south of ATEC, is popular with surfers and tight-budget travelers. Dark rooms without fans are musty and graffiti-ridden, but those with fans are more merciful. Bright, immaculate communal baths. Try for a room away from the kitchen, which is open for your use. ₡1500 per person, ₡1900 with fan. ❶

Cabinas Ritz (☎750 0176). Rickety rooms, but cheap and perfectly located on the beach, next door to the police station. ₡4000 for 2 beds, ₡6000 for 4 beds. ❶

Cabinas Yoli (☎750 0090), 250m inland from the bus stop, is unexciting but clean with private bathrooms. Guests have key to outer and inner doors for added safety. Owner allows guests to use the kitchen in his house. Singles ₡2000-3000; ₡doubles 4000. ❶

Miss Iris's Camping. The adventurous may want to head toward this camping area outside of town, about 350m east of ATEC on the main road, behind restaurant Salsa Brava. Miss Iris offers simple bathrooms and an outdoor kitchen with pans, wood-burning stove, and refrigerator access. Some people stay for months, forming their own little community. Miss Iris stresses that she wants to keep Puerto Viejo affordable for everyone. Camping and rental camp gear available. Campers' bags should be safely stored indoors. ₡500 per night, including tent equipment, while supplies last. ❶

FOOD

Food in Puerto Viejo is often not authentically Caribbean and aims to please (and overcharge) tourists. However, the few listed below have local ownership and fabulous local cuisine.

Soda Isma, a block west of ATEC on the main road. Famous for its *rondon,* a local dish of fish in coconut sauce that must be ordered a day in advance (₡2500). More spur-of-the-moment types can feast on tasty *gallo pinto* (₡550-700), tiny sandwiches (₡500), or a *casado* (₡900-2000). Try the coconut bread (₡100). Open daily 8am-9pm. ❶

Soda Lidia, one block east and 2 blocks south of ATEC, is an open-air restaurant with a thatched roof, offering great *casados* drizzled in Caribbean sauce (chicken ¢1000). A favorite for cheaper prices, but frequented mostly by tourists. Hours vary. ❶

Miss Sam's (☎750 0101), less cheery decor than Lidia's next door. More local customers. Breakfast ¢200-800; lunch and dinner ¢600-1400. Open M-Sa 7am-9:30pm. ❷

The Garden, attached to Jacaranda Cabinas, is a step above what you might expect to find in this tiny village. Owner and chef Vera (who also runs the *cabinas*) makes dishes with an Asian twist. Spending a few extra bucks here is worth it. Island curry chicken ¢2400; grilled red snapper ¢3200. Open only in high season (Dec.-Apr.). ❸

Momchie's, a half-block west and 1 block south of ATEC. A fantastic Caribbean bakery. Try the mango pie (¢300) or *pan bon*, a traditional Caribbean cake (¢300). Ricardo paints with as much flavor as he bakes. Check out the art gallery he's built next door. Bakery open Su-F 6:30am-noon, 3-6pm. ❶

Super Buen Precio (☎750 0060), the grocery store opposite the bus stop, faces the beach. Accepts payment in dollars and gives colones in change for a decent rate. Open M-Th 6:30am-8pm, F-Su 8:30am-8:30pm. AmEx/MC/V.

👁 SIGHTS

FINCA LA ISLA'S BOTANICAL GARDEN. Finca La Isla's Botanical Garden, a 20min. walk west of town (there are numerous signs), is an abandoned cacao plantation that has been transformed into a working tropical farm. Tours are comprehensive and focus on education regarding the varieties of spices (including chocolate, black pepper, and cinnamon), herbs, and medicines that are produced on the farm. Organic permaculture is stressed. Tours last 2½hr. and end with a demonstration table with juice and fruit samples. Labels are helpful for those opting to skip the tour. Look out for the infamous poison dart frogs underfoot. (☎750 0046; jardbot@racsa.co.cr; www.greencost.com\garden.html. Open F-M 10am-4pm. Admission US$3; 2½hr. guided tour including entrance US$8.)

RESERVA INDÍGENA COCLES/KEKOLDI. The majority of Costa Rica's indigenous population (less than 1% of the total population) resides on reservations throughout this region. The most accessible to outsiders is the Reserva Indígena Cocles/Kekoldi, 4km west of Puerto Viejo. Established in 1977, it is home to approximately 40 Bribrí and Cabécar families. To tour the reservation, you must have an authorized guide, available through ATEC, Puerto Viejo Tours, and Terraventuras (one-day trips US$25-45). The ATEC guides, Gloria Mayorga and Lucas Chávez, are members of the reservation. Tours include a hike on ancient trails through old cacao plantations, secondary forests, and farms. Many stop for lunch at an impressive waterfall in the center of the reservation. Tours concentrate more on nature than culture to create a relationship of privacy and respect between the community and the tourist. For this reason, most tours begin at Luca's house for a meeting with the family and short sensitivity introduction. Tours are conducted in Spanish. English speakers can pick up a copy of "Taking Care of Sibu's Gifts," which tells many of the same stories that the guides will share. Located at the entrance to the reservation is the **Iguana Farm,** two Bribrí women's project to bolster the reservation's declining iguana population. A guide is not necessary to visit the farm, which is actually a series of cages and pens housing thousands of the reptiles. (To get there, take the bus headed for Bribrí and ask the driver to let you off at the Iguana Farm (15min., ¢100). To get back, catch the 12:45pm bus coming from Bribrí. If you miss the bus, your best bet is to walk the 4km back to Puerto Viejo, though some travelers report hitching is possible. Let's Go does not recommend hitchhiking. Farm admission ¢400.)

⚠🏄 OUTDOOR ACTIVITIES AND GUIDED TOURS

SURFING

Most surfers head straight over to **La Salsa Brava,** an extraordinary surf-hole east of the village, where waves break over a coral reef. However, if you're less experienced with a board, and getting drilled into the coral doesn't sound "far-out," a 15min. walk east along the beach is **Beach Break,** where comparable waves break on soft sand. Hotel Puerto Viejo (see **Accommodations,** above) rents surfboards and boogie boards (¢3000 per day with ¢5000 deposit). **Peter's Place,** next to Ferretería Ivon and Soda Palmer, rents snorkeling equipment, bikes, and boogie boards. (US$5. Open 7:15am-6pm.)

TOUR OPERATORS

Terraventuras (☎ 750 0426), a half-block west of ATEC and 2 blocks north, rents snorkeling gear (US$5 per day) and offers tours, including horseback riding (US$10 per hr.), snorkeling in Parque Nacional Cahuita (US$35), a hiking tour of Gandoca-Manzanillo Wildlife Refuge (US$40), and a tour of the Kekoldi and Talamanca Bribrí Indian reserves (US$40), as well as trips to Tortuguero (US$81), Bocas del Toro (US$205), and Panama. All tours include transportation and fruit. Bike rental US$5 per day. Open daily 8am-1pm and 3:30-6:30pm; closed W during wet season months might be helpful. AmEx/MC/V.

Reef Runner Divers (☎ 750 0480), a half-block west of ATEC and 2 blocks north, specializes in scuba diving and offers all types of PADI certification courses and runs diving excursions. Open water certification US$275. Excursions 3hr. US$75. All dives include full equipment, guide, boat, fruits, and beverages. Open daily 8am-6 or 7pm. AmEx/MC/V (8% charge).

Puerto Viejo Tours (☎ 750 0411; fax 755 0082), across from the bus stop, offers informal tours similar to Terraventura plus surfing lessons and gear rental. Surf boards US$10 per day. Scooters US$7.49 per hr., US$30 per day. All rentals include helmet.

Costa Rica Caribbean Adventure (☎ 750 0576; getwet@cs.com; www.costarica-adventures.com). One of the favorite adventures of tourists is a night-time kayak tour; ask for "Tiki Torch" along the Río Cocles.

ATEC (see **Practical Information,** above) offers tours similar to Terraventuras and Puerto Viejo as well as a half-day trip to Punta Uva (US$15), an Afro-Caribbean Farm tour (US$15), and a 3-4 day leatherback turtle watch (prices vary). The Moín-Tortuguero Canal boat trip is with a Tortuguero native guide (US$50).

Atlántico Adventures—Tours and Toys (☎ 750 0004), a half-block east and a half-block north of ATEC, has the same deals as the other 3, and rents bikes (¢3000 per day), boogie boards, and snorkel gear (¢3000 per day, weekly/monthly rates available). The Oklahoma-born owner will accompany you on the public bus for cheaper tour prices.

🎵 NIGHTLIFE

True to its reputation, Puerto Viejo is a party town, and locals and tourists pack the hot spots night after night from 10:30pm until the early morning. Every Monday and Friday, the bar/dance club ▪**Bambú,** 300m east of ATEC on the main road on the beach, explodes in a crazed orgy of dancing, drinking, and smoking until 2am. For a less intense experience, make a cameo at cocktail hour from 4-7pm or eat anytime from 8am-7pm (Caribbean *casado* ¢900-1500). From Bambú, groove at ▪**Discoteca Stanford** next door (2 beers ¢600). On Mondays and Fridays the two open-air floors of dancing pour out onto the beach. **Johnny's Place,** a half-block west of ATEC and two blocks north along the beach, is the place to be on Saturday nights, when it becomes a pulsing disco blasting rock, *salsa*, reggae, and techno.

SOUTH OF PUERTO VIEJO

If Puerto Viejo seems too crowded, no need to fuss: a sublimely secluded beach with perfect waves awaits somewhere down the coast. Moving southeast, the closest beach to Puerto Viejo is **Playa Cocles,** 2km away, which many claim offers the best surfing on the Caribbean. Two kilometers south is **Playa Chiquita.** Another 8km from Puerto Viejo lie the gorgeous white-sand beaches of **Punta Uva,** and another 4km of beach lead to the town of **Gandoca.** Each town has accommodation and dining options, though none are particularly conducive to budget travel. Past Puerto Viejo, ethnicity becomes even more diverse along the costal villages. The vast majority of the proprietors are European, though the towns still maintain their distinctly Caribbean feel.

GANDOCA

Twenty years ago, this isolated town would have been completely overlooked by tourists. Now it is one of the most popular destinations of the Southern Caribbean coast for nature-conscious travelers. The village is tucked near the border with Panama; **Sixaola** offers the closest phone and **Changuinola** the closest bank. These inconveniences hardly disuade legions of volunteers (over 300 during turtle season) from spending a week to six months participating in a project to save the endangered population of leatherback turtles. Others are attracted by Gandoca's extensive coral reefs, 37 species of algae, and 34 mollusks. If midnight beach vigils and marine life aren't your thing, check out the **Refugio Nacional de Vida Silvestre Gandoca-Manzanillo,** which extends from Playa Cocles to the Panama border. The ranger station is located in Gandoca and tours are available.

TRANSPORTATION. Depending on the weather, Gandoca can be reached by two equally difficult routes. To hike the route, follow the dirt trail between **Maxi's** restaurant and the beach for a few hundred meters past a soccer field, until you reach a small lagoon. From there, cross a small stream, and you'll see the trail begin amid a forest of coconut-laden palms. Wear sturdy shoes, use insect repellent, and bring bottled water. It's a bad idea to try this hike shortly after rainfall, as it is easy to lose the trail in the undergrowth and fallen leaves. After about 10min., the trail climbs uphill and reaches an excellent lookout—a modest but defiant precipice that leans over the water.

The trail continues another 8km to **Punta Mona,** entering the beach at times, but often hugging the shade of the nearby forest. This spot is named for the persistent presence of howler monkeys. At Punta Mona there is an **organic farm** run by Steve Brooks. Most people end their walk here, but it's possible to continue another 8km to the **Gandoca ranger station** or another 2km to the **Sixaola.** You'll probably want a guide for this hike.

From Punta Mona, continuing along the beach for 3km, you will pass the dolphin observation area and finally reach the turtle-breeding haven of **Gandoca.** Taking a right off the beach at the first sign of civilization will land you in the heart of the town of Gandoca. Five hundred meters inland along this road is the ranger station. This trail, however, is nearly impossible after heavy rainfall. The trail gets lost and the uphill climbs become complicated by deep puddles and heavy mud. Also, the wet sand can be as difficult to trudge through as mud. The other option is to take a bus heading to or coming from Sixaola, and ask to be dropped at the entrance to Gandoca or "Finca 96" (12km from the border along the highway). From Finca 96, it is a 10km walk to the beach along a small unpaved road within banana plantations. Hitchhiking is occasionally possible, though cars infrequently enter this road. *Let's Go* does not recommend hitchhiking. Taxis can also be hired in Sixaola, but charge between US$25-30.

◼️🔼 ORIENTATION AND PRACTICAL INFORMATION. Gandoca is along a single road running from the beach to the ranger station, continuing inland to Finca 96. To either side of the road are wetlands and the forest. There are no trails extending from Gandoca, but locals know how to navigate the nearby area. There is a single **police officer** in the town, usually posted from the ranger station. Next door to the police station is **Centro de Salud**, visited by a doctor every eight days. **Cabinas Restaurante Las Orquideas** offers laundry service (¢100 per item). There are two unlabeled *pulperías* in town; ask around to get one opened for you.

🔼🔽 ACCOMMODATIONS AND FOOD. Volunteers are assigned random accommodations with a local family. (US$14 for a room, access to bathroom, and 3 meals.) For tourists, the only option is **Cabinas Restaurante Las Orquideas ❶**, labeled by a wooden sign 100m from the shore. Rooms are slightly musty, but the beautifully carved wooden beds and doors and sparkling private baths give it a nice feel. (Breakfast ¢700, lunch ¢1000, dinner ¢1500. US$28 per person includes 3 meals.) The **ranger station** has beds and cooking facilities, but permission to stay must be obtained in advance from the MINAE office in Cahuita or Limón. **Camping** for volunteers is available behind the ANAI station (US$7). Camping facilities have access to shower and comfortable locations. Camping on the beach is strictly forbidden. For non-volunteer camping options, speak to the rangers.

🔽 ACTIVITIES. You can visit Gandoca as a **volunteer** for the ANAI sea turtle project, but the responsibilities are demanding. (See **Alternatives to Tourism**, p. 84.) Volunteers usually serve alone in 6hr. shifts, guarding the eggs from poachers, who can earn up to US$5 per egg on the black market. Patrols over the three sectors last between 8am and midnight and midnight to 4am. Patrols tag the turtles, install microchips, take tissue samples, and measure females who emerge from the sea to lay eggs. Patrols also relocate the eggs to the hatchery and camouflage the nest. ANAI provides a manual, as well as an Investigative Assistant (usually a local student) with each group in order to teach volunteers the correct techniques for the delicate work. Because of night work done on the beach, entrance after 6pm is forbidden for all except volunteers and those accompanied by a ranger. Though swimming and resting on the beach is allowed during the day, officials ask that the area be treated with the utmost respect. Littering is deadly for the turtles.

Other ways to get to know the area include hiring a local guide to explore **trails** in the Refugio. Monkeys are everywhere (spider, howler, and white-throated capuchin monkeys) and crocodiles lurk in the nearby lagoon, which can be explored by canoe. It is also the location of the last surviving red mangrove trees in Costa Rica. This lagoon begins 200m from the ranger station and spills into the ocean and is often frequented by manatees looking for food. For all these activities, guides, boats, and directions can be obtained through MINAE rangers.

To volunteer, show up at the ANAI headquarters, labeled "Private Property" 150m down a small trail off the main entrance to Gandoca. Registration is US$25. One weeks' accommodations and food fees (US$98) up front are also required. There is no cap on volunteers and no requirements except enthusiasm and commitment to the project. To arrange in advance, contact Didher Chacón, the marine biologist coordinating such conservation efforts in the WIDECAST Foundation. (Wider Caribbean Sea Turtle Conservation Network; snail mail Apdo. 170-2070, Sabanilla, San José, CR. ☎224 3570; fax 253 7524; tortugas@sol.racsa.co.cr.)

◢ PUNTA UVA

Buses from **Puerto Viejo** *head for* **Manzanillo** *via Punta Uva (7:20am, 4, 7:30pm; return 5:15, 8:45am, 5:15pm). Other options for getting to Punta Uva are* **walking** *(about 2hr.),* **taxi** *(₡3000-3500), or renting a* **bike** *or* **horse** *in Puerto Viejo. Hitchhiking is also possible and fairly easy, although one should always consider the risk.*

The water is perfect for swimming, and the small waves that break close to shore are ideal for body surfing. Palm and mango trees line the beach only 50m from the water's edge. Look to the east to see the actual "grape point" for which Punta Uva is named—a small peninsula juts offshore, with a natural tunnel that acts as a window to the ocean. From the main road there are three entrances to the beach: one at the sign for Selvin's, one a 7min. walk later at Restaurant Punta Uva, and the third 3min. after that at the sign for Restaurant La Arrecife.

Most people visiting quiet Punta Uva stay in **Selvin's Cabinas ❶** (look for the sign off the road, on the western end of Punta Uva). At friendly Selvin's, doubles are basic and well-maintained. Clean, large mosquito nets are draped on every bed. The 100m path to the beach is just a few steps away from the cabins and there is a great restaurant on the premises. (*Casados* ₡1300-2000. Restaurant open F-Su low season; W-Su high season. Singles ₡2500; doubles ₡3500; for private bath and fan add ₡500. More luxurious apartments with kitchenettes and 2 double beds ₡7000.) **Cabinas Punta Uva ❸** has the advantage of being located exactly on the beach, 100m past Selvin's on the left (follow the signs). Each beautifully decorated double has an outdoor kitchenette and access to a communal kitchen. (☎ 750 0431. US$35 per room, with bath US$40. Traveler's checks.) Another option is **Cabinas Casa Ángelas ❶**, on the main road 10min. past Selvin's. Turn left at the sign for La Arrecife, and follow the road for 600m. The modern cabins have Aztec statues and hammocks in a lush garden. Rooms come with private hot-water baths and fully equipped kitchens, but are a bit expensive unless you come with a group. (☎ 750 0291. Triples without kitchen US$20; 4 or 5 people US$40-50.)

There isn't a wide array of dining opportunities in Punta Uva. **La Arrecife Marisquería ❷**, an open-air bar/restaurant on the beach (you'll see a sign pointing the way 10min. past Selvin's on the main road), specializes in seafood. Tasty mounds of rice with shrimp or octopus (₡1800) are accompanied by crispy fries. (☎ 759 0700. Open daily 7:30am-9pm.) Another pleasant place to sit and enjoy the sea breeze is **Ranchito Beach Restaurant ❶**, a bar on the beach about 7min. past Selvin's. This resort also rents out **kayaks** (₡1500 per hr.), provides guided **snorkeling** (US$25 for 8hr.), and can arrange beach and jungle tours. (Open daily 11am-5pm.) Several hundred meters before Selvin's, you will encounter a sign for a **Butterfly Garden.** Follow the signs uphill and bearing to the left. This garden distinguishes itself from the others in the area as a center for butterfly reproduction. The owner provides a tour that points out eggs, cocoons, and the plants that caterpillars eat. The garden has up to 80 butterfly species, depending on the season. Many come here for meditation. (Open daily 8am-3pm. US$5, children free.)

◤ MANZANILLO

Buses run daily from Puerto Viejo to **Manzanillo** *(7:20am, 3:30, 4, 7:30pm; returns 5am, 8:30pm), passing through Punta Uva and the other beaches. You can also take a* **taxi** *(₡4500), rent a* **bike** *or* **horse** *(see* **Orientation and Practical Information,** *p. 373), or* **walk** *(3hr.) from Puerto Viejo. The walk along the beach, though lengthy, is gorgeous and peaceful. A bright green* **MINAE office** *is located on the bend of the road in Manzanillo, facing the beach. (☎ 759 0600, fax 759 0601. Open M-F 8am-4pm.) The rangers can provide details on the park and the preservation efforts inside the refuge (including dolphin* *and turtle projects often looking for **volunteers**). A map and history of the refuge are available with donation. The rangers are not as active with tourists because of the well-organized coalition of local guides (see below). Rangers offer beds and baths for students looking to volunteer in the Refugio.*

Bordered by a spectacular beach, the seaside village of Manzanillo is 6km southeast of Punta Uva. The original *manzanillo* tree for which the town is named fell into the sea in 1957, and the species has not been spotted since. Maybe it's for the best though, since the tree was known to be poisonous. Carelessly falling asleep beside the toxic bark meant an eternal rest for the hapless napper.

The main reason to come to Manzanillo is to visit the breathtaking **Refugio Nacional Gandoca-Manzanillo.** This dense jungle path stretches from the village through the Refuge all the way to Panama. Founded in 1985 to protect endangered flora and fauna, the refuge includes 5013 hectares of private and public land, 65% of which is tropical rainforest, and 4436 hectares of ocean. The wetlands teem with crocodiles, alligators, sloths, pumas, and monkeys, while the coastal areas accent the refuge with five types of coral reefs, sandy beaches, and fossil-lined coral caves. A red mangrove tree swamp, unique to the Costa Rican Caribbean, sits beside the **Gandoca Lagoon** protecting the only natural population of mangrove oysters on the coast and the home of the nearly extinct manatee. The waters off rocky **Punta Mona** are frequented by tucuxi, bottlenose, and Atlantic spotted dolphins. This uniquely isolated marine and coastal ecosystem richly rewards visitors willing to get a little muddy, bug-bitten, and wet. One of the only drawbacks of the Refugio is that trails are not well-marked and heavy rains year-round make them very poorly maintained. A guide is almost always necessary.

The **police station** is behind Maxi's (see below). Make **phone calls** from the phones in front of Maxi's. **La Caribeña Lavandera** is 50m behind La Selva Restaurant in a residential house labeled "Local Guide" (☎759 0643; see below). The cheapest place to stay in town is **Cabinas Maxi ❶** (☎759 0661), behind Restaurante Maxi at the end of the town road. It has basic, clean digs with rugged private bathrooms, no mosquito netting, and mattresses doing their best bed impersonations, as well as large windows that open right onto the beach. (¢5000 per room with single and double bed; ¢4000 for solo traveler.) Another option is the colorful **Pangea Bed and Breakfast ❷;** look 100m down from Aquamor for a sign pointing inland on a sidestreet between the MINAE office and Maxi's. A vibrant garden leads to two artfully decorated double rooms with ceiling fans, beautiful wood floors and walls, hot-water baths, and brightly woven comforters. (☎759 0604; pangqecr@racsa.co.cr. US$25 per room includes breakfast. AmEx/MC/V.) Next to Pangea Bed and Breakfast, the recently opened **Cabinas Something Different ❸** does as its name suggests, offering modern, airy, luxurious cabins with cable TV, fridge, and private bath with hot water. Each cabin sleeps up to four people on two double beds (☎759 0614. US$25 for one person, $5 for each additional person). In the Refugio itself, it's possible to camp in certain areas designated by rangers. Camping areas vary by season and other factors, so be sure to speak to a ranger before heading in with a tent. You can also camp in **Steve Brooks' organic farm** in Punta Mona. (☎391 2116. US$5 per person; volunteer and he'll waive the fee.)

🍴**Restaurant Maxi ❸,** in front of Cabinas Maxi in town, serves delicious, fresh seafood from a lovely upstairs porch (catch of the day ¢2300-2700, veggie dish ¢1000) and is the center of the town's social life with a full page mixed drink menu. Maxi's lobster is famous throughout the region. (Lobster ¢3900. Open daily noon-10pm.) Down the road as you enter Manzanillo is **Restaurant La Selva ❷,** which has a large open-air patio set among a humid, green jungle garden. Keep an eye out for the owner's pet toucan and the howler monkeys that are frequently seen in the trees across the street. (☎759 0633. Seafood dishes ¢1800-3000; lobster $5000-7000.

Open daily noon-9pm.) The cheapest food in town is 50m down the street from Aquamor at **Soda Rinconato Alegre ❷,** where generous portions of pancakes and fruit (¢500) and sizable menus (¢1200-2000) attract tourists and locals. (☎759 0640. Open daily 7am-7pm.) **Abastecedor Más X Menos** is located on the main road 50m past **Restaurant La Selva.** (☎759 0621. Open daily 7am-noon and 2pm-7pm.)

S GUIDED TOURS. Guides from other Caribbean towns are often denied access, as MINAE requests that tourists only employ local guides. Local guides can be found in the office across the street from **Abastecedor Más X Menos.** Almost all guides are native to the region and have recently founded the establishment Guis MANT (☎759 0643), a coalition uniting their profession and their devotion to conserve land in Manzanillo. A portion of their earnings goes to support local farmers to minimize their need for agricultural expansion (and forest destruction). The extremely friendly and personable Abel Bustamante, president of the organization, is willing to answer questions on this new project. The guides give various tours, including trips to the refuge, turtle watching, night walks, horseback rides, snorkeling, fishing, and just about any other adventure a traveler might want to tackle in Manzanillo. Most tours go for US$15-20 per person. To get in touch with Abel after hours, go to the house that offers laundry service.

The 9km beach off Gandoca is the site of **marine turtle** nesting grounds. Four species colonize here: leatherback, green, hawksbill, and loggerhead. Only visitors with a guide are permitted to enter the beach and observe the turtles during nesting season (Mar. 1-Oct. 31). For more information contact **ANAI** (National Association of Indigenous Affairs; ☎750 0020; anaital@sol.racsa.co.cr).

◪ WATERSPORTS. If you want to explore the park from the water, check with the watersports shop **Aquamor,** the last right off the main road before Maxis in Manzanillo. They rent kayaks and snorkeling gear and offer diving trips and dolphin observation excursions. (☎359 0612; aquamorl@racsa.co.cr. Kayaks US$6 per hr., US$15 per hr. with guide. Snorkel gear US$3 per hr., US$15 per hr. with guide. Beach dives US$30. Kayak dives US$37. Dolphin tours US$30. Open daily 7am-6pm.) Aquamor also serves as a coral reef educational center, and is one of the founders of the Talamanca Dolphin Foundation, an organization that researches and protects the region's dolphins and their ecosystem. Get in touch with Aquamor for information on how to volunteer for the TDF or contact them directly (☎586 9942; fax 586 0995; info@dolphinlink.org).

SIXAOLA

This small, dusty border town serves as little more than a stop to or from Panama (see below). Buses from Sixaola head back to **San José** (6hr.; 5, 7:30, 9:30am, 2:30pm; ¢2815) and **Limón** (3hr., 8 per day 5am-5pm, ¢930). The 3pm bus enters **Puerto Viejo de Talamanca** (2hr., ¢500), while the others will drop you at the intersection 5km from the town. Frequent buses cover the remaining distance (15min., ¢200). Passengers leaving Sixaola must show their papers, so don't tuck your passport away.

There are a limited number of services in town. Right after the bridge on the main road is **Mercado California,** which sells the Red Cross stamps and changes US dollars to colones at a bad rate. (☎754 2030. Open 8am-9pm.) Next door is a **Western Union.** The nearest **bank** is in the town of Bribrí (see p. 371). Costa Rican police sit right opposite the Migración office. (☎754 2160.) **Phones** are right before the bridge on the left-hand side of the tracks. If you have to stay in Sixaola overnight, walk 400m down from the bridge on the left-hand side of the tracks and bear right until the end of the road to **Hotel Doris ❶.** The musty rooms have collective baths. (*Soda* downstairs 8am-11pm; breakfast ¢600. Singles ¢2000; doubles ¢2500.)

⚔ BORDER WITH PANAMA

The Panamanian side of the border in Guabito (see below) is open daily from 8am to 6pm. The Costa Rican side, in Sixaola (see above), is open daily from 7am to 5pm; the time zone difference assures the two coincide. Both close for lunch (noon-12:30pm). To leave Costa Rica you will need to buy a Red Cross exit stamp (¢200) and show an onward ticket. A tourist card is also needed (US$5). Officials reserve the right to ask for proof of economic independence. (☎ 754 2044.) For all practical purposes Panama uses US dollars, which makes handling money very convenient.

BOCAS DEL TORO, PANAMA

The Bocas del Toro archipelago is made up of six large islands and many smaller ones. Sometimes called "Bocas Isla," charming Isla Colón is the main base for people visiting the archipelago. Besides the town of Bocas itself, Isla Colón has a few other tiny settlements (notably Boca del Drago on the opposite side) and plenty of natural attractions. For visitors, the islands' diving, hiking, beaches, and lifestyle are the main attractions. Getting to Bocas from Costa Rica is straightforward. After crossing the border, continue to Almirante via Guabito and Changuinola, then take a water taxi to the islands.

GUABITO

For those entering Panama, the first, hopefully brief, stop will be Guabito. Frequent **buses** run from Gaubito to Changuinola (15min., US$0.70) until about 7pm. Collective **taxis** cost US$1 and leave from in front of Kiosco Dalys, on the left side of the crossing entering from Costa Rica.

Comercial Tucán, on the left side of the border crossing, changes money, but often runs out of colones. (☎ 759 7944. Open 9am-8pm.) A single phone sits in front of the **Aduanas** (customs), next to the migration office. The **migration offices** are across the street from national **police** posts (☎ 759 7940, emergency ☎ 104), which are connected by a decrepit bridge. Guabito has no accommodations and almost no restaurants. **Kiosco Dalys ❶**, in Guabito, serves *comida corriente* (US$2), to the right of the border crossing. (Open 5:30am-10pm.)

CHANGUINOLA

Changuinola offers very basic services and accommodations, but there is no reason why you should ever have do anything but change buses there. **Terminal La Piquera**, next to the Shell station in the center of town, handles short-distance travel. There is no office and schedules vary significantly. **Collective taxis** are parked under specific destination signs. **Buses** leave from the terminal to the **Costa Rican border at Guabito** (35min., every 45min. 7am-7:45pm, US$0.70); **El Silencio** (40min., every 15min. 6am-7pm, US$0.50); **Finca 44** (25min., every 30min. 5am-9pm, US$0.65) via **Almirante** (45min., US$1); and many other destinations in the surrounding farmland. **Taxis** to Guabito take 20min, and cost US$1.

Changuinola is strung out along the road from Guabito and the border in the northwest to Almirante in the southeast. The road to Almirante curves along a traffic circle around a large white statue. The northern end of town is full of enormous inexpensive stores, while the southern end hosts expensive hotels.

CARIBBEAN LOWLANDS

ALMIRANTE

From the terminal, **buses** leave for **Changuinola** (30min., every 30min. 6am-9pm, US$1). Two **water taxi** companies, Taxi 25 (☎757 9062) and Galapago's Tours (☎757 9073), take passengers to **Bocas del Toro** (30min.; every hr. or when boats are full 6am-6pm; US$5 each way). Alternatively, a **ferry** leaves from the opposite side of town four days a week. (1½hr; M, W, F, Sa 9am; US$1.) For the ferry, turn right at the T across the tracks and take the first left. Follow that road along the tracks and turn right just before the road crosses back over the tracks. **Taxis** charge US$1 to run from the bus station to the water taxi docks.

BOCAS DEL TORO AND ISLA COLÓN

Bocas is the essence of small-town Caribbean life, seamlessly melding a welcoming atmosphere of easy aimlessness with the energy and drive of a tightly-knit community. It's also the best place in Panama to launch for a tropical reef-and-beach vacation without the ritzy resorts. Throw your watch off the ferry and get ready for real relaxation—breathe deeply, slice open a mango, and stare at the sea and the palms. Ambitious visitors can work a few side trips into their visit, including Isla Bastimentos, Boca del Drago, and other nearby islands.

▐ TRANSPORTATION

Water Taxis: Galápagos Tours (☎757 9073), next to Bar Le Pirate in the middle of Calle 3, and **Taxi 25** (☎757 9062), next to the police station on Calle 1, have water taxis about every hr. to **Almirante** (30min., 6am-6pm, US$5 one-way). Because of the new road between Almirante and Chiriquí Grande, there are no boats from Chiriquí Grande.

Ferry: (☎758 3731), leaves from the dock at the southern end of Calle 3 for **Almirante** (W and F-Su 5pm, US$1).

Local Boats: Locals with *botes* hang out at the **public docks** south of the police station or at the **pier** next to Le Pirate Bar on Calle 3 (especially in the morning). Prices are negotiable, though the price to Old Bank on Isla Bastimentos is set (US$2).

▐▌ ORIENTATION AND PRACTICAL INFORMATION

Tiny Bocas is laid out in an L-shaped grid; numbered *calles* run north-south and lettered *avenidas* run east-west. With the docks at your back, north is to the right and south to the left. Just about everything is on **Calle 3,** the main street, or on **Calle 1,** further east. The water cuts across the grid from Calle 3 at the South end of town to Calle 1 at the East end. A small park lies between Calles 2 and 3 and Av. D and F. **Av. G,** at the northern end of town, is the only route out to the rest of the island. Billboard maps are posted around town.

Immigration: (☎757 9263), in the government building north of the *parque*. Open M-F 9am-noon and 12:30-4pm.

Tourist Information: IPAT (☎757 9871), near the police station, in a large yellow house on Calle 1, has a small exhibition about the history and ecology of Bocas and provides cheap Internet access (US$1.50 per hr., students US$0.75). Open M-F 8:30am-4:30pm. **ANAM** (☎757 9244; www.bocas.com), on Calle 1 north of the police station, with info and permits for Parque Nacional Isla Bastimentos. Open M-F 8am-4pm.

Banks: Banco Nacional, Av. F, Calles 1/2, a block north and 1½ blocks east of the park. Cashes traveler's checks. Open M-F 8am-2pm. **ATM** one block north of the *parque*, near La Ballena.

Laundry: Don Chicho's restaurant on Calle 3, across from the *parque.*

Supermarkets: Av. H and Calle 6. Open M-Sa 9am-8pm, Su noon-7pm. Scattered fruit and vegetable markets on Calle 3, just south of the *parque.*

Police: (☎ 757 9217; emergency 104), on Calle 1 by the water.

Hospital: (☎ 757 9201), on Av. H, a few blocks west of town. 24hr. emergency.

Internet Access: El Mirador (☎ 757 9834), across from the water taxis on Calle 3, has fast connections and a pleasant balcony cafe that serves breakfast and sandwiches for US$2-3. Internet US$1.50 per hr. Open M-Sa 8am-9pm, Su 8am-8pm. Also available at the **IPAT** office (see above).

Post Office: in the government building just north of the *parque.*

ACCOMMODATIONS

Bocas is strewn with tons of excellent, inexpensive hotels (US$5-10), but they fill up in high season (make reservations in advance). There are also a number of relatively high-end places that offer breezy, polished luxury for very reasonable prices. Another option is to find a house or small family establishment that rents rooms, either on Calle 3 or around the northern corner along Av.'s G and H.

▧ **Casa Max** (☎ 757 9120), on Av. G 50m west of Calle 3, has perfected the higher end of the classic backpacker hostel. Live the sweet life in the multi-colored hammocks and dreamy rooms of this "old Caribbean house put in a new coat." Book exchange and common stereo. Private baths. Singles US$18; doubles US$20. ❸

▧ **Modo Taitú,** (☎ 757 9425), across from Casa Max on Av. G. If Casa Max perfects the fancy side of backpacker lodging, friendly and communal Modo Taitú does the same for the budget set. Dorm US$5 per person; private doubles US$7 per person. ❶

Hotel Swan's Cay (☎ 757 9090), on Calle 3, a block north of the *parque,* has a selection of carpeted, wood-paneled rooms with cable TV, phone, and A/C, built around a flower-filled courtyard. The hotel runs tours to the nearby beaches (US$5-10), and fishing excursions (US$115). Snorkel equipment free for all guests. Singles US$40.50; doubles US$60.70; triples US$80.90. AmEx/MC/V. ❹

Hostal Familiar La Concha, on Calle 3 across from the *parque.* Five rooms with communal or private bath, A/C, TV, and kitchen access. Common space upstairs doubles as a pleasant 4-bed dorm room (US$5 per person). Bring ear plugs if you plan to stay in the dorm beds. Singles US$5.50-15; doubles US$11-28.50; triples US$22. ❶

FOOD AND NIGHTLIFE

Restaurants, almost all on Calle 3 or just off of it, range from *típico* to classy Italian. *Bocatareño* food means lots of seafood with spicy coconut-lime juice flavoring. Bocas doesn't have clean tap-water, but some places have a filter on their tap. To paraphrase the advice of the Peace Corps: peel it, wash it, cook it, or vom-it.

▧ **The Reef,** at the far southern end of Calle 3, is one of the few places left in Bocas Town to get tasty *bocatareño* food. Excellent meals of seafood accompanied by rice, potatoes or *patacones* can be had for US$5-7. After 8pm or so, the restaurant shifts into bar mode. Open daily 9am-midnight. ❷

La Ballena (☎ 989 9089), on Av. F, just off Calle 3. Authentic Italian food known as the best on the island. La Ballena imports the food, the cooks, and the owners directly from Italy. Dinners, from butterfly pastas to lobster *risotto* are US$10-15. Reservations necessary during high season. Open daily 8-11:30am, 12-2:30pm, and 7-10pm. ❹

Buena Vista Deli & Bar (takeout ☎757 9035), next to Starfleet on Calle 2. A foreigner favorite, with great sandwiches (US$4.50-5), veggie treats, clean water and ice, DirecTV athletics, mellow music, and mean margaritas (US$3.50). Open W-M noon-10pm. ❷

Don Chicho's, on Calle 3 across from the *parque*. This mini-empire (laundry, Internet, and cafeteria) is a popular local hangout with the cheapest meals around. *Comida* US$2. Big breakfasts US$1-3. Open daily 6:30am-midnight. ❶

The bar scene, like everything in Bocas town, swells hugely in the winter months (especially around Christmas). But even the rainy summer nights bring an amiable mix of locals, tourists, and ex-pats out to the dock-side *cabañas* and comfortable pool halls. Things generally pick up (if they pick up at all) around 9 or 10pm, and run until 1 or 2am. Sunday nights are often quiet. **Loop,** across from the park, has pool tables and a cool indoor/outdoor bar. Farther down Calle 3, across from Hospedaje EYL, is **Bar El Encanto,** a local favorite which cranks thunderous dance hall and *cumbia*. On Calle 1, near Taxi 25, is **Barco Hundido** (aka Wreck Bar), a great place to dry off after snorkeling. If you're in luck you might catch the **Beach Boys de Bastimentos,** the local calypso band known to have jammed for 15hr. straight.

⚐ ⚠ WATERSPORTS AND OUTDOOR ACTIVITIES

In a local economy almost entirely dependent on tourism, nearly every hotel, restaurant, dock, shack, and patch of grass offers some form of tour or rental. The listings here provide an overview of what's available and a few unique or particularly dependable businesses.

For **diving,** the best rental/tour operator is PADI-certified **Starfleet Eco-Adventures** (☎/fax 757 9630), on Calle 1 where it curves east at the southern end of town. A 2-tank dive costs US$45, including boat and all equipment. A PADI open water certification course is also offered (3-4 days about US$195, half/full-day crash course US$65-95). Dive also vary depending on the time of year, time of day, and weather—though operators can try to arrange your choice. The **Playground** is an open-water dive just 5min. from Bocas town with tons of standard reef fish (angels, damsels, butterflyfish, hamlets, and triggerfish) as well as the occasional giant moray eel. **Big Bank** is for advanced divers, with coral formations as deep as 40m that eagle rays, jewfish, and standard reef fish call home. **Hospital Point,** on Cayo Nancy, is a shallow wall dive offering scorpionfish, toadfish, octopi and Giant Brain coral. **Dolphin Rock,** another open-water dive, has some of the largest, brightest schools of fish around, including parrotfish and barracuda. Also ask about **Bahía Bocatorito,** south of Isla Cristóbal, directly south of Bocas town, to see **bottle-nose dolphins** year-round.

For **snorkeling,** most dive shops rent gear (US$5-8 per day) and offer tours (US$15-20, equipment included). At **Bocas' Best Tour** (☎620 5130), Christian, a knowledgeable guide, captains one of the area's better boats. Local boat owners who hang out by the Le Pirate Bar docks on Calle 3, are often cheaper than tour companies—try to bargain a little.

Another popular activity is renting recreational equipment. Always check rentals, especially bikes, for quality. Rent **bikes** at: Galápagos Tours (US$2.50 per hr., US$10 per day); Hotel Laguna, on Calle 3 by the park (☎757 9091; US$2 per hr.); and **Spanish by the Sea Language School,** behind the Hotel Bahía at the southern end of Calle 4 (US$4 per half-day, US$6 per day); or the stand near Modo Taitú on Av. G. Rent **kayaks** at **Galápagos Tours** and **Bocas Water Sports** (US$5 and US$10 per half-day, respectively). Spanish by the Sea also rents **canoes** (US$10 per day, US$7.50 per half-day). A few beat-up **motorcycles,** dirt bikes, and surf boards can be rented on a patch of grass next to the handicrafts stands across from the *parque* on Calle 3 (motorcycles US$8 per hr., surfboards US$2 per hr.).

🎯 SIGHTS AROUND THE ISLAND

From Bocas Town, Av. H leads west across a small isthmus to the main body of the island. From here, the road forks; the left side leads 15km through the middle of the island past La Gruta to Boca del Drago, and the right fork follows the eastern coast, passing Big Creek, Punta Puss Head, Playa Paunch, and Playa Bluff along the way. Many of these beaches are infested with *chitras* (tiny sandflies with an irritating bite), especially in the late afternoon. Walking and biking are the cheapest transportation options around the island, but roads are alternately bumpy and muddy—bring sturdy shoes or a well-maintained bike, especially after rain.

EASTERN BEACHES. The best of these beaches is relatively *chitra*-free **Playa Bluff.** The sand beach stretches almost 2km, with good surfing and casual swimming on more mellow days. Between March and September (especially June-July) the beach attracts **sea turtles** laying their eggs. To arrange a trip to see nesting turtles on the island's eastern coast, go to the CARIBARO office, 2 blocks north of the park on Calle 3, across from the church in an unmarked green-and-yellow building. *(Trips depart 8pm or midnight; stop by earlier in the day. Office is sporadically closed off-season (June-Aug.). Playa Bluff is on the eastern shore about 8km north of Bocas town; biking takes about 45min.)*

LA GRUTA CAVE. A small cave with plenty of bats and bat guano, **La Gruta** is considered a religious shrine and is the site of a annual pilgrimage celebrating *Nuestra Señora de la Gruta*, the Virgen del Carmen. A torchlight parade down Calle 3 takes place every July 16th in celebration of the Virgin; the pilgrimage to her cave happens the following Sunday. *(La Colonia Santeña, where a trail leads to the cave, is about a 45min. bike ride from town. Bring a flashlight and good boots.)*

BOCA DEL DRAGO. On the western side of the island, 8km past La Gruta on a hilly road, sits the little town of Boca del Drago. Here you'll find beautiful beaches and a coral reef walkable at low tide. The town has lodging and food, but no services in town. Look left near the end of the road for **Cabañas Estefany ❷**, where most cabins have their own kitchen, bath, and mosquito nets. From May 15 to August 15, they are generally rented out to a school program, but you may be able to scrounge an extra room or camp on the property. (☎ 626 7245. Ask for Chino Fátima. 5-person *cabaña* US$30.25; 6-person US$38.50; 8-person US$60.50. Reservations recommended.) Next door is the gringo-tour favorite **Restaurante Yarisnari ❷**, which also rents snorkel gear and a paddle boat. (Lentils and rice US$3.50; seafood US$7-10. Open daily 7:30-9:30am and noon-7:30pm.)

About 15min. by *bote* from Boca del Drago sits **Isla de Pájaros**, or **Swan Caye**, where hundreds of seabirds circle a huge rock and a few hardy trees. There's a coral reef with excellent deep-water snorkeling right off Isla de Pájaros, although the water isn't always that clear, particularly after rain. Tour operators in Bocas all offer trips here. Just past Swan Cay are two smaller rocky islands: **Wreck Rock,** which looks like the wreck of a ship, and **Sail Rock,** a phallic rock sticking straight out of the water. *(A taxi between Boca del Drago and Bocas del Toro runs round-trip US$25. There's also a bus that leaves Drago at 7:30am, waits in front of the mercado in Bocas, and returns to Drago at about 2pm (US$3 each way). If there are a few people who want to go, you might be able to convince the driver to make another run. Otherwise, hire a bote for the day—a trip to Boca del Drago and Isla de Pájaros costs US$25.)*

ISLA BASTIMENTOS

For a little less of the touristy, gringoesque flavor of Bocas, and more Caribbean authenticity, head to Bastimentos, only 10min. from Bocas. Here you'll find the small village of **Old Bank** (where most boats arrive), oodles of beautiful, deserted beaches, an indigenous Ngöbe village, and **Parque Nacional Marino Isla Bastimentos,** the region's largest and most important protected natural area. In fair weather, Bastimentos hosts a party on Monday nights—ask in Bocas town for the latest.

OLD BANK

The village of Old Bank (also known as **Bastimentos**) has no roads, only a semi-paved 1km footpath running along the water. With your back to the water, east is to your right and west to your left. The little park is toward the western end, as are most of the docks, where you can catch a *bote* to Bocas del Toro.

Getting to Isla Bastimentos from **Bocas del Toro** is easy. Regular boats leave Bocas del Toro from the pier next to Le Pirate Bar and head to Old Bank (more frequent in the morning, 6am-6pm; US$2). To reach **Cayos Zapatillas** or the other side of the island or your best bet is one of the tour operators. An equally dependable option is to ask around near the docks for a boat—independent operators are everywhere. Agree on a fare beforehand.

All the accommodations in town are fairly budget, though facilities vary widely. **Pensión "Tío Tom" Bastimentos ❷,** near the park in a green building with a red roof, has pleasant wooden rooms on stilts over the water. (☎/fax 757 9831. www.puntacaracol.com. Singles US$10; doubles US$10, in high season US$12, with private bath US$20; each additional person US$7.) **Pelícano Cabinas ❷,** at the far eastern end of the path, has the nicest rooms in town. (☎757 9830. Singles US$10; doubles US$16; triple with bunk beds US$18.) Between Tío Tom and Pelícano is **Hospedaje Sylvia ❷,** with fanned rooms, shared baths, and a basic restaurant run by a local family. (☎757 9442. US$10 per room.)

🏖 **BEACHES.** The island's beautiful beaches lie in a string on the northern and eastern coasts, connected by trails. To get to **Playa Primera,** take the path (marked with a sign for "1st Beach") that branches inland near the eastern end of Old Bank's main cement path and proceed for 20min.; after rain, it might be worth taking a boat to avoid the 1½hr. walk through mud (US$2). Beware: extremely strong currents make swimming dangerous. The next beach to the east is **Playa Segunda,** also known as Red Frog Beach for the little red frogs found only here (harder to spot on sunny days). This is a favorite tour destination from Bocas and a good surfing spot during the dry season. Two beaches farther is **Playa Cuarto,** one of the best beaches in the entire archipelago. Also known as Ola Chica or Don Polo, the eastern end of the beach is sheltered by **Wild Cane Key,** a small offshore island.

At the opposite end of the island from the town of Old Bank lies **Punta Vieja,** a secluded beach that offers astonishingly clear water and awesome snorkeling. Not only do many turtles nest here during the night, but there is an awesome reef right out front and the Ngöbe village of **Salt Creek** is nearby. Many of the tour operators in Bocas run tours to both the reef and Salt Creek (US$15-25).

🏞 **PARQUE NACIONAL MARINO ISLA BASTIMENTOS.** After a 3hr. hike along the beach and trails from Old Bank, you'll reach the spectacular 14km **Playa Larga,** an important **turtle nesting** site. The beach holds a ranger station and an entrance to **Parque Nacional Marino Isla,** which protects Playa Larga, the interior of Isla Bastimentos, the extensive mangrove swamps on the island's western side, and the two **Cayos Zapatillas** farther out in the ocean to the southeast. The inland forest on Isla Bastimentos is home to fantastic wildlife, and the southern of the two Cayos

Zapatillas has a forest trail that leads to golden beaches and underwater cave formations. The crowded ranger stations on the island and on the southern Cayo Zapatillas both have simple **refugios** and allow **camping.** There are no facilities; bring everything you need, including mosquito nets (or heavy-duty repellent) and something to purify water. Before heading to the park, you have to get permission from ANAM in Bocas and pay an entrance fee. They can ensure that rangers will be there. Park rangers guide for no fee, although a tip is expected. Talk to the Ancon office at the Bocas Inn (see **Watersports and Guided Tours,** above) for info on turtle-watching. (Camping US$5 per person. Park admission US$10.)

OTHER ISLANDS

ISLA CARENERO
Isla Carenero is just a few hundred meters east of the docks on Calle 3 in Bocas. There are three good seafood **restaurants** on the island, all along the beach (meals US$5-8; all open daily 1-9pm): **Restaurante Pargo Rojo** (☎ 757 9649), **Restaurante Ocean Queen** (☎ 757 9360), and **Doña Mara** (☎ 757 9552). All restaurants will pick you up at the public dock in Bocas if you call, and *botes* make the trip as well (US$2). To get back, ask at the restaurants or stand on the dock and wave to catch passing boats. For groups, Pargo Rojo and Doña Mara also offer good deals on *cabinas.* Pargo Rojo's are larger and cheaper (cabin for up to 5 people US$25), but Doña Mara's are newer with more facilities (quads with A/C, TV, hot water US$50). On the eastern end of Carenero is a small point with decent snorkeling and a few good breaks for surfing. New construction is at full-tilt in this part of the island, however, and it can get noisy.

CAYO NANCY
Cayo Nancy is famous for **Hospital Point,** near one of the best, most accessible snorkeling spots. You'll find a variety of corals, some barely submerged, others 100 ft. deep, and enough bright fish to keep you ooohing and aaahing all day. Any *bote* can transport you, but bring your own snorkeling gear. There are a few good places to snorkel in the protected waters between Bocas, Isla Carenero, Isla Bastimentos, and Cayo Nancy. If you go by private boat, ask the driver to wait rather than return, because these are open-water sites.

CARIBBEAN LOWLANDS

ELECTIONS IN COSTA RICA
A national celebration of peace and democracy

Election Day in Costa Rica is a time when all Costa Ricans come together to celebrate peace and democracy. On this day, a spirit of celebration and pride comes with each step of the election process. The ballot boxes, often located in small schools and staffed by representatives of each of the parties, open from 6am to 6pm on the first Sunday in February every four years. Costa Ricans, dressed in their party's colors, passionately go out onto streets already lined with houses displaying party flags. Parents will often take their children by hand and go voting as a family. The cars on the streets bear colored flags, and drivers honk their horns and cheer for their favorite candidate. Even spouses who support different candidates walk hand in hand. Their party flags and colors show their political differences, but they respect and tolerate each other's opinions. This tolerance is displayed by all *ticos*, who walk to and from the ballot boxes alongside their opponent's supporters. They may shout their support for different candidates, but they all celebrate and cheer for peace and democracy together. The following are some important facts about elections in Costa Rica.

The vote in Costa Rica is direct and obligatory. Every four years, *ticos* vote for their president (who cannot be reelected) and for representatives of the Legislative Assembly.

For the past five decades, Costa Rica has set an example of "clean" elections to many nations in the world. A big part of this success is due to the *Tribunal Supremo de Elecciones* (Supreme Electoral Tribunal), an independent body which organizes, directs, and watches over the country's elections. The Electoral Tribunal was put together by the Constitution of 1949 to free the electoral process from any interference by the State, which was originally in charge of elections and had invested interests in the process.

A Dry Law strictly prohibits the sale of liquor the day prior to, of, and following Election Day. To enforce the law, Tribunal delegates go around the country at midnight on Friday closing and sealing the doors of bars and taverns; the seals aren't removed until 3 days later.

Even though children in Costa Rica already participate in elections by helping and ushering people to the ballot boxes, the Supreme Electoral Tribunal also holds a Children's Election that parallels the official election in all senses. Children over 5 years of age also vote for the different presidential candidates in their own ballot boxes, staffed by other children involved in running the election. After all ballot boxes close, the votes are counted, and the results are announced on TV alongside the official results.

The most recent elections were held on February 3, 2002. For the first time in 50 years, Costa Rica had a second round of elections because a minority party, *Partido Acción Ciudadana*, won a large enough percentage of the popular vote to prevent either of the two main parties, *Partido Unidad Social Cristiana* and *Partido Liberación Nacional*, from receiving the required 40% of the electorate needed to win the election. Costa Rica's 29th president, Dr. Abel Pacheco from the *Partido Unidad Social Cristiana*, was elected on April 7th, 2002.

Shannon Music was born and raised in Costa Rica. Currently a psychology concentrator at Harvard University, she is planning on pursuing her career in Latin America.

JUNGLE RAVES
Raves with a tropical flavor

Raves have been a worldwide phenomenon since the 80s, but did not appear in Costa Rica until a decade later. Ever since the first raves were carried out in Sapo Verde, a humble club in Escazú, the rave scene has developed a flavor of its own. A new breed of rave, jungle raves, has emerged in Costa Rica because of the natural surroundings and much lower prices. The location and the weather complement the unique dance experience, adding a new flare to the eco-tourism industry. This type of outdoor party received worldwide exposure in singer/actress Jennifer Lopez's video for her single "Waiting for Tonight," which featured a jungle rave celebration right before the turn of the century. Costa Rica's outdoor settings offer an atmosphere of freedom unparalleled by the standard warehouses where raves are usually held.

One of the most memorable raves took place near Tamarindo, on the northern Nicoya Peninsula, this past New Year's Eve. The party featured internationally renowned DJ John Creamer, and hosted thousands of people from all over the world for over 10 hours of dancing under the stars. As Melania Gamboa, a regular raver, points out, "The spirit at these parties is always amazing. There are people from different corners of the world, all here to have fun and enjoy the music. The energy is so upbeat that you can't help but get carried away." Already, many North American and European DJs have gravitated to Costa Rica, like Anthony Pappa and Luis Diaz, New York power players Sasha and John Digweed, and British underground stars like Nick Warren.

The jungle rave industry is still in its infancy. Until recently, only one promotion company, 979 Conexión, was involved in organizing the events. They handled everything from location scouting and bringing the DJs, to setting up security for the events. The raves proved so successful, however, that other production companies are now vying for a piece of the fortune. One of the most successful raves held this year was organized by a new organization called Promotion; it attracted over 1000 people and was headlined by DJ Sean Kusick.

Many bars and clubs now cater to the local electronic music culture at beach towns and in San José. There are big venues like Planet Mall in San José and Noai in Tamarindo, as well as at small techno bars like Regina. However, the national media attention that has helped mainstream this movement has also been quick to point out the controversial drug-taking and the increase in ecstasy consumption that often occurs at outdoor raves. Even so, it is mild compared to other parties of this sort around the world. As Carmen Farach, a party insider, describes, "Organizers go to great lengths to ensure a safe party environment. Bags are checked as people are coming in, there's tight security, and a Red Cross ambulance is on call in case anything happens."

Costa Rica's raves have opened doors for many national DJs, allowing them to make a name for themselves internationally. DJ Tekes, who started at the early raves in Escazú, now DJs in Barcelona. DJ Dr. Leo plays all over Central America and attracts the biggest crowds in Costa Rica. Other Costa Rican DJs trying to make it big include DJ Patrice, who performed with DJ Karlos and Tini Tun of Mexico at a lakeside mountain rave, and DJ Diego López, who accompanied DJ Sean Kusick at the successful Promotion event.

These types of parties are definitely on the rise. In the end, the jungle raves add to the image and vibrancy of this small Central American country. Whether you enjoy hiking through the forest or dancing in it, Costa Rica now offers a chance to do both. These days, Costa Rica is not only an ecologically rich destination but also a party hot-spot.

Oscar Arias, a native of Costa Rica, studies applied math and economics at Harvard College...Juan Pastor, also born and raised in Costa Rica, studies journalism and international relations at New York University.

LA POBLACIÓN INDÍGENA
From golden bands to government branding

Ever since Europeans discovered Costa Rica, the Costa Rica's indigenous populations have struggled for recognition and protection. On September 18, 1502, Columbus landed on Isla Uvita, near Puerto Limón, on his fourth and final voyage to the New World and observed an indigenous population that numbered a quarter of a million and spanned eight different ethnic groups. Upon witnessing the golden bands that adorned the ears and noses of the region's inhabitants, Columbus returned to Europe spinning tales of untold wealth in the New World. Although similar accounts inspired Gil Gonzalez Dávila to refer to the land as the "Rich Coast," the subsequent invasion by the Spanish conquistadors did not yield the sought-after gold deposits. As the Spaniards exerted their influence in Costa Rica, the indigenous population slowly dwindled due to European diseases. By the sixteenth century, the few remaining members of the indigenous population fled to the highlands to escape the slavery of the Spanish lords.

Based on archaeological evidence, it is believed that humans first occupied the environs of Costa Rica over 10,000 years ago. The cultural mysteries left behind by the region's pre-Columbian inhabitants include thousands of perfectly spherical granite *bolas* (balls) that dot the entire Caribbean coast, the ruins of an ancient city complete with still-functional aqueducts near Turrialba, and sophisticated gold and jade ceremonial pieces believed to have been constructed as early as 1000 AD.

Unlike the native empires of Mexico and Perú, the indigenous population of Costa Rica can be divided into distinct cultural groups. Since Costa Rica is part of the bridge between North and South America, each group displays a unique combination of traits characteristic to several geographic locales. In the north, the Chorotega thrived under Aztec and Maya influence. Other ethnic groups like the Boruca, Bribri, Cabecar, Guaymi, Huetar, and Guatuso spoke languages that incorporated the same compositional elements as the Incas. As Arawak and Caribe cultures established permanent settlements along the Caribbean Coast, the addition of new phonetic sounds resulted in a more complex linguistic structure. Although few words from this ancestral tongue are in common use today, many topographic features retain their native names. For example, Volcán Poas is named after the yellow flowers that grow at the summit of the volcano.

The Bribrí and the Cabecar remain today as the only two native groups that have been successful in maintaining their religious myths and isolation from outside social and cultural influences. More than 20 generations of story-telling, as well as a fierce resistance to the promises of the Christian missionaries, have preserved the collective faith in Sibú, the supreme god and creator of the universe. Today, the government of Costa Rica estimates that there are around nine thousand Bribrí and Cabecar inhabiting the mountainous Cordillera de Talamanca.

In the early 1970s, Costa Rica established the National Commission for Indigenous Affairs (CONAI). The loosely structured aims of this government-sponsored organization were to improve the social, economic, and cultural situations of the native populations. Although CONAI was pressured by native groups to purchase indigenous lands from the government, the organization never received proper funding and ultimately failed to perform this fundamental task.

Due to the failure of CONAI, Costa Rica enacted legislation in 1977 to permanently establish 22 *Reservas Indígenas* (Indigenous Reserves) for the remaining eight native groups. The bill awarded indigenous populations the right to self-governance within their communities as long as the government retained the land titles. Unfortunately, the Costa Rican government has allowed interest groups to enter the reserve and exploit the land for agriculture and mining. In the early 90s, the government finally began the distribution of national identification cards within the reserves. This awarded the indigenous population the same benefits as Costa Rican citizens, including voting rights and access to health care from the *Caja Costarricense del Seguro Social* (CCSS).

Despite the country's progressive legislation, a lot of work remains to be done in the field of indigenous rights in Costa Rica. The growing apathy of the government regarding the protection of reserve borders coupled with the increasing pressure to profit from eco-tourism through the construction of resort lodges and transit grids have threatened the indigenous people with the potential loss of their native lands. In addition to being financially and politically constrained, indigenous populations must also contend with the rising percentage of alcoholism and drug-use within the reserves.

Fortunately, one benefit of the recent tourism boom in Costa Rica has been an increase in the awareness of the general public regarding the plight of the indigenous population as well as the formation of various worldwide non-government organizations (NGOs) dedicated to protecting the human rights of the native peoples of Latin America. Although a significant amount of work still needs to be done, NGOs have thus far been successful in arbitrating disputes over boundaries, securing reparations for previous land encroachments and encouraging the formation of mixed governmental committees to ensure that the indigenous population can actively participate in the legislative process. If you are planning to spend more then a month's time in Costa Rica, consider the wide range of volunteer programs available through both student travel agencies in your home country and NGOs operating within Latin America. In addition to helping improve the lives of the población indígena, you will also experience a dimension of Costa Rica that few travelers witness.

Matthew Firestone was a Research-Writer for Let's Go: Britain & Ireland 2002. *He has studied post-weaning nutrition among indigenous populations in Costa Rica, traveling to various clinics and interviewing clinical doctors and natives. He is currently in Sub-Saharan Africa researching the dietary practices of hunter-gatherer populations inhabiting the Kalahari.*

LIGHTS, CAMERA, ACTION!
The film industry boom in Costa Rica

While Costa Rica is known for many things, it is not usually associated with the glitz and glamour of Hollywood. This small, humble country, wedged in the narrow Central American isthmus, at times seems to be detached from the hustle and bustle of the rest of the world. However, in recent years, it has become an unlikely hotspot for filmmakers who want to take advantage of the country's beautiful landscape and reliable people.

This current trend has followed the tourism boom in the area for the last 15 years. The attractions are the usual: beautiful beaches, teeming rainforests, diverse landscapes, and a cosmopolitan flare. Costa Rica stands apart from other nearby tropical locations because of its peaceful history, democratic nature, developed infrastructure, and educated workforce. These characteristics have allowed filmmakers to explore and take advantage of the country's scenery with unusual ease.

From small Canadian and European independent films, to big budget Hollywood productions, the number of films shot in Costa Rica has steadily increased over the years. In the early 90s with the film *1492*, it became evident that Costa Rica, mysterious yet inviting, had a lot to offer to the film industry. Since then, many productions have found a home in this vibrant country, from big blockbusters like *Congo* to comedies like *Nuns on the Run* and sequels like *Endless Summer 2*. These productions have also inspired *ticos* themselves to take part in filmmaking; since the 90s, many national films have been produced in the country, and some, like Oscar Castillo's *Asesinato en el Meneo*, have enjoyed commercial success.

Costa Rica is, undeniably, a developing country and, at times, filmmakers and actors have had to cope with unusual conditions. As María Cristina González, who has served as assistant location manager and local contact person on many of the shoots, describes it, "Actors are always startled when they first see iguanas running across a hotel lobby or howler monkeys on the trees by the swimming pool." Other challenges include pesky mosquitoes, untimely rain showers, and remote locations. Even natives have had to adapt by brushing up on their English while hotels, transportation companies, and catering services feel the need to improve services to accommodate the production teams.

In the end, it is a win-win situation for the country and the filmmakers. The country benefits economically, the filmmakers shoot their productions, and the rest of the world gets to enjoy the beautiful scenery. Because shoots usually occur in remote locations, small towns benefit most from film projects. Hotels and restaurants that would otherwise remain empty for most of the year suddenly find themselves accommodating over 100 people for weeks and months at a time. Rosalía Morales, a resident of Puerto Viejo, one of the these towns, describes, "There is definitely a change, but it is a change for the better. The filmmakers not only leave revenue, but they are genuinely excited to be here. For us, it is always exciting to be part of something like this."

One of the most recent productions to be shot in Puerto Viejo is a joint Canadian and British film entitled *The Blue Butterfly*. The story features a boy (actor William Hurt) with terminal cancer who is searching for a mysterious butterfly. The production team spent about six months in the area and employed over 50 Costa Ricans, both as part of the production team and as extras in the film. Another production, *Spy Kids 2*, wrapped up production in early spring and hit theaters in the USA in Summer 2002.

Shooting on location abroad can be a daunting task, but thanks to Costa Rica's infrastructure, stability, and level of development, production companies have found an opportunity to make their films with ease. Undeniably, this trend has helped Costa Rica stand out and has further fueled the tourism industry.

Oscar Arias, a native of Costa Rica, studies applied math and economics at Harvard College.

PRACTICAL AESTHETICS
From transportation to art

For one weekend in March, the *campo* descends on Escazú, and the annual Día de los Boyeros parade brings teams of oxen and brightly painted *carretas* (oxcarts) to the town's narrow streets. Following performers on stilts, who amble through the crowds in an astonishing array of scary or goofy costumes, the *boyeros* (oxcart drivers), usually dressed in jeans and red bandanas, skillfully control the muscular beasts, who trod slowly past delighted observers. Most people mill about the streets, delighting in flavored ice and pastries; some pay attention to the official competition, but the main spectacle is the oxcarts.

Painted in vibrant hues and geometrical patterns which can be traced back to the Moors, the *carreta* is a source of national pride. Adopted as the symbol for the National Labor Party in 1988, the oxcart serves as a reminder of Costa Rica's campesino past. Rustic vehicles, oxcarts are essentially large wooden storage compartments with extremely large wheels (suitable for tackling most rough terrain and even small rivers) pulled by a pair of oxen. The invention of the oxcart allowed Costa Rica to integrate into world trade in the mid-19th century by allowing farmers to transport their products from interior mountainous regions to ports through formerly impassable terrain. The first sign of success, in 1843, was the transportation of a shipment of coffee to Puntarenas where it was then shipped to London. Following this delivery, oxcarts were regularly used as a method of transportation until World War II, when they were rendered obsolete by increasingly available trucks and cars.

With *carretas* serving an important role in international commerce, farmers had little time for decoration. Local lore holds that wives would recognize the sound of a husband's oxcarts and rush to meet them upon their return from the port (a journey that could take several weeks). Now, the exquisitely designed exteriors are a fool-proof way to distinguish the oxcarts. Artisans claim that no two are alike. This tradition began in the early 20th century when some *boyeros* painted the carts' wheels with simple patterns derived from Spanish colonial designs—color scheme and geometric arrangement were region-specific. The trend caught on and spawned generations of craftsmen who spend months perfecting intricate designs, which cover not only the cart's wheels but also its main storage area. These ornate designs, the most famous examples of Costa Rican artistry, are responsible for the *carreta's* fame.

As a result of the *carreta's* popularity, Sarchí (and other areas where artisans have historically converged to craft these rustic masterpieces) has become inundated with tourists searching for a unique Costa Rican souvenir. The craftsmen are more than willing to comply—miniature oxcarts, oxcarts that have been converted into bars, and full-sized carts are readily available for purchase. Be prepared to pay (a lot) for a piece of this genuine *tico* craftsmanship.

Despite, their commercial success, the oxcarts are most impressive in action. One can see the rich symbolism of the *carreta* embodied by the harmony between the serene rotation of the enormous colorful wheels, the oblivious oxen, and the masterful *boyero*. In addition to illustrating Costa Rica's pastoral past, the *carreta* also attests the hardworking, peaceful nature of Costa Ricans; if nothing else it speaks highly of the artisans' dedication to and expertise in preserving and celebrating rustic traditions.

Amber Musser, currently editing for Let's Go, lived in Costa Rica for four years.

DEMILITARIZATION
A leading nation in an insecure world

Costa Rica garners widespread praise for its eco-friendly development policies and maintenance of political stability amid general Central American tempestuousness. Within elite international circles, Costa Rica has earned praise for its role in resolving armed conflict and its advocacy of demilitarization, a policy it has maintained within its own borders since 1948. In the late 80s, Costa Rican president Oscar Arias (1986-90) challenged US and Soviet military-aid policies, which fueled civil conflict in El Salvador and Nicaragua, by presenting a non-violent alternative for the negotiating table. Success earned Arias a Nobel Peace Prize. Arias has since utilized the political credibility won for himself and for Costa Rica to promote the virtues of negotiation and demilitarization.

Demilitarization involves both political and economic factors. The degree of demilitarization is a function of administrative authority and division of resources. A highly demilitarized state is characterized by considerable civilian control over security forces and relatively low allocation of funds to security. Arias, when urging other nations to demilitarize, focuses on social implications, which ensue from the political and economical decisions of military expenditure. According to Arias, in 1994 developing nations accounted for 70 percent of world arms sales, 90 percent of the purchases being supplied by the five permanent members of the UN Security Council plus Germany. In 1995 Arias claimed that 12 percent of annual military expenditure by developing nations would pay for health care for everyone in the world. (Robert Collier, "Sunday Interview: Oscar Arias," *San Francisco Chronicle*, 10/29/1995.) Arias can point to his nation: Costa Rican citizens enjoy both universal health care and education.

Disproportionate power concentrated in the hands of the military has traditionally plagued Central American—indeed, most Latin American—states. Civilian authority has neither been successful in stimulating economic development nor in suppressing internal security threats. As civilian-led police forces have failed to protect citizens or state apparatuses, the military has been called upon to restore order. The military—an armed group—is thus presented with opportunities to assume political authority and garner popular support in the absence of a state power, leading to further degradation of democratic institutions and of society's respect for the rule of law.

Throughout the 70s and 80s, Costa Rica—with overwhelming popular support up to 77 percent—resisted pressures to militarize despite the threat of Nicaraguan invasion. It remained demilitarized in the 1990s despite dramatic increases in criminal activity, which were largely due to illegal drug trade. Strategic military aid from the US during the 70s and 80s was politically motivated and did not reach Costa Rica. Support now flows to Costa Rica for anti-drug security programs, to put down the internal threat of drug trafficking. The US has expanded joint efforts with Costa Rica because of the relationship between drugs and terrorism. Some say the US might even call on Costa Rica to take an even more independent role.

Arias has not achieved his goal of making all of Central America the world's first demilitarized region, but individual nations have made significant strides. Panama, since its military was eliminated by US invasion in 1989, has emulated the Costa Rican model. Says Arias, "The safest border in the region is between Costa Rica and Panama, because neither has an army." (Douglas Farah, "Central American Armies Get Down to Business," *The Washington Post*, 6/4/1996.) Greater civilian control and a reduction of fear by politicians have characterized the gradual trends toward demilitarization in nations such as El Salvador, Honduras, Nicaragua, and Guatemala.

Arias envisions widespread demilitarization not so much as a state-by-state effort than as the use of incentives and/or coercion by the international community. In the terminology of international relations theory, Arias is known as an "internationalist." Internationalists believe in the power of international bodies to establish and enforce regional and global norms and regulations. They desire to augment the jurisdiction of organizations like the United Nations (UN) and the Organization of American

States (OAS). The UN's International Criminal Court is an excellent example of an internationalist vision—it is meant to enforce international human rights codes that would allow the court's jurisdiction to override the jurisdiction of state judicial mechanisms in instances of alleged crimes against humanity. This challenges traditional realms of state sovereignty.

One can certainly understand why a Latin American would take such a world-view. Dictatorships and economic crises have led to infringements on human rights, perpetrated even by the states themselves. Furthermore, unequal bilateral relations between weak and strong states—like the US's and Soviet Union's relationships with Central American armed groups in the 1980s—allow strong states to impose self-interested policies. In theory, regional alliances put more power into the hands of small states as they mobilize to bargain with large states; they allow them to pool resources for security, for example. Critics often point out that, in practice, a regional power comes to dominate these organizations anyway.

The viability of demilitarization as widespread policy depends on significant internationalist progress; the only way to protect a demilitarized state from a national security threat is through an international body. But that never frightened Arias. "The Sandinistas never dared to invade Costa Rica (during the 1980s)," he says, "because the whole world was watching to make sure that they didn't." (Collier—SF Chronicle article, 1995.)

Derek Glanz was the Editor of Let's Go: Spain, Portugal & Morocco 1998. *He is now a freelance journalist who recently began pursuing postgraduate studies in international relations. He has been published in* The Associate Press *and* The Miami Herald *(via AP), and has appeared as a guest TV analyst on Colombia's* TeleCartagena.

APPENDIX

CLIMATE

Avg. Temp. (lo/hi), Precipitation	January			April			July			October		
	°C	°F	mm	°C	°F	mm	°C	°F	mm	°C	°F	mm
Caribbean Lowlands	21/29	69/84	300	22/31	71/87	270	23/31	73/87	450	22/30	71/86	220
Northern Lowlands	19/27	66/80	120	23/30	73/86	75	24/31	75/87	400	22/30	71/86	425
San José and Central Valley	17/26	62/78	20	19/28	66/82	60	19/27	66/80	160	18/26	64/78	280
Northwestern Costa Rica	21/33	69/91	10	23/36	73/96	45	23/32	73/89	150	22/31	71/87	275
Central Pacific Coast	21/31	69/87	50	23/32	73/89	110	23/31	73/87	450	23/30	73/86	550
Southern Costa Rica	21/33	69/91	100	23/33	73/91	250	22/31	71/87	450	22/31	71/87	600

LANGUAGE

Spanish pronunciation is very straightforward. Each vowel is pronounced only one way: **a** ("ah" in father); **e** ("e" in "convey"); **i** ("ee" in "beet"); **o** ("oh" in "tote"); **u** ("oo" in "boot"); **y**, by itself, is pronounced like the English "ee." Most consonants are pronounced the same as in English. Important exceptions are: **j** ("h" in "hello"), ll ("y" in "yes"); **ñ** ("ny" in "canyon"); **rr** (trilled "r"); **h** (always silent); **x** (either "h" when in the middle of a word or like in English when at the end). The letter **c** is pronounced like an English s before "soft vowels"—e and i—and like the English k before "hard vowels"—a, o, and u. Z sounds like the English s.

By rule, the stress of a Spanish word falls on the second-to-last syllable if the word ends in a vowel, n, or s. If the word ends in any other consonant, the stress is on the last syllable. Any word in which the accent does not follow the rule carries an accent mark over the stressed syllable.

BASICS

ENGLISH	SPANISH	ENGLISH	SPANISH
Hello. [informal]	Hola/Buenas.	**How are you?**	¿Cómo está?
Good morning.	Buenos días.	**I'm fine, thanks.**	(Estoy) bien, gracias.
Good afternoon.	Buenas tardes.	**Please/Thank you.**	Por favor/Gracias.
Good evening/night.	Buenas noches.	**You're welcome!**	De nada/Con mucho gusto.
Good-bye.	Adiós.	**Yes/no.**	Sí/no.
Sorry. Forgive me.	Lo siento. Perdón.	**I would like...**	Quisiera.../Me gustaría
What's your name?	¿Cómo se llama?	**I need...**	Me falta.../Necesito...

ENGLISH	SPANISH	ENGLISH	SPANISH
My name is Gabrielle.	Me llamo Gabrielle.	I don't speak Spanish.	No hablo español.
I'm from...	Soy de...	I don't understand.	No entiendo.
No problem.	No hay problema.	Please repeat.	Repita, por favor.
OK.	OK. Perfecto. Muy bien.	Let go of me.	Suélteme.
Who?	¿Quién?	I don't know.	No sé.
When?	¿Cuándo?	Go away/Leave me alone.	Váyase/Déjeme.
What (did you say)?	¿Cómo?	Stop/enough.	Pare/Basta.
Where is...?	¿Dónde está...?	Help!	¡Socorro! ¡Ayuda!
Why?	¿Por qué?	I would like to make a call to the US	Quisiera llamar a los Estados Unidos.
Do you accept traveler's checks?	¿Acepta cheques viajeros?	Where is the bathroom?	¿Dónde está el baño?
How much does it (this) cost?	¿Cuánto vale (esto)?	Excuse me.	Con permiso/Perdón.
That's too much.	Eso es demasiado.	I like *Let's Go.*	Me gusta *Let's Go.*
What time is it?	¿Qué hora es?	several	varios, algunos
many/few	muchos/pocos	a ton of	un montón de
a couple	un par de		

DIRECTIONS AND TRANSPORTATION

ENGLISH	SPANISH	ENGLISH	SPANISH
(to the) right	a la derecha	(to the) left	a la izquierda
next to	a la par de/al lado de	across from	en frente de
straight ahead	recto/derecho	to turn	doblar
near	cerca	far	lejos
above	arriba/encima de	below	abajo/debajo de
traffic light	semáforo	corner	esquina
street/avenue	calle/avenida	block	cuadra
How do I get to...?	¿Cómo llego a...?	Where is...street?	¿Dónde está la calle...?
How far is...?	¿Qué tan largo queda...?	What bus line goes to...?	¿Cuál bus tiene servicio a...?
When does the bus leave for...?	¿A qué hora sale el bus para...?	From where does the bus leave?	¿De dónde sale el bus?
I'm getting off at...	Me bajo en...	Is this bus going to...?	¿Este bus va para...?
How long does it take?	¿Cuánto dura/tarda?	I'm lost.	Estoy perdido(a).

ACCOMMODATIONS AND FOOD

ENGLISH	SPANISH	ENGLISH	SPANISH
I'd like to see a room with one bed.	Quisiera ver un cuarto con una cama.	Is there a fan/private bath/hot water?	¿Hay abanico/baño privado/agua caliente?
Are there rooms?	¿Hay habitaciones?	I would like a room.	Quisiera una habitación.
Where is the bathroom?	¿Dónde está el baño?	Check, please.	La cuenta, por favor.
breakfast	desayuno	lunch	almuerzo
dinner	cena	Bon apetit	Buen provecho
drink	bebida	water (purified)	agua (purificada)
bread	pan	rice	arroz
vegetables	verduras/vegetales	chicken	pollo
meat	carne	milk	leche

APPENDIX

ENGLISH	SPANISH	ENGLISH	SPANISH
eggs	huevos	coffee	café
juice	jugo	tea	té
wine	vino	beer	cerveza
ice cream	helado	fruit	fruta
soup	sopa/caldo	vegetarian	vegetariano(a)
fork	tenedor	cup	taza/copa
spoon	cuchara	knife	cuchillo

GLOSSARY

aduana: customs
aeropuerto: airport
agua pura/purificada: purified water
aguas calientes: hot springs
aire acondicionado: air-conditioner
alcadía: mayoral district
altiplano: plateau
arena: sand
arroz: rice
artesanía: handicrafts
asado: (n. adj.) roast(ed)
autobús: bus
avenida: avenue
avería: (car) breakdown
avión: airplane
aviso: warning, advisory
bahía: bay
baleada: a soft, taco-like food
balneario: bathing area
banano: banana
baño: bathroom
barrio: neighborhood
batido: milkshake
bebida: drink
borracho: drunk
bote: boat
cabina: cabin
caliente: hot
calle: street
cama: bed
cambio: change
camioneta: small truck
campamento: camp area
candado: padlock
candela: candle
cantina: rowdy bar
carne: meat
caro/a: expensive
carretera: highway
casado/a: married
casado: rice, beans, & meat dish
cascada: waterfall
catarata: waterfall
catedral: cathedral
cayuco: dugout canoe
cena: dinner
cenote: sinkhole
centro: city center
cerveza: beer

cheques viajeros: traveler's checks
chichas: sandflies
chicle: chewing gum
chófer: driver
ciudad: city
coche: car
colectivo: bus/van
colón: name of currency
comida: food, meal
comedor: a small diner
compartido: shared (bath)
conductor: driver
consulado: consulate
correo: post office
córdobas: Nicaraguan currency
coyotes: money changers
cuadra: (street) block
cuarto: room
cuenta: restaurant bill
cuevas: caves
de ida y vuelta: round-trip
desayuno: breakfast
día: day
dinero: money
discoteca: disco
dorado: fried
edificio: building
embajada: embassy
emergencia: emergency
enfermo/a: sick
entrada: entrance, admission
estación: station
este: east
extranjera/o: foreign(er)
farmacia: pharmacy
finca: plantation-like farm
fría: cold
frijoles: beans
frito: fried
frontera: border
fuego: fire
fútbol: soccer (football)
gallo pinto: fried rice & beans
Garífuna: Caribbean ethnic group
gaseosa: soft drink
grande: big
gringo/a: white person, North American
grutas: caves
hacienda: ranch
hombre: man

hospedaje: inn
hospital: hospital
huipil: an embroidered garment
iglesia: church
isla: island
indígena/o: indigenous
inundacíon: flood
invierno: winter; rainy season
ladrón: thief
lancha: launch (boat)
lago: lake
laguna: lagoon, lake
lavandería: laundromat
licuado: fruity shake
linterna: flashlight
llamada por cobrar: collect call
llanuras: plains
lista de correos: *poste restante*
llave: key
malecón: boardwalk
manglar: mangrove
mañana: morning, tomorrow
marisco: shellfish, seafood
matrimonial: bed for two
médico: doctor
menú del día: meal of the day
mercado: market
merendero: snack bar
MINAE: national park info
mirador: view, lookout
Miskito: indigenous group
molas: patched cloth panels
mondongo: innards
montaña: mountain
monte: mountain
moto: motorcycle
mujer: woman, wife
niño: child
norte: north
novio/a: fiancé/fiancée
oeste: west
ola: wave
oriente: eastern
palapa: palm-thatched hut
pan: bread
panadería: bakery
panga: skiff (boat)
parada: stop, bus stop
páramo: barren plain
parque: park; plaza
pasaporte: passport
peligroso/a: dangerous

pensión: hostel
pequeño: small
picop: pickup truck
pledra: stone, rock
pincho: meat shish kebab
pipa: green coconut, pipe
playa: beach
pollo: chicken
poniente: western
pueblo: town
pulpería: grocery store
pupusa: fried tortilla with beans and cheese
pupsería: vendor of *pupusas*
privado: private (bath)

rebaja: bargain
refugio: shelter
resaca: hangover
restaurante: restaurant
río: river
ropa: clothes
sábanas: sheets
salida: exit
santo: saint
semana: week
sendero: path
soda: roadside eatery
sopa: soup
stela: stele, stone monument
sur: south

taquería: taco stand
tico/a: Costa Rican
tienda: store
típico: traditional (food)
tortuga: turtle
vegetales: vegetables
verano: summer
verde: green
vuelo: flight
zapatos: shoes
zona rosa: red light district; prostitution zone

TICO TALK: COSTA RICAN LANGUAGE QUIRKS

¡OJO! Using local colloquialisms is a great way to build a cultural bridge and befriend the *ticos* you encounter on the road. Politeness is a central value of Costa Rican culture, however, so refrain from using any of this slang in formal or business settings or when dealing with people of authority or respect (such as elders). Talking to young people in a casual setting can be very relaxed, yet some of these terms are potentially inappropriate even with young people. To avoid making any cultural faux pas, refrain from directly referring to someone with any words in the list that have negative or possibly offensive meanings.

agarrado: (adj.) greedy, stingy.
agüevarse: to become sad, bored.
armarse la gorda: a fight, brawl.
bañazo: (m.) something (or someone) ridiculous or embarrassing.
birra: (f.) beer.
bostezo: (m.) something (or someone) that is boring.
buena nota: (adj.) someone who is nice, kind, pleasant.
cabanga: (f.) sadness from missing someone; sometimes used to describe homesickness.
cañas: (f.) colones (Costa Rican currency).
casado: (noun.) Costa Rican lunch that usually includes rice and beans, a steak, two eggs, and plantains.
chao: good bye (from Italian "ciao").
chapulín: young thief.
chavalo: (noun.) young boy, guy.
Chepe: Costa Rica's capital, San José.
chiva, chivísima: expression used amongst youths that denotes liking.
ponerse chiva: get mad.
con toda la pata: 1) satisfied; 2) very good; 3) in a good state of health.
corrongo: (adj.) funny, pretty.
dicha: (f.) luck.
diez con hueco: deception, fraud (allusion to a perforated coin with no value).
dolor de huevos: 1) someone who is vain or presumptuous; 2) a tedious chore or activity.
echar(le) un ojo (a algo): (v.) observe, take care, guard.
enjache: (m.) to observe (someone) with attention or malice.
filo: (m.) hunger.
fregar: (v.) bother, annoy.
gallo pinto: (m.) typical Costa Rican breakfast made with rice and black beans.
gato: (noun) 1) person with green or blue eyes. 2) someone who's talented at something.

guachimán: (m.) guardian. Generally the person who takes care of cars parked on the street.
guacho: (m.) watch.
guachos: eyes.
lo estoy guachando: (v.) I am watching over/supervising it.
guaro: (m.) liquor made from sugar cane (Costa Rican national drink); by extension, any alcoholic beverage, liquor.
guava: (f.) luck.
güeiso: (m.) 1) something ugly, bad; 2) when you are left alone.
güila: (noun) young boy/girl.
hablar paja: to speak trivialities, say nothing of importance.
hablar (hasta) por los codos: (v.) to speak too much, to chatter.
harina: (f.) money, "dough".
importar un comino/pepino: of no importance.
jacha: (f.) face.
jalar: (v.) to be boyfriend and girlfriend.
jalarse la torta: to get pregnant without being married.
joder: (v.) bother, annoy, drive someone crazy.
jugar de vivo: to try to be very clever.
jumas: in a drunken state.
jupa: (f.) head.
jupón: (m.) someone who is stubborn.
lata: (f.) bus.
lavado: (adj.) without money.
ligar: (v.) to flirt, to seek someone's company with romantic/emotional intentions.
limpio: (adj.) with no money.
macho, machito: someone with light colored skin and hair.
mae/maje: used amongst young people to address each other.
hacerse el maje: to pretend it has nothing to do with you. Also "hacerse el ruso."
media teja: (f.) 50 colon bill.
mejenga: (f.) pick-up or neighborhood soccer match; depreciative when a professional team does not show much talent on the field.
menear: (v.) to "shake it," dance.
menudo: bunch of coins.
meter la pata: make an error, commit an impropriety or indiscretion.
montado: (noun/adj.) self seeking, a person that takes advantage of others (verb: montarse).
mosca/mosquita muerta: (f.) person that feigns innocence or weakness.
mota: (m.) marijuana.
nerdo: (noun.) nerd.
ni papa: nothing.
nica: (noun) Nicaraguan.
¡ojo!: Watch out!
olla de carne: typical soup made with meat and vegetables.
pa'l tigre: to feel or be bad for some reason; opposite of "pura vida."
pachanga: (f.) party, celebration.
pacho: (m.) comical situation.
pachuco: (noun) young vagrant, that does not study, is rude and vulgar.
paja: (f.) trivialities.
palmar: to die.
paracaidista: person who shows up at a party without having been invited.
pelada: (f.) embarrassing, to do something wrong.
pendejo: (noun/adj.) strong term for fearful, dumb, or incompetent at certain things.
pinche: greedy, stingy, avaricious.
plata: (f.) money.

playo: (m.) homosexual.
ponerse las pilas: 1) to hurry, do something with more effort or will; 2) to become ready, attentive.
polada: (f.) something that denotes bad taste.
porfa: please (abbreviated form of "por favor").
pringa pie: (m.) diarrhea.
¡pura vida!: general expression of satisfaction.
quitarse: (v.) to go back on something previously said or agreed upon.
rajón: (adj.) presumtuous (verb: rajar).
rata: thief.
un rico: (m.) good-looking, attractive man.
una rica: (f.) good-looking, attractive, sexy woman, with a really nice body.
roco: (m.) old person.
rojo, rojito: (m.) 1) 1000 colon bill; 2) taxi.
rulear: (v.) to sleep.
salado: (adj.) without luck.
sobre: (m.) bed.
soda: modest restaurant.
soplado: very quick.
¡soque!: expression used to ask someone to hurry.
¡suave!: expression used to ask someone to wait or stop.
tanate: (m.) a lot.
tatas: parents.
teja: 100 colon bill.
tico/a: (noun/adj.) Costa Rican.
tigra: (adj.) bored.
timba: (f.) the stomach, abdomen.
Tiquicia: Costa Rica.
tombo: policeman.
toque: (m.) 1) a brief time interval, a little while; 2) a little bit (quantity).
torta: (f.) problem.
tortillera: (f.) lesbian.
troliar: (v.) to walk.
tuanis: (adj.) good, wonderful.
tucán: 5000 colon bill.
turno: (m.) party, specific fair of some community.
la U: the University.
¡upe!: Expression used in place of knocking at the door.
vacilón: (m.) fun, comical, entertaining.
verde: someone who studies a lot or is very responsible with his/her studies.
vino: (m.) (noun) someone who gossips.
volado: (m.) crazy.
vuelto: (m.) change (of money) when buying something.
wuata (güater): water.
wuatear (güatear): shower.
¿Y diay?: What's up? What happened? How have you been? What's wrong?
zaguate: (m.) mutt, street dog. Also used to describe a sexually very active man.

INDEX

A

A2Z Languages 77
Academia Latinoamericana de Español S.A. 77
accommodations 26
adapters 25
adventure trips 31
aerogrammes 31
AIDS 24
airplane travel
  fares 36
  standby 38
Alajuela 107
  Butterfly Farm 112
  Zoo-Ave 112
alcohol 19
Alliances Abroad 81
alligators 57
Almirante (P) 384
alternatives to tourism 74–84
  getting started 74
  studying abroad 74–78
  volunteering 80–84
  working 78–80
altitude, high 22
American Express 14, 15, 25, 33, 43
American Field Service (AFS) 75
American Institute for Foreign Study 75
American Red Cross 21
AmeriSpan Study and Work Abroad 79
AmeriSpan Unlimited 77
Amigos de las Americas 81
Amity Institute, Amity Volunteer Teachers Abroad Programs 80
animals. See environment.
anteaters 56
appendix 398–403
  climate 398
  glossary 400
  language 398
Archaeological Institute of America 78
armadillos 56
army ants 57
Ashley xi
Asociación de Voluntario de Areas Protegias Silvestres (ASVO) 83
Asociación Preservacionista de Flora y Fauna Silvestre (APREFLOFAS) 83
Atenas 113
ATM cards 15
Avancari Eco-Camp 83

B

backpacks 30
Bagaces 160–161
  Parque Nacional Palo Verde 161
  Reserva Biológica Lomas Barbudal 162
Bahía Drake 322–326
Baird's tapir 56
bargaining 16
Barra del Colorado 362–365
Barva 131–132
beaches
  Bahía Bocarito (P) 386
  Bluff (P) 387
  Cuarto (P) 388
  Larga (P) 388
  Primera (P) 388
  Punta Vieja (P) 388
  Red Frog (P) 388
  Segunda (P) 388
beetles 57
Ben xi
Bijagua 158
biodiversity law 62
boas 57
Boca del Drago (P) 387
Bocas del Toro (P) 384
Bocas del Toro Province (P) 384–389
border crossings
  to Nicaragua 172, 200
  to Panama 318
Boruca 309
Brasilito 211
budgeting your trip 16
Buenos Aires 307–308
butterflies 57
Butterfly Farm 112

C

Cabuya 255–256
Cahuita 366–369
caimans 57
Caldera 269
calling cards 33
camping 28
Cañas 154–155
Cañas-Juarez Treaty 63
Caño Negro 197
Caño Negro Wildlife Refuge 197–200
Caño Palma Biological Station 362
car
  rental 42–44
car insurance 45
car rental 42
Cariari 356
Caribbean Lowlands 342–382
  Barra del Colorado 362–365
  Bribrí 371
  Cahuita 366–369
  Gandoca 378–379
  Guácimo 346
  Guápiles 343–345
  Manzanillo 380
  Parismina 351–354
  Parque Nacional Cahuita 369–371
  Parque Nacional Tortuguero 354–362
  Puerto Limón 348–351
  Puerto Viejo de Talamanca 373–377
  Reserva Biológica Hitoy-Cerere 372
  Siquirres 347–348
Carmona 243
Cartago 132–136
Cascada Verde 77, 82
cash advances 15
Cavernas de Venado 191–192
caves
  Cavernas de Venado 191
  La Gruta (P) 387
  Terciopelo 229
Cayo Nancy (P) 389
Cayos Zapatillas (P) 388
Centers for Disease Control (CDC) 20
Central Pacific Coast 262–299
  Esparza 270
  Hacienda Barú 297
  Iguana Park 265
  Jacó 272–278
  Orotina 262–265
  Parque Nacional Manuel Antonio 290–294

Parque Nacional Marino
  Ballena 299
Parrita 281
Puntarenas 266–270
Quepos 284–290
Uvita 297–299
Central Valley 107–145
  Barva 131–132
  Grecia 117–118
  Heredia 125–129
  Naranjo 118–120
  Reserva Santa Elena 152
  San Ramón 120–122
  Sarchí 114–116
  Tilarán 156
  Volcán Barva 130
  Zarcero 122–124
Centro de Educación Creativo
  (Creative Learning Center) 82
Centro de Nutrición y
  Educación (CEN) 82
Centro Neotrópico Sarapiquis
  183
Cerro Kámuk 318
Cerro Tortuguero 362
changing money 14
Changuinola (P) 383
Charlene xi
children and travel 49
CHIP card 33
Chirripó 304
cholera 23
Cirrus 15
Ciudad Quesada 176–179
climate 398
clothing 25
cloud forests 55
Cóbano 257
Comisión Salvemos Las
  Tortugas de Parismina 83
community service 81
Comunicare 77
con artists 19
conifers 55
conservation work 83
consulates 11
contact lenses 25
Converters 25
converting currency 14
coral snake 57
Cordillera Central 54
Cordillera de Guanacaste 54
Cordillera de Talamanca 54
Cordillera de Tilarán 54
Costa Rica Rainforest Outward
  Bound School 78
Costa Rica today 61–64
  Costa Rica and Nicaragua
    63
  Costa Rica in the World 63

The unspectacular record
  elections of 2002 64
Costa Rican Language
  Academy 77
costs 16
Council on International
  Educational Exchange (CIEE)
  75
Council Travel 36
credit cards 15
crocodiles 57
Cross-Cultural Solutions 81
Cuarto beach (P) 388
Cultural Experiences Abroad
  76
currency exchange 14
customs 13

D

dangerous plants 56
debit cards 15
deciduous forests 55
dehydration 21
dengue fever 22
diarrhea 23
dietary concerns 49
disabled travelers 48
Discover Costa Rica 1–4
diseases
  food- and water-borne 22
  insect-borne 22
dolphins 57
Dominical 294
doxycycline 22
driving permits 45
drugs 19
dry season 1
dysentery 23

E

Earthwatch 83
ecotourism 62
Elderhostel, Inc. 83
elevation, high 22
email 34
embassies 11
emergency medical services
  21
endangered plants 56
entrance requirments 11
environment
  animals 56
  plants 55
epiphytes 56
Erin xi
ervice Civil International
  Voluntary Service (SCI-IVS)
  82
Escazú 104

Escuela Idiomas d'Amore 77
Esparza 270
essentials 11–53
Estación Biológica La Selva
  184
evergreen forests 55
exchange rates 14
exhaustion, heat 21
Experiment in International
  Living 75

F

features
  A jungle adventurer's dream
    come true... 326
  Cocolores 250
  demilitarization 396
  Drugs in Caribbean paradise
    344
  Elections in Costa Rica 390
  Hotel the Place 244
  Hydroelectric power, Project
    Boruca 306
  Jungle Raves 391
  La población indígena 392
  Life lessons from the
    Caribbean 364
  Lights, camera, action! 394
  Luz de Mono 249
  New royalty, new loyalty 308
  Ox-carts 395
  Parrot Bay Village 332
  Project Boruca 306
  Rain, rain come back again
    334
  The women of Boruca
    Reserve 316
Federal Express 32
female travelers 45
fer-de-lance 57
festivals 69
Filadelfia 213–214
film 26
Finca la Isla's Botanical
  Garden 376
Finca Lomas 84
flora & fauna 55–58
Forester Instituto
  Internacional 77
Fortuna 187–190
frostbite 21
Fulbright English Teaching
  Assistantship 80

G

Gandoca 378–379
gay travelers 48
geckos 57
General Delivery 32

Global Routes 81
glossary 400
GO25 card 13
golden orb spider 57
golden toads 57
Golfito 326–330
grayboxes
    "Black and yellow kill a
    fellow, red and black,
    friend of jack" 303
    Flora, fauna, and...pottery?
    327
    Lending a helping hand 368
    Saving Parismina's turtles
    352
    What is the largest land
    mammal in Central and
    South America? 341
    What's love got to do with it
    313
Grecia 117–118
Guabito (P) 383
Guácimo 346
Guaitil, Pottery Village of 216
Guanacaste 146–175
Guápiles 343–345
Guayabo National Monument
144

H

Habitat for Humanity
    International 81
Hacienda Barú 297
harpy eagle 56
health 20
    sexually transmitted
    diseases 24
    women 24
heatstroke 21
hepatitis A 20, 23
hepatitis B 20, 24
hepatitis C 24
Heredia 125–129
high altitude 22
high season 1
hitchhiking 45
HIV 24
hospedajes 26
hostels
    Hostelling International (HI)
    27
hot springs
    Orosi 139
    Parque Nacional Rincón de
    la Vieja 168, 170
    Tabacón 190, 191
hotels 26
hummingbirds 56
Hurricane Cesar 55

Hurricane Mitch 55
hypothermia 21

I

identification 13
iguanas 57
immunizations 20
inoculations 20
Instituto Monteverde 76
insurance 24, 43
Intern Abroad 79
international calls 33
International Driving Permit
    (IDP) 45
International School Services
    80
International Student Identity
    Card (ISIC) 13
International Teacher Identity
    Card (ITIC) 13
International Volunteer
    Programs Association 81
International Youth Discount
    Travel Card (IYTC) 13
internet 34
ISIC card 13
islands
    Bastimentos (P) 388
    Carenero (P) 389
    de Uvita 351
    Pájaros (P) 387
ITIC card 13

J

Jacó 272–278
jaguars 56
Jardín Botánico Lankester 136

K

keeping in touch 31
kosher 50

L

La Cruz 173–175
La Escuela del Mundo 77
La Virgen 185
Laguna de Cote 192
land 54–58
    Cordillera Central 54
    Cordillera de Guanacaste
    54
    Cordillera de Tilarán 54
    flora & fauna 55–58
language 398
Language Immersion Institute
    77
language quirks 401

Languages Abroad 77, 81
Lariam 22
leaf-cutter ants 57
lesbian travelers 48
Liberia 163–167
lizards 57
Lomas Barbudal 162–163
Los Chiles 196–197
Luggage 25

M

macaws 56
mail 31
Mal País 244, 244–249
malaria 22
Maleku 192
manatees 57
mangroves 55
MasterCard 15
measles 20
Medic Alert 21
medical assistance 21
medical insurance 24
mefloquine 22
Meseta Central. See Central
    Valley.
Model Mugging 18
money 14
money belt 19
monkeys 56
Montana Linda Spanish
    School 78
Monteverde 147–154
Montezuma 249
moors 55
Moravia 103
mosquito net 26

N

Nandayure (Carmona) 243
Naranjo 118–120
national parks
    Isla Bastimentos (P) 388
Neily 314–316
Nicoya 226–229
Nicoya Peninsula 201–261
    Cabuya 255–256
    Cóbano 257
    Filadelfia 213–214
    Mal País 244–249
    Nicoya 226–229
    Paquera 260
    Parque Nacional Barra
    Honda 229
    Parque Nacional Marino Las
    Baulas 216–218
    Refugio Nacional Curú 261
    Reserva Natural Absoluta
    Cabo Blanco 256

Santa Cruz 214–216
Santa Teresa 244–249
Tambor 257–259
Northern Lowlands 176–200
  Caño Negro Wildlife Refuge 197–200
  Cavernas de Venado 191–192
  Ciudad Quesada 176–179
  Estación Biológica La Selvaí 184
  Fortuna 187–190
  La Virgen 185
  Los Chiles 196–197
  Parque Nacional Juan Castro Blanco 179
  Parque Nacional Volcán Arenal 190
  Puerto Viejo de Sarapiquí 180–183
  San Rafael de Guatuso 192–194
  Vara Blanca 185–187
Northwestern Costa Rica 146–175
  Bagaces 160–161
  Cañas 154–155
  La Cruz 173–175
  Liberia 163–167
  Lomas Barbudal 162–163
  Monteverde 147–154
  Parque Nacional Palo Verde 161–162
  Parque Nacional Rincón de la Vieja 168–170
  Parque Nacional Santa Rosa 170–171
  Reserva Biológica Monteverde 151
  Reserva Forestal Bosque Eterno de los Niños 152
  Volcán Tenorio 158–159

O

ocelots 56
Ocotal 207
Office of Overseas Schools 80
Old Bank (P) 388
older travelers 46
orchids 56
Orosi 137
  Purisil Park 140
Orotina 262–265
Ostional 233
outdoors 28
outdoors equipment 26

P

Pacheco, Abel 64
packing 25
Palmar Norte 310–311
Palmares 122
Paquera 260
parasites 23
Pargos. See Playa Negra.
Parismina 351–354
Parque Internacional La Amistad 316–318
Parque Nacional Manuel Antonio 290–294
Parque Nacional
  Barra Honda 229
  Braulio Carrillo 129
  Cahuita 369
  Chirripó 305
  Corcovado 339
  Guanacaste 172
  Juan Castro Blanco 179
  La Amistad 316
  Manuel Antonio 290
  Marino Ballena 299
  Marino Las Baulas 216
  Palo Verde 161
  Piedras Blancas 331
  Rincón de la Vieja 168
  Santa Rosa 170
  Tapantí 140
  Tortuguero 354
  Volcán Arenal 190
  Volcán Poás 111
Parque Nacional Palo Verde 161–162
Parque Nacional Rincón de la Vieja 168–170
Parque Nacional Santa Rosa 170–171
Parrita 281
Partido de Liberacion Nacional (PLN) 64
Partido Unidad Social Cristiana (PUSC) 64
Paso Canoas 318, 327
Paso Llano 129
passports 12
Peace Corps 82
Peace Studies and Peace Journalism 78
Peñas Blancas 172
Península de Osa y Golfo Dulce 321–341
  Bahía Drake 322–326
  Golfito 326–330
  Parque Nacional Corcovado 339–341
  Parque Nacional Piedras Blancas 331

Puerto Jiménez 335–339
Sierpe 321–322
Personal Identification Number (PIN) 15
phone cards 33
phones 33
pickpockets 19
plants and animals. See environment.
plate tectonics 55
playa
  Avellana 226
  Bahía Uvita 297
  Bandera 284
  Beach Break 377
  Bejuco 242, 284
  Boca Barranca 269
  Bonita 351
  Brasilito 211
  Cabuya 256
  Cahuita 366
  Caldera 269
  Camaronal 242
  Carmen 245
  Carrillo 239
  Cedros 253
  Chiquita 378
  Cocles 378
  Conchal 212
  Corozalito 242
  Coyote 243
  de Cacao 330
  de Doña Ana 269
  del Coco 204
  Dominical 294
  El Carmen 247
  Escondida 270, 293
  Espadilla 293
  Espadilla Sur 293
  Esterillos Centro 283
  Esterillos Este 284
  Esterillos Oeste 282
  Flamingo 209
  Grande 216, 253
  Guiones 231
  Hermosa 201, 247, 279
  Herradura 278
  Jacó 272
  Junquillal 223
  La Salsa Barva 377
  Los Suecos 248
  Mal País 244, 247
  Manuel Antonio 293
  Manzanillo 243, 248
  Montezuma 249
  Nancite 171
  Naranjo 171
  Negra 224
  Nosara 229
  Ocotal 207

Ostional 233
Palma 284
Pan de Azúcar 208
Panamá 204
Pavones 331
Pelada 231
Penca 208
Potrero 208
Prieta 208
Punta Banco 332
Punta Islita 242
Puntarenas 269
Sámara 234
San Miguel 242
Santa Teresa 245, 247
Tamarindo 218
Tambor 257
Tivives 270
Uvita 297
Valor 270
Vuelta del Sur 242
Zancudo 333
PLUS 15
Pochote 259
poison-dart frogs 57
post 31
Poste Restante 32
Potrero 208
Programa Voluntarios para la Conservación del Ambiente (PROVCA) 84
Puerto Jiménez 335–339
Puerto Limón 348–351
Puerto Viejo de Sarapiquí 180–183
Centro Neotrópico Sarapiquis 183
Río Sarapiquí 184
Puerto Viejo de Talamanca 373–377
pumas 56
Punta Mona Center 82
Punta Uva 380
Puntarenas 266–270
Purisil Park 140

Q

Quepos 284–290
quetzal 56

R

Rabies 20
rainy season 1
Red Cross 21
Refugio Nacional
Curú 261
Golfito 330
Nacional Gandoca-Manzanillo 381

rental agencies 42
rental cars 42
renting a car 42
Reserva
Biológica Hitoy-Cerere 372
Biológica Lomas Barbudal 162
Biológica Monteverde 151
Forestal Bosque Eterno de los Niños 152
Indígena Boruca 309
Indígena Cocles/Kekoldi 376
Los Ángles Cloud Forest 122
Natural Absoluta Cabo Blanco 256
Santa Elena 152
Reserve. See Reserva.
Río Parismina 351
Río San Juan 184, 200
Río Sarapiquí 184
robbery 19
roundworms 22

S

safety 18
San Carlos. See Ciudad Quesada.
San Francisco de Coyote 243
San Gerardo de Rivas 304, 304–307
San José 85–106
Centro Nacional de Arte y Cultura 99
Museo de Arte Costarricense 99
Museo de Criminología 99
Museo de Jade 98
Museo de Oro 98
Museo Nacional 98
Parque de España 99
Parque Morazón 99
Parque Zoológico y Jardín Botánico Nacional Simón Bolívar 99
Serpentarium 98
Teatro Nacional 98
San José de la Montaña 129
San Pedro 95, 97, 101
San Rafael de Guatuso 192–194
San Ramón 120–122
San Vito 311–313
Wilson Botanical Gardens 313
Santa Cruz 214–216
Pottery Village of Guaitil 216
Santa Teresa 244–249
Sarchí 114–116

savannas 55
scams 19
School for International Training, College Semester Abroad 75
scuba
Bahía Drake 322
Parque Nacional Manuel Antonio 290
Playa del Coco 204
Playa Hermosa 201
Playa Junquillal 224
Puerto Viejo de Talamanca 377
scuba diving
Bocas del Toro (P) 386
Isla Colón (P) 386
Semana Santa 1
senior travelers 46
sexually transmitted diseases 24
sharks 57
Sierpe 321–322
Siquirres 347–348
Sixaola 382
sloths 56
snake bites 29
snakes 57
snorkeling
Bahía Drake 322
Bocas del Toro (P) 386
Cahuita 366
Conchal 212
Hospital Point (P) 389
Isla Colón (P) 386
Junquillal 223
Parque Nacional Cahuita 369
Parque Nacional Manuel Antonio 290
Parque Nacional Marino Ballena 299
Playa del Coco 204
Playa Hermosa 201, 204
Playa Tamarindo 218
solo travelers 46
South of Puerto Viejo 378–383
Southern Costa Rica 300–320
Buenos Aires 307–308
Neily 314–316
Palmar Norte 310–311
Parque Internacional La Amistad 316–318
Parque Nacional Chirripó 305
Reserva Indígena Boruca 309
San Gerardo de Rivas 304–

307
San Vito 311–313
Wilson Botanical Gardens 313
souvenirs 103
special concerns
  dietary concerns 49
specific concerns
  bisexual, gay, and lesbian travelers 48
  children and travel 49
  disabled travelers 48
  senior travelers 46
  solo travel 46
  women travelers 45
spiders 57
STA Travel 38
standby flights 38
STDs 24
studying abroad 74–78
  language schools 76
  study programs 75
sunburn 21
sunscreen 21
SUNY Brockport International Education 79
surfing
  Jacó 277
  La Roca Loca 277
  Pavones 331
  Playa Avellana 226
  Playa Bandera 284
  Playa Bejuco 284
  Playa Boca Barranca 269
  Playa Camaronal 242
  Playa Coyote 243
  Playa Dominical 294
  Playa Escondida 270
  Playa Esterillos Oeste 282
  Playa Guiones 231
  Playa Hermosa 279, 281
  Playa Junquillal 223
  Playa Mal País 247
  Playa Naranjo 171
  Playa Negra 224
  Playa Palma 284
  Playa Tamarindo 218
  Playa Tivives 270
  Playa Valor 270
  Puerto Viejo de Talamanca 377
  Swan Caye (P) 387

T

Tambor 257–259
tarantulas 57
Taxes 17
Teacher Workshops Abroad 80
teaching english 79

telephones 33
terrorism 18
tetanus-diphtheria 20
theft 19
this 341
Thomas Cook 15
Tilarán 156
time 34
time differences 34
time zones 34
tipping 16
tips for saving money 16
Tortuguero 354
Tortuguero Village 354
toucans 56
tourist offices 12
transportation
  boats 45
  cars 42
  planes 36
  trains 40
travel advisories 18
travel agencies 36
traveler's checks 14
tree frogs 57
tropical rainforests 55
turtles 56
  Bluff (P) 387
  Gandoca 378
  Ostional 233
  Parismina 351, 353
  Parque Nacional Marino Las Baulas 216
  Playa Camaronal 242
  Playa Grande 216
  Playa Hermosa 280
  Playa Larga (P) 388
  Playa Nancite 171
  Playa Tamarindo 218
  Puerto Viejo de Talamanca 377
  Tortuguero National Park 354
Typhoid 20
Typhoid fever 23

U

University of Costa Rica Field Ecology 76
Upala 194
US State Department 16
Uvita 297–299

V

vaccinations 20
valuables, protecting 19
Vara Blanca 185–187
vegetarians 50
vegetation zones 55

Visa 14, 15
volcán
  Arenal 190
  Barva 129, 130
  Cacho Negro 129
  Irazú 136
  Miravalles 159
  Poás 111
  Rincón de la Vieja 168
  Tenorio 158, 159
Volcán Tenorio 158–159
volcanic eruptions 55
volunteering 80–84
  community service 81
  conservation work 83

W

waterfalls
  Escondidas 169
  Fortuna 190
  La Cangreja 169
  Montezuma 254
  Near Nosara 233
  Reserva Biológica Hitoy-Cerere 372
  Reserva Indígena Cocles/Kekoldi 376
weather 398
Western Union 16
whales 57
WIDECAST Foundation 84
Wild Cane Key (P) 388
Wilson Botanical Gardens 313
windsurfing
  Tilarán 157
wiring money 16
women travelers 45
  health 24
work permits 13
working 78–80
  long-term work 78
  short-term work 80
  teaching english 79
World Wide Web 52
WorldTeach, Inc. 80

Z

Zarcero 122–124
Zoo-Ave 112

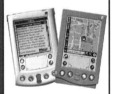

WHO WE ARE

A NEW LET'S GO

With a sleeker look and innovative new content, we have revamped the entire series to reflect more than ever the needs and interests of the independent traveler. Here are just some of the improvements you will notice when traveling with the new *Let's Go*.

MORE PRICE OPTIONS

Still the best resource for budget travelers, *Let's Go* recognizes that everyone needs the occassional indulgence. Our "Big Splurges" indicate establishments that are actually worth those extra pennies (pulas, pesos, or pounds), and price-level symbols (❶ ❷ ❸ ❹ ❺) allow you to quickly determine whether an accommodation or restaurant will break the bank. We may have diversified, but we'll never lose our budget focus—"Hidden Deals" reveal the best-kept travel secrets.

BEYOND THE TOURIST EXPERIENCE

Our Alternatives to Tourism chapter offers ideas on immersing yourself in a new community through study, work, or volunteering.

AN INSIDER'S PERSPECTIVE

As always, every item is written and researched by our on-site writers. This year we have highlighted more viewpoints to help you gain an even more thorough understanding of the places you are visiting.

IN RECENT NEWS. *Let's Go* correspondents around the globe report back on current regional issues that may affect you as a traveler.

CONTRIBUTING WRITERS. Respected scholars and former *Let's Go* writers discuss topics on society and culture, going into greater depth than the usual guidebook summary.

THE LOCAL STORY. From the Parisian monk toting a cell phone to the Russian *babushka* confronting capitalism, *Let's Go* shares its revealing conversations with local personalities—a unique glimpse of what matters to real people.

FROM THE ROAD. Always helpful and sometimes downright hilarious, our researchers share useful insights on the typical (and atypical) travel experience.

SLIMMER SIZE

Don't be fooled by our new, smaller size. *Let's Go* is still packed with invaluable travel advice, but now it's easier to carry with a more compact design.

FORTY-THREE YEARS OF WISDOM

For over four decades *Let's Go* has provided the most up-to-date information on the hippest cafes, the most pristine beaches, and the best routes from border to border. It all started in 1960 when a few well-traveled students at Harvard University handed out a 20-page mimeographed pamphlet of their tips on budget travel to passengers on student charter flights to Europe. From humble beginnings, *Let's Go* has grown to cover six continents and *Let's Go: Europe* still reigns as the world's best-selling travel guide. This year we've beefed up our coverage of Latin America with *Let's Go: Costa Rica* and *Let's Go: Chile*; on the other side of the globe, we've added *Let's Go: Thailand* and *Let's Go: Hawaii*. Our new guides bring the total number of titles to 61, each infused with the spirit of adventure that travelers around the world have come to count on.

Members SAVE More

Join the Student Advantage® Membership Program to save hundreds of dollars a year on food, clothing, travel and more! Members enjoy ongoing, exclusive savings at more than 15,000 locations around campus, online, and throughout the U.S.A. Here are just a few:

U·S AIRWAYS

Member-only discounts and
bonus Dividend Miles®

Foot Locker

$10 OFF purchases of $50 or more
(some exclusions may apply)

Booking fee waived

15% OFF walk-up fares

Plus, receive the **Student Advantage Bonus Savings Book** with over $200 in additional savings from J.Crew, Timberland®, Student Advantage Tech Store and more!

JOIN TODAY!

Go to studentadvantage.com or call 1.877.2JOINSA and reference promotion code LET88P9001. This code entitles you to special Membership pricing.

1-year Membership: $15.00*   (SAVE $5)

4-year Membership: $50.00* (SAVE $10)

*Plus $2.50 shipping and handling for 1-year Membership and $5.00 for 4-year Membership. Student Advantage® is a registered trademark and product of Student Advantage, Inc.

studentadvantage.com

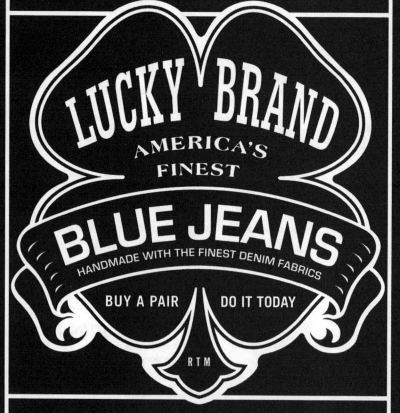

Book your air, hotel, and transportation all in one place.

Hotel or hostel? Cruise or canoe? Car? Plane? Camel?
Wherever you're going, visit Yahoo! Travel and get total control
over your arrangements. Even choose your seat assignment.
So. One hump or two? travel.yahoo.com

powered by *hp*

YAHOO!
Travel

MAP INDEX

Alajuela 110
Bahía Drake Area 324
Barra del Colorado Area 363
Cahuita 367
Cañas 155
Caribbean Lowlands 342
Cartago 134
Central Pacific Coast 263
Central Valley 109
Costa Rica xii-xiii
Costa Rica: Watersports xiv-xv
Escazu 105
Fortuna 189
Golfito 328
Heredia 125
Jacó Area 273
Jacó Center 274
Liberia 165
Manuel Antonio Area 292
Monteverde & Santa Elena 149
Montezuma 251
Neily 315
Nicoya 227
Northern Lowlands 177

Northwestern Costa Rica 146
Palmar Norte 310
Parque Nacional Cahuita 370
Parque Nacional Tortuguero 355
Parque Viejo de Talamanca 374
Peninsula de Nicoya 202
Peninsula de Osa and Golfo Dulce 323
Playa del Coco 205
Playa Samara 235
Playa Tamarindo 219
Puerto Jiménez 337
Puerto Limón Area 349
Puntarenas 267
Puerto Viejo de Talamanca 374
Quepos 285
Regions of Costa Rica viii
San Isidoro 302
San José Center 87
San José Overview 86
San Vito 313
Southern Costa Rica 301
Suggested Itineraries 6-7
Turrialba 143

MAP LEGEND

Hospital	Building	Thermal Bath	
Hotel/Hostel	Police	Park: city, other	Cave
Camping	Post Office	Plaza/other area	Waterfall
Food	Tourist Information	Beach	Pass
Nightlife	Point of Interest	Water	Peak
Museum	Embassy/Consulate	Swamp	Mountain Range
Church	Telephone Office	Pedestrian Zone	Ranger Station
Synagogue	Airport	Steps	Archaeological Site
Theater	Bus Station	Trail	Monastery
Internet Café	Train Station	Ferry Route/Stop	Border Crossing
Bank	Shopping		

ABBREVIATIONS:

Lg.   Laguna, Lago
M.N.   Monumento Nacional
PL.   Plaza
Pq.   Parque
P.I.   Parque Internacional
P.N.   Parque Nacional
Q.   Quebrada
R.   Río
R.B.   Reserva Biológica
R.E.   Reserva Ecológica
R.F.   Reserva Forestal
R.F.S. Refugio de Fauna Silvestre
R.V.S. Refugio de Vida Silvestre
R.I.   Reserva Internacional

The Let's Go compass
always points NORTH.